Marketing
Research
Essentials

Seventh Edition

John Wiley & Sons, Inc

Dedicated to
the market research instructors and students
who make this book a part of their
professional lives

VICE PRESIDENT & EXECUTIVE PUBLISHER   George Hoffman
SENIOR EDITOR   Franny Kelly
EXECUTIVE MARKETING MANAGER   Diane Mars
ASSISTANT EDITOR   Maria Guarascio
SENIOR DESIGNER   Madelyn Lesure
PHOTO EDITOR   Sheena Goldstein
SENIOR PRODUCTION EDITOR   Trish McFadden
PRODUCTION MANAGEMENT SERVICES   Kate Boilard, Laserwords Maine
EDITORIAL ASSISTANT   Emily McGee
MARKETING ASSISTANT   Laura Finley
MEDIA EDITOR   Allie K. Morris
COVER PHOTO   Masterfile

This book was set in Adobe Garamond by Laserwords, Chennai and printed and bound by
RRD VHP. The cover was printed by RRD VHP.

This book is printed on acid free paper. ∞

To order books or for customer service, please call 1-800-CALL WILEY (225-5945).

ISBN-13 978-0470-16970-4

Printed in the United States of America

10 9 8 7 6 5 4 3 2 1

CONTENTS IN BRIEF

CONTENTS

PREFACE

Making Marketing Research Real

The world of marketing research is fast-paced, dynamic, and always in a state of change. Understanding the complexities and rapid development of marketing research today requires an insider's perspective. This text is co-authored by a full-time market researcher. It is the only marketing research text written by the president and CEO of a large, very successful research organization. Thus, we continue offering you **Real Data, Real People,** and **Real Research** like no one else. By keeping our fingers on the pulse of marketing research today we can offer insights into qualitative and quantitative methods unmatched by other texts.

Our Most Thorough Revision Ever!

Each chapter has been thoroughly revised to reflect the latest thinking and trends in marketing research. **We have consolidated Internet research into a single, new chapter.** We begin by discussing traditional survey research in Chapter 5. Next, the new Chapter 6 explains how the Internet has impacted not only survey research, but virtually all aspects of marketing research.

 More than half of the end-of-chapter cases are new! Every chapter has a new case. Some of the organizations and products include: the Food and Drug Administration, Scottish Bureau of Tourism, and Glad Trash Bags, to name a few. Each case concludes with critical thinking questions designed to stimulate thinking about the material in the chapter.

 All new opening vignettes! We offer something new with many of the seventh edition opening vignettes. Where practical, we decided to feature actual research studies by some of America's largest marketing research firms. Some of the firms are Harris Interactive study on materialism; Luth Research study on happiness; Decision Analyst study on health and nutrition; NPD Group study on outdoor grilling; and Research International's study on Baby Boomers. In some cases, research firms asked us to disguise both their name and the clients. **But, as always, the data are real.** Some opening vignettes feature well-known organizations and products. A few examples are: Bertolli Foods (think olive oil), Staples, and the Monterrey Bay Aquarium. **We believe that the best learning experiences come through true experiences.**

New Content in Every Chapter That Offers Cutting-Edge Trends and Methodology

New Content by Chapter:

Chapter 1—The Role of Marketing Research in Management Decision Making
New AMA definition of marketing research; new examples throughout.

Chapter 2—Problem Definition, Exploratory Research, and the Research Process
New discussion of creating action-producing research; new exhibit on benefits of a good proposal; new material on doing marketing research in China.

Chapter 3—Secondary Data and Databases
New discussion on behavioral targeting; new material on the Children's Online Privacy Protection Act.

Chapter 4—Qualitative Research
New discussion on group moderating skills; new example of a focus group discussion guide; new material on planning global focus groups; new material on getting quality information and decision-making results from focus groups; new section on cost of focus groups versus independent depth interviews; new material on writing a focus group report; new section on the Delphi method; new material on projection techniques; new projective techniques—analogies and personification.

Chapter 5—Traditional Survey Research
New section on cell phone surveys.

Chapter 6—Online Marketing Research
New material on using the Internet for secondary data; online focus groups' best practices; web community research; new material on web survey software; new section on gaining online survey completions; new material on formatting an online survey; new material on timing survey invitations; major new section on commercial online panel providers; major new section on panel management; new material on eliminating professional survey takers.

Chapter 7—Primary Data Collection: Observation
New material on ethnographic research; online ethnography; new material on mystery shopping; new section on eye-tracking; new section on GPS measurement; new material on Project Apollo; new material on "click-streams."

Chapter 8—Primary Data Collection: Experimentation and Test Markets
New material on psychographics; new material on selection bias; new material on product-specific test markets.

Chapter 9—The Concept of Measurement and Attitude Scales
New discussion of construct validity.
Introduce new two-stage scaling format; new section on the popular Net Promoter Score (NPS); new section on scale conversions.

Chapter 10—Questionnaire Design

New material on "heavy responders"; new material on survey response errors; new discussion on ethnicity and gender bias; new material on survey contamination from national differences in response styles.

Chapter 11—Basic Sampling Issues

New discussion of cell phone only households; new discussion on using driver's licenses and voter registration lists as sampling frames; new material on sampling frames to collect global data; new discussion on when address-based telephone surveys outperform random-digit dialing; new material on snowball sampling.

Chapter 12—Sample Size Determination

New discussion on planning the sample size; new thoughts on determining the optimal sample size; new material on nonresponse bias; new discussion on small samples; new material on the relationship between confidence level and sample size.

Chapter 13—Data Processing, Fundamental Data Analysis, and the Statistical Testing of Differences

New material on fake interviews and avoiding interview fraud; new discussion on push polling; new material on practical applications of the Z test; new discussion of the T test; new examples of ANOVA.

Chapter 14—Bivariate Correlation and Regression

New material on avoiding bias when using least-squares regression; new discussion on Pearson's product–moment correlation.

Chapter 15—Communicating Research Results and Managing Marketing Research

Major rewrite on how marketing research reporting is done today; new section on the PowerPoint deck; new section on the relationship between the research report and the RFP; new section on "margin of error" misconceptions; new section on marketing research outsourcing; major new section on managing the marketing research department, including discussion of allocating the budget, prioritizing projects, and retaining good staff.

You Can Bring Internet Research Alive with Vovici WebResearcher

Your students can use the same marketing research Web application as professional marketing researchers. You will have the capability of assigning multiple class projects and conducting real Internet marketing research surveys. You can create, implement, and manage surveys using only a Web browser. There is nothing to download or install. Vovici question logic capabilities such as branching, linking, and piping make creating simple or complex questionnaires easy. You can even set quotas for your surveys to reach your target demographics. *In short, you can make Internet marketing research come alive for your students!*

Great Resources to Meet Your Teaching Needs

Redesigned Instructor's Manual

We know how busy you are with teaching and research commitments, therefore we have done everything possible to facilitate your teaching marketing research with our new Instructors Manual. Each chapter offers the following:

- ☐ *Suggested Lesson Plans.* Suggestions are given on dividing up the chapter material, based on the frequency and duration of your class period.

- ☐ *Chapter Scan.* A quick synopsis highlights the core material in each chapter.

- ☐ *Learning Objectives.* The list of learning objectives found in the text is repeated here.

- ☐ *General Chapter Outline.* The main headers provide a quick snapshot of all the content areas within the chapter.

- ☐ *List of Key Terms.* The key terms introduced to the students in the text are repeated here.

- ☐ *Detailed Chapter Outline.* This outline fleshes out the general outline given previously. It also indicates where ancillary materials fit into the discussion: PowerPoint slides, exhibits from the text, learning objectives, and review questions. Opening vignettes and boxed features are also included in this outline.

- ☐ *Summary Explaining Learning Objectives.* An explanation of how the learning objectives are satisfied by chapter material is the basis of the Instructor's Manual summary.

- ☐ *Answers to Pedagogy.* Suggested answers and approaches to the critical thinking questions, the Internet activities, the cases, the cross-functional questions, and the ethical dilemmas are offered at the end of each chapter or part.

  Instructors can access the electronic files on the Instructor Companion Site at *www.wiley.com/college/mcdaniel.*

New Comprehensive PowerPoint Package

For this edition, we have created a comprehensive, fully interactive PowerPoint presentation with roughly 400 slides in the package. You can tailor your visual presentation to include the material you choose to cover in class. This PowerPoint presentation gives you the ability to completely integrate your classroom lecture with a powerful visual statement of chapter material. Keep students engaged and stimulate classroom discussion! The entire collection of slides will be available for download from our website at *www.wiley.com/college/mcdaniel.*

New Classroom-Tested Comprehensive Test Bank

Our test bank is comprehensive and thoroughly classroom-tested. The questions range from definitions of key terms to basic problem-solving questions to creative-thinking problems. This new and improved test bank includes approximately 60 questions per chapter consisting of multiple-choice, true/false, and essay questions. Regardless of the type and level of knowledge you wish to test, we have the right questions for your students. A computerized version of this newly created test bank is also available on the book's companion Web site so that you can customize your quizzes and exams. Instructors can access the electronic files on the Instructor Companion Site at *www.wiley.com/college/mcdaniel*.

New Personal Response System (PRS)

Our personal response system questions for each chapter of this textbook are designed to spark discussion and debate in the Marketing Research classroom. For more information on PRS, please contact your local Wiley representative.

Focus Group Video and Lecture Launches

Additional *Real Research* is offered through a focus group video conducted by another one of our research partners, Jerry Thomas, president of Decision Analyst (www.decisionanalyst .com). Decision Analyst, Incorporated is a large international marketing research firm. The focus group subject is online dating and ties in with the online dating data case. We also offer several interviews featuring Jerry Thomas and your author, Carl McDaniel, discussing key topics in marketing research. For more information on this 45-minute video, available on DVD, please contact your local Wiley representative.

Acknowledgments

This book could not have been written and published without the generous expert assistance of many people. We would like to thank Joshua Been for his excellent assistance in preparing the material on geographic information systems (GIS); Richard Leviton for his extensive assistance in a number of areas and experienced input on editorial issues; Jerry Thomas for providing the focus group research; and Craig Stevens, Senior Vice President, e-Rewards Market Research for providing material on online panels. We also thank Joe Cangelosi of University of Central Arkansas for preparing the Instructor's Manual, Test Bank, and PowerPoint Slide.

Our deepest gratitude goes to the team at John Wiley and Sons for continuing the trend of excellence established by this text. Special thanks to Franny Kelly, Maria Guarascio, and Emily McGee, and to Ellinor Wagner for the photo research, and Kate Boilard, our production editor.

Finally, we'd like to thank the following reviewers for their valuable comments throughout the revision process:

Paul Boughton, Saint Louis University
Haim Mano, University of Missouri, St. Louis
Carolyn E. Predmore, Manhattan College
Louis A. Tucci, The College of New Jersey
Michael Tsiros, University of Miami
Robert Watson, Quinnipiac University

Felipe Rodriguez Fernandez/Getty Images

THE ROLE OF MARKETING RESEARCH IN MANAGEMENT DECISION MAKING

LEARNING OBJECTIVES

1.	To review the marketing concept and the marketing mix.
2.	To comprehend the marketing environment within which managers must make decisions.
3.	To define marketing research.
4.	To understand the importance of marketing research in shaping marketing decisions.
5.	To learn when marketing research should and should not be conducted.
6.	To learn how the Internet is changing marketing research.
7.	To examine marketing research ethics.

The Monterey Bay Aquarium, considered a great family entertainment and educational experience, was not achieving the growth in visitors it had targeted. Aquarium management performed customer satisfaction market research to find out if there were service problems that, if corrected, would increase attendance.

But that's not what they found. People who visited actually rated their experiences as excellent. Instead, the survey revealed an untapped potential group of future visitors: It showed that the best future visitors were past visitors who lived within driving distance. The survey also showed that the more these people had visited in the past, the more likely they were to visit in the future. In addition, ongoing surveys show that Monterey Bay area residents are the most likely to return in a year, followed in order by San Francisco Bay area residents, California residents, and visitors from other states.

The aquarium then created marketing programs targeted at the potentially "best" visitors. Efforts included building mailing lists, focusing on converting this segment into aquarium members, and advertising with "come back" messages, rather than "here's what we are and where we are." Since families typically rate their experience higher than adult-only groups, advertising focused specifically on families in the Bay area.

The aquarium achieved its targets by offering incremental benefits to "average" local visitors to convert them into "excellent" repeat advocates.[1] This was made possible through marketing research. So what exactly is marketing research? And how important is it in shaping marketing decisions? When should marketing research be conducted? These are some of the questions we will address in Chapter 1.

Nature of Marketing

Marketing is the activity, set of institutions, and processes for creating, communicating, delivering, and exchanging offerings that have value for customers, clients, partners, and society at large.[2] Good customer relationships often result in exchanges; that is, a good or service is exchanged for money. The potential for exchange exists when there are at least two parties and each has something of potential value to the other. When the two parties can communicate and deliver the desired goods or services, exchange can take place. How do marketing managers attempt to stimulate exchange? They follow the "right" principle. They attempt to get the right goods or services to the right people at the right place at the right time at the right price, using the right promotion techniques. The "right" principle describes how marketing managers control the many factors that ultimately determine marketing success. To make the "right" decisions, management must have timely decision-making information. Marketing research is a primary channel for providing that information.

The Marketing Concept

To efficiently accomplish their goals, firms today have adopted the **marketing concept**, which requires (1) a consumer orientation, (2) a goal orientation, and (3) a systems orientation. A **consumer orientation** means that firms strive to identify the people (or firms) most likely to buy their product (the target market) and to produce a good or offer a service that will meet the needs of target customers most effectively in the face of

> **marketing**
> The process of planning and executing the conception, pricing, promotion, and distribution of ideas, goods, and services to create exchanges that satisfy individual and organizational objectives.

> **marketing concept**
> A business philosophy based on consumer orientation, goal orientation, and systems orientation.

> **consumer orientation**
> The identification of and focus on the people or firms most likely to buy a product and the production of a good or service that will meet their needs most effectively.

> **goal orientation**
> A focus on the accomplishment of corporate goals; a limit set on consumer orientation.

> **systems orientation**
> The creation of systems to monitor the external environment and deliver the desired marketing mix to the target market.

competition. The second tenet of the marketing concept is **goal orientation**; that is, a firm must be consumer-oriented only to the extent that it also accomplishes corporate goals. The goals of profit-making firms usually center on financial criteria, such as a 15 percent return on investment.

The third component of the marketing concept is **systems orientation**. A system is an organized whole—or a group of diverse units that form an integrated whole—functioning or operating in unison. It is one thing for a firm to say it is consumer oriented and another actually to *be* consumer oriented. First, systems must be established to find out what consumers want and to identify market opportunities. As you will see later, identifying target market needs and finding market opportunities are the tasks of marketing research. Next, this information must be fed back to the firm. Without feedback from the marketplace, a firm is not truly consumer oriented.

Opportunistic Nature of Marketing Research

Marketing research is an excellent tool for discovering opportunities in the market place. For example, DVD recorders have enabled consumers to zap commercials as they watch their favorite programs. Moreover, as people get more of their news from the Internet, newspaper readership has gone into a free fall. The plethora of cable channels has splintered and reduced viewership at the traditional television networks. Blogs and podcasts have further confused the advertising picture. Marketers are asking, "How can we efficiently and effectively reach our target audience?"

Marketing research recently found that frequent moviegoers say commercials before the flick starts are more acceptable than commercials on television. According to an Arbitron study, over half (53 percent) of frequent moviegoers (people who attended more than five movies in the past three months) find advertising before the movie to be acceptable versus 46 percent who find television advertising to be acceptable.

The study also revealed that 59 percent of moviegoers recall having watched on-screen commercials before the movie began on their most recent trip to the theater. This is a particularly impressive number considering that not all movie theaters run on-screen ads.

One of the central themes that arose from the national survey of Americans age 12 or older is that a significant number of moviegoers accept on-screen commercials as part of the total entertainment experience.

Cinema advertising connects with the youth market. Advertising in movie theaters reaches over 124 million or 45 percent of Americans 12 or older in a month. Eighty-one percent of teens and 67 percent of young adults age 18–24 have been to the movies in the past 30 days. Not only do movie theaters reach a high concentration of young people, but these consumers are also more likely to embrace cinema commercials than ads targeting them on the Internet, before programming on DVDs, and embedded in video games.

Movie theater advertising can provide an antidote for commercial avoidance. Moviegoers are more likely to use technology that allows them to avoid advertising such as digital video recorders (DVR) for television or pop-up blockers on the Internet. Moviegoers are more than twice as likely to use a DVR, such as TiVo, compared to nonmoviegoers (26 percent vs. 11 percent).

The modern cinema environment provides advertisers with multiple opportunities to connect with consumers. Eighty percent of moviegoers looked at posters while in the lobby or concession area on their most recent trip to the theater, and 54 percent noticed advertising on concession stand food and drink containers regardless of whether or not they consumed any of the items. Forty percent of moviegoers heard music playing overhead, and 28 percent saw video programming in the lobby or concession area. These multiple touchpoints open the door for advertisers and marketers to create complete brand experiences within the theater setting.[3] Thus, marketing research has uncovered an opportunity for marketers to get their messages across in the radically changing promotional environment.

External Marketing Environment

Over time, the **marketing mix** must be altered because of changes in the environment in which consumers and businesses exist, work, compete, and make purchasing decisions. Some new consumers and businesses will become part of the target market, while others will drop out of the market; those who remain may have different tastes, needs, incomes, lifestyles, and purchase habits than the original target consumers.

> **marketing mix**
> The unique blend of product/service, pricing, promotion, and distribution strategies designed to meet the needs of a specific target market.

Although managers can control the marketing mix, they cannot control elements in the external environment that continually mold and reshape the target market. Unless management understands the external environment, the firm cannot intelligently plan its future, and organizations are often unaware of the forces that influence their future.

Marketing research is a key means for understanding the environment. Knowledge of the environment helps a firm not only to alter its present marketing mix, but also to identify new opportunities. For example, when Ann Arbor, Michigan-based Domino's Pizza introduced its pizza delivery in Japan, a major change in Japanese consumers' behavior was needed as well. Yet Domino's managed to rise to the challenge successfully. If Domino's had merely tested the acceptability of the service it delivered in other parts of the world, it never would have entered Japan. Japanese consumers typically don't eat tomato-based food, and Asians tend to have allergies to milk products. Home delivery was not widely accepted, housewives were reluctant to give up cooking, houses were small, and finding customers in the labyrinthine streets of Tokyo seemed impossible. A market for pizza didn't exist, nor did any sign of hope in creating one.

Instead of trying to sell its existing product and service to the market, Domino's used its marketing research about customers to design a new product and service offering for Japan. It introduced toppings such as fish and sushi. To sustain its 30-minute delivery, Domino's developed a complex address database and small scooters to navigate the narrow streets in Tokyo. Through this research process this pizza-delivery service that no one asked for became a big hit in Japan.[4]

Marketing Research and Decision Making

Marketing research plays two key roles in the marketing system. First, as part of the marketing intelligence feedback process, marketing research provides decision makers with data on the effectiveness of the current marketing mix and offers insights into necessary changes. Second, marketing research is the primary tool for exploring new opportunities in the marketplace. Segmentation research and new product research help identify the most lucrative opportunities for a firm.

Marketing Research Defined

Now that you have an understanding of how marketing research fits into the overall marketing system, we can proceed with a formal definition of the term, as stated by the American Marketing Association:

Marketing research is the function that links the consumer, customer, and public to the marketer through information—information used to identify and define marketing opportunities and problems; generate, refine, and evaluate marketing actions; monitor marketing performance; and improve understanding of marketing as a process. Marketing research specifies the information required to address these issues, designs the method for collecting information, manages and implements the data collection process, analyzes the results, and communicates the findings and their implications.

We prefer another definition: **Marketing research** is the planning, collection, and analysis of data relevant to marketing decision making and the communication of the results of this analysis to management.

Importance of Marketing Research to Management

Marketing research can be viewed as playing three functional roles: descriptive, diagnostic, and predictive. Its **descriptive function** includes gathering and presenting statements of fact. What is the historic sales trend in the industry? What are consumers' attitudes and beliefs toward a product? Opening a pack of bacon is a messy job. Bacon lovers have to reach into the package, and if they only pull out a few slices, there's no easy way to store the remainder. Oscar Mayer marketing researchers hear plenty from consumers about what they disliked about its former bacon packaging. So marketers figured the best solution would be a packaging innovation that eliminated the chore of placing the opened pack in a resealable plastic bag or wrapping it in plastic or foil. This unwanted task was done so that the last piece of bacon would be as fresh as the first.

Recently, Oscar Mayer Center Cut Bacon was introduced in a new "Stay-Fresh Reclosable Tray." The flip top lid allows easy access to the bacon inside. The top snaps closed, making it readily resealable. The flat tray makes for simplified storage in the refrigerator.[5]

The second role of research is the **diagnostic function**, wherein data and/or actions are explained. For example, what was the impact on sales when the Oscar Mayer package design was changed? How can product/service offerings be altered to better serve customers and potential customers? Since kids eat over 5 billion ounces of ketchup each year, Heinz decided that the heavy users (kids) should have a lot to say (via marketing research) about how to make ketchup fun. Heinz listened and watched children using ketchup, which resulted in a new bottle design, name selection, and color. The true ketchup connoisseurs helped create Heinz EZ Squirt green ketchup! More than 10 million bottles were sold in the first seven months! This was followed up a year later with "Funky purple" ketchup.

The final role of research is the **predictive function**. How can the firm best take advantage of opportunities as they arise in the ever-changing marketplace? Kraft Foods noticed that consumers were flocking to "low-carb" diets. The company used marketing research to determine if this was a fad or long-term trend. Determining that "low carb" was more than a fad, it entered into an alliance with Arthur Agatston, the creator of *The South Beach Diet*. The result was certain Kraft products being labeled "South Beach Diet Recommended." Further marketing research led to a broad line of products entitled "The South Beach Diet" brand. Products include cereal, meal replacement and cereal bars, refrigerated sandwich wraps, frozen entrees, and frozen pizza.

The Unrelenting Drive for Quality and Customer Satisfaction
Quality and customer satisfaction have become the key competitive weapons of the decade. Few organizations can prosper in today's environment without a focus on quality, continual improvement, and customer satisfaction. Corporations across the globe have implemented quality improvement and satisfaction programs in an effort to reduce costs, retain customers, increase market share, and, last but not least, improve the bottom line.

Ritz-Carlton is the only service company to have won the prestigious Malcolm Baldrige National Quality Award twice. The chain placed first in guest satisfaction among

---

marketing research
The planning, collection, and analysis of data relevant to marketing decision making and the communication of the results of this analysis to management.

descriptive function
The gathering and presentation of statements of fact.

diagnostic function
The explanation of data or actions.

predictive function
Specification of how to use descriptive and diagnostic research to predict the results of a planned marketing decision.

luxury hotels in the most recent J.D. Power and Associates hotel survey. Ritz-Carlton spends about $5,000 to train each new hire. First is a two-day introduction to company values (it's all about the service) and the 20 Ritz-Carlton "basics." (Basic 13 is "Never lose a guest.") Next comes a 21-day course focused on job responsibilities, such as a bellman's 28 steps to greeting a guest. Each employee carries a plastic card imprinted with the credo and the basics, as well as the "employee promise" and the three steps of service. Step 1: "A warm and sincere greeting. Use the guest's name, if and when possible."

Porters and doormen wear headsets, so when they spot your name on luggage tags, they can radio the information to the front desk. In addition, an in-house database called the Customer Loyalty Anticipation Satisfaction System stores guest preferences, such as whether an individual likes Seagram's ginger ale or Canada Dry. The software also alerts front-desk clerks when a guest who's stayed at other Ritz-Carltons has a habit of inquiring about the best sushi in town.[6]

Where does marketing research come into play at Ritz-Carlton? The company continually measures customer satisfaction to make certain that it is meeting the high standards that the firm has set. And delighted customers typically means repeat customers in high-end hotel chains.

Quality that means little to customers usually doesn't produce a payoff in improved sales, profits, or market share; it represents wasted effort and expense. Today, the new mantra is **return on quality**, which means that (1) the quality being delivered is the quality desired by the target market and (2) the added quality must have a positive impact on profitability. For example, banking giant NationsBank Corporation measures every improvement in service quality, from adding more tellers to offering new mortgage products, in terms of added profitability.

> **return on quality**
> Management objective based on the principles that (1) the quality being delivered is at a level desired by the target market and (2) that level of quality must have a positive impact on profitability.

The passion to drive down costs can destroy the delicate balance between efficiency and service. For example, the University of Michigan annual marketing research survey entitled the American Customer Satisfaction index revealed that Home Depot slipped to dead last among major U.S. retailers.[7] Cost cutting, including replacing many full-time workers with part-timers and reducing the profit-sharing pool for all workers, created a customer service disaster. As a result, same-store sales at Home Depot now lag far behind the much better liked Lowe's.

Paramount Importance of Keeping Existing Customers An inextricable link exists between customer satisfaction and customer loyalty. Long-term relationships don't just happen; they are grounded in the delivery of service and value. Customer retention pays big dividends for firms. Powered by repeat sales and referrals, revenues and market share grow. Costs fall because firms spend less funds and energy attempting to replace defectors. Steady customers are easy to serve because they understand the modus operandi and make fewer demands on employees' time. A firm's ability to retain customers also drives job satisfaction and pride, which leads to higher employee retention. In turn, long-term employees acquire additional knowledge that increases productivity. A Bain & Company study estimates that a 5 percent decrease in the customer defection rate can boost profits by 25 to 95 percent.[8] Another study found that the customer retention rate has a major impact on the value of the firm.[9]

The ability to retain customers is based on an intimate understanding of their needs. This knowledge comes primarily from marketing research. For example, British Airways recast its first-class transatlantic service based on detailed marketing research. Most airlines stress top-of-the-line service in their transatlantic first-class cabins. However, British Air research found that most first-class passengers simply want to sleep. British Air now gives premium flyers the option of dinner on the ground, before takeoff, in the first-class lounge. Then, once on board, they can slip into British Air pajamas, put their heads on real pillows, slip under blankets, and enjoy an interruption-free flight. On arrival at their

Asking the right questions in marketing research can be as important as getting good answers. UPS found that customers wanted more interaction with their UPS driver. Go to http://www.ups .com to find out how UPS uses marketing research to better serve its customers.

PhotoDisc, Inc./Getty Images

destination, first-class passengers can have breakfast, use comfortable dressing rooms and showers, and even have their clothes pressed before they set off. These changes in British Air's first-class service were driven strictly by marketing research.

Understanding the Ever-Changing Marketplace

Marketing research also helps managers to understand trends in the marketplace and to take advantage of opportunities. Marketing research has been practiced for as long as marketing has existed. The early Phoenicians carried out market demand studies as they traded in the various ports on the Mediterranean Sea. Marco Polo's diary indicates he was performing a marketing research function as he traveled to China. There is evidence that the Spanish systematically conducted marketing surveys as they explored the New World, and examples exist of marketing research conducted during the Renaissance.

All during the 1990s, the market share for Campbell soups slipped. Soup wasn't "cool," and consumers turned to other foods. Campbell's turned to marketing research to better understand consumers' fast-paced lifestyles. The first new product was Soup at Hand, a "shippable" product that was easily portable. Soon after, changes began inside the test kitchen. The flavor profiles of nearly every soup in the portfolio got an upgrade. Building on the launch of Campbell's Select Gold Label, the company began touting a top-tier line of restaurant-style soups to introduce the notion that soup will actually make a sophisticated meal. Its new choices included Golden Butternut Squash and Creamy Portobello Mushroom. "We want to start to create a premium tier for people who want to trade up," said Denise Morrison, president of U.S. Soup, Sauce and Beverages. "We're bringing luxury to the soup aisle."[10] Thanks to marketing research and Campbell's creativity, sales are now growing briskly!

Proactive Role of Marketing Research

Understanding the nature of the marketing system is a necessity for a successful marketing orientation. By having a thorough knowledge of factors that have an impact on the target market and the marketing mix, management can be proactive rather than reactive. Proactive management alters the marketing mix to fit newly emerging patterns in economic, social, and competitive environments, whereas reactive management waits for change to have a major impact on the firm before deciding to take action. It is the difference between viewing the turbulent marketing environment as a threat (a reactive stance) and as an opportunity (a proactive stance). Companies like UPS, Apple, and FedEx were largely proactive in Internet marketing and customer service. A proactive position would have been to become cutting-edge Internet marketers. Marketing research plays a key role in proactive management by allowing managers to anticipate changes in the market and customer desires and then design goods and services to meet those changes and needs.

A proactive manager not only examines emerging markets but also seeks, through strategic planning, to develop a long-run **marketing strategy** for the firm. A marketing strategy guides the long-term use of the firm's resources based on the firm's existing and projected internal capabilities and on projected changes in the external environment.

> **marketing strategy**
> A plan to guide the long-term use of a firm's resources based on its existing and projected internal capabilities and on projected changes in the external environment.

A good strategic plan is based on good marketing research. It helps the firm meet long-term profit and market share goals.

Applied Research versus Basic Research

Virtually all marketing research is conducted to better understand the market, to find out why a strategy failed, or to reduce uncertainty in management decision making. All research conducted for these purposes is called **applied research**. For example, should the price of DiGiorno frozen pizza be raised 40 cents? What name should Toyota select for a new sedan? Which commercial has a higher level of recall: A or B? On the other hand, **basic**, or **pure**, **research** attempts to expand the frontiers of knowledge; it is not aimed at a specific pragmatic problem. Basic research is conducted to validate an existing theory or learn more about a concept or phenomenon. For example, basic marketing research might test a hypothesis about high-involvement decision making or consumer information processing. In the long run, basic research helps us understand more about the world in which we live. The findings of basic research usually cannot be implemented by managers in the short run. Most basic marketing research is now conducted in universities; the findings are reported in such publications as *The Journal of Marketing Research* and *The Journal of Marketing*. In contrast, most research undertaken by businesses is applied research because it must be cost-effective and of demonstrable value to the decision maker.

Nature of Applied Research

Marketing research studies can be classified into three broad categories: programmatic, selective, and evaluative. **Programmatic research** is conducted to develop marketing options through market segmentation, market opportunity analysis, or consumer attitude and product usage studies. **Selective research** is used to test decision alternatives. Some examples are testing concepts for new products, advertising copy testing, and test marketing. **Evaluative research** is done to assess program performance; it includes tracking advertising recall, doing organizational image studies, and examining customer attitudes on a firm's quality of service.

Programmatic research arises from management's need to obtain a market overview periodically. For example, product management may be concerned that the existing market information base is inadequate or outdated for present decision making, or marketing plans may call for the introduction of new products, ad campaigns, or packaging. Whatever the specific situation, current information is needed to develop viable marketing options. Typical programmatic research questions include the following:

- ☐ Has its target market changed? How?
- ☐ Does the market exhibit any new segmentation opportunities?
- ☐ Do some segments appear to be more likely candidates than others for the firm's marketing efforts?
- ☐ What new product or service opportunities lie in the various segments?

Equidistant between Los Angeles and San Francisco in the Eastern Sierra Nevada Mountains, Mammoth Mountain has been serving the skiers and snowboarders of central California for 50 years. With the summit reaching above 11,000 feet and average annual snowfall hitting 400 inches, thousands of customers flock to the slopes and the lodges annually.

Yet, the resort's longstanding direct-mail program just wasn't driving the traffic. While the resort wasn't losing visitors (most resort traffic industrywide comes from existing skiers and

applied research Research aimed at solving a specific, pragmatic problem—better understanding of the marketplace, determination of why a strategy or tactic failed, or reduction of uncertainty in management decision making.

basic, or pure, research Research aimed at expanding the frontiers of knowledge rather than solving a specific, pragmatic problem.

programmatic research Research conducted to develop marketing options through market segmentation, market opportunity analyses, or consumer attitude and product usage studies.

selective research Research used to test decision alternatives.

evaluative research Research done to assess program performance.

"I don't *know* what I'm doing — this is pure research!"

Rex F. May

snowboarders rather than those new to the sports), executives hoped to gain some ground in an overall stable market by injecting some life into what had become an out-of-date marketing campaign—and to increase the frequency of visits by the 900,000 customers in its database.

Resort executives used programmatic research collected from an annual survey, the National Skier and Snowboarder Opinion Survey conducted on behalf of resorts across the country, and found that 94 percent of Mammoth's users in particular acknowledge using the Internet to find information about everything from weather advisories to checking room rates at one of Mammoth's lodges.

This information led to the creation of an e-mail marketing system that reaches 18,000 subscribers. The format is chatty and informing. For example, "The weather has been beautiful here lately, and with a 12- to 14-foot base you can't go wrong anywhere on the mountain. At 1:15 p.m. the temperature is 34 degrees at Main Lodge with clear skies and moderate to gusty winds. It's extremely windy and cold on top at 17 degrees, so be sure to bundle up." Skier visit numbers have been increasing 5 percent or more annually as a result of the programmatic research![11]

Selective research typically is conducted after several viable options have been identified by programmatic research. If no one alternative is clearly superior, product management usually will wish to test several alternatives. However, selective research may be required at any stage of the marketing process, such as when advertising copy is being developed, various product formulations are being evaluated, or an entire marketing program is being assessed, as in test marketing.

The need for evaluative research arises when the effectiveness and efficiency of marketing programs must be evaluated. Evaluative research may be integrated into programmatic research when program changes or entirely new options are demanded because of present performance such as at Mammoth Mountain.

Decision to Conduct Marketing Research

A manager who is faced with several alternative solutions to a particular problem should not instinctively call for applied marketing research. In fact, the first decision to be made is whether to conduct marketing research at all. In a number of situations, it is best not to conduct research.

☐ *Resources are lacking.* There are two situations in which a lack of resources should preclude marketing research. First, an organization may lack the funds to do the research properly. If a project calls for a sample of 800 respondents but the budget allows for only 50 interviews, the quality of the information would be highly suspect. Second, funds may be available to do the research properly but insufficient to implement any decisions resulting from the research. Small organizations in particular sometimes lack the resources to create an effective marketing mix. In one case, for example, the director of a performing arts guild was in complete agreement with the recommendations that resulted from a marketing research project. However, two years after the project was completed, nothing had been done because the money was not available.

☐ *Research results would not be useful.* Some types of marketing research studies measure lifestyle and personality factors of steady and potential customers. Assume that a study finds that introverted men with a poor self-concept, yet a high need for achievement, are most likely to patronize a discount brokerage service. The management of Charles Schwab discount brokerage service might be hard-pressed to use this information.

- [ ] *The opportunity has passed.* Marketing research should not be undertaken if the opportunity for successful entry into a market has already passed. If the product is in the late maturity or decline stage of the product life cycle (such as cassette recorders or black-and-white television sets), it would be foolish to do research on new product entry. The same may be true for markets rapidly approaching saturation, such as super-premium ice cream (Häagen-Dazs, Ben and Jerry's). For products already in the market, however, research is needed to modify the products as consumer tastes, competition, and other factors change.

- [ ] *The decision already has been made.* In the real world of management decision making and company politics, marketing research has sometimes been used improperly. Several years ago, a large marketing research study was conducted for a bank with over $800 million in deposits. The purpose of the research project was to guide top management in mapping a strategic direction for the bank during the next five years. After reading the research report, the president said, "I fully agree with your recommendations because that was what I was going to do anyway! I'm going to use your study tomorrow when I present my strategic plan to the board of directors." The researcher then asked, "What if my recommendations had been counter to your decision?" The bank president laughed and said, "They would have never known that I had conducted a marketing research study!" Not only was the project a waste of money, but it also raised a number of ethical questions in the researcher's mind.

- [ ] *Managers cannot agree on what they need to know to make a decision.* Although it may seem obvious that research should not be undertaken until objectives are specified, it sometimes happens. Preliminary or exploratory studies are commonly done to better understand the nature of the problem, but a large, major research project should not be. It is faulty logic to say "Well, let's just go ahead and do the study and then we will better understand the problem and know what steps to take." The wrong phenomena might be studied or key elements needed for management decision making may not be included.

- [ ] *Decision-making information already exists.* Some companies have been conducting research in certain markets for many years. They understand the characteristics of their target customers and what they like and dislike about existing products. Under these circumstances, further research would be redundant and a waste of money. Procter & Gamble, for example, has extensive knowledge of the coffee market. After it conducted initial taste tests, P&G went into national distribution with Folger's Instant Coffee without further research. The Sara Lee Corporation did the same thing with its frozen croissants, as did Quaker Oats with Chewy Granola Bars. This tactic, however, does not always work. P&G thought it understood the pain reliever market thoroughly, so it bypassed marketing research for Encaprin, encapsulated aspirin. The product failed because it lacked a distinct competitive advantage over existing products and was withdrawn from the market.

- [ ] *The costs of conducting research outweigh the benefits.* There are rarely situations in which a manager has such

The super-premium ice cream market is reaching saturation. At this point, it might not be wise to enter this market. However, marketing research is necessary to keep products already in the market ahead of the competition.

PhotoDisc, Inc./Getty Images

EXHIBIT 1.1	Deciding Whether to Conduct Marketing Research	
Market Size	**Small Profit Margin**	**Large Profit Margin**
Small	Costs likely to be greater than benefits (e.g., eyeglass replacement screw, tire valve extension). DON'T CONDUCT MARKETING RESEARCH.	Benefits possibly greater than cost (e.g., ultra-expensive Lamborghini-type sportswear, larger specialized industrial equipment like computer-aided metal stamping machines). PERHAPS CONDUCT MARKETING RESEARCH. LEARN ALL YOU CAN FROM EXISTING INFORMATION PRIOR TO MAKING DECISION TO CONDUCT RESEARCH.
Large	Benefits likely to be greater than costs (e.g., Stouffers frozen entrees, Crest's teeth whitener strips). PERHAPS CONDUCT MARKETING RESEARCH. LEARN ALL YOU CAN FROM EXISTING INFORMATION PRIOR TO MAKING DECISION TO CONDUCT RESEARCH.	Benefits most likely to be greater than costs (e.g., medical equipment like CAT scanners, Toshiba's high-definition television). CONDUCT MARKETING RESEARCH.

tremendous confidence in her or his judgment that additional information relative to a pending decision would not be accepted if it were available and free. However, the manager might have sufficient confidence to be unwilling to pay very much for it or wait long to receive it. Willingness to acquire additional decision-making information depends on a manager's perception of its quality, price, and timing. The manager would be willing to pay more for perfect information (that is, data that leave no doubt as to which alternative to follow) than for information that leaves uncertainty as to what to do. Therefore, research should be undertaken only when the expected value of the information is greater than the cost of obtaining it.

Two important determinants of potential benefits are profit margins and market size. Generally speaking, new products with large profit margins are going to have greater potential benefit than products with smaller profit margins, assuming that both items have the same sales potential. Also, new product opportunities in large markets are going to offer greater potential benefits than those in smaller markets if competitive intensity is the same in both markets (see Exhibit 1.1).

Profound Impact of the Internet on Marketing Research

The Internet has turned the world of marketing research upside down. Current methods of conducting some types of research soon may seem as quaint as a steam-engine train. New techniques and strategies for conducting traditional marketing research are appearing online in increasing numbers every day. Today, Internet marketing research accounts for about 50 percent of all marketing research revenue in the United States. Following are some growth drivers of such research:

☐ The Internet provides more rapid access to business intelligence and thus allows for better and faster decision making.

- ☐ The Internet improves a firm's ability to respond quickly to customer needs and market shifts.

- ☐ The Internet facilitates conducting follow-up studies and longitudinal research.

- ☐ The Internet slashes labor- and time-intensive research activities (and associated costs), including mailing, telephone solicitation, data entry, data tabulation, and reporting.

With the mushrooming number (currently over 75 percent) of Americans with Internet access, researchers are finding that online research and offline research yield the same results. Moreover, 82 percent of active Internet users have broadband.[12] America Online's (AOL) Digital Marketing Services (DMS), an online research organization, has done a number of surveys with both online and offline samples for clients such as IBM, Eastman Kodak, and Procter & Gamble. Side-by-side comparison of over 100 online and offline studies showed that both techniques led clients to the same business decisions.[13] That is, the guidance provided by both sets of data was the same.

Conducting surveys is not the sum total of the Internet revolution in marketing research. Management of the research process and dissemination of information also have been greatly enhanced by the Internet. Several key areas have been greatly affected by the Internet:

- ☐ *Libraries and various printed materials, which may be virtually replaced as sources of information.* On its website, the Bureau of Census (*www.census.gov*) indicates that it plans to gradually make the Internet the major means of distributing census data. The same is true for a number of other government agencies. Information from countless databases (both governmental and nongovernmental) can be called up almost instantaneously on the user's desktop, notebook, Blackberry, or even some cell phones!

- ☐ *The distribution of requests for proposals (RFPs) and the proposals themselves.* Companies can now quickly and efficiently send RFPs to a select e-mail list of research suppliers. In turn, the suppliers can develop proposals and e-mail them back to clients. A process that used to take days now occurs in a matter of hours.

- ☐ *Collaboration between the client and the research supplier in the management of a research project.* Both the researcher and the client might look at a proposal, RFP, report, or some type of statistical analysis at the same time on their computer screens while discussing it over the telephone. This is very effective and efficient, as changes in sample size, quotas, and other aspects of the research plan can be discussed and changes made immediately.

- ☐ *Data management and online analysis.* Clients can access their survey via the research supplier's secure website and monitor the data gathering in real time. The client can use sophisticated tools to actually carry out data analysis as the survey develops. This real-time analysis may result in changes in the questionnaire, sample size, or types of respondents interviewed. The research supplier and the client become partners in "just-in-time" marketing research.

- ☐ *Publishing and distribution of reports.* Reports can be published directly to the Web from such programs as PowerPoint and all the latest versions of leading word processing, spreadsheet, and presentation software packages. This means that results are available to appropriate managers worldwide on an almost instantaneous basis. Reports can be searched for content of specific interest, with the same Web browser used to view the report.

- ☐ *Oral presentations of marketing research surveys,* which now can be viewed by widely scattered audiences. Managers throughout the world can see and hear the actual client presentation on password-protected websites. This saves firms both time and money, as managers no longer need to travel to a central meeting site.

As we pointed out earlier, the Internet represents the present and the future of a significant portion of the world of marketing research. Its impact is limited only by the researcher's imagination. In this edition of *Marketing Research*, we have pulled all aspects of Internet marketing research into a new chapter (6) to illustrate how the Internet impacts the world of marketing research.

PRACTICING MARKETING RESEARCH

What Is Good about Marketing Research Today

William D. Neal is founder and senior executive officer of SDR Consulting in Atlanta. Bill talks about what he believes is good about marketing research today.

Looking back over the last 40 years, marketing research on the whole has contributed significantly to business success. Investments in marketing research have continued to increase far above the rate of inflation, and operational marketing managers depend more on marketing research to reduce the risks in undertaking new marketing initiatives.

Voice of the customer. More than ever, businesses and other institutions are measuring and monitoring customer satisfaction and loyalty on a continuous basis, using that information to improve processes and stem defections. Fifteen years ago, very little customer satisfaction and loyalty tracking research was supported or funded at all. Now, most major firms and many smaller firms track their customers' levels of satisfaction. And a smaller number are tracking customers' attitudinal and/or behavioral loyalty. Clearly, both the organization and the customer benefit from this revived focus on customer care.

Management metrics. Slowly, but surely, marketing research is beginning to provide some of the key metrics to senior management. Long the exclusive territory of the purveyors of financial numbers, management metrics are beginning to include marketing components—brand health measures, changes in brand equity, advertising and promotional effectiveness measures, indices of customer satisfaction, and several other measures of marketing impact.

New products. Research has often been blamed for the historically abysmal rate of new product failures. However, some of the more recent investigations into new product failures tend to exonerate at least some of the research. More often, the failures occur because (1) there were inadequate investments in research, (2) the research was ignored, (3) what was researched was not what was launched, (4) there was inadequate marketing and promotional support, or (5) there was inadequate sales or fulfillment support. We have several new tools for testing new products, from concept to prelaunch. When used properly, these newer tools greatly reduce the risks inherent in a new product launch and accurately predict trial and repurchase rates under different levels of marketing support.

Branding. After the branding debacles of the early 1990s, many firms began to recognize that their greatest asset is their brands. Unlike any other aspect of the marketing mix, brands represent a component of value that can't be replicated by a competitor. Thus it represents a unique, defensible asset for the owner and a launch pad for new product development and deployment. Unfortunately, branding has long been resistant to the imposition of scientific investigation, relying too much on the creative arts of advertising and promotion. But that is changing. There are now several research-based models for measuring brand value and brand equity and uncovering their key drivers. Quantifiable changes in brand equity represent the ultimate measure of return on marketing investment.[14]

Marketing is an organizational function and a set of processes for creating, communicating, and delivering value to customers and for managing customer relationships in ways that benefit the organization and its stockholders. Marketing managers attempt to get the right goods or services to the right people at the right place at the right time at the right price, using the right promotion technique. This may be accomplished by following the marketing concept, which is based on consumer orientation, goal orientation, and systems orientation.

The marketing manager must work within an internal environment of the organization and understand the external environment over which he or she has little, if any, control. The primary variables over which the marketing manager has control are distribution, price, promotion, and product/service decisions. The unique combination of these four variables is called the *marketing mix*.

Marketing research plays a key part in providing the information for managers to shape the marketing mix. Marketing research has grown in importance because of management's focus on customer satisfaction and retention. It also is a key tool in proactive management. Marketing research should be undertaken only when the perceived benefits are greater than the costs.

A marketing research study can be described as programmatic, selective, or evaluative. Programmatic research is done to develop marketing options through market segmentation, market opportunity analysis, or consumer attitude and product usage studies. Selective research is used to test decisional alternatives. Evaluative research is done to assess program performance.

The Internet has had a major impact on the marketing research industry. The use of Internet surveys has increased dramatically because they can be quickly deployed, cost significantly less, are readily personalized, have high response rates, and provide the ability to contact the hard-to-reach respondent. Most importantly, as Internet participation by households has increased, identical online and offline surveys have been shown to produce the same business decisions.

Marketing research has also found other uses for the Internet. It serves as a major information source, aids in the distribution of RFPs and proposals, facilitates collaboration between the client and the research supplier in the management of a research project, provides data management and online analysis, and allows for the publication and distribution of reports and the viewing of oral presentations by a widely scattered audience. The Internet represents the present and the future of marketing research.

marketing An organizational function and a set of processes for creating, communicating, and delivering value to customers and for managing customer relationships in ways that benefit the organization and its shareholders.

marketing concept A business philosophy based on consumer orientation, goal orientation, and systems orientation.

consumer orientation The identification of and focus on the people or firms most likely to buy a product and the production of a good or service that will meet their needs most effectively.

goal orientation A focus on the accomplishment of corporate goals; a limit set on consumer orientation.

systems orientation The creation of systems to monitor the external environment and deliver the desired marketing mix to the target market.

marketing mix The unique blend of product/service, pricing, promotion, and distribution strategies designed to meet the needs of a specific target market.

marketing research The planning, collection, and analysis of data relevant to marketing decision making and the communication of the results of this analysis to management.

descriptive function The gathering and presentation of statements of fact.

diagnostic function The explanation of data or actions.

predictive function Specification of how to use descriptive and diagnostic research to predict the results of a planned marketing decision.

return on quality Management objective based on the principles that (1) the quality being delivered is at a level desired by the tar-

get market and (2) that level of quality must have a positive impact on profitability.

marketing strategy A plan to guide the long-term use of a firm's resources based on its existing and projected internal capabilities and on projected changes in the external environment.

applied research Research aimed at solving a specific, pragmatic problem—better understanding of the marketplace, determination of why a strategy or tactic failed, or reduction of uncertainty in management decision making.

basic, or pure, research Research aimed at expanding the frontiers of knowledge rather than solving a specific, pragmatic problem.

programmatic research Research conducted to develop marketing options through market segmentation, market opportunity analyses, or consumer attitude and product usage studies.

selective research Research used to test decision alternatives.

evaluative research Research done to assess program performance.

QUESTIONS FOR REVIEW & CRITICAL THINKING

1. The role of marketing is to create exchanges. What role might marketing research play in facilitating the exchange process?
2. Marketing research traditionally has been associated with manufacturers of consumer goods. Today, an increasing number of organizations, both profit and nonprofit, are using marketing research. Why do you think this trend exists? Give some examples.
3. Explain the relationship between marketing research and the marketing concept.
4. Comment on the following statement by the owner of a restaurant in a downtown area: "I see customers every day whom I know on a first-name basis. I understand their likes and dislikes. If I put something on the menu and it doesn't sell, I know that they didn't like it. I also read the magazine *Modern Restaurants* to keep up with industry trends. This is all the marketing research I need to do."
5. Why is marketing research important to marketing executives? Give several reasons.
6. What differences might you note among marketing research conducted for (a) a retailer, (b) a consumer goods manufacturer, (c) an industrial goods manufacturer, and (d) a charitable organization?

7. Comment on the following: Ralph Moran is planning to invest $1.5 million in a new restaurant in Saint Louis. When he applied for a construction financing loan, the bank officer asked whether he had conducted any research. Ralph replied, "I checked on research, and a marketing research company wanted $20,000 to do the work. I decided that with all the other expenses of opening a new business, research was a luxury that I could do without."

8. What is meant by "return on quality"? Why do you think that the concept evolved? Give an example.

9. Describe three situations in which marketing research should not be undertaken. Explain why this is true.

10. Give an example of (a) the descriptive role of marketing research, (b) the diagnostic role of marketing research, and (c) the predictive function of marketing research.

11. Using the Internet and a Web browser, visit a search engine such as Google or Yahoo! and type, "marketing research." From the thousands of options you are offered, pick a website that you find interesting and report on its content to the class.

12. Divide the class into groups of four. Each team should visit a large organization *(Team Exercise)* (profit or nonprofit) and conduct an interview with a top marketing executive to discover how this firm is using marketing research. Each team then should report its findings in class.

13. How is the Internet changing the field of marketing research?

Young Consumers Searching for a Bank Still Want the Personal Touch

REAL-LIFE RESEARCH • 1.1

Raised in an age of evolving technology, many young consumers are still banking the way their parents historically have done, according to a report by Chicago research firm Mintel. The firm found that only 33 percent of consumers 18–34 are using online banking services. In addition, 37 percent of those ages 18–34 say that "better customer service" would cause them to switch banking providers.

With numerous financial service options available, Mintel's research also shows that younger consumers still have concerns about the security of online banking. Some 40 percent of those who do not use online banking state it is because they "don't trust transactions on the Internet."

"Financial services companies continue to elevate their level of safety and security messaging to their consumers, but it is interesting that the Echo Boom and Gen X groups have not necessarily had their fears laid to rest," says Susan Menkie, senior financial services analyst for Mintel. "The fact that many of them still rely upon human interaction for their banking is actually surprising, given the fact that these generations have grown up with the Internet already being a staple in American culture."

In addition, with 80 percent of respondents in the 18–24 range and 83 percent of those ages 25–34 owning debit cards, credit card ownership has been dropping in recent years for these age groups. However, contactless credit cards provide a new outlet for attracting new consumers, with over 60 percent of consumers in this age range showing interest in the newer option.

"Young consumers understand that many of their parents have dealt with credit card debt, specifically during the boom of these types of products and services," says Menke. "Because they have been able to see older consumers dealing with potential debt challenges, it has made some younger consumers more cautious when it comes to using credit cards. Over 70 percent of respondents in the 22–24 age range stated that they do not like the idea of being in debt, and that can significantly impact their relationship with credit card companies."[15]

Questions

1. How might a bank use this information?
2. Could this research have been conducted over the Internet? What other means might have been used to gather the data?
3. Is this basic or applied research? Why?
4. What other type of marketing research information might a bank need to effectively market to young consumers?

APPENDIX 1-A
CAREERS IN MARKETING RESEARCH

Marketing research offers a variety of career paths depending upon one's education level, interests, and personality. Most jobs are to be found with either research suppliers (firms that conduct research for clients) or research users (corporations that depend on marketing research for decision-making guidance). A limited number of marketing research positions are also available with advertising agencies, nonprofit organizations, associations, and various branches of government

Positions with research suppliers (or research firms) tend to be concentrated in a few large cities; for example, New York, Chicago, Los Angeles, San Francisco, and Dallas. Although research suppliers are found throughout the country, a majority of the larger firms (and entry-level jobs) are found in these cities. Research users (corporations, organizations, etc.), on the other hand, tend to be more widely scattered and found in communities of various size; for example, General Mills in Minneapolis; Tyson in Springdale, Arkansas.

Women have long been accepted as equals in the marketing research industry, and some of the larger research firms were founded by women. At the college entry-level position of junior analyst, women are twice as prevalent as men! Obviously, young women increasingly are recognizing the opportunities that await them in the exciting field of marketing research.

There was a time when a decision to go into marketing research represented a lifetime career commitment. Once you were a marketing researcher, there was a good chance you would always be a marketing researcher. Today this inflexibility is not so prevalent. Now it is more common to see people transfer into and out of the marketing research department as part of a career in marketing.

Exhibit 1-A.1 presents a comparative summary of career positions within the research industry. Not all companies have all positions, but you will find people with these titles across the industry. The table also lists the minimum experience and education typical for each position.

EXHIBIT 1-A.1	Career Opportunities in Marketing Research: General Duties and Qualifications		
Positions	**Level of Responsibility**	**Minimum Experience**	**Minimum Education**
Director or vice president	Department administration	10+ years	Graduate degree
Assistant director	Projects administration	5+ years	Graduate degree
Senior analyst	Project supervision	3–5 years	College degree (may require graduate degree)
Analyst	Project analysis and expediting	2–4 years	College degree (may require graduate degree)
Statistician	Statistical analysis	0 years	College degree (may require graduate degree)
Clerical	Office management	3–5 years	Vocational
Junior analyst	Project assistance	0 years	College degree
Field director	Data collection supervisor	3–5+ years	High school diploma
Librarian	Library management	0 years	College degree
Interviewer	Questionnaire administration	0 years	Some high school
Tabulator	Simple tabulation, filing, and organizing	0 years	Some high school

Positions within Supplier Organizations

Research suppliers offer a majority of the entry-level career positions in the marketing research field. Many of the newer firms are entrepreneurial in nature and headed by a founder or partners. In smaller companies the founder-owner not only manages the company but typically is involved in selling and conducting research projects. Owners of larger supplier organizations perform basically the same functions as top managers in other large corporations, such as creating strategic plans and developing broad corporate polices. It is also common in large supplier organizations to have managers that specialize in either a specific industry or type of research; for example, manager of healthcare research, manager of financial research, or political polling. Firms also may have a director of qualitative research or a director of multivariate studies. A list of jobs found in supplier firms follows.

Statistician: A person holding this position is viewed as an internal expert on statistical techniques, sampling methods, and statistical software programs such as SPSS, SAS, or R-Language. Normally, a master's degree or even a PhD is required.

Tabulation programmer: A person holding this position uses tabulation software such as Quantum or UNCLE to create cross-tabulations of survey data. Tabulation programmers are often involved in data cleaning and data management functions, and they may need knowledge of database systems. Normally a bachelor's degree is required.

Senior analyst: A senior analyst is usually found in larger firms. The individual typically works with an account executive to plan a research project and then supervises several analysts who execute the projects. Senior analysts work with a minimal level of supervision themselves. They often work with analysts in developing questionnaires and may help in analyzing difficult data sets. The final report is usually written by an analyst but reviewed, with comments, by the senior analyst and/or account executive. This position is usually given budgetary control over projects and responsibility for meeting time schedules.

Analyst: The analyst usually handles the bulk of the work required for executing research projects. An analyst normally reports to a senior analyst. He or she assists in questionnaire preparation, pretests, then does data analysis, and, finally, writes the preliminary report. Much of the secondary data work is performed by the analyst.

Junior analyst: This is typically an entry-level position for a person with a degree. A junior analyst works under close supervision on rather mundane tasks; for example, editing and coding questionnaires, performing basic statistical analysis, conducting secondary data searches, and writing rough draft reports on simple projects.

Project director: The project director actively manages the flow of research projects, works out schedules, performs quality assurance checks, and provides information and directions to subcontractors and operations. Sometimes the project director is also involved in questionnaire design development of a tabulation plan, and report preparation.

Account executive: An account executive is responsible for making sales to client firms and keeping client organizations satisfied enough to continue funneling work to the research supplier. An account executive works on a day-to-day basis with clients and serves as liaison between the client and the research organization. Account managers must understand each client's problems and know what research techniques should be employed to provide the right data. He or she must be able to explain to the client what research techniques are needed in a nontechnical manner. Moreover, the account executive must be able to sell the firm's services and abilities over competing suppliers. Account executives work hand in hand with research analysts to develop the research methodology to solve the client's problems. This position often requires an MBA or master's degree.

Senior executive (vice president, senior vice president, executive vice president): Typically, this executive oversees several departments or teams of account executives and also has business development responsibilities in addition to managerial responsibilities. These executives are responsible for the hiring, training, and development of account executives, analysts, and project directors; in addition, they spend much of their time in high-level meetings with major clients.

Field work director: Most market research firms do not have their own interviewers. Instead, they rely on market research field services throughout the United States to conduct the actual interviews. Field services are the production line of the market research industry. They hire, train, and supervise interviewers within a specific geographic area. A field work director is responsible for obtaining completed interviews in the proper geographic area, using the specified sampling instructions, within a specified budget and on time. Field work directors keep in close touch with field services thoughout the United States. They know which field services have the best interviewers and can maintain time schedules. After a study has been fielded, the field service director obtains daily reports from the field service. Typical data reported include the number of completed interviews; the number of refusals; interviewing hours, travel time, and mileage; and problems, if any.

Director of operations: Larger research firms will have a large operations function with a number of departments (data preparation, sampling, data entry, tabulation, questionnarie programming, control center, and so on). The director oversees these departments, schedules projects, ensures quality assurance, hires and trains staff, and makes sure that research projects are properly executed.

Positions within Research Departments and Advertising Agencies

Many manufactures, retailers, and other organizations have marketing research departments, although the fashion these days is to call these "consumer insights" departments. These companies, like Kraft, Wal-Mart, Frito-Lay, Sears, and Procter & Gamble, have research groups of varying sizes and responsibilities. Some research departments act like internal research companies, while other research departments function as internal consultants but subcontract all the work to research suppliers. Corporate research departments will often have internal teams headed by directors or managers. Some research departments are organized by brand, while others are organized by research technique specialization. In some companies, competitive intelligence is a separate function, and in others it is a part of the research department. Also, in some companies, strategic planning is a subgroup within the research function, while in others it is a separate department. Organizational structure varies from company to company. Descriptions of some positions follow.

Research director: The research director (sometimes vice president of research or even senior vice president) is responsible for the entire research program of the company. The director may conduct strategic research for top management or accept work from new product managers, brand managers, or other internal clients. In some cases, the director may initiate proposals for studies but typically just responds to requests. He or she has full responsibility for the market research budget and, since resources are limited, may have to set priorities regarding projects undertaken. The director hires the professional staff and exercises general supervision of the research department. He or she normally presents the findings of strategic research projects to top management. This position often requires a master's degree and, in some companies, a PhD. The director is often viewed as the top technical expert in the department as well.

Assistant research director: This position is normally found only in large, full-scale research departments. The person is second in command and reports to the research director. Senior analysts, statisticians, database analysts, syndicated data analysts, secondary data analysts and data processing specialists usually report to the assistant director, who performs many of the same functions as the director.

Research Directors and Others in Limited-Function Research Departments

Most research departments in corporations or advertising agencies are limited in their functions. Therefore, they do not conduct the research or analyze the data. Instead, they formulate requests for research proposals, analyze the proposals, award contracts to research suppliers, and evaluate the supplier's work. Internally, they work with brand managers and new product specialists in formulating research problems and interpreting and implementing the recommendations of the research reports provided by the suppliers.

The research director and assistant director (if any) function in a manner as described earlier. Analysts formulate and evaluate proposals and the work of research suppliers. They also help implement the recommendations. With the exception of a secretary, there is usually no other personnel in a limited-function research department.

Some of the most effective departments in corporate settings and advertising agencies are organized by *brand* or *business unit,* rather than by *function* or *method.* Researchers who are assigned to specific brands are expected to have a working knowledge of many different research processess and approaches. This broad knowledge, as well as daily involvement with a given brand or business unit, creates greater value for the organization as a whole. This person essentially becomes an integral part of a brand or account team, affording him or her a greater understanding of the business issues. In turn, research-based recommendations are often more relevant and actionable.

A Career in Marketing Research at 3M

In order to gain an appreciation for a career in marketing research, we'll examine the career path in one company.

The challenges are tough, but the opportunities available to marketing researchers at 3M are almost limitless. The biggest challenge is that each researcher has an annual goal of a set percentage of time that must be spent on approved projects. The opportunities presented by a large number of businesses, with thousands of products that need research information, are obvious.

The corporate marketing research department consists of about 29 people, organized as in Exhibit 1-A.2. The marketing research project work is carried out by the analysts, senior analysts, supervisors, and the two research managers. (The research manager for corporate planning services works solely for the corporate planning and strategy committee.)

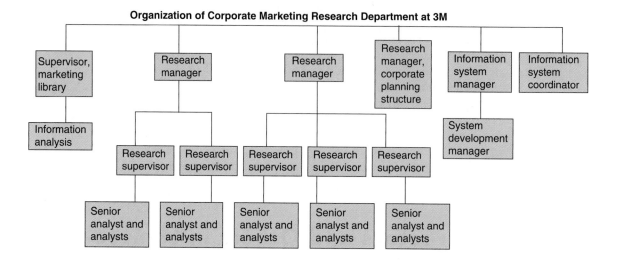

Organization of Corporate Marketing Research Department at 3M

Exhibit 1-A.2

Using Marketing Research—A Corporate Perspective

Projects are obtained through requests from marketing personnel in the operating units or from sales calls made by analysts and senior analysts. A sales call may be the result of follow-up from a previous project, introduction of a new research service, information on new or expanded activity in the operating unit, or the introduction of a new analyst. All project requests take the form of a proposal that outlines the marketing situation, the information needed, how the information will be obtained, timing, and costs. The signed proposal, with an operating unit designated to be charged for the costs, is the authorization to proceed with the project.

The analysts are recruited from university MBA programs and from among 3M employees in other disciplines (e.g., engineering, laboratory) who have obtained an MBA while working at 3M and want to make a career change. Analysts' career goals are in marketing management, but they are interested in, and have an aptitude for, spending three years in marketing research. Just about all of the analysts have post-baccalaureate business experience with 3M or other companies.

In the first year about 60 percent of an analyst's time is spent on research projects for operating units. The remainder of the time is spent in development seminars and classes covering sampling, study design, questionnaire design, focus groups, and other relevant subjects. The classes taken depend on prior experience and aptitude. All analysts take sales training from one of 3M's divisional sales trainers. (They are expected to sell their time to cover their costs, so they are given sales training. Also, managers believe that sales training is very beneficial in developing the personal interviewing techniques required in many projects.)

One year as an analyst, with good performance, qualifies a person for a position as a senior analyst. This is a promotion, and the senior positions require selling close to 100 percent of one's time. The senior analyst is the workhouse of the project system, devoting time entirely to getting projects sold, completed, and reported.

Researchers' projects, for the most part, are divided along sector and group lines. Therefore, an individual's work will have an emphasis in a particular area such as industrial, healthcare, or imaging. However, if a project in one sector calls for an area of expertise that someone assigned to another sector has, that person can cross over for the project. Flexibility is an important element in the personal development of the analysts.

The senior analyst becomes a supervisor in about one year, or sometimes two, and is given a beginning analyst to develop into a competent researcher and future 3M marketer. The supervisor still does operating unit work, handling some of the more complex projects, selling time in the 60 to 80 percent range.

Supervisors will have developed a special rapport with several operating units over the years and will invariably be offered a marketing position in one of the line units at about the time three years have been completed. Alternatively, the managers of corporate marketing research will be asked for a recommendation to fill an operating unit marketing position, and the available supervisors will be recommended for interviews.

As you consider a career in marketing research, there are advantages to gaining experience on both sides of the industry. Here is a brief summary of some key considerations:

Advantages of supplier-side experience:

- ☐ Exposure to a variety of research needs and projects across a wide array of industries

- ☐ Expertise in questionnaire design and project execution gained at every stage

- ☐ Understanding of the detailed technical aspects of the production side of research, including theories behind the approaches

- ☐ Long-term career opportunities; room for advancement within research field

Advantages of corporate and advertising agency experience:

- ☐ Exposure to the broader marketing function

- ☐ Visibility of research results and how they are utilized within client organizations

- ☐ Less need for involvement in "production" issues related to research projects

- ☐ Opportunities to advance either into research or marketing or brand management

To learn about salaries of marketing researchers, go to www.marketingpower.com. Click on "marketing jobs" and then "salary survey." Scroll down to "marketing research," and then select the area of the country or/area of interest to you.

APPENDIX 1-B
MARKETING RESEARCH ETHICS

The two most important factors for research clients in their relationships with research departments/suppliers are client confidentiality and honesty. Each is a question of ethics. **Ethics** are moral principles or values generally governing the conduct of an individual or group. Ethical behavior is not, however, a one-way relationship. Clients, suppliers, as well as field services, must also act in an ethical manner.

 ethics
Moral principles or values, generally governing the conduct of an individual or group.

Ethical questions range from practical, narrowly defined issues, such as a researcher's obligation to be honest with its customers, to broader social and philosophical questions, such as a company's responsibility to preserve the environment and protect employee rights. Many ethical conflicts develop from conflicts between the differing interests of company owners and their workers, customers, and surrounding community. Managers must balance the ideal against the practical—the need to produce a reasonable profit for the company's shareholders with honesty in business practices, and larger environmental and social issues.

Ethical Theories

People usually base their individual choice of ethical theory on their life experiences. The following are some of the ethical theories that apply to business and marketing research.[1]

Deontology

The deontological theory states that people should adhere to their obligations and duties when analyzing an ethical dilemma. This means that a person will follow his or her obligations to another individual or society because upholding one's duty is what is considered ethically correct. For instance, a deontologist will always keep his promises to a friend and will follow the law. A person who follows this theory will produce very consistent decisions since they will be based on the individual's set duties. Note that this theory is not necessarily concerned with the welfare of others. Say, for example, a research supplier has decided that it's his ethical duty (and very practical!) to always be on time to meetings with clients. Today he is running late. How is he supposed to drive? Is the deontologist supposed to speed, breaking his duty to society to uphold the law, or is the deontologist supposed to arrive at his meeting late, breaking his duty to be on time? This scenario of conflicting obligations does not lead us to a clear ethically correct resolution, nor does it protect the welfare of others from the deontologist's decision.

Utilitarianism

The utilitarian ethical theory is founded on the ability to predict the consequences of an action. To a utilitarian, the choice that yields the greatest benefit to the most people is the choice that is ethically correct. One benefit of this ethical theory is that the utilitarian can compare similar predicted solutions and use a point system to determine which choice is more beneficial for more people. This point system provides a logical and rational argument for each decision and allows a person to use it on a case-by-case context.

There are two types of utilitarianism: act utilitarianism and rule utilitarianism. *Act utilitarianism* adheres exactly to the definition of utilitarianism as described in the above section. In act utilitarianism, a person performs the acts that benefit the most people, regardless of personal feelings or the societal constraints such as laws. *Rule utilitarianism*, however, takes into account the law and is concerned with fairness. A rule utilitarian seeks to benefit the most people but through the fairest and most just means available. Therefore, added benefits of rule utilitarianism are that it values justice and doing good at the same time.

As is true of all ethical theories, however, both act and rule utilitarianism contain numerous flaws. Inherent in both are the flaws associated with predicting the future. Although people can use their life experiences to attempt to predict outcomes, no human being can be certain that his predictions will be true. This uncertainty can lead to unexpected results, making the utilitarian look unethical as time passes because his choice did not benefit the most people as he predicted.

Another assumption that a utilitarian must make is that he has the ability to compare the various types of consequences against each other on a similar scale. However, comparing material gains such as money against intangible gains such as happiness is impossible since their qualities differ so greatly.

Casuist

The casuist ethical theory compares a current ethical dilemma with examples of similar ethical dilemmas and their outcomes. This allows one to determine the severity of the situation and to create the best possible solution according to others' experiences. Usually, one will find examples that represent the extremes of the situation so that a compromise can be reached that will hopefully include the wisdom gained from the previous situations.

One drawback to this ethical theory is that there may not be a set of similar examples for a given ethical dilemma. Perhaps that which is controversial and ethically questionable is new and unexpected. Along the same line of thinking, this theory assumes that the results of the current ethical dilemma will be similar to results in the examples. This may not be necessarily true and would greatly hinder the effectiveness of applying this ethical theory.

Understanding ethical theories will help us better decide how certain unethical practices in marketing research should be resolved. Exhibit 1-B.1 details some of the unethical practices most common among the various groups involved in marketing research.

Research Supplier Ethics

Unethical research supplier practices range from low-ball pricing to violating client confidentiality.

Low-Ball Pricing

A research supplier should quote a firm price based on a specific incidence rate (percentage of the respondents in the sample that will qualify to complete the survey) and

EXHIBIT 1-B.1	Unethical Practices in Marketing Research	
Research Suppliers	**Research Clients**	**Field Services**
Low-ball pricing	Issuing bid requests when a supplier has been predetermined	
Allowing subjectivity into the research	Soliciting free advice and methodology via bid requests	Using professional respondents
Abusing respondents		Not validating data
Selling unnecessary research	Making false promises	
Violating client confidentiality	Issuing unauthorized requests for proposal	
Black box branding		

questionnaire length (time to complete). If either of the latter two items changes, then the client should expect a change in the contract price. Low-ball pricing in any form is unethical. In essence, **low-ball pricing** is quoting an unrealistically low price to secure a firm's business and then using some means to substantially raise the price. For example, quoting a price based on an unrealistically high incidence rate is a form of low-ball pricing. Offering to conduct a focus group at $6,000 a group and, after the client commits, saying, "The respondents' fees for participating in the group discussion are, of course, extra" is a form of low-balling.

> **low-ball pricing**
> Quoting an unrealistically low price to secure a firm's business and then using some means to substantially raise the price.

Allowing Subjectivity into the Research

Research suppliers must avoid using biased samples, misusing statistics, ignoring relevant data, and creating a research design with the goal of supporting a predetermined objective. One area of research today is so-called *advocacy studies*. These studies are commissioned by companies or industries for public relations purposes or to advocate or prove a position. For example, Burger King once used positive responses to the following question in an advocacy study in an attempt to justify the claim that its method of cooking hamburgers was preferred over that of McDonald's: "Do you prefer your hamburgers flame-broiled or fried?" When another researcher rephrased the question—"Do you prefer a hamburger that is grilled on a hot stainless-steel grill or cooked by passing the meat through an open gas flame?"—the results were reversed: McDonald's was preferred to Burger King.

Kiwi Brands, a shoe polish company, commissioned a study on the correlation between ambition and shiny shoes. The study found that 97 percent of self-described ambitious young men believe polished shoes are important. In many cases, advocacy studies simply use samples that are not representative of the population. For example, a news release for a diet products company trumpeted: "There's good news for the 65 million Americans currently on a diet." A company study had shown that people who lose weight can keep it off—the sample consisted of 20 graduates of the company's program, who also endorsed its products in commercials.

When studies are released to the news media, the methodology should be readily available to news reporters. Typically, this information is withheld, often on the ground that the material is proprietary. A survey done for Carolina Manufacturer's Service, a coupon redemption company, found that "a broad cross-section of Americans find coupons to be true incentives for purchasing products." The description of the methodology was available only at a price: $2,000.

Abusing Respondents

Respondent abuse can take several forms. Perhaps the most common is lengthy interviews. This problem stems in part from the "as long as you're asking questions" mentality of many product managers. It is not uncommon for clients to request additional "nice to know" questions, or even exploratory questions on an entirely separate project. This leads to lengthy questionnaires, 30-minute telephone or Internet interviews, and 40-minute mall-intercept interviews. As a result of long interviews and telephone sales pitches, more and more Americans are refusing to participate in survey research. The refusal rate for telephone surveys now averages 60-plus percent, an increase of 10 percent over 10 years. Forty-nine percent of the people who do participate say the surveys are "too personal."

Predictive dialers are tremendous productivity tools for survey research telephone call centers. They remove much of the idle time an interviewer would otherwise spend manually dialing numbers and recording call dispositions, such as no-answer and busy signals.

When studies are released to the news media, the methodology should be readily available to news reporters. A survey done for a coupon redemption company found that "a broad cross-section of Americans find coupons to be true incentives for purchasing products." The description of the methodology, however, was available only for a price of $2,000.

PhotoDisc, Inc./Getty Images

By definition, predictive dialers dial phone numbers ahead of available interviewers, predicting when an interviewer will become available. Adjusting the pacing manually sets the aggressiveness of this dial-ahead capability. Obviously, there is strong motivation for call-center managers to increase the pacing and minimize the time an interviewer spends between calls. However, this action has undesirable consequences because some respondents are contacted before an interviewer is available. In most cases, the dialer than places the respondent on hold or disconnects the call. Both actions decrease respondent goodwill.[2]

Interest in a product or service is often discerned during the interviewing process, and the researcher knows the interviewees' potential purchasing power from their answers to income and other pertinent financial questions. Although the introduction phase of the questionnaire usually promises confidentiality, some researchers have sold names and addresses of potential customers to firms seeking sales leads. Individuals willing to participate in the survey research process have a right to have their privacy protected.

The state of New York sued Student Marketing Group for selling information on a broad scale to direct marketers. The survey filled out by students included age, gender, religious affiliation, career interests, and grade point average. The company said that it was gathering the data to provide to universities to help the students gain admission and financial aid. Direct marketers used the information to sell credit cards, magazines, videos, cosmetics, and other products.[3]

Selling Unnecessary Research

A research supplier dealing with a client who has little or no familiarity with marketing research often has the opportunity to "trade the client up." For example, if a project called for four focus groups and an online survey of approximately 350 consumers, the research supplier might sell eight groups and 1,000 Internet interviews, with a 400-interview telephone follow-up in six months.

It is perfectly acceptable to offer a prospective client several research designs with several alternative prices when and if the situation warrants alternative designs. The supplier should point out the pros and cons of each method, along with sample confidence intervals. The client, in consultation with the supplier, then can decide objectively which design best suits the company's needs.

Violating Client Confidentiality

Information about a client's general business activities or the results of a client's project should not be disclosed to a third party. The supplier should not even disclose the name of a client unless permission is received in advance.

The thorniest issue in confidentiality is determining where "background knowledge" stops and conflict arises as a result of work with a previous client. One researcher put it this way:

I get involved in a number of proprietary studies. The problem that often arises is that some studies end up covering similar subject matter as previous studies. Our code of ethics states that you cannot use data from one project in a related project for a competitor. However, since I often know some information about an area, I end up compromising my original client. Even though upper management formally states that it should not be done, they also expect it to be done to cut down on expenses. This conflict of interest situation is difficult to deal with. At least in my firm, I don't see a resolution to the issue. It is not a onetime situation, but rather a process that perpetuates itself. To make individuals redo portions of studies which have recently been done is ludicrous, and to forgo potential new business is almost impossible from a financial perspective.[4]

Black Box Branding

Marketing research suppliers have discovered branding. Synovate has over 25 branded product offerings, including Brand Vision and M2M. Maritz Research offers Loyalty Maximizer, and Harris Interactive has TRBC, a scale bias correction algorithm. Go to virtually any large marketing research firm's website, and you'll see a vast array of branded research products for everything from market segmentation to customer value analysis—all topped off with a diminutive [SM], [TM], or ®.

A common denominator across some of these products is that they are proprietary, which means the firms won't disclose exactly how they work. That's why they're also known pejoratively as black boxes. A black box method is proprietary—a company is able to protect its product development investment. And if customers perceive added value in the approach, suppliers can charge a premium price to boot. (Black boxes and brand names are not synonymous. Almost all proprietary methods have a clever brand name, but there are also brand names attached to research methods that are not proprietary.)

At least two factors have given rise to this branding frenzy. First, competitive pressures force organizations to seek new ways to differentiate their product offerings from those of their competitors. Second, many large research companies are publicly held, and publicly held companies are under constant pressure to increase sales and profits each quarter. One way to do this is to charge a premium price for services. If a company has a proprietary method for doing a marketing segmentation study, presumably it can charge more for this approach than another firm using publicly available software such as SPSS or SAS.

Clients have no objective way of determining whether the results of a proprietary method would vary significantly from those of more standard approaches, and neither have we. Go to five different companies that have five different black boxes for choice modeling, for example. Each company claims its method is superior, yet it's impossible to assess, from a psychometric perspective, which possesses the highest level of validity.

Of course, no one is forcing clients to purchase a black box method, and they can always contact other organizations that have used a supplier's proprietary method to assess its effectiveness. Often clients will obtain multiple bids on a project so that they can select from a variety of approaches to help them answer their research questions.[5]

Client Ethics

Like research suppliers, clients (or users) also have a number of ethical do's and don'ts. Some of the more common client problems are requesting bids when a supplier has been predetermined, requesting bids to obtain free advice and methodology, making false promises, and issuing unauthorized RFPs.

Requesting Bids When a Supplier Has Been Predetermined

It is not uncommon for a client to prefer one research supplier over another. Such a preference may be due to a good working relationship, cost considerations, ability to make deadlines, friendship, or quality of the research staff. Having a preference per se is not unethical. It is unethical, however, to predetermine which supplier will receive a contract and yet ask for proposals from other suppliers to satisfy corporate requirements. Requiring time, effort, and money from firms that have no opportunity to win the contract is very unfair. Why more than a single RFP? Some corporations require more than one bid.

Requesting Bids to Obtain Free Advice and Methodology

Client companies seeking bargain-basement prices have been known to solicit detailed proposals, including complete methodology and a sample questionnaire, from a number of suppliers. After "picking the brains" of the suppliers, the client assembles a questionnaire and then contracts directly with field services to gather the data. A variation of this tactic is to go to the cheapest supplier with the client's own proposal, derived by taking the best ideas from the other proposals. The client then attempts to get the supplier to conduct the more elaborate study at the lower price.

Making False Promises

Another technique used by unethical clients to lower their research costs is to hold out a nonexistent carrot. For example, a client might say, "I don't want to promise anything, but we are planning a major stream of research in this area, and if you will give us a good price on this first study, we will make it up to you on the next one." Unfortunately, the next one never comes—or if it does, the same line is used on another unsuspecting supplier.

Requesting Proposals without Authorization

In each of the following situations, a client representative sought proposals without first receiving the authority to allocate the funds to implement them:

1. A client representative decided to ask for proposals and *then* go to management to find out whether she could get the funds to carry them out.

2. A highly regarded employee made a proposal to management on the need for marketing research in a given area. Although managers were not too enthused about the idea, they told the researcher to seek bids so as not to dampen his interest or miss a potentially (but, in their view, highly unlikely) good idea.

3. A client representative and her management had different ideas on what the problem was and how it should be solved. The research supplier was not informed of the

management view, and even though the proposal met the representative's requirements, management rejected it out of hand.

4. Without consulting with the sales department, a client representative asked for a proposal on analyzing present sales performance. Through fear of negative feedback, corporate politics, or lack of understanding of marketing research, the sales department blocked implementation of the proposal.

Field Service Ethics

Marketing research field services are the production arm of the research industry requiring telephone or face-to-face interviews. They are the critical link between the respondent and the research supplier. It is imperative that they properly record information and carefully follow sampling plans. Otherwise, even the best research design will produce invalid information (garbage in; garbage out). Maintaining high ethical standards will aid a field service in procuring good raw data for the research firm.

Using Professional Respondents

The problem of professional respondents arises most often in the recruitment of focus group participants. Virtually all field services maintain a database of people willing to participate in qualitative discussion groups, along with a list of their demographic characteristics. Maintaining such a list is good business and quite ethical. When qualifications for group participants are easy (for example, pet owners, persons who drive SUVs), there is little temptation to use professional respondents. However, when a supplier wants, for example, persons who are heavy users of Oxydol detergent or who own a Russian Blue cat, it is not unheard of for a group recruiter to call a professional respondent and say, "I can get you into a group tomorrow with a $75 respondent fee and all you need to say is that you own a Russian Blue cat."

In an attempt to weed out professional respondents, a research supplier may specify that the participant must not have been a member of a qualitative discussion group within the past six months. However, dishonest field services will simply tell the professional respondent to deny having participated in a group within the past six months.

Data Collection Code of Ethics

The Marketing Research Association (MRA) is an association to which many field services belong. The organization is dedicated to promoting excellence in data collection. To this end, it recently enacted the following code of ethics:

Companies Engaged in Data Collection . . .

1. will treat the respondent with respect and not influence a respondent's opinion or attitude on any issue through direct or indirect attempts, including the framing of questions.

2. will conduct themselves in a professional manner and ensure privacy and confidentiality.

3. will ensure that all formulas used during bidding and reporting during the data collection process conform with the MRA/Council of American Survey Research Organizations (CASRO) Incidence Guidelines.

4. will make factually correct statements to secure cooperation and will honor promises made during the interview to respondents, whether verbal or written.

5. will give respondents the opportunity to refuse to participate in the research when there is a possibility they may be identifiable even without the use of their name or address (e.g., because of the size of the population being sampled).

6. will not use information to identify respondents without the permission of the respondent except to those who check the data or are involved in processing the data. If such permission is given, the interviewer must record it, or a respondent must do so, during all Internet studies, at the time the permission is secured.

7. will adhere to and follow these principles when conducting online research:

   ☐ Respondents' rights to anonymity *must* be safeguarded.

   ☐ Unsolicited e-mail *must not* be sent to those requesting not to receive any further e-mail.

   ☐ Researchers interviewing minors *must* adhere to the Children's Online Privacy Protection Act (COPPA).

   ☐ Before collecting, using, or disclosing personal information from a child, the researcher must obtain verifiable parental consent from the child's parent.

   Refer to MRA Internet Ethics Guidelines "Use of the Internet for Conducting Opinion and Marketing Research" for more educational information. www.mra-net .org/codes/internet_ethics_guidelines.PDF.

8. for Internet research, will not use any data in any way contrary to the provider's published privacy statement without permission from the respondent.

9. will respect the respondent's right to withdraw or refuse to cooperate at any stage of the study and will not use any procedure or technique to coerce or imply that cooperation is obligatory.

10. will obtain and document respondent consent when it is known that the personally identifiable information of the respondent may be passed by audio, video, or Interactive Voice Response to a third party for legal or other purposes.

11. will obtain permission and document consent of a parent, legal guardian, or responsible guardian before interviewing children 13 years of age or younger. Prior to obtaining permission, the interviewer should divulge the subject matter, length of interview, and other special tasks that may be required of the respondent.

12. will ensure that all interviewers comply with any laws or regulations that may be applicable when contacting or communicating to any minor (18 years old or younger) regardless of the technology or methodology utilized.

13. will not reveal any information that could be used to identify clients without their written authorization.

14. will ensure that companies, their employees, and subcontractors involved in the data collection process adhere to reasonable precautions so that multiple surveys are not conducted at the same time with a specific respondent without explicit permission from the sponsoring company or companies.

15. will consider all research materials provided by the client or generated as a result of materials provided by the client to be the property of the client. These materials will not be disseminated or disposed of without the verbal or written permission of the client.

16. will, as time and availability permit, give their client the opportunity to monitor studies in progress to ensure research quality.

17. will not represent a nonresearch activity to be opinion and marketing research, such as:

   ☐ the compilation of lists, registers, or data banks of names and addresses for any nonresearch purposes (e.g., canvassing or fund raising).

- ☐ industrial, commercial, or any other form of espionage.
- ☐ the acquisition of information for use by credit rating services or similar organizations.
- ☐ sales or promotional approaches to the respondent.
- ☐ the collection of debts.[6]

Respondents' Rights

Respondents in a marketing research project typically give their time and opinions and receive little or nothing in return. These individuals, however, do have certain rights that should be upheld by all marketing researchers. All potential participants in a research project have the right to choose, the right to safety, the right to be informed, and the right to privacy.

Right to Choose

Everyone has the right to determine whether or not to participate in a marketing research project. Some people, such as poorly educated individuals or children, may not fully appreciate this privilege. A person who would like to terminate an interview or experiment may give short, incomplete answers or even false data.

The fact that a person has consented to be part of an experiment or to answer a questionnaire does not give the researcher carte blanche to do whatever she or he wants. The researcher still has an obligation to the respondent. For example, if a person participating in a taste test involving a test product and several existing products prefers the test product, the researcher does not have the right to use the respondent's name and address in a promotion piece, saying that "Ms. Jones prefers new Sudsies to Brand X."

Right to Safety

Research participants have the right to safety from physical or psychological harm. While it is unusual for a respondent to be exposed to physical harm, there have been cases of persons becoming ill during food taste tests. Also, on a more subtle level, researchers rarely warn respondents that a test product contains, say, a high level of salt. An unwitting respondent with hypertension could be placed in physical danger if the test ran several weeks.

It is much more common for a respondent to be placed in a psychologically damaging situation. Individuals might experience stress when an interviewer presses them to participate in a study. Others might experience stress when they cannot answer questions or are given a time limit to complete a task (for example, "You have five minutes to browse through this magazine, and then I will ask you a series of questions").

Right to Be Informed

Research participants have the right to be informed of all aspects of a research task. Knowing what is involved, how long it will take, and what will be done with the data, a person can make an intelligent choice as to whether to participate in the project.

Often, it is necessary to disguise the name of the research sponsor to avoid biasing the respondent. For example, it is poor research practice to say, "We are conducting a survey for Pepsi; which brand of soft drink do you consume most often?" In cases in which disguising the sponsor is required, a debriefing should take place following the completion of the interview. The debriefing should cover the study's purpose, the sponsor, what happens next with the data, and any other pertinent information. A debriefing can reduce respondent stress and build goodwill for the research industry. Unfortunately, taking the time to debrief a respondent is a cost that most companies are unwilling to incur.

In some business and academic research, the researcher may offer to provide the respondent with a copy of the research results as an incentive to obtain his or her participation in the project. When a commitment has been made to disseminate the findings to survey respondents, it should be fulfilled. On more than one occasion, we have participated in academic surveys where the carrot of research results was offered but never delivered.

Right to Privacy

All consumers have the right to privacy. All major research organizations, including the MRA (discussed above), CASRO, the Internet Marketing Research Association (IMRO), the American Marketing Association (AMA), and the Advertising Research Foundation (ARF), have privacy codes. For example, with online research, lists of potential respondents must have one of two characteristics. Potential respondents must have either a prior opt-in for contact or they must have an existing business relationship with the sender through which an e-mail contact would not be considered a random, unsolicited e-mail (spam).

Consumer privacy can be defined in terms of two dimensions of control. The first dimension includes control of unwanted telephone, mail, e-mail, or personal intrusion in the consumer's environment, and the second concerns control of information about the consumer. Consumer privacy can be viewed in the context of any interaction, profit or nonprofit, between marketer and consumer, including (but not limited to) credit and cash sales, consumer inquiries, and marketer-initiated surveys. The very nature of the marketing research business requires interviewers to invade an individual's privacy. An interviewer calls or approaches strangers, requests a portion of their limited free time, and asks them to answer personal questions—sometimes *very* personal questions. Perhaps the greatest privacy issue for consumers today is the role of marketing databases (see Chapter 3).

A number of laws have been passed in recent years dealing with various aspects of privacy as it relates to the marketing research industry. Diane Bowers, president of the CASRO, poses the following questions to marketing researchers:

Did you know. . . .

You may be violating the law if you interview customers of financial institutions who have not consented to that research? (Federal regulations require opt-out; some states require opt-in.)

You may be violating the law if patients you interview for health care research have not consented to that research? (Federal regulations require opt-in.)

You may be violating the law if telephone customers you interview for telecommunications research have not consented to that research? (Federal regulations require opt-out.)

You may be violating the law if you exchange personal data about respondents with someone in Europe without complying with the U.S. Safe Harbor and the EU Directive on Data Protection? (U.S. Safe Harbor principles must be verifiably adhered to, or contractually met, or you must be EU-certified.)

You may be violating the law if you disclose personal information about respondents to a subcontractor, including interviewers and data processors? (Privacy laws require binding confidentiality agreements before any "onward transfer" of such information.)

*You are violating the law if you fail to comply with any material aspect of your online privacy statement or offline privacy policy? (The FTC, for example, has the ability to impose fines of up to several thousands of dollars **per day** for such violations.)*

You are legally and professionally liable for the privacy and confidentiality of your research respondents and the integrity of your research?[7]

Ethics and Professionalism

Today's business ethics are actually a subset of the values held by society as a whole. The values that underlie marketing decisions have been acquired through family, educational, and religious institutions, and social movements (for example, women's rights, environmental protection). A marketing researcher with a mature set of ethical values accepts personal responsibility for decisions that affect the community. Considerations include the following:

☐ Employees' needs and desires and the long-range best interests of the organization

☐ The long-range goodwill and best interests of people who are directly affected by company activities (a bonus: good publicity for the firm)

☐ The societal values and conditions that provide the basis for the social structure in which the company exists

High standards of ethics and professionalism go hand in hand. Good ethics provide a solid foundation for professionalism, and striving for a lofty level of professionalism requires ethical behavior on the part of researchers.

A profession and membership in it are objectively determined; professionalism is evaluated on more personal and subjective levels.

Digital Vision/Getty Images

Fostering Professionalism

Because of the specialized knowledge and expertise they possess, members of a profession have influence and power over those for whom they provide a particular service. The tools of a doctor or lawyer cannot easily be obtained and sold in the marketplace; these professions guard their knowledge and control who has access to it. Although marketing researchers and marketers wield power and influence over their customers and even society, the marketing industry does not have a credentialing process or high entry barriers. The argument can be made that the marketers who most need to think, believe, and behave with professionalism are those in marketing research.

The distinction between a profession and professionalism is important: a **profession** and membership in it are objectively determined (for example, by medical board exams), whereas **professionalism** is evaluated on more personal and subjective levels. A study designed to measure the level of professionalism in marketing research found that researchers had autonomy in their jobs, were permitted to exercise judgment, and were recognized for their level of expertise and ability to work independently. These characteristics are marks

▷ **profession**
Organization whose membership is determined by objective standards, such as an examination.

professionalism
Quality said to be possessed by a worker with a high level of expertise, the freedom to exercise judgment, and the ability to work independently.

of professionalism. However, most researchers did not readily identify the contribution that marketing makes to society, nor did most firms tend to reward researchers' participation in professional organizations. These characteristics do not indicate a high level of professionalism.

Several steps have been taken recently to improve the level of professionalism in the marketing research industry. For example, CASRO has sponsored symposia dealing with ethical issues in survey research. CASRO also has created a code of ethics that has been widely disseminated to research professionals. The CASRO board has worked with groups such as the Marketing Research Association to provide input to legislatures considering antimarketing research legislation.

Researcher Certification

Today, it is far too easy to begin practicing marketing research. We have seen several "fast talkers" convince unwary clients that they are qualified researchers. Unfortunately, relying on poor information to make major decisions has resulted in loss of market share, reduction in profits, and, in some cases, bankruptcy.

Certification has generated a great deal of debate among members of the marketing research industry. It should be noted that certification is not licensing. *Licensing* is a mandatory procedure administered by a governmental body that allows one to practice a profession. *Certification* is a voluntary program administered by a nongovernmental body that provides a credential for differentiation in the marketplace. The issue of certification is sensitive because it directly affects marketing researchers' ability to practice their profession freely.

The MRA has launched a Professional Researcher Certification program. The objectives, according to the MRA, are "to encourage high standards within the profession in order to raise competency, establish an objective measure of an individual's knowledge and proficiency, and to encourage continued professional development."[8] The program allows for certification as a research user, supplier, or data collector. The process requires a series of continuing education credits and then passing an exam. Researchers can be grandfathered into certification if they meet the MRA's standards for a specific research job. The grandfathering period ended on February 28, 2007.

CHAPTER 2

Jetta Productions/Getty Images

PROBLEM DEFINITION, EXPLORATORY RESEARCH, AND THE RESEARCH PROCESS

LEARNING OBJECTIVES

1.	To understand the problem definition process.
2.	To learn the steps involved in the marketing research process.
3.	To understand the components of the research request.
4.	To learn the advantages and disadvantages of survey, observation, and experiment research techniques.
5.	To become familiar with how the marketing research process is initiated.

Today's youth population, the so-called Net Generation born between 1980 and 1996, is undoubtedly of great interest to the consumer electronics industry. They are the first to grow up in the digital world, with the proliferation of the Internet and the introduction of such consumer technologies as wireless phones and DVDs. Since this population segment represents the first tech-savvy generation to enter the consumer buying population, it is of great interest to companies involved in the consumer technologies industries. In particular, the Consumer Electronics Association (CEA), a trade association promoting growth in the consumer technology industry, is very interested in gaining insight into the Net Generation. Among CEA's unanswered questions surrounding this generational group are their attitudes, behaviors, and interests with regard to wireless phones.

CEA's market research department set out to answer those questions by designing a study of the youth population with the following research objectives:

- ☐ Understand usage behaviors among young wireless users, including time devoted to wireless activities, types of activities, and environment (i.e., location and social circumstance).

- ☐ Explore the attitudes, behaviors, and desires around various phone features such as text messaging, Web access, mobile instant messaging, photos, or other features.

- ☐ Define the attitudes, behaviors, and desires around wireless phone personalizations such as skins, ring tones, and custom personalizations (i.e., glitter).

- ☐ Develop insight into behaviors and preferences regarding transporting wireless phones.

The study's participants consisted of both girls and boys across the United Sates, from a mix of urban, suburban, and rural environments, and from a mix of household income levels. In addition to recording their daily phone usage—which included the type of phone activities they were engaging in (voice calls, text messaging, game playing, etc.); the duration of those activities; who they were interacting with; where those activities took place and the total minutes used—they were also asked about phone personalization, transportation, and accessories.

Overall, the project proved extremely successful. It fully met CEA's research objectives.[1]

Gathering data about the Net Generation's cell phone usage (or any other subject) requires marketing research. Conducting marketing research involves a series of logical steps, beginning with problem definition and research objectives. Notice the careful definition of research objectives in the cell phone study. What are the steps in the marketing research process? How is the research process initiated? These are the issues we will address in this chapter.

Critical Importance of Correctly Defining the Problem

Correctly defining the problem is the crucial first step in the marketing research process. If the research problem is defined incorrectly, the research objectives will also be wrong, and the entire marketing research process will be a waste of time and money. A large consumer packaged goods company wanted to conduct a study among a brand's heavy users in order to understand the brand's equity. More specifically, it wanted to expand that equity into new products. The brand had very low penetration, so the company needed new products to meet the upcoming fiscal year's volume goal of double-digit growth. Notice the absence of tying research learning—understanding the brand's equity—to the business objective.

The brand had a small base from which to grow, so simply investigating the brand's equity among its most loyal users wouldn't help decision makers reach a double-digit growth rate. Upon reflection, the business objective focused on identifying marketing levers that would increase brand penetration—and thus growth. Accordingly, the research objectives transformed into understanding barriers to current brand purchase and identifying bridges that would motivate category users to buy the brand.

Study results showed that the brand chiefly suffered from awareness problems. Both brand and category users liked the product, but didn't use it as often as others in the category because they simply forgot about the brand. Reminders—in the form of advertising, incentives, and new products—became the levers that could improve brand penetration and growth. Conducting an equity study among heavy users clearly wouldn't have caught this.[2]

The process for defining the problem is shown in Exhibit 2.1. Note that the ultimate goal is to develop clear, concise, and meaningful marketing research objectives. Researching such objectives will yield precise decision-making information for managers.

Recognize the Problem or Opportunity

The marketing research process begins with the recognition of a marketing problem or opportunity. As changes occur in the firm's external environment, marketing managers are faced with the questions "Should we change the existing marketing mix?" and, if so, "How?" Marketing research may be used to evaluate products and services, promotion, distribution, and pricing alternatives. In addition, it may be used to find and evaluate new opportunities, in a process called **opportunity identification**.

Let's look at an example of opportunity identification. In 2005, online travel spending surpassed offline travel spending for the first time. During that year, $66 billion of leisure and unmanaged business trips were bought through the Internet.[3] Yet, the landscape for consumers is confusing because there are so many sites out there. For savvy marketers, this information represents an opportunity. Marketing research can hone in and clarify where the best opportunities lie.

Marketing research led to the creation of sites like Cheapflights, FareCompare, Kayak, Mobissimo, Ziso, SideStep, and Yahoo's Farechase. These so-called aggregators do what consumers have attempted with their own manual comparison shopping: open several browsers on a computer screen to check multiple travel sites. Aggregators simultaneously scour the websites of airlines, hotels, car rental companies, and consolidators, and present data along with the special deals.

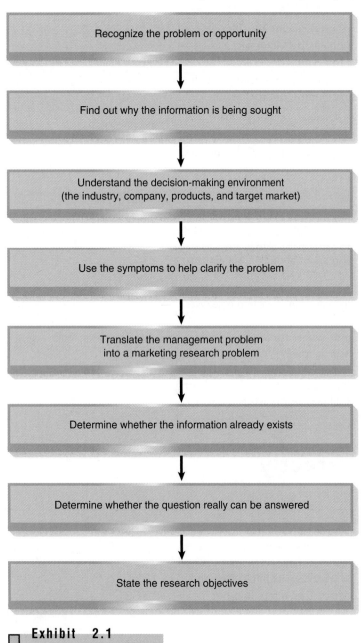

Recognize the problem or opportunity

↓

Find out why the information is being sought

↓

Understand the decision-making environment (the industry, company, products, and target market)

↓

Use the symptoms to help clarify the problem

↓

Translate the management problem into a marketing research problem

↓

Determine whether the information already exists

↓

Determine whether the question really can be answered

↓

State the research objectives

Exhibit 2.1

Problem Definition Process

Mobissimo noticed that other aggregators targeted the U.S. market. Again, this presented an opportunity to fill a niche in the marketplace. Mobissimo offers access to international hotels and many low-fare international carriers that the other aggregators lack. A direct flight from New York to Athens, for instance, may be too expensive. But Mobissimo can fly these travelers to Amsterdam and connect with one of Europe's 50 discount airlines. Marketing research helps firms like Mobissimo understand online travel purchasers' needs and what features they want on an online aggregator website. Satisfaction studies, done every quarter, help track the online travel purchasers' level of satisfaction and loyalty to a site.

> **opportunity identification**
> Using marketing research to find and evaluate new opportunities.

Of course, marketing research doesn't always deal with opportunities. Managers may want to know, for example, "Why are we losing marketing share?" or "What should we do about Ajax Manufacturing lowering its prices by 10 percent?" In these instances, marketing researchers can help managers solve problems.

Find Out Why the Information Is Being Sought

Large amounts of money, effort, and time are wasted because requests for marketing information are poorly formulated or misunderstood. For example, managers may not have a clear idea of what they want or may not phrase their questions properly. Therefore, marketing researchers often find the following activities helpful:

☐ Discuss what the information will be used for and what decisions might be made as a result of the research. Work through detailed examples to help clarify the issue.

☐ Try to get the client or manager to prioritize their questions. This helps sort out central questions from those of incidental interest.

☐ Rephrase the questions in several slightly different forms and discuss the differences.

☐ Create sample data and ask if such data would help answer the questions. Simulate the decision process.

☐ Remember that the more clear-cut you think the questions are and the more quickly you come to feel that the questions are straightforward, the more you should doubt that you have understood the real need.

Understand the Decision-Making Environment with Exploratory Research

Once researchers understand the motivation for conducting the research, often they need additional background information to fully comprehend the problem. This may mean simply talking to brand managers or new product managers, reading company reports, visiting production facilities and retail stores, and perhaps talking with suppliers. If the industry has a trade association, researchers might peruse its website for information published by the association. The better the marketing researcher understands the decision-making environment, including the industry, the firm, its products or services, and the target market, the more likely it is that the problem will be defined correctly. This step may be referred to as conducting a **situation analysis**.

> **situation analysis**
> Studying the decision-making environment within which the marketing research will take place.

Sometimes informed discussions with managers and suppliers and on-site visits aren't enough. **Exploratory research** may be conducted to obtain greater understanding of a concept or to help crystallize the definition of a problem. It is also used to identify important variables to be studied. Exploratory research is preliminary research, not the definitive research used to determine a course of action.

> **exploratory research**
> Preliminary research conducted to increase understanding of a concept, to clarify the exact nature of the problem to be solved, or to identify important variables to be studied.

Exploratory research can take several forms: pilot studies, experience surveys, secondary data analysis, pilot studies case analysis, and focus groups. **Pilot studies** are surveys using a limited number of respondents and often employing less rigorous sampling techniques than are employed in large, quantitative studies.

Nickelodeon, for example, was well aware of the new baby boom and wanted to know what it meant for the network. Exploratory research found that a long-held assumption about kids' attitudes was not accurate: the belief that female images in TV programming generally work with girls but alienate boys. The exploratory research consisted of a small-scale pilot study on the Internet and focus groups in which children were brought together to discuss their attitudes toward television. Like Nickelodeon's research, much exploratory research is highly flexible, with researchers following ideas, clues, and hunches as long as time and money constraints permit. Often ideas are obtained from so-called experts in the field. Nickelodeon, for example, could have spoken with child psychologists.

As the researcher moves through the exploratory research process, a list of marketing research problems and subproblems should be developed. The investigator should identify all factors that seem to be related to the problem area, as these are probable research topics. This stage of problem definition requires a brainstorming-type approach, but one guided by the previous stage's findings. All possibilities should be listed without regard to the feasibility of addressing them via research. Nickelodeon ultimately decided to define the marketing research problem as determining whether a live-action show with girls as the protagonists would appeal to both sexes. Quantitative marketing research results showed that such a program would have dual appeal. Managerial action taken as a result yielded a program where the star was female, but the audience was 53 percent male.[4]

Experience Surveys Analysis

A second form of exploratory research is experience surveys. **Experience surveys** involve talking with knowledgeable individuals, both inside and outside the organization, who may provide insights into the problem. Rarely do experience surveys include a formal questionnaire. Instead, the researcher may simply have a list of topics to be discussed. The survey, then, is much like an informal discussion. For example if Jet Blue is redesigning the interior of its aircraft, it may use experience surveys to speak with interior designers, frequent flyers, flight attendants, and pilots.

Secondary Data Analysis

Secondary data analysis is another form of exploratory research. Because secondary data analysis is covered extensively in Chapter 3, we will touch on it only lightly here. *Secondary data* are data that have been gathered for some purpose other than the one at hand. Today, marketing researchers can use the Internet to access countless sources of secondary data quickly and at minimal expense. There are few subjects that have not been analyzed at one time or another. With a bit of luck, the marketing researcher can use secondary data to help precisely define the problem.

Case Analysis

Case analysis represents the fourth form of exploratory research. The purpose of **case analysis** is to review information from a few other situations that are similar to the present research problem. For example, electric utilities across America are scrambling to adopt the marketing concept and to become customer oriented; these utilities are conducting market segmentation research, customer satisfaction studies, and customer loyalty surveys. To better understand the deregulation of the electric utility industry, marketing researchers are examining case studies on the deregulation of the airline industry. Researchers, however, must always take care to determine the relevancy of any case study to the present research problem.

Focus Groups

Focus groups are in-depth discussions, usually consisting of 8 to 12 participants, which are led by a moderator and are generally limited to one particular concept, idea, or theme. The general idea is to have what one person says generate thoughts and comments by others, therefore creating group dynamics. That is, the interplay of responses will yield more information than if the same number of persons had contributed in individual interviews. Focus groups are the primary topic of discussion in Chapter 4, so they will be lightly covered here. We mention them now because they are probably the most popular form of exploratory research.

Focus groups can, and do, cover just about any topic imaginable. Your authors, unlike all other marketing research text authors, have conducted over 2,000 focus group sessions. When used in exploratory research, focus groups are used to help clarify and understand the problem and issues involved. A few examples of topics that we have covered include: what creates the Harley-Davidson mystique, what happens when you discover head lice in your children, whether having a tequila made in America is a problem, what kitchen item is most difficult to clean, and the list goes on.

Using Intranets for Exploratory Research   The computer can be a very powerful tool for doing exploratory research. In very large organizations with intranets, the researcher has the capability of determining whether needed or relevant information is available somewhere inside the organization. The corporate marketing research department at Texas Instruments (TI), for example, has developed a powerful intranet application that permits TI managers worldwide to search for past research studies and those currently in progress on the basis of key words. They have immediate online access to a brief description of each study and can send e-mail seeking permission to view the full text of reports on old projects. Permission can be granted electronically via e-mail by the owner of the report (the person who paid for it), and the full text can be accessed online.

More and more organizations are developing similar systems to permit much more effective managerial use of information resources. In large organizations, it is not uncommon for a group in one part of the organization to conduct a research project that might have great value to managers in another part of the organization. Too often, there is no way for one group to find out what another group has already done. Intranet systems like the one at Texas Instruments will help organizations get the most mileage out of their research dollars.

While intranets provide easy access to internal data, the Internet is an invaluable resource for searching tens of millions of external sources for the information needed. At the exploratory stage, a researcher might use any one or several of the online search engines to find information needed. This type of search not only is much faster than a traditional library search but also provides access to an incredible array of information that is not available in any library. The researcher can perform an Internet search and point out or download the desired information in a matter of hours rather than the days or weeks a standard library search might require. Finally, the researcher can identify a range of discussion or special-interest groups on the Internet that may be relevant to a research project.

Completing Exploratory Research   The end of exploratory study comes when the marketing researchers are convinced that they have found the major dimensions of the problem. They may have defined a set of questions that can be used as specific guides to a detailed research design. Or they may have developed a number of potential ideas about possible causes of a specific problem of importance to management. They may also have determined that certain other factors are such remote possibilities that they can be safely ignored in any further study. Finally, the researchers may end exploration because they feel that further research is not needed or is not presently possible due to time, money, or other constraints.

Use the Symptoms to Clarify the Problem

Marketing researchers must be careful to distinguish between symptoms and the real problem. A symptom is a phenomenon that occurs because of the existence of something else. For example, managers often talk about the problem of poor sales, declining profits, increased customer complaints, or defecting customers. Each of these is a symptom of a deeper problem. That is, something is causing a company's customers to leave. Is it lower prices offered by the competition? Or is it better service? Focusing on the symptoms and not the true problem is often referred to as the *iceberg principle*. Approximately 10 percent of an iceberg rises out of the ocean; the remaining 90 percent is below the surface. Preoccupied with the obstacle they can see, managers may fail to comprehend and confront the deeper problem, which remains submerged. Marketing researchers Terry Grapentine, president of Grapentine Company and Dianne Weaver, owner of Strategy Resource Company, discuss the role of marketing researchers in problem definition in the Practicing Marketing Research box on page 47.

Ensuring that the true problem has been defined is not always easy. Managers and marketing researchers must use creativity and good judgment. Cutting through to the heart of a problem is a bit like peeling an onion—you must take off one layer at a time. One approach to eliminating symptoms is to ask, "What caused this to occur?" When the researcher can no longer answer this question, the real problem is at hand. For example, when a St. Louis manufacturer of pumps faced a 7-percent decline in sales from the previous year, managers asked, "What caused this?" A look at sales across the product line showed that sales were up or about the same on all items except large, heavy-duty submersible pumps, whose sales were down almost 60 percent. They then asked, "What caused this?" Sales of the pump in the eastern and central divisions were about the same as in the previous year. However, in the western region, sales were zero! Once again they asked, "What caused this?" Further investigation revealed that a Japanese manufacturer was dumping a similar submersible pump in western markets at about 50 percent of the St. Louis manufacturer's wholesale price. This was the true problem. The manufacturer lobbied the Justice Department to fine the Japanese company and to issue a cease and desist order.

> **marketing research problem**
> A statement specifying the type of information needed by the decision maker to help solve the management decision problem and how that information can be obtained efficiently and effectively.

Translate the Management Problem into a Marketing Research Problem

Once the true management decision problem has been identified, it must be converted into a marketing research problem. The **marketing research problem** specifies what information is needed to solve the problem and how that information can be obtained efficiently and effectively. The **marketing research objective**, then, is the goal statement, defining the specific information needed to solve the marketing research problem. Managers must combine this information with their own experience and other related information to make a proper decision.

> **marketing research objective**
> A goal statement, defining the specific information needed to solve the marketing research problem.

In contrast to the marketing research problem, the **management decision problem** is action oriented. Management decision problems tend to be much broader in scope and far more general than marketing research problems, which must be narrowly defined and specific if the research effort is to be successful. Sometimes several research studies must be conducted to solve a broad management decision problem.

> **management decision problem**
> A statement specifying the type of managerial action required to solve the problem.

Determine Whether the Information Already Exists

It often seems easier and more interesting to develop new information than to delve through old reports and data files to see whether the required information already exists.

PRACTICING MARKETING RESEARCH

Driving Action-Producing Research

If researchers conduct research and marketers run the business, then should researchers be responsible for clarifying management objectives? Yes, because corporate researchers ultimately are responsible for the research-yielding action. This role shouldn't be relegated to marketers (who aren't as well versed in research) or research suppliers (who are less familiar with the business as "outsiders," and don't know how the research fits into a larger research and business plan).

Therefore, to design actionable research, researchers must play both marketing and market research roles. If you ran the business, then what would you need to know to make it successful? Starting with this question—and knowing how to answer it—will help you better define management objectives in the absence of clear definition from others.

Putting yourself in the decision maker's shoes is the first step in understanding what information to gather. Albert Einstein was known for doing "mind experiments," in which he would think through the effects of gravity on time and the speed of light. Our goals might not be as lofty, but engaging in this activity can be just as useful. Ask yourself questions such as, "If the research study discovered 'X,' then what decision would I make and how would it affect the business?"

In addition to mind experiments, referring to the business basics can guide your thinking on research design. The following primer covers most strategic business issues that clients face, as well as the levers at their disposal for addressing them. Understanding the specific business issues that the research will address brings clarity to the management objective and, thus, the research.

Basic Business Objectives. Volume loss or desire to gain volume is the crux of most business issues. Three basic objectives and corresponding strategies can gain volume, depending on the business's nature.

- ☐ *Increase penetration*: Grow awareness and trial of new or existing low-penetration products.
- ☐ *Increase buy rate*: Grow usage or loyalty among current customers for high-penetration products.
- ☐ *Steal/stave off competitive volume*: This usually occurs as a share-defense strategy, or a way to increase buy rate in a competitive, mature product category.

Ask yourself, or your client, under which category the business problem falls; the answer will help guide not only the development of research objectives, but also sample composition. To increase penetration, talk to consumers who are in the category but not currently using the brand. To increase buy rate, talk to current customers. To steal or stave off competitive volume, talk to competitive brand users and brand switchers.[5]

Questions

1. Is it the sole responsibility of marketing researchers to define the management problem? Why?
2. What happens if the management problem is defined incorrectly?

There is a tendency to assume that current data are superior to data collected in the past, as current data appear to be a "fix on today's situation." And because researchers have more control over the format and comprehensiveness of fresh data, they promise to be easier to work with. Yet, using existing data can save managers time and money if such data can answer the research question.

Research objectives must be as specific and unambiguous as possible. Remember that the entire research effort (in terms of time and money) is geared toward achieving the objectives. When the marketing researcher meets with a committee to learn the goals of a particular project, committee members may not fully agree on what is needed. We have learned from experience to go back to a committee (or the individual in charge) with a written list of research objectives. The researcher should then ask the manager, "If we accomplish the objectives on this list, will you have enough information to make informed decisions about the problem?" If the reply is yes, the manager should be asked to sign off on the objectives. The researcher should then give the manager a copy and keep a copy for the research files. Putting the agreed-on objectives in writing prevents the manager from saying later, "Hey, this is not the information I wanted." In a busy and hectic corporate environment, such misunderstandings happen more frequently than one might imagine.

Avoiding the Nice-to-Know Syndrome   Even after conducting exploratory research, managers often tend to discuss research objectives in terms of broad areas of ignorance. They say, in effect, "Here are some things I don't know." A Starbucks executive might wonder: "You know, we already sell fresh-baked goods in our stores. . . . I wonder if people would buy frozen Starbucks pastries and rolls in supermarkets?" Maybe I'll ask this question on our out-of-home advertising media study." Unfortunately, this scenario usually leads to disappointment. There is nothing wrong with interesting findings, but they must also be *actionable*. That is, the findings must provide decision-making information. Accomplishment of a research objective has to do more than reduce management's level of ignorance. Unless all the research is exploratory, it should lead to a decision. Perhaps the best way to assure that research is actionable is to determine how the research results will be implemented. Asking a single question about purchase intent of Starbucks frozen baked goods in a grocery store is not actionable. So much more would have to be known—for example, type of goods, price points, packaging design, and so forth. Numerous taste tests would also have to be conducted.

Determine Whether the Question Can Be Answered

When marketing researchers promise more than they can deliver, they hurt the credibility of marketing research. It is extremely important for researchers to avoid being impelled—either by overeagerness to please or by managerial macho—into an effort that they know has a limited probability of success. In most cases, you can discern in advance the likelihood of success by identifying the following:

- Instances in which you know for certain that information of the type required exists or can be readily obtained
- Situations in which you are fairly sure, based on similar prior experiences, that the information can be gathered
- Cases in which you know that you are trying something quite new and there is a real risk of drawing a complete blank

State the Research Objectives

The culmination of the problem definition process is a statement of the research objectives. These objectives are stated in terms of the precise information necessary to address the marketing research problem/opportunity. Well-formulated objectives serve as a road map in pursuing the research project. They also serve as a standard that later will enable managers to evaluate the quality and value of the work by asking "Were the objectives met?" and "Do the recommendations flow logically from the objectives and the research findings?"

Research Objectives as Hypotheses Often researchers state a research objective in the form of a hypothesis. A **hypothesis** is a conjectural statement about a relationship between two or more variables that can be tested with empirical data; it is considered to be plausible, given the available information. A good hypothesis will contain clear implications for testing stated relationships. For example, based on exploratory research, a researcher might hypothesize that a doubling of expenditures for billboards in cities of 300,000 or more population will increase the sales of Starbucks' summer drinks by 15 percent. Alternatively, a second hypothesis might be that spending $30,000 for vehicle wraps in cities of 300,000 or more will have no significant impact on the sales of Starbucks' summer drinks.

> **hypothesis**
> A conjectural statement about a relationship between two or more variables that can be tested with empirical data.

Marketing Research Process

We have just discussed the first step in the marketing research process: identifying the problem/opportunity and stating the marketing research objectives. The other steps in the process are creating the research design, choosing the method of research, selecting the sampling procedure, collecting the data, analyzing the data, writing and presenting the report, and following up on any recommendations that were made as a result of the report (see Exhibit 2.2). The overview of the process in this section forms the foundation for the remainder of the text. The following chapters examine specific aspects of the marketing research process.

Creating the Research Design

The **research design** is a plan for addressing the research objectives or hypotheses. In essence, the researcher develops a structure or framework to answer a specific research problem/opportunity. There is no single best research design. Instead, different designs offer an array of choices, each with certain advantages and disadvantages. Ultimately, trade-offs are typically involved. A common trade-off is between research costs and the quality of the decision-making information provided. Generally speaking, the more precise and error-free the information obtained, the higher the cost. Another common trade-off is between time constraints and the type of research design selected. Overall, the researcher must attempt to provide management with the best information possible, subject to the various constraints under which he or she must operate. The researcher's first task is to decide whether the research will be descriptive or causal.

> **research design**
> The plan to be followed to answer the marketing research objectives.

Descriptive Studies **Descriptive studies** are conducted to answer who, what, when, where, and how questions. Implicit in descriptive research is the fact that management already knows or understands the underlying relationships among the variables in the problem. A **variable** is simply a symbol or concept that can assume any one of a set of values.

A descriptive study for Starbucks might include demographic and lifestyle characteristics of typical, light, and heavy patronizers of Starbucks stores, purchasers of Starbucks baked goods, purchasers of Starbucks sandwiches, and buyers of coffee to take home. Other questions might determine drive time from work or home to the nearest Starbucks and if purchasers pay by cash or credit.

Descriptive research can tell us that two variables, such as advertising and sales, seem to be somehow associated, but it cannot provide convincing evidence that high levels of advertising cause high sales. Because descriptive research can shed light on associations or relationships, it helps the researcher select variables for a causal study.

> **descriptive studies**
> Research studies that answer the questions who, what, when, where, and how.

> **variable**
> A symbol or concept that can assume any one of a set of values.

Exhibit 2.2

Marketing Research Process

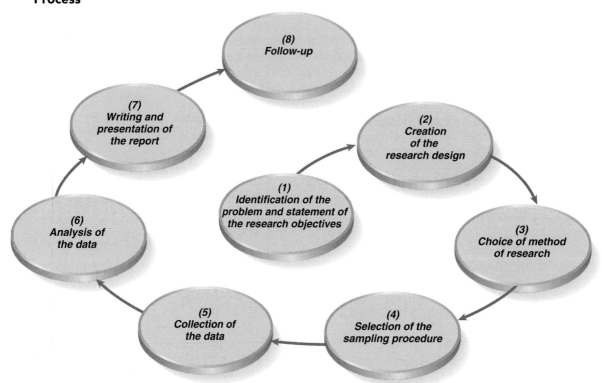

causal studies
Research studies that examine whether the value of one variable causes or determines the value of another variable.

dependent variable
A symbol or concept expected to be explained or influenced by the independent variable.

independent variable
A symbol or concept over which the researcher has some control and that is hypothesized to cause or influence the dependent variable.

Causal Studies In **causal studies**, the researcher investigates whether the value of one variable causes or determines the value of another variable, in an attempt to establish linkage between them. Experiments (see Chapter 7) often are used to measure causality. A **dependent variable** is a symbol or concept expected to be explained or affected by an independent variable. In contrast, an **independent variable** is a variable that the market researcher can, to some extent, manipulate, change, or alter. An independent variable in a research project is a presumed cause of or influence on the dependent variable, the presumed effect. For example, Starbucks would like to know whether the level of advertising (independent variable) determines the level of sales (dependent variable).

A causal study for Starbucks might involve changing one independent variable (for example, the number of direct mailings offering a 10-percent discount on a one-pound bag of coffee over a six-month period to target customers) and then observing the effect on coffee sales. Here, there is an appropriate causal order of events, or **temporal sequence**; the effect follows closely the hypothesized cause. Temporal sequence is one criterion that must be met for causality.

A second criterion for causality is **concomitant variation**—the degree to which a presumed cause (direct-mail promotion) and a presumed effect (coffee sales) occur together or vary together. If direct-mail promotions are a cause of increased coffee sales, then when the number of direct-mail promotions is increased, coffee sales should go up, and when the number of promotions is decreased, sales should fall. If, however, an increase in direct-mail promotions does not result in an increase in coffee sales, the researcher

must conclude that the hypothesis about the relationship between direct-mail promotions and coffee sales is not supported.

An ideal situation would be one in which sales of coffee increased markedly every time Starbucks increased its direct-mail promotions (up to a saturation level). But, alas, we live in a world where such perfection is rarely achieved. One additional bulk mailing might bring a small increase in sales and the next mailing a larger increment, or vice versa. And, during the next six-month period, an increase in direct-mail promotions might produce no increase or even a decline in sales.

Remember, even perfect concomitant variation would not prove that A causes B. All the researcher could say is that the association makes the hypothesis more likely.

An important issue in studying causality is recognizing the possibility of **spurious association**, in which other variables are actually causing changes in the dependent variable. In an ideal situation, the researcher would demonstrate a total absence of other causal factors. However, in the real world of marketing research, it is very difficult to identify and control all other potential causal factors. Think for a moment of all the variables that could cause sales of one-pound bags of coffee to increase or decrease—for example, prices, newspaper and television advertising, coupons, discounts, and weather. The researcher may be able to lower spurious associations by trying to hold constant these other factors. Alternatively, the researcher may look at changes in sales in similar socioeconomic areas.

Choosing a Basic Method of Research

A research design, either descriptive or causal, is chosen based on a project's objectives. The next step is to select a means of gathering data. There are three basic research methods: (1) survey, (2) observation, and (3) experiment. Survey research is often descriptive in nature but can be causal. Observation research is typically descriptive, and experiment research is almost always causal.

Surveys **Survey research** involves an interviewer (except in mail and Internet surveys) who interacts with respondents to obtain facts, opinions, and attitudes. A questionnaire is used to ensure an orderly and structured approach to data gathering. Face-to-face interviews may take place in the respondent's home, a shopping mall, or a place of business.

Observations **Observation research** is examining patterns of behavior as opposed to asking consumers why they do what they do. This may involve people watching consumers or the use of a variety of machines. Since 2000, Kimberly-Clark, the maker of Huggies, Kleenex, and other household staples, has outfitted consumers with mini video

temporal sequence An appropriate causal order of events.

concomitant variation The degree to which a presumed cause and a presumed effect occur or vary together.

Survey research is the most popular form of marketing research.

Jeffrey Greenberg/Photo Researchers, Inc

spurious association A relationship between a presumed cause and a presumed effect that occurs as a result of an unexamined variable or set of variables.

survey research Research in which an interviewer (except in mail and Internet surveys) interacts with respondents to obtain facts, opinions, and attitudes.

observation research Typically, descriptive research that monitors respondents' actions without direct interaction.

cameras mounted to visors and linked to a recording device. Paid participants wear the somewhat strange-looking eye gear, known internally as the Consumer Vision System (CVS), while doing chores or shopping.

Under the system, K-C discovered that mothers who used Huggies Baby Wash, a bathing lotion, had trouble holding the bottle and needed two hands to open and dispense its contents. "[Moms] almost always have to have one hand on the baby at one time," said Becky Walter, K-C director–innovation, design and testing.[6]

K-C redesigned the product with a grippable bottle and a large lid that could easily be lifted with a thumb. The result was a significant increase in market share. Observation research is discussed in detail in Chapter 6.

> **experiments**
> Research to measure causality, in which the researcher changes one or more independent variables and observes the effect of the changes on the dependent variable.

Experiments **Experiments** are the third method researchers use to gather data. Experiment research is distinguished by the researcher's changing one or more independent variables—price, package, design, shelf space, advertising theme, or advertising expenditures—and observing the effects of those changes on a dependent variable (usually sales). The objective of experiments is to measure causality. The best experiments are those in which all factors other than the ones being manipulated are held constant. This enables the researcher to infer with confidence that changes in sales, for example, are caused by changes in the amount of money spent on advertising.

Holding all other factors constant in the external environment is a monumental and costly, if not impossible, task. Factors such as competitors' actions, weather, and economic conditions in various markets are beyond the control of the researcher. One way researchers attempt to control factors that might influence the dependent variable is to use a laboratory experiment—that is, an experiment conducted in a test facility rather than in the natural environment. Researchers sometimes create simulated supermarket environments, give consumers scrip (play money), and then ask them to shop as they normally would for groceries. By varying package design or color over several time periods, for example, the researcher can determine which package is most likely to stimulate sales. Although laboratory techniques can provide valuable information, it is important to recognize that the consumer is not in a natural environment; how people act in a test facility may differ from how they act in an actual shopping situation. Experiments are discussed in detail in Chapter 7.

Selecting the Sampling Procedure

A sample is a subset from a larger population. Although the basic nature of the sample is specified in the research design, selecting the sampling procedure is a separate step in the research process. Several questions must be answered before a sampling procedure is selected. First, the population or universe of interest must be defined. This is the group from which the sample will be drawn. It should include all the people whose opinions, behaviors, preferences, attitudes, and so on will yield information needed to answer the research problem—for example, all persons who eat Mexican food at least once every 60 days.

> **probability sample**
> A subset of a population where every element in the population has a known nonzero chance of being selected.

> **nonprobability sample**
> A subset of a population in which the chances of selection for the various elements in the population are unknown.

After the population has been defined, the next question is whether to use a probability sample or a nonprobability sample. A **probability sample** is a sample for which every element in the population has a known nonzero probability of being selected. Such samples allow the researcher to estimate how much sampling error is present in a given study. All samples that cannot be considered probability samples are nonprobability samples. **Nonprobability samples** are those in which the chances of selection for the various elements in the population are unknown. Researchers cannot statistically calculate the reliability of a nonprobability sample; that is, they cannot determine the degree of sampling error that can be expected. Sampling is the topic of Chapter 11.

Collecting the Data

Most survey-based data are now collected on the Internet. Interviewer-based data collection is done by marketing research field services. Field service firms, found throughout the country, specialize in collecting data through personal and telephone interviewing on a subcontract basis. A typical interviewer-based research study involves data collection in several cities and requires working with a comparable number of field service firms. To ensure that all subcontractors do everything exactly the same way, detailed field instructions should be developed for every job. Nothing should be left to chance; in particular, no interpretations of procedures should be left to the subcontractors.

In addition to doing interviewing, field service firms often provide group research facilities, mall intercept locations, test product storage, and kitchen facilities for preparing test food products. They may also conduct retail audits (counting the amount of product sold from retail shelves).

Analyzing the Data

After the data have been collected, the next step in the research process is data analysis. The purpose of this analysis is to interpret and draw conclusions from the mass of collected data. The marketing researcher may use a variety of techniques, beginning with simple frequency analysis and culminating in complex multivariate techniques. Data analysis will be discussed later in the text.

Writing and Presenting the Report

After data analysis is completed, the researcher must prepare the report and communicate the conclusions and recommendations to management. This is a key step in the process because a marketing researcher who wants project conclusions acted on must convince the manager that the results are credible and justified by the data collected.

The researcher usually will be required to present both written and oral reports on a project. The nature of the audience must be kept in mind when these reports are being prepared and presented. The oral report should begin with a clear statement of the research objectives, followed by an outline of the methodology. A summary of major findings should come next. The report should end with a presentation of conclusions and recommendations for management. In today's fast-paced world of marketing research, long, elaborately written reports are virtually a thing of the past. Decision makers today typically want only a copy of the PowerPoint presentation.

Judging the Quality of a Report Because most people who enter marketing become research users rather than research suppliers, it is important to know what to look for in a research report. The ability to evaluate a research report is crucial. As with many other items we purchase, the quality of a research report is not always readily apparent. Nor does paying a high price for a project necessarily guarantee superior quality. The basis for measuring a report's quality lies in the research proposal. Does the report meet the objectives established in the proposal? Has the methodology outlined in the proposal been followed? Are the conclusions based on logical deductions from the data analysis? Do the recommendations seem prudent, given the conclusions?

Using the Internet to Disseminate Reports It is becoming increasingly commonplace for research suppliers and clients to publish reports directly to the Web. All of the latest versions of major word-processing, spreadsheet, and presentation packages have the capability to produce Web-ready material, which simplifies the process of putting reports on the Web. Most companies, such as Texas Instruments, locate this material not in public areas on the Web but on corporate intranets or in password-protected locations on websites. Publishing reports on the Web has a number of advantages:

1. The reports become immediately accessible to managers and other authorized and interested parties worldwide.
2. The reports can incorporate full multimedia presentation, including text, graphs, various types of animation, audio comments, and video clips.
3. The reports are fully searchable. Suppose a manager is interested in any material relating to advertising. Instead of manually scanning a long and detailed report for such mentions, he or she can search the report for comments relating to advertising.

Following Up

After a company has spent a considerable amount of effort and money on marketing research and the preparation of a report, it is important that the findings be used. Management should determine whether the recommendations were followed and, if not, why not. As you will learn in the next section, one way to increase the likelihood that research conducted by a corporate marketing department will be used is to minimize conflict between that department and other departments within the company.

Managing the Research Process

The Research Request

> **research request**
> An internal document used by large organizations that describes a potential research project, its benefits to the organization, and estimated costs; it must be formally approved before a research project can begin.

Before conducting a research project, a company such as Microsoft might require approval of a formal research request. Moderate- and large-size retailers, manufacturers, and nonprofit organizations often use the **research request** as a basis for determining which projects will be funded. Typically, in larger organizations there are far more requests by managers for marketing research information than monies available to conduct such research. Requiring a research request is a formalized approach to allocating scarce research dollars.

It is very important for the brand manager, new product specialist, or whoever is in need of research information to clearly state in the formal research request why the desired information is critical to the organization. Otherwise, the person with approval authority may fail to see why the expenditure is necessary.

In smaller organizations, the communication link between brand managers and marketing researchers is much closer. Their day-to-day contact often removes the need for a formal research request. Instead, decisions to fund research are made on an ad hoc basis by the marketing manager or the director of marketing research.

Completion and approval of the request represent a disciplined approach to identifying research problems and obtaining funding to solve them. The degree of effort expended at this step in the research process will be reflected in the quality of the information provided to the decision maker because a well-conceived research request will guide the design, data-gathering, analysis, and reporting processes toward a highly focused objective. The sections of a formal research request are as follows:

1. *Action.* The decision maker should describe the action to be taken on the basis of the research. This will help the decision maker focus on what information should be obtained and guide the researcher in creating the research design and in analyzing the results.
2. *Origin.* The decision maker should state the events that led to a need for a decision. This will help the researcher understand more deeply the nature of the management decision problem.

3. *Information.* The decision maker should list the questions that she or he needs to have answered to take action. Carefully considering the questions will improve the efficiency of the research.

4. *Use.* This section should explain how each piece of information will be used to help make the actual decision. By giving logical reasons for each part of the research, it will ensure that the questions make sense in light of the action to be taken.

5. *Target groups and subgroups.* By describing those from whom information must be gathered to address the research problem, this section will help the researcher design the sample procedure for the research project.

6. *Logistics.* Time and budget constraints always affect the research technique chosen for a project. For this reason, approximations of the amount of money available and the amount of time left before results are needed must be included as a part of the research request.

7. *Comments.* Any other comments relevant to the research project must be stated so that, once again, the researcher can fully understand the nature of the problem.

Request for Proposal

The research request is an internal document used by management to determine which projects to fund. A **request for proposal (RFP)** is a solicitation sent to marketing research suppliers inviting them to submit a formal proposal, including a bid. An actual RFP, adapted slightly for the purposes of this text, is shown in Exhibit 2.3. The RFP is the lifeblood of a research supplier. Receiving it is the initial step in getting new business and, therefore, revenue.

> **request for proposal (RFP)**
> A solicitation sent to marketing research suppliers inviting them to submit a formal proposal, including a bid.

A typical RFP provides background data on why a study is to be conducted, outlines the research objectives, describes a methodology, and suggests a time frame. In some RFPs, the supplier is asked to recommend a methodology or even help develop the research objectives. Most RFPs also ask for (1) a detailed cost breakdown, (2) the supplier's experience in relevant areas, and (3) references. Usually, a due date for the proposal will be specified.

Suppliers must exercise care in preparing their proposals in response to the RFP. More than one client has said, "We find the quality of the proposals indicative of the quality of work produced by the firm." Thus, a research supplier that doesn't have the necessary time to adequately prepare a proposal should simply not submit a bid.

The Marketing Research Proposal

When marketing research suppliers receive an RFP, they respond to the potential client with a research proposal. The **research proposal** is a document that presents the research objectives, research design, time line, and cost of a project. We have included an actual proposal (disguised) prepared by two project managers at Decision Analyst (a large international marketing research firm) in Appendix 2-A. Most research proposals today are short (3 to 5 pages) and are transmitted back to the potential client as an e-mail attachment. A proposal for the federal government can run 50 pages or longer. The federal proposal will include a number of standard forms mandated by the government.

> **research proposal**
> A document developed, usually in response to an RFP, that presents the research objectives, research design, time line, and cost of a project.

Most proposals contain the following elements:

I. Title Page
This includes the title of the project from the RFP; the names of the preparers of the proposal, and contact information; who the proposal is being prepared for; and the date.

Exhibit 2.3

An RFP to Conduct an Image Benchmark Study

Background

Mega Health has been tracking consumers' awareness and image of our plan on an annual as well as monthly basis for many years. These studies have been conducted for the purpose of understanding our brand awareness, brand image, and brand benchmarking vs. the competition. As we plan for advertising and public communication, we first need to determine how Mega Health is perceived in the marketplace. The annual Brand Image Benchmarking study allows Mega Health to assess its brand image in a competitive context.

Issue

Assess overall Mega Health brand strength by surveying individuals (in MD/DC/VA regions) in the 3rd–4th quarter of 2009, using a version of the current survey instrument.

Objectives

- Assess brand awareness and image of Mega Health in the MD/DC/VA regions.
- Benchmark Mega Health awareness and image vs. competitors in all regions.
- Determine importance of health insurance company/HMO attributes.
- Assess rating of Mega Health and competitor performance on health insurance company/HMO attributes.
- Assess reaction to attributes of Mega Health.
- Profile insured population.
- Create comprehensive brand image analysis.

Methodology

Quantitative telephone survey with the general public and business decision makers.*

Sample:
- Total interviews: 1950.
  General public: approx. 1250 interviews (may need as many as 300 over sample—1550 total—to improve representation in harder-to-recruit areas). RDD methodology. *Business decision makers:* approx. 400 interviews.
- List sources and detailed sampling methodology: to be determined.
- Quota for the study should be representative of 5 mid-Atlantic regions: Baltimore Metro, DC Metro, Eastern Shore MD, Southern MD, and Western MD (Southern and Western MD may be combined after study completion). Mega Health will provide zip codes in order to delineate regions.

Questionnaire: This study is being conducted for benchmarking and tracking purposes. Thus, the questionnaire that has previously been used to conduct this research has been included (see attachment). Some modifications to this questionnaire may be necessary for improved analysis.

Proposed Timing

Develop RFP for research	8/11/09
Select vendor	8/17/09
Sample and survey adjusted/finalized	8/30/09
Initiate interviews (including recruiting)	9/1/09
Complete interviews	10/4/09
Topline analysis	10/15/09
Final analysis†	11/1/09

We would like to begin the preparation for this study, so please expedite the return of proposals as soon as possible. Thank you for your consideration. Please contact Joe Bedlow at 999-998-7513 (fax: 999-998-7660; email: joebedlow@megahealth.com) with any questions or proposals.

*Sample of general public and decision makers subject to change. *Note*: The population from which to sample business decision makers is typically not very large and can be more difficult to recruit, especially larger businesses (1000+ employees).

†It is most important that the "general public" sample be completed within this time frame. Business decision makers' results may be afforded a later date, if needed.

Note: *The real company name, contract name, and phone numbers have been disguised.*

II. Statement of the Research Objectives

These are often stated in the RFP. If not, they must be determined as described earlier in the chapter.

III. Study Design

This presents a statement of how the data will be gathered and who will be sampled and the sample size.

IV. Areas of Questioning

This is not found in all proposals, but in our experience we have found it to be very helpful. It is a tentative list of survey topics based on the research objectives.

V. Data Analysis

This states which techniques will be used to analyze the data.

VI. Personnel Involved

This provides a complete list of all supervisory and analytical personnel who will be involved in the project and a short vita of each. Each person's responsibility is also outlined. This element is typically not included when the client and supplier have an ongoing relationship. It is mandatory in most government work.

VII. Specifications and Assumptions

Most RFPs are relatively short and don't spell out every detail. In order to make certain that the supplier and potential client are on the same page, it is a good idea to list the specifications and assumptions that were made when creating the proposal (see Appendix 2-A).

Exhibit 2.4 details the benefits of a good proposal to both the client and the supplier.

VIII. Services

This spells out exactly what the research supplier will do (see Appendix 2-A). For example, who is designing the questionnaire? Is it the client, the supplier, or is it a joint effort? Again, the purpose is to make sure that the client and the research supplier operate from the same set of expectations.

IX. Cost

This specifies the cost and payment schedule.

X. Timing

This states when various phases of the project will be completed and provides a final completion date.

Preparing proposals may be the most important function a research supplier performs inasmuch as proposals, and their acceptance or rejection, determine the revenue of the firm. If a research firm's proposals are not accepted, the company will have no funds and will ultimately go out of business! Moreover, if the price that is quoted is too low, the researcher may get the job but lose money. If the price is too high, the proposal may be outstanding, but the researcher will lose the work to a competitor.

What to Look for in a Marketing Research Supplier

Market Directions, a Kansas City marketing research firm, asked marketing research clients around the United States to rate the importance of several statements about research companies and research departments. Replies were received from a wide range of industries, resulting in the following top 10 list of desirable qualities in marketing researchers:

1. Maintains client confidentiality

2. Is honest

3. Is punctual

EXHIBIT 2.4	Benefits of a Good Proposal
Client	**Supplier**
Serves as a road map for the project	Serves as a road map for the project
☐ specifies research methodology ☐ specifies time line ☐ specifies deliverables ☐ specifies projected costs ☐ allows for planning-team member involvement and resource allocation	☐ identifies specific responsibilities of the vendor ☐ identifies the role the client has in fielding the research ☐ allows for planning-team member involvement and resource allocation
Ensures that competing vendors carefully consider:	Serves as a valuable tool for managing client expectations, especially when the client:
☐ project specifications ☐ research design/methodology ☐ project cost	☐ contributes to delays or revises project timeline ☐ mandates changes to project scope ☐ requests additional or alternative deliverables ☐ cancels the project
Ensures that the selected vendor has an explicit understanding of business decisions the research will affect	Provides an objective method for clients to examine vendor qualifications
Prompts the client to consider unique capabilities that individual firms offer, which might contribute to project success	

Source: Matthew Singer, "Writer's Lock," *Marketing Research* (Fall 2006), p. 38.

4. Is flexible

5. Delivers against project specifications

6. Provides high-quality output

7. Is responsive to the client's needs

8. Has high quality-control standards

9. Is customer oriented in interactions with client

10. Keeps the client informed throughout a project[7]

The two most important qualities, confidentiality and honesty, are ethical issues; the remaining factors relate to managing the research function and maintaining good communications.

Good communications are a necessity. Four of the qualities on the top 10 list—flexibility, responsiveness to clients' needs, customer orientation, and keeping the client informed—are about good communications. A successful marketing research organization requires good communications both within the research company and with clients.

How important is communication? Consider this: Managers spend at least 80 percent of every working day in direct communication with others. In other words, 48 minutes of every hour are spent in meetings, on the telephone, or talking informally. The other 20 percent of a typical manager's time is spent doing desk work, most of which is communication in the form of reading and writing.[8] Communications permeate every aspect of managing the marketing research function.

One of the hottest markets in the world today is China. The accompanying Global Research box discusses conducting marketing research in this rapidly developing market.

GLOBAL RESEARCH

Tapping the China Market

Matthew Harrison is a director of B2B International, a United Kingdom-based marketing research firm that has recently set up an office in Beijing. He discusses conducting marketing research in China below.

To most Western companies, the idea of commissioning market research in China can be daunting. Frequently, they see the perceived barriers of researching a Chinese market as so insurmountable that they make no serious consideration of the potential benefits. For companies wishing to conduct or commission research, however, the opportunity in China is enormous. This is a huge, diverse, growing, and increasingly affluent and innovative economy eager to share its ideas with potential investors. China might not be the easiest country in which to conduct research, but for the research buyer, the value of the obtained information can be enormous.

Market Size and Sectors

Although the Chinese market research industry has existed for about two decades, its development has been relatively slow. Even today, the value of market research commissioned in China is worth approximately 5,000 million renminbi (RMB), or $636.1 million. However, the market is growing rapidly—at around 20 percent per annum.

B2B Research. B2B is defined as market research in which an organization seeks the views of businesspeople to facilitate a business decision. It also incorporates projects in which organizations seek the views of government officials, and medical or pharmaceutical projects in which organizations seek the views of physicians, for example.

Estimates of the proportion of the Western market research industry that is composed of B2B research are usually at about 10 percent. In China, however, the proportion is at about 25 to 30 percent, putting its value at about $180.3 million. This B2B sector of the market is expected to experience the most growth over the coming years—with Chinese companies increasingly open to the idea of obtaining the views of businesspeople and Western companies ever hungrier for Chinese business opinions. Estimates of current growth in this part of the market are at about 25 percent per annum.

In terms of the industries in which an organization conducts most market research, the picture is changing rapidly. Nevertheless, some clear patterns are emerging—for example, the fast-moving consumer goods sector is progressively more buoyant. In business research, the level of commissioned work can be ranked as:

1. automotive
2. petrochemical
3. information technology (IT)
4. pharmaceutical and medical
5. financial

Foreign-owned companies with joint ventures or subsidiaries within China commission most automotive and petrochemical research. In the telecom and IT markets, indigenous companies increasingly have the budgets and strategic vision to recognize the benefits of business research. The pharmaceutical/medical and financial markets are both significant and have huge potential. The financial market is now exposed to increasing competition, with state-owned companies registered on the Chinese stock exchange and permitted to commission market research. And the pharmaceutical and medical market is growing rapidly, with domestic and foreign companies seeking information to be able to profit from the huge Chinese market.

Across industries, the type of research that an organization commissions is markedly different from that in Europe and North America. In the West, research reflects the objectives of companies operating in mature markets, which want to establish customer loyalty, achieve differentiation through branding, monitor the satisfaction of their employees, develop new concepts, or segment their target audiences. Typical research projects are therefore customer and employee satisfaction studies, branding studies, concept tests, and segmentations. In China, however, about 60 percent of research projects are focused on market assessment studies in which clients (often foreign companies) ask for a comprehensive explanation of market size and structure. In the Western economies, research buyers generally seek intelligence that will help them progress in existing markets—whereas in China, much of the research is about entering new markets.

Active Market Companies

Identifying the correct agency is difficult for any company aiming to conduct market research in China. There are a number of impediments, including the absence of a comprehensive English-language directory of the key players. The website of ESOMAR, the World Association of Research Professionals, is currently the best English-language source of contact details for research agencies in China—but even this contains the particulars of only about 50 agencies from the 1,000-plus active in the country. It is fair to state, however, that this list contains both the majority of the main full-service agencies and agencies with a cross-China capability. The website of the Chinese Market Research Association (CMRA), in Chinese, provides a far more comprehensive list (www.cmra.org.cn).[9]

Questions

1. What might be some of the problems one could encounter in conducting marketing research in China?
2. What problems might different languages between the client and supplier pose?

What Motivates Decision Makers to Use Research Information?

When research managers communicate effectively, generate quality data, control costs, and deliver information on time, they increase the probability that decision makers will use the research information they provide. Yet academic research shows that political factors and preconceptions can also influence whether research information is used. Specifically, the determinants of whether or not a manager uses research data are (1) conformity to prior expectations, (2) clarity of presentation, (3) research quality, (4) political acceptability within the firm, and (5) lack of challenge to the status quo.[10] Managers and researchers both agree that technical quality is the most important determinant of research use. However, managers are less likely to use research that does not conform to preconceived notions or is not politically acceptable.[11] This does not mean, of course, that researchers should alter their findings to meet management's preconceived notions.

Marketing managers in industrial firms tend to use research findings more than do their counterparts in consumer goods organizations.[12] This tendency among industrial managers is attributed to a greater exploratory objective in information collection, a greater degree of formalization of organizational structure, and a lesser degree of surprise in the information collected.

The process for correctly defining the research problem consists of a series of steps: (1) recognize the problem or opportunity, (2) find out why the information is being sought, (3) understand the decision-making environment, (4) use the symptoms to help clarify the problem, (5) translate the management problem into a marketing research problem, (6) determine whether the information already exists, (7) determine whether the question can really be answered, and (8) state the research objectives. If the problem is not defined correctly, the remainder of the research project will be a waste of time and money.

The steps in the market research process are as follows:

1. Identification of the problem/opportunity and statement of the marketing research objectives
2. Creation of the research design
3. Choice of the method of research
4. Selection of the sampling procedure
5. Collection of data
6. Analysis of data
7. Preparation and presentation of the research report
8. Follow-up

In specifying a research design, the researcher must determine whether the research will be descriptive or causal. Descriptive studies are conducted to answer who, what, when, where, and how questions. Causal studies are those in which the researcher investigates whether one variable (independent) causes or influences another variable (dependent). The next step in creating a research design is to select a research method: survey, observation, or experiment. Survey research involves an interviewer (except in mail and Internet surveys) interacting with a respondent to obtain facts, opinions, and attitudes. Observation research, in contrast, monitors respondents' actions and does not rely on direct interaction with people. An experiment is distinguished by the fact that the researcher changes one or more variables and observes the effects of those changes on another variable (usually sales). The objective of most experiments is to measure causality.

A sample is a subset of a larger population. A probability sample is one for which every element in the population has a known nonzero probability of being selected. All samples that cannot be considered probability samples are nonprobability samples. Any sample in which the chances of selection for the various elements in the population are unknown can be considered a nonprobability sample.

In larger organizations, it is common to have a research request prepared after the statement of research objectives. The research request generally describes the action to be taken on the basis of the research, the reason for the need for the information, the questions management wants to have answered, how the information will be used, the target groups from whom information must be gathered, the amount of time and money available to complete the project, and any other information pertinent to the request. The request for proposal (RFP) is the document used by clients to solicit proposals from marketing research suppliers.

Marketing research proposals are developed in response to an RFP. In some cases, the proposals are created based on an informal request such as in a telephone conversation between a client and research supplier. The research proposal gives the research objectives, research design, time line, and cost. Research proposals are the tool that generates revenue for the research firm.

SUMMARY ☐

Good communications are the foundation of research management and the basis for getting decision makers to use research information. The information communicated to a decision maker depends on the type of research being conducted.

KEY TERMS & DEFINITIONS

opportunity identification Using marketing research to find and evaluate new opportunities.

situation analysis Studying the decision-making environment within which the marketing research will take place.

exploratory research Preliminary research conducted to increase understanding of a concept, to clarify the exact nature of the problem to be solved, or to identify important variables to be studied.

pilot studies Surveys using a limited number of respondents and often employing less rigorous sampling techniques than are employed in large, quantitative studies.

experience surveys Discussions with knowledgeable individuals, both inside and outside the organization, who may provide insights into the problem.

case analysis Reviewing information from situations that are similar to the current one.

marketing research problem A statement specifying the type of information needed by the decision maker to help solve the management decision problem and how that information can be obtained efficiently and effectively.

marketing research objective A goal statement, defining the specific information needed to solve the marketing research problem.

management decision problem A statement specifying the type of managerial action required to solve the problem.

hypothesis A conjectural statement about a relationship between two or more variables that can be tested with empirical data.

research design The plan to be followed to answer the marketing research objectives.

descriptive studies Research studies that answer the questions who, what, when, where, and how.

variable A symbol or concept that can assume any one of a set of values.

causal studies Research studies that examine whether the value of one variable causes or determines the value of another variable.

dependent variable A symbol or concept expected to be explained or influenced by the independent variable.

independent variable A symbol or concept over which the researcher has some control and that is hypothesized to cause or influence the dependent variable.

temporal sequence An appropriate causal order of events.

concomitant variation The degree to which a presumed cause and a presumed effect occur or vary together.

spurious association A relationship between a presumed cause and a presumed effect that occurs as a result of an unexamined variable or set of variables.

survey research Research in which an interviewer (except in mail and Internet surveys) interacts with respondents to obtain facts, opinions, and attitudes.

observation research Typically, descriptive research that monitors respondents' actions without direct interaction.

experiments Research to measure causality, in which the researcher changes one or more independent variables and observes the effect of the changes on the dependent variable.

probability sample A subset of a population where every element in the population has a known nonzero chance of being selected.

nonprobability sample A subset of a population in which the chances of selection for the various elements in the population are unknown.

research request An internal document used by large organizations that describes a potential research project, its benefits to the organization, and estimated costs; it must be formally approved before a research project can begin.

request for proposal (RFP) A solicitation sent to marketing research suppliers inviting them to submit a formal proposal, including a bid.

research proposal A document developed, usually in response to an RFP, that states the research objectives, research design, time line, and cost.

QUESTIONS FOR REVIEW & CRITICAL THINKING

1. The definition of the research problem is one of the critical steps in the research process. Why? Who should be involved in this process?
2. What role does exploratory research play in the marketing research process? How does exploratory research differ from other forms of marketing research?
3. Give some examples of symptoms of problems and then suggest some underlying real problems.
4. Give several examples of situations in which it would be better to take a census of the population than a sample.
5. Critique the following methodologies and suggest more appropriate alternatives:
   a. A supermarket is interested in determining its image. Cashiers drop a short questionnaire into the grocery bag of each customer prior to bagging the groceries.
   b. To assess the extent of its trade area, a shopping mall stations interviewers in the parking lot every Monday and Friday evening. After people park their cars, interviewers walk up to them and ask them for their zip codes.
   c. To assess the potential for new horror movies starring alien robots, a major studio invites people to call a 900 number and vote yes if they would like to see such movies or no if they would not. Each caller is billed a $2 charge.
6. You have been charged with determining how to attract more business majors to your school. Outline the steps you would take, including sampling procedures, to accomplish this task.
7. What can researchers do to increase the chances that decision makers will use the marketing research information they generate?
8. Explain the critical role of the research proposal.
9. Divide the class into teams of four or five. Half of the teams should prepare short *(Team Exercise)* RFPs on the following topics:
   a. food on campus
   b. role of fraternities and sororities on campus
   c. entertainment in your city
   d. your university website
   e. role of student internships in education
   f. online purchasing of school supplies
   g. purchasing music on the Internet

   The RFPs should state clearly and precisely the research objectives and other pertinent information. The remaining teams should create proposals in response to the RFPs.

WORKING THE NET

1. Go to the Internet and search on "intranet + future." Report your findings to the class.
2. Describe how putting research reports on the Web can benefit managers.
3. Go to a search engine and type "writing RFPs." Explain what kind of help is available to prepare RFPs.

REAL-LIFE RESEARCH • 2.1

The Food and Drug Administration Finds Consumers Aren't up to Speed on Nutritional Matters

With the FDA mulling a "report card" to be printed on foods that make health claims, a new study found that most consumers are "nutritionally naïve" when it comes to reading nutrition food labels.

The *Food for Life* study was conducted by research firm Yankelovich, Chapel Hill, North Carolina, to assess consumers' attitudes and behaviors about nutrition, diet, and healthcare. "Consumers need better tools to make intelligent decisions," said Steve Bodhaine, Yankelovich group president. "The data show a glaring lack of understanding of the basics of nutrition and why the right messages aren't getting through. We've taught people how to compare labels when shopping for food but not to understand what they are reading."

The study was conducted online among 2,200 adults age 18 and older. Among the findings:

- 72% of Americans say if food does not taste good, they won't eat it, no matter how healthy and nutritious it is.

- 43% support legislation to ban vending machines from schools.

- 63% said they have a fair to very good grasp of nutritional information on labels. But half didn't know how many calories they should consume daily and 80% did not know how much fat, carbs, or sodium to consume in a 2,000-calorie diet.

That contradiction is somewhat explained by the fact that, when asked which was bigger, an ounce or a gram, nearly a third incorrectly said a gram. "If people don't know how much fat should be in their diets, how is it helpful to look at the fat content as a source of information?" asked Bodhaine.

Food companies should not feel their marketing efforts are being wasted. Among those surveyed, the top five reasons for shopping for healthy foods were freshness, whole grain, low fat, high in fiber, and low cholesterol. Marketers like General Mills and Kellogg leverage such buzz words on-pack and in advertising for their whole-grain cereals and snacks.

Bodhaine offered ways for marketers to become part of the solution. First, scrap the metric system and use a standard with which Americans are familiar. He feels the FDA's "report card" (*Brandweek*, February 2006) is a good idea. It would designate health claims with A, B, C, and D, in descending order of scientific evidence, backing the claims on labels. But even that might not work. Bodhaine said studies show consumers are more apt to trust a brand that aligns itself with a medical group, such as the American Heart Association, than the government. Among others, Campbell's Healthy Request soups, ConAgra's Egg Beaters and Healthy Choice, and Kellogg's Smart Start Healthy Heart cereal all sport the AHA's "heart check mark." Also, PepsiCo's SmartSpot program has an icon on more than 100 products that communicates they meet nutritional standards set by the National Academy of Sciences and the FDA.

If companies are seeking one gem from the survey, it might be this: Almost 60 percent of respondents said they would support legislation to force marketers to make food labels more understandable if marketers don't do it themselves.[13]

Questions

1. Would you say that this was an exploratory study? If not, what are the research questions?
2. Is this research causal or descriptive? Why?
3. Explain how the FDA might use this information. Kellogg's?
4. What might be included in an RFP to do further research?

APPENDIX 2-A
A MARKETING RESEARCH PROPOSAL

Decision Analyst, Inc. Proposal to Conduct a Brand Equity Study

Confidential

Prepared For:
Fun City Gaming, Inc.

Prepared by:
Kathi McKenzie & Sally Danforth
January 2009

Background

Fun City Gaming, Inc. currently operates a multilevel dockside riverboat casino and a land-based pavilion with three restaurants and a hotel, all located on the Arlen River. The casino offers 1500 slot machines and 70 table games, and is the "flagship" of the Fun City franchise.The Fun City Casino has four primary competitors currently operating in the area, all within a roughly 30-mile radius of the Fun City. The Fun City Casino ranks second in revenue, but first in profit among these competitors. In addition to these competitors, additional competition will be provided by the planned "River Wild" casino, which will likely begin construction in about a year. This casino will be located in St. George, minutes from the Fun City Casino.

Fun City is currently undergoing a large redevelopment, involving construction of a completely new gaming vessel, significant upgrades to the pavilion, addition of new restaurants, and a new parking garage. The gaming vessel will feature 2500 slot machines, 84 table games, high-limit gaming areas, and upgraded décor. The new Fun City will offer superior features to the current product as well as to primary competitors.

In order to be financially feasible, this project must increase business from current customers as well as attract customers from competitive casinos, some of whom may have to travel past competitive casinos to arrive at Fun City. In addition, the new offering should be especially attractive to premium casino players.

Objectives

The overall objective of this study would be to help management position the new Fun City offering. Key questions to be addressed include:

- What should be the positioning of the new casino?
- Should the Fun City name be used, or should it be rebranded?
- If rebranded, what name should be used?

Study Design

This study would be conducted using a targeted telephone survey among 800 gamblers within a 100-mile radius of the Fun City Casino location. Specifically, we will survey 400 within the Arlen Valley portion of this area and 400 in the area eastward, where the majority of current/future competition lies. Respondents will be screened based on past 12-month casino usage.

Areas of Questioning

Decision Analyst would work closely with Fun City Gaming in developing the questionnaire. Assuming that we have three to four potential positionings to test, tentative survey topics would include:

- Current casino usage and gambling behavior.
- Awareness and overall rating for Fun City name, as well as names of key competitors and other names owned by Fun City Gaming which might be used for the new casino.

- [ ] Rating of Fun City and key competitors on several (8 to 10) image attributes.
- [ ] Exposure to brief description of the "new" (redeveloped) casino. Each respondent would be exposed to the description with *one* of the potential positionings. This will result in a readable sample size for each positioning.
- [ ] Overall rating and rating on key image attributes for the "new" casino.
- [ ] Rating of Fun City name and other potential names on overall appeal and fit with this description.
- [ ] Projected use of new casino; effect on gambling habits and share of casino visits.

Data will be analyzed both by area of residence and by gambling value (high/medium/low value gamblers).

Data Analysis

Factor analysis will be conducted, and the factors that are most related to the overall rating of the casino will be identified. On the basis of these factors, a perceptual map will be created to show visually the relationship between the current Fun City and competitive brands, based on brand image. The image projected by the new casino description will also be shown on this map, and a gap analysis conducted to highlight possible differences in image projected by each of the three to four positionings.

Personnel Involved

This project will be supervised by Kathi McKenzie and Sally Danforth. Kathi will be the overall supervisor and Sally will be responsible for the data analysis and presentation. *(Note: A short bio of each person would normally be attached.)*

Specifications/Assumptions

The cost estimate is based on the following assumptions:

- [ ] Number of completed interviews = 800
- [ ] Average interview length = 20 minutes
- [ ] Average completion rate = 0.62 completes per hour
- [ ] Assumed incidence = 25%
- [ ] No open-ended questions
- [ ] Type of sample: targeted random digit
- [ ] Up to two banners of statistical tables in Word format
- [ ] Factor analysis, two perceptual maps (total sample and high-value gambler), and gap analysis
- [ ] Report
- [ ] Personal presentation, if desired

Services

Decision Analyst, Inc. would:

- ☐ Develop the questionnaire, in conjunction with Fun City Gaming management
- ☐ Generate sample within the target area
- ☐ Program the survey
- ☐ Manage and administer the project
- ☐ Monitor and oversee all telephone interviewing
- ☐ Process data, specify cross-tabulations, and compile statistical tables
- ☐ Analyze the data and prepare presentation-style report, if desired

Cost

The cost to conduct this study, as described, would be $61,900, plus a minimum 10 percent contingency fee, which would only be spent with specific prior approval of Fun City Gaming. This cost estimate does not include the cost of any travel outside of the Dallas-Fort Worth area. Any overnight deliveries or travel expenses would be billed at cost at the end of the study.

Decision Analyst would closely monitor data collection. If the actual data collection experience differed from the stated specifications and assumptions, we would notify you immediately to discuss the options available.

Timing

After approval of the final questionnaire, the project would require approximately five to six weeks, as outlined below:

Survey programming and quality control	3–4 days
Data collection	3 weeks
Final data tabulations	3 days
Final report	1–2 weeks

Ryan McVay/Getty Images

SECONDARY DATA
AND DATABASES

LEARNING OBJECTIVES

1.	To understand how firms create an internal database.
2.	To learn about the advantages of creating a database from website visitors.
3.	To become familiar with data mining.
4.	To understand the advantages and disadvantages of using secondary data.
5.	To understand the role of the Internet in obtaining secondary data.
6.	To learn about types of information management systems.

Research International, a global marketing research firm, recently conducted a major study on baby boomers. Boomers are those people who were born between 1946 and 1964. Interviews were conducted in 16 different countries ranging from Australia and Finland to Turkey and the United States.

Some of the key findings of the study are:

☐ Baby boomers do not always recognize themselves as a cohesive generation, partly due to their wide variations of life stage and style.

☐ However, they share history and common experiences, especially in terms of battling for personal freedom and economic improvement in their youth. They also share a current unease about the state of the world around them.

☐ They all have a need to face the future, which is generally thought to be economically bleak, albeit more so in some countries than others. The need to make more provisions for self in old age is becoming increasingly common across markets.

☐ The pace of life is fast for all boomers, and they can find it disturbing to live in a multicultural and "over-informed" world; this leads them to be selective and cautious in relation to "communications," brand values, and the world around them in general.

☐ Financial and work security, and notably the lack of them, is paramount in the boomers' outlooks. They feel they deserve to keep the benefits of their work and battles—but many are now confronting the fact that they may not be able to do so.

☐ In this respect, Northern Europe faces its own future, but not that of its children, with more optimism than does Southern Europe and the United States, with Japan and Australia less certain about how things will go. This is as much a psychological as an actual position for boomers, and those communicating with them need to be aware of this, particularly with regard to the tone of voice they use to address them. Despite the fact that experts believe boomers are the wealthiest generation this century (except perhaps in the United States), boomers themselves see their hard-earned financial security potentially being lost.

☐ Modern-day cares and concerns are common to all 16 markets, and are first parochial, second national, and only third global. Fear for personal safety and health, and a lack of trust in national and international institutions, has led boomers to look inward and to friends and family for peace of mind. They are suspicious and feel let down by society at large; they no longer feel they have the power to change things as they did in their youth. In an ideal world, they would like something halfway between the social structure of their early years and the openness of today. Boomers want to hold on to their hard-won freedom, but in the context of a more moral world, where people care more deeply for the rights and feelings of others. In approaching boomers, communicators would do best to avoid any element of patronization and should show respect for boomers' achievements.

☐ For boomers, advertising must treat them as adults, be honest, clever, and funny, but not overestimating of problems. Above all, it must respect people and *never* patronize.

☐ Marketers and advertisers must recognize that boomers are *not* defined by brands. If they buy into comfort or image, for example, they do so knowingly. Relations with brands are based on the intrinsic worth and integrity of the brand rather than pure status. Longevity and consistency of communication and product qualities are reassuring in a volatile world. New brands can be accepted, providing they meet the needs of boomers for product (rather than pure image) integrity and must adopt a nonpatronizing approach.

☐ Boomers believe they have a better diet than either their parents or their children, through (claimed) adherence to fresh, natural produce, which is now available in infinite variety all year round. They are conscious of the need to avoid excesses of sugar, salt, and fat. "Natural" is a key word in the vocabulary of food for boomers. Only in Greece and Turkey is there admitted resistance: the traditional diet is preferred, and boomers can rationalize that there are worse problems than diet and there are other priorities in life. However, in all markets, supplements are used extensively, especially by women. They are used specifically to help or prevent ailments of aging such as painful joints, osteoporosis, dry skin and hair, and so on. While it would seem that there is awareness of diet, exercise is another issue. Only in the United States did we encounter more fanatical exercisers: in most other markets, only more leisurely exercise such as walking and swimming are mentioned.[1]

When Research International conducted this study, it was gathering primary data. When your authors received a copy of the research, they were examining secondary data. What is the difference between the two? What are the pros and cons of using secondary data? These are some of the questions we will answer in Chapter 3. We will also explain databases and data mining.

Nature of Secondary Data

> **secondary data**
> Data that have been previously gathered.

> **primary data**
> New data gathered to help solve the problem under investigation.

Secondary data consist of information that has already been gathered and *might* be relevant to the problem at hand. **Primary data**, in contrast, are survey, observation, and experiment data collected to solve the particular problem under investigation. It is highly unlikely that any marketing research problem is entirely unique or has never occurred before. It also is probable that someone else has investigated the problem or one similar to it in the past. Therefore, secondary data can be a cost-effective and efficient means of obtaining information for marketing research. There are two basic sources of secondary data: the company itself (internal databases, like Bud Net) and other organizations or persons (external databases).

Secondary information originating within the company includes annual reports, reports to stockholders, sales data, customer profiles, purchase patterns, product testing results (perhaps made available to the news media), and house periodicals composed by company personnel for communication to employees, customers, or others. Often all this information is incorporated into a company's internal database.

Outside sources of secondary information include innumerable government (federal, state, and local) departments and agencies that compile and publish summaries of business data, as well as trade and industry associations, business periodicals, and other news media that regularly publish studies and articles on the economy, specific industries, and even individual companies. When economic considerations or priorities within the organization preclude publication of summaries of the information from these sources, unpublished summaries may be found in internal reports, memos, or special-purpose analyses with limited circulation. Most of these sources can be found on the Internet.

Advantages of Secondary Data

Marketing researchers use secondary information because it can be obtained at a fraction of the cost, time, and inconvenience associated with primary data collection. Additional advantages of using secondary information include the following:

❑ *Secondary data may help to clarify or redefine the problem during the exploratory research process* (see Chapter 2). Consider the experience of a local YMCA. Concerned about a stagnant level of membership and a lack of participation in traditional YMCA programs, it decided to survey members and nonmembers. Secondary data revealed that there had been a tremendous influx of young single persons into the target market, while the number of "traditional families" had remained constant. The problem was redefined to examine how the YMCA could attract a significant share of the young single adult market while maintaining its traditional family base.

☐ *Secondary data may actually provide a solution to the problem.* It is highly unlikely that the problem is unique; there is always the possibility that someone else has addressed the identical problem or a very similar one. Thus, the precise information desired may have been collected, but not for the same purpose.

Many states publish a directory of manufacturers (typically available online) that contains information on companies: location, markets, product lines, number of plants, names of key personnel, number of employees, and sales levels. When a consulting company specializing in long-range strategic planning for members of the semiconductor industry needed a regional profile of its potential clients, it used individual state directories to compile the profile; no primary data collection was necessary.

☐ *Secondary data may provide primary data research method alternatives.* Each primary data research endeavor is custom-designed for the situation at hand; consequently, the marketing researcher should always be open to sources that suggest research alternatives. For example, when we (the authors) started work on a research project for a large southwestern city's convention and visitor's bureau, we obtained a research report prepared by *Meeting and Convention Planners* magazine. In designing our questionnaire, we used a series of scales from the magazine's questionnaire. Not only were the scales well designed, but results from our study could be compared with the magazine's data.

☐ *Secondary data may alert the marketing researcher to potential problems and/or difficulties.* In addition to alternatives, secondary information may divulge potential dangers. Unpopular collection methods, sample selection difficulties, or respondent hostility may be uncovered. For example, examination of a study of anesthesiologists by a researcher planning to conduct a study of their satisfaction with certain drugs discovered a high refusal rate in a telephone survey. The researcher had planned to use a telephone study but instead switched to a mail questionnaire with a response incentive.

☐ *Secondary data may provide necessary background information and build credibility for the research report.* Secondary information often yields a wealth of background data for planning a research project. It may offer a profile of potential buyers versus nonbuyers, industry data, desirable new product features, language used by purchasers to describe the industry, and the advantages and disadvantages of existing products. Language used by target consumers can aid in phrasing questions that will be meaningful to respondents. Sometimes background data can satisfy some of the research objectives, eliminating the need to ask certain questions; shorter questionnaires typically have higher completion rates. And secondary data can enrich research findings by providing additional insights into what the data mean or by corroborating current findings. Finally, secondary data can serve as a reference base for subsequent research projects.

☐ *Secondary data may provide the sample frame.* If a company, such as UPS, wants to track its levels of customer satisfaction each quarter, the names of customers must come from its database. Thus, the customer list is the sample frame, and the sample frame is the list or device from which a sample is drawn.

Limitations of Secondary Data

Despite the many advantages of secondary data, they also pose some dangers. The main disadvantages of secondary information are lack of availability, lack of relevance, inaccuracy, and insufficiency.

Lack of Availability   For some research questions, there are simply no available data. Suppose Kraft Foods wants to evaluate the taste, texture, and color of three new gourmet brownie mixes. No secondary data exist that can answer these questions; consumers must try each mix and then evaluate it. If McDonald's wants to evaluate its image in Phoenix, Arizona, it must gather primary data. If BMW wants to know the reaction of college students to a new two-seater sports car design, it must show prototypes to the students and evaluate their opinions. Of course, secondary data may have played a major role in the engineer's design plan for the car.

Lack of Relevance   It is not uncommon for secondary data to be expressed in units or measures that cannot be used by the researcher. For example, Joan Dermott, a retailer of oriental rugs, determined that the primary customers for her rugs were families with a total household income of $40,000 to $80,000. Higher-income consumers tended to purchase pricier rugs than those Dermott carried. When she was trying to decide whether to open a store in another Florida city, she could not find useful income data. One source offered class breakdowns of $30,000 to $50,000, $50,000 to $70,000, $70,000 to $90,000, and so forth. Another secondary source broke down incomes into less than $15,000, $15,000 to $30,000, and more than $30,000. Even if the given income brackets had met Joan's needs, she would have faced another problem: outdated information. One study had been conducted in 1995 and the other in 2001. In Florida's dynamic markets, the percentages probably were no longer relevant. This is often the case with U.S. Census data, which are nearly a year old before they become available.

Inaccuracy   Users of secondary data should always assess the accuracy of the data. There are a number of potential sources of error when a researcher gathers, codes, analyzes, and presents data. Any report that does not mention possible sources and ranges of error should be suspect.

   Using secondary data does not relieve the researcher from attempting to assess their accuracy. A few guidelines for determining the accuracy of secondary data are as follows:

1.   *Who gathered the data?* The source of the secondary data is a key to their accuracy. Federal agencies, most state agencies, and large commercial marketing research firms generally can be counted on to have conducted their research as professionally as possible. Marketing researchers should always be on guard when examining data in which a hidden agenda might be reflected. A chamber of commerce, for instance, is always going to put its best foot forward. Similarly, trade associations often advocate one position over another.

2.   *What was the purpose of the study?* Data are always collected for some reason. Understanding the motivation for the research can provide clues to the quality of the data. A chamber of commerce study conducted to provide data that could be used to attract new industry to the area should be scrutinized with a great deal of caution. There have been situations in which advertising agencies have been hired by clients to assess the impact of their own advertising programs. In other words, they have been asked to evaluate the quality of the job they were doing for their clients!

3.   *What information was collected?* A researcher should always identify exactly what information was gathered and from whom. For example, in a dog food study, were

purchasers of canned, dry, and semimoist food interviewed, or were just one or two types of dog food purchasers surveyed? In a voters' survey, were only Democrats or only Republicans interviewed? Were the respondents registered voters? Was any attempt made to ascertain a respondent's likelihood of voting in the next election? Were self-reported data used to infer actual behavior?

4. *When was the information collected?* A shopping mall study that surveyed shoppers only on weekends would not reflect the opinions of "typical" mall patrons. A telephone survey conducted from 9:00 a.m. to 5:00 p.m. would vastly underrepresent working persons. A survey of Florida visitors conducted during the summer probably would reveal motivations and interests different from those of winter visitors.

5. *How was the information collected?* Were the data collected by mail, telephone, Internet, or personal interview? Each of these techniques offers advantages and disadvantages. What was the refusal rate? Were decision makers or their representatives interviewed? In short, the researcher must attempt to discern the amount of bias injected into the data by the information-gathering process. A mail survey with a 1 percent response rate (that is, only 1 percent of those who received the survey mailed it back) probably contains a lot of self-selection bias.

6. *Is the information consistent with other information?* A lack of consistency between secondary data sets should dictate caution. The researcher should delve into possible causes of the discrepancy. Differences in the sample, time frame, sampling methodology, questionnaire structure, and other factors can lead to variations in studies. If possible, the researcher should assess the validity of the different studies as a basis for determining which, if any, study should be used for decision making.

Insufficiency A researcher may determine that available data are relevant and accurate but still not sufficient to make a decision or bring closure to a problem. For example, a manager for Wal-Mart may have sufficient secondary data on incomes, family sizes, number of competitors, and growth potential to determine in which of five Iowa towns Wal-Mart wishes to locate its next store. But if no traffic counts exist for the selected town, primary data will have to be gathered to select a specific site for the store.

Internal Databases

For many companies, a computerized database containing information about customers and prospects has become an essential marketing tool. An **internal database** is simply a collection of related information developed from data within the organization.

Creating an Internal Database

A firm's sales activities can be an excellent source of information for creating an internal database. A traditional starting point has been the firm's sales or inquiry processing and tracking system. Typically, such a system is built on salespersons' "call reports." A call report provides a blueprint of a salesperson's daily activities. It details the number of calls made, characteristics of each firm visited, sales activity resulting from the call, and any information picked up from the client regarding competitors, such as price changes, new products or services, credit term modifications, and new product or service features.

An internal marketing database built on sales results and customer preferences can be a powerful marketing tool.

internal database
A collection of related information developed from data within the organization.

Growing Importance of Internal Database Marketing

Perhaps the fastest growing use of internal databases is database marketing. **Database marketing** relies on the creation of a large computerized file of customers' and potential customers' profiles and purchase patterns to create a targeted marketing mix. A recent study found that 94 percent of the large companies in America have a marketing database.[2]

> **database marketing**
> Marketing that relies on the creation of a large computerized file of customers' and potential customers' profiles and purchase patterns to create a targeted marketing mix.

In the 1950s, network television enabled advertisers to "get the same message to everyone simultaneously." Database marketing can get a customized, individual message to everyone simultaneously through direct mail. This is why database marketing is sometimes called *micromarketing*. Database marketing can create a computerized form of the old-fashioned relationship that people used to have with the corner grocer, butcher, or baker. "A database is sort of a collective memory," says Richard G. Barlow, president of Frequency Marketing, Inc., a Cincinnati-based consulting firm. "It deals with you in the same personalized way as a mom-and-pop grocery store, where they knew customers by name and stocked what they wanted."[3]

The size of some databases is impressive: Ford Motor Company's is about 50 million names; Kraft Foods, 30 million; Citicorp, 30 million; and Kimberly-Clark, maker of Huggies diapers, 10 million new mothers. American Express (AmEx) can pull from its database all cardholders who made purchases at golf pro shops in the past six months, who attended symphony concerts, or who traveled to Europe more than once in the past year, as well as the very few people who did all three.

The San Diego Padres baseball team used database marketing to attract 60,000 new fans and collected about $400,000 in revenues from new season ticket sales. This was accomplished by marrying the database with customer relationship marketing (CRM) software. New, powerful CRM software is helping marketers enhance their recruitment of new customers and also keep current clients.

Aided by technology, sports-specific strategies are helping marketers reconnect with their fans. Even when a team is winning and stadiums are packed, CRM helps identify those fans most likely to buy season tickets or ticket packages in advance by creating databases on fan attendance. A team can then target these prospects for season tickets the following year. Advance ticket sales are extremely valuable to sports teams since they guarantee a certain revenue level for the season.

"Club cards," similar to ATM cards, are at the heart of fan loyalty programs these days. Although programs vary slightly from team to team, the idea is pretty much the same: Each time fans use their card, they rack up attendance points redeemable for promotional coupons or items such as food, drinks, and souvenirs. The more points they compile, the more "rewards" they receive. In return, the teams get a database filled with information on their fans, which could lead to additional revenue streams.[4]

Data Mining

> **neural network**
> A computer program that mimics the processes of the human brain and thus is capable of learning from examples to find patterns in data.

American Express uses a neural network to examine the hundreds of millions of entries in its database that tell how and where individual cardholders transact business. A **neural network** is a computer program that mimics the processes of the human brain and thus is capable of learning from examples to find patterns in data. The result is a set of *purchase propensity scores* for each cardholder. Based on these scores, AmEx matches offers from affiliated merchants to the purchase histories of individual cardholders and encloses these offers with their monthly statements. The benefits are reduced expenses for AmEx and information of higher value for its cardholders; American Express is engaged in data mining.

Data mining is the use of statistical and other advanced software to discover nonobvious patterns hidden in a database. The objective is to identify patterns that marketers can use in creating new strategies and tactics to increase a firm's profitability. Camelot Music Holdings used data mining to identify a group of high-spending, 65+ customers (members of its frequent shopper club) who were buying lots of classical and jazz music and movies. Further data mining revealed that a large percentage were also buying rap and alternative music; these were grandparents buying for the grandkids. Now, Camelot tells the senior citizens what's hot in rap and alternative music, as well as in traditional music.

Data mining involves searching for interesting patterns and following the data trail wherever it leads. The discovery process often requires sifting through massive quantities of data; electronic point-of-sale transactions, inventory records, and online customer orders matched with demographics can easily use up hundreds of gigabytes of data storage space. Probability sampling, descriptive statistics, and multivariate statistics are all tools of data mining that make the task manageable. (Probability sampling was discussed in Chapter 2; descriptive statistics programs and multivariate statistics will be covered in Chapters 12, 13 and 14.) Other more advanced data mining tools, such as genetic algorithms and case-based reasoning systems, must be left for an advanced text.

Data mining has many potential uses in marketing. Those with widest application include the following:

☐ *Customer acquisition.* In the first stage of a two-stage process, direct marketers apply data mining methods to discover customer attributes that predict their responses to special offers and communications such as catalogues. In the second stage, attributes that the model indicates make customers most likely to respond are matched to the attributes appended to rented lists of noncustomers in order to select noncustomer households most likely to respond to a new offer or communication.

> **data mining**
> The use of statistical and other advanced software to discover nonobvious patterns hidden in a database.

Farmers Group Insurance used data mining to find out that, as long as a sports car wasn't the only vehicle in a household, the accident rate for sports cars wasn't much greater than that for regular cars. This information led to lower insurance rates for sports cars in this category.

John Prescott/Stockphoto

- *Customer retention.* In a typical marketing application, data mining identifies those customers who contribute to the company's bottom line but who are likely to leave and go to a competitor. With this information, the company can target the vulnerable customers for special offers and other inducements not available to less vulnerable customers.

- *Customer abandonment.* Some customers cost more than they contribute and should be encouraged to take their business elsewhere. At Federal Express, customers who spend a lot with little service and marketing investment get different treatment from, say, those who spend just as much but cost more to keep. If their shipping volume falters, "good" clients can expect a phone call, which can head off defections before they occur. As for the "bad" clients—those who spend but are expensive to the company—FedEx is turning them into profitable customers, in many cases, by charging higher shipping prices. And the "ugly" clients, those customers who spend little and show few signs of spending more in the future? They can catch the TV ads. "We just don't market to them anymore," says Sharanjit Singh, managing director for marketing analysis at FedEx. "That automatically brings our costs down."[5]

- *Market basket analysis.* By identifying the associations among product purchases in point-of-sale transactions, retailers and direct marketers can spot product affinities and develop focused promotion strategies that work more effectively than traditional one-size-fits-all approaches. The American Express strategy of selectively stuffing offers in monthly statements is an example of how market basket analysis can be employed to increase marketing efficiency.

The Farmers Group has used data mining to better understand its customers. A few years ago, owning a Porsche or a Corvette almost guaranteed that you would pay more for car insurance. Conventional wisdom and decades of data collected by insurers suggested that drivers of high-performance sports cars were more likely to have accidents than were other motorists. But, by using data mining, the Farmers Group discovered something interesting: as long as the sports car wasn't the only vehicle in a household, the accident rate actually wasn't much greater than that for a regular car. Based on that information, Farmers changed its policy that had excluded sports cars from its lowest-priced insurance rates. By eliminating that rule, "we figured out that we could almost double our sports-car market," says Melissa McBratney, vice president of personal lines at the Los Angeles insurer.[6] Farmers estimates that just letting Corvettes and Porsches into its "preferred premium" plan could bring in an additional $4.5 million in premium revenue over the next two years, without a significant rise in claims. The pattern Farmers discovered isn't intuitive—it had eluded most insurance veterans.

Battle over Privacy

Acxiom is one of America's largest database marketing firms. The company knows a lot about you and me. It has scoured public records for how many cars you own and what your house is worth. It has accumulated surveys that show if you are married and how many children you have.

And for years Acxiom sold that information to marketers eager to use it to send mailings and make telephone pitches to consumers most likely to buy. Now the company is putting those hundreds of millions of bits of data in the service of customizing which display ads to show people browsing the Web—a development that has raised red flags with some privacy advocates.

Yahoo! Inc. and Microsoft Corp. are among the Internet companies that engage in so-called behavior targeting, using information such as users' Web search habits and the pages they visit to pick which ads to show them when they visit their own or partner websites.

Behavioral targeting allows a Web publisher, for example, to charge premium rates for a luxury car ad even on a lightly visited site about needlepoint, if the user's previous Web activity shows an interest in buying an automobile.

In the United States in 2007, advertisers spent $575 million on these behaviorally targeted ads, and are a projected to spend $3.8 billion in 2011, according to research firm eMarketer Inc.[7]

Acxiom's service, Relevance-X, goes further, drawing on the company's database of 133 million households to determine which ads to show. Acxiom's consumer database includes information gleaned from sources such as public real estate and motor vehicle records, surveys, and warranty cards consumers fill out. Estimates of annual income, marital status, average ages of kids, home ownership and property value, educational level, and travel histories are also available.

The company classifies each U.S. household into 70 clusters based, it says, "on that household's specific consumer and demographic characteristics, including shopping, media, lifestyle, and attitudinal information." Clusters ranged from "Married Sophisticates" to "Penny Pinchers."

Acxiom contracts with websites that collect consumer addresses, such as online retailers and those offering sweepstakes and surveys. In a blink, Acxiom looks up the people who provide their addresses in its database, matches them with their demographic and lifestyle clusters and places "cookies," or small pieces of tracking data, on their computer hard drives.

When those people visit Acxiom partner websites in the future, Acxiom can read cluster codes embedded in the cookies and use them to pick which ads to show. The company doesn't disclose the sites that carry such targeted ads, but says they reach 60 percent of U.S. Internet users.

That allows a company selling an expensive antiwrinkle cream, for example, to contract with Acxiom to display its ads to affluent women 40 years or older in the "Skyboxes and Suburbans" or "Summit Estates" clusters.

Some privacy advocates say they are concerned that Acxiom risks going too far with its Internet ad targeting. "You're potentially seeing a link between very sophisticated offline databases being used to target online advertising," says Jeff Chester, executive director of the Center for Digital Democracy, a nonprofit consumer-advocacy group focused on digital media. "That's precisely the objection that privacy advocates had back in 2000."[8]

Then, the Federal Trade Commission investigated the data-collection practices of Double-Click Inc., one of the biggest Internet ad companies at the time. The company had announced plans to link consumers' names and addresses with Web-surfing habits, but the company renounced the plans after criticism. The FTC dropped the investigation.[9]

The concept of privacy is changing radically as a result of our new computer-based lives. Privacy used to be achieved through the sheer friction of everyday life: distance, time, and lack of records. Information didn't travel well, and most people who wanted to escape their past could simply move to a new location. Now the picture has changed. People can escape their surroundings through the Internet, but their actions can easily catch up with them. And it's not just the Internet; it's electronic toll roads (exactly *when* did you leave that party?), credit card transactions (we know what hotel you went to), vendor databases (and what book you bought), cell phone records (and whom you called), and more. At work, employee arrival and departure times may be recorded, along with their Web searches, e-mail messages, and sick days.

What makes all this troubling to privacy advocates is the growing ability of technology to combine information: the products you bought from a variety of different merchants; your sick days plus someone else's hotel bills. It's not the routine use of this information for marketing purposes that people find troubling; it's the way someone with an agenda might put the pieces together.

Identity Theft   People have a right to be concerned. Identity theft cost $55 billion annually.[10] One company that has come under fire is ChoicePoint. Since spinning off from the credit bureau Equifax in 1997, it has been buying up databases and data mining operations. Businesses, individuals, even the FBI, now rely on its storehouse. Other customers: Nigerian scammers who apparently used the data to steal people's identities.

The problem was unreliable safeguards. To ensure that only certain businesses had access to its data, ChoicePoint set up certain requirements that potential customers must meet. A man named Olatunji Oluwatosin—and possibly others—used fake names and a Hollywood copy shop fax machine to create fictitious small businesses requesting Choice-Point service. Before Oluwatosin was caught—after someone at ChoicePoint grew suspicious about one of his applications—he accessed at least 145,000 names. (Oluwatosin pleaded no contest to felony identity theft in California in February 2005; he is serving a 16-month sentence.)[11] ChoicePoint announced in 2005 that it will no longer sell consumer data that includes drivers license numbers and Social Security numbers.[12]

An organization has recently been formed to protect consumer privacy. Its motto is "No E-Commerce without E-Privacy." You can learn more about its efforts at www.privacy.org.

Governmental Actions   Three key laws (one a state law) have been passed to protect consumers from identity theft. These are:

Federal Laws

> **Gramm-Leach-Bliley Act (Financial Services Modernization Act):** aimed at financial companies. Requires those corporations to tell their customers how they use their personal information and to have policies that prevent fraudulent access to it. Partial compliance has been required since 2001.

> **Health Insurance Portability and Accountability Act:** aimed at the healthcare industry. Limits disclosure of individuals' medical information and imposes penalties on organizations that violate privacy rules. Compliance required for large companies since 2003.

> **The Fair Credit Reporting Act (FCRA):** enforced by the Federal Trade Commission, promotes accuracy in consumer reports and is meant to ensure the privacy of the information in them.

> **The Children's Online Privacy Protection Act (COPPA):** Aims to give parents control over what information is collected from their children online and how such information may be used.

COPPA applies to:

- ☐ Operators of commercial websites and online services directed to children under 13 that collect personal information from them.
- ☐ Operators of general audience sites that knowingly collect personal information from children under 13.
- ☐ Operators of general audience sites that have a separate children's area and that collect personal information from children under 13.

COPPA requires operators to:

- ☐ Post a privacy policy on the homepage of the website and link to the privacy policy on every page where personal information is collected.

☐ Provide notice about the site's information collection practices to parents and obtain verifiable parental consent before collecting personal information from children.

☐ Give parents a choice as to whether their child's personal information will be disclosed to third parties.

☐ Provide parents access to their child's personal information and the opportunity to delete the child's personal information and opt out of future collection or use of the information.

☐ Not condition a child's participation in a game, contest, or other activity on the child's disclosing more personal information than is reasonably necessary to participate in that activity.

☐ Maintain the confidentiality, security and, integrity of personal information collected from children.

State Laws

California's Notice of Security Breach Law: if any company or agency that has collected the personal information of a California resident discovers that nonencrypted information has been taken by an unauthorized person, the company or agency must tell the resident. Compliance required since 2003. (Some 30 other states are considering similar laws.)

Getting Paid to Give Up Your Privacy   A number of marketing research firms are paying people to participate in online surveys, to track their click streams, or to evaluate websites. This, of course, is legitimate research. Usually, consumers are willing to give up their right to privacy quite cheaply. A recent Jupiter report said that 82 percent of respondents would give personal information to new shopping sites to enter a $100 sweepstakes.[13] There is also a dark side to getting paid for online surveys. Many websites, such as Express Paid Surveys, Get Cash for Surveys, and Opinion Paycheck, promise money for taking surveys. The catch is that you must first pay a membership fee; such fees range from $25 to $37. Donna Gillin and Jane Sheppard, both directors of the Council for Marketing and Opinion Research, discuss the membership fee in the Practicing Marketing Research box on page 82.

Marketing Research Aggregators

The **marketing research aggregator** industry is a $100 million business that is growing about 6 percent a year. Companies in this field acquire, catalogue, reformat, segment, and resell reports already published by large and small marketing research firms. Even Amazon.com has added a marketing research aggregation area to its high-profile e-commerce site.

> **marketing research aggregator**
> A company that acquires, catalogues, reformats, segments, and resells reports already published by large and small marketing research firms.

The role of aggregator firms is growing because their databases of research reports are getting bigger and more comprehensive—and more useful—as marketing research firms get more comfortable using resellers as a sales channel. Meanwhile, advances in Web technology are making the databases easier to search and deliveries speedier. And aggregators are slicing and repackaging research reports into narrower, more specialized sections for resale to better serve small- and medium-sized clients who often cannot afford to commission their own studies or buy full reports—essentially nurturing a new target market for the information.

Research aggregators are indirectly tapping new markets for traditional research firms. Selling smaller chunks of data at a lower price point is putting big research firms' results into the hands of small- and medium-sized business clients, who often cannot afford to spend more than a few hundred dollars for a report.

PRACTICING MARKETING RESEARCH

Have you recently received e-mail that offers to pay you for your opinions, "turn your opinions into cash," or the like? If the answer to this question is yes, you're not alone. Many in the survey research industry have received and expressed concern over similar e-mails with offers to pay members of the public for their opinions (usually for a membership fee). In reality, these websites sell their "members" a database of industry members they claim will "pay" respondents for their opinions. This type of offer raises several concerns. First, a legitimate survey researcher (focus group or otherwise) never asks respondents to pay to become research participants. Second, with the publicity of these offers, respondents may become uniformly accustomed to being "paid for their opinions," rather than, in some cases, being paid as an incentive or a thank you for participation by legitimate industry members.

Moreover, although incentives may be used in focus groups, mall studies, customer satisfaction studies, Web surveys, or others, incentives normally are not used in telephone studies where telephone numbers have been randomly generated by a computer. Since telephone studies make up a considerable amount of the survey research conducted in our industry, the respondent is left with an unrealistic expectation of being offered or receiving an incentive whenever he or she participates in survey research. In addition, given the reality that all potential respondents won't fit the desired demographic for all studies, the materials (generally) don't clearly notify potential respondents that they may never be chosen to participate in any survey research and therefore may never be provided with an incentive to participate in the research process.

Lastly, as industry members have reported, one net effect of such "offers" is the creation of "professional respondents" or "professional survey takers." Such individuals who frequent group discussions have views that may not be wholly representative of the group and are more familiar with group discussion practice—which may result in uncharacteristic and unrepresentative behavior.[14]

Questions

1. Do you think that it is ethical to pay for someone's opinion?
2. How can paying for opinions influence data quality?

Prior to the emergence of research aggregators, a lot of marketing research was only available as premium-priced subscription services. For example, a $2,800 report from Wintergreen Research, Inc. (based in Lexington, Massachusetts) was recently broken up and sold (on internetnews.com) for $350 per chapter for the report's 17 chapters, significantly boosting the overall revenue generated by the report.

In addition to iternetnews.com, other major aggregators are, Bitpipe.com, USA DATA, and MarketResearch.com.

Information Management

Computerized databases, secondary data published or posted on the Internet, and internal databases are important parts of an organization's information system. Intelligent decision making is always predicated on having good information. The problem today is how to manage all the information available. It was sometime after the middle of the twentieth

century that—for the first time in human history—we began to produce information faster than we could process it. Various innovations—computers, microwave transmissions, television, satellites, and the like—have pushed us from a state of information scarcity to a state of information surplus in a very short time.

The need to make better decisions requires that emphasis move from the problems of data acquisition to the problems of effectively managing and utilizing the vast sea of data available. Everyone who has been faced with a decision recognizes that information is the single most important input influencing the quality of that decision. Information is necessary to define the problem, to determine its scope and magnitude, and to generate and evaluate alternatives. Poor decisions are usually the result of using incorrect information, making invalid assumptions, or inappropriately analyzing the information available.

Today, most managers in large and medium-size organizations and progressive smaller ones are bombarded with information. The concern at firms such as American Airlines, Pfizer, and Citicorp has shifted from the generation of information to the shaping and evaluation of information to make it useful to decision makers.

Geographic Information Systems

A **geographic information system (GIS)** provides both a means of maintaining geographic databases and a tool capable of complex spatial analysis to provide information for a decision support system. Spatial analysis is the analysis of phenomena distributed in space and having physical dimensions (the location of, proximity to, or orientation of objects, such as stores, with respect to one another). A geographic database can store and provide access to corporate data, such as customer locations, facilities, logistic routes, and competitors. As a spatial analysis tool, this corporate data can be immersed with secondary demographic data and digitized maps to analyze and maximize the effects of locations. Utilities, oil companies, large retailers, and government agencies have long used these

> **geographic information system (GIS)** Computer-based system that uses secondary and/or primary data to generate maps that visually display various types of data geographically.

systems. Today the technology accounts for several billion dollars a year in hardware, software, and consulting sales. There are three reasons for this boom. The cost of a GIS has fallen dramatically, the ease of use for business-related analysis has improved, and GIS data can now be transmitted over the Internet fairly easily. GIS is now one of the hottest business information tools. Companies as diverse as Chase Manhattan, Domino's Pizza, Ace Hardware, Gold's Gym, and Subaru America have embraced mapping as an easier and more powerful way to manage geographic data than mind-numbing printouts, spreadsheets, and charts. GIS offers researchers, managers, and clients an intuitive way to organize data and to see relationships and patterns.[15]

Avon Products, Inc.'s sales rose 29 percent. One reason for this success could be its extensive use of GIS software to identify sales opportunities, manage market penetration, and territory realignment. Avon uses a GIS product called Territory Manager from Tactician Corporation. This software assists Avon to identify new sales opportunities by combining secondary demographic data with their internal corporate sales data to segment the U.S. market. For example, the software helped Avon to pinpoint a growing Asian American population in the Southeast. The maps produced are then used to further penetrate the market and to identify new sales representatives. After using the Territory Manager software, some sales areas saw recruitment increase up to 138 percent over the previous year during the same time period. The GIS is then used to create maps ranking sales territories to optimize the distribution and alignment of sales areas. These maps are made available to sales representatives over the Internet.[16]

GIS analysts and geographers talk about lines, points, and polygons (areas), while marketing researchers talk about roads, stores, and sales territories. But lines, points, and polygons are how business data are represented within a geographic database. Applications using lines include finding the quickest truck routes for long-haul freight companies and the shortest routes for local delivery trucks. Sears Roebuck calculates daily delivery routes, based on "estimated travel times, in-home time, truck capacity, optimal stop sequence." GPS (global positioning system) receivers in the vehicles can communicate with a GIS to receive real-time weather and road conditions to the drivers. Applications involving points focus on finding the best potential sites for retail bank branches and devising the best strategy for a network of miniwarehouses. Applications involving areas range from finding the best markets for hardware sales to identifying the best location for a new Taco Bell. A GIS can also answer detailed marketing questions. If a marketing researcher for Target wants to know how many of the company's high-performance stores have trading areas that overlap by at least 50 percent with trading areas for Wal-Mart, a GIS analyst can run a *spatial query* on a geographic database to address the question.

Aftermarket auto repair is a highly competitive $90 billion-a-year business in which dealerships have improved their services and market share. To stay ahead of the competition, Meineke Discount Muffler Corporation has turned to GIS. Meineke's 900 franchisees continuously send detailed customer and service records to Meineke headquarters in Charlotte, North Carolina. Records include customer's name and home address; vehicle make, model, and year; work performed; and payment method. They also explain how the customer learned about Meineke. This data is integrated with demographics, average commute times, market area incomes, and the like, within a geographic database. Meineke can then map its stores, competitors, and other retail outlets in relation to its customer base. GIS analysis is used to compute site selection, market share analysis, and inventory management.

Using TargetPro GIS software from MapInfo Corporation, Meineke analysts have developed GIS models (geographic formulas), allowing them to specify an actual or proposed retail location and then create an easy-to-understand report. Meineke can customize trade areas as it sees fit. If marketing research shows that some customers will not cross a river or a state boundary to get to the nearest outlet but will drive 2 miles farther to another Meineke franchise in a different zip code, the company can use TargetPro to create a map that reflects those shopping patterns. Meineke uses GIS to determine optimal inventory levels by analyzing demographics, commute times, and historical sales figures, which can point to short- and long-term potential business.

"We can place a store on the map, draw a radius around it, then ask the system how many vehicles are in the area," said Paul Baratta, director of real estate and international development for Meineke. "There might be 75,000 cars in a given neighborhood, but another layer of data might show that 6,500 of those are Lexus brands. How many people are going to put mufflers on a car that they're trading in every two years? [GIS] looks at the information in a different way."[17]

MapInfo is now combining GIS, data mining, and predictive analysis software to predict not only which markets offer the best potential for expansion—down to specific intersections—but also how each new store will affect revenue across the chain, generating color-coded maps of the best locales. For example, in the fast-food business, clustering with similar merchants is often beneficial, because diners typically will drive only five minutes for quick food and tend to go where they have myriad options. But as Arby's learned, specific products can affect behavior. MapInfo discovered that diners drove as much as 20 percent farther for an Arby's roast beef sandwich than for the chain's chicken offering. The reason? Shoppers could get chicken elsewhere but considered roast beef a "destination" product.[18]

Decision Support Systems

A **decision support system (DSS)** is designed to support the needs and styles of individual decision makers. In theory, a DSS represents something close to the ultimate in data management. We say "in theory" because, for the most part, the ideal has not been realized in practice. However, there have been some notable exceptions that have provided a glimpse of how a DSS can truly support the decision-making process. Characteristics of a true DSS are as follows:

> **decision support system (DSS)**
> An interactive, personalized information management system, designed to be initiated and controlled by individual decision makers.

- ☐ *Interactive.* The manager gives simple instructions and sees results generated on the spot. The process is under the manager's direct control; no computer programmer is needed, and there is no need to wait for scheduled reports.

- ☐ *Flexible.* It can sort, regroup, total, average, and manipulate data in a variety of ways. It will shift gears as the user changes topics, matching information to the problem at hand. For example, the chief executive can see highly aggregated figures, while the marketing analyst can view detailed breakouts.

- ☐ *Discovery oriented.* It helps managers probe for trends, isolate problems, and ask new questions.

- ☐ *Easy to learn and use.* Managers need not be particularly knowledgeable about computers. Novice users can elect a standard, or default, method of using the system, bypassing optional features to work with the basic system immediately. The opportunity to gradually learn about the system's possibilities minimizes the frustration that frequently accompanies use of new computer software.

Managers use a DSS to conduct sales analyses, forecast sales, evaluate advertising, analyze product lines, and keep tabs on market trends and competitors' actions. A DSS not only allows managers to ask "what if" questions but enables them to view any given slice of the data.

Here's a hypothetical example of using a DSS provided by a manager of new products:

To evaluate sales of a recently introduced new product, we can "call up" sales by the week, then by the month, breaking them out at [the vice president's] option by, say, customer segments. As he works at his terminal, his inquiries could go in several directions depending on the decision at hand. If his train of thought raises questions about monthly sales last quarter compared to forecasts, he wants his decision support system to follow along and give him answers immediately.

He might see that his new product's sales were significantly below forecast. Forecasts too optimistic? He compares other products' sales to his forecasts and finds that the targets were very accurate. Something wrong with the product? Maybe his sales department is getting insufficient leads, or is not putting leads to good use? Thinking a minute about how to examine that question, he checks ratios of leads converted to sales, product by product. The results disturb him. Only 5 percent of the new product's leads generate orders compared to the company's 12 percent all-product average. Why? He guesses that the sales force is not supporting the new product vigorously enough. Quantitative information from the DSS perhaps could provide more evidence to back that suspicion. But already having enough quantitative knowledge to satisfy himself, the VP acts on his intuition and experience and decides to have a chat with his sales manager.

☐ SUMMARY

Secondary data are previously gathered information that *might* be relevant to the problem at hand. They can come from sources internal to the organization or external to it. Primary data are survey, observation, or experiment data collected to solve the particular problem under investigation.

A database is a collection of related data. A traditional type of internal marketing database is founded on customer information. For example, a customer database may have demographic and perhaps psychographic information about existing customers and purchase data such as when the goods and services were bought, the types of merchandise procured, the dollar amount of sales, and any promotional information associated with sales. A database can even be created from recorded conversations. An internal database also may contain competitive intelligence, such as new products offered by competitors and changes in competitors' service policies and prices.

Data mining has dramatically increased users' ability to get insightful information out of databases. It can be used to acquire new customers, retain existing customers, abandon accounts that are not cost-effective, and engage in market-based analyses.

The proliferation of databases on and off the Internet has raised consumer and government concerns over privacy. Several laws have been passed to protect our privacy. These include the Gramm-Leach-Bliley Act, the Health Insurance Portability and Accountability Act, the Fair Credit Reporting Act, the Children's Online Privacy Protection Act, and California's Notice of Security Breach Law.

Using secondary data has several advantages. Secondary data may (1) help to clarify or redefine the problem during the exploratory research process, (2) actually provide a solution to the problem, (3) provide primary data research method alternatives, (4) alert the marketing researcher to potential problems and difficulties, and (5) provide necessary background data and build credibility for the research report. The disadvantages of using secondary data include lack of availability, lack of relevance, inaccuracy, and insufficient data.

Geographic information systems, which consist of a demographic database, digitized maps, and software, enable users to add primary data from a current study (or secondary corporate data) to the mix. The result is computer-generated maps that can reveal a variety of strategic findings to marketing managers; for example, a map may indicate an optimal location for a new retail store.

Decision support systems are designed from the individual decision maker's perspective. DSS systems are interactive, flexible, discovery oriented, and easy to learn; they can offer many benefits to small and large firms alike.

KEY TERMS & DEFINITIONS

secondary data Data that have been previously gathered.

primary data New data gathered to help solve the problem under investigation.

internal database A collection of related information developed from data within the organization.

database marketing Marketing that relies on the creation of a large computerized file of customers' and potential customers' profiles and purchase patterns to create a targeted marketing mix.

neural network A computer program that mimics the processes of the human brain and thus is capable of learning from examples to find patterns in data.

data mining The use of statistical and other advanced software to discover nonobvious patterns hidden in a database.

marketing research aggregator A company that acquires, catalogs, reformats, segments, and resells reports already published by large and small marketing research firms.

geographic information system (GIS) Provides both a means of maintaining geographic databases and a tool capable of complex spatial analysis to provide information for a decision support system.

decision support system (DSS) An interactive, personalized information management system, designed to be initiated and controlled by individual decision makers.

QUESTIONS FOR REVIEW & CRITICAL THINKING

1. Why should companies consider creating an internal marketing database? Name some types of information that might be found in this database and the sources of this information.

2. Why has data mining become so popular with firms such as United Airlines, American Express, and Ford Motor Company?

3. What are some of the keys to ensuring the success of an internal database?

4. Why are secondary data often preferred to primary data?

5. What pitfalls might a researcher encounter in using secondary data?

6. In the absence of company problems, is there any need to conduct marketing research or develop a decision support system?

7. What is a marketing research aggregator? What role does it play in marketing research?

8. Divide the class into groups of four or five. Each team should go to the Internet and look up database marketing. Each team should then report to the class on how a specific company is effectively using databases to improve their marketing efficiency.

(Team Exercise)

WORKING THE NET

1. What makes vendors' websites a desirable tool for creating an internal database?

2. Go to *www.yankelovich.com*. Explain to the class the nature and scope of the Yankelovich MONITOR. How can marketing researchers use the data from this research?

3. Go to the National Opinion Research Center at *www.norc.uchicago.edu* and describe what new reports are available for researchers.

4. You are interested in home-building trends in the United States, as your company, Whirlpool, is a major supplier of kitchen appliances. Go to *www.nahb.com* and describe what types of information at this site might be of interest to Whirlpool.

5. Go to *www.claritas.com*. Describe types of secondary data available at this site.

6. Go to *www.marketresearch.com* and explain what types of reports are available.

REAL-LIFE RESEARCH • 3.1

Sanitized to Perfection[19]

Marketing research firm Yankelovich's *Monitor Minute* newsletter has been tracking a growing segment of the American population it has dubbed "Neatniks"—those who agree that "having a clean, spotless home is important in personal life today." The group comprised 35 percent of those surveyed; Non-Neatniks made up 63 percent.

But consumers are seeking more from the act of cleaning than simply streak-free windows. Yankelovich examined the deeper dimensions today's consumers associate with cleaning, and how cleaning satisfies their emotional needs.

"As people increasingly look to gain control over what they can in the world, there is a growing minority of consumers focusing on the importance of maintaining a clean house," the report stated. "Cleaning today fills a multidimensional role in people's lives."

In other words, average American citizens can't create a cure for the bird flu; they do, however, have dominion over dust bunnies.

Being clean has taken on a more elevated status in maintaining one's overall well-being in the minds of consumers, who believe good grooming is a crucial component to staying healthy: The *Yankelovich Preventive Health and Wellness in America* study reports that two-thirds of respondents (68 percent) cited "personal hygiene and cleanliness" as the best way to maintain one's good health.

Three-quarters (72 percent) of the population said housecleaning is a regular physical activity, even when it's a drag. A year earlier, 63 percent of parents with kids under age 18 said keeping up with housework caused a fair amount to a great deal of stress in their lives.

While Neatniks may believe cleanliness is next to Godliness, it's more of an aspiration than an actual exertion for many of them. Only 22 percent of Americans surveyed said they have a clean and spotless home, and less than half (45 percent) of so-called Neatniks said this accurately describes the state of their domicile.

In order to provide the biggest payoff from consumers' investment of time and elbow grease, Yankelovich suggests that marketers position cleaning tools as fulfilling a lot of other needs in their lives. Products and services that satisfy these higher-level cravings can gain a competitive advantage.

Neatniks's lives aren't solely about dusting and polishing the surfaces, but research suggests that such tasks may represent deeper themes. For example, the propensity for one to value cleaning correlates with a high premium on self-reliance. And Neatniks are more concerned than Non-Neatniks about how others view their personal style and in-the-know status. Here are partial results from the Yankelovich study.

Being as self-reliant as possible is important in my personal life today

Neatniks 81%
Non-Neatniks 66%

Extremely/very important for others to see me as:

Having a sense of style

Neatniks 50%
Non-Neatniks 31%

Someone with "the inside scoop"

Neatniks 39%
Non-Neatniks 25%

Concerned with buying products that express my own style and personality

Neatniks 34%
Non-Neatniks 30%

Questions

1. Is the Yankelovich study primary or secondary data? Why?
2. How might someone like Procter & Gamble use this information? Hoover (vacuum cleaners)?
3. Are psychographic data as helpful to marketers as demographic data?
4. What other sources might a company like Hoover use to help develop new products/product modifications, identify target customers, and develop a promotional strategy?

Charles Krupa/©Ap/Wide World Photos

QUALITATIVE RESEARCH

LEARNING OBJECTIVES

1.	To define qualitative research.
2.	To explore the popularity of qualitative research.
3.	To learn about focus groups and their tremendous popularity.
4.	To gain insight into conducting and analyzing a focus group.
5.	To learn about other forms of qualitative research.

Eight to one. That was the abysmal ratio of customer complaints to kudos at Staples stores in 2001. The company's slogan—"Yeah, we've got that"—had become laughable. Customers griped that items were often out of stock and said the sales staff was unhelpful to boot. After weeks of focus groups and interviews, Staples' executive VP for marketing, Shira Goodman, had a revelation. "Customers wanted an easier shopping experience," she says. "It became clear that's where the opportunities were."

Staples' subsequent rebranding effort is one of the most successful mass-marketing campaigns in recent memory, and one of the most holistic. Rather than simply bombarding customers with a new slogan—"Staples: That was easy"—Goodman and her team led a companywide overhaul that actually simplified the shopping experience. Better yet, the marketers created an iconic object, the Easy Button, which customers are now buying at Staples stores in droves, helping to spread the marketing message, not to mention bringing in some extra cash.

Customer research conducted by Goodman and her team revealed that while shoppers expected Staples and its competitors to have everything in stock, they placed little importance on price. Instead, customers overwhelmingly requested a simple, straightforward shopping experience. "They wanted knowledgeable and helpful associates and hassle-free shopping," Goodman says. The "That was easy" tagline was the simple—yet inspired—outgrowth of that realization.

The Easy Button soon gave birth to a string of humorous and popular television commercials. In one spot, called "The Wall," an emperor uses the button to erect a giant barrier as marauders approach; another shows an office worker causing printer cartridges to rain down from above. Online, Staples created a downloadable Easy Button toolbar, which took shoppers directly from their desktops to Staples.com, while billboards reminded commuters that an Easy Button would be helpful in snarled traffic.

The payoff is striking. In addition to the viral success of the buttons, Staples says customer recall of its advertising has doubled to about 70 percent, compared with the industry average of 43.[1]

What is qualitative research? How is it conducted? Is one form of qualitative research more popular than others? What makes qualitative research controversial? These are some of the issues we will explore in this chapter. ▪

Nature of Qualitative Research

Qualitative research is a term used loosely to refer to research whose findings are not subject to quantification or quantitative analysis. A quantitative study may determine that a heavy user of a particular brand of tequila is 21 to 35 years of age and has an annual income of $18,000 to $25,000. While **quantitative research** might be used to find statistically significant differences between heavy and light users, qualitative research could be used to examine the attitudes, feelings, and motivations of the heavy user. Advertising agencies planning a campaign for tequila might employ qualitative techniques to learn how heavy users express themselves and what language they use—essentially, how to communicate with them.

The qualitative approach was derived from the work of the mid-eighteenth-century historian Giambattista Vico. Vico wrote that only people can understand people and that they do so through a faculty called *intuitive understanding*. In sociology and other social sciences, the concept of *Verstehen*, or the intuitive experiment, and the use of empathy have been associated with major discoveries (and disputes).

> **qualitative research**
> Research whose findings are not subject to quantification or quantitative analysis.

> **quantitative research**
> Research that uses mathematical analysis.

Qualitative Research versus Quantitative Research

Exhibit 4.1 compares qualitative and quantitative research on several levels. Perhaps most significant to managers is the fact that qualitative research typically is characterized by small samples—a trait that has been a focal point for criticism of all qualitative techniques. In essence, many managers are reluctant to base important strategy decisions on small-sample research because it relies so greatly on the subjectivity and interpretation of the researcher. They strongly prefer a large sample, with results analyzed on a computer and summarized into tables. These managers feel comfortable with marketing research based on large samples and high levels of statistical significance because the data are generated in a rigorous and scientific manner.

Popularity of Qualitative Research

Companies are now spending over $4.6 billion annually on qualitative research.[2] Why does the popularity of qualitative research continue to grow? First, qualitative research is usually much cheaper than quantitative research. Second, there is no better way to understand the in-depth motivations and feelings of consumers. When, in a popular form of qualitative research, product managers unobtrusively observe from behind a one-way mirror, they obtain firsthand experiences with flesh-and-blood consumers. Instead of plodding through a computer printout or consultant's report that requires them to digest reams of numbers, the product manager and other marketing personnel observe consumers' reactions to concepts and hear consumers discuss their own and their competitors' products at length, in their own language. Sitting behind a one-way mirror can be a humbling experience for a new product-development manager when the consumer begins to tear apart product concepts that were months in development in the sterile laboratory environment.

A third reason for the popularity of qualitative research is that it can improve the efficiency of quantitative research. Reckitt Benckiser PLC, the maker of Woolite and Lysol, knew women were not happy with how glasses were cleaned in a dishwasher.

EXHIBIT 4.1	**Qualitative versus Quantitative Research**	
	Qualitative Research	**Quantitative Research**
Types of questions	Probing	Limited probing
Sample size	Small	Large
Amount of information from each respondent	Substantial	Varies
Requirements for administration	Interviewer with special skills	Interviewer with fewer special skills or no interviewer
Type of analysis	Subjective, interpretive	Statistical, summation
Hardware	Tape recorders, projection devices, video recorders, pictures, discussion guides	Questionnaires, computers, printouts
Degree of replicability	Low	High
Researcher training	Psychology, sociology, social psychology, consumer behavior, marketing, marketing research	Statistics, decision models, decision support systems, computer programming, marketing, marketing research
Type of research	Exploratory	Descriptive or causal

Focus groups learned that, over time, glasses washed in a dishwasher tended to become cloudy and stained. The company decided to embark on a major quantitative study to determine the extent of the perceived "staining" problem among households with dishwashers. The quantitative study verified that consumers were indeed unhappy with how their glasses looked after numerous rounds in the dishwasher. They also were willing to pay a reasonable price to find a solution. Reckitt Benckiser recently introduced Finish Glass Protector, a dishwasher detergent that protects glassware from mineral corrosion. Thus qualitative research led to a well-conceived quantitative study that verified demand for the new product.

It is becoming more common for marketing researchers to combine qualitative and quantitative research into a single study or a series of studies. The Finish Glass example showed how qualitative research can be used prior to quantitative research; in other research designs, the two types of research are conducted in the reverse order. For instance, the patterns displayed in quantitative research can be enriched with the addition of qualitative information on the reasons and motivations of consumers. One major insurance company conducted a quantitative study in which respondents were asked to rank the importance of 50 service characteristics. Later, focus groups were conducted in which participants were asked to define and expound on the top 10 characteristics. Most of these characteristics dealt with client–insurance agent interactions. From these focus groups the researchers found that "agent responds quickly" may mean either a virtually instantaneous response or a response within a reasonable time; that is, it means "as soon as is humanly possible for emergencies" and "about 24 hours for routine matters." The researchers noted that had they not conducted focus groups after the quantitative study, they could only have theorized about what "responds quickly" means to customers.[3]

In the final analysis, all marketing research is undertaken to increase the effectiveness of decision making. Qualitative research blends with quantitative measures to provide a more thorough understanding of consumer demand. Qualitative techniques involve open-ended questioning and probing. The resulting data are rich, human, subtle, and often very revealing.

Limitations of Qualitative Research

Qualitative research can and does produce helpful and useful information—yet it is held in disdain by some researchers. One drawback relates to the fact that marketing successes and failures many times are based on small differences in attitudes or opinions about a marketing mix, and qualitative research does not distinguish those small differences as well as large-scale quantitative research does. However, qualitative research is sometimes able to detect problems that escape notice in a quantitative study. For example, a major manufacturer of household cleaners conducted a large quantitative study in an effort to learn why its bathroom cleanser had lackluster sales when in fact its chemical compound was more effective than those used by leading competitors. The quantitative study provided no clear-cut answer. The frustrated product manager then turned to qualitative research, which quickly found that the muted pastel colors on the package did not connote "cleansing strength" to the shopper. In light of this finding and the finding that a number of people were using old toothbrushes to clean between their bathroom tiles, the package was redesigned with brighter, bolder colors and with a brush built into the top.

A second limitation of qualitative studies is that they are not necessarily representative of the population of interest to the researcher. One would be hard-pressed to say that a group of 10 college students was representative of all college students, of college students at a particular university, of business majors at that university, or even of marketing majors! Small sample size and free-flowing discussion can lead qualitative research projects down many paths. Because the subjects of qualitative research are free to talk about what interests them, a dominant individual in a group discussion can lead the group into areas of only tangential interest to the researcher. It takes a highly skilled researcher to get the discussion back on track without stifling the group's interest, enthusiasm, and willingness to speak out.

The Importance of Focus Groups

focus group
Group of 8 to 12 participants who are led by a moderator in an in-depth discussion on one particular topic or concept.

Focus groups had their beginnings in group therapy used by psychiatrists. Today, a **focus group** consists of 8 to 12 participants who are led by a moderator in an in-depth discussion on one particular topic or concept. The goal of focus group research is to learn and understand what people have to say and why. The emphasis is on getting people to talk at length and in detail about the subject at hand. The intent is to find out how they feel about a product, concept, idea, or organization; how it fits into their lives; and their emotional involvement with it.

Focus groups are much more than merely question-and-answer interviews. A distinction is made between *group dynamics* and *group interviewing*. The interaction associated with **group dynamics** is essential to the success of focus group research; this interaction is the reason for conducting research with a group rather than with individuals. One idea behind focus groups is that a response from one person will become a stimulus for another person, thereby generating an interplay of responses that will yield more information than if the same number of people had contributed independently.

group dynamics
Interaction among people in a group.

The idea for group dynamics research in marketing came from the field of social psychology, where studies indicated that, unknown to themselves, people of all walks of life and in all occupations would talk more about a topic and do so in greater depth if they were encouraged to act spontaneously instead of reacting to questions. Normally, in group dynamics, direct questions are avoided. In their place are indirect inquiries that stimulate free and spontaneous discussions. The result is a much richer base of information, of a kind impossible to obtain by direct questioning.

Popularity of Focus Groups

The terms *qualitative research* and *focus groups* are often used as synonyms by marketing research practitioners. Popular writing abounds with examples of researchers referring to qualitative research in one breath and focus groups in the next. Although focus groups are but one aspect of qualitative research, the overwhelming popularity of the technique has virtually overshadowed the use of other qualitative tools.

How popular are focus groups? Most marketing research firms, advertising agencies, and consumer goods manufacturers use them. Today, most of all marketing research expenditures for qualitative research is spent on focus groups. The majority of focus research projects in the United States take place in over 750 focus facilities and are directed by over 1,000 moderators. The most common formats of qualitative research are focus groups and individual depth interviews (IDIs).

Focus group research is a globally accepted form of marketing research. In 2007, there were an estimated 350,000 focus groups and equivalent individual depth interview sessions conducted outside the United States throughout Europe, Latin America, and the Asia-Pacific. This makes a worldwide total of 600,000 sessions.[4]

Focus groups tend to be used more extensively by consumer goods companies than by industrial goods organizations, as forming industrial groups poses a host of problems not found in consumer research. For example, it is usually quite easy to assemble a group of 12 homemakers; however, putting together a group of 10 engineers, sales managers, or financial analysts is far more costly and time-consuming.

Lewis Stone, former manager of Colgate-Palmolive's Research and Development Division, says the following about focus groups:

If it weren't for focus groups, Colgate-Palmolive Co. might never know that some women squeeze their bottles of dishwashing soap, others squeeeeeze them, and still others squeeeeeeeeze out the desired amount. Then there are the ones who use the soap "neat." That is, they put the product directly on a sponge or washcloth and wash the dishes under running water until the suds run out. Then they apply more detergent.

Stone was explaining how body language, exhibited during focus groups, provides insights into a product that are not apparent from reading questionnaires on habits and practices. Focus groups represent a most efficient way of learning how one's products are actually used in the home. By drawing out the panelists to describe in detail how they do certain tasks . . . you can learn a great deal about possible need-gaps that could be filled by new or improved products, and also how a new product might be received.[5]

Thus, an "experiencing" approach represents an opportunity to learn from a flesh-and-blood consumer. Reality in the kitchen or supermarket differs drastically from that in most corporate offices. Focus groups allow the researcher to experience the emotional framework in which the product is being used. In a sense, the researcher can go into a person's life and relive with him or her all the satisfactions, dissatisfactions, rewards, and frustrations experienced when the product is taken home.

Robert L. Wehling, senior vice president of global marketing and consumer knowledge at the Procter & Gamble Company, issued the following mandate to researchers: "Know the individual consumer's heart and you will own the future! Get to know this changing consumer personally. Not as an average but as a person."[6]

Conducting Focus Groups

On the following pages, we will consider the process of conducting focus groups, illustrated in Exhibit 4.2. We devote considerable space to this topic because there is much potential for researcher error in conducting focus groups.

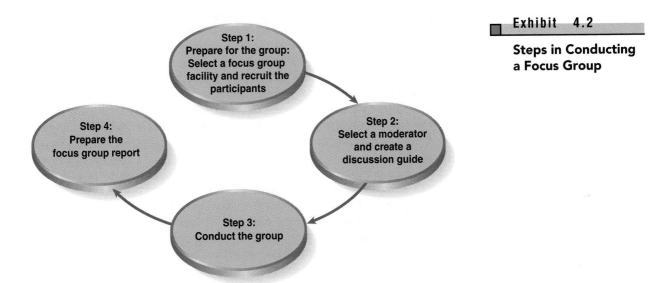

Exhibit 4.2

Steps in Conducting a Focus Group

Exhibit 4.3

A Focus Group in Progress

Setting Focus groups are usually held in a **focus group facility**. The setting is often a conference room, with a large one-way mirror built into one wall. Microphones are placed in an unobtrusive location (usually the ceiling) to record the discussion. Behind the mirror is the viewing room, which holds chairs and note-taking benches or tables for the clients. The viewing room also houses the recording or videotaping equipment. The photo in Exhibit 4.3 illustrates a focus group in progress.

Some research firms offer a living-room setting as an alternative to the conference room. It is presumed that the informality of a living room (a typical homelike setting) will make the participants more at ease. Another variation is to televise the proceedings to a remote viewing room rather than use a one-way mirror. This approach offers clients the advantage of being able to move around and speak in a normal tone of voice without being heard through the wall. On more than one occasion, focus groups have been distracted by a flash seen through the mirror when a client moved too suddenly while watching the group.

Participants Participants for focus groups are recruited from a variety of sources. Two traditional procedures are mall-intercept interviewing and random telephone screening. (Both methods are described in detail in Chapter 5.) Researchers normally establish criteria for the group participants. For example, if Quaker Oats is researching a new cereal, it might request as participants mothers who have children between 7 and 12 years old and who have served cold cereal, perhaps of a specific brand, in the past three weeks.

Some progressive focus group researchers are now combining psychographics and demographics to recruit group participants. For example, RoperASW in New York City has studied a consumer segment it calls "the Influentials"—the one American in every 10 who has significant word-of-mouth clout. Drawing on a database of more than 10,000 questions and interviews with more than 50,000 Influentials and 500,000 other Americans, RoperASW uses its knowledge of this segment to help its clients recruit candidates for qualitative research, says RoperASW CEO Ed Keller.[7]

"Influentials are two to five years ahead of the curve in their involvement with new trends and new products and lifestyle choices. They have this bellwether nature to them," explains Keller. Recruiting Influentials is particularly useful when a marketer is trying to determine how to launch a new product or how a product's use is changing over time, he says. "We'd never say that this is a panacea for every eventuality, but to the extent that you're looking for people knowledgeable, informed and open-minded, and ahead of the curve, Influentials are very appropriate to study in qualitative research," adds Keller.[8]

Other focus group recruiters go to where the target market is to find qualified respondents. This type of recruiting means going to nursery schools to find moms with kids, health clubs to find people with active lifestyles, the home improvement center to find do-it-yourselfers, supermarkets to find primary food shoppers, and community centers to find senior citizens.

Usually, researchers strive to avoid repeat, or "professional," respondents in focus groups. Professional respondents are viewed by many researchers as actors or, at the very least, less-than-candid participants. Questions also may be raised regarding the motives of the person who would continually come to group sessions. Is she or he lonely? Does she or he really need the respondent fee that badly? It is highly unlikely that professional respondents are representative of many, if any, target markets. Unfortunately, field services find it much easier to use repeat respondents than to recruit a new group of individuals each time. Sample screening questions to identify repeat respondents are shown in Exhibit 4.4.

Ken Berwitz, president of Ken Berwitz Marketing Research, offers a few hints on how to get qualified respondents to attend focus groups in the Practicing Market Research feature on page 98.

---

1. Past Participation Series

Sometimes it is important to talk with people who have participated in previous research because they have experience talking about certain topics. At other times, it is important to talk with people who have never participated in an opinion study. Often we are looking for a mix of different experiences. What type of opinion studies, if any, have you ever participated in? (DO NOT READ LIST.)

	CIRCLE ALL MENTIONS
One-on-one in-person depth interview	1
Group interview with two or more participants	2
Mock jury or trial	3
Product placement test with a follow-up interview	4
Mall interview	5
Internet survey	6
Phone survey	7
Other (SPECIFY)	8
None	9

1A. When was the last time you participated in a

_____ Group interview with two or more participants

_____ (LIST ANOTHER TYPE OF RESEARCH YOU MIGHT CONSIDER INAPPROPRIATE.)

IF WITHIN THE LAST SIX MONTHS, THANK AND TERMINATE.

1B. What were the topics of all of the group interviews in which you have participated?

_____

_____

IF ONE OF THE TOPICS LISTED BELOW IS MENTIONED, THANK AND TERMINATE.

(   ) MP3 Players

(   ) Camera Cell Phones

1C. Are you currently scheduled to participate in any type of market research study?

	CIRCLE	
Yes	1	→ (THANK AND TERMINATE)
No	2	→ (CONTINUE)

Exhibit 4.4

Sample Screening Questions for Identifying Professional Focus Group Participants

---

Source: Merrill Shugoll and Nancy Kolkebeck, "You Get What You Ask For," *Quirk's Marketing Research Review* (December 1999), pp. 61–65. Reprinted by permission.

Recruiting Tricks of the Trade

Here are a few things that I have learned over the years:

1. *The multiple incentive; or, how to turn the same amount of money into more than it is, even though it isn't.*

   You have a qualified respondent who is interested in attending your session. So your recruiter offers the $75 incentive and waits for him/her to stop drooling long enough to gasp out a delighted "Yes!" But that "Yes!" doesn't come. Instead there is a refusal because the money isn't enough, along with comments like "It's too far to drive," or "Do you realize how much parking costs in that part of town?"

   What do you do? Well, here's something that has worked for me many times: Offer them a different $75. You do this by splitting the total into two components: an incentive and an allowance for gas and parking. At $75, a logical breakdown would be $50 incentive and $25 travel.

   The reason this works is because prospective group members see it as being two payoffs instead of one. They get an amount of money that, by itself, is not enough to entice them (in this regard, $50 is no different than $75). But they also get a second amount of money for gas and parking that almost certainly will exceed their actual out-of-pocket expenditure. Suddenly they're hitting for the daily double, and it feels really good. Your show rate goes up, and it didn't cost a penny more.

2. *Stealth qualifiers.*

   A very easy and very effective recruiting trick that I've used for many years is to get at least one or two qualifying criteria out of the way before the screener is actually administered.

   Let's say you need to recruit female heads of household, 25–49 years of age, who are employed outside the home, drink at least two cups of coffee a day, and use a certain brand most often. You certainly don't want to ask about the coffee usage before a security screening has been performed. That would, er, spill the beans, so to speak. But what in the world would prevent you from determining age and employment status before that security screening takes place?

   The way you do it is via judicious use of the introduction statement. Instead of simply asking to speak with the female head of the household, you would say "We are conducting a study among female heads of household, 25–49 years of age, who are employed outside their homes. If the female head of household fits this description, may I speak to her for just a few moments?"

   Voilà! If there is such a person in the household, you have met the age and employment criteria before you ever speak to her. Now you can ask all those other questions, without the prospect of losing your potential group member at the end because she is the wrong age or has the wrong employment status. And security has not been breached in any way. This makes recruiting faster, less expensive, and doesn't in any way compromise quality. Win, win, and win.

3. *A lottery that you always win.*

   I cheerfully concede that I did not personally come up with this technique. But it's so good I decided to pass it along anyway.

   You nervously check your watch again. It's 5:58 p.m., two minutes to show time. And you have three, maybe four, group members in the reception area. The client is starting to throw funny looks your way, and you're reduced to asking the hostess if she is sure your people were properly re-screened, or that they were told the right time and day, or that they weren't inadvertently spirited into someone else's group, etc.

   What's happening is that you're suffering through the fabled 6:00 p.m. Lateness Syndrome. There are a hundred excuses for people to stroll in after the start of that early-evening group—"There was too much crosstown traffic," "I had a last-minute office crisis,"—and you've heard them all.

Want to avoid this? Spring for one extra incentive and you are likely to at least lessen the problem, or even make it go away altogether. Here's how:

After a screening questionnaire has been successfully administered, interviewers, of course, tell recruited group members what day and time the session will take place. But instead of ending with "Thanks, we'll see you at the group session," they are also told that "For everyone who shows up 15 minutes or more before the session starts, their names will be put into a bowl and there will be a drawing. The winner gets a second incentive, and winds up with double the amount."

The result is astounding. Suddenly cross-town traffic evaporates, office work is completed at 5:00 p.m. on the button, and you have the maximum number of people who really, truly could get to the facility on time. Is this worth an extra incentive? You tell me.[9]

Questions

1. Is it okay to have "professional" focus group respondents that participate continually just for the money?
2. Would you like to participate in a focus group? Why or why not?

Although there is no ideal number of participants, a typical group will contain eight participants. If the group contains more than eight people, group members will have little time to express their opinions. Rarely will a group last more than two hours; an hour and a half is more common. The first 10 minutes is spent on introductions and an explanation of procedures. This leaves about 80 useful minutes in the session, and up to 25 percent of that time may be taken by the moderator. With 10 people in the group, an average of only six minutes per individual is left for actual discussion. If the topic is quite interesting or of a technical nature, fewer than eight respondents may be needed. The type of group will also affect the number recruited.

Why do people agree to participate in focus groups? Research shows that the number one reason is money.[10] Other motivations, in rank order, are (2) the topic was interesting, (3) it was a convenient time, (4) focus groups are fun, (5) respondent knew a lot about the product, (6) curiosity, and (7) focus groups offer an opportunity to express opinions. The study also found that participants who came only for the money were less committed to research and tended to fulfill their roles in a more perfunctory way.

Moderator   Having qualified respondents and a good focus group moderator are the keys to a successful focus group. A **focus group moderator** needs two sets of skills. First, the moderator must be able to conduct a group properly. Second, he or she must have good business skills in order to effectively interact with the client. Key attributes for conducting a focus group include the following:

1. Genuine interest in people, their behavior, emotions, lifestyles, passions, and opinions
2. Acceptance and appreciation for the differences in people, especially those whose lives vary greatly from your own
3. Good listening skills: the ability both to hear what is being said and to identify what is not being said
4. Good observation skills: the ability to see in detail what is happening or not happening and to interpret body language
5. Interest in a wide range of topics and the ability to immerse yourself in the topic and learn the necessary knowledge and language quickly
6. Good oral and written communication skills: the ability to clearly express yourself and to do so confidently in groups of all types and sizes

> **focus group moderator**
> Person hired by the client to lead the focus group; this person should have a background in psychology or sociology or, at least, marketing.

7. Objectivity: the ability to set your personal ideas and feelings aside and remain open to the ideas and feelings of others

8. Sound knowledge of the basic principles, foundations, and applications of research, marketing, and advertising

9. Flexibility, ability to live with uncertainty, make fast decisions, and think on your feet (or the part of your anatomy that is seated in the moderator's chair)

10. Good attention to detail and organizational ability[11]

Rapport is the medium that makes research work. A moderator develops a free and easy sense of discourse about anything with respondents. These strangers meet and are helped to a common ground through the ease of rapport. In a comfortable, nonthreatening, lively place, they can talk about anything at all—about sausage, insurance, tires, baked goods, magazines. In research the moderator is the bridge builder, and rapport is the bridge between people's everyday lives and the client's business interest.

Jeff Eschrich, president of Catalyst Qualitative Research, offers a few techniques for building rapport:

1. Ask personal questions during warm-up. Get to know them as people first, then as consumers. Ask about their kids, applaud their anniversaries or birthdays. Inquire about the schools they attend, the courses they're taking. Get personal.

2. By the same token, it helps for the moderator to include personal information in the first round of introductions. If you expect revelations from them, you should reveal a bit about yourself. I usually say where I'm from, that I'm married for 10 years, and that I have two girls aged eight and four and reside in Kansas City.

3. Don't be afraid to ask respondents for assistance in the process of the research. It helps rapport if they're up and moving around and feel comfortable in the space. Ask them to pass out stimulus, keep time, pin things to the wall, or take notes. This small involvement opens the two-way involvement in the relationship.

Dilbert

DILBERT reprinted by permission of United Features Syndicate, Inc.

4. Lighten things up with humor. Laughter is energy. It goes a long way to helping break the ice and pick up the pace. Encourage humor from others and enjoy yourself as well. Self-deprecating humor can be more successful than focusing on any of the respondents.[12]

In addition to the above, a moderator needs the following client-focused skills:

1. An ability to understand the client's business in more than just a cursory fashion, to become an integral part of the project team, and to have credibility with senior management

2. The ability to provide the strategic leadership in both the planning and the execution phases of a project in order to improve the overall research design and provide more relevant information on which to base decisions

3. The ability to provide feedback to and be a sounding board for the client at every stage of the research process, including before, during, and after the groups. This includes being able to turn the research findings into strategically sound implications for the client at the end of the project

4. Reliability, responsiveness, trustworthiness, independence, and a dogged determination to remove obstacles in order to get the job done

5. A personal style that is a comfortable match with the client[13]

In the past few years, there has been an increase in the number of formal moderator training courses offered by advertising agencies, research firms, and manufacturers with large marketing research departments. Most programs are strictly for employees, but a few are open to anyone. Also, there is the Qualitative Research Consultants Association that promotes professionalism in a qualitative research. The association has a quarterly publication, *QRCA Views*, that features ideas and tools for qualitative research. In addition, the organization holds an annual conference dedicated to improving qualitative research. You can learn more at www.qrca.org.

Discussion Guide   Regardless of how well trained and personable the moderator is, a successful focus group requires a well-planned discussion guide. A **discussion guide** is a written outline of the topics to be covered during the session. Usually the guide is generated by the moderator based on the research objectives and client information needs. It serves as a checklist to ensure that all salient topics are covered and in the proper sequence. For example, an outline might begin with attitudes and feelings toward eating out, then move to fast foods, and conclude with a discussion of the food and decor of a particular chain. It is important to get the research director and other client observers, such as a brand manager, to agree that the topics listed in the guide are the most important ones to be covered. It is not uncommon for a team approach to be used in generating a discussion guide.

The guide tends to lead the discussion through three stages. In the first stage, rapport is established, the rules of group interactions are explained, and objectives are given. In the second stage, the moderator attempts to provoke intensive discussion. The final stage is used for summarizing significant conclusions and testing the limits of belief and commitment.

Exhibit 4.5 shows an actual discussion guide for diet breads by a Decision Analyst moderator. The groups were held in several cities around the country.

> **discussion guide**
> Written outline of topics to be covered during a focus group discussion.

Exhibit 4.5

Decision Analyst, Inc. Discussion Outline: Diet Breads

I. Introduction

   A. Tape recording/observers
   B. Casual, relaxed, informal
   C. No right or wrong answers
   D. Be honest. Tell the truth.
   E. Discussion rules
      • Talk one at a time
      • Don't dominate the discussion
      • Talk in any order
      • Listen to others

II. General Attitudes Toward Bread

   A. Eating more or less bread now, compared to two years ago? Explore reasons.
   B. Advantages of bread, compared to other foods?
   C. Disadvantages of bread, compared to other foods?
   D. Words/mental images associated with great tasting bread?
   E. Foods bread goes with best? Why?

III. Usage/Purchase of Bread

   A. When and where is bread consumed most often?
   B. How does bread usage vary by household member? Why?
   C. Types of bread used most frequently?
   D. Likes/dislikes of each type of bread?
   E. Brands preferred? Why these brands? Vary by family member?

IV. Bread Consumption When Dieting

   A. Changes in bread consumption related to dieting? Why?
   B. Types of bread eaten when dieting, if any. Reasons?
   C. Role of bread in dieting?

V. Attitudes Toward Diet Breads

   A. Awareness of diet breads/brands?
   B. Experiences with diet breads/brands?
   C. Satisfaction with each brand? Why like or not like? Brand perceptions?
   D. Important factors/product attributes associated with preferred brands?

VI. The Perfect Diet Bread

   A. Product characteristics?
      • Taste
      • Texture
      • Color
      • Crust
   B. Nutritional benefits?
   C. Packaging preferences?

VII. Show and Discuss Advertising Concepts

   A. Overall reactions to each concept?
   B. Likes/dislikes for each concept?
   C. Main idea for each concept?
   D. Believability?

VIII. Reactions to Diet Bread Samples

   A. Overall reactions to each bread?
   B. Reactions to taste?

C. Reactions to texture and mouth feel?
D. Reaction to slice shape and thickness?
E. Reaction to loaf shape and size?
F. Reaction to color?
G. Reaction to feel in hand?

www.decisionanalyst.com

Exhibit 4.5

Decision Analyst, Inc. Discussion Outline Diet Breads
(continued)

Focus Group Length   Many managers today prefer shorter (around an hour) focus groups. Yet the average group today is still about 90 minutes. Although shorter groups may be the trend, there is much to be said for longer focus groups. By a longer group we mean two hours or longer. A long group helps managers get more things done in a single session, and it also allows the respondents to get more involved, participate in more time-consuming tasks, and interact more extensively.

The group length issue is not an isolated one; rather, it is intertwined with a second key factor: the number of questions in the discussion guide. One of the biggest problems with focus groups today, in our opinion, is the tendency to prepare discussion guides that pose far too many questions, which virtually precludes any depth of coverage or any significant group interactions. Managers want to get their money's worth, so it makes sense for them to ask every possible question. The "focus group" turns into a group interrogation or survey but without the controls and statistical power of scientific surveys.

In order to think more explicitly and logically about the number of questions to ask, managers should examine the interactions between the length of the focus group and the size of the discussion guide. As illustrated in Exhibit 4.6, more questions and less time combine to create a research environment that elicits responses that are mere survey-like sound bites. Also, moderators who have to plow through 40 questions in 90 minutes are likely to feel rushed, unable to probe interesting responses, and inclined to be abrupt with long-winded or slow individuals. As we move up and to the right in the table, these pressures and constraints diminish. With fewer questions and more time, respondents can elaborate their answers, moderators can probe more effectively, and the pace becomes more relaxed, natural, and humanistic.[14]

EXHIBIT 4.6	Response Time per Question per Respondent		
	Focus Group Length		
Number of Questions	75 min.	90 min.	120 min.
15	:30	:36	:48
20	:23	:27	:36
25	:18	:22	:29
30	:15	:18	:24
35	:13	:15	:21
40	:11	:14	:18

Note: The analysis assumes a group comprising 10 respondents.

Source: Dennis Rook, "Out of Focus Groups," *Marketing Research* (Summer 2003), p. 13.

> **instant analysis**
> Moderator debriefing, offering a forum for brainstorming by the moderator and client observers.

Focus Group Report   Typically, after the final group in a series is completed, there will be a moderator debriefing, sometimes called **instant analysis**. This tradition has both pros and cons. Arguments for instant analysis include the idea that it serves as a forum for combining the knowledge of the marketing specialists who viewed the group with that of the moderator. It gives the client an opportunity to hear and react to the moderator's initial perceptions, and it harnesses the heightened awareness and excitement of the moment to generate new ideas and implications in a brainstorming environment.

The shortcomings include the possibility of biasing future analysis on the part of the moderator with this "hip-shooting commentary," conducted without the benefit of time to reflect on what transpired. Instant analysis will be influenced by recency, selective recall, and other factors associated with limited memory capabilities; it does not allow the moderator to hear all that was said in a less than highly involved and anxious state. There is nothing wrong with a moderator debriefing as long as the moderator explicitly reserves the right to change her or his opinion after reviewing the tapes.

Today, a formal focus group report is typically a PowerPoint presentation. The written report is nothing more than a copy of the PowerPoint slides.

Jacob Brown of In-Depth Research discusses conducting focus groups in the accompanying Global Research box.

GLOBAL RESEARCH

Planning Global Focus Groups

Consistency is best achieved by building a well-defined research template that clearly communicates research guidelines but still allows each moderator to adapt the process to fit local culture and individual style. Clearly articulating these ground rules will eliminate much of the ambiguity and reduce opportunities for misunderstanding. Some simple suggestions include:

- Start the research in your home country (we'll assume you're a U.S.-based company). That way all the stakeholders have a chance to attend the groups and agree on how the research "should" look before you fan out across the globe.
- Send copies of the U.S. videotapes to each foreign moderator. Remember that you may have to have the tapes converted to the appropriate video format for each country and pay to have a translator watch the video with the moderator.

- Have the U.S. moderator schedule conference calls with each moderator to discuss the research process and answer questions—after they have watched the videos.
- If your budget allows it, have the U.S. moderator travel to each country. The U.S. moderator can manage the process locally, give consistent direction to each moderator, and ensure that the research doesn't get off course.

Internationally, most moderators have a more passive moderating style. They generally like a more leisurely pace and a more open group environment. As a result, you may not be able to cover as many topics as you might in the United States, nor will you be able to drill down quite as deeply.

Tips for Some Major Countries

Here are a few facts about conducting research in some of the major markets.

Japan

Scheduling a large number of B2B groups can be a challenge in Japan since you can only do one focus group each night, not two as we do in the United States. Professionals have long commutes, they work late, and they can't leave early or do a lunch group. However, they are willing to come in and do groups or interviews on the weekend. So, if you need to do six groups, think of doing three on Saturday and three on Sunday. But remember, there's a lot of competition for space at facilities on the weekend, so book early.

Germany

When doing any research in Germany, be aware that the privacy laws are probably the most restrictive in the world. Your ability to get names from e-mail lists, publication lists, or other databases can be severely constrained. Even using names from your own company database may be an issue.

France

Paris is famous for strikes, especially among the transportation workers. Check with the recruiter to see if there are any strikes on the horizon. If strikes have been in the news, make sure you schedule enough replacements and expect some delays. If a transportation strike is expected, you can still do the research, but have the recruiter check with each respondent about his or her ability to get to the facility if there is a strike. And make sure your hotel is within walking distance of the facility.

England

There is a wide mix of educational levels among UK businesspeople. Leaving school early is not uncommon in England, and many successful businesspeople have relatively little formal education. If a degree is important, make sure to include it in the screener—don't assume it the way you would in the United States. Conversely, don't require a degree in the screener unless you really feel it's important.

Scandinavia

Companies often overlook the Scandinavian countries when planning European research. But remember: Scandinavia has the best technology infrastructure and the most educated and fluent English-speaking professionals in Europe.[15]

Questions

1. Can focus groups be conducted the same all over the world?
2. How might culture impact a focus group?

Benefits and Drawbacks of Focus Groups

The benefits and drawbacks of qualitative research in general also apply to focus groups. But focus groups have some unique pros and cons that deserve mention.

Advantages of Focus Groups The interactions among respondents can stimulate new ideas and thoughts that might not arise during one-on-one interviews. And group pressure can help challenge respondents to keep their thinking realistic. Energetic interactions among respondents also make it likely that observation of a group will provide firsthand consumer information to client observers in a shorter amount of time and in a more interesting way than will individual interviews.

Another advantage focus groups offer is the opportunity to observe customers or prospects from behind a one-way mirror. In fact, there is growing use of focus groups to expose a broader range of employees to customer comments and views. "We have found that the only way to get people to really understand what customers want is to let them see customers, but there are few people who actually come in contact with customers," says Bonnie Keith, corporate market research manager at Hewlett-Packard. "Right now, we are getting people from our manufacturing and engineering operations to attend and observe focus groups."

Another advantage of focus groups is that they can be executed more quickly than many other research techniques. In addition, findings from groups tend to be easier to understand and to have a compelling immediacy and excitement. "I can get up and show a client all the charts and graphs in the world, but it has nowhere near the impact of showing 8 or 10 customers sitting around a table and saying that the company's service isn't good," says Jean-Anne Mutter, director of marketing research at Ketchum Advertising.[16]

Disadvantages of Focus Groups Unfortunately, some of the strengths of focus groups also can become disadvantages. For example, the immediacy and apparent understandability of focus group findings can cause managers to be misled instead of informed. Mutter says, "Even though you're only getting a very small slice, a focus group gives you a sense that you really understand the situation." She adds that focus groups can strongly appeal to "people's desire for quick, simple answers to problems, and I see a decreasing willingness to go with complexity and to put forth the effort needed to really think through the complex data that will be yielded by a quantitative study."[17]

This sentiment is echoed by Gary Willets, director of marketing research for NCR Corporation. He notes, "What can happen is that you will do the focus group, and you will find out all of these details, and someone will say, 'OK, we've found out all that we need to know.' The problem is that what is said in a focus group may not be all that typical. What you really want to do is do a qualitative study on the front end and follow it up with a quantitative study."[18] Focus groups, like qualitative research in general, are essentially inductive in approach. The research is data-driven, with findings and conclusions being drawn directly from the information provided. In contrast, quantitative studies generally follow a deductive approach, in which formulated ideas and hypotheses are tested with data collected specifically for that purpose.

Other disadvantages relate to the focus group process. For example, focus group recruiting may be a problem if the type of person recruited responds differently to the issues being discussed than do other target segments. White middle-class individuals, for example, participate in qualitative research in numbers disproportionate to their presence in the marketplace. Also, some focus group facilities create an impersonal feeling, making honest conversation unlikely. Corporate or formal settings with large boardroom tables and unattractive or plain decor may make it difficult for respondents to relax and share their feelings.

The greatest potential for distortion is during the group interview itself. As a participant in the social interaction, the moderator must take care not to behave in ways that prejudice responses. The moderator's style may contribute to bias. For example, an aggressive, confronting style may lead respondents to say whatever they think the moderator wants them to say, to avoid attack. Or "playing dumb" may create the perception that the moderator is insincere or phony and cause respondents to withdraw.

Respondents also can be a problem. Some individuals are simply introverted and do not like to speak out in group settings. Other people may attempt to dominate the discussion. These are people who know it all—or think they do—and answer every question first, without giving others a chance to speak. A dominating participant may succeed in swaying other group members. If a moderator is abrupt with a respondent, it can send the wrong message to other group members—"You'd better be cautious, or I will do the same thing to you." Fortunately, a good moderator can stifle a dominant group member and not the rest of the group. Simple techniques used by moderators include avoiding eye contact with a dominant person; reminding the group that "we want to give everyone a chance to talk;" saying "Let's have someone else go first;" or if someone else is speaking and the dominant person interrupts, looking at the initial speaker and saying, "Sorry, I cannot hear you."

Video Transmission of Focus Groups   Live video transmissions of focus groups has occurred for the past 20 years. The advantage for researchers and clients is that not everyone has to travel to every focus group to participate. A survey found that users of video focus groups were typically quite pleased. Sixty-seven percent rated the experience excellent or good. Approximately 22 percent of all U.S. focus groups involve video transmissions.[19]

Other Qualitative Methodologies

Most of this chapter has been devoted to focus groups because of their pervasive use in marketing research. However, several other qualitative techniques are also used, albeit on a much more limited basis.

Individual Depth Interviews

Individual depth interviews (IDI) are relatively unstructured one-on-one interviews. The interviewer is thoroughly trained in the skill of probing and eliciting detailed answers to each question. Sometimes psychologists are used as depth interviewers: They may employ nondirective clinical techniques to uncover hidden motivations. IDIs are the second most popular form of qualitative research.

> **individual depth interviews**
> One-on-one interviews that probe and elicit detailed answers to questions, often using nondirective techniques to uncover hidden motivations.

The direction of a depth interview is guided by the responses of the interviewee. As the interview unfolds, the interviewer thoroughly probes each answer and uses the replies as a basis for further questioning. For example, a depth interview might begin with a discussion of snack foods. The interviewer might follow each answer with "Can you tell me more?" "Would you elaborate on that?" or "Is that all?" The interviewer might then move into the pros and cons of various ingredients, such as corn, wheat, and potatoes. The next phase could delve into the sociability of the snack food. Are Fritos, for example, more commonly eaten alone or in a crowd? Are Wheat Thins usually reserved for parties? When should you serve Ritz crackers?

The advantages of depth interviews over focus groups are as follows:

1. Group pressure is eliminated, so the respondent reveals more honest feelings, not necessarily those considered most acceptable among peers.

2. The personal one-on-one situation gives the respondent the feeling of being the focus of attention—that his or her thoughts and feelings are important and truly wanted.

3. The respondent attains a heightened state of awareness because he or she has constant interaction with the interviewer and there are no group members to hide behind.

4. The longer time devoted to individual respondents encourages the revelation of new information.

5. Respondents can be probed at length to reveal the feelings and motivations that underlie statements.

6. Without the restrictions of cultivating a group process, new directions of questioning can be improvised more easily. Individual interviews allow greater flexibility to explore casual remarks and tangential issues, which may provide critical insights into the main issue.

7. The closeness of the one-on-one relationship allows the interviewer to become more sensitive to nonverbal feedback.

8. A singular viewpoint can be obtained from a respondent without influence from others.

9. The interview can be conducted anywhere, in places other than a focus group facility.

10. Depth interviews may be the only viable technique for situations in which a group approach would require that competitors be placed in the same room. For example, it might be very difficult to do a focus group on systems for preventing bad checks with managers from competing department stores or restaurants.

The disadvantages of depth interviews relative to focus groups are as follows:

1. The total cost of depth interviews can be more expensive than focus groups, but not on a cost per respondent minute (see the next heading).

2. Depth interviews do not generally get the same degree of client involvement as focus groups. It is difficult to convince most client personnel to sit through multiple hours of depth interviews so as to benefit firsthand from the information.

3. Because depth interviews are physically exhausting for the moderator, they do not cover as much ground in one day as do focus groups. Most moderators will not do more than four or five depth interviews in a day, whereas they can involve 20 people in a day in two focus groups.

4. Focus groups give the moderator an ability to leverage the dynamics of the group to obtain reactions that might not be generated in a one-on-one session.[20]

The success of any depth interview depends mainly on the skills of the interviewer. Good depth interviewers, whether psychologists or not, are hard to find and expensive. A second factor that determines the success of depth research is proper interpretation. The unstructured nature of the interview and the clinical nature of the analysis increase the complexity of the task. Small sample sizes, the difficulty of making comparisons, the subjective nature of the researcher's interpretations, and high costs have all contributed to the lack of popularity of depth interviewing. Classic applications of depth interviews include:

☐ Communication checks (for example, review of print, radio, or TV advertisements or other written materials)

☐ Sensory evaluations (for example, reactions to varied formulations for deodorants or hand lotions, sniff tests for new perfumes, or taste tests for a new frosting)

☐ Exploratory research (for example, defining baseline understanding or a product, service, or idea)

☐ New product development, prototype stage

☐ Packaging or usage research (for example, when clients want to "mirror" personal experience and obtain key language descriptors)[21]

A variation of the depth interview is called customer care research (CCR). The basic idea is to use depth interviewing to understand the dynamics of the purchase process. The following seven questions are the basis for CCR:

1. What started you on the road to making this purchase?

2. Why did you make this purchase now?

3. What was the hardest part of this process? Was there any point where you got stuck?

4. When and how did you decide the price was acceptable?

5. Is there someone else with whom I should talk to get more of the story behind this purchase?

6. If you've purchased this product before, how does the story of your last purchase differ from this one?

7. At what point did you decide you trusted this organization and this person to work with in your best interests?[22]

Cost of Focus Groups versus IDI In a standard, eight-person, 90-minute focus group, there are nine people (eight participants plus moderator) sharing the floor. On average, therefore, each respondent is allotted 10 minutes of talk time across those 90 minutes (90 minutes divided by nine people).

The cost of a focus group of this type is about $6,000. That number includes everything: recruiter, moderator, participant stipend, food, facility, report write-up, and the cost of getting a few observers to the event. Divide 80 minutes of participant talk time (the moderator doesn't count) into the $6,000 expense, and your cost per respondent minute in this case is $75 ($6,000/80).

If, however, a typical in-depth interview runs 30 minutes and costs between $400 and $500 (including recruiting, interviewing, participant stipend, and reporting), the cost per respondent minute is in the range of $16 to $25. The big difference results from the amount of time the respondent spends talking, which is typically about 20 to 25 of those 30 minutes in an in-depth phone interview.

Thus, when considering the cost per respondent minute, in-depth interviews can provide much greater value.[23] Of course, the quality of both the focus groups and the IDI determines the real value of the research.

Using Hermeneutics Some IDI researchers use a technique called hermeneutic research to achieve their goals. **Hermeneutic research** focuses on interpretation as a basis of understanding the consumer. Interpretation comes about through "conversations" between the researcher and the participant. In hermeneutic research, the researcher answers the participant's questions and, as in the traditional method, the researcher only questions the respondent. There are no predetermined questions, but questions arise spontaneously as the conversation unfolds.

> **hermeneutic research**
> Research that focuses on interpretation through conversations.

For example, a researcher and consumer in conversation about why that individual purchased a high-end home theater system may discuss the reasons for making the purchase, such as holding movie parties, enjoying a stay-at-home luxury, or immersing oneself in sporting events. The researcher may interpret "holding movie parties" as a reason for purchase to mean that without the system, the consumer would not hold the parties at all, and so the researcher will return to the consumer for additional information. Upon reviewing the data and talking more, the researcher and consumer determine that why the item was purchased and why it is used (which may or may not be the same) are not as telling as how the product makes its owner feel. In this case, the owner may feel confident as an entertainer, more social, powerful, wealthy, relaxed, or rejuvenated. Talking and probing more about the use of the home theater, the researcher uncovers both new data and new issues to address or consider moving forward.[24]

Using the Delphi Method The **Delphi Method** is often used in new product development when firms are looking for creative new ideas to incorporate in products or services. The term *Delphi* has its roots in Greek history. The city of Delphi was a hub of activity, combining culture, religion, and perspective into one highly populated area of information. Delphi was also home to the Oracle of Pythia, a woman believed to offer great insight into the future. The Oracle was a great influence to visitors, who believed this knowledge of the future would help them succeed in life.

> **Delphi Method**
> Rounds of individual data collection from knowledgeable people; results are summarized and returned to participants for further refinement.

Typically, the Delphi Method relies on people who are experts in some area. It may be product development researchers, marketing managers, professional people (doctors, engineers, etc.), magazine editors, executives, priests, and so forth. Obviously, the type of experts used depends on the objectives of the Delphi session. If one is looking for more efficient ways to handle materials management in a warehouse, the experts may simply be the workers in the warehouse.

The Delphi Method involves a number of rounds of data collection. In the classical Delphi procedure, the first round is unstructured, in order to allow individual experts relative freedom to identify and elaborate the pertinent issues from their point of view. These issues are then consolidated by the researcher(s) into a structured questionnaire. This questionnaire is subsequently used to elicit the opinions and judgments of the panel of experts in a quantitative form. The responses are analyzed and statistically summarized and presented back to the panelists for further consideration. Respondents are then given the opportunity to alter prior opinions on the basis of feedback. The number of rounds varies from two to ten, but seldom goes beyond one or two iterations.

The key characteristics of Delphi are anonymity, iteration, feedback, and aggregation of group responses. The objective is to obtain the most reliable consensus of opinion via a series of intensive questionnaires, interspersed with opinion feedback.

The purpose of anonymity in a Delphi study is to exclude group interaction, which can cause a number of problems, such as group conflict and individual dominance. Delphi relies on a structured, indirect approach to group decision making; that is, participants don't meet, relying instead on statistical aggregation of individual predictions and ideas.

Controlled feedback, developed from the results of a round, is presented back to the panel of experts at the start of the next round. The form of the feedback varies depending on the topic. It may simply be an aggregation of ideas, or, if the group is estimating sales of a proposed new product, then quantitative estimates, for example, medians, may be given. Sometimes the Delphi Method creates scenarios—for example, how can we create a better customer relationship management (CRM) software that will enable us to take market share from the two market leaders? Scenarios can be used to answer two types of questions: (1) Precisely how might some hypothetical situation come about, step by step? and (2) What alternatives exist, for each actor, at each step, for preventing, diverting, or facilitating the process?

The iteration, controlled feedback, and aggregation of group responses aim to produce as many high-quality responses and opinions as possible on a given issue(s) from a panel of experts to enhance decision making. By feeding back responses from the panel to each member in the group, through a series of iterations, experts are able to adjust their estimates on the basis of others' comments.

Projective Tests

Projective techniques are sometimes incorporated into depth interviews. The origins of projective techniques lie in the field of clinical psychology. In essence, the objective of any **projective test** is to delve below surface responses to obtain true feelings, meanings, and motivations. The rationale behind projective tests comes from the knowledge that people are often reluctant or unable to reveal their deepest feelings. In some instances, they are unaware of those feelings because of psychological defense mechanisms.

Projective tests are techniques for penetrating a person's defense mechanisms to allow true feelings and attitudes to emerge. Generally, a respondent is presented with an unstructured and nebulous situation and asked to respond. Because the situation is ill-defined and has no true meaning, the respondent must impose her or his own frame of reference. In theory, the respondent "projects" personal feelings into the unstructured situation, bypassing defense mechanisms because the respondent is not referring directly to herself or himself. As the individual talks about something or someone else, her or his inner feelings are revealed.

projective test
Technique for tapping respondents' deepest feelings by having them project those feelings into an unstructured situation.

Why is projection important? Consumers (or doctors, voters, managers, or whomever we are studying) may not tell us everything that influences them. Three obstacles stand in the way:

1. Respondents may be unconscious or unaware of a particular influence.

2. They may be aware of an influence, but feel it is too personal or socially undesirable to admit (e.g., prestige image or racial bias).

3. They may be aware that they perceive a product a particular way, but they may not bother to mention this because, in their view, it is not a logical, rational reason for buying or not buying the product. Some doctors, for example, are adamant that what they prescribe has nothing to do with the sound of a drug's name or the attractiveness of the manufacturer's logo, and is based solely on decision-making factors such as research findings, clinical experience, and patient compliance.[25]

Most projective tests are easy to administer and are tabulated like other open-ended questions. They are often used in conjunction with nonprojective open- and closed-ended questions. A projective test may gather "richer," and perhaps more revealing, data than do standard questioning techniques. Projective techniques are used often in image questionnaires and concept tests, and occasionally in advertising pretests. It is also common to apply several projective techniques during a depth interview.

The most common forms of projective techniques used in marketing research are word association tests, sentence and story completion tests, cartoon tests, photo sorts, consumer drawings, storytelling, and third-person techniques. Other techniques, such as psychodrama tests and the Thematic Apperception Test (TAT), have been popular in treating psychological disorders but of less help in marketing research.

Word Association Tests   **Word association tests** are among the most practical and effective projective tools for marketing researchers. An interviewer reads a word to a respondent and asks him or her to mention the first thing that comes to mind. Usually, the individual will respond with a synonym or an antonym. The words are read in quick succession to avoid allowing time for defense mechanisms to come into play. If the respondent fails to answer within three seconds, some emotional involvement with the word is assumed.

> **word association test**
> Projective test in which the interviewer says a word and the respondent must mention the first thing that comes to mind.

Word association tests are used to select brand names, advertising campaign themes, and slogans. For example, a cosmetic manufacturer might ask consumers to respond to the following words as potential names for a new perfume: infinity, encounter, flame, desire, precious, erotic. One of these words or a synonym suggested by respondents might then be selected as the brand name.

Analogies   Slightly different from word associations, **analogies** draw a comparison between two items in terms of their similarities. For example, a researcher investigating consumers' perceptions of Ford automobiles may ask: "I'm going to read you a list of stores, and then I'd like you to tell me which of these is most similar to Ford cars. If possible, try to give the first answer that comes to mind. The stores are: Neiman Marcus, Wal-Mart, Macy's, JC Penney, Kmart, Nordstrom, Target, and Lord & Taylor." As a follow-up, the researcher would then ask: "What is it about [Store X] that is most similar to Ford cars? How are the qualities of Ford cars similar to this store?" This line of questioning induces the respondent to talk (indirectly) about his or her perceptions of Ford cars.

> **analogy**
> Drawing a comparison between two items in terms of their similarities.

The use of analogies in this instance is not to determine which store(s) people associate with Ford cars but rather to get people to talk about their perceptions of Ford cars in ways they might otherwise be unable to do. Because perceptions of stores vary, some respondents may choose Store A, and some may choose Store B. The researcher should be less concerned with identifying the store(s) that respondents tend to select and more concerned with determining the reasons respondents give for the choices they make. Person A may select a different store from Person B, but this is of little significance if these two individuals share similar perceptions of the stores they chose, and hence of the Ford brand.[26]

> **personification**
> Drawing a comparison between a product and a person.

Personification   A technique similar to analogies, **personification** involves drawing a comparison between a product and a person. To continue with the example from above, the researcher might say, "Think about the Ford brand, and imagine it were a person. Who would this brand be? How would you describe this person? What personality characteristics would this person have? In what ways do you associate this person with the brand?"

During this type of exercise, the researcher should encourage the participant to discuss such things as the person's values, beliefs, goals, lifestyle, appearance, age, occupation, socioeconomic status, hobbies, and interests. All of these can speak volumes about the respondent's attitudes toward the brand and can go significantly beyond the output of standard lines of questioning.[27]

> **sentence and story completion tests**
> Projective tests in which respondents complete sentences or stories in their own words.

Sentence and Story Completion Tests   **Sentence and story completion tests** can be used in conjunction with word association tests. The respondent is furnished with an incomplete story or group of sentences and asked to complete it. A few examples of incomplete sentences follow:

1. Best Buy is . . .
2. The people who shop at Best Buy are . . .
3. Best Buy should really . . .
4. I don't understand why Best Buy doesn't . . .

Here's an example of a story completion test:

Sally Jones just moved to Chicago from Los Angeles, where she had been a salesperson for IBM. She is now a district manager for the Chicago area. Her neighbor Rhonda Smith has just come over to Sally's apartment to welcome her to Chicago. A discussion of where to shop ensues. Sally notes, "You know, I've heard some things about Best Buy. . . ." What is Rhonda's reply?

As you can see, story completion tests provide a more structured and detailed scenario for the respondent. Again, the objective is for the interviewees to put themselves in the role of the imaginary person mentioned in the scenario.

Sentence and story completion tests have been considered by some researchers to be the most useful and reliable of all the projective tests. Decision Analyst is now offering both online sentence completion and online word association research to its clients.

> **cartoon test**
> Projective test in which the respondent fills in the dialogue of one of two characters in a cartoon.

Cartoon Tests   The typical **cartoon test** consists of two characters with balloons, similar to those seen in comic books; one balloon is filled with dialogue, and the other balloon is blank (see Exhibit 4.7). The respondent is asked to fill in the blank balloon. Note that the cartoon figures in Exhibit 4.7 are left vague and without expression so that the respondent is not given clues regarding a suggested type of response. The ambiguity is designed to make it easier for the respondent to project his or her feelings into the cartoon situation.

Cartoon tests are extremely versatile and highly projective. They can be used to obtain differential attitudes toward two types of establishments and the congruity or lack of congruity between these establishments and a particular product. They can also be used to measure the strength of an attitude toward a particular product or brand, or to ascertain what function is being performed by a given attitude.

Exhibit 4.7

Cartoon Test

Photo Sorts

With **photo sorts**, consumers express their feelings about brands by manipulating a specially developed photo deck depicting different types of people, from business executives to college students. Respondents connect the individuals in the photos with the brands they think they would use.

BBDO Worldwide, one of the country's largest advertising agencies, has developed a trademarked technique called Photosort. A Photosort conducted for General Electric found that consumers thought the brand attracted conservative, older, business types. To change that image, GE adopted the "Bring Good Things to Life" campaign. A Photosort for Visa found the credit card to have a wholesome, female, middle-of-the-road image in customers' minds. The "Everywhere You Want to Be" campaign was devised to interest more high-income men.

Another photo sort technique, entitled Pictured Aspirations Technique (PAT), was created by Grey Advertising, a large New York advertising agency. The technique attempts to uncover how a product fits into a consumer's aspirations. Consumers sort a deck of photos according to how well the pictures describe their aspirations. In research done for Playtex's 18-hour bra, this technique revealed that the product was out of sync with the aspirations of potential customers. The respondents chose a set of pictures that depicted "the me they wanted to be" as very energetic, slim, youthful, and vigorous. But the pictures they used to express their sense of the product were a little more old-fashioned, a little stouter, and less vital and energetic looking. Out went the "Good News for Full-Figured Gals" campaign, with Jane Russell as spokesperson, and in came the sexier, more fashionable concept of "Great Curves Deserve 18 Hours."

> **photo sort**
> Projective technique in which a respondent sorts photos of different types of people, identifying those people who she or he feels would use the specified product or service.

Consumer Drawings

Researchers sometimes ask consumers to draw what they are feeling or how they perceive an object. **Consumer drawings** can unlock motivations or express perceptions. For example, McCann-Erickson advertising agency wanted to find out why Raid roach spray outsold Combat insecticide disks in certain markets. In interviews, most users agreed that Combat is a better product because it kills roaches without any effort on the user's part. So the agency asked the heaviest users of roach spray—low-income women from the southern United States—to draw pictures of their prey (see Exhibit 4.8). The goal was to get at their underlying feelings about this dirty job.

> **consumer drawings**
> Projective technique in which respondents draw what they are feeling or how they perceive an object.

"One night I just couldn't take the horror of these bugs sneaking around in the dark. They are always crawling when you can't see them. I had to do something. I thought wouldn't it be wonderful if when I switch on the light the roaches would shrink up and die like vampires to sunlight. So I did, but they just all scattered. But I was ready with my spray so it wasn't a total loss. I got quite a few . . . continued tomorrow night when nighttime falls."

"A man likes a free meal you cook for him; as long as there is food he will stay."

"I tiptoed quietly into the kitchen, perhaps he wasn't around. I stretched my arm up to turn on the light. I hoped I'd be alone when the light went on. Perhaps he is sitting on the table I thought. You think that's impossible? Nothing is impossible with that guy. He might not even be alone. He'll run when the light goes on I thought. But what's worse is for him to slip out of sight. No, it would be better to confront him before he takes control and 'invites a companion'."

Exhibit 4.8

Consumer Drawings That Helped Identify Respondents' Need for Control

Source: Courtesy of McCann-Erickson, New York.

All of the 100 women who participated in the agency's interviews portrayed roaches as men. "A lot of their feelings about the roach were very similar to the feelings that they had about the men in their lives," said Paula Drillman, executive vice president at McCann-Erickson. Many of the women were in common-law relationships. They said that the roach, like the man in their life, "only comes around when he wants food." The act of spraying roaches and seeing them die was satisfying to this frustrated, powerless group. Setting out Combat disks may have been less trouble, but it just didn't give them the same feeling. "These women wanted control," Drillman said. "They used the spray because it allowed them to participate in the kill."

storytelling
Projective technique in which respondents are required to tell stories about their experiences, with a company or product, for example; also known as the *metaphor technique*.

Storytelling As the name implies, **storytelling** requires consumers to tell stories about their experiences. It is a search for subtle insights into consumer behavior.

Gerald Zaltman, a Harvard Business School professor, has created a metaphor laboratory to facilitate the storytelling process. (A metaphor is a description of one thing in terms that are usually used to describe another; it can be used to represent thoughts that are tacit, implicit, and unspoken.) Zaltman elicits metaphors from consumers by asking them to spend time over several weeks thinking about how they would visually represent their experiences with a company. To help them with the process, he asks them to cut out magazine pictures that somehow convey those experiences. Then, consumers come to his lab and spend several hours telling stories about all of the images they chose and the connections between the images and their experiences with the firm.

One metaphor study was conducted on pantyhose. "Women in focus groups have always said that they wear them because they have to, and they hate it," says Glenda Green, a marketing research manager at DuPont, which supplies the raw material for many pantyhose manufacturers. "We didn't think we had a completely accurate picture of their feelings, but we hadn't come up with a good way to test them."[28] DuPont turned to storytelling for better insights. Someone brought a picture of a spilled ice cream sundae, capturing the rage she feels when she spots a run in her hose. Another arrived with a picture of a beautiful woman with baskets of fruit. Other photos depicted a Mercedes and Queen Elizabeth. "As we kept probing into the emotions behind the choice of these photos, the women finally began admitting that hose made them feel sensual, sexy, and more attractive to men," says Green. "There's no way anyone would admit that in a focus group." Several stocking manufacturers used this information to alter their advertising and package design.

Third-Person Technique   Perhaps the easiest projective technique to apply, other than word association, is the **third-person technique**. Rather than directly asking respondents what they think, researchers couch the question in terms of "your neighbor," "most people," or some other third party. Rather than asking a mother why she typically does not fix a nutritionally balanced breakfast for her children, a researcher might ask, "Why don't many people provide their families nutritionally balanced breakfasts?" The third-person technique is often used to avoid questions that might be embarrassing or evoke hostility if posed directly to a respondent.

> **third-person technique**
> Projective technique in which the interviewer learns about respondents' feelings by asking them to answer for a third party, such as "your neighbor" or "most people."

Future of Qualitative Research

The rationale behind qualitative research tests is as follows:

1. The criteria employed and the evaluations made in most buying and usage decisions have emotional and subconscious content, which is an important determinant of buying and usage decisions.

2. Such content is adequately and accurately verbalized by the respondent only through *indirect* communicative techniques.

To the extent that these tenets remain true or even partially correct, the demand for qualitative applications in marketing research will continue to exist. But the problems of small sample sizes and subjective interpretation will continue to plague some forms of qualitative research. Inability to validate and replicate qualitative research will further deter its use.

On the positive side, the use of focus groups will grow. Focus group research can provide data and insights not available through any other techniques. Low cost and ease of application will lend even greater impetus to use online focus groups. Finally, the qualitative–quantitative split will begin to close as adaptations and innovations allow researchers to enjoy the advantages of both approaches simultaneously.

SUMMARY

Qualitative research refers to research whose findings are not subject to quantification or quantitative analysis. It is often used to examine consumer attitudes, feelings, and motivations. Qualitative research, particularly the use of focus groups, continues to grow in popularity for three reasons. First, qualitative research is usually cheaper than quantitative studies. Second, it is an excellent means of understanding the in-depth motivations and feelings of consumers. Third, it can improve the efficiency of quantitative research.

Qualitative research is not without its disadvantages. Sometimes, qualitative research does not distinguish small differences in attitudes or opinions about a marketing mix as well as large-scale quantitative studies do. Also, respondents in qualitative studies are not necessarily representative of the population of interest to the researcher. And the quality of the research may be questionable, given the number of individuals who profess to be experts in the field, yet lack formal training.

Focus groups are the most popular type of qualitative research. A focus group typically consists of 8 to 12 paid participants who are led by a moderator in an in-depth discussion on a particular topic or concept. The goal of the focus group is to learn and understand what people have to say and why. The emphasis is on getting people to talk at length and in detail about the subject at hand. The interaction associated with group dynamics is essential to the success of focus group research. The idea is that a response from one person will become a stimulus for another person, thereby generating an interplay of responses that will yield more information than if the same number of people had contributed independently.

Most focus groups are held in a group facility, which is typically set up in a conference room, with a large one-way mirror built into one wall. Microphones are placed in unobtrusive locations to record the discussion. Behind the mirror is a viewing room. The moderator plays a critical role in the success or failure of the group and is aided in his or her efforts by a well-planned discussion guide.

A number of other qualitative research methodologies are used but on a much more infrequent basis. One such technique is depth interviews. Individual depth interviews are unstructured one-on-one interviews. The interviewer is thoroughly trained in the skill of probing and eliciting detailed answers to each question. He or she often uses nondirective clinical techniques to uncover hidden motivations. Other qualitative techniques are hermeneutics and the Delphi Method. The use of projective techniques represents another form of qualitative research. The objective of any projective test is to delve below the surface responses to obtain true feelings, meanings, or motivations. Some common forms of projective techniques are word association tests, analogies, personification sentence and story completion tests, cartoon tests, photo sorts, consumer drawings, storytelling, and third-person techniques.

KEY TERMS & DEFINITIONS

qualitative research Research findings that are not subject to quantification or quantitative analysis.

quantitative research Research that uses mathematical analysis.

focus group Group of 8 to 12 participants who are led by a moderator in an in-depth discussion on one particular topic or concept.

group dynamics Interaction among people in a group.

focus group facility Research facility consisting of a conference room or living room setting and a separate observation room with a one-way mirror or live audio-visual feed.

focus group moderator Person hired by the client to lead the focus group; this person should have a background in psychology or sociology or, at least, marketing.

discussion guide Written outline of topics to be covered during a focus group discussion.

instant analysis Moderator debriefing, offering a forum for brainstorming by the moderator and client observers.

individual depth interviews (IDI) One-on-one interviews that probe and elicit detailed answers to questions, often using nondirective techniques to uncover hidden motivations.

hermeneutic research Research that focuses on interpretation through conversations.

Delphi Method Rounds of individual data collection from knowledgable people. Results are summarized and returned to the participants for further refinement.

projective test Technique for tapping respondents' deepest feelings by having them project those feelings into an unstructured situation.

word association test Projective test in which the interviewer says a word and the respondent must mention the first thing that comes to mind.

analogies Comparison of two items based on similarities.

personification Drawing a comparison between a product and a person.

sentence and story completion tests Projective tests in which respondents complete sentences or stories in their own words.

cartoon test Projective test in which the respondent fills in the dialogue of one of two characters in a cartoon.

photo sort Projective technique in which a respondent sorts photos of different types of people, identifying those people who she or he feels would use the specified product or service.

consumer drawings Projective technique in which respondents draw what they are feeling or how they perceive an object.

storytelling Projective technique in which respondents are required to tell stories about their experiences, with a company or product, for example; also known as the *metaphor technique*.

third-person technique A projective technique in which the interviewer learns about respondents' feelings by asking them to answer for a third party, such as "your neighbor" or "most people."

QUESTIONS FOR REVIEW & CRITICAL THINKING

Team Exercise

1. What are the major differences between quantitative and qualitative research?
2. What are some of the possible disadvantages of using focus groups?
3. Create a story completion test for downloading music from the Internet.
4. What can the client do to get more out of focus groups?
5. What is the purpose of a projective test? What major factors should be considered in using a projective technique?
6. Divide the class into groups of four and eight. The groups of four will select a topic below (or one suggested by your instructor) and create a discussion guide. One of the four will then serve as the group moderator. One of the groups of eight will then serve as participants in the focus group. The groups should last at least 20 minutes and be observed by the remainder of the class. Suggested topics:
   a. New video games
   b. Buying a hybrid gasoline/electric car

c. Student experiences at the student union

d. The quality of existing frozen dinners and snacks and new items that would be desired by students

e. How students spend their entertainment dollars and what additional entertainment opportunities they would like to see offered

7. What are some major issues in conducting international focus groups?

8. Take a consumer drawing test—draw a typical Pepsi drinker and a typical Coke drinker. What do the images suggest about your perceptions of Coke and Pepsi drinkers?

9. Use the metaphor technique to tell a story about going to the supermarket.

WORKING THE NET

Go to *www.researchconnections.com*. Under "Demos," look at the information available at Virtual Focus Facility. Report your findings to the class.

REAL-LIFE RESEARCH• 4.1

Repositioning Scotland

The proliferation of low-cost air carriers and the expansion of their pan-European route network means European consumers now have a greater choice of vacation destinations than ever before. Consequently, the need for established tourist destinations to market themselves appropriately, and to communicate their unique "reasons to visit" clearly and effectively to their audience, has become requisite.

As tourist destinations face up to increased competition for market share, VisitScotland, Scotland's national tourism agency, approached UK-based Nunwood Consulting to develop and instigate a qualitative research program. The research was intended to determine consumer wants and current brand perceptions within the three key markets of France, Germany, and Spain. The resulting insights would then be used to adapt and refine the group's future marketing and creative communications strategy, with the ultimate goals of repositioning the brand "Scotland" within the tourism sector and reigniting consumer interest within the three stated key territories.

The Process

Nunwood carried out a series of in-depth, qualitative workshops (focus groups) at six different locations within the three countries. The research utilized existing imagery of Scotland to elicit spontaneous responses based on emotional experience. Overall, it could be broken down into a series of key questions:

• What are the current consumer perceptions of the brand "Scotland"?

• Which aspects of the country are most appealing/would motivate a person to visit?

- Which of these aspects then appeal specifically to each of their market target countries, and thus, would a generic, pan-European communications strategy be feasible? (This would represent a huge cost saving.)

Unmet Needs

Once the research was completed, the debrief—in this case, a facilitated workshop-style process with a carefully constructed audience—yielded remarkable insight and identified three core and as-yet-unmet consumer needs:

- *Social engagement/cultural immersion.* Ad executions should advance from traditional, purely landscape-oriented messages to create the expectation within a visitor that they'll experience high levels of social interaction with the archetypal friendly, welcoming, indigenous people.
- *Discovery and learning.* The brand should communicate feelings of unique discovery, surprise, and the capacity for personal learning.
- *Flexibility and independence.* Future communications should appeal to more spontaneous, proactive, "flexible" tourists with few preordained plans.

Another important piece of information to emerge from the data was that these needs were consistent across all of the defined national markets, allowing for the generic, pan-European campaign that VisitScotland had hoped for.

The Rebrand

The next step was to utilize these findings to develop and refine a new, effective and creative promotional compaign. The old campaign was based on a traditional and generic approach to advertising vacation/short-break destinations: a simple but heart-stoppingly beautiful picture of the destination, plus an image of a calm and relaxed vacationer. The new campaign, called "the white line concept," answered the brief, as defined by the research recommendations. Any engaging creative mock-ups for Visit Scotland needed to underline elements of sociability and cultural immersion, discovery and learning, and freedom and independence. Nunwood tested the creative mock-ups across the three nations in a second wave of qualitative workshops several months later and made final edits based on this. The designs and the concept researched remarkably well, with the friendly and informal tone really appealing to the tourist segment.

"White lines" consist of a series of panoramic, visually rich landscape/scenery shots, featuring the tagline "Scotland, Welcome to Our Life."

While the comparison of these images hints at the wealth of things to discover in Scotland, a white, hand-drawn line runs through the scene, tracing the path a visitor could take. Short, scribbled stories, written in the first-person tense and dotted at points on the line, are indicative of the situations a visitor could experience during their time in Scotland.

Story examples include:

"I spoke to a lovely lady, thought she was the gardener, but turned out she owns the castle."

"Got stuck in a herd of sheep—the Scottish way to slow down your life."

Scotland, Welcome to
Our Life.

Douglas McGlviray/iStockphoto

Well Received

To substantiate initial positive feedback, and to make sure that this line of creative was
on-track, on-brand, and effectively delivering the key messages all parties had agreed
upon, Nunwood conducted a series of one-on-one conversation studies in France,
Germany, and Spain in order to gauge direct consumer response on the new campaign.
With the exception of a few small refinements, the creative was very well received and the
new campaign was promptly rolled out across all three European markets.[29]

Questions

1. The rebranding used focus groups and individual depth interviews. What other
   qualitative techniques could have been used?
2. Was the qualitative research done here sufficient to make decisions regarding the rebranding campaign?
3. What else could the researchers have determined if they had done a quantitative
   study?
4. How might one measure the success of the campaign?

Brooklyn Productions/Getty Images, Inc.

TRADITIONAL SURVEY RESEARCH

LEARNING OBJECTIVES

1.	To understand the reasons for the popularity of survey research.
2.	To learn about the types of errors in survey research.
3.	To learn about the types of surveys.
4.	To gain insight into the factors that determine the choice of particular survey methods.

According to the NPD Group, Port Washington, New York, grilling in America has nearly doubled in 20 years, reaching an all-time high. And while summer is still the most popular time of year to barbecue, grilling throughout the year is on the rise.

In 1985, 17 percent of households used a grill at dinner at least once during an average two-week period throughout the year; in 2006, it was 32 percent.

Summer remains the most popular season for grilling, with about 50 percent of households using their grills. Although summer grilling has remained steady over the last 10 years, grilling throughout the year has grown. Fall in particular has grown by 6 percent over the past decade in terms of household grill usage. Spring has grown by 5 percent, winter by 4 percent.

Undoubtedly, the reason for off-season increases in usage is due to the increase in grill ownership. According to NPD's Kitchen Audit data, the majority of consumers now own an outdoor gas grill over a charcoal grill.

According to NPD's 21st annual Eating Patterns in America survey, 35 percent of women say they "never" prepare meals on the grill, while 40 percent of men say they "always" prepare meals on the grill.[1]

Survey research, such as the survey of consumer grilling habits, is the use of a questionnaire to gather facts, opinions, and attitudes; it is the most popular way to gather primary data. What are the various types of survey research? As noted previously, not everyone is willing to participate in a survey. What kinds of errors does that create? What are the other types of errors encountered in survey research? Why has Internet survey research become so popular, and what are its drawbacks? These questions are answered in this chapter.

Popularity of Survey Research

Some 126 million Americans have been interviewed at some point in their lives. Each year, about 70 million people are interviewed in the United States, which is the equivalent of over 15 minutes per adult per year. Surveys have a high rate of usage in marketing research compared to other means of collecting primary data, for some very good reasons.

- ☐ *The need to know why.* In marketing research, there is a critical need to have some idea about why people do or do not do something. For example, why did they buy or not buy a particular brand? What did they like or dislike about it? Who or what influenced them? We do not mean to imply that surveys can prove causation, only that they can be used to develop some idea of the causal forces at work.

- ☐ *The need to know how.* At the same time, the marketing researcher often finds it necessary to understand the process consumers go through before taking some action. How did they make the decision? What time period passed? What did they examine or consider? When and where was the decision made? What do they plan to do next?

- ☐ *The need to know who.* The marketing researcher also needs to know who the person is, from a demographic or lifestyle perspective. Information on age, income, occupation, marital status, stage in the family life cycle, education, and other factors is necessary for the identification and definition of market segments.

A new survey of marketing research professionals found that the most common source of market research information is survey data, used by 94 percent of companies surveyed. Other sources include: syndicated research (78 percent); focus groups (74 percent);

company sales data (67 percent); and scanner data (16 percent). Also, 88 percent of corporations use online methods to conduct survey-based market research. Sixty-five percent of those surveyed agree that the speed of online research has helped accelerate the pace of their business. Half of all online research dollars are spent on projects transitioning from traditional (i.e., telephone, mail, mall) research methods.[2]

Types of Errors in Survey Research

When assessing the quality of information obtained from survey research, the manager must determine the accuracy of those results. This requires careful consideration of the research methodology employed in relation to the various types of errors that might result (see Exhibit 5.1).

Sampling Error

Two major types of errors may be encountered in connection with the sampling process. They are random error and systematic error, sometimes referred to as bias.

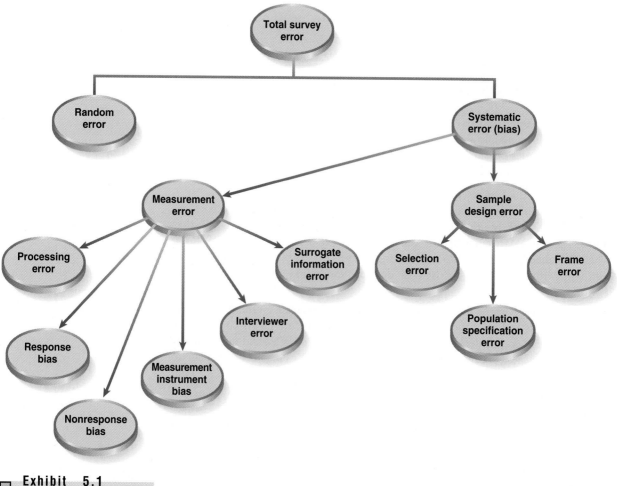

Exhibit 5.1

Types of Survey Error

Surveys often attempt to obtain information from a representative cross section of a target population. The goal is to make inferences about the total population based on the responses given by respondents sampled. Even when all aspects of the sample are investigated properly, the results are still subject to a certain amount of **random error** (or **random sampling error**) because of chance variation. **Chance variation** is the difference between the sample value and the true value of the population mean. This error cannot be eliminated, but it can be reduced by increasing the sample size. It is possible to estimate the range of random error at a particular level of confidence. Random error and the procedures for estimating it are discussed in detail in Chapters 11 and 12.

Systematic Error

Systematic error, or **bias**, results from mistakes or problems in the research design or from flaws in the execution of the sample design. Systematic error exists in the results of a sample if those results show a consistent tendency to vary in one direction (consistently higher or consistently lower) from the true value of the population parameter. Systematic error includes all sources of error except those introduced by the random sampling process. Therefore, systematic errors are sometimes called *nonsampling errors*. The nonsampling errors that can systematically influence survey answers can be categorized as *sample design error* and *measurement error*.

Sample Design Error

Sample design error is a systematic error that results from a problem in the sample design or sampling procedures. Types of sample design errors include frame errors, population specification errors, and selection errors.

Frame Error. The **sampling frame** is the list of population elements or members from which units to be sampled are selected. **Frame error** results from using an incomplete or inaccurate sampling frame. The problem is that a sample drawn from a list that is subject to frame error may not be a true cross-section of the target population. A common source of frame error in marketing research is the use of a published telephone directory as a sampling frame for a telephone survey. Many households are not listed in a current telephone book because they do not want to be listed or are not listed accurately because they have recently moved or changed their telephone number. Research has shown that those people who are listed in telephone directories are systematically different from those who are not listed in certain important ways, such as socioeconomic levels.[3] This means that if a study purporting to represent the opinions of all households in a particular area is based on listings in the current telephone directory, it will be subject to frame error.

Population Specification Error. **Population specification error** results from an incorrect definition of the population or universe from which the sample is to be selected. For example, suppose a researcher defined the population or universe for a

A population must be defined before research can begin. Errors can occur if a population is not defined correctly or if selection procedures are not followed properly.

PhotoDisc, Inc./Getty Images

> **random error**, or **random sampling error**
> Error that results from chance variation.

> **chance variation**
> The difference between the sample value and the true value of the population mean.

> **systematic error**, or **bias**
> Error that results from problems or flaws in the execution of the research design; sometimes called *nonsampling error*.

> **sample design error**
> Systematic error that results from an error in the sample design or sampling procedures.

> **sampling frame**
> The list of population elements or members from which units to be sampled are selected.

> **frame error**
> Error resulting from an inaccurate or incomplete sampling frame.

> **population specification error**
> Error that results from incorrectly defining the population or universe from which a sample is chosen.

study as people over the age of 35. Later, it was determined that younger individuals should have been included and that the population should have been defined as people 20 years of age or older. If those younger people who were excluded are significantly different in regard to the variables of interest, then the sample results will be biased.

> **selection error**
> Error that results from incomplete or improper sample selection procedures or not following appropriate procedures.

Selection Error. Selection error can occur even when the analyst has a proper sampling frame and has defined the population correctly. **Selection error** occurs when sampling procedures are incomplete or improper or when appropriate selection procedures are not properly followed. For example, door-to-door interviewers might decide to avoid houses that do not look neat and tidy because they think the inhabitants will not be agreeable to doing a survey. If people who live in messy houses are systematically different from those who live in tidy houses, then selection error will be introduced into the results of the survey. Selection error is a serious problem in nonprobability samples, a subject discussed in Chapter 11.

Measurement Error Measurement error is often a much more serious threat to survey accuracy than is random error. When the results of public opinion polls are given in the media and in professional marketing research reports, an error figure is frequently reported (say, plus or minus 5 percent). The television viewer or the user of a marketing research study is left with the impression that this figure refers to total survey error. Unfortunately, this is not the case. This figure refers only to random sampling error. It does not include sample design error and speaks in no way to the measurement error that may exist in the research results. **Measurement error** occurs when there is variation between the information being sought (true value) and the information actually obtained by the measurement process. Our main concern in this text is with systematic measurement error. Various types of error may be caused by numerous deficiencies in the measurement process. These errors include surrogate information error, interviewer error, measurement instrument bias, processing error, nonresponse bias, and response bias.

> **measurement error**
> Systematic error that results from a variation between the information being sought and what is actually obtained by the measurement process.

> **surrogate information error**
> Error that results from a discrepancy between the information needed to solve a problem and that sought by the researcher.

Surrogate Information Error. **Surrogate information error** occurs when there is a discrepancy between the information actually required to solve a problem and the information being sought by the researcher. It relates to general problems in the research design, particularly failure to properly define the problem. A few years ago, Kellogg spent millions developing a line of 17 breakfast cereals that featured ingredients that would help consumers cut down on their cholesterol. The product line was called Ensemble. It failed miserably in the marketplace. Yes, people want to lower their cholesterol, but the real question was whether they would purchase a line of breakfast cereals to accomplish this task. This question was never asked in the research. Also, the name "Ensemble" usually refers to either an orchestra or something you wear. Consumers didn't understand either the product line or the need to consume it.

> **interviewer error**, or **interviewer bias**
> Error that results from the interviewer's influencing—consciously or unconsciously—the answers of the respondent.

Interviewer Error. **Interviewer error**, or **interviewer bias**, results from the interviewer's influencing a respondent—consciously or unconsciously—to give untrue or inaccurate answers. The dress, age, gender, facial expressions, body language, or tone of voice of the interviewer may influence the answers given by some or all respondents. This type of error is caused by problems in the selection and training of interviewers or by the failure of interviewers to follow instructions. Interviewers must be properly trained and supervised to appear neutral at all times. Another type of interviewer error occurs when deliberate cheating takes place. This can be a particular problem in door-to-door interviewing, where interviewers may be tempted to falsify interviews and get paid for work they did not actually do. The procedures developed by the researcher must include safe-guards to ensure that this problem will be detected (see Chapter 15).

Measurement Instrument Bias.   **Measurement instrument bias** (sometimes called *questionnaire bias*) results from problems with the measurement instrument or question-naire (see Chapter 10). Examples of such problems include leading questions or elements of the questionnaire design that make recording responses difficult and prone to record-ing errors. Problems of this type can be avoided by paying careful attention to detail in the questionnaire design phase and by using questionnaire pretests before field interviewing begins.

> **measurement instrument bias**
> Error that results from the design of the question-naire or measurement in-strument; also known as *questionnaire bias*.

Processing Error.   **Processing errors** are primarily due to mistakes that occur when in-formation from survey documents is entered into the computer. For example, a docu-ment may be scanned incorrectly.

> **processing error**
> Error that results from the incorrect transfer of infor-mation from a survey doc-ument to a computer.

Nonresponse Bias.   Ideally, if a sample of 400 people is selected from a particular population, all 400 of those individuals should be interviewed. As a practical matter, this will never happen. Response rates of 5 percent or less are common in mail sur-veys. The question is "Are those who did respond to the survey systematically differ-ent in some important way from those who did not respond?" Such differences lead to **nonresponse bias**. We recently examined the results of a study conducted among customers of a large savings and loan association. The response rate to the question-naire, included in customer monthly statements, was slightly under 1 percent. Analy-sis of the occupations of those who responded revealed that the percentage of retired people among respondents was 20 times higher than in the local metropolitan area. This overrepresentation of retired individuals raised serious doubts about the accu-racy of the results.

> **nonresponse bias**
> Error that results from a systematic difference be-tween those who do and those who do not re-spond to a measurement instrument.

Obviously, the higher the response rate, the less the possible impact of nonresponse because nonrespondents then represent a smaller subset of the overall picture. If the de-crease in bias associated with improved response rates is trivial, then allocating resources to obtain higher response rates might be wasteful in studies in which resources could be used for better purposes.

Nonresponse error occurs when the following happens:

☐ A person cannot be reached at a particular time.

☐ A potential respondent is reached but cannot or will not participate at that time (for example, the telephone request to participate in a survey comes just as the family is sitting down to dinner).

☐ A person is reached but refuses to participate in the survey. This is the most serious problem because it may be possible to achieve future participation in the first two circumstances.

The **refusal rate** is the percentage of persons contacted who refused to participate in a survey. Today, the overall refusal rate is approximately 60 percent—up from 52 percent in 1992, according to the Council for Marketing and Opinion Research (CMOR). Most refusals (68 percent) occur before the survey introduction (initial re-fusals); only one-quarter (26 percent) occur after the introduction is read (qualified refusals). Few (6 percent) terminate once the survey is under way. While most individu-als (71 percent) express a willingness to participate in future surveys, this willingness is lukewarm (nearly three times as many are "fairly willing" compared to "very willing").[4] While these percentages are based on a study by the CMOR and are not necessarily re-flective of the entire industry, they do reflect the significant increase in the refusal rate.

> **refusal rate**
> Percentage of persons contacted who refused to participate in a survey.

EXHIBIT 5.2	Types of Errors and Strategies for Minimizing Errors

I. Random error — This error can be reduced only by increasing sample size.

II. Systematic error — This error can be reduced by minimizing sample design and measurement errors.

A. Sample design error

Frame error — This error can be minimized by getting the best sampling frame possible and doing preliminary quality control checks to evaluate the accuracy and completeness of the frame.

Population specification error — This error results from incorrect definition of the population of interest. It can be reduced or minimized only by more careful consideration and definition of the population of interest.

Selection error — This error results from using incomplete or improper sampling procedures or not following appropriate selection procedures. It can occur even with a good sampling frame and an appropriate specification of the population. It is minimized by developing selection procedures that will ensure randomness and by developing quality control checks to make sure that these procedures are followed in the field.

B. Measurement error

Surrogate information error — This error results from seeking and basing decisions on the wrong information. It results from poor design and can be minimized only by paying more careful attention to specification of the types of information required to fulfill the objectives of the research.

Interviewer error — This error occurs because of interactions between the interviewer and the respondent that affect the responses given. It is minimized by careful interviewer selection and training. In addition, quality control checks should involve unobtrusive monitoring of interviewers to ascertain whether they are following prescribed guidelines.

Measurement instrument bias — Also referred to as *questionnaire bias,* this error is minimized only by careful questionnaire design and pretesting.

Processing error — This error can occur in the process of transferring data from questionnaires to the computer. It is minimized by developing and following rigid quality control procedures for transferring data and supporting quality control checks.

Nonresponse bias — This error results from the fact that those people chosen for the sample who actually respond are systematically different from those who are chosen and do not respond. It is particularly serious in connection with mail surveys. It is minimized by doing everything possible (e.g., shortening the questionnaire, making the questionnaire more respondent friendly, doing callbacks, providing incentives, contacting people when they are most likely to be at home) to encourage those chosen for the sample to respond.

Response bias — This error occurs when something about a question leads people to answer it in a particular way. It can be minimized by paying special attention to questionnaire design. In particular, questions that are hard to answer, might make the respondent look uninformed, or deal with sensitive issues should be modified (see Chapter 10).

▷ response bias
Error that results from the tendency of people to answer a question incorrectly through either deliberate falsification or unconscious misrepresentation.

Response Bias. If there is a tendency for people to answer a particular question in a certain way, then there is **response bias**. Response bias can result from deliberate falsification or unconscious misrepresentation.

Deliberate falsification occurs when people purposefully give untrue answers to questions. There are many reasons why people might knowingly misrepresent information in a survey. They may wish to appear intelligent, not reveal information that they feel is embarrassing, or conceal information that they consider to be personal.

For example, in a survey about fast-food buying behavior, the respondents may have a fairly good idea of how many times they visited a fast-food restaurant in the past month. However, they may not remember which fast-food restaurants they visited or how many times they visited each restaurant. Rather than answering "Don't know" in response to a question regarding which restaurants they visited, the respondents may simply guess.

Unconscious misrepresentation occurs when a respondent is legitimately trying to be truthful and accurate but gives an inaccurate response. This type of bias may occur because of question format, question content, or various other reasons.

Strategies for minimizing survey errors are summarized in Exhibit 5.2.

Types of Surveys

Asking people questions is the essence of the survey approach. But what type of survey is best for a given situation? The non-Internet survey alternatives discussed in this chapter are door-to-door interviews, executive interviews, mall-intercept interviews, telephone interviews, self-administered questionnaires, and mail surveys.

Door-to-Door Interviews

Door-to-door interviews, in which consumers are interviewed in person in their homes, were at one time thought to be the best survey method. This conclusion was based on a number of factors. First, the door-to-door interview is a personal, face-to-face interaction with all the attendant advantages—immediate feedback from the respondent, the ability to explain complicated tasks, the ability to use special questionnaire techniques that require visual contact to speed up the interview or improve data quality, and the ability to show the respondent product concepts and other stimuli for evaluation. Second, the participant is at ease in a familiar, comfortable, secure environment.

> **door-to-door interviews**
> Interviews conducted face to face with consumers in their homes.

Door-to-door interviews began a steep decline in the early 1970s and have now virtually disappeared altogether from the U.S. marketing research scene. The primary reason is the cost of paying an interviewer's travel time, mileage, and survey time as well as ever-rising refusal rates. Door-to-door interviewing, however, is still used in developing countries. Matthew Harrison, a director of B2B International, an English marketing research firm, talks about door-to-door and other forms of marketing research in the accompanying Global Research box.

Executive Interviews

Executive interviews are used by marketing researchers as the industrial equivalent of door-to-door interviews. This type of survey involves interviewing businesspeople at their offices concerning industrial products or services. For example, if Hewlett-Packard wants information about user preferences for features that might be offered in a new line of office computer printers, it needs to interview prospective user-purchasers of the printers. It would thus be appropriate to locate and interview these people at their offices.

> **executive interviews**
> Industrial equivalent of door-to-door interviewing.

This type of interviewing is expensive. First, individuals involved in the purchasing decision for the product in question must be identified and located. Sometimes lists can be obtained from various sources, but more frequently screening must be conducted over the telephone. A particular company may indeed have individuals of the type being sought, but locating them within a large organization can be expensive and time-consuming. Once a qualified person is located, the next step is to get that person to agree to be interviewed and to set a time for the interview. This is not usually as hard as it might seem because most professionals seem to enjoy talking about topics related to their work.

GLOBAL RESEARCH

Conducting Marketing Research in China

Data collection in China has traditionally given significant weight to face-to-face interviewing, in consumer and B2B research alike. In 2000, marketing research firms conducted about 90 percent of all research interviews in China this way. Since then, the role of face-to-face interviewing has decreased; current estimates are at just more than 60 percent. Of course, this is considerably higher than most Western research firms, which conduct less than 10 percent of all interviews face-to-face.

Face-to-face interviewing is prominent in relation to certain target respondent groups. In B2B research, the more senior the respondent, the more likely he or she will require a meeting to discuss his or her views on the market. Middle- to senior-level managers and government officials are the main respondent groups in the face-to-face category. This is partly due to respondents' natural curiosity about to whom they are giving information. But it's also due to a cultural perception that high-level discussions merit a face-to-face meeting. This perception is often as prominent within the research firms as it is among respondents.

The main reason for the trend away from face-to-face interviews is the growing understanding and acceptance of market research among Chinese target respondents; they are increasingly willing to discuss business and other matters over the telephone. And in contrast to Western markets, access to respondents is increasing.

Marketing research firms use the focus group methodology in China, albeit less than in Western markets. There's an almost unanimous view that Chinese respondents—particularly businesspeople—prefer to provide information on a one-to-one basis rather than in groups. The exact reason for this preference is unclear, although the balance of opinion suggests this is more a cultural than a confidentiality issue. When researchers conduct focus groups, they commonly do so in a "mini-group" format of three or four people; groups of six to eight people are also fairly common. Groups of more than eight are very rare.

Although Chinese agencies are extremely technologically savvy, they tend to lag behind their Western counterparts in their use of online data-collection techniques. This appears to be due to the relatively low Internet penetration in China. Currently, online surveys are limited to certain groups such as IT managers and teenagers, and online focus groups are yet to be introduced to any audience.

Data collection into the future. By 2010, two important trends will become evident in terms of data collection. First, the move toward more telephone-based fieldwork will continue—as acceptance increases among the target market and clients alike and as demand for research grows outside of the main cities. By 2010, telephone interviewing will constitute the main data-collection method. And face-to-face interviewing will remain significant, as it is entrenched in China's culture of research.

Second, the emergence of the Internet as a viable means of data collection appears certain, again based on the acceptability of this method to both clients and respondents. The high demand for large-sample projects within China means that the Web survey will be the most widespread of these techniques, with substantial growth predicted to begin by 2008.[5]

Finally, an interviewer must go to the particular place at the appointed time. Long waits are frequent; cancellations are common. This type of survey requires highly skilled interviewers because they are frequently interviewing on topics they know little about. Executive interviews have essentially the same advantages and disadvantages as door-to-door interviews. More and more executive interviews are moving online.

Mall-Intercept Interviews

Mall-intercept interviews are a popular survey method for conducting personal interviews. This survey approach is relatively simple. Shoppers are intercepted in public areas of shopping malls and either interviewed on the spot or asked to come to a permanent interviewing facility in the mall. Approximately 500 malls throughout the country have permanent survey facilities operated by marketing research firms. An equal or greater number of malls permit marketing researchers to interview on a daily basis. Many malls do not permit marketing research interviewing, however, because they view it as an unnecessary nuisance to shoppers.

> mall-intercept interviews
> Interviews conducted by intercepting mall shoppers (or shoppers in other high-traffic locations) and interviewing them face to face.

Mall surveys are less expensive than door-to-door interviews because respondents come to the interviewer rather than the other way around. Interviewers spend more of their time actually interviewing and less of their time hunting for someone to interview. Also, mall interviewers do not have the substantial travel time and mileage expenses associated with door-to-door interviewing. In addition to low cost, mall-intercept interviews have many of the advantages associated with door-to-door interviews in that respondents can try test products on the spot.

However, a number of serious disadvantages are associated with mall-intercept interviewing. First, it is virtually impossible to get a sample representative of a large metropolitan area from shoppers at a particular mall. Even though malls may be large, most of them draw shoppers from a relatively small local area. In addition, malls tend to attract certain types of people, based on the stores they contain. Studies also show that some people shop more frequently than others and therefore have a greater chance of being selected. Finally, many people refuse mall interviews. In summary, mall-intercept interviewing cannot produce a good or representative sample except in the rare case in which the population of interest is coincident with or is a subset of the population that shops at a particular mall.

Second, the mall environment is not always viewed as a comfortable place to conduct an interview. Respondents may be ill at ease, in a hurry, or preoccupied by various distractions outside the researcher's control. These factors may adversely affect the quality of the data obtained. Even with all its problems, the popularity of mall-intercept interviews has only slightly declined in recent years.

Rather than interview in the public areas of malls, some researchers are conducting surveys in stores at the point-of-purchase. Firms such as Marketing Research Services, Inc. (www.mrsi.com), specialize in in-store interviewing. The company notes:

When a consumer reaches for a product on a store shelf, the eye of market research should be wide open. This is the only time and place that consumers' purchase interest and motivations are well defined and readily expressed. The moment of purchase is the most critical point in the entire marketing cycle. It is the moment when shoppers best recall why they made the choice to put a particular item in their shopping cart.[6]

Various companies, including Procter & Gamble, General Mills, Starbucks, McDonald's, and Walgreens, currently conduct in-store studies.

Telephone Interviews

Until 1990, telephone interviewing was the most popular form of survey research. The advantages of telephone interviewing are compelling. First, telephoning is a relatively inexpensive way to collect survey data. Second, the telephone interview has traditionally produced a high-quality sample. Ninety-five percent of all Americans have a telephone. *Random-digit sampling*, or *random-digit dialing*, is a frequently used sampling approach (see Chapter 11). The basic idea is simple: Instead of drawing a sample from the phone book or other directory, researchers use telephone numbers generated via a random-number procedure. This approach ensures that people with unlisted numbers and those who have moved or otherwise changed their telephone numbers since the last published phone book are included in the sample in the correct proportion.

A major problem with telephone surveys today is that 12.8 percent of U.S. households cannot now be reached by the typical telephone survey because they have only a cell phone and no landline telephone. In early 2003, just 3.2 percent of households were cell only. Twenty years ago the survey research profession worried mostly about the roughly 7 percent of U.S. households that could not be interviewed because they had no telephone.[7]

If people who can only be reached by cell phone were just like those with landlines, their absence from surveys would not create a problem for polling. But cell-only adults are very different.

A recent survey found them to be much younger, more likely to be African American or Hispanic, less likely to be married, and less likely to be a homeowner than adults with landline telephones. These demographic characteristics are correlated with a wide range of social and political behaviors.[8]

Given the speed with which the number of cell-only households has increased, there is growing concern within the marketing research industry about how long the landline telephone survey will remain a viable data-collection tool, at least by itself. At the annual meeting of the American Association for Public Opinion Research, a government researcher told the audience that the size of the cell-only group could approach 25 percent by the end of 2008 if the current rate of increase is sustained.[9]

The Pew Research Center conducted four studies that included samples of cell phone numbers as well as landline numbers.[10] The surveys covered a wide range of topics, including use of technology, media consumption, political and social attitudes, and electoral engagement. Comparing the cell-only respondents with those reached on landlines allowed an assessment of the degree to which traditional surveys are biased by the absence of the cell-only respondents.

The good news, says the report, is that none of the measures would change by more than 2 percentage points when the cell-only respondents were blended into the landline sample and weighted according to U.S. Census parameters on basic demographic characteristics.

While the cell-only problem is currently not biasing polls based on the entire population, it may very well be damaging estimates for certain subgroups in which the use of only a cell phone is more common. According to the most recent government estimate, more than 25 percent of those under age 30 use only a cell phone.

Perhaps, says the report, excluding the cell-only respondents also yields lower estimates of technological sophistication. For example, the overall estimate for the proportion of 18- to 25-year-olds using social networking sites is 57 percent when the cell-only sample is blended with the landline samples, while the estimate based only on the landline sample is 50 percent.

Including a cell-only sample with a traditional landline-based poll is feasible, but cell-only surveys are considerably more difficult and expensive to conduct than landline surveys. Because federal law prohibits the use of automated dialing devices when calling cell phones, each number in the cell phone sample must be dialed manually.

Besides the cell phone problem, the telephone survey approach has several inherent disadvantages. First, respondents cannot be shown anything in a typical telephone interview. This shortcoming ordinarily eliminates the telephone survey as an alternative in situations that require respondents to comment on visual product concepts, advertisements, and the like.

Second, some critics have suggested that telephone interviewers are unable to make the various judgments and evaluations that can be made by in-home interviewers (for example, evaluations concerning income, based on what the respondent's home looks like and other outward signs of economic status). In reality, marketing research interviewers are almost never called on to make such judgments.

A third disadvantage of the telephone interview is that it limits the quantity and types of information that can be obtained. A respondent's patience wears thin more easily over the phone, and it is easy to hang up the phone. The telephone is also a poor vehicle for conducting a depth interview or a long interview with many open-ended questions.

A fourth disadvantage of telephone interviewing is associated with the increased use of screening devices. These include answering machines, do-not-call lists, call blocking, caller ID, and distinctive ringing. On the average, for every hour an interviewer spends on the phone, 30 minutes is spent just trying to find a person who will agree to be surveyed.[11] This, of course, drives up the cost of telephone surveys.

A fifth disadvantage is that research has shown the potential for personality bias in phone surveys. That is, persons who agree to participate in a telephone interview may be more outgoing, confident, conscientious, and agreeable than those who will not.[12]

Today, nearly all telephone interviews are central-location telephone interviews. In some cases, firms are further centralizing the process by conducting completely automated telephone surveys but only from landlines.

Central-Location Telephone Interviews

Central-location telephone interviews are conducted from a facility set up for that purpose. The reason for the popularity of central-location phone interviews is fairly straightforward—in a single word, control. First, the interviewing process can be monitored; most central-location telephone interviewing facilities have unobtrusive monitoring equipment that permits supervisors to listen in on interviews as they are being conducted. Interviewers who are not doing the interview properly can be corrected, and those who are incapable of conducting a proper interview can be terminated. One supervisor can monitor from 10 to 20 interviewers. Ordinarily, each interviewer is monitored at least once per shift. Second, completed interviews are edited on the spot as a further quality control check. Interviewers can be immediately informed of any deficiencies in their work. Finally, interviewers' working hours are controlled.

Most research firms have computerized the central-location telephone interviewing process. In **computer-assisted telephone interviews (CATI)**, each interviewer is seated in front of a computer terminal or a personal computer. When a qualified respondent gets on the line, the interviewer starts the interview by pressing a key or series of keys on the keyboard. The questions and multiple-choice answers appear on the screen one at a time. The interviewer reads the question and enters the response, and the computer skips ahead to the appropriate next question. For example, the interviewer might ask whether the respondent has a dog. If the answer is yes, there might be a series of questions regarding what type of dog food the person buys. If the answer is no, those questions would be inappropriate. The computer takes into account the answer to the dog ownership question and skips ahead to the next appropriate question.

In addition, the computer can help customize questionnaires. For example, in the early part of a long interview, a respondent is asked the years, makes, and models of all the cars he or she owns. Later in the interview, questions might be asked about each specific car owned. The question might come up on the interviewer's screen as follows: "You said you own a 2009 GMC truck. Which family member drives this vehicle most often?" Other questions about this vehicle and others owned would appear in similar fashion.

Another advantage of CATI is that computer tabulations can be run at any point in the study. This luxury is not available with a pencil-and-paper interview. Based on preliminary tabulations, certain questions might be dropped, saving time and money in subsequent interviewing. If, for example, 98.3 percent of those interviewed answer a particular question in the same manner, there is probably no need to continue asking the question.

central-location telephone interviews Interviews conducted by calling respondents from a centrally located marketing research facility.

computer-assisted telephone interviews (CATI) Central-location telephone interviews in which interviewers enter respondents' answers directly into a computer.

Kiosk-based computer interviewing is a relatively new and successful way of capturing data on consumers' recent experiences. Go to www.intouchsurvey.com to find out more about the kiosk-based offerings of In-Touch Survey Systems, Inc.

Courtesy of In-Touch survey systems

⬅ **self-administered questionnaires**
Questionnaires filled out by respondents with no interviewer present.

Tabulations may also suggest the need to add questions to the survey. If an unexpected pattern of product use is uncovered in the early stages of interviewing, questions can be added that delve further into this behavior. Finally, management may find the early reporting of survey results useful in preliminary planning and strategy development.

Self-Administered Questionnaires

The self-administered and mail survey methods explained in this section have one thing in common. They differ from the other survey methods discussed in that no interviewer—human or computer—is involved. The major disadvantage of **self-administered questionnaires** is that no one is present to explain things to the respondent and clarify responses to open-ended questions. For example, if someone were asked via an open-ended question why he or she does not buy a particular brand of soft drink, a typical answer might be "because I don't like it." From a managerial perspective, this answer is useless. It provides no information that can be used to alter the marketing mix and thereby make the product more attractive. An interviewer conducting the survey, however, would "probe" for a response—after receiving and recording the useless response, the interviewer would ask the respondent what it was that he or she did not like about the product. The interviewee might then indicate a dislike for the taste. Next, the interviewer would ask what it was about the taste that the person did not like. Here the interviewer might finally get something useful, with the respondent indicating that the product in question was, for example, "too sweet." If many people give a similar response, management might elect to reduce the sweetness of the drink. The point is that, without probing, management would have only the useless first response.

Some have argued that the absence of an interviewer is an advantage in that it eliminates one source of bias. There is no interviewer whose appearance, dress, manner of speaking, or failure to follow instructions may influence respondents' answers to questions.

Self-administered interviews are often used in malls or other central locations where the researcher has access to a captive audience. Airlines, for example, often have programs in which questionnaires are administered during the flight. Passengers are asked to rate various aspects of the airline's services, and the results are used to track passenger perceptions of service over time. Many hotels, restaurants, and other service businesses provide brief questionnaires to patrons to find out how they feel about the quality of service provided (see Exhibit 5.3).

A recent development in the area of direct computer interviewing is kiosk-based computer interviewing. Kiosks are developed with multimedia, touch-screen computers contained in freestanding cabinets. These computers can be programmed to administer complex surveys, show full-color scanned images (products, store layouts), and play sound and video clips. Kiosks have been used successfully at trade shows and conventions and are now being tested in retail environments, where they have many applications. From a research standpoint, kiosk-based interviewing can be used in place of exit interviews to capture data on recent experiences. Kiosks have other definite advantages: This form of interviewing tends to be less expensive, people tend to give more honest answers

Exhibit 5.3

Self-Administered Questionnaire

Source: Courtesy of Accent Marketing & Research, Ltd., London.

GATWICK EXPRESS

Customer Survey

+ [0 1 2 3 4 5 6 7 8 R]

Please complete this questionnaire by ticking the appropriate boxes or by writing in your answer in the space provided. A separate questionnaire should be completed by EACH member of your travelling party aged 14 and over.

Veuillez compléter le questionnaire suivant en cochant les cases appropriées ou en écrivant votre réponse dans l'espace prévu. Un questionnaire séparé devrait être complété par CHAQUE membre de votre groupe de voyage âgé de 14 ans et au-delà.

Bitte füllen Sie den nachfolgenden Fragebogen durch Ankreuzen der entsprechendenb Kästchen bzw. schriftlich an den vorgesehenen Stellen aus. JEDES Mitglied Ihrer Reisegruppe über 14 Jahren sollte einen separaten Fragebogen ausfüllen.

Q1 Are you sitting in Club (1st) class or Express (2nd) class on this train?
Etes vous assis en classe Club (1ère) ou Express (2ème) dans ce train?
Sitzen Sie in der Club-Klasse (1. Kl) oder in der Express-Klasse (2. Kl) dieses Zuges?
Club (1st) ☐
Express (2nd) ☐

Q2 Are you flying or have you flown today?
Est-ce vous partez en voyage ou avez-vous voyagé par avion aujourd'hui?
Fliegen Sie heute oder Sie heute schon geflogen?
I will fly /*Je vais voyager par avion /Ich fliege* ☐
I have flown / *J'ai voyagé par avion /Ich bin geflogen* ☐
I am not flying (GO TO Q11) ☐
Je ne voyage pas par avion /Ich fliege nicht (ALLEZ A /WEITER ZU Q11)

Q3a Please write in the origin and destination of your flight and the scheduled arrival and departure times.
Veuillez inscrire l'origine et la destination de votre vol ainsi que les heures prévues de départ et d'arrivée.
Bitte geben Sie Ihren Abflug- und Zielort und die planmäßige Abflug- und Ankunftszeit an.
From / *De /Von* ....
To / *A /Zu* ....
Departure time / *Départ /Abflugzeit* ....
Arrival time / *Arrivée /Ankunftzeit* ....

Q3b Do you know your flight number?
Connaissez-vous le numéro de votre vol?
Wissen Sie Ihre Flugnummer?
If yes PLEASE WRITE IN ....

Q3c Which airline will/did you fly with?
Avec quelle compagnie aérienne volerez-vous/avez-vous volé?
Mit welcher Fluggesellschaft fliegen Sie/sind Sie geflogen?
....

OFFICE USE ONLY
[0 1 2 3 4 5 6 7 8 9] 1000
[ ] 100
[ ] 10
[ ] 1
[0 1 2 3 4 5 6 7 8 9]
[ ] 100
[ ] 10
[ ] 1

Q4 Are/were you on the outward or return leg of your air journey?
Outward ☐   Return ☐
Single leg journey ☐

Q5a Is/was this flight a direct one or will/did you change planes en route?
Direct flight (GO TO Q6) ☐
Will/did change planes en route ☐

Q5b Please write in your ultimate origin and ultimate destination airports of this trip.
Origin [ ]   Destination [ ]

Q6 What flight ticket type do/did you have?
Economy Full Fare ☐   First Class ☐
Stand-by/Apex ☐   Business/Club ☐
Staff-Discount ☐   Don't know ☐
Other discount ☐   Other ☐

Q7 What is the UK origin/destination of your journey today?
Central London ☐   Outer London (North) ☐
Outer London (South) ☐   Other South East ☐
East Anglia ☐   South West ☐
Midlands ☐   Northern England ☐
Scotland ☐   Wales ☐
N.Ireland ☐   Other ☐
Don't know ☐

Q8 What is your usual country of residence?
Mainland UK ☐   Northern Ireland/Eire ☐
Channel Islands ☐   Other ☐

Q9 How many **adults** are in your party (including yourself)?
One adult ☐   Two adults ☐
Three adults ☐   More than three adults ☐

PLEASE TURN OVER

(continued)

than they would to a human interviewer, and internal control is higher because the survey is preprogrammed.[13]

Mail Surveys

Two general types of mail surveys are used in marketing research: ad hoc mail surveys and mail panels. In **ad hoc mail surveys** (sometimes called *one-shot mail surveys*), the researcher selects a sample of names and addresses from an appropriate source and mails questionnaires to the people selected. Ordinarily, there is no prior contact, and the sample is used only for a single project. However, the same questionnaire may be sent to

> **ad hoc mail surveys**
> Questionnaires sent to selected names and addresses without prior contact by the researcher; sometimes called *one-shot mail surveys*.

Exhibit 5.3

Self-Administered Questionnaire
(continued)

Q10 How many **children** (aged 2-14) are in your party?

	None ☐
One child ☐	Two children ☐
Three children ☐	More than three ☐

Q11 What is/was the nature of your journey today?

Flying on business ☐
Flying for a conference/trade fair/exhibition ☐
Flying for a holiday (package) ☐
Flying for a holiday (arranged independently) ☐
Flying to visit friends/relatives ☐
Flying to/from work ☐
Flying for other purposes ☐

Meeting friends/relatives at the airport ☐
Business at the airport ☐
Travel to/from work at the airport ☐
Travel to/from work in London ☐
Other reason, but not flying ☐

Q12 How many times in the last 12 months have you travelled by air? (PLEASE INCLUDE ALL YOUR FLIGHTS TO/FROM ANY AIRPORT)

None ☐	Once only ☐
2-3 times ☐	4-5 times ☐
6-10 times ☐	11-40 times ☐
41-50 times ☐	More than 50 times ☐

Q13 Where did you hear about Gatwick Express?

In Britain ☐   Outside Britain ☐

Q14 How did you **first** hear about the Gatwick Express? (TICK ONE BOX ONLY)

Advert in newspaper/magazine ☐
Poster/Leaflet ☐
Article in newspaper/magazine ☐
British Rail ☐
Word of mouth ☐
Signs at Gatwick Airport ☐
Signs at Victoria Station ☐
Travel guide ☐
Travel Agency information ☐
Airline leaflet or Airline Offices ☐
In-flight magazine ☐
In-flight announcement or flight staff ☐
Other ☐

Q15 Did you consider an alternative way of travelling between London and Gatwick Airport?

Yes ☐   No (GOTO Q17) ☐

Q16 Which alternative(s) did you consider? (YOU MAY TICK MORE THAN ONE BOX)

Taxi ☐	Car ☐
Coach ☐	South Central Trains ☐
Thameslink Trains ☐	Other ☐

Q17 What was the **main** reason you chose to travel **by rail** to/from Gatwick for your journey today? (TICK ONE BOX ONLY)

Speed ☐	Convenience ☐
Comfort ☐	Reliability ☐
Cost ☐	Other ☐

Q18 Why did you choose to travel **on the Gatwick Express** rather than any other train service between London and Gatwick Airport? (YOU MAY TICK MORE THAN ONE BOX)

Speed ☐	Convenience ☐
Comfort ☐	Reliability ☐
Frequency ☐	Cost ☐
Always a train ready to join ☐	
Didn't know about other train service ☐	
Other ☐	

Q19 What is your age?

Under 14 ☐	14-17 ☐
18-24 ☐	25-34 ☐
35-44 ☐	45-54 ☐
55-64 ☐	65 or over ☐

Q20 Are you male or female?

Male ☐   Female ☐

Q21 Do you have any other comments to make about the Gatwick Express service?

THANK YOU FOR YOUR COOPERATION, PLEASE HAND THIS QUESTIONNAIRE TO THE INTERVIEWER WHEN THEY RETURN OR LEAVE IT ON YOUR SEAT WHEN YOU LEAVE THE TRAIN.
MERCI DE VOTRE COOPERATION, VEUILLEZ REMETTRE CE QUESTIONNAIRE A L'ENQUETEUR A SON RETOUR OU LE LAISSER SUR VOTRE SIEGE AVANT DE SORTIR DU TRAIN.
WIR DANKEN IHNEN FÜR IHRE FREUNDLICHE HILFE. BITTE HÄNDIGEN SIE DIESEN FRAGEBOGEN AN DEN INTERVIEWER ZURÜCK, WENN DIESE/R ZU IHREM ABTEIL ZURÜCKKEHRT ODER LASSEN SIE IHN AUF DEM SITZ LIEGEN, WENN SIE SIE DEN ZUG VERLASSEN.

> **mail panels**
> Precontacted and prescreened participants who are periodically sent questionnaires.

nonrespondents several times to increase the overall response rate. In contrast, **mail panels** operate in the following manner:

1. A sample group is precontacted by letter. In this initial contact, the purpose of the panel is explained, and people are usually offered a gratuity.

2. As part of the initial contact, consumers are asked to fill out a background questionnaire on the number of family members, their ages, education level, income, types of pets, types of vehicles and ages, types of appliances, and so forth.

3. After the initial contact, panel participants are sent questionnaires from time to time. The background data collected on initial contact enable researchers to send questionnaires only to appropriate households. For example, a survey about dog food usage and preferences would be sent only to dog owners.

A mail panel is a type of longitudinal study. A **longitudinal study** is one that questions the same respondents at different points in time. Several companies, including Synovate, NPD Research, and The Gallop Panel, operate large (more than 100,000 households) consumer mail panels.

➤ longitudinal study
Study in which the same respondents are resampled over time.

On first consideration, mail appears to be an attractive way to collect survey data. There are no interviewers to recruit, train, monitor, and pay. The entire study can be sent out and administered from a single location. Hard-to-reach respondents can be readily surveyed. Mail surveys appear to be convenient, efficient, and inexpensive. The promise of anonymity is another benefit. While personal and telephone interviews may indicate that all information collected will be kept confidential, blind mail surveys absolutely guarantee it. This is particularly important to someone who may be asked to provide information of a confidential or personal nature.[14]

Like self-administered questionnaires, mail surveys of both types encounter the problems associated with not having an interviewer present. In particular, no one is there to probe responses to open-ended questions, a real constraint on the types of information that can be sought. The number of questions—and, consequently, the quantity of obtainable information—is usually more limited in mail surveys than in surveys involving interviewers.

Ad hoc mail surveys suffer from a high rate of nonresponse and attendant systematic error. Nonresponse in mail surveys is not a problem as long as everyone has an equal probability of not responding. However, numerous studies have shown that certain types of people—such as those with more education, those with high-level occupations, women, those less interested in the topic, and students—have a greater probability of not responding than other types. Response rates in ad hoc mail surveys may run anywhere from less than 5 percent to more than 50 percent, depending on the length of the questionnaire, its content, the group surveyed, the incentives employed, and other factors. Those who operate mail panels claim response rates in the vicinity of 70 percent.

Many strategies designed to enhance response rates have been developed. Some of the more common ones are summarized in Exhibit 5.4. The question must always be, "Is the cost of the particular strategy worth the increased response rate generated?" Unfortunately, there is no clear answer to this question that can be applied to all procedures in all situations.

EXHIBIT 5.4	Tactics Employed to Increase Mail Survey Response Rates

☐ Advance postcard or telephone call alerting respondent to survey

☐ Follow-up postcard or phone call

☐ Monetary incentives (half-dollar, dollar)

☐ Premiums (pencil, pen, keychain, etc.)

☐ Postage stamps rather than metered envelopes

☐ Self-addressed, stamped return envelope

☐ Personalized address and well-written cover letter

☐ Promise of contribution to favorite charity

☐ Entry into drawings for prizes

☐ Emotional appeals

☐ Affiliation with universities or research institutions

☐ Personally signed cover letter

☐ Multiple mailings of the questionnaire

☐ Reminder that respondent participated in previous studies (for mail panel participants)

EXHIBIT 5.5	Non-Internet Forms of Survey Research
Type of Interview	**Description**
Door-to-door interviews	Interviews are conducted in respondents' homes (rarely used today in the United States).
Executive interviews	Interviews of industrial product users (e.g., engineers, architects, doctors, executives) or decision makers are conducted at their place of business.
Mall-intercept interviews	Interviews with consumers are conducted in a shopping mall or other high-traffic location. Interviews may be done in a public area of the mall, or respondents may be taken to a private test area.
Central-location telephone interviews	Interviews are conducted from a telephone facility set up for that purpose. These facilities typically have equipment that permits supervisors to unobtrusively monitor the interviewing while it is taking place. Many of these facilities do national sampling from a single location. An increasing number have computer-assisted interviewing capabilities. At these locations, the interviewer sits in front of a computer terminal with a personal computer. The questionnaire is programmed into the computer, and the interviewer uses the keyboard to directly enter responses.
Self-administered questionnaires	Self-administered questionnaires are most frequently employed at high-traffic locations such as shopping malls or in captive audience situations such as classrooms and airplanes. Respondents are given general information on how to fill out the questionnaire and expected to fill it out on their own. Kiosk-based point-of-service touch screens provide a way to capture information from individuals in stores, health clinics, and other shopping or service environments.
Ad hoc (one-shot) mail surveys	Questionnaires are mailed to a sample of consumers or industrial users, without prior contact by the researcher. Instructions are included; respondents are asked to fill out the questionnaire and return it via mail. Sometimes a gift or monetary incentive is provided.
Mail panels	Questionnaires are mailed to a sample of individuals who have been precontacted. The panel concept has been explained to them, and they have agreed to participate for some period of time, in exchange for gratuities. Mail panels typically generate much higher response rates than do ad hoc mail surveys.

Even with its shortcomings, mail surveying remains a popular data collection technique in commercial marketing research. In fact, more people participate in mail surveys than in any other type of traditional survey research.

Non-Internet survey alternatives discussed in this section are summarized in Exhibit 5.5.

Determination of the Survey Method

A number of factors may affect the choice of a survey method in a given situation. The researcher should choose the survey method that will provide data of the desired types, quality, and quantity at the lowest cost. The major considerations in the selection of a survey method are summarized in Exhibit 5.6.

Sampling Precision

The required level of sampling precision is an important factor in determining which survey method is appropriate in a given situation. Some projects by their very nature require a high level of sampling accuracy, whereas this may not be a critical consideration

EXHIBIT 5.6	Factors That Determine the Selection of a Particular Survey Method
Factor	**Comment**
Sampling precision	If the need for accuracy in the study results is not great, less rigorous and less expensive sampling procedures may be appropriate.
Budget	It is important to determine how much money is available for the survey portion of the study.
Need to expose respondent to various stimuli and have respondent perform specialized tasks	Taste tests and prototype usage tests usually require face-to-face contact. Card sorts, certain visual scaling methods, and the like require either face-to-face contact or the Internet.
Quality of data required	It is important to determine how accurate the results of the study need to be.
Length of questionnaire	Long questionnaires are difficult to do by mail, over the phone, or in a mall.
Incidence rate	Are you looking for people who make up 1 percent of the total population or 50 percent of the population? If you are looking for a needle in a haystack, you need an inexpensive way to find it. The Internet is probably the best source.
Degree of structure of questionnaire	Highly unstructured questionnaires may require data collection by personal interview.
Time available to complete survey	There may not be time to wait for responses via snail-mail. The Internet is the fastest way to go.

in other projects. If sampling accuracy were the only criterion, the appropriate data-collection technique would probably be central-location telephone interviewing, an on-line survey of a sample drawn from a huge Internet panel, or some other form of polling of a sample drawn from customer lists. The appropriate survey method for a project not requiring a high level of sampling accuracy might be the mail approach or some type of mall survey.

The trade-off between the central-location telephone survey, Internet panel, and the mail survey methods in regard to sampling precision is one of accuracy versus cost. A central-location telephone survey employing a random-digit dialing sampling procedure will probably produce a better sample than the mail survey method. However, the mail survey will most likely cost less. In some cases, Internet samples will provide both lower cost and greater accuracy.

Budget

The commercial marketing researcher frequently encounters situations in which the budget available for a study has a strong influence on the survey method used. For example, assume that for a particular study the budgetary constraint for interviewing is $10,000 and the sample size required for the necessary accuracy is 1,000. If the cost of administering the questionnaire using the mall-intercept method is $27.50 per interview and the cost of administering it via Internet survey is $.50 per interview, the

Taste tests are most often conducted in a controlled environment because of their unique requirements. Can you imagine conducting this type of research through a mail survey?

Norbert Schwerin/The Image Works

choice is fairly clear—assuming that nothing about the survey absolutely requires face-to-face contact.

Requirements for Respondent Reactions

In some studies, the marketing researcher needs to get respondent reactions to various marketing stimuli—perhaps product prototype usage (a new style of PC keyboard) or a taste test. In these cases, the need to get respondent reactions to stimuli normally requires personal contact between interviewer and respondent.

Taste tests typically require food preparation. This preparation must be done under controlled conditions so that the researcher can be certain that each person interviewed is responding to the same stimulus. The only viable survey alternative for tests of this type is the mall-intercept approach or some variant. One variant, for example, is recruiting people to come to properly equipped central locations, such as community centers, to sample products and be interviewed.

Some surveys require face-to-face interviewing because of the need to use special measurement techniques or obtain specialized forms of information. The tasks are so complex that the interviewer must be available to explain the tasks and ascertain whether the respondents understand what is required of them.

Quality of Data

The quality of data required is an important determinant of the survey method. Data quality is measured in terms of validity and reliability. (These two concepts are discussed in detail in Chapter 9.) *Validity* refers to the degree to which a measure reflects the characteristic of interest. In other words, a valid measure provides an accurate reading of whatever the researcher is trying to measure. *Reliability* refers to the consistency with which a measure produces the same results with the same or comparable populations.

Many factors beyond the interviewing method affect data quality. Sampling methods, questionnaire design, specific scaling methods, and interviewer training are a few of them. However, each of the various interviewing methods has certain inherent strengths and weaknesses in terms of data quality. These strengths and weaknesses are summarized in Exhibit 5.7.

The important point here is that the issue of data quality may override other considerations such as cost. For example, although the least expensive way to get responses to a long questionnaire with many open-ended questions might be via a mall-intercept interview, the data obtained by this method might be so biased—because of respondent fatigue, distraction, and carelessness—that the results would be worthless at best and misleading at worst.

Length of the Questionnaire

The length of the questionnaire—the amount of time it takes the average respondent to complete the survey—is an important determinant of the appropriate survey method to use. If the questionnaire for a particular study takes an hour to complete, the choices of survey method are extremely limited. Telephone, mall-intercept, and most other types of surveys, with the exception of personal interviews, will not work. People shopping at a mall ordinarily do not have an hour to spend being interviewed. Terminations increase

EXHIBIT 5.7	Strengths and Weaknesses of Selected Data-Collection Methods in Terms of Quality of Data Produced	
Method	**Strengths**	**Weaknesses**
Mall-intercept interview	Interviewer can show, explain, and probe.	Many distractions are inherent in the mall environment; respondent may be in a hurry, not in proper frame of mind to answer survey questions; there is more chance for interviewer bias; nonprobability sampling problems arise.
Central-location telephone interview	Supervisor can monitor the interviewing process easily; excellent samples can be obtained; interviewer can explain and probe.	Respondent may be distracted by things going on at their location; problems arise in long interviews and interviews with many open-ended questions. Many refuse to participate.
Self-administered questionnaire	Interviewer and associated biases are eliminated; respondent can complete the questionnaire when convenient; respondent can look up information and work at own pace.	There is no interviewer to show, explain, or probe; sample may be poor because of nonresponse; who actually completes the questionnaire cannot be controlled.
Mail survey	Same strengths as for self-administered method.	Same weaknesses as for self-administered questionnaire; sample quality is better with mail panel.

and tempers flare when interviewers must try to keep respondents on the phone for an hour. Response rates plummet when people receive through the mail questionnaires that take an hour or more to complete. The trick is to match the survey technique to the length of the questionnaire.

SurveySpot, SSI's huge Internet panel, asked its panel members what was the ideal survey length. The responses were as follows:[15]

- ☐ Less than 2 minutes   2%
- ☐ 2 to 5 minutes   21%
- ☐ 6 to 10 minutes   44%
- ☐ 11 to 15 minutes   21%
- ☐ 16 to 25 minutes   3%
- ☐ 26 minutes or more   0%
- ☐ No ideal length   8%
- ☐ Not sure   1%

Incidence Rate

Recall that the incidence rate refers to the percentage of people, households, or businesses in the general population that would qualify as interviewees in a particular study. Search costs, which correlate with the time spent trying to locate qualified respondents, sometimes exceed the costs of interviewing. In situations where the researcher expects incidence rates to be low and search costs high, it is important to select the method or combination of methods that will provide the desired survey results at a reasonable cost.

Doing a low-incidence rate study in a mall would be very expensive. This approach should be taken only if there is some compelling reason for doing so—a long in-depth interview, for example. The lowest-cost survey alternative for the low-incidence study is probably the Internet panel, assuming that this approach meets the other data collection requirements of the study. One advantage of the Internet panel is that it can be prescreened; people can be asked a number of questions, usually including some on product usage. For example, if panel members were asked during prescreening whether anyone in their household participated in downhill or alpine skiing, the Internet panel operator could—at very low cost—pull out only those households with one or more skiers for a survey of Alpine skiers.

Structure of the Questionnaire

In addition to the length of the questionnaire, the degree of structure required in the questionnaire may be a factor in determining which survey method is most appropriate for a given study. *Structure* refers to the extent to which the questionnaire follows a set sequence or order, has a predetermined wording of questions, and relies on closed-ended (multiple-choice) questions. A questionnaire that does all these things would be structured; one that deviates from these set patterns would be considered unstructured. A questionnaire with little structure is likely to require a face-to-face interview. Very brief, highly structured questionnaires do not require face-to-face contact between interviewer and respondent. Mail, telephone, self-administered, and online surveys are viable options for studies of this type.

Time Available to Complete the Survey

If the client needs to have survey results quickly, the Internet is the best choice. Generally, central-location telephone and mall-intercept interviews can also be completed in a timely manner.

Marketing Research Interviewer

No discussion of survey research in marketing would be complete without considering the person who actually does the interviewing. As noted in Chapter 2, most marketing research in-person interviewing is still done under the direct supervision of field service firms. The actual interviewing is conducted, to a large extent, by individuals who work part-time for relatively low wages. A new, totally inexperienced interviewer works at a rate somewhere between minimum wage and minimum wage plus 20 percent. It is unusual to find even the most experienced interviewers earning more than minimum wage plus 50 percent. The pay is not good, and fringe benefits are minimal. Ordinarily, an interviewer's involvement with an interviewing assignment begins when he or she is asked by a supervisor at a field service firm to work on a particular job. If the interviewer accepts the assignment, he or she will be given a date and time for a briefing about the job. At the briefing, the questionnaire for the study and all deadlines and requirements for the job are discussed.

Interviewers are typically the main interface with consumers and are, therefore, a vital link to consumer cooperation. Their skill level and pay level are areas of concern now being addressed by the Marketing Research Association, which has several suggestions for developing and strengthening interviewers' consumer interaction skills: good training programs that cover ways to establish consumer rapport and a basic understanding of "cooperation turning points," frequent monitoring of interviewers' interaction skills to evaluate their impact on consumer cooperation, and feedback to interviewers on monitoring results.

SUMMARY

Surveys are popular for several reasons. First, managers need to know why people do or do not do something. Second, managers need to know how decisions are made. Third, managers need to know what kind of person, from a demographic or lifestyle perspective, is making the decision to buy or not to buy a product.

There are two major categories of errors in survey research: random error and systematic error, or bias. Systematic error can be further broken down into measurement error and sample design error. Types of sample design error include selection, population specification, and frame errors. Frame error results from the use of an incomplete or inaccurate sampling frame. Population specification error results from an incorrect definition of the universe or population from which the sample is to be selected. Selection error results from adopting incomplete or improper sampling procedures or not properly following appropriate selection procedures.

The second major category of systematic error is measurement error. Measurement error occurs when there is a discrepancy between the information being sought (true value) and the information actually obtained by the measurement process. Measurement error can be created by a number of factors, including surrogate information error, interviewer error, measurement instrument bias, processing error, nonresponse bias, and response bias. Surrogate information error results from a discrepancy between the information actually required to solve a problem and the information sought by the researcher. Interviewer error occurs when an interviewer influences a respondent to give untrue or inaccurate answers. Measurement instrument bias is caused by problems within the questionnaire itself. Processing error results from mistakes in the transfer of information from survey documents to the computer. Nonresponse bias occurs when a particular individual in a sample cannot be reached or refuses to participate in the survey. Response bias arises when interviewees tend to answer questions in a particular way, whether out of deliberate falsification or unconscious misrepresentation.

There are several types of traditional surveys. Mall-intercept interviews are conducted with shoppers in public areas of shopping malls, either by interviewing them in the mall or by asking them to come to a permanent interviewing facility within the mall. Executive interviews are the industrial equivalent of door-to-door interviews; they involve interviewing professional people at their offices, typically concerning industrial products or services. Central-location telephone interviews are conducted from a facility set up for the specific purpose of doing telephone survey research. Computer-assisted telephone interviewing (CATI) is a form of central-location interviewing. Each interviewer is seated in front of a computer terminal or personal computer. The computer guides the interviewer and the interviewing process by exhibiting appropriate questions on the computer screen. The data are entered into the computer as the interview takes place. A self-administered questionnaire is filled out by the respondent. The big disadvantage of this approach is that probes cannot be used to clarify responses. Mail surveys can be divided into ad hoc, or one-shot, surveys and mail panels. In ad hoc mail surveys, questionnaires are mailed to potential respondents without prior contact. The sample is used for only a single survey project. In a mail panel, consumers are precontacted by letter and are offered an incentive for participating in the panel for a period of time. If they agree, they fill out a background questionnaire. Then, periodically, panel participants are sent questionnaires.

The factors that determine which survey method to use include the degree of sampling precision required, budget size, whether respondents need to react to various stimuli or to perform specialized tasks, the quality of data required, the length of the questionnaire, the degree of structure of the questionnaire, and the time available to complete the survey.

KEY TERMS & DEFINITIONS

random error, or **random sampling error** Error that results from chance variation.

chance variation Difference between the sample value and the true value of the population mean.

systematic error, or **bias** Error that results from problems or flaws in the execution of the research design; sometimes called non-sampling error.

sample design error Systematic error that results from an error in the sample design or sampling procedures.

sampling frame List of population elements or members from which units to be sampled are selected.

frame error Error resulting from an inaccurate or incomplete sampling frame.

population specification error Error that results from incorrectly defining the population or universe from which a sample is chosen.

selection error Error that results from incomplete or improper sample selection procedures or not following appropriate procedures.

measurement error Systematic error that results from a variation between the information being sought and what is actually obtained by the measurement process.

surrogate information error Error that results from a discrepancy between the information needed to solve a problem and that sought by the researcher.

interviewer error, or **interviewer bias** Error that results from the interviewer's influencing—consciously or unconsciously—the respondent.

measurement instrument bias Error that results from the design of the questionnaire or measurement instrument; also known as questionnaire bias.

processing error Error that results from the incorrect transfer of information from a survey document to a computer.

nonresponse bias Error that results from a systematic difference between those who do and those who do not respond to a measurement instrument.

refusal rate Percentage of persons contacted who refused to participate in a survey.

response bias Error that results from the tendency of people to answer a question incorrectly through either deliberate falsification or unconscious misrepresentation.

door-to-door interviews Interviews conducted face-to-face with consumers in their homes.

executive interviews Industrial equivalent of door-to-door interviewing.

mall-intercept interviews Interviews conducted by intercepting mall shoppers (or shoppers in other high-traffic locations) and interviewing them face-to-face.

central-location telephone interviews Interviews conducted by calling respondents from a centrally located marketing research facility.

computer-assisted telephone interviews (CATI) Central-location telephone interviews in which interviewers enter respondents' answers directly into a computer.

self-administered questionnaires Questionnaires filled out by respondents with no interviewer present.

ad hoc mail surveys Questionnaires sent to selected names and addresses without prior contact by the researcher; sometimes called one-shot mail surveys.

mail panels Precontacted and prescreened participants who are periodically sent questionnaires.

longitudinal study Study in which the same respondents are resampled over time.

1. The owner of a hardware store in Eureka, California, is interested in determining the demographic characteristics of people who shop at his store versus those of people who shop at competing stores. He also wants to know what his image is relative to the competition. He would like to have the information within three weeks and is working on a limited budget. Which survey method would you recommend? Why?

2. Discuss this statement: "A mall-intercept interview is representative only of people who shop in that particular mall. Therefore, only surveys that relate to shopping patterns of consumers within that mall should be conducted in a mall-intercept interview."

3. A colleague is arguing that the best way to conduct a study of attitudes toward city government in your community is through a mail survey because it is the cheapest method. How would you respond to your colleague? If time were not a critical factor in your decision, would your response change? Why?

4. Discuss the various types of sample design errors and give examples of each.

5. Why is it important to consider measurement error in survey research? Why is this typically not discussed in professional marketing research reports?

6. What types of error might be associated with the following situations?
   a. Conducting a survey about attitudes toward city government, using the telephone directory as a sample frame.
   b. Interviewing respondents only between 8:00 a.m. and 5:00 p.m. on features they would like to see in a new condominium development.
   c. Asking people if they have visited the public library in the past two months.
   d. Asking people how many tubes of toothpaste they used in the past year.
   e. Telling interviewers they can probe using any particular example they wish to make up.

Dairy Management Inc.

Dairy Management Inc. (DMI) is the domestic and international planning and management organization responsible for increasing demand for U.S.-produced dairy products on behalf of America's dairy farmers.* DMI and state and regional organizations manage the programs of the American Dairy Association, the National Dairy Council, and the U.S. Dairy Export Council. The mission of DMI is to increase demand for dairy products through the development and execution of an industrywide, market-driven business plan that invests resources in a strategic manner and provides the best possible economic advantage to dairy farmers.

Since 1997, DMI's national dairy marketing efforts have specifically targeted kids (6 to 12 years of age) and their moms. Four elements comprised these marketing efforts. First, "got milk?" ads on kids' favorite TV shows depicted milk as hip, cool, and fun. Second, the dairy promotions in retail stores have included a joint promotion

*http://www.dairycheckoff.com

with Kellogg's cereals that aims to involve kids in milk purchasing decisions and increase white gallon milk sales. The promotion is prominently featured on several Kellogg's brand cereals, with in-store displays and other point-of-sale materials. Third, national, state, and regional dairy promotion organizations have aggressively implemented programs to improve kid's milk-drinking experiences in schools. Cafeteria promotions use fun, hip posters that promote milk's many great-tasting flavors. Fourth, milk publicity and special events have taken the theme of making the "Great Soda Swap." In this way, nutrient-deficient soft drinks would be replaced with fun, nutrient-rich flavored milks.

Now, DMI managers would like to evaluate some of the effects of these marketing efforts. They are considering buying syndicated research on beverage consumption produced by the National Family Opinion (NFO) WorldGroup research agency. The NFO SIP (Share of Intake Panel) is a special panel of U.S. consumers who record their consumption of beverages in a diary for two weeks at a time. Typically, 12,000 consumers participate in the NFO SIP panel each year. NFO SIP reveals both at-home and away-from-home beverage consumption (excluding tap water) by household members during any two-week period. This database has more than 20 years of data gathered from more than 12,000 respondents a year including kids, teens, and adults.

Upon contacting NFO WorldGroup's SIP team, DMI managers discovered that 90 percent of all kids (ages 6 to 12) drank at least one serving of milk as a beverage during an average two-week period and that kids consumed 28 gallons of milk annually per capita.

Questions

1. If you were working for the DMI research team, what questions would you want to ask the NFO WorldGroup team about its data and the methods used in collecting this data in deciding whether to purchase a complete report from NFO World Group or to purchase part of the database?

2. What are the advantages and disadvantages of mail panel research? What other survey methods could have been used to gather the information? Why do you think NFO chose a mail panel?

© Terrell Creative/StockFood America

ONLINE MARKETING RESEARCH

LEARNING OBJECTIVES

1.	To understand the online world as it applies to marketing research.
2.	To learn about using the Internet to gather secondary data for marketing research.
3.	To appreciate Internet search strategies.
4.	To understand the popularity and types of online focus groups.
5.	To gain insights into survey research on the Internet.
6.	To appreciate the importance of panel management in maintaining data quality.

Most Americans believe some restaurants serve portions that are too large. In an ongoing Health and Nutrition Strategist syndicated study, Decision Analyst asked 4,156 survey respondents about the amount of food they are served by restaurants. Among all surveyed, 57 percent agreed completely or agreed somewhat that some restaurants often serve portions that are too large. About 23 percent of respondents neither agreed nor disagreed, and 20 percent disagreed completely or disagreed somewhat that restaurant portions are too large.

By gender, 67 percent of female respondents said restaurant portions are too large, while 47 percent of male respondents felt the same way. Older respondents (over 65) also tended to think portions are too large (68 percent), while only 55 percent of younger people (18–24) agree.

The survey shows that the higher one's income, the more likely she or he is to believe that portions are too large. For example, 45 percent of respondents earning under $25,000 annually said food portions are sometimes too large, while 70 percent of respondents earning at least $150,000 said portions are sometimes too large.

Those respondents who "don't worry about nutrition when they eat out" are much less likely to agree that portions are too large (53 percent) than those who "try to make healthy choices when they eat out" (70 percent).

Decision Analyst's Health and Nutrition Strategist was conducted online via its American Consumer Opinion panel.[1]

Decision Analyst is one of the featured marketing research companies in this text because your authors have a very close relationship with the firm's management. The study on restaurant portions was conducted using one of Decision Analyst's online panels.

Chapter 6 explores the ever-increasing role of the Internet in secondary data search, qualitative research, and survey research. Online observation research, another form of research growing at a sizzling pace, is covered in Chapter 7.

The Online World

The world's Internet population will total about 1.3 billion users by the time you read this paragraph. That's right, about one-fifth of the world's population is online. In the United States, 70 percent of the population is online spanning every ethnic, socioeconomic, and educational divide. It is no wonder then that most managers accept the idea that online research can, under appropriate conditions, accurately represent U.S. consumers as a whole.[2] Nonadopters of the Internet tend to be older, low-income consumers (aged 65+ and with household income less than $30,000).[3] These consumers are not the target market for many companies' goods and services.

The popularity of online research continues to grow, with the vast majority of America's marketing research companies conducting some form of online research.[4] Today online survey research has replaced computer-assisted telephone interviewing (CATI) as the most popular mode of data collection.[5] Internet data collection is also rated as having the greatest potential for further growth. Having made this observation, we must also report that there is no sign that paper surveys are disappearing as two-thirds of the market research companies are still relying on them.[6]

Using the Internet for Secondary Data

Recall from Chapter 3 that secondary data can play a key role early in the marketing research process. It can clarify the problem, perhaps suggest a methodology for approaching the problem, and, if you are really lucky, provide a solution so that the time and cost of primary research is avoided.

Sites of Interest to Marketing Researchers

Exhibit 6.1 details a number of different sites where researchers can go to obtain secondary information, including competitive intelligence. You will note that a rich variety of data is available on many different topics. Although a lot of information is free, some, such as that offered by Claritas International, must be purchased.

Periodical, Newspaper, and Book Databases   Several excellent periodical, newspaper, and book databases are available to researchers. We have also posted these on our website at www.wiley.com/college/McDaniel. Some can be directly accessed via the Internet and others through your local library's website.

Newsgroups

A primary means of communicating with other professionals and special-interest groups on the Internet is through newsgroups. With an Internet connection and newsreader software, you can visit any newsgroup supported by your service provider. If your service provider does not offer newsgroups or does not carry the group in which you are interested, you can find one of the publicly available newsgroup servers that does carry the group you'd like to read.

> **newsgroup**
> An Internet site where people can read and post messages devoted to a specific topic.

Newsgroups function much like bulletin boards for a particular topic or interest. A newsgroup is established to focus on a particular topic. Readers stop by that newsgroup to read messages left by other people, post responses to others' questions, and send rebuttals to comments with which they disagree. Generally, there is some management of the messages to keep discussions within the topic area and to remove offensive material. However, readers of a newsgroup are free to discuss any issue and communicate with anyone in the world who visits that group. Images and data files can be exchanged in newsgroups, just as they can be exchanged via e-mail.

With over 250,000 newsgroups currently in existence and more being added every day, there is a newsgroup for nearly every hobby, profession, and lifestyle. Both Netscape Navigator and Microsoft Internet Explorer, as well as other browsers, come with newsgroup readers. If you do not already have a newsgroup reader, you can go to one of the search engines and search for a freeware or shareware newsgroup reader. These newsgroup readers function much like e-mail programs. To find a particular newsgroup, follow these steps:

1. Connect to the Internet in your usual way.

2. Open your newsreader program.

3. Search for the topic of interest. Most newsreaders allow you to search the names of the newsgroups for keywords or topics. Some newsreaders, like Microsoft Internet Explorer, also allow you to search the brief descriptions that accompany most newsgroups.

4. Select the newsgroup of interest.

5. Begin scanning messages. The title of each message generally gives an indication of its subject matter.

Newsgroup messages look like e-mail messages. They contain a subject title, author, and message body. Unlike normal e-mail messages, however, newsgroup messages are threaded discussions. This means that any reply to a previous message will appear linked to that message. Therefore, you can follow a discussion between two or more people by starting at the original message and following the links (or threads) to each successive reply. Images, sound files, and video clips can be attached to messages for anyone to download and examine.

Blogs

The traditional definition of a blog, or Web log, was a frequent, chronological publication of personal thoughts and Web links. Now companies are also using blogs

EXHIBIT 6.1	Secondary Data Available Online for Marketing Researchers	
Organization	URL	Description
American Marketing Association	www.marketingpower.com	Enables users to search all of the AMA's publications by using keywords.
BLS Consumer Expenditure Surveys	stats.bls.gov/csxprod.htm	Provides information on the buying habits of consumers, including data on their expenditures, income, and credit ratings.
Bureau of Economic Analysis	www.bea.doc.gov	Offers a wide range of economic statistics.
Bureau of Transportation Statistics	www.bts.gov	Is a comprehensive source for a wide range of statistics on transportation.
American City Business Journals	bizjournals.com/journals/demographics	Offers a wealth of articles, reports, news, and data on everything from ratings of America's best small cities to statistics on men's and women's salaries. Current articles and reports, as well as an extensive archive dating back to 1994, provide insight and analysis of key business and economic trends. Sample hundreds of spreadsheets with demographic and economic statistics on topics such as race, families, and children, and population projections; get up-to-date demographic news from around the nation; or find out each month how your city or state rates economically, based on population, income and employment trends.
Center for International Earth Science Network	ciesin.org	Is an excellent source of demographic information concerning the United States.
Centers for Disease Control/National Center for Health Statistics	www.cdc.gov/nchs	Maintains data on vital events, health status, lifestyle, exposure to unhealthy influences, onset and diagnosis of illness and disability, and use of health care, through the National Center for Health Statistics. The NCHS, a subdivision of the Centers for Disease Control and Prevention, is the federal government's principal agency for vital and health statistics.
Claritas International	www.claritas.com	Provides access to a wide range of secondary data on many topics. Most must be purchased.
Clickz.com	www.clickz.com	Statistics on Internet research: weekly usage statistics, online populations, browser statistics and more.
Decision Analyst	www.secondarydata.com	Organizes, indexes, and links to the very best sources of free economic and marketing data available online.
The Dismal Scientist	www.dismal.com	Provides timely economic information, with comprehensive data and analyses at the metro, state, and national levels. This authoritative site also has data and analyses of global issues, including situations facing Asia, South America, and Europe. Visitors can rank states and metro areas on more than 100 economic, socioeconomic, and demographic categories.

(continued)

EXHIBIT 6.1 *(continued)*

Organization	URL	Description
Easy Analytic Software, Inc./The Right Site	www.easidemographics.com	Offers demographic site reports, or three-ring studies, including current estimates for population and households. Each three-ring study has census estimates for race, ethnicity, age distribution, and income distribution, as well as weather data. The New York City-based developer and marketer of demographic data also offers one million pages of demographic reports for zip codes, counties, metropolitan areas, cities, states, sectional centers, television markets, and other geographic areas.
EconData.Net	www.econdata.net	Enables users to access a tremendous number of links to government, private, and academic data sources. Check out the list of top 10 data sources at this premier site for researchers interested in economics and demographics.
Encyclopedia Britannica	www.britannica.com	Provides free online access to the entire 32-volume encyclopedia.
FIND/SVP	www.findsvp.com	Offers consulting and research services. The site claims to offer access to the largest private information center in the United States.
Harris InfoSource	www.harrisinfo.com	Provides business-to-business data on American manufacturers and key decision makers.
Jupiter Media Corporation	www.internetnews.com/stats	A cross between an online magazine and a data dump, the site is a compilation of short articles written around the latest Internet research from the top names in the industry. Also, the stats tab offers lots of good online data.
Marketing Research Association	www.mra-net.org	Offers causes and solutions of "declining respondent cooperation" and links to research suppliers.
Mediamark Research/ Top-Line Reports	www.mediamark.com/mri/ docs/toplinereports.html/	Allows marketers and researchers to access demographic data on magazines, cable TV, and 53 different product or service categories. Top-Line Reports breaks down cable TV networks' viewers according to age, sex, and income. Magazines are listed by total audience, circulation, readers per copy, median age, and income.
Nielsen/NetRatings	www.nielsen-netratings.com	Is a source of Internet audience information. Researchers can find data on Internet growth and user patterns.
Population Reference Bureau	www.prb.org	Is a source of demographic information on population issues.
Service Intelligence	www.serviceintelligence.com	Has an area devoted to customer stories of unpleasant experiences with airlines, banks, restaurants, and other service businesses. However, "hero" stories are also included.
Social Security Administration	www.ssa/gov/statistics/ supplement/2000	Provides a range of government statistics.

(continued)

EXHIBIT 6.1	(continued)	
Organization	**URL**	**Description**
Tetrad Computer Applications, Inc./Census	www.tetrad.gov	Provides detailed information about the population of metropolitan areas.
U.S. Census Bureau	www.census.gov	Is a very useful source of virtually all census data.
U.S. Department of Agriculture/ Economic Research Service	www.ers.usda.gov	Offers a wide range of agricultural statistics.
USAData	www.usadata.com	Provides access to consumer lifestyle data on a local, regional, and national basis.
U.S. Government	www.fedstats.gov	Source for statistics and reports for more than 100 government agencies. Also links to other sources of relevant information. Highly recommended site but you may have to dig a little.
WorldOpinion	www.worldopinion.com	Offers thousands of marketing research reports. This is perhaps the premier site for the marketing research industry.

to talk to customers and to other businesses. Blogging gained popularity with the introduction of automated published systems, most notably Bloggeratblogger.com. Marketing researchers are finding blogs to be an important source of information on just about any topic imaginable. Researchers have also used them to recruit respondents for surveys. Although blogs can be found on most search engines, several engines, such as blogsearchengine.com, are dedicated to blog searches.

Internet Search Strategies

There is perhaps no single best way to search the Web, but we recommend a five-step strategy.[7]

> **Step One:** Analyze your topic to decide where to begin. A suggested worksheet is shown in Exhibit 6.2.

> **Step Two:** Test run a word or phrase in a search engine such as Google. Consider synonyms or equivalent terms.

> **Step Three:** Learn as you go and vary your approach with what you learn. Don't assume that you know what you want to find. Look at the search results and see what else you might use in addition to what you thought of.

> **Step Four:** Don't get bogged down in any strategy that doesn't work. Consider using a subject directory. A few of the best are the Librarian's Index, lii.org; Infomine, infomine.ucr.edu; Academic Info, www.academicinfo.net; Google Directory, directory .google.com; About.com, www.about.com; and Yahoo Directory, dir.yahoo.com. Many researchers switch back and forth between directories and search engines.

> **Step Five:** If you haven't found what you want, go back to earlier steps better informed.

Evaluating Web Pages   Once you have found what you were looking for, the next step is to evaluate the quality. Things are not always as they seem. For example, recall the

| **EXHIBIT 6.2** | **Internet Search Topic Worksheet** |

Jot down a topic or subject you'd like to explore on the Web:

BEGIN THE PRE-SEARCHING ANALYSIS

1. **What UNIQUE WORDS, DISTINCTIVE NAMES, ABBREVIATIONS, or ACRONYMS are associated with your topic?**
   These may be the place to begin because their specificity will help zero in on relevant pages.

2. **Can you think of societies, organizations, or groups that might have information on your subject via their pages?**
   Search these as a "phrase in quotes," looking for a homepage that might contain links to other pages, journals, discussion groups, or databases on your subject. You may require the "phrase in quotes" to be in the documents' titles by preceding it by **title:** (no space)

3. **What other words are likely to be in ANY Web documents on your topic?**
   You may want to require these by joining them with **AND** or preceding each by + (no space)

4. **Do any of the words in 1, 2, or 3 belong in phrases or strings—together in a certain order, like a cliché?**
   Search these as a "phrase in quotes" (e.g., "observation research" or "marketing research aggregator").

5. **For any of the terms in #4, can you think of synonyms, variant spellings, or equivalent terms you would also accept in relevant documents?**
   You may want to allow these terms by joining them by **OR** and including each set of equivalent terms in ( ) (e.g., surveys or interviews).

6. **Can you think of any extraneous or irrelevant documents these words might pick up?**
   You may want to exclude terms or phrases with—**[no space] before each term**, or **AND NOT** (e.g., surveys or interviews—job).

7. **What BROADER terms could your topic be covered by?**
   When browsing subject categories or searching sites of webliographies or databases on your topic, try broader categories (e.g., marketing research).

websites that want you to pay a membership fee to become an online survey respondent. There is a website that supposedly ranks websites that provide an entrée to earning cash through completing interviews. All of the sites ranked required a membership fee, and no real marketing research firms, such as Greenfield Online or Harris Interactive, were included. Of course, legitimate researchers don't charge a fee to become a panel member. The ranking site was probably created by one of the sites that charge a membership fee. No criteria were given for how the rankings were determined.

Techniques for evaluating Web pages are detailed in Exhibit 6.3.

Creating a Database from a Website— A Marketer's Dream[8]

If a person today were opening, say, a wine shop, which of the following would give the owner the best opportunity to build a database—a traditional store or a Web retailer such as wine.com?

A Web merchant like wine.com has access to data about its clients that would make its physical-world counterparts very envious. A customer's conduit to an online store is a two-way electronic link, allowing the online merchant to gather all sorts of information, particularly if that customer has shopped with that merchant before.

Getting the customer's name, address, and purchasing history is only the beginning. A Web merchant can record the customer's actions as he or she moves through the merchant's site, taking note not only of purchases but also of window shopping. The end result is a file that allows the merchant to determine what that customer is most likely to purchase next—and then offer inducements to make it happen.

Meanwhile, back in the physical world, the wine store owner sits behind the register, eyeing the anonymous customer who just went out empty-handed. Had the customer visited the site before? If so, what did he or she buy? Did the customer even see the new Chardonnay that just came in? Unfortunately, the owner was too busy to ask those questions (and the customer would have been offended if the owner had). Maybe the customer will come back—maybe not.

Preview Travel Inc., an online travel agency based in San Francisco, determined that Las Vegas, Orlando, and Cancun were the top three vacation spots among its customers. The firm quickly purchased keywords for the three destinations on several Internet directory

---

EXHIBIT 6.3 | **How to Evaluate Web Pages**

1. What can the URL tell you?
Techniques for Web Evaluation:
1. Before you leave the list of search results—before you click and get interested in anything written on the page—glean all you can from the URLs of each page.
2. Then choose pages most likely to be reliable and authentic.

Questions to ask:
Is it somebody's *personal page*?
- Read the URL carefully:
  - Look for a personal name (e.g., *jbarker* or *barker*) following a tilde (~), a percent sign (%), or the words "users," "members," or "people."
  - Is the server a commercial *ISP* * or other provider mostly of Web page hosting (like aol.com or geocities.com)

What are the implications?
Personal pages are not necessarily "bad," but you need to investigate the author very carefully. For personal pages, there is no publisher or domain owner vouching for the information in the page.

Look for appropriateness and fit. What kind of information source do you think is most reliable for your topic?

(continued)

EXHIBIT 6.3 *(continued)*

What type of *domain* does it come from?
(educational, nonprofit, commercial, government, etc.)

- Is the domain appropriate for the content?
  ○ Government sites: look for .gov, .mil, .us, or other country code
  ○ Educational sites: look for .edu

2. Scan the perimeter of the page, looking for answers to these questions.
Techniques for Web Evaluation:

1. Look for links that say **"About us," "Philosophy," "Background," "Biography," "Who am I,"** etc.
2. If you cannot find any links like these, you can often find this kind of information if you trucate back URL.
   INSTRUCTIONS for Truncating back a URL: In the top Location Box, delete the end characters of the URL stopping just before each / (leave the slash). Press enter to see if you can see more about the author or the origins/nature of the site providing the page. Continue this process, one slash (/) at a time, until you reach the first single / which is preceded by the domain name portion. This is the page's server or "publisher."
3. Look for the date "last updated"—usually at the bottom of a Web page.
   Check the date on all the pages on the site.
   Do not rely on a date given in IE's File|Properties or Netscape/Mozilla's View|Page Info displays. These dates can be automatically kept current and are useless in critical evaluation.

Questions to ask:
Who wrote the page?

- Look for the name of the author, or the name of the organization, institution, agency, or whatever, who is responsible for the page
  ○ An e-mail contact is not enough.
- If there is no personal author, look for an agency or organization that claims responsibility for the page.
  ○ If you cannot find this, locate the publisher by truncating back the URL (see technique above). Does this publisher claim responsibility for the content? Does it explain why the page exists in any way?

What are the implications?
Web pages are all created with a purpose in mind by some person or agency or entity. They do not simply "grow" on the Web like mildew grows in moist corners.

You are looking for someone who claims accountability and responsibility for the content.

An e-mail address with no additional information about the author is not sufficient for assessing the author's credentials.

If this is all you have, try e-mailing the author and asking politely for more information about him/her.

3. Look for indicators of quality information:
Techniques for Web Evaluation:

1. Look for a link called "links," "additional sites," "related links," etc.
2. In the text, if you see little footnote numbers or links that might refer to documentation, take the time to explore them. What kinds of publications or sites are they? reputable? scholarly? Are they real? On the Web (where no publisher is editing most pages), it is possible to create totally fake references.
3. Look at the publisher of the page (first part of the URL).
   Expect a journal article, newspaper article, and some other publications that are recent to come from the original publisher IF the publication is available on the web. Look at the bottom of such articles for copyright information or permissions to reproduce.

Question to ask:
Are sources documented with footnotes or links?

- Where did the author get the information?
  ○ As in published scholarly/academic journals and books, you should expect documentation.
- If there are links to other pages as sources, are they to reliable sources?
- Do the links work?

What are the implications?
In scholarly/research work, the credibility of most writings is proven through footnote documentation or other means of revealing the sources of information. Saying what you believe without documentation is not much better than just expressing an opinion or a point of view.

EXHIBIT 6.3 *(continued)*

4. What do others say?
Techniques for Web Evaluation:
1. Find out what other Web pages link to this page.
   a. Use alexa.com URL information:
   Simply paste the URL into alexa.com's search box.
   You will see, depending on the volume of traffic to the page:
   - Traffic rank
   - Subjective reviews
   - "Site statistics" including some page history, sites that link to the page
   - Contact/ownership info for the domain name

5. Does it all add up?
Techniques for Web evaluation:
1. Step back and think about all you have learned about the page. Listen to your gut reaction. Think about why the page was created, the intentions of its author(s).
   If you have doubts, ask your instructor or come to one of the library reference desks and ask for advice.
2. Be sensitive to the possibility that you are the victim of irony, spoof, fraud, or other falsehood.
3. Ask yourself if the Web is truly the best place to find resources for the research you are doing.

Questions to ask:
Why was the page put on the Web?
- Inform, give facts, give data?
- Explain, persuade?
- Sell, entice?
- Share?
- Disclose?

So what? What are the implications?
These are some of the reasons to think of. The Web is a public place, open to all. You need to be aware of the entire range of human possibilities of intentions behind Web pages.

sites; when a Web surfer performs a search for any of the three vacation spots, a Preview Travel advertising banner accompanies the list of results. Karen Askey, senior vice president of consumer marketing at Preview Travel, says traditional travel agencies could employ the same promotional tactics, but she doubts they could spot top destinations as quickly. "When you're online, the speed at which you can get that data is basically instantaneous," she says.

Once Web surfers start clicking around the virtual aisles of an online store, merchants can monitor their every move. The best known method of doing so involves a **cookie**, a text file that sits on a user's computer and identifies that user when she or he revisits a website.

Even some privacy advocates admit that cookies have beneficial uses. For instance, they can store passwords, sparing users the hassle of having to identify themselves every time they go to a website, and they allow online shopping carts to work. Despite what some Net users believe, a site can read only the cookie that site put on the user's system, not any other cookies the user has collected from other websites.

Cookies are a powerful device for monitoring a user's behavior within a site, one that can tell a merchant whether the user lingers in lingerie or lawn chairs. "What it's like," says Nick Donatiello, president of Odyssey, a marketing research firm based in San Francisco, "is every time you walk into Macy's, they put a little tracker on you that follows you everywhere you go, how long you look at perfume and blue jeans."[9]

Cookies give Web merchants an advantage over their competitors in traditional retailing. Web merchants can follow window shoppers and then use the information they

cookie
A text file placed on a user's computer in order to identify the user when she or he revisits the website.

obtain to target promotions to them on return visits. And, unlike traditional counterparts, an online merchant can rearrange the entire layout of a store in real time, sticking an advertisement for, say, parkas on the front door when an avid skier comes calling.

Online Qualitative Research

The primary form of online qualitative research is focus groups. These come in two categories in the online world: *traditional,* sometimes referred to as synchronous groups, and *online bulletin boards,* sometimes referred to as asynchronous groups. You will learn that online focus groups can take several forms. Traditional online groups are what the name implies. The goal is to get 8 to 10 participants online at the same time, a moderator to send questions to the participants, and the participants to provide their comments. Special software from companies such as Itracks (see www.itracks.com/qual) provides the environment for these groups. Online bulletin boards are a new form of qualitative research that takes advantage of the online medium. In these groups, questions are posted for participants each day, and they have all day to provide their responses. They usually run for two to three days, sometimes longer. The moderator answers questions from participants throughout the day. Questions for the next day can be modified based on what participants have to say. Probing questions can be sent to individual participants or to all. Supporting software can permit participants to see what others had to say after they respond. An even newer twist on online focus groups are Web communities, which we will also exam in this section. We conclude with a brief look at online individual depth interviewing.

The Popularity of Online Focus Groups

> **online focus groups**
> Focus groups conducted via the Internet.

Perhaps the hottest area in qualitative research today is **online focus groups**. Many marketing researchers, such as Greenfield Online, NFO Interactive, and Harris Black International, believe that Internet focus groups can replace face-to-face focus groups, although they acknowledge that online research has limitations. Others that are moving aggressively into online marketing research, such as Millward Brown International and Digital Marketing Services (DMS), were slower to use online focus groups.

Advantages of Online Focus Groups
Marketers who have used online focus groups, and the marketing researchers conducting them, say that benefits far outweigh limitations. Those benefits include lack of geographic barriers, much lower costs (about half as much), faster turnaround time, respondents can be geographically separate and be located anywhere, and intangibles such as increased openness on the part of respondents when they do not have an interviewer staring them in the face.

"I think [the panelists] were more definite about things they didn't like than they'd be in front of a moderator," said Lisa Crane, vice president of sales and marketing for Universal Studios Online, which used an online focus group to test a redesigned site it's developing for Captain Morgan Original Spiced Rum, a brand of its parent company, Seagram Company. Rudy Nadilo, president and CEO of Greenfield Online, which conducted the online focus groups for Universal, said they are meant "to complement, not replace" traditional panels.[10]

Not only are the costs lower for online focus groups, but there are substantial travel savings for the client as well. Expenditures for round-trip airline tickets to distant cities, meals, hotels, and taxis are avoided. Clients merely log on in their own office, or even at home, to observe the research in progress.

Another advantage of online focus groups lies in access to the hard-to-reach target population. Online, it's possible to reach populations that are traditionally inaccessible because of time or professional constraints—groups such as physicians, lawyers, and senior business executives. Chances are higher that they will be available to participate, too, since they do not need to take time from their busy schedules to visit a focus group facility but, rather, can participate from the privacy of their own homes.

Another advantage claimed for online focus groups is efficient moderator–client interaction. During the traditional focus group, the client observes the discussion from behind a one-way glass; communication with the moderator is impossible without interfering with the discussion. An online focus group, however, offers a remarkable opportunity for two-way interaction between the moderator and the client. This direct interaction, while the moderator conducts the group, has become a necessity in operating a fully effective online focus group discussion. Rather than sneaking into the room with a note scribbled on a piece of paper, the client can address the moderator directly, clearly, and efficiently, without interrupting the group dynamic.

Traditional focus groups always include "natural talkers," who dominate the discussion, despite a good moderator's attempt to equalize participant contributions. Other participants will be less comfortable voicing opinions in a group; they may express themselves more freely when not face to face with their peers. The online focus group has a built-in leveling effect, in the sense that shy participants can express themselves as freely as more outgoing participants. One participant points out why he likes participating in online focus groups, explaining, "I can be honest without the face-to-face peer pressure of focus groups"; another offers, "I get to express my opinion without having to hear someone's reaction."[11] At least in terms of honesty and willingness to offer genuine ideas and opinions, respondents tend to feel more comfortable participating from the privacy of their own homes.

Disadvantages of Online Focus Groups

Critics say that the research community does itself an injustice by calling qualitative research sessions conducted over the Internet "focus groups." Their criticisms include the following:

- *Group dynamics.* One of the key reasons for using traditional focus groups is to view the interactions among the group participants, as they can provide excellent insights. In cyberspace, it is difficult, if not impossible, to create any real group dynamics, particularly when the participants are reading from computer screens rather than interacting verbally. *Note:* new systems such as those offered by M2 overcome this problem.

- *Nonverbal inputs.* Experienced moderators use nonverbal inputs from participants while moderating and analyzing sessions. It is not always possible to duplicate the nonverbal input in an online environment.

- *Client involvement.* Many organizations use the focus group methodology because it gives clients an opportunity to experience some direct interface with consumers in an objective environment. Nothing can replace the impact of watching focus groups from behind a one-way mirror, no matter how good the videotapes, remote broadcast facilities, streaming video, or reports written by moderators.

- *Exposure to external stimuli.* A key use of focus groups is to present advertising copy, new product concepts, prototypes, or other stimuli to the participants in order to get their reactions. In an online chat situation, it is almost impossible to duplicate the kind of exposure to external stimuli that occurs in the live focus group environment. As a result, the value of the input received online is more questionable than that of input coming from a live environment.

- *Role and skill of the moderator.* Most marketing professionals agree that the most important factor in the quality of traditional focus group research is the skill of the moderator. Experienced moderators do more than simply ask questions of participants. A good moderator uses innovative techniques to draw out quiet or shy participants, energize a slow group, and delve a little deeper into the minds of the participants. The techniques available to a moderator sitting at a computer terminal are not the same as face-to-face involvements.

Exhibit 6.4 summarizes the advantages and disadvantages of traditional and online focus groups.

Using Channel M2 to Conduct Online Focus Groups Channel M2 provides market researchers with user-friendly virtual interview rooms, recruiting, and technical support for conducting virtual qualitative research efficiently and effectively. By using Channel M2, the moderator and client can see and hear every respondent. You can see a demo at www.channelM2.com.

EXHIBIT 6.4	**Advantages and Disadvantages of Traditional and Online Focus Groups**	
	Traditional Focus Groups	**Online Focus Groups**
Basic costs	More expensive.	Cheaper.
Participants	Participants are locally based, because of travel time and expense.	Anyone in the world with a computer and modem can participate.
Time commitment	Approximately 3½-hour time commitment. Busy respondents are less likely to be available.	No driving to facility, approximately 60-minute time commitment. Busy respondents are more likely to be available.
Openness of respondents	Some respondents are intimidated and afraid to speak openly in a face-to-face group setting.	Lack of direct face-to-face contact may lead respondents to express true feelings in writing if no Web cam is available.
Group dynamics	What one person says and does (gestures and expressions) can lead others to react.	None, according to critics.
Nonverbal communication	Body language can be observed.	Body language can only be observed if Web cameras are used.
Transcripts	Transcript is time-consuming and expensive to obtain; often not in complete sentences or thoughts.	Word-for-word transcripts are available almost immediately, usually in complete sentences/thoughts.
Respondent recruiting	Recruiting certain types of respondents (e.g., physicians, top managers) is difficult.	It is easier to obtain all types of respondents.
Client travel costs	Very expensive when client must go to several cities for one or two days each.	None.
Communication with moderator	Observers can send notes into focus group room.	Observers can communicate privately with moderator on a split screen.
Respondent security	Participants are accurately identified.	It is sometimes more difficult to ascertain who is participating.
Client involvement	Client can observe flesh-and-blood consumers interacting.	Client can observe via Web cameras.
Exposure to external stimuli	Package designs, advertising copy, and product prototypes with demonstrations can be shown to participants.	Ability to show stimuli is somewhat limited.

Focus group recruiting at M2 uses a blend of e-mail recruitment (from a global panel with access to over 15 million online consumers) and telephone verification and confirmation. Specifically, e-mails elicit involvement and direct participants to an online qualification questionnaire to ensure that each meets screening criteria. Telephone follow-up confirms that respondents qualify. Prior to the interview, respondents know they must show photo ID on camera so as to verify identity. Specifically, respondents are directed to show their driver's license to their Web cam.

Channel M2 focus groups begin by the participants logging onto a Web page where everyone sees and hears each other, and communicates in a group setting. Participants are recruited using traditional methods and are then sent a Web camera so that both verbal and nonverbal reactions can be recorded. Installation of the Web cam is simple, aided by Channel M2 tech support 1 to 2 days prior to the interview.

Participants are then provided instructions via e-mail, including a link to the Channel M2 interviewing room and a toll-free teleconference number to call. Upon clicking on the link, participants sign on and see the Channel M2 interview room, complete with live video of the other participants, text chat, screen or slide sharing, and whiteboard.

Once the focus group is underway, questions and answers occur in "real time" in a lively setting. Participants comment spontaneously, both verbally or via text messaging, yet the moderator can provide direction exactly as they would in a traditional setting.[12]

Types of Online Focus Groups Decision Analyst, one of America's most progressive firms in applying Internet technology to marketing research, offers two types of online focus groups:

1. **Real-Time Online Focus Groups.** These are live, interactive sessions with four to six participants and a moderator in a chat room format. The typical session lasts no longer than 45 to 50 minutes. The technique is best for simple, straightforward issues that can be covered in a limited time. The results tend to be superficial compared to in-person focus groups—but this is acceptable for certain types of projects. Typically, three to four groups are recommended as a minimum. Clients can view the chat room as the session unfolds and communicate with the moderator.

2. **Time-Extended Online Focus Groups.** These sessions, sometimes called Bulletin Board Focus Groups, follow a message board format and usually last 5 to 10 days. The 15 to 20 participants must comment at least two or three times per day, and spend 15 minutes a day logged in to the discussion. The moderator reviews respondents' comments several times per day (and night) and probes or redirects the discussion as needed. This technique provides three to four times as much content as the average in-person focus group. Time-extended online focus groups, also called asynchronous focus groups, give participants to reflect, to talk to others, to visit a store, or time to check the pantry. This extra time translates into richer content and deeper insights. Clients can view the online content as it is posted and may communicate with the moderator at any time.

Berni Stevens, of Tech Focus Research, discusses best practices in online qualitative research in the accompanying Practicing Marketing Research box.

Using the Web to Find Focus Group Participants The Internet is proving to be an excellent tool to locate group participants that fit a very specific set of requirements. Researchers are tapping online bulletin boards such as Craigslist, which attracts 20 billion page views each month to its classified advertisements. The site is most useful "when you're trying to find niche users to a small population of users that is hard to find," says Tim Plowman, an anthropologist who works at Redwood Shores, California's Cheskin, a marketing consulting firm.[13]

PRACTICING MARKETING RESEARCH

Online Focus Group Best Practices

Recruiting for online is different than for in-person interviewing because there are no restricting geographical boundaries and those who are recruiting are not working off their local databases. Here are some tips on how to effectively manage your online qualitative recruitment, payment of respondents, and group composition.

1. *Evaluate your source of recruits carefully.*

For those instances in which you aren't using a list of your own customers, you should choose your recruiting source carefully because the quality of sample sources varies quite a lot. For in-person qualitative research, focus group facilities have typically handled the recruiting, relying on their database of potential participants (which is fraught with problems, but that's another story).

With online focus groups, where there are no geographical boundaries, recruiting organizations rely on purchased samples from firms like Survey Sampling International (SSI) or online consumer or business panels like those from SSI, Greenfield Online, or e-Rewards. These sample sources are fine as long as they approximate random samples from sample frames that are representative of the population of interest.

2. *Over-recruit.*

Even though your participants won't have to travel and have the comfort and convenience of participating from wherever they want, it's unlikely that everyone is going to show up, despite your best efforts. People forget or have something come up that's a higher priority. Our general rule of thumb is to over-recruit by 10 to 20 percent.

3. *Offer an incentive high enough to ensure a high participation rate.*

If you want a good show rate and a sample that is not skewed to those who are less busy or of lower incomes, you are going to have to compensate participants fairly for their time. What is fair and enticing is going to vary according to how valuable someone's time is; the amount of effort that will be required; the convenience of participation; and how relevant the topic is to them.

4. *Require full participation for incentive payment.*

Those who agree to participate in multisession/day discussions must be clearly instructed that they will only be paid for participation in all sessions. A participant's input won't be of much value if he or she drops out after day 2 of a three-day interview. If you expect a high dropout rate, you should over-recruit to compensate for this, or better yet, redesign the discussion guide so that it's more engaging and enjoyable.

5. *Take advantage of the ability to efficiently interview large numbers of respondents but don't overdo it.*

One of the key benefits of online interviewing is the ability to conduct either large-group interviews or very large numbers of in-depth interviews simultaneously. If you want group interaction in a synchronous session, stick to the maximum of 8 to 10 that is conventional for in-person groups.

For asynchronous groups where respondents have the time to digest more information, you can safely increase this to 20–25. And for asynchronous groups in which respondents cannot see others' responses and are not interacting at all with one another, you can have as many as your software will allow.

Our ability to digest such large volumes of data is limited, however, and you have to ask why you are doing a qualitative exploration among so many in the first place. The exception is when we are collecting information from a number of segments or conducting a hybrid quantitative/qualitative session.[14]

Questions

1. Would you like to participate in an online focus group? Why or why not?

2. Do you think that a company gets just as much quality information from an online group as a traditional focus group?

Point Forward, Inc., a Redwood City, California, marketing research firm, has used Craigslist to find people who fit very specific categories, such as people who travel frequently between the United States and Mexico, says Vice President Michael Barry.

A recent Craigslist posting by a different marketing research firm offered $350 to $900 to New York residents willing to give researchers a tour of their liquor cabinets, take them on a liquor-shopping trip, or make a video-based documentary of a social event they were planning.

Screening questions included: "When you are out for drinks or purchasing alcohol in a store, do people tend to ask for your advice on which brands of liquor to buy? If yes, how often does that happen?"

Web Community Research[15] A **Web community** is a carefully selected group of consumers who agree to participate in an ongoing dialogue with a particular corporation. All community interaction takes place on a custom-designed website. During the life of the community—which may last anywhere from six months to a year or more—community members respond to questions posed by the corporation on a regular basis. These discussions, which typically take the form of qualitative "dialogues," are augmented by the ability of community members to talk to one another about topics that are of interest to them as well.

The popularity and power of Web communities initially came from several key benefits. Web communities:

> **web community**
> Carefully Selected group of consumers who agree to participate in an ongoing dialogue with a corporation.

- Engage customers in a space where they are most comfortable, allowing clients to interact with them on a deeper level.
- Uncover "exciters" and "eureka moments," resulting in customer-derived innovations.
- Establish brand advocates who are emotionally invested in a company's success.
- Offer real-time results, enabling clients to explore ideas that normal time constraints prohibit.
- Create a forum where natural dialogue allows customers to initiate topics important to them.[16]

In addition, Web communities help companies create a customer-centered organization by putting employees into direct contact with consumers from the comfort of their own desks.

Since communities provide advantages in speed, flexibility, and 24/7 access to consumers, they let the organization be agile in its research decision making and prudent in its spending.

By adding a research focus to the Web community environment, this holistic perspective deepens as the community becomes a way to:

- Map the psyche of consumer segments.
- Brainstorm new ideas.
- Co-create and test new products.

- ☐ Observe natural consumer behavior.
- ☐ Rally the company around a customer-centered perspective.[17]

Beyond that, communities provide even greater value when the insights gained can be quickly shifted from the community space to the traditional market research space. This tight integration with more mainstream research approaches ensures that the community is both feeding new research initiatives and being fueled by insights gained from traditional research projects.

This type of cross-pollination takes another step toward a new research paradigm, one that integrates Web communities and traditional research. This new paradigm offers the potential to:

- ☐ Increase the efficiency of research by quickly finding the most appropriate forum for exploration of new insights.
- ☐ Reduce costs by using the community to follow up on questions left unanswered from ad hoc research studies.
- ☐ Improve the way consumer insights and implications are shared across organizational departments.[18]

Online Individual Depth Interviewing   A few marketing research firms are experimenting with online individual depth interviews (IDIs). After respondents are recruited, each participant is given a private blog where they can create their online journal for the project. Over a period of days, the respondents are given a series of questions to ponder in their blogs. A second phase of the research may feature a telephone, e-mail, or bulletin-board in-depth discussion. The discussion topics are derived from the blogs.

Survey Research on the Internet

The Internet has forever changed the way we conduct survey research. As noted earlier, a vast majority of all U.S. research firms are now conducting online research. In the United States, the online population is now closely tracking the U.S. population in most key demographic areas. Moreover, the number of Internet users around the world continues to explode. As the number of users grows worldwide, characteristics of a country's population and Internet user characteristics tend to meld. The reason for the phenomenal growth of online research is straightforward. The advantages far outweigh the disadvantages.

Advantages of Online Surveys

Most companies today face shorter product life cycles, increased competition, and a rapidly changing business environment. Management decision makers are having to make complex, rapid-fire decisions, and Internet research can help by providing timely information. The specific advantages of online surveys include the following:[19]

- ☐ *Rapid deployment, real-time reporting.* Online surveys can be broadcast to thousands of potential respondents simultaneously. Respondents complete surveys, and the results are tabulated and posted for corporate clients to view as the returns arrive. Thus, Internet survey results can be in the decision maker's hands in significantly less time than traditional survey results.

- *Reduced costs.* The use of electronic survey methods can cut costs by 25 to 40 percent and provide results in half the time it takes to do traditional telephone surveys. Data-collection costs account for a large proportion of any traditional marketing research budget. Telephone surveys are labor-intensive efforts incurring training, telecommunications, and management costs. Online surveys eliminate these costs almost completely. Although the costs of traditional survey techniques rise in proportion to the number of interviews desired, electronic solicitations can grow in volume with less increase in project costs.

- *Ready personalization.* Internet surveys can be highly personalized for greater relevance to each respondent's own situation, thus speeding up the response process. Respondents appreciate being asked only pertinent questions, being able to pause and then resume the survey as needed, and having the ability to see previous responses and correct inconsistencies.

- *High response rates.* Busy respondents may be growing increasingly intolerant of "snail mail" or telephone-based surveys. Online surveys take less time to complete than phone interviews do, can be accomplished at the respondent's convenience (after work hours), and are much more stimulating and engaging. Graphics, interactivity, links to incentive sites, and real-time summary reports make the interview more enjoyable. The result: much higher response rates.

- *Ability to contact the hard-to-reach.* Certain groups are among the most difficult to reach (doctors, high-income professionals, CIOs in Global 2000 firms). Most of these groups are well represented online. Internet surveys provide convenient anytime/anywhere access that makes it easy for busy professionals to participate.

- *Simplified and enhanced panel management.* Internet panels are electronic databases, linked via the Internet, that are committed to providing feedback and counsel to research firms and their clients. They may be large or small, syndicated or proprietary, and they may consist of customers, potential customers, partners, or employees. Internet panels can be built and maintained at less cost and time required for traditional panels. Once a panel is created and a questionnaire is finalized, surveys can be deployed, data are collected, and top-level results are reported within days.

  A sophisticated database tracks panelist profile data and survey responses, facilitating longitudinal studies and data mining to yield insights into attitudes and behaviors over time and across segments. Response rates are high, typically 20 to 60 percent, because respondents have agreed in advance to participate in the survey. These participants tend to provide more detailed and thoughtful answers than do those in traditional surveys, because they don't have to provide demographic and lifestyle information (it's already been captured) and because they become engaged in the panel over time.

- *External Internet panels simplify life for research suppliers.* The availability of huge Internet panels maintained by firms such as Harris Interactive, SSI, Greenfield Online, e-Rewards, and Decision Analyst makes the sampling process much easier for research companies that utilize these panels. We will discuss these panels in detail later in the chapter. Moreover, the cost to use the panels has dropped as the number of panel suppliers has increased.

Disadvantages of Online Surveys

The most common complaint about the use of online surveys traditionally was that Internet users are not representative of the population as a whole. As mentioned earlier, this comment has largely disappeared in the United States. Harris Interactive and DSS

Research have conducted over 300 surveys using parallel modes (telephone and Internet) and found that the research produced similar results. In all of the studies, it was rare to find a statistically significant difference between the sampling modes.[20] DSS concluded that the Internet panel methodology offered the best alternative for market share measurement and competitive benchmarking objectives based on cost (half the cost of telephone), speed (can be completed in less than half the time of telephone), and accuracy of measurement.

Lee Smith, COO of Insight Express, conducted a side-by-side comparison of online research and mail surveys. He found that online research delivered data of the same quality as using mail surveys in one-eighth the time and at one-eighth the cost.[21] Other research has shown that in most countries where the Internet penetration rate exceeds 20 percent, online surveys tend to yield results similar to those found in traditional methods such as telephone or paper-and-pencil survey research.[22]

> **unrestricted Internet sample**
Self-selected sample group consisting of anyone who wishes to complete an Internet survey.

A second problem exists when an **unrestricted Internet sample** is set up on the Internet. This means anyone who wishes to complete the questionnaire can do so. It is fully self-selecting and probably representative of no one except Web surfers. The problem gets worse if the same Internet user can access the questionnaire over and over. For example, the first time *InfoWorld,* a computer user magazine, conducted its Readers' Choice survey on the Internet, the results were so skewed by repeat voting for one product that the entire survey was publicly abandoned and the editor had to ask for readers' help to avoid the problem again. All responsible organizations conducting surveys over the Internet easily guard against this problem by providing unique passwords to those individuals they invite to participate. These passwords permit one-time access to the survey.

A third problem is that the sample frame needed may not be available on the Internet. Assume that Guido's, a popular Italian restaurant in Dayton, Ohio, wanted to know how its customers perceived the food quality and service compared with that of the big chains, such as Olive Garden. A large Internet panel, such as Greenfield Online, is probably not going to have enough members in Dayton, Ohio, that patronize Guido's to give a representative sample. If Guido's doesn't have customer e-mail addresses, then an Internet sample isn't feasible.

Other problems include a lack of "call back" procedures to clarify open-ended responses, potential for questionnaire programming errors, and a lack of bandwidth (some potential respondents can't complete the survey or download photos and video quickly). Some companies may view Internet research as fast and simple, and software to conduct basic surveys is readily available. However, some research companies don't have the technical expertise to conduct survey research properly.

Methods of Conducting Online Surveys

There are several basic methods for conducting online surveys: Web survey software, survey design Web sites, and Web hosting.

Web Survey Software

Web survey software is software systems specifically designed for Web questionnaire construction and delivery. In a typical use, the questionnaire is constructed with an easy-to-use edit feature, using a visual interface, and then automatically transmitted to a Web server system. The Web server distributes the questionnaire and files responses in a database. The user can query the server at any time for completion statistics, descriptive statistics on responses, and graphical displays of data. Several popular online survey research software packages are SPSS Quanquest, Inquisite, Sawtooth CiW, Infopoll, Designer, and SurveyGold.

Gaining Survey Completions

Doing-it-yourself software, such as SPSS Quanquest, requires that you offer the respondent a good experience if you expect the person to complete the survey. The more engaged respondents are, the better quality insights they will provide. The following tips can help create a better experience for the interviewee:

- ☐ As with any questionnaire, use language that is less "research-ese" and more conversational.

- ☐ Be honest and upfront about the time required to complete a study.

- ☐ Provide more opportunities for participants to provide open-ended answers and truly express themselves.

- ☐ Ensure that all possible answer choices are given; avoid overuse of "other."

- ☐ Keep survey to less than 20 minutes in length, and provide participants with progress information as they advance through the survey.

- ☐ Consider using graphics when possible or appropriate to make the experience more visually engaging.

- ☐ Explore new ways to facilitate interaction between respondents and a researcher.

- ☐ Make studies more informative—participants are particularly motivated by acquiring new knowledge and information about a product or topic.

- ☐ Offer participants the opportunity to be contacted again to receive updates on projects of products being tested.[23]

How important are incentives in online research? And does the cosmetic appearance of the questionnaire have an impact on completion rates? Decipher, Inc. conducted an online study to address these questions.[24] It conducted a survey using a domestic customer list provided by eBay Inc. Over 1,900 eBay members participated in a seven-minute online survey. The recruits were sent an e-mail invitation containing a link that directed them to the survey. The study employed four parallel cells:

	Survey Design	**Incentive**
Cell 1	Plain	None
Cell 2	Fancy	None
Cell 3	Fancy	1 in 500 chance to win $1,000
Cell 4	Fancy	Guaranteed $2 cash to first 500 qualified completes

As can be seen from the setup, a comparison between Cell 1 and Cell 2 measured the effect of a plain versus fancy survey design. Color, the use of tables, and the right-aligned buttons distinguished the fancy from the plain survey design (see Exhibit 6.5).

A comparison between Cells 2 and 3 or Cells 2 and 4 measured incentive effects. Finally, a comparison between Cells 3 and 4 measured the effects of the different types of incentive: a cash prize drawing or a smaller, guaranteed cash incentive.

The appearance of the survey had no measurable impact on the completion rate (in both instances about 77 percent completed the survey). Nor did the type of incentive affect completion rates. However, either incentive boosted completion rates about 10 percent. For all four cells dropouts occurred primarily over the first 90 seconds after a respondent entered the survey. Persons offered an incentive were significantly less likely to drop out during this period.[25]

Giselle Lederman, of Zoomerang Marketing Research, discusses formatting an Internet survey in the accompanying Practicing Marketing Research box on page 169. Another issue involving Internet surveys is whether timing is important in sending out survey invitations. It is in the United Kingdom, as explained in the Global Research box on page 171.

Exhibit 6.5

Does a Fancy Survey Design Matter?

Source: Jamin Brazil, Aaron Jue, Chandra Mullins, and Jamye Plunkett, "Capture Their Interest," *Quirk's Marketing Research Review* (July/August 2006), p. 48.

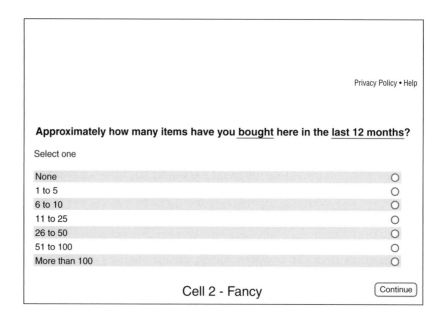

Survey Design and Web Hosting Sites   Many Web sites allow the researcher to design a survey online without loading design software. The survey is then administered on the design site's server. Some offer tabulation and analysis packages as well. Popular sites that offer Web hosting are WebSurveyor, Perseus Survey Monkey, e-Rewards, and Zoomerang.

Commercial Online Panels

Many researchers turn to commercial online panel providers to assist in the process of completing a market research study, often by hosting a survey on their website. Commercial online panels are not created for the exclusive use of any one specific

PRACTICING MARKETING RESEARCH

Formatting a Survey for Success

Research on research suggests that appropriate formatting is vital to successful Web-based surveys. The right formatting engages your respondents, makes it easier for them to navigate through surveys, and maximizes your return rates. Correct formatting also helps elicit unbiased opinions so that you can collect highly accurate feedback that supports your critical decisions.

Radio Buttons

Traditionally, radio buttons are represented as small round circles in Web design. Radio buttons should be used when there is only one answer from a predefined set of options. In other words, responses should be mutually exclusive. Radio buttons are also the best choice for either/or items. Here are a few findings.

- An experiment in Belgium revealed the advantages of using radio buttons. Two groups were given the same survey: one with radio buttons and the other with drop-downs. Participants using radio buttons were more likely to complete the survey (88.37 percent) than those using drop-downs (84.07 percent).

- The use of radio buttons that offer the user noncommittal answers such as "don't know" did not increase the likelihood of such nonsubstantial answers being selected.

Checkboxes

Checkboxes are similar to multiple-choice categories, which are often used in paper-based surveys. These response categories can be mutually exclusive or can be used when multiple answers exist for a single question. Some findings are as follows.

- Recent research on Internet surveys and response categories tends to treat radio buttons and checkboxes as one and the same,

so conclusions regarding the impact of using a checkbox versus a radio button are not yet definitive.

- It appears that stationary, visible checkboxes may reduce end-user mistakes.

- The use of multiple-option "check all that apply" questions in Web surveys may result in respondents filling out what they perceive to be the "appropriate" number of responses, then skipping to the next question. The use of this special type of checkbox may result in measurement error. Published research regarding these issues is minimal, and as a result, multiple checkboxes in Web surveys should be used with caution.

Drop-downs

Drop-down boxes can initially appear in your survey as a blank box with instructions to scroll down. This type of response format requires the user to locate the answer, click on the box, and/or scroll down to locate their answer.

- Because response categories are not totally visible on the initial screen, drop-down options should be used for fields with which respondents are already familiar (such as their state of residence). If drop-downs are used, it's important to organize response options in a logical way (e.g., alphabetical listings).

- Research indicates that the presence of drop-downs or radio buttons does not impact users' tendency to give "don't know" responses or leave items blank. However, drop-downs have been found to take more time for users to complete.

- Visibility and primacy are key factors in influencing choice on both Web- and paper-based surveys. When comparing two different response formats—radio buttons and drop-downs—the order in which the answer options are presented impacts the likelihood of one being chosen over the other. This ordering effect seems to be magnified when using drop-boxes, especially when not all options are initially visible. Ordering effects may be more pronounced when the first five options are displayed initially and the rest are hidden.

Fill-in Boxes

Text or fill-in boxes are blank spaces in which users can enter free-form answers. Based on our field experiences, text boxes are ideal when you either have more answers than can be accommodated by a drop-down box or want to hear exactly what users have to say. Here are a few recommendations.

- Providing clear, concise directions to users gets the best results.
- Motivation levels may play a stronger part in getting users to complete text boxes than multiple-choice boxes, since they require more effort and thought.
- Placement of fill-in boxes may also be important. Using them earlier in the survey is generally better than later. However, you should avoid using fill-in boxes at the top of the survey, as many respondents want to start with easy, noncontroversial questions.

- Fill-in boxes may have higher skip rates, so it's wise to use them sparingly.
- Users typically fill the space provided. So when using fill-in boxes, it's important to allow sufficient space. If you want shorter answers, limit the space provided. If you want longer responses, use larger boxes to accommodate wordier responses.
- As many survey designers already know, informing subjects that fill-in answers are optional may increase the likelihood they will not complete those areas of the survey.[26]

Questions

1. Don't you think that someone who is good at creating paper questionnaires should be good at creating online questionnaires? Why or why not?

2. Do you think that only one style, such as drop-downs, should be used in a survey if possible? Why?

commercial online panel Group of individuals who do online surveys from a particular panel company. The company charges organizations doing surveys for access to the panel.

company, or for any one particular project. Instead, **commercial online panels** are created for the use of multiple projects by many different companies. The companies providing access to the online panels have invested in the pre-recruitment of people who opt to participate in online market research surveys. Some online panels are for use by a specific industry, such as construction, medical, or technology industries, and may have a few thousand panel members, while the large commercial online panels have millions of people who have opted to participate in online surveys of varying topics. When people join most online panels, they answer an extensive profiling questionnaire that records demographic, lifestyle, and psychographic information, typically with hundreds of dimensions. This profiling information enables the panel provider to record detailed information on every panel member. Using this information, the panel provider can then target research efforts to panel members who meet specific criteria.

For example, a research study may require surveying avid golfers who play golf at least once a week, people who own an HDTV, or people who make decisions regarding information technology and work in companies with over 1,000 employees. Finding people who meet these criteria can be difficult, but online panel providers may be able to more easily identify these people based on their profiling information. By having millions of people pre-recruited and engaged in the research process, online panels help reduce recruitment cost and field time needed to complete a research project. For the really low-incidence groups, many of the larger panel providers, such as e-Rewards or Harris Interactive, are able to develop specialty panels for hard-to-reach audiences, such as small-business owners, affluent consumers, and healthcare providers.

Panel Management

While online panels are quite effective at reducing costs and field time, the quality of the data is dependent on how well the panel is managed. Several factors influence the quality of an online panel. These include the recruitment methods, respondent participation, panel management practices, and types of incentives offered.

Panel Recruitment   The method of recruitment of panel members is critical to the quality of the panel. If the panel is to meet a researcher's needs for a study requiring a general audience of consumers, it is important to evaluate whether the panel's recruitment method draws from a representative audience of consumers. Likewise, if a researcher's project requires business professionals, the panel's recruitment methods should draw from a universe of business professionals. Ideally, a panel should represent a diverse sampling of the population under study. Panel member recruitment methodology is a key distinction among online panels. There are essentially two methods for recruiting for an online panel: open source and by invitation only.

Intercepting people as they surf the Internet through ads is known as open recruitment. **Open online panel recruitment** allows any person who has access to the Internet to "self-select" and enroll in a market research panel. This provides the benefit of building a panel quickly with people who are Internet-savvy and responsive to online advertising.

A key drawback is the lack of control over who is recruited. A panel with open recruitment may sign up millions of Web surfers who share similar characteristics, but may include only people who are responsive to Web ads and/or "seek out" an opportunity to

A research study may focus on people who meet a specific criteria such as golfing once a week.

Terrell Creative/Stock Food America

▶ **open online panel recruitment**
Any person with Internet access can self-select to be in a research panel.

GLOBAL RESEARCH

Timing Is Everything in Survey Invitations

Although respondents to online surveys can choose when to complete surveys, the time at which the invitation is sent can have a major impact on the number of responses, according to findings from London-based Lightspeed Research.

The firm sent out invitations to an online survey to 7,440 of its panelists in the UK at different times during the week. Overall, the results showed that invitations sent on a Monday afternoon achieved the best response rates, at up to 39 percent. Surveys sent at 5:30 p.m. on Friday afternoon resulted in relatively low response rates of 28 percent for women and 29 percent for men.

In addition, the research showed that external events could have a dramatic impact on response rates for online surveys. A major soccer game on Wednesday night had an impact on response rates, in particular among male respondents. Only 11 percent of male invitees from the Wednesday 5:30 p.m. invitation group responded to the survey, compared to 31 percent of women.

The research also showed that the majority of responders are likely to respond in the first 24 hours, with only around a third responding after this period. In other words, if the response rate is quite low within the first 24 hours, it is unlikely to recover in the following days. Invitations sent on Monday at 5:30 p.m. achieved a response rate of 26 percent within the first 24 hours and ended with a total response rate of 38 percent after six days. On the other hand, an invitation sent on Wednesday at 5:30 p.m. achieved only a 14 percent response rate after 24 hours and a total rate of 22 percent after six days.[27]

join an online panel by using search engines. This leaves out a large percentage of the general population.

In many cases, open recruitment leads to an overabundance of panel members who participate in many different panels and complete an inordinate amount of surveys. These are known in the industry as "professional survey takers"—people who sign up to take hundreds of surveys in order to enter into sweepstakes drawings or other types of incentives. The primary concerns associated with professional survey takers are (1) they can give false or misleading information in an attempt to get through a survey quickly without regard to providing well-considered responses; (2) they tend to go through surveys in a perfunctory manner, which shows up in the time they take to complete the survey; and (3) they can make up a disproportionate amount of survey responders, leading to biased and unrepresentative research data. To the detriment of Internet marketing research, some websites have been developed to recruit people to sign up for several panels at one time. One study found that more than 30 percent of all online surveys are completed by less than 1 percent of the population. The study also found that professional survey takers respond to an average of 80 surveys over a 90-day period—with some taking several surveys per day.[28] However, it is important to consider that not all online panels are made up of professional survey takers. This is why it is so important to understand the recruitment methods used by an online panel before employing them in the research process.

Craig Stevens, Executive Vice President of e-Rewards, one of America's largest commercial online panel providers, discusses how to prevent "professional survey takers" in the Practicing Marketing Research box: Preventing Professional Survey Takers.

The other method used for recruiting respondents to an online panel, the "by-invitation-only" method, was first used by e-Rewards, Inc. **Closed online panel recruitment,** or "by invitation only," invites only pre-validated individuals, or individuals who share known characteristics, to enroll in a market research panel. Most often, this is accomplished by inviting customers from large, highly trusted leading brands who collectively have a large, diverse base of customers in a given population (i.e., general consumers or business professionals). In recruiting for its consumer panel, for example, e-Rewards has partnered with large, well-known companies that have large, diverse customer bases. Similarly, in recruiting for its panel of business professionals, e-Rewards has partnered with major airlines, hotels, and car rental companies. There is some natural overlap in the recruiting since business professionals who travel are also consumers, but e-Rewards pays close attention to panelist enrollment to ensure there isn't panelist duplication.

> **closed online panel recruitment**
> Invited only pre-validated individuals or those with shared known characteristics to enroll in a research panel.

The "by-invitation-only" method enables a panel researcher to recruit people with specific demographics into the panel in order to meet a client's needs for a representative sample of the understudy population, or to meet specific needs. For example, in order to recruit affluent panel members, the panel provider may recruit customers from upscale retailers to join the panel. To recruit teenagers, a panel provider may recruit customers of specific clothing retailers that specialize in the teen market. To recruit business decision makers, a panel provider may recruit customers from companies that cater to businesspeople, such as airlines, hotels, car rental companies, and subscribers to business publications.

Using a "by-invitation-only" recruitment method gives a panel provider greater control over who is invited to the panel and greatly reduces the likelihood of professional survey takers. One particular area that requires attention with this approach is that the panel composition is dependent on the people who are invited to join the panel and may be biased by customers of a specific recruitment source. Thus, it is important that a "by-invitation-only" panel have a large number of diverse recruitment sources by working with companies in many different areas to ensure balanced representation in the panel.

Open versus Closed Recruitment

e-Rewards, Inc., conducted a study of recruitment methods to compare "open" versus "closed" recruitment. During a six-month test, e-Rewards Market Research, which recruits exclusively with a closed-loop recruitment approach, enrolled 38,162 panel members into an experimental consumer panel using an open enrollment methodology. e-Rewards then conducted a parallel tracking experiment that compared closed-sourced panelists to these open-sourced panelists (see Exhibit 6.6).

PRACTICING
MARKETING RESEARCH

Preventing Professional Survey Takers

Professional survey takers (PSTs) have become a concern for online research. PSTs join panels, often many panels, to take as many surveys as possible. Often, their goal is to cash in on sweepstakes or other incentives offered for surveys. The more surveys they take, the greater their odds of winning a drawing or accumulating more incentives. Normally, researchers desire survey participation, but PSTs pose a unique problem. PSTs can bias market research data if they represent a disproportionate percentage of respondents in the survey data. Worse, PSTs will often give misleading or false information about themselves in order to qualify for more surveys. A single PST may claim to own every product ever made, suffer from a wide range of health ailments, and hold multiple positions in several different industries. Preventing this behavior is a key goal of marketing research companies.

The following presents some of the methods employed by e-Rewards to stop professional survey takers:

- Using the "by-invitation-only" recruitment method to invite panel members with known characteristics—this helps to close the door on PSTs who might try to self-select into an online panel.
- Requiring a valid e-mail and physical address, verify against postal records.

- Performing blind and double-blind screening, which screens respondents for qualifications repeatedly.
- Limiting the frequency of survey invitations to specific individuals.
- Not "telegraphing" survey requirements, such as asking "If you are age 18–24 and shop online for cell phones, please take this survey."
- Identifying PSTs using survey responses, specifically looking for behavior such as
  - Straight-lining answers
  - Inconsistent profiling answers
  - Illogical answers
  - Speeders—People who answer surveys too quickly
- Employing a Veracity Assessment System that observes a respondent's survey-taking behavior and "grades" the respondents accordingly. Members whose score falls below a specific threshold are then removed from the active panel.

Questions

1. How do you think a Veracity Assessment System might work?
2. Do you think PSTs are a threat to online survey research? Why?

EXHIBIT 6.6	Open versus Closed Panel ("by-invitation-only") Recruitment Methods	
	Open Recruitment	Closed Recruitment
Percent working outside of the home	45.6%	77.0%
Percent homemaker	15.7%	4.4%
Percent female	73.7%	47.5%
Percent participate in multiple survey panels	87.3%	39.5%
Percent participate in five or more panels	55.2%	19.6%
Mean number of online panels joined	5.4	1.4
Mean time to take survey	8 min: 22 sec	9 min: 45 sec

Source: e-Rewards 2008.

The experiment revealed that open-sourced panelists are often quite different from closed-sourced panelists. Open-sourced panelists were much more likely to be home-makers, retired people, students, and unemployed. They were also more likely to exhibit the behaviors of professional survey takers, including enrollment in multiple panels, a preference for multiple surveys each week, and a tendency to complete surveys more quickly, indicating a lack of thoughtful participation.

Respondent Cooperation

Respondent participation is critical to the success of the research process in order to minimize nonresponse bias. Therefore, it is important to understand the panel management practices and incentives employed by an online panel. Response rates for online surveys can vary dramatically, with some populations having average response rates less than 5 percent, others with response rates closer to 30 percent, and sometimes well over 60 percent for prescreened individuals, who have been alerted to expect to receive a survey at a specific time or date. The diminishing response rates observed with telephone interviewing have played a key role in the increased usage of online panels.

Ensuring participation is a function of several factors, including to what extent panel members are engaged in the research process, their experience with surveys and the panel in general, and the topic of the research. Of course, one of the primary drivers of participation is the incentive program.

Generally, online panels use two incentive models: the sweepstakes model and the pay-all model. The sweepstakes model offers survey participants a chance to be entered into a drawing for a prize, often hundreds or thousands of dollars, albeit with extremely low odds of winning. Pay-all incentive models pay each respondent a small incentive for their time and participation each time they take part in a survey.

The choice of incentive model is not trivial. A sound incentive model influences not only survey response rates, but also retention rates for panel members—which becomes very important when there is a need to use profiling information for targeting a specific type of respondent. Panel members who do not feel adequately compensated for their time and effort are much less likely to participate in research studies.

A study conducted by e-Rewards in 2006, using a third-party online panel, compared sweepstakes and pay-all incentive methods. For a three-minute survey about books and music with 100 percent qualifying incidence, 40,000 people were invited to complete the survey in order to be entered into a sweepstakes drawing of $2,500 for one winner. An additional 4,000 people were invited to complete the same survey in exchange for $2.00 in cash. Both groups were selected randomly and then invited on the same day of the week and at the same time of day (Wednesday afternoon), and both were given seven days to complete the survey.

The study found that the pay-all model was much more effective than the sweepstakes method (see Exhibit 6.7). People who were offered the pay-all incentive responded more quickly, and the response rate for the pay-all incentive group was 58 percent higher than that of the sweepstakes group (19.3 percent response rate vs. 12.2 percent response rate). While response rate is not the only measure of the quality of an online panel, it is a key metric.

Controlling the Panel

In addition to effective panel recruitment and respondent cooperation programs, online panel providers must have effective ongoing management of their panel to ensure a high level of quality. Panels must continually see that that their participants have positive experiences with every research project. Among other components, good panel management includes frequency controls to see that panel members are not surveyed too little or too much. Panel members should be given enough survey opportunities to stay effectively engaged in the research process, but not surveyed too much as to be burdened with survey invitations. Other keys to guaranteeing a positive panel member's experience is providing respondent privacy, safeguarding personal information, and protecting members from bogus research that attempts to use online surveys as a sales channel (this is the practice of "sugging"—selling under the guise of research).

Panel providers are continually recruiting new members to keep up with the growth in demand for online samples, as well as replace any panel members who may drop out. Even with exceptional panel member retention, some panel members will become less active in responding to surveys. In addition, panels will often recruit new members to assist in growing certain hard-to-reach segments and/or balancing the panel to have maximum representation of the overall population. Ensuring a growing supply of engaged, active panel members is a constant goal of every panel provider.

Finally, panel management includes ensuring panel freshness. As panel members change, their profiles must be updated. A single, 25-year-old college student with an annual income of $12,000 from last year may now be a married 26-year-old accountant with a new baby and a household income of $45,000. Updating profiles ensures that panel providers are able to consistently target qualified people for surveys.

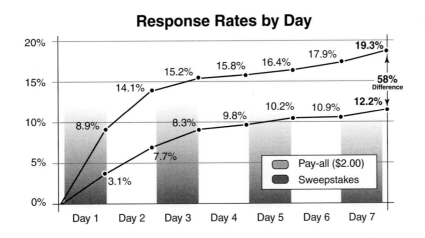

Response Rates by Day

Exhibit 6.7

Pay-all versus Sweepstakes

Source: e-Rewards, 2007.

When evaluating the quality of an online panel, there are several key drivers that contribute toward a panel's overall methodologies. If a panel does not have well-defined guiding principles to help deliver the highest level of quality, a sample purchaser should beware of the potential negative implications for the quality of the data. e-Rewards, for example, utilizes its *15 Points of Quality Differentiation* (see Exhibit 6.8) to see that every aspect of their panel's operation delivers the highest level of quality.

Mobile Internet Research—The Next Step

Approximately 76 percent of all consumers in the United States and Western Europe have Internet access on their mobile device, and about one-third use it. Among those with mobile access, the UK leads in usage (54 percent), followed by the United States at 41 percent.[29]

Lightspeed Research has undertaken research studies in the United States, UK, and Australia to measure the willingness of respondents to take part in mobile surveys. The survey used in the U.S. study focused on personal healthcare matters, whereas the UK and Australia studies focused on media-related topics. Each survey included no more than 10 questions with different routes, in which varying types of questions (e.g., single or multipunch, open-ended) were tested. Each study was conducted with approximately 1,000 panelists, who received incentives for their participation in the survey.

In the United States, the overall response rate to the mobile survey was 28 percent. About one-third of the responses to the survey invitation message were received within the first hour (and 61 percent within the first 12 hours), suggesting that mobile surveys could potentially generate a quick response.[30]

Mobile research offers:

☐ An alternative way to conduct research with hard-to-reach groups.

☐ Increased respondent cooperation from all demographic groups.

Exhibit 6.8

e-Rewards' 15 Points of Quality Differentiation

Quality makes our panels perform

At e-Rewards® Market Research we've built the industry's most comprehensive and deeply profiled panels as a result of our dedication to quality. In fact, we've implemented *15 points of quality differentiation* that are applied to all aspects of panel management—recruitment, composition, maintenance, screening, and incentives. These 15 points of quality ensure the integrity of our sample and set the industry standard.

1. *"By-Invitation-Only" Acquisition*
   Since we started in 1999, every e-Rewards member has been exclusively invited into the panel and has experienced the same standardized enrollment process. By avoiding "open" recruitment, we do not attract the undesirable "professional survey takers" that many other panels do.

2. *Multichannel Recruitment*
   We invite our panel members through a controlled mix of both online and offline methods, including e-mail and direct mail invitations for hard-to-reach respondents such as physicians. We vary the mix of our invitation methods based on the different types of respondents we seek— whether for our Business, Consumer, or Specialty Panels.

3. *Fraud Prevention*
   We employ an arsenal of leading-edge techniques to eliminate professional survey-taking behavior within our panels. We check for the following bad behaviors:

   ☐ Inconsistent profiling answers
   ☐ Straight-lining answers
   ☐ Answering surveys too quickly
   ☐ Member duplication

4. *Normalized Panel Recruitment*
   We work with our diverse set of sourcing partners "upfront" to invite only the types of individuals that fit the current normalization needs of our Consumer and Business Panels.

5. *300+ Segmentation Variables*
   The more that is known about a panelist upfront, the more relevant and accurate research can be. That's why we're committed to maintaining the deepest panelist profiling information (using over 300 segmentation variables).

6. *Quality Control System*
   Our veracity assessments allow us to measure the desirability of panelists through the life of their panel participation. We also track the activity levels of each of our panelists to ensure that inactive panelists are periodically phased out from receiving survey opportunities.

7. *Member Verification Process*
   We require a physical address from each member, and we verify its validity against government postal information. We also require a valid and unique e-mail address in order for panelists to receive surveys. Lastly, we do not re-send to addresses that have ever "bounced back."

8. *Dynamic Profile Enrichment*®
   We use our proprietary Dynamic Profile Enrichment capabilities to achieve industry-leading quality levels of panel maintenance and data freshness. Our Dynamic Profile Enrichment is an intelligent database algorithm that periodically presents panelists with opportunities to update key aspects of their profile.

9. *Managed Participation Levels*
   Our average e-Rewards member qualifies and participates in less than five full surveys each year. Other sample vendors allow annual survey participation rates to exceed 12–24 surveys each year.

10. *High-Level Member Retention*
    We have a high level of member retention. This retention rate underscores our commitment to quality communications, panel design, and customer service.

11. *Leading Response Rates*
    We are able to maintain industry-leading response rates due to our panel management practices, recruitment, and incentive methodologies.

12. *Commitment to Privacy*
    We respect our panel members' privacy and adhere to a highly ethical privacy policy. This allows us to build a stronger trust with panel members, which leads to more honest quality responses to survey questions.

13. *"Double Blind" Screening*
    When appropriate, we use a two-step "blind screener" approach to identify qualified respondents. This approach controls against any respondents who wish to provide false screener answers to qualify for the study.

14. *Rewarding Respondents with a Fair-Value Exchange*
    We believe that the best way to establish and maintain long-term relationships with our panel members is to truly value their time. Our panel members earn e-Rewards currency for the time they spend answering market research surveys. Members can redeem this currency for valuable rewards.

15. *Industry Involvement*
    As an active member organization of CASRO, ESOMAR and MRA we continuously strive to meet and exceed all industry guidelines and standards. We also promote and support the active involvement of our employees within each of these organizations. Currently, over 75 e-Rewards Market Research employees have earned Professional Researcher Certification (PRC) from the Market Research Association (MRA), and continue to participate in conferences, workshops, and other educational events to maintain their Certification status and achieve higher levels of Certification.

Exhibit 6.8

e-Rewards' 15 Points of Quality Differentiation

(continued)

☐ Immediate feedback on research questions concerning marketing campaigns, ad testing, and more.

☐ Cost savings—faster reply to surveys, shorter project completion time.

☐ Use as a mobile recruiting tool to direct respondents to online surveys.

☐ Another way of reaching people on the go.[31]

A few disadvantages of mobile Internet surveys are as follows.

☐ Lightspeed found that the response rate decreased with age due to lower usage of mobile Internet services among older people. Thus, the profile doesn't reflect the average consumer.

☐ Questionnaires must be short.

☐ Question types are limited, as is the length of questions.

☐ Higher incentives must be offered to remove the financial burden of receiving and completing mobile surveys from the respondent.[32]

Mobile Internet technologies provide an exciting new channel for marketing researchers. However, their limitations will mean that traditional online marketing research will be the channel of choice for most survey research.

Interactive Marketing Research Organization

> **Interactive Marketing Research Organization (IMRO)**
> Organization dedicated to the development, dissemination, and implementation of interactive marketing research concepts, practice, and information.

In 2001, a new organization called the **Interactive Marketing Research Organization (IMRO)** was formed. The first objective of IMRO is to be "a confederation of world leaders among firms involved in new technology marketing research, to lead in the development, dissemination, and implementation of interactive marketing research concepts, practice, and information."[33] Thirteen Internet marketing research suppliers, including Modalis Research Technologies, Greenfield Online, Market Facts, NPD Online, NFO Interactive, and Cyber Dialogue, along with eight client companies, including Dell Computer, IBM, Intel, and Time Warner, helped to found the organization.

IMRO's initial efforts focused on spam and the misuse of personal data. The organization hosts conferences, debates, and workshops and publishes a quarterly newsletter called *The Edge*. It also publishes the *Journal of Online Research* in conjunction with the Advertising Research Foundation.

SUMMARY

About one-fifth of the world's population is online. In the United States, the figure approaches 70 percent. Over 90 percent of America's research firms are conducting online research.

Secondary data can play a key role in the marketing research process. It can clarify a problem, suggest a particular research methodology, or sometimes actually provide a solution to the problem. Exhibit 6.1 offers an extensive list of online sources of secondary data. The Internet has, in many ways, revolutionized the gathering of secondary data. Now, rather than wait for replies from government agencies or other sources, users can find millions of pieces of information on the Internet. Trips to the library may become a thing of the past for many researchers. Search engines and directories contain links to millions of documents throughout the world. Special-interest discussion groups, and blogs, on the Internet can also be valuable sources of secondary data.

A five-step approach to searching the Internet is presented. This is followed by a detailed procedure that explains how to evaluate the quality of Web pages.

Website databases can produce important insights. A Web merchant can track a person as he or she clicks through a site. The merchant can examine what was looked at and what was bought. The screen the customer will see first on the next visit to the site can be tailored to the customer's past purchase and browsing behavior. Cookies are an important tool for monitoring a user's behavior within a site.

More and more focus groups are being conducted online because online focus groups are fast and cost-effective; they also reach populations that are typically inaccessible. However, there are several problems associated with online focus groups. Channel M2 provides virtual focus group interview rooms where respondents participate via a webcam. Questions and answers occur in real time, thus simulating a traditional focus group. Asynchronous focus groups are time-extended focus groups conducted much like an online chat group. Web community research is where a group of consumers agree to participate in an ongoing dialogue with a company. The discussion may last a year or more, and participants respond to questions that are regularly posted to the community. Insights from the community can be used as a basis for traditional marketing research.

Some firms are experimenting with individual depth interviews online. Each participant creates an online journal based on a series of questions provided by the researcher.

Internet surveys offer rapid deployment and real-time reporting, dramatically reduced costs, ready personalization, high response rates, ability to reach low-incidence respondents, simplified and enhanced panel management, and profitability for survey research firms. The disadvantages are the potential nonrepresentativeness of Internet users, lack of callback procedures to clarify open-ended responses, bandwidth problems, and the sample frame needed may not be available on the Internet.

A number of tips are given for improving completion rates for online surveys. One study found that appearance had no impact, but financial incentives did improve completions. When formatting a survey, radio buttons should be used with a predetermined set of options. Drop-down boxes are appropriate when respondents are familiar with the categories, such as the state where you live. Fill-in boxes require clear, concise directions. They should be used sparingly because they have a high skip rate.

Commercial online panels are used for multiple projects by many different companies. While panels reduce cost and field time, the quality of the data requires good panel management. Panel recruitment can be by open source or "by invitation only." The by-invitation-only method is highly preferred for quality purposes. Good panel management requires the blocking of professional survey takers. Typically, Internet panels use either a "pay-all" or a sweepstakes strategy to gain respondent cooperation. Pay-all tends to be much more effective. Mobile Internet technologies will probably be the next platform in Internet survey research.

KEY TERMS & DEFINITIONS

newsgroup An Internet site where people can read and post messages devoted to a specific topic.

cookie A text file placed on a user's computer in order to identify the user when she or he revisits the Web site.

online focus groups Focus groups conducted via the Internet.

web community Carefully selected group of consumers who agree to participate in an ongoing dialogue with a corporation.

unrestricted Internet sample Self-selected sample group consisting of anyone who wishes to complete an Internet survey.

commercial online panel Group of individuals who have agreed to receive invitations to do online surveys from a particular panel company such as eRewards or SSI. The panel company charges organizations doing surveys for access to the panel. Charges are usually so much per survey depending on survey length and the type of people being sought for the survey. The panel company controls all access to the members of its panel.

open online panel recruitment Any person with Internet access can self-select to be in a research panel.

closed online panel recruitment Inviting only pre-validated individuals or those with shared known characteristics to enroll in a research panel.

Interactive Marketing Research Organization (IMRO) Organization dedicated to the development, dissemination, and implementation of interactive marketing research concepts, practice, and information.

QUESTIONS FOR REVIEW & CRITICAL THINKING

1. Do you think that eventually all marketing research will be done on the Internet? Why or why not?
2. Explain the relationship between blogs and marketing research.
3. How can a researcher evaluate the quality of a Web page?
4. How can a company benefit from building an internal database from its website visitors? Is there an advantage that a Web retailer might have over a traditional store?
5. Discuss the advantages and disadvantages of online focus groups.
6. Explain the differences between real-time focus groups and asynchronous focus groups.
7. Do you think that a company such as Caterpillar could benefit from Web community research? Ford? United Airlines?
8. Discuss the popularity of online survey research. Why is it so popular?
9. What are some techniques for increasing survey completion rates?
10. Describe some ways to recruit for online panels.
11. How does one avoid professional survey takers with online panels?
12. Is panel management a critical task for a quality online panel?

WORKING THE NET

Go to Exhibit 6.1 and using it as a resource, determine the 10 highest income counties in the United States; where the highest ratio of pickup trucks per capita is found; the oldest median age zip code in America; a list of key decision makers in the U.S. steel industry; a reader profile on *Time* magazine; where most avocados are grown; and this week's Internet usage in the United States.

Compare and contrast the offerings of *www.surveysampling.com*; *info.zoomerang .com*; *www.e-rewards.com/researchers*; and *www.websurveyor.com*.

Grocery Shoppers Just Want to Save Money

In a study of grocery shopping by Vertis Research, it was found that just under half (49 percent) of the adults queried said they prefer a discount on specific products during each store visit, compared to 34 percent who would rather accumulate points for a larger reward or payoff at stores that offer a frequent-buyer or loyalty card program.

Fifty-one percent of professional/white-collar adults would prefer a discount on specific products during each visit, compared to 46 percent of blue-collar adults surveyed. Of Baby Boomers, 51 percent prefer immediate discounts on specific products or services, compared to 45 percent of Generation X (1965–1976) consumers. Forty-two percent of Hispanic consumers prefer to accumulate points for a larger reward or payoff.

The survey of 3,000 adults was conducted via phone and the Internet. Respondents were asked which one type of media most influenced their buying decisions. Among men 18–34, TV (25 percent), advertising inserts/circulars (18 percent), and the Internet (17 percent) topped the list. Among men 35–49, the top three were inserts/circulars (32 percent), TV (17 percent), and newspaper ads (16 percent). For women 18–34, the breakdown was inserts/circulars (31 percent), TV (24 percent) and newspaper ads (11 percent). For women 35–49, preference was for inserts/circulars (40 percent), TV (20 percent), and newspaper ads (16 percent).

Other tidbits:

- The influence of inserts among women 50+ has grown. Today, 33 percent say inserts have had the most influence, up from 28 percent in 2004.

- Eighty-four percent of grocery insert readers use circulars to compare prices, while 52 percent use them to decide where to shop for groceries.

- And among male weekday newspaper readers who are 50+, weekday advertising insert readership increased to 68 percent in 2008 from 52 percent in 2002.

Still Clipping Coupons

The old-fashioned paper coupon is alive and well, according to the study. Of the grocery ad insert readers surveyed, 51 percent of men 35–49 said they regularly use coupons they receive from grocery advertising inserts or circulars, compared to 45 percent of women in the same age group. Of the women aged 50 and over who said they were ad insert readers, 36 percent said they occasionally use coupons they receive from grocery advertising inserts or circulars, compared to 45 percent of men in the same age group. Of the women aged 50 and over who said they were ad insert readers, 36 percent said they occasionally use coupons they receive from grocery advertising inserts or circulars, compared to 30 percent of men 50+ in the same category. Twenty-seven percent of men and 23 percent of women aged 18–34 who are grocery ad insert readers rarely use coupons they receive from grocery advertising inserts or circulars.

Some questions looked at the types of stores shoppers prefer for different types of foodstuffs. Respondents were asked, "In the past two weeks, other than at a traditional grocery store, what type of store did you visit most often to purchase nonperishable products, such as rice, pasta, canned goods, cereals, etc.?" (Choices included drug store, convenience store, dollar store, wholesale/warehouse club, regular discount store, super-sized grocery store, super discount store.) Twenty-three percent of women grocery shoppers 18–34 cited a super discount store compared to 12 percent of women in the same category who visited a super-sized grocery store. Among women grocery shoppers 35–49, 21 percent indicated they had visited a super discount store, compared to 16 percent who shopped at super-sized grocery stores.

Twenty-four percent of women grocery shoppers 18–34 said they had visited a super discount store most often to purchase perishable products (such as meat, produce, dairy, or bakery items), compared to 17 percent in the same age group who visited a super-sized grocery store.

You Say Deli, I Say Bakery

In addition to the meat and produce departments, respondents were asked to cite two other departments that most influence where they choose to buy groceries. Thirty-three percent of men 18–34 said the deli is the most important department to consider. Other consumers leaned toward the bakery department: 26 percent of women grocery shoppers and 26 percent of men grocery shoppers aged 35–49 tabbed it as most important. Only 9 percent of women and 7 percent of men 18–34 labeled the canned goods department as a prime influence.[34]

Questions

1. This survey was conducted by both telephone and the Internet. Could it have been done quicker and more cheaply only on the Internet? Would telephone-only have been more efficient?

2. Could this survey have been performed by an open Internet panel since everyone shops for groceries? Why or why not?

3. How might Kroger, Safeway, or Wal-Mart have used this data?

4. If this survey was only done in the Baltimore area, the location of the research firm, would it be projectable to the entire country? The sample size was 3,000 consumers.

Adrian Weinbrecht/Getty Images

PRIMARY DATA COLLECTION: OBSERVATION

LEARNING OBJECTIVES

1.	To develop a basic understanding of observation research.
2.	To learn the approaches to observation research.
3.	To understand the advantages and disadvantages of observation research.
4.	To explore the types of human observation.
5.	To understand the types of machine observation and their advantages and disadvantages.
6.	To explore the tremendous impact of scanner-based research on the marketing research industry.
7.	To learn about observation research on the Internet.

Baby Boomers and Gen Xers have been cocooning and nesting since the 1990s—fueling, among other trends, a voracious appetite for savory meals prepared at home that are as convenient as take-out.

Bertolli Brand North America has had a name in the U.S. market since the 1890s with its pasta sauces and olive oils. But scanning sales figures for prepared meals, Bertolli executives saw a fast-growing segment where the company had zero presence.

"It was very clear to us that we were not playing in an area that was really growing up," says Lori Zoppel, brand development director of marketing for Bertolli Brand North America, based in Englewood Cliffs, New Jersey. "All the food trends were toward convenience and serving working-couple homes. Here was an area that fit consumer desires, but there was no brand with an upscale name."

The largest section of the overall frozen meal category is single-serve options, with about 75 percent of the category. Multiserve frozen entrées and dinner—the market eyed by Bertolli—represents about 20 percent of the category but is the fastest-growing segment.

Once the decision to enter the frozen entrée fray was made, Bertolli turned to ethnographic research in 2000 to help design meals that would stand out from competitors—that would mark its products as an upscale, luxurious end to a busy day, not just a convenience. Zoppel worked closely with Debbie Weiss Clark, a research manager at Unilever, Bertolli's parent company.

"There is no substitute, when you want to learn about how people eat and cook, than going and observing them and talking to them while they are eating and cooking and experiencing things," Clark says. "It's so much better than a laboratory setting, where it's all so artificial and you cannot capture what is turning them on and turning them off."

Teams of Bertolli researchers hired subcontractors to identify families willing to participate in the research; participants were paid about $150. Researchers accompanied them to grocery stores to observe their shopping habits, and watched them cook and eat traditional frozen meals to learn areas of complaint and dissatisfaction.

What Bertolli heard was that polybag meals already on the market had mushy pasta and didn't taste fresh. Participants also complained that the packaging was unappealing and seemed downscale.

Meanwhile, other researchers visited traditional Italian restaurants in Manhattan's Little Italy and the Bronx's Arthur Avenue, to see what kinds of ingredients chefs used in their dishes. Researchers also visited popular Italian chain restaurants, including Romano's Macaroni Grill and Olive Garden.

"We were looking for trends and the little things, the key ingredients, that add something," Clark says. "For example, using portabello mushrooms instead of standard mushrooms, or pecorino Romano instead of Parmesan cheese."

With the market research complete, the Bertolli team decided to bring the Dinner for Two concept to market. The product's initial offerings—such as Chicken Parmigiana & Penne—were test-marketed in New England for two years. While under development, Bertolli's marketing team made sure it paid equal attention to the packaging of the meals as was paid to the recipes. Designers placed a photograph of the cooked entrée against a sepia-toned background of the hills of Tuscany. There's also a glass of wine on the package, meant to underscore the idea that the food inside is on a par with a restaurant meal. "The message is that this product is worth paying more for because there is better quality inside," Clark says.

Consumers and food experts alike raved about the taste and the convenience, even as they cringed at the products' nutritional information in nearly the same breath.

Since launching nationwide, Bertolli-brand frozen entrées have carved out a 38.6 percent share of the multiserve polybag market, besting both Stouffer's and Birds Eye. In U.S. grocery stores, Bertolli accounts for 8 of the top 11 best-selling polybag dinners, according to ACNielsen.[1]

The Bertolli story describes a form of observation research. What is observation research? What are its advantages and limitations? Are mechanical devices used in observation research? These are some of the questions we will consider in this chapter.

Nature of Observation Research

> **observation research**
> Systematic process of recording patterns of occurrences or behaviors without normally communicating with the people involved.

Instead of asking people questions, as a survey does, observation research depends on watching what people do. Specifically, **observation research** can be defined as the systematic process of recording patterns of occurrences or behaviors without normally questioning or communicating with the people involved. (Mystery shopping is an exception.) A marketing researcher using the observation technique witnesses and records events as they occur or compiles evidence from records of past events. The observation may involve watching people or watching phenomena, and it may be conducted by human observers or by machines. Exhibit 7.1 gives examples of some common observation situations.

Conditions for Using Observation

Three conditions must be met before observation can be successfully used as a data collection tool for marketing research:

1. The needed information must be either observable or inferable from behavior that is observable. For example, if a researcher wants to know why an individual purchased a new Jeep rather than an Explorer, observation research will not provide the answer.
2. The behavior of interest must be repetitive, frequent, or in some manner predictable. Otherwise, the costs of observation may make the approach prohibitively expensive.
3. The behavior of interest must be of relatively short duration. Observation of the entire decision-making process for purchasing a new home, which might take several weeks or months, is not feasible.

Approaches to Observation Research

Researchers have a variety of observation approaches to choose from. They are faced with the task of choosing the most effective approach for a particular research problem, from the standpoint of cost and data quality. The dimensions along which observation approaches

EXHIBIT 7.1	**Observation Situations**
Situations	**Example**
People watching people	Observers stationed in supermarkets watch consumers select frozen Mexican dinners, with the purpose of seeing how much comparison shopping people do at the point of purchase.
People watching phenomena	Observers stationed at an intersection count vehicles moving in various directions to establish the need for a traffic light.
Machines watching people	Movie or video cameras record consumers selecting frozen Mexican dinners.
Machines watching phenomena	Traffic-counting machines monitor the flow of vehicles at an intersection.

vary are (1) natural versus contrived situations, (2) open versus disguised observation, (3) human versus machine observers, and (4) direct versus indirect observation.

Natural versus Contrived Situations   Counting how many people use the drive-in window at a particular bank during certain hours is a good example of a completely natural situation. The observer plays no role in the behavior of interest. Those being observed should have no idea that they are under observation. At the other extreme is recruiting people to do their shopping in a simulated supermarket (rows of stocked shelves set up in a field service's mall facility) so that their behavior can be carefully observed. In this case, the recruited people must be given at least some idea that they are participating in a study. The participants might be given grocery carts and told to browse the shelves and pick out items that they might normally use. The researchers might use alternative point-of-purchase displays for several products under study. To test the effectiveness of the various displays, the observers would note how long the shopper paused in front of the test displays and how often the product was actually selected. Today, many firms, such as Frito-Lay and Procter & Gamble, use online simulated environments.

A contrived environment enables the researcher to better control extraneous variables that might have an impact on a person's behavior or the interpretation of that behavior. Use of such an environment also tends to speed up the data-gathering process. The researcher does not have to wait for natural events to occur but instead instructs the participants to perform certain actions. Because more observations can be collected in the same length of time, the result will be either a larger sample or faster collection of the targeted amount of data. The latter should lower the costs of the project.

The primary disadvantage of a contrived setting is that it is artificial, and thus the observed behavior may be different from what would occur in a real-world situation. The more natural the setting, the more likely it is that the behavior will be normal for the individual being observed.

Open versus Disguised Observation   Does the person being observed know that he or she is being observed? It is well known that the presence of an observer may have an influence on the phenomena being observed.[2] Two general mechanisms work to bias the data. First, if people know they are being observed (as in **open observation**), they may behave differently. Second, the appearance and behavior of the observer offers a potential for bias similar to that associated with the presence of an interviewer in survey research.

Disguised observation is the process of monitoring people who do not know they are being watched. A common form of disguised observation is observing behavior from behind a one-way mirror. For example, a product manager may observe respondent reactions to alternative package designs from behind a one-way mirror during a focus group discussion.

open observation
Process of monitoring people who know they are being watched.

disguised observation
Process of monitoring people who do not know they are being watched.

Human versus Machine Observers   In some situations, it is possible and even desirable to replace human observers with machines—when machines can do the job less expensively, more accurately, or more readily. Traffic-counting devices are probably more accurate, definitely cheaper, and certainly more willing than human observers. It would not be feasible, for example, for ACNielsen to have human observers in people's homes to record television viewing habits. Movie cameras and audio-visual equipment record behavior much more objectively and in greater detail than human observers ever could. Finally, the electronic scanners found in most retail stores provide more accurate and timely data on product movement than human observers ever could.

Direct versus Indirect Observation   Most of the observation carried out for marketing research is direct observation of current behavior. However, in some cases, past behavior must be observed. To do this, the researcher must turn to some record of

Sylvain Grandadam/Robert Harding/
Getty Images, Inc.

Exhibit 7.2

Pictures Can Help Understand Global Consumers

> **garbologists**
> Researchers who sort through people's garbage to analyze household consumption patterns.

the behavior. Archaeologists dig up sites of old settlements and attempt to determine the nature of life in early societies from the physical evidence they find. **Garbologists** sort through people's garbage to analyze household consumption patterns. Marketing research usually is much more mundane. In a product prototype test, it may be important to learn how much of the test product the consumer used. The most accurate way to find this out is to have the respondent return the unused product so that the researcher can see how much is left. If a study involved the in-home use of a laundry soil and stain remover, it would be important to know how much of the remover each respondent actually used. All of the respondents' answers to questions would be considered from this usage perspective.

Pictures can also be used to see what people have done in certain situations. For example, a global study conducted by New York-based GfK NOP created a massive visual database with the goal of better understanding global consumers. Part of that research was photographing people's kitchens, which in many cultures is the "heart of the home." Examples of the kind of understanding the researchers gleaned from the photos are shown in Exhibit 7.2.

Advantages of Observation Research

Watching what people actually do rather than depending on their reports of what they did has one very significant and obvious advantage: Firsthand information is not subject to many of the biasing factors associated with the survey approach. Specifically, the researcher avoids problems associated with the willingness and ability of respondents to answer questions. Also, some forms of data are gathered more quickly and accurately by observation. Letting a scanner record the items in a grocery bag is much more efficient than asking the shopper to enumerate them. Similarly, rather than asking young children which toys they like, major toy manufacturers prefer to invite target groups of children into a large playroom and observe via a one-way mirror which toys are chosen and how long each holds the child's attention.

Disadvantages of Observation Research

The primary disadvantage of observation research is that only behavior and physical personal characteristics usually can be examined. The researcher does not learn about motives, attitudes, intentions, or feelings. Also, only public behavior is observed; private behavior—such as dressing for work or committee decision making within a company—is beyond the scope of observation research. A second problem is that present observed behavior may not be projectable into the future. The fact that a consumer purchases a certain brand of milk after examining several alternatives does not mean that he or she will continue to do so in the future.

Observation research can be time-consuming and costly if the observed behavior occurs rather infrequently. For example, if observers in a supermarket are waiting to watch the purchase behavior of persons selecting Lava soap, they may have a long wait. And if the choice of consumers to be observed is biased (for example, shoppers who go grocery shopping after 5:00 p.m.), distorted data may be obtained.

Human Observation

As noted in Exhibit 7.1, people can be employed to watch other people or certain phenomena. For example, people can act as mystery shoppers, observers behind one-way mirrors, or recorders of shopper traffic and behavior patterns. Researchers also can conduct retail and wholesale audits, which are types of observation research.

Ethnographic Research

Ethnographic research comes to marketing from the field of anthropology. The popularity of the technique in commercial marketing research is increasing. **Ethnographic research,** or the study of human behavior in its natural context, involves observation of behavior and physical settings. Ethnographers directly observe the population they are studying. As "participant observers," ethnographers can use their intimacy with the people they are studying to gain richer, deeper insights into culture and behavior—in short, what makes people do what they do. Over $100 million annually is spent on ethnographic research.[3] Today corporations such as Eastman Kodak and Microsoft have their own in-house ethnographers. Ethnographic studies can cost anywhere from $5,000 to as much as $800,000, depending on how deeply a company wants to delve into its customers' lives.

> **ethnographic research**
> Study of human behavior in its natural context, involving observation of behavior and physical setting.

One of the first uses of ethnographic research in an informal manner goes back to the Spanish Civil War in the 1930s. Forrest Mars Sr., when he wasn't dodging bullets, was observing soldiers coating their chocolate with sugar. The result of this observational or ethnographic research? M&M's, named for Mars and business associate Bruce Murrie.[4]

Advantages of Ethnographic Research

Both focus groups and individual depth interviews rely on retrospection. That is, they ask respondents to recall their behavior and the behavior of others. Human memory, of course, can sometimes be faulty. In addition, respondents sometimes reply in a socially desirable manner. A man may be reading adult magazines but claims to be reading *Fortune* and *BusinessWeek*.

With ethnographic research, observers can record:

- ☐ What is happening, including what objects are being created or manipulated.
- ☐ Where it is happening.
- ☐ The flow of what is happening.
- ☐ The order of what is happening.
- ☐ The time spent on what is happening.

Early Ethnographic Research led to the creation of M&M's.

Richard B. Levine/NewsCom

- ☐ Who is doing what.
- ☐ What is being communicated verbally and nonverbally.
- ☐ The reactions of the various participants, which are critical.[5]

Because individuals generally acclimate to an observer's presence over time (often quickly), their behavior becomes relatively unbiased by the observer—resulting in a more accurate characterization of behavior.

Although the ethnographic researcher's principal activity is observing behavior, active interviews or discussion with respondents is a key component. Getting respondents' perspectives on actions, through dialogue, is informative. Furthermore, the ethnographic data can be utilized in mixed method studies, for comparing and contrasting it with data from other sources. For example, a research manager could leverage observational data of the sales reps interacting with customers and prospects, and compare it with information from in-depth district and regional sales manager interviews—identifying any disconnects between what's being done and what's expected.[6]

Conducting Ethnographic Research   The first step of the research is to find an informant. An informant is a participant who can introduce the researchers to a particular group of people and explain the meaning behind the rituals, language, and general goings on. After entering a social group, ethnographers keenly observe activities, listen to conversation, conduct ongoing informal interviews, and participate in meaningful activities. Interactions are also observed to ascertain the effects of social influence.

Data is recorded in the form of field notes, jotted down in a notebook whenever researchers get a chance. The researchers may also use photographs, audio, and video. There is an attempt to build a collection of artifacts—items that represent particular meaning to the people being studied. A researcher's own experiences—reactions, feelings, thoughts—are also important data. There are some things researchers can't fully understand until they experience them themselves.

The next step is to analyze and interpret all of the data collected to find themes and patterns of meaning. This is no simple task. Hours and hours of audio and video must be transcribed and re-studied. Even for the well-trained and experienced ethnographer, the amount of data can at times be overwhelming. But through careful and thorough analysis of the data, themes and categories emerge and applicable findings become clear. Ethnographers usually create frameworks to help companies think about their consumers and understand what it all means.

Triangulation, the process of checking findings against what other people say and against similar research already conducted, is a way to verify the accuracy of collected data. While traditional ethnography stops with the description of the group studies, this is not sufficient for businesses. They need actionable guidelines, recommendations, and an outline of strategy. The findings must be presented in a fashion to enable companies to create innovative and successful solutions.[7]

For managers at Cambridge SoundWorks, it was a perplexing problem: in retail outlets across the country, men stood wide-eyed when sales reps showed off the company's hi-fi, "blow-your-hair-back" stereo speakers. So why didn't such unabashed enthusiasm for the product translate into larger—and bigger ticket—sales?

To find out, the Andover, Massachusetts, manufacturer and retailer of stereo equipment hired research firm Design Continuum, in West Newton, Massachusetts, to follow a dozen prospective customers over the course of two weeks. The researchers' conclusion: the high-end speaker market suffered from something referred to as "the spouse acceptance factor." While men adored the big black boxes, women hated their unsightly appearance. Concerned about the way the speakers would "look" in the living room, women would talk their husbands out of buying a cool but hideous and expensive piece of stereo equipment. Even those who had purchased the product had trouble showing it off: Men would attempt to display the loudspeakers as trophies in living rooms, while women would hide them behind plants, vases, and chairs. "Women would come into the store, look at the speakers and say, 'that thing is ugly,'" says Ellen Di Resta, principal at Design Continuum. "The men would lose the argument and leave the store without a stereo. The solution was to give the target market what men and women *both* wanted: a great sound system that looks like furniture so you don't have to hide it."

Armed with this knowledge, Cambridge SoundWorks unveiled a new line. The furniture-like Newton Series of speakers and home theater systems comes in an array of colors and finishes. The result: The Newton Series is the fastest growing and best-selling product line in the firm's 14-year history.[8]

Marriott hired IDEO Inc. to rethink the hotel experience for an increasingly important customer: the young, tech-savvy road warrior. "This is all about looking freshly at business travel and how people behave and what they need," explains Michael E. Jannini, Marriott's executive vice president for brand management.[9]

To better understand Marriott's customers, IDEO dispatched a team of seven consultants, including a designer, anthropologist, writer, and architect, on a six-week trip. Covering 12 cities, the group hung out in hotel lobbies, cafés, and bars, and asked guests to graph what they were doing hour by hour.

This is what they learned: Hotels are generally good at serving large parties but not small groups of business travelers. Researchers noted that hotel lobbies tend to be dark and better suited to killing time than conducting casual business. Marriott lacked places where guests could comfortably combine work with pleasure outside their rooms. IDEO consultant and Marriott project manager Dana Cho recalls watching a female business traveler drink wine in the lobby while trying not to spill it on papers spread out on a desk. "There are very few hotel services that address [such] problems," says Cho.[10]

Having studied IDEO's findings, in January Marriott announced plans to reinvent the lobbies of its Marriott and Renaissance Hotels, creating for each a social zone, with small tables, brighter lights, and wireless Web access, that is better suited to meetings. Another area will allow solo travelers to work or unwind in larger, quiet, semiprivate spaces where they won't have to worry about spilling coffee on their laptops or papers.[11]

Jim Stengel, Procter & Gamble's chief marketing officer, notes, "I'm a big observational guy." So he has urged the P&G marketers to spend lots of time with consumers in their homes, watching the ways they wash their clothes, clean their floors, and diaper their babies, and asking them about their habits and frustrations. Back in 2000, the typical brand marketer spent less than four hours a month with consumers. Says Stengel: "It's at least triple that now."[12]

Martha Rivera, with Doyle Research Associates, Chicago, talks about how ethnography complements and expands other forms of research in the accompanying Global Research box.

Jerry Thomas, CEO of Decision Analyst, discusses "online ethnography" in the accompanying Practicing Marketing Research box.

Mystery Shoppers

Mystery shoppers are used to gather observational data about a store (for example, are the shelves neatly stocked?) and to collect data about customer–employee interactions. In the latter case, of course, there is communication between the mystery shopper and the employee. The mystery shopper may ask, "How much is this item?" "Do you have this in blue?" or "Can you deliver this by Friday?" The interaction is not an interview, and

> **mystery shoppers**
> People who pose as consumers and shop at a company's own stores or those of its competitors to collect data about customer–employee interactions and to gather observational data; they may also compare prices, displays, and the like.

GLOBAL RESEARCH

Ethnographics Are an Enriching Process

Some of the insights resulting from the use of ethnography as a key element of consumer insights research are as follows.

- *No person can fully report his or her own unconscious behavior.* During a research study conducted in Venezuela, in an ordinary bathroom I saw a large multicolored, perfectly round sphere made of small bits of body soap. The interviewee explained that he usually compressed together these bits of body soap when they had become too small. None of the previous interviewees had reported something like that, but all subsequent participants were asked what they regularly did with the last pieces of their body soap. Most of them automatically placed the old small piece onto the new soap bar without another thought. Supplementary questions revealed that the flat form of the client's soap bar was thought to facilitate this, and that these consumers actually looked for that particular brand for that reason. Hence the client abandoned its plan to change the shape of its soap.
- *People's reports of their own behavior always contain at least a small portion of biases and inaccuracies.* While testing a new type of package for pre-prepared meat, Mexican housewives claimed that they would readily buy any pre-prepared food item because it offered the convenience that they reportedly expected from all types of products. However, it was observed that their refrigerators were filled exclusively with fresh food items, thus suggesting that these housewives habitually prepared their meals from scratch and did not consume any form of pre-prepared food. Further questions about such apparent incongruity confirmed this inference.
- *Researchers' unfamiliarity with the product makes it hard to interpret verbal reports from consumers.* We were commissioned to investigate the general mind-set of Venezuelan truck drivers in regards to air filters, and so short in-truck trips were performed. The truck drivers were requested to teach the ethnographers about the replacement of an external air filter on the truck's exhaust system. As a result, the researchers were able to remove the air filters from their cases and to identify the right moment to replace them. Most drivers used their air filters far longer than recommended by the manufacturer. The truckers waited until the filters got to a particular tone of gray, which we were able to reproduce for the written report. The manufacturer was able to prepare a simple sheet correlating the different degrees of gray with increasingly adverse consequences for the truck's performance.[13]

communication occurs only so that the mystery shopper can observe the actions and comments of the employee. Mystery shopping is, therefore, classified as an observational marketing research method, even though communication is often involved. It is estimated that 70 percent of America's national retailers use the technique: Wal-Mart, McDonald's, Starbucks, Blockbuster, Jiffy Lube, Rite Aid, PF Chang's restaurants, and Whole Foods Markets are some of the big-name clients that rely on mystery shoppers.[15]

"The No. 1 thing we're trying to do is reinforce a company's training," explains David Rich, president of ICC/Decision Services, which deploys mystery shoppers for such clients as Levi's and Godiva.[16] Mystery shopping gives managers nearly instant feedback on whether their underlings are smiling when they ought to, making customers feel at ease, or inviting them to get fries with that. Many companies tie bonuses to performance on mystery inspections, giving employees an incentive to be nice.

PRACTICING MARKETING RESEARCH

Taking Ethnography Online

Online ethnography begins by pulling a sample that is representative of the target market, typically from an online panel. One of the advantages here is that panel members are accustomed to surveys and therefore are more likely to participate than the average man or woman on the street. Moreover, since no one is visiting their homes or offices, a higher share of potential subjects will agree to participate, which creates a more representative sample.

Beyond the sampling advantages, another benefit of this approach is that the online environment promotes a sense of anonymity and safety, which encourages a high level of self-disclosure. In the online environment, participants feel comfortable expressing their feelings. With guidance from experienced moderators, respondents can explore and describe all the behaviors, routines, thoughts, feelings, and experiences they believe are most relevant to their purchasing decisions.

The respondents' normal routines are not disrupted. They can provide their detailed responses at a convenient time and over a span of several days (or sometimes weeks). This expanse of time also gives the respondents an opportunity to reflect on the questions posed and to give detailed descriptions of their thoughts, feelings, and experiences.

So, how does online ethnography work? How is it conducted? The exact design of the project and its execution depend on the product or service category and the objectives of the research. As a general rule, some or all of the following steps are involved:

- *Respondents might be asked to keep diaries* (either online or offline) to record their behaviors, routines, thoughts, and observations related to the purposes of the study.
- *Participants might be asked to take digital pictures* related to the focus of the study (it could be photos of their refrigerators, pantries, backyards, or bedrooms). And with

the spread of digital cameras (even cell phones now have digital cameras), digital photos are relatively easy for most people to take and send (with the moderator subsequently uploading the pictures for discussion).

- *One member of the household could be asked to take photos or videos* of other members of the household at certain times or to record specific behaviors, events, and so on.
- *Participants' stories or explanations typically accompany the photos,* telling us what is in the picture, who is in the picture, what is happening, and perhaps even what it means to the respondent.
- *Projective techniques can be employed* as well (for example, respondents might search and select online photos or be instructed to take photos that represent the personality of a brand, or that bring to mind memories of the brand).

Typically, the digital photos or videos are sent to the moderator via e-mail for review and uploading to the online depth interview. The diaries and photos are studied by the analyst and then used as stimulus in conducting the follow-up online depth interviews. These are typically described as "time-extended" depth interviews since the project unfolds over a period of several days (5 to 10 days, but longer time periods are possible). In fact, the term *time-extended* should be used to describe the whole online ethnography process. Indeed, this is one of the major advantages of the method: the respondent's concentration on a topic for a period of several days sensitizes her to the subject and reveals her own feelings and motives related to the topic.

Example of an Online Ethnography Project

Decision Analyst conducted an online ethnographic project on health and beauty products among women and men from the United States,

UK, and France. All participants were medium to heavy users of skin-care products.

Study Methodology:

- Respondents were asked to take *digital pictures of their skin-care products and other health and beauty products* in their normal storage place. They were also asked to add stories of "what's in the pictures" to accompany the pictures.

- To record *daily diary entries* of their morning/evening routines when using health and beauty products.

- *To provide detailed descriptions* of their experiences from a regular shopping occasion for health and beauty products.

- To keep a *log of advertising* they noticed related to health and beauty.

Follow-up *depth interviews* focused on the following types of questions: How do you define beauty? What motivates your interest in skin beauty? How would you feel if your favorite skin-care lotion should vanish from the marketplace? How much time do you spend daily caring for your skin? What are your favorite brands, and why?

Some comments and pictures from one participant, Sally, in Chicago:

Obviously my medicine cabinet is filled with a variety of products at various price points. I admit that I like to try the high-end brands, but I'm on a budget and also *take advantage of the less pricey products one finds at drugstores and stores like Body Shop. So that's why Crème de la Mer is elbowing for room with Olay, and Kinerase is cheek-and-jowl with Ponds.*

Once all of the photos, diaries, stories, and interview transcripts are finished, the next step is the analysis, which is the most time-consuming and brain-intensive part of the process. There are no shortcuts. The analyst must comb and recomb through all of the raw data (photos, videos, diaries, transcripts) and try to understand what it all means. Certainly, some understanding of cultural anthropology is helpful to the analyst, as is some knowledge of psychology, sociology, economics, history, and so on. The most important background, however, is knowledge of the target industry, the product category, and previous experience with marketing and marketing research related to the product or service. If all of these knowledge sets can be integrated, the analysis is apt to be much better than an analysis based on a single academic discipline.[14]

Questions

1. Which do you think reveals the most insights—traditional ethnography or online ethnography?

2. Which is most difficult to conduct?

3. Would you rather participate in an online or traditional ethnographic study?

The mystery shopping concept has four basic levels, which differ in the depth and type of information collected:

- ❑ *Level 1*—The mystery shopper conducts a mystery telephone call. Here, the mystery shopper calls the client location and evaluates the level of service received over the phone, following a scripted conversation.

- ❑ *Level 2*—The mystery shopper visits an establishment and makes a quick purchase; little or no customer–employee interaction is required. For example, in a level 2 mystery shop, a mystery shopper purchases an item (for example, gas, a hamburger, or a lottery ticket) and evaluates the transaction and image of the facility.

- ❑ *Level 3*—The mystery shopper visits an establishment and, using a script or scenario, initiates a conversation with a service and/or sales representative. Level 3 mystery shopping usually does not involve an actual purchase. Examples include discussing different cellular telephone packages with a sales representative, reviewing services provided during an oil change, and so forth.

PRACTICING MARKETING RESEARCH

Advances in Mystery Shopping

Integrated, total-customer-experience evaluations that measure what happens at every possible touchpoint. Automated, fast report distribution via e-mail. Web-based reporting. Digitally recorded phone call evaluations. Hidden-video captures. High-resolution digital photos, embedded directly in online reports. Reports, call recordings, and photos burned onto CDs. Rewards presented on the spot to client employees who perform well. Palm Pilots and laptop computers. Certified professional evaluators. Same-day report turnaround. Instantaneous, online summary capabilities presenting over 40 different formats, for true, real-time reporting. These are just some of the latest advances in mystery shopping.

Recently, an industrywide effort to help improve overall skills and assist members in improving the quality of reporting was undertaken by the Mystery Shopping Providers Association (MSPA), which began offering a certification process for interested mystery shoppers. Currently, two certifications are available: silver and gold.

Silver certification requires a shopper to attend an online educational program, followed by a comprehensive test about general mystery shopping skills. If they pass, they are awarded silver certification. Gold certification is open only to shoppers with silver certification and requires shoppers to attend a one-day seminar, held in approximately 25 locations annually throughout the United States. These seminars cover the issues shoppers are required to know and comply with in the course of their duties. In 2005, almost 22,000 shoppers were awarded silver certification, and more than 2,000 were awarded gold certification.[18]

Questions

1. Would you like to be a mystery shopper?
2. What can a retailer learn from mystery shopping?

☐ *Level 4*—The mystery shopper performs a visit that requires excellent communication skills and knowledge of the product. Discussing a home loan, the process for purchasing a new car, or visiting apartment complexes serve as examples. The "HotelSpy" in the Practicing Market Research box is another example of Level 4 mystery shopping.

Mystery shopping can have one or several objectives. As mentioned earlier, a common objective is measuring employee training. Other objectives are:

☐ Enabling an organization to monitor compliance with product/service delivery standards, and specifications.

☐ Enabling marketers to examine the gap between promises made through advertising/sales promotion and actual service delivery.

☐ Helping monitor the impact of training and performance improvement initiatives on compliance with or conformance to product/service delivery specifications.

☐ Identifying differences in the customer experience across different times of day, locations, product/service types, and other potential sources of variation in product/service quality.[17]

Ron Welty, president of Intell.Shop, a mystery shopping firm, discusses how technology has changed mystery shopping in the last few years in the Practicing Marketing Research box on page 195.

One-Way Mirror Observations

one-way mirror observation
Practice of watching behaviors or activities from behind a one-way mirror.

The discussion of focus groups in Chapter 4 noted that focus group facilities almost always provide **one-way mirror observation,** which allows clients to observe the group discussion as it unfolds. New product development managers, for example, can note consumers' reactions to various package prototypes as they are demonstrated by the moderator. (One researcher spent 200 hours watching mothers change diapers to gather information for the redesign of disposable diapers.) In addition, the clients can observe the degree of emotion exhibited by the consumer as he or she speaks. One-way mirrors are also sometimes used by child psychologists and toy designers to observe children at play. At the Fisher-Price Play Lab some 3,500 children per year pass through. It is set up like a preschool classroom. On the other side of the glass is a narrow carpeted room with about 10 chairs and two video cameras. Nearly all Fisher-Price toys have been taken for a spin in the Play Lab at some point in their development.[19]

The lighting level in the observation room must be very dim relative to that in the focus group room. Otherwise, the focus group participants can see into the observation room. Several years ago, we (the authors) were conducting a focus group of orthopedic surgeons in St. Louis, Missouri. One physician arrived approximately 20 minutes early and was ushered into the group room. A young assistant product manager for the pharmaceutical manufacturer was already seated in the observation room. The physician, being alone in the group room, decided to take advantage of the large framed mirror on the wall for some last-minute grooming. He walked over to the mirror and began combing his hair. At the same time, the assistant product manager, sitting about a foot away on the other side of the mirror, decided to light a cigarette. As the doctor combed his hair, there was suddenly a bright flash of light, and another face appeared through the mirror. What happened next goes beyond the scope of this text. In recent years, the trend has been to inform participants of the one-way mirror and to explain who is in the other room watching and why.

Audits

audit
Examination and verification of the sales of a product.

Audits are another category of human observation research. An **audit** is the examination and verification of sales of a product. Audits generally fall into two categories: retail audits, which measure sales to final consumers, and wholesale audits, which determine the amount of product movement from warehouses to retailers. Wholesalers and retailers allow auditors into their stores and stockrooms to examine the company's sales and order records in order to verify product flows. In turn, the retailers and wholesalers receive cash compensation and basic reports about their operations from the audit firms.

Because of the availability of scanner-based data (discussed later in this chapter), physical audits at the retail level may someday all but disappear. The largest nonscanner-based wholesale audit company, SAMI, has already gone out of business. Its client list was sold to Information Resources, Incorporated (IRI), a company that specializes in providing scanner-based data. ACNielsen, the largest retail audit organization, no longer uses auditors in grocery stores. The data are entirely scanner-based. Currently, ACNielsen uses both auditors and scanner-based data for some other types of retail outlets. However, the data probably will be scanner-based only in the near future.

Machine Observation

The observation methods discussed so far have involved people observing things or consumers. Now we turn our attention to observation by machines, including traffic counters, physiological measurement devices, opinion and behavior management devices, and scanners.

Traffic Counters

Among the most common and popular machines in observation research are **traffic counters**. As the name implies, traffic counters measure vehicular flow over a particular stretch of roadway. Outdoor advertisers rely on traffic counts to determine the number of exposures per day to a specific billboard. Retailers use the information to ascertain where to locate a particular type of store. Convenience stores, for example, require a moderately high traffic volume to reach target levels of profitability.

> **traffic counters**
> Machines used to measure vehicular flow over a particular stretch of roadway.

Physiological Measurement Devices

When an individual is aroused or feels inner tension or alertness, his or her condition is referred to as *activation*. Activation is stimulated via a subcortical unit called the *reticular activation system* (*RAS*), located in the human brain stem. The sight of a product or advertisement, for example, can activate the RAS. When the arousal processes in the RAS are directly provoked, the processing of information increases. Researchers have used a number of devices to measure the level of a person's activation.

Electroencephalograph   An **electroencephalograph (EEG)** is a machine that measures electric pulses on the scalp and generates a record of electrical activity in the brain. Although electroencephalography probably is the most versatile and sensitive procedure for detecting arousal, it involves expensive equipment, a laboratory environment, and complex data analysis requiring special software programs. Using EEG technology developed by NASA to monitor astronauts' alertness levels, Capita Corporation measures respondents' reactions to advertisements. Capita uses a headset that reads electrical signals coming from a subject's scalp five times per second, as the person interacts with media such as a television program, a commercial, a Web page, or a banner ad. These brain waves are converted into a scrolling graph synchronized with the visual stimuli on the screen, giving the marketer a play-by-play view of which segments excite the viewer and which ones don't.

> **electroencephalograph (EEG)**
> Machine that measures electrical pulses on the scalp and generates a record of electrical activity in the brain.

With the help of U.S. Interactive, an Internet services company that tracks Web ads, Capita tested the system's reliability. Capita monitored the brain waves of 48 respondents as they confronted four banner ads with strong click-through rates and four ads with low rates. In three of four tests, Capita's measure correctly identified the "strong" banners.[20]

The ability to accurately translate the data is what troubles one cable network executive. "An ad might get someone to perspire or their eyes to dilate or their brain waves to peak, but the resounding issue is, what does that really tell you?" he says. "Just because the needles are moving does not mean that it will affect their behavior, get them to purchase something, or improve their brand awareness."[21]

> **galvanic skin response (GSR)**
> Change in the electric resistance of the skin associated with activation responses; also called *electrodermal response*.

Galvanic Skin Response   **Galvanic skin response (GSR)**, also known as *electrodermal response,* is a change in the electric resistance of the skin associated with activation responses. A small electric current of constant intensity is sent into the skin through electrodes attached to the palmar side of the fingers. The changes in voltage observed between the electrodes indicate the level of stimulation. Because the equipment is portable and not expensive, measuring GSR is the most popular way to assess emotional reaction to a stimulus. GSR is used primarily to measure stimulus response to advertisements but is sometimes used in packaging research.

Inner Response, Incorporated uses GSR to evaluate commercials. In tests of an Eastman Kodak Company digital photo processing ad, Inner Response determined that viewers' interest levels built slowly in the opening scenes, rose when a snapshot of an attractive young woman was shown, but spiked highest when a picture appeared of a smiling, pigtailed girl. Knowing which scenes had the highest impact helped Kodak in making changes in the spot's content and cutting its length.

Eye Tracking The PreTesting Company has long been a leader in eye-tracking research in advertising. A new system offered by the research company is called eMotion. eMotion uses a PC-connected camera to measure the rapid motion of viewers' eyes—the subtle eyeball vibrations that increase when we see something of interest. The system allows viewers to move their heads naturally, thanks to a special computer-driven camera mount that is able to distinguish eye movement from head movement. PreTesting follows up with an interview to determine how much the viewers remember. Then a proprietary algorithm gives advertising executives instant feedback on how well the spot worked.

Lee Weinblatt of PreTesting believes that viewers should be engaged but not so visually stimulated for the full 30 seconds that they don't take in any verbal information. "This could be revolutionary," he says. "Advertisers will finally be able to understand which ads are working."[22] Weinblatt's favorite example, from his beta-testing, was an ad for Dr. Scholl's massaging gel insoles. It featured a leggy model emerging from a swimming pool, which sent the eyes of his male subjects vibrating. When the model turned out to be wearing high-heel shoes, his female subjects got excited. Then the ad cut to nothing but text and voice-over, letting the information sink in.

Facial Action Coding Service (FACS) Researchers at the University of California at San Francisco identified the 43 muscle movements responsible for all human facial expression (see Exhibit 7.3). They spent seven years categorizing roughly 3,000 combinations of such movements and the emotions they convey—the "eyelid tightener" expresses anger, for instance, and the "nasolabial fold deepener" manifests sadness. The system has proved to be highly accurate; the FBI and CIA reportedly use the FACS method to determine the emotions of suspects during interrogations.[23]

Sensory Logic, a St. Paul, Minnesota, research firm, uses FACS to get to the "truth." The firm's clients include Target, Nextel, General Motors, and Eli Lilly, according to Don Hill, the firm's president (see www.sensorylogic.com). To measure initial gut reactions to a commercial or ad, Hill first attaches electrodes to the side of a subject's mouth (monitoring the zygomatic muscle, for smiles), above the eyebrow (corrugator muscle, for frowns), and on two fingers (for sweat). He says the facial muscle movements reflect appeal, whereas perspiration translates into what he calls "impact"—emotional power. After Hill takes initial readings, he removes the electrodes and he videotapes an interview with each subject. Later, his FACS-trained team reviews the video, second by second, cataloguing emotions.

Even some of Hill's happy customers say that face reading has limitations. For one thing, not everyone believes that pitches have to aim for the heart. "A lot of the advertising we do is a more rational sell," a General Motors researcher says, "so emotional research doesn't apply."[24]

Which One Is Fake?
Is it ever really clear if consumers like what you're selling? Some might tell you they like your product even if they don't. Who's really interested and who's just being polite? Can you tell? The areas around the eyes and around the mouth are the places to look for clues. A true smile will involve the eyes (a reaction of an involuntary nerve) as well as the mouth. Also, a true smile will curve the lips while a fake smile won't. In a fake smile, the corners of the mouth will move outward, not upward.

Opinion and Behavior Measurement Devices

GPS Measurement   Nielsen Outdoor and its technology partner, RDP Associates, have developed a proprietary GPS device—the Nielsen Personal Outdoor Device, or Npod—about the size of a cell phone, which people carry in their pockets, purses or wear like a cell phone. Members of a randomly chosen sample carry an Npod as they move about on foot or in vehicles; the device is linked to orbiting satellites that enable Nielsen Outdoor to identify their location, speed and direction of travel, passively, continuously, easily, and affordably.

To determine actual exposure to outdoor displays, we gather travel information of the routes taken by an individual, which are matched to a list of geo-coded outdoor sites to obtain passages, or the opportunity to see specific outdoor sites. When the respondent's travel path intersects with a known outdoor site, an "intercept" is recorded, with each event dated and time-stamped, and the direction and speed of travel noted. This provides a robust set of data with the "opportunity to see" an outdoor display. This unique technology also enables Nielsen Outdoor to accurately measure exposure to transit advertising, or opportunity to see the outside advertising on any bus. Thus, Nielsen Outdoor measures kiosks, bus shelters, billboards, and buses.[25]

People Reader   The PreTesting Company has invented a device called the **People Reader,** which looks like a lamp. When respondents sit in front of it, they are not aware that it is simultaneously recording both their reading material and the activity of their eyes. The self-contained unit is totally automatic and can record any respondent—with or without glasses—without the use of attachments, chin rests, helmets, or special optics. It allows respondents to read any size magazine

Exhibit   7.3

Which One Is Blowing Smoke?

Dan Hill, president of Sensory Logic, says that some of the consumers who tell you they like what you're selling don't really mean it. Here he shows us how to tell who's being genuine and who's just making nice.

Elle Wagner/Copyright John Wiley & Sons, Inc.

The People Reader, an opinion and behavior measurement device developed by the PreTesting Company, unobtrusively records reading material and readers' eye activity to determine readers' habits as well as the stopping power and brand-name recall associated with different-sized ads. Go to *www.pretesting.com* to learn about the products and services this company offers.

Courtesy The Pretesting Co., Tenafly, N.J.

> **People Reader**
> Machine that simultaneously records the respondent's reading material and eye reactions.

or newspaper and lets them spend as much time as they want reading and rereading the publication. Through use of the People Reader and specially designed hidden cameras, the PreTesting Company has been able to document both reading habits and the results of different-sized ads in terms of stopping power and brand-name recall. The company's research has found the following:

☐ Nearly 40 percent of all readers either start from the back of a magazine or "fan" a magazine for interesting articles and ads. Fewer than half the readers start from the very first page of a magazine.

☐ Rarely does a double-page ad provide more than 15 percent additional top-of-mind awareness than a single-page ad. Usually, the benefits of a double-page spread are additional involvement and communication, not top-of-mind awareness.

☐ In the typical magazine, nearly 35 percent of each of the ads receive less than two seconds' worth of voluntary examination.

☐ The strongest involvement power recorded for ads has been three or more successive single-page ads on the right-hand side of a magazine.

☐ Because most ads "hide" the name of the advertisers and do not show a close-up view of the product package, brand-name confusion is greater than 50 percent on many products such as cosmetics and clothing.

☐ A strong ad that is above average in stopping power and communication will work regardless of which section in the magazine it is placed. It will also work well in any type of ad or editorial environment. However, an ad that is below average in stopping power and involvement will be seriously affected by the surrounding environment.[26]

The Portable People Meter and Project Apollo

For the past decade or so, watching television in America has been defined by the families recruited by Nielsen Media Research who have agreed to have an electronic meter attached to their televisions or to record in a diary what shows they watch. Traditional "people meters" are electronic TV-set-top boxes that continually record which channel is tuned in. Nielsen uses people meters in the top media markets such as Chicago, New York, and Los Angeles. Outside the 10 or so major markets, Nielsen still uses the old paper diary system where viewers log what they are watching in a notebook. This approach may not last much longer because technology demands it. Bob Luff, the chief technology officer at Nielsen, views the modern American home as a digital zoo: radio is going on the Web, TV is going on cell phones, the Web is going on TV, and everything, it seems, is moving to video-on-demand (VOD), the iPod, and the PlayStation Portable. "Television and media," Luff said over the noise of five sets tuned to five different channels, "will change more in the next three or five years than it's changed in the past 50."[27]

Arbitron has counted radio listeners—and, at various times, television viewers—since the late 1940s. It has harnessed new technology to measure audiences. Participants wear a black plastic box that looks like a pager, 3 inches by 2 inches by ½ inch, whose circuitry is roughly as complex as that of a cell phone. The device is called the **portable people meter,** or the PPM.

> **portable people meter**
> Device worn by people that measures the radio and TV programming to which the participant was exposed during the day.

Participants clip the PPM to their belts, or to any other article of clothing, and wear it throughout their waking hours. Before going to bed, they dock the PPM in a cradle so that overnight it can automatically send its data to a computer center in Maryland, where marketing researchers can download and review the information. The PPM will tell Arbitron exactly what kind—and exactly how much—television and radio programming a person was exposed to during the day. Eventually, the PPM may also tell the researchers at Arbitron a host of other things too, such as whether a PPM-wearer heard any Web streaming, or supermarket Muzak, or any electronic media with audible sound that someone might encounter on a typical day.

Project Apollo is a venture between ACNielsen and Arbitron in conjunction with Procter & Gamble, Unilever, Kraft, and four other major advertisers. The idea can be thought of as "a day in the life of" thousands of consumers. The project uses Arbitron's personal people meters to learn about media habits and exposure; then it follows up with Nielsen's Homescan consumer panel. The panel uses scanner data to monitor participants' purchases of all scanned consumer goods. (*Note:* We will describe Information Resources' scanner-based panel in detail later in the chapter.) In addition, Project Apollo will conduct print (e.g., magazines and newspapers) readership studies and purchase behavior and attitude studies across a variety of industries and product categories. The object of Project Apollo is to accomplish marketing's holy grail, that is, how did the marketing mix influence the purchase of specific goods and services.[28]

To illustrate how Apollo works, data was collected through the portable people meter and Homescan on how effective a cable-TV ad campaign for an unidentified painkiller was in reaching the painkiller's target audience of 25- to 54-year-olds. After monitoring which media outlets the target audience was exposed to, the study concluded that the painkiller would reach 16 percent more of its target audience by making certain changes to its ad program.

The changes in the painkiller ad program were based on specific findings about the participants' shopping and TV viewing habits. With the data from Project Apollo, the maker of the painkiller learned which ads on the cable networks and what times of the day would reach more buyers.

It's easier, after all, to get existing buyers to purchase more of a brand than to enlist a new buyer for the brand. A consumer who already uses the brand for headaches can be reminded that it works for muscle aches, too.[29]

Scanner-Based Research

Two electronic monitoring tools comprise the basic scanner-based research system: television meters and laser scanners, which "read" the UPC codes on products and produce instantaneous information on sales. Separately, each monitoring device provides marketers with current information on the advertising audience and on sales and inventories of products. Together, television meters and scanners measure the impact of marketing. Has scanner-based research been of much benefit to marketers? The top executive of one manufacturer estimates that one-third to one-half of its gains in profitability in the past several years can be attributed to scanner-based research.[30]

The marriage of scanners, database management, telecommunications, artificial intelligence, and computing gives hope for a "brave new world" of marketing.

The two major scanner-based research suppliers are Information Resources, Incorporated (IRI) and ACNielsen; each has about half the market. So that you can gain an appreciation of scanner-based research, we will discuss the product offerings of IRI in detail.[31]

BehaviorScan   IRI is the founder of scanner-based research and the developer of **BehaviorScan,** which has a household panel in each of five markets. The BehaviorScan markets are geographically dispersed cities: Pittsfield, Massachusetts; Eau Claire, Wisconsin; Cedar Rapids, Iowa; Grand Junction, Colorado; and Midland, Texas (see Exhibit 7.4).

> **BehaviorScan**
> Scanner-based research system that can manipulate the marketing mix for household panels in geographically dispersed markets and then electronically track consumer purchases.

Exhibit 7.4

BehaviorScan Market Map

Source: www.infores.com

◼ Converter (Panel HH) Targetable TV
▲ Checkerboard (Cable Zone) Targetable TV

Panel members shop with an ID card, which is presented at check-outs in supermarkets, drugstores, and mass merchandisers. This card allows IRI to electronically track each household's purchases, item by item, over time. For nonparticipating retailers, panel members use a hand-held scanner at home to record their purchases. With such a measure of household purchasing, it is possible to analyze real changes in consumer buying behavior associated with manipulating marketing variables (such as TV advertising or consumer promotions) or introducing a new product.

For strategic tests of alternative marketing plans, the BehaviorScan household panels are split into two or more subgroups, balanced on past purchasing, demographics, and stores shopped. A test commercial can be broadcast over the cable network to one group of households, while the other group gets a control ad, without the consumer even realizing that the commercial is only a test ad. Alternatively, three different test ads per city can be used simultaneously to see which ad generates the greatest demand. This feature makes BehaviorScan a most effective means of evaluating changes in advertising. In each market, IRI maintains permanent warehouse facilities and staff to control distribution, price, and promotions. Competitive activity is monitored, and a record of pricing, displays, and features permits an assessment of the responsiveness to a brand promotion.

For testing consumer promotions such as coupons, product samples, and refund offers, balanced panel subsamples are again created within each market. Then, through direct mail or split newspaper-route targeting, a different treatment is delivered to each group. Both sales and profits are analyzed.

In-store variables may also be tested. Within the markets, split groups of stores are used to read the effect on sales of a change in packaging, shelf placement, or pricing. Tests are analyzed primarily on a store movement basis, but purchasing by panel shoppers in the test and control stores can also be analyzed. With the BehaviorScan system, it is possible to evaluate alternative advertising levels while simultaneously varying in-store prices or consumer promotions, thereby testing a completely integrated marketing plan.

In summary, BehaviorScan allows marketing managers to answer critical marketing questions such as the following:

- What is the impact of our new advertising program?
- How can we minimize incremental media costs?
- What happens to sales if we change the ad frequency or day part?
- How many units of our new product will we sell in a year?
- How many units will be cannibalized from existing products by the new product?
- What is the effectiveness of each marketing mix element in driving trial and repeat purchasing?
- What is the impact of an alternative marketing program on results?

Frito-Lay senior vice president Dwight Riskey said, "BehaviorScan is a critical component of Frito-Lay's go-to-market strategy for a couple of reasons. First, it gives us absolutely the most accurate read on the sales potential of a new product, and a well-rounded view of consumer response to all elements of the marketing mix. Second, BehaviorScan TV ad testing enables us to significantly increase our return on our advertising investment. We definitely plan to continue using BehaviorScan."[32]

InfoScan   **InfoScan Custom Store Tracking** provides the retail sales and causal information essential to developing, implementing, and evaluating marketing programs. InfoScan is based on all-store, census scanner data, which are collected weekly from more than 70,000 supermarkets, drugstores, and mass merchandiser outlets across the United States. InfoScan gives manufacturers and retailers access to detailed information on sales, share, distribution, pricing, and promotion for hundreds of product categories. InfoScan Custom Store Tracking can help marketing managers:

> **InfoScan Custom Store Tracking**
> Scanner-based data system that collects information on consumer packaged goods.

- Understand and track categories, products, and competitive factors for effective marketing and sales planning.
- Identify opportunities for new product development and marketing mix improvements for existing products.
- Monitor and evaluate promotions and new product launches and execute timely modifications to plans.
- Implement sales and broker compensation programs based on measurable objectives.
- Increase sales force efficiency by allocating resources to critical sales drivers and local opportunities.
- Maximize return on trade promotion spending by evaluating compliance and response at the retail level.
- Strengthen manufacturer/retailer relationships by developing and implementing category management programs that maximize joint profitability.[33]

InfoScan Syndicated Store Tracking is a common source of retail scanner-based information for manufacturers, retailers, and brokers. In addition, financial analysts, trade publications, and the business media use InfoScan Syndicated Store Tracking to gain consumer packaged goods (CPG) industry understanding. InfoScan Syndicated Store Tracking provides the tools needed to develop targeted marketing strategies based on product performance, distribution, and promotion responsiveness across a wide range of geographical areas. InfoScan Syndicated Store Tracking provides:

- ☐ 266 InfoScan categories reflecting a standard view of the CPG industry.
- ☐ Product details including category, type (segment) parent company, manufacturer, brand, and UPC.
- ☐ Customized product groupings via IRI's software tools.
- ☐ Data on supermarkets, drugstores, mass merchandisers, and a three-outlet combination; eight IRI regions per outlet; 64 supermarket outlet markets; census and sample key accounts; and drugstore census accounts.
- ☐ A comprehensive list of retail measures covering sales, share, distribution, pricing, and promotion activities.
- ☐ Annual, quarterly, monthly, and weekly time periods, many of which cover the last five calendar years. Year-ago comparisons are also available for many time periods.
- ☐ Monthly database updates.
- ☐ User access via IRI's timeshare environment using Oracle Sales Analyzer, the Internet via ReviewNet, or data delivery on CD-ROM, in spreadsheet format or on hard copy.
- ☐ Data available on a subscription or one-time basis.[34]

Observation Research on the Internet

Clickstream data represent the idiosyncratic steps and behaviors of consumers on their way to information and entertainment as well as online purchase decisions. Assume a firm has clickstream data from its current customers. Clickstream data initially are collected in Web logs. Different methods exist for collecting clickstream data (for example, cookies, tracking software, proxy servers), and pulling and manipulating this online data is typically a large undertaking that is unique to every site. Depending on the website, a researcher can capture codes about clicks, rotating offers, banners, page sequences, duration, and product configuration.

The first question an online marketer might ask is, "How many people visited my site in a month?" Even this question is subject to controversy. For example, if one asked, "How many people visited Yahoo in June 2007?" you would not get a unified answer. About 133 million in the United States, says ComScore, a Web measurement company. No, says its chief rival, Nielsen//NetRatings, it was 108 million. The difference—25 million people—is hardly a rounding error. It's larger than the population of Texas.[35]

And that's the problem. The Internet bills itself as the most accountable ad medium in history. But it's not as precise as it seems, and companies want proof that the $20 billion they spent in 2007 to advertise online was worth it.

The established players, ComScore and Nielsen//NetRatings, which together hold the majority of the market, know they have a problem. They support the idea of a public audit. But they stand by the current method, in which global panels of thousands of volunteers agree to download tracking software.

Even so, new public ComScore has announced a half-dozen features to better track Web behavior. Among the improvements are measuring widgets, counting video downloads, and expanding their search categories to include sites like Amazon and eBay. Nielsen//NetRatings is also raising its game. The company, which counts Time Inc. (*Fortune*'s publisher) among its clients, recently began measuring how much time consumers spend on sites. It also bought Telephia, which tracks Web behavior on cell phones.[36]

Just 2 percent of the Web surfers who are exposed to an ad will click on them—(and even fewer will actually make a transaction).[37] Fetchback is a firm that engages in ad retargeting. Fetchback works like this: Say you find yourself on the website of Discover Card, a Fetchback client. After a few seconds, you get bored and move on. Later in the day, while you're browsing Amazon.com for the latest Harry Potter book, an ad for Discover Card pops up—encouraging you to visit the company's site for a special deal. You decide not to. The next day, you're sifting through your LinkedIn page, and another ad for Discover Card appears—this time offering you a $20,000 limit on your next card if you click now. That does the trick. You give in and click.

Retargeted advertising converts people who are already interested—you were visiting the Discover Card site for a reason, right?—into buyers.[38]

Predictive Customer Intelligence

The clickstream data can be a vital foundation of a predictive customer intelligence system. **Predictive customer intelligence** involves modeling surfing patterns along with demographic and psychographic data to predict consumer behavior. Two components are needed to build a predictive customer intelligence system. The first required component involves the way the website is designed. Website design should be matched up with the buying process (for example, need recognition, searching, comparing, purchasing, after-sales service), and the Web pages should be categorized accordingly.

The second required component involves the modeling of clickstream and other customer data. The first objective is to increase understanding of the online customer base and use this to customize the website and improve the website experience. A second objective of this modeling stage is to develop predictive models. This entails predicting who are the most likely purchasers and who will respond best to which marketing action. By relating purchasing data to the sequences of the clickstream, as well as to the additional information included on the customer, it's possible to derive models to help predict future visits and help predict what customers are most likely to do during these future visits. This also can help determine whether the clicker's path through the website indicates that the visit is a research visit, support-seeking visit, or a purchasing visit. If it is a purchasing visit, this data can indicate when, what, and how much the customer is likely to buy.

As the most visited destination on the Web, Yahoo has an estimated 131 million monthly unique visitors to its sites. By dropping cookie files onto every Web browser that calls up one of its sites, Yahoo has amassed a staggering amount of data about its users. Yahoo gathers 12 terabytes of user information that flow into Yahoo's servers every day, more than the entire inventory of the Library of Congress. The data is crunched, blended with information about what people do on Yahoo's search engine, and fed into models that predict consumer behavior.

Fayyad, a former rocket scientist at NASA's Jet Propulsion Lab, is in charge of Yahoo's predictive intelligence. A recent experiment has led him to an important conclusion: What you do on the Web reveals far more about you than what you type into a search box. Fayyad ran a test with brokerage Harris Direct (now part of E-Trade) to gauge how display ads affect brand awareness. Using Yahoo visitors as guinea pigs, Fayyad served some of them Harris Direct ads, and others house ads, and followed their behavior. The data that came back was anything but subtle: Those who saw the brokerage ads were 160 percent more likely to search in that category over the next three weeks, typing in keywords like "online brokerages." And they overwhelmingly clicked on a text ad for Harris Direct when it popped up in the paid research results. How can search advertising compete with that? Says Fayyad, "Search is broken in some ways, because the advertiser only gets one shot."[39]

> **predictive customer intelligence**
> Modeling surfing patterns along with demographic and psychographic data to predict consumer behavior.

Tacoda, purchased by AOL, is one of the largest predictive intelligence firms in the world with partnerships with over 4,000 Web sites and reaching 122 million unique visitors a month. Tacoda worked with Pepsi when it brought out Aquafina Alive, a vitamin-enhanced water. Tacoda identified health-conscious people by looking at traffic to sites about healthy lifestyles over a month-long period. Then Pepsi arranged to place Aquafina Alive ads on some of the Web sites affiliated with Tacoda so that the ads would pop up whenever these health-conscious consumers visited.

Pepsi recorded a threefold increase in the number of people clicking on its Aquafina Alive ads compared with previous campaigns. "We've never been able to get to this level of granularity," says John Vail, director of the interactive marketing group at Pepsi-Cola North America.[40]

Revcube, a recent start-up consisting of math PhDs, Web application designers, and, yes, rocket scientists, developed a system that looks at 5,000 attributes in ads from across the Web—everything from color to keywords to image sizes. Identifying surfers by their IP addresses, it grabs details such as gender, age, and political affiliation from behavioral networks like Tacoda and Revenue Science and data services like Quantcast. These profiles are then analyzed by Revcube's proprietary system, allowing the firm to predict which text ad, banner ad, or marketing e-mail is most likely to make each potential new customer click.

With client LiveCareer, for example, Revcube designed about 100 different banner and text ads and 40 landing pages (where customers are sent after clicking on an ad) and tested them against thousands of demographic and environmental attributes. In this case, nothing mattered as much as the day of the week. A green banner and a photo of a woman were most popular on Sunday; a man on a blue background worked best on Monday. Overall, Revcube's campaign more than doubled LiveCareer's revenue.[41]

DoubleClick DoubleClick, purchased by Google, is the largest company tracking clickstreams on the Internet. Clicks are only the most basic way to measure online marketing programs. The following are among the metrics sophisticated advertisers are now using to measure the effectiveness of their online campaigns:

- ☐ post-click conversions
- ☐ cost per conversion
- ☐ unique reach of ads delivered
- ☐ average frequency of exposures
- ☐ frequency-to-conversion ratio
- ☐ ad exposure time (rich media)
- ☐ ad interaction rate (rich media)
- ☐ brand impact lift versus control ad (including ad recall, brand awareness, message association, brand favorability, purchase intent)
- ☐ view-through rate (i.e., delayed visits to advertiser's site without a direct ad click-through)
- ☐ Web page eye tracking
- ☐ offline sales lift[42]

Two of the most important developments in online advertising in the past decade also play directly to the Internet's strength of measurability: rich media and search engine advertising.

The term *rich media* describes a variety of online advertising media experiences, including high-quality animation, streaming audio and video, and software-like features that can be embedded in relatively small ad files, such as games, registration forms, and detailed marketing information. A user can explore all of those features in the ad unit without ever leaving the content page on which the ad appears.

DoubleClick's Motif platform can report, for example, the total time the ad is displayed on the user's page, any interactions the reader makes with her mouse over the ad, and the total time she spends exploring features of the ad. Rich media has risen steadily in popularity with online advertisers, now accounting for over 35 percent of all ad impressions.[43]

Observation Research and Virtual Shopping

Advances in computer technology have enabled researchers to simulate an actual retail store environment on a computer screen. Depending on the type of simulation, a shopper can "pick up" a package by touching its image on the monitor and rotate it to examine all sides. Like buying on most online retailers, the shopper touches the shopping cart to add an item to the basket. During the shopping process, the computer unobtrusively records the amount of time the consumer spends shopping in each product category, the time the consumer spends examining each side of a package, the quantity of product the consumer purchases, and the order in which items are purchased.

Computer-simulated environments like this one offer a number of advantages over older research methods. First, unlike focus groups, concept tests, and other laboratory approaches, the virtual store duplicates the distracting clutter of an actual market. Consumers can shop in an environment with a realistic level of complexity and variety. Second, researchers can set up and alter the tests very quickly. Once images of the product are scanned into the computer, the researcher can make changes in the assortment of brands, product packaging, pricing, promotions, and shelf space within minutes. Data collection is also fast and error-free because the information generated by the purchase is automatically tabulated and stored by the computer. Third, production costs are low because displays are created electronically. Once the hardware and software are in place, the cost of a test is largely a function of the number of respondents, who generally are given a small incentive to participate. Fourth, the simulation has a high degree of flexibility. It can be used to test entirely new marketing concepts or to fine-tune existing programs. The simulation also makes it possible to eliminate much of the noise that exists in field experiments.[44]

Kimberly-Clark has refined the virtual shopping experience even more. Located in Appleton, Wisconsin, the firm's virtual testing lab has a woman standing in a room surrounded by three screens showing a store aisle, a retina-tracking device recording her every glance.

Asked by a Kimberly-Clark researcher to find a "big box" of Huggies Natural Fit diapers in size three, the woman pushed forward on a handle like that of a shopping cart, and the video simulated her progress down the aisle. Spotting Huggies' red packages, she turned the handle to the right to face a dizzying array of diapers. After pushing a button to get a kneeling view of the shelves, she reached forward and tapped the screen to put the box she wanted in her virtual cart.

Kimberly-Clark hopes these virtual shopping aisles will provide better understanding of consumer behavior and make the testing of new products faster, more convenient, and more precise.[45]

Kimberly-Clark's lab also features a U-shaped floor-to-ceiling screen that re-creates in vivid detail interiors of the big retailers that sell the company's products—a tool that the company will use in presentations to executives in bids to win shelf space. A separate area is reserved for real replicas of store interiors, which can be customized to match the flooring, light fixtures, and shelves of retailers such as Target Corp. and Wal-Mart Stores, Inc.[46]

Kimberly-Clark says its studio allows researchers and designers to get a fast read on new product designs and displays without having to stage real-life tests in the early stages of development. Doing the research in a windowless basement, rather than an actual test market, also avoids tipping off competitors early in the development process.

"We're trying to test ideas faster, cheaper, and better," says Ramin Eivaz, a vice president at Kimberly-Clark focusing on strategy. Formerly, new product testing typically took eight months to two years. Now, that time is cut in half, he says. Projects that test well with the virtual-reality tools will be fast-tracked to real-store trials, Mr. Eivaz says.[47]

Virtual shopping research is growing rapidly as companies such as Frito-Lay, Goodyear, Procter & Gamble, General Mills, and Coca-Cola realize the benefits from this type of observation research. About 40,000 new consumer package goods are introduced in the United States each year.[48] All are vying for very limited retail shelf space. Any process, such as virtual shopping, that can speed product development time and lower costs is always welcomed by manufacturers.

To sell retailers on new products, manufacturers are revealing more about their product pipelines to drum up interest early on. Over the past several months, Kimberly-Clark says it has brought in executives from major chains, including Target, Wal-Mart, and Kroger, to see the Appleton facility. Kimberly-Clark uses the data from its virtual-reality tests with consumers to tout the performance of products in development.

"It no longer works to show up on a retailer's doorstop with your new product and say, 'Isn't this pretty?'" Mr. Eivaz says. "We need to be an indispensable partner to our retailers and show we can do more for them."[49]

SUMMARY

Observation research is the systematic process of recording patterns of occurrences or behaviors without questioning or normally communicating with the people involved. For observation to be used successfully, the needed information must be observable and the behavior of interest must be repetitive, frequent, or in some manner predictable. The behavior of interest also should be of a relatively short duration. There are four dimensions along which observation approaches vary: (1) natural versus contrived situations, (2) open versus disguised observation, (3) human versus machine observers, and (4) direct versus indirect observation.

The biggest advantage of observation research is that researchers can see what people actually do rather than having to rely on what they say they did, thereby avoiding many biasing factors. Also, some forms of data are more quickly and accurately gathered by observation. The primary disadvantage of this type of research is that the researcher learns nothing about motives, attitudes, intentions, or feelings.

People watching people or objects can take the form of ethnographic research, mystery shopping, one-way mirror observations (for example, child psychologists might watch children play with toys), shopper pattern and behavior studies, and audits.

Machine observation may involve traffic counters, physiological measurement devices, opinion and behavior measurement devices, or scanners. The use of scanners in carefully controlled experimental settings enables the marketing researcher to accurately and objectively measure the direct causal relationship between different kinds of marketing efforts and actual sales. The leaders in scanner-based research are Information Resources, Incorporated and ACNielsen.

Observation research on the Internet originally focused on tracking the surfing patterns of Internet users. A major growth area is predictive customer intelligence. It involves modeling surfing patterns along with demographic and psychographic data to predict consumer behavior. The goal is to create more effective online advertising.

Virtual shopping using advanced computer technology to create a simulated shopping environment is a rapidly growing form of observation research. It reduces the cost and time it takes to bring new products to the market.

KEY TERMS & DEFINITIONS

observation research Systematic process of recording patterns of occurrences or behaviors without normally communicating with the people involved.

open observation Process of monitoring people who know they are being watched.

disguised observation Process of monitoring people who do not know they are being watched.

garbologists Researchers who sort through people's garbage to analyze household consumption patterns.

ethnographic research Study of human behavior in its natural context, involving observation of behavior and physical setting.

mystery shoppers People who pose as consumers and shop at a company's own stores or those of its competitors to collect data about customer–employee interactions and to gather observational data; they may also compare prices, displays, and the like.

one-way mirror observation Practice of watching behaviors or activities from behind a one-way mirror.

audit Examination and verification of the sales of a product.

traffic counters Machines used to measure vehicular flow over a particular stretch of roadway.

electroencephalograph (EEG) Machine that measures electrical pulses on the scalp and generates a record of electrical activity in the brain.

galvanic skin response (GSR) Change in the electric resistance of the skin associated with activation responses; also called *electrodermal response*.

People Reader Machine that simultaneously records the respondent's reading material and eye reactions.

portable people meter Device worn by people that measures the radio and TV programming to which the participant was exposed during the day.

BehaviorScan Scanner-based research system that can manipulate the marketing mix for household panels in geographically dispersed markets and then electronically track consumer purchases.

InfoScan Custom Store Tracking Scanner-based data system that collects information on consumer packaged goods.

predictive customer intelligence Modeling surfing patterns along with demographic and psychographic data to predict consumer behavior.

QUESTIONS FOR REVIEW & CRITICAL THINKING

1. You are charged with the responsibility of determining whether men are brand conscious when shopping for racquetball equipment. Outline an observation research procedure for making that determination.

2. Fisher-Price has asked you to develop a research procedure for determining which of its prototype toys is most appealing to 4- and 5-year-olds. Suggest a methodology for making this determination.

3. What are the biggest drawbacks of observation research?

4. Compare the advantages and disadvantages of observation research with those of survey research.

5. It has been said that "people buy things not for what they will do, but for what they mean." Discuss this statement in relation to observation research.

6. You are a manufacturer of a premium brand of ice cream. You want to know more about your market share, competitors' pricing, and the types of outlets where your product is selling best. What kind of observation research data would you purchase? Why?

7. How might a mystery shopper be valuable to the following organizations?
   a. JetBlue Airlines
   b. Macy's Department Store
   c. H&R Block

8. Use ethnographic research to evaluate the dining experience at your student center. What did you learn?

9. Why has Project Apollo been seen as "the ultimate answer" for marketing researchers? Do you see any disadvantages of this methodology?

10. Describe how clickstream research can benefit an online retailer.

11. Do you think that virtual shopping will replace other forms of marketing research? Why or why not?

(Team Exercise) 12. Divide the class into teams of five. Each team should select a different retailer (services are okay for mystery shopping). Two members of the team should prepare a list of 10 to 15 questions to be answered. A sample of questions for an Eye Care Clinic are shown below. The remaining three members of the team should become mystery shoppers with the goal of answering the questions created by the team. After the shopping is complete, the team should combine their findings and make a report to the class.

Sample Mystery Shopping Questions for an Eye Care Clinic

1. Was the phone answered within three rings?
2. How long did you have to wait for an appointment?
3. Were you given clear directions to the office?
4. Did you receive a new patient packet in the mail?
5. Were signs directing you to the office clear and visible?
6. Did the receptionist greet you when you entered the office?
7. How long did you wait before being taken into a room for the pre-exam?
8. Did all staff members have a name tag on?
9. Was the facility clean?

10. Were your eyes dilated before you saw the doctor?

11. Were exam procedures explained clearly?

12. Were you given an opportunity to ask the doctor questions?

13. Were your questions answered promptly and respectfully?

14. Were you directed to the optical shop after your exam?

15. Were your glasses/contacts ready when promised?

WORKING THE NET

1. Go to *acnielsen.com* and *www.infores.com* and determine what ACNielsen and IRI are saying on the Web about their latest scanner-based research technology.

2. Go to *www.doubleclick.com* and read its latest research findings. Make an oral presentation to your class.

3. Go to *www.mysteryshop.org* to learn more about mystery shopping.

REAL-LIFE RESEARCH • 7.1

A Glad Trash Bag Breakthrough

Previous innovation in the $1.03 billion trash bag category has focused on the act of tieing: First there was the twist tie, then there were plastic ties, then bags with longer flaps that you could tie and, finally, the drawstring. Other enhancements, such as bags that absorbed or limited smells, haven't sparked much consumer interest. And while companies have made stronger bags that could carry larger loads, "there hadn't been much focus on tensile strength," said Ken Harris of Cannondale Associates, Evanston, Illinois.

The problem was that, as bags got stronger and thicker, they also got less flexible and more likely to tear. And that is where Glad found its, pardon the phrase, opening.

Glad Products (a subsidiary of Clorox, Oakland, California) launched ForceFlex, a bag that stretches to accommodate the bulky items that consumers tend to throw away. The *New York Times* called ForceFlex "the Mercedes of trash bags." Subsequent sales confirmed that Glad had a winner on its hands.

With a price tag of $6.50–$7.99 for a 28-count with drawstring (versus $4.50–$6.00 for the regular product), ForceFlex cleaned up with $108.4 million in sales for the year ended August 13, posting a 38.9 percent increase in unit sales in the same period, per Information Resources. ForceFlex's performance was no small marketing feat, given that consumers don't usually contemplate their trash bags longer than it takes to haul out the garbage. "If you are actually spending time with your trash, there's something wrong," said Audy Baack, marketing manager for Glad Trash.

To avoid a "trash disaster" (i.e., a broken bag), companies had made bags that were thicker, heavier, and stronger, said Alan Savicki, Glad's group manager for trash business R&D. "They needed to be, because the trash composition was heavily laden with big glass bottles and cardboard boxes. So we're saying we ought to look at the design of our bag," said Savicki. "Is it meeting today's consumer needs?"

Glad went straight to the source for answers by conducting ethnographic studies, which Baack said was every bit as odd as it sounds. "You go to peoples' homes and say, 'Can I ask you about your trash?' and you get some funny looks."

Nevertheless, researchers found that consumers were putting more items into their trash bags that were leaky, including food leftovers, or were big but light, such as pizza boxes and hangers. Because those latter objects tend to have sharp points and edges, they easily punctured the bags—creating a sticky situation. Armed with enough evidence, Glad turned to a partner with the scientific expertise necessary to implement a new technology.

Enter Procter & Gamble, which owned a 10 percent stake in Glad and was trying to figure out what to do with a new, stretchable plastic it had developed for some of its baby products. "P&G had some interesting ideas it didn't know what to do with," said Baack. "Glad had the marketing and category expertise to turn some of those into [trash bag] products."[50]

Questions

1. How else might the decision-making information have been gathered besides ethnographics?
2. What are the disadvantages to Glad if they only used ethnographics?
3. Could this research have been done using virtual reality? Why or why not?
4. Could the location of the ethnographic research influence the research outcome? Explain.

Michael Poehlman/Getty Images

PRIMARY DATA COLLECTION: EXPERIMENTATION AND TEST MARKETS

LEARNING OBJECTIVES

1.	To understand the nature of experiments.
2.	To gain insight into requirements for proving causation.
3.	To learn about the experimental setting.
4.	To examine experimental validity.
5.	To learn the limitations of experimentation in marketing research.
6.	To compare types of experimental designs.
7.	To gain insight into test marketing.

Texas Star is the oldest brewing company in Texas or, at least, the oldest beer brand in Texas. During the 1980s, the company went through bankruptcy because of its inability to compete with the big national beer brands. In the 1990s, a group of investors purchased the brand name from the bankruptcy court and reincarnated it as a microbrewery with retail locations offering a brew pub atmosphere and casual dining. In addition, Texas Star distributed its products through specialty liquor stores that offer an extensive assortment of specialty beers, including imported and microbrewery beers. The company currently has 18 brew pub locations and distribution in 243 liquor stores across Texas.

The company has experienced solid growth and financial performance over its 25-year history. However, the competitive environment remains tough with the big national brands at one end of the spectrum and other microbreweries and brew pubs at the other end. It is critical that Texas Star spend its limited marketing budget in the most efficient manner to drive business to its brew pubs and the sale of its products through liquor stores.

The management team at Texas Star has been divided in regard to the best marketing strategy for the company. One contingent wants to pursue a strategy based on a low price, relative to imports and other microbrews. The other group wants to focus on enhancing the image of Texas Star with a focus on its long history in the state of Texas and the artisanal nature of its brewing process. The difference of opinion between the two factions has become heated and somewhat divisive. Furthermore, time is running out to get their marketing strategy in place for the coming year.

Toby Geren, director of marketing, knows that it is important to make the right decision and to break the deadlock quickly so that the company can move on with its plans and business development activities. He wants to design a test that will settle the issue, once and for all, in a scientific manner. Texas Star has always focused on college markets across the state with a brew pub in the vicinity of every major college in Texas. Toby's research plan calls for testing the price-oriented campaign in one market and the image-oriented campaign in another. The impact on sales in the respective markets will indicate the effectiveness of the two approaches. He faces a number of decisions. First, he is considering using Bryan-College Station and Lubbock as the two test markets. His logic is that they are both somewhat isolated markets and what Texas Star does in these markets will not likely spill over into other areas. Second, there is the question of how long to run the test. Finally, it is necessary to sort out what happens in the two test markets from the general trend for Texas Star in the rest of the state.

Chapter 8 explores the use of experimental designs in marketing research and speaks to all these issues.

What Is an Experiment?

Research based on experimentation is fundamentally different from research based on surveys or observation.[1] In the case of both survey and observation research, the researcher is, in essence, a passive assembler of data. The researcher asks people questions or observes what they do. In experimental research, the situation is very different: the researcher becomes an active participant in the process.

In concept, an **experiment** is straightforward. The researcher changes or manipulates one thing (called an *experimental, treatment, independent,* or *explanatory variable*) to observe the effect on something else (referred to as a *dependent variable*). In marketing experiments, the dependent variable is frequently some measure of sales, such as total sales, market share, or the like; experimental variables are typically marketing mix variables, such as price, amount or type of advertising, and changes in product features.

> **experiment**
> Research approach in which one variable is manipulated and the effect on another variable is observed.

Demonstrating Causation

> **causal research**
> Research designed to determine whether a change in one variable likely caused an observed change in another.

Experimental research is often referred to as **causal** (not casual) **research** because it is the only type of research that has the potential to demonstrate that a change in one variable *causes* some predictable change in another variable. To demonstrate causation (that *A* likely caused *B*), one must be able to show three things:

1. Concomitant variation (correlation)
2. Appropriate time order of occurrence
3. Elimination of other possible causal factors

Please note that we are using the terms *causation* and *causality* in the scientific sense.[2] The scientific view of causation is quite different from the popular view, which often implies that there is a single cause of an event. For example, when someone says in everyday conversation that *X* is the cause of some observed change in *Y*, he or she generally means that *X* is the only cause of the observed change in *Y*. But the scientific view holds that *X* is only one of a number of possible determining conditions that caused the observed change in *Y*.

In addition, the everyday view of causality implies a completely deterministic relationship, while the scientific view implies a probabilistic relationship. The popular view is that if *X* is the cause of *Y*, then *X* must always lead to *Y*. The scientific view holds that *X* can be a cause of *Y* if the presence of *X* makes the occurrence of *Y* more probable, or likely.

Finally, the scientific view holds that one can never definitively prove that *X* is a cause of *Y* but only infer that a relationship exists. In other words, causal relationships are always inferred and never demonstrated conclusively beyond a shadow of a doubt. Three types of evidence—concomitant variation, appropriate time order of occurrence, and elimination of other possible causal factors—are used to infer causal relationships.

Concomitant Variation

> **concomitant variation**
> Statistical relationship between two variables.

To provide evidence that a change in *A* caused a particular change in *B*, one must first show that there is **concomitant variation**, or correlation, between *A* and *B*; in other words, *A* and *B* must vary together in some predictable fashion. This might be a *positive* or an *inverse* relationship. Two variables that might be related in a positive manner are advertising and sales. They would be positively related if sales increased by some predictable amount when advertising increased by a certain amount. Two variables that might be related in an inverse manner are price and sales. They would be inversely (negatively) related if sales increased when price decreased and decreased when price increased. The researcher can test for the existence and direction of statistical relationships by means of a number of statistical procedures, including chi-square analysis, correlation analysis, regression analysis, and analysis of variance to mention a few. All of these statistical procedures are discussed later in the text (chi-square, correlation analysis, regression analysis, and analysis of variance in Chapter 14).

However, concomitant variation by itself does not prove causation. Simply because two variables happen to vary together in some predictable fashion does not prove that one causes the other. For example, suppose you found a high degree of correlation between sales of a product in the United States and the GDP (gross domestic product) of Germany. This might be true simply because both variables happened to be increasing at a similar rate. Further examination and consideration might show that there is no true link between the two variables. To infer causation, you must be able to show correlation—but correlation alone is not proof of causation.

Appropriate Time Order of Occurrence

The second requirement for demonstrating that a causal relationship likely exists between two variables is showing that there is an **appropriate time order of occurrence.** To demonstrate that A caused B, one must be able to show that A occurred before B occurred. For example, to demonstrate that a price change had an effect on sales, you must be able to show that the price change occurred before the change in sales was observed. However, showing that A and B vary concomitantly and that A occurred before B still does not provide evidence strong enough to permit one to conclude that A is the likely cause of an observed change in B.

> ▷ **appropriate time order of occurrence**
> Change in an independent variable occurred before an observed change in the dependent variable.

Elimination of Other Possible Causal Factors

The most difficult thing to demonstrate in marketing experiments is that the change in B was not caused by some factor other than A. For example, suppose a company increased its advertising expenditures and observed an increase in the sales of its product. Correlation and appropriate time order of occurrence are present. But has a likely causal relationship been demonstrated? The answer is "no." It is possible that the observed change in sales is due to some factor other than the increase in advertising. For example, at the same time advertising expenditures were increased, a major competitor may have decreased advertising expenditures, or increased price, or pulled out of the market. Even if the competitive environment did not change, one or a combination of other factors may have influenced sales. For example, the economy in the area might have received a major boost for some reason that has nothing to do with the experiment. For any of these reasons or many others, the observed increase in sales might have been caused by some factor or combination of factors other than or in addition to the increase in advertising expenditures. Much of the discussion in this chapter is related to designing experiments so as to eliminate or adjust for the effects of other possible causal factors.

> ▷ **elimination of other possible causal factors**
> Hard to prove that something else did not cause change in B.

Experimental Setting

Experiments can be conducted in a laboratory or a field setting.[3] Most experiments in the physical sciences are conducted in a laboratory setting; many marketing experiments are field experiments.

Laboratory Experiments

Laboratory experiments provide a number of important advantages.[4] The major advantage of conducting experiments in a laboratory is the ability to control extraneous causal factors—temperature, light, humidity, and so on—and focus on the effect of a change in A on B. In the lab, the researcher can effectively deal with the third element of proving causation (elimination of other possible causal factors) and focus on the first two elements (concomitant variation and appropriate time order of occurrence). This additional control strengthens the researcher's ability to infer that an observed change in the dependent variable was caused by a change in the experimental, or treatment, variable. As a result, laboratory experiments are viewed as having greater internal validity (discussed in greater detail in the next section). On the other hand, the controlled and possibly sterile environment of the laboratory may not be a good analog of the marketplace. For this reason, the findings of laboratory experiments sometimes do not hold up when transferred to the marketplace. Therefore, laboratory experiments are seen as having greater problems with external validity (see the next section). However, laboratory experiments are probably being used to a greater extent in marketing research today than in the past because of their many advantages.

> ▷ **laboratory experiments**
> Experiments conducted in a controlled setting.

Field Experiments

> **field experiments**
> Tests conducted outside the laboratory in an actual environment, such as a marketplace.

Field experiments are conducted outside the laboratory in an actual market environment. Test markets, discussed later in this chapter, are a frequently used type of field experiment. Field experiments solve the problem of the realism of the environment but open up a whole new set of problems. The major problem is that in the field the researcher cannot control all the spurious factors that might influence the dependent variable, such as the actions of competitors, the weather, the economy, societal trends, and the political climate. Therefore, field experiments have more problems related to internal validity, whereas lab experiments have more problems related to external validity.

Experimental Validity

Validity is defined as the degree to which an experiment actually measures what the researcher was trying to measure (see Chapter 9). The validity of a measure depends on the extent to which the measure is free from both systematic and random error. Two specific kinds of validity are relevant to experimentation: internal validity and external validity.

> **internal validity**
> Extent to which competing explanations for the experimental results observed can be ruled out.

Internal validity refers to the extent to which competing explanations for the experimental results observed can be ruled out. If the researcher can show that the experimental, or treatment, variable actually produced the differences observed in the dependent variable, then the experiment can be said to be internally valid. This kind of validity requires evidence demonstrating that variation in the dependent variable was caused by exposure to the treatment variable and not other possible causal factors.

> **external validity**
> Extent to which causal relationships measured in an experiment can be generalized to outside persons, settings, and times.

External validity refers to the extent to which the causal relationships measured in an experiment can be generalized to outside persons, settings, and times.[5] The issue here is how representative the subjects and the setting used in the experiment are of other populations and settings to which the researcher would like to project the results. As noted earlier, field experiments offer a higher degree of external validity and a lower degree of internal validity than do laboratory experiments. See the following Practicing Marketing Research feature.

PRACTICING MARKETING RESEARCH

Know Your Potential Customers, Psychologically Speaking

Put aside demographics; a better way to know test market customers in advance might be psychographics, based on real-life psychological and lifestyle portraits. Researchers at Wayne State University in Detroit, Michigan, used a random sample of 1,000 applicants for various bank services to come up with what they thought would

be a "superior predictor" of market behavior, combining the benefits of demographics with "the richness and dimensionality of psychological characteristics" of target customers. Product-specific psychological profiles, they report, increase marketers' ability to predict customer behavior by getting a more refined analysis of its people makeup.

Out of 1,000 people polled, 350 filled out the researchers' special questionnaires, which queried respondents on standard demographic variables and 53 psychographic items. The questions were presented in 10 categories, such as price consciousness, dynamic leadership, credit use, and innovation, with typical questions such as: "I usually shop a lot for 'specials.'" Or "I often try new brands before my friends and neighbors do." The results were calculated using discriminant analysis to show how "relatively stable" consumer characteristics (the psychographics) were linked to and thereby predictive of service usage, in this case, bank credit cards. These results then gave marketers solid data on *exactly who* the users of the intended services are and how best to service them.

The researchers discovered that lifestyle variables, culled from the 53 psychographic inventory questions, proved to be excellent predictors of user patterns. In all, 55 to 56 percent of credit card users were correctly classified and predicted this way. Heavy credit card users, contrasted with light and medium users, scored highest in the categories of fashion consciousness, income level,

dynamic leadership, and financial satisfaction; second lowest in community mindedness; and lowest in price consciousness. In summary, the researchers found that heavy credit card users had much higher incomes and self-confidence levels than people who used their cards less.[6]

Questions

1. In developing an experimental design and identifying key variables to manipulate, how could you take maximum advantage from the fact that heavy credit card users are not concerned with price?

2. Identify several factors among heavy credit card users that contradict the psychographic findings and reduce the degree to which they match the profile presented (e.g., the correlation of heavy credit card usage with personal debt and bankruptcy).

Experimental Notation

In our discussion of experiments, we will use a standard system of notation, described as follows:

☐ *X* is used to indicate the exposure of an individual or a group to an experimental treatment. The experimental treatment is the factor whose effects we want to measure and compare. Experimental treatments may be factors such as different prices, package designs, point-of-purchase displays, advertising approaches, or product forms.

☐ *O* (for observation) is used to refer to the process of taking measurements on the test units. *Test units* are individuals, groups of individuals, or entities whose response to the experimental treatments is being tested. Test units might include individual consumers, groups of consumers, retail stores, total markets, or other entities that might be the targets of a firm's marketing program.

☐ Different time periods are represented by the horizontal arrangement of the *X*s and *O*s. For example,

$$O_1 \quad X \quad O_2$$

would describe an experiment in which a preliminary measurement O_1 was taken of one or more test units, then one or more test units were exposed to the experimental variable *X*, and then a measurement O_2 of the test units was taken. The *X*s and *O*s can be arranged vertically to show simultaneous exposure and measurement of different test units. For example, the following design involves two different groups of test units:

$$X_1 \quad O_1$$
$$X_2 \quad O_2$$

The two groups of test units received different experimental treatments at the same time (X_1 and X_2), and then the two groups were measured simultaneously (O_1 and O_2).[7]

Extraneous Variables

In interpreting experimental results, the researcher would like to be able to conclude that the observed response is due to the effect of the experimental variable. However, many things stand in the way of the ability to reach this conclusion. In anticipation of possible problems in interpretation, the researcher needs to design the experiment so as to eliminate as many extraneous factors as possible as causes of the observed effect.

Examples of Extraneous Variables

Examples of extraneous factors or variables that pose a threat to experimental validity are history, maturation, instrument variation, selection bias, mortality, testing effects, and regression to the mean.[8]

history
Intervention, between the beginning and end of an experiment, of outside variables or events that might change the dependent variable.

History **History** refers to the intervention, between the beginning and end of the experiment, of any variable or event—other than those manipulated by the researcher (experimental variables)—that might affect the value of the dependent variable. Early tests of Prego spaghetti sauce by the Campbell Soup Company provide an example of a possible problem with extraneous variables. Campbell executives claim that Ragu, a competing brand, greatly increased its advertising levels and use of cents-off deals during their Prego tests. They believe that this increased marketing activity was designed to get shoppers to stock up on Ragu and make it impossible for Campbell to get an accurate reading of potential sales for its Prego product.

maturation
Changes in subjects occurring during the experiment that are not related to the experiment but which may affect subjects' response to the treatment factor.

Maturation **Maturation** refers to changes in subjects during the course of the experiment that are a function of time; it includes getting older, hungrier, more tired, and the like. Throughout the course of an experiment, the responses of people to a treatment variable may change because of these maturation factors and not because of the treatment variable. The likelihood that maturation will be a serious problem in a particular experiment depends on the length of the experiment. The longer the experiment runs, the more likely it is that maturation will present problems for interpreting the results.

instrument variation
Changes in measurement instruments (e.g., interviewers or observers) that might affect measurements.

Instrument Variation **Instrument variation** refers to any changes in measurement instruments that might explain differences in the measurements taken. It is a serious problem in marketing experiments where people are used as interviewers or observers to measure the dependent variable. If measurements on the same subject are taken by different interviewers or observers at different points in time, differences between measurements may reflect variations in the way the interviewing or observation was done by different interviewers or observers. On the other hand, if the same interviewer or observer is used to take measurements on the same subject over time, differences may reflect the fact that the particular observer or interviewer has become less interested and is doing a sloppier job.

selection bias
Systematic differences between the test group and the control group due to a biased selection process.

Selection Bias The threat to validity posed by **selection bias** is encountered in situations where the experimental or test group is systematically different from the population to which the researcher would like to project the experimental results or from the control group. In projecting the results to a population that is systematically different from the test group, the researcher may get results very different from those obtained in the test because of differences in the makeup of the two groups. Similarly, an observed difference between a test group and an untreated control group (not exposed to the experimental variable) may be due to differences between the two groups and not to the effect of the experimental variable. Researchers can ensure equality of groups through either randomization or matching. *Randomization* involves assigning subjects to test groups and control groups at random. *Matching* involves what the name suggests—making sure that there is a one-to-one match between people or other units in the test and control groups in regard to key characteristics (e.g., age). Specific matching procedures are discussed later in this chapter.

Mortality   **Mortality** refers to the loss of test units during the course of an experiment. It is a problem because there is no easy way to know whether the lost units would have responded to the treatment variable in the same way as those units that remained throughout the entire experiment. An experimental group that was representative of the population or that matched a control group may become nonrepresentative because of the systematic loss of subjects with certain characteristics. For example, in a study of music preferences of the population, if nearly all the subjects under the age of 25 were lost during the course of the experiment, then the researcher would likely get a biased picture of music preferences at the end of the experiment. In this case, the results would lack external validity.

Testing Effects   **Testing effects** result from the fact that the process of experimentation may produce its own effect on the responses observed. For example, measuring attitude toward a product before exposing subjects to an ad may act as a treatment variable, influencing perception of the ad. Testing effects come in two forms:

- *Main testing effects* are the possible effects of earlier observations on later observations. For example, students taking the GMAT for the second time tend to do better than those taking the test for the first time, even though the students have no information about the items they actually missed on the first test. This effect also can be reactive in the sense that responses to the first administration of an attitude test have some actual effect on subjects' attitudes that is reflected in subsequent applications of the same test.

- *Interactive testing effect* is the effect of a prior measurement on a subject's response to a later measurement. For example, if subjects are asked about their awareness of advertising for various products (pre-exposure measurement) and then exposed to advertising for one or more of these products (treatment variable), postmeasurements would likely reflect the joint effect of the pre-exposure and the treatment condition.

Regression to the Mean   **Regression to the mean** refers to the observed tendency of subjects with extreme behavior to move toward the average for that behavior during the course of an experiment. Test units may exhibit extreme behavior because of chance, or they may have been specifically chosen because of their extreme behavior. The researcher might, for example, have chosen people for an experimental group because they were extremely heavy users of a particular product or service. In such situations, their tendency to move toward the average behavior may be interpreted as having been caused by the treatment variable when in fact it has nothing to do with the treatment variable.

Controlling Extraneous Variables

Causal factors that threaten validity must be controlled in some manner to establish a clear picture of the effect of the manipulated variable on the dependent variable. Extraneous causal factors are ordinarily referred to as *confounding variables* because they confound the treatment condition, making it impossible to determine whether changes in the dependent variable are due solely to the treatment conditions.

Four basic approaches are used to control extraneous factors: randomization, physical control, design control, and statistical control.

Randomization is carried out by randomly assigning subjects to treatment conditions so that extraneous causal factors related to subject characteristics can reasonably be

mortality
Loss of test units or subjects during the course of an experiment, which may result in a nonrepresentativeness.

testing effect
Effect that is a by-product of the research process itself.

regression to the mean
Tendency of subjects with extreme behavior to move toward the average for that behavior during the course of an experiment.

randomization
Random assignment of subjects to treatment conditions to ensure equal representation of subject characteristics.

> **physical control**
> Holding constant the value or level of extraneous variables throughout the course of an experiment.

> **design control**
> Use of the experimental design to control extraneous causal factors.

> **statistical control**
> Adjusting for the effects of confounded variables by statistically adjusting the value of the dependent variable for each treatment condition.

assumed to be represented equally in each treatment condition, thus canceling out extraneous effects.

Physical control of extraneous causal factors may involve somehow holding constant the value or level of the extraneous variable throughout the experiment. Another approach to physical control is matching respondents in regard to important personal characteristics (e.g., age, income, lifestyle) before assigning them to different treatment conditions. The goal is to make sure there are no important differences between characteristics of respondents in the test and control groups.

Design control is the control of extraneous factors by means of specific types of experimental designs developed for this purpose. Such designs are discussed later in this chapter.

Finally, **statistical control** can be used to account for extraneous causal factors if these factors can be identified and measured throughout the course of the experiment. Procedures such as analysis of covariance can adjust for the effects of a confounded variable on the dependent variable by statistically adjusting the value of the dependent variable for each treatment condition.

Experimental Design, Treatment, and Effects

> **experimental design**
> Test in which the researcher has control over and manipulates one or more independent variables.

In an **experimental design**, the researcher has control over and manipulates one or more independent variables. In the experiments we discuss, typically only one independent variable is manipulated. Nonexperimental designs, which involve no manipulation, are often referred to as *ex post facto* (after the fact) research—an effect is observed, and then some attempt is made to attribute this effect to some causal factor.

An experimental design includes four factors:

1. The *treatment,* or experimental, *variable* (independent variable) that is manipulated
2. The *subjects* who participate in the experiment
3. A *dependent variable* that is measured
4. Some *plan or procedure* for dealing with extraneous causal factors

> **treatment variable**
> Independent variable that is manipulated in an experiment.

The **treatment variable** is the independent variable that is manipulated. *Manipulation* refers to a process in which the researcher sets the levels of the independent variable to test a particular causal relationship. To test the relationship between price (independent variable) and sales of a product (dependent variable), a researcher might expose subjects to three different levels of price and record the level of purchases at each price level. As the variable that is manipulated, price is the single treatment variable, with three treatment conditions or levels.

An experiment may include a test, or treatment, group, and a control group. A *control group* is a group in which the independent variable is not changed during the course of the experiment. A *test group* is a group that is exposed to manipulation (change) of the independent variable.

> **experimental effect**
> Effect of the treatment variable on the dependent variable.

The term **experimental effect** refers to the effect of the treatment variable on the dependent variable. The goal is to determine the effect of each treatment condition (level of treatment variable) on the dependent variable. For example, suppose that three different markets are selected to test three different prices, or treatment conditions. Each price is tested in each market for three months. In Market 1, a price 2 percent lower than existing prices for the product is tested; in Market 2, a price 4 percent lower is tested; and in Market 3, a price 6 percent lower is tested. At the end of the three-month test, sales in Market 1 are observed to have increased by less than 1 percent over sales for the preceding three-month period. In Market 2, sales increased by 3 percent; and in Market 3, sales increased by 5 percent. The change in sales observed in each market is the experimental effect.

Limitations of Experimental Research

As the preceding discussion shows, experiments are an extremely powerful form of research—the only type of research that can truly explore the existence and nature of causal relationships between variables of interest. Given these obvious advantages over other research designs for primary data collection, you might ask why experimental research is not used more often. There are many reasons, including the cost of experiments, the issue of security, and problems associated with implementing experiments.

High Cost of Experiments

To some degree, when making comparisons of the costs of experiments with the costs of surveys or observation-based research, we are comparing apples to oranges. Experiments can be very costly in both money and time. In many cases, managers may anticipate that the costs of doing an experiment would exceed the value of the information gained. Consider, for example, the costs of testing three alternative advertising campaigns in three different geographic areas. Three different campaigns must be produced; airtime must be purchased in all three markets; the timing in all three markets must be carefully coordinated; some system must be put into place to measure sales before, during, and after the test campaigns have run; measurements of other extraneous variables must be made; extensive analysis of the results must be performed; and a variety of other tasks must be completed in order to execute the experiment. All of this will cost a bare minimum of $1 million for a low-profile product and as much as tens of millions for a high-profile brand.

Security Issues

Conducting a field experiment in a test market involves exposing a marketing plan or some key element of a marketing plan in the actual marketplace. Undoubtedly, competitors will find out what is being considered well in advance of full-scale market introduction. This advance notice gives competitors an opportunity to decide whether and how to respond. In any case, the element of surprise is lost. In some instances, competitors have actually "stolen" concepts that were being tested in the marketplace and gone into national distribution before the company testing the product or strategy element completed the test marketing.

Implementation Problems

Problems that may hamper the implementation of an experiment include difficulty gaining cooperation within the organization, contamination problems, differences between test markets and the total population, and the lack of an appropriate group of people or geographic area for a control group.

It can be extremely difficult to obtain cooperation within the organization to execute certain types of experiments. For example, a regional marketing manager might be very reluctant to permit her market area to be used as a test market for a reduced level of advertising or a higher price. Quite naturally, her concern would be that the experiment might lower sales for the area.

contamination
Inclusion in a test of a group of respondents who are not normally there—for example, buyers from outside the test market who see an advertisement intended only for those in the test area and enter the area to purchase the product being tested.

Contamination occurs when buyers from outside the test area come into the area to purchase the product being tested, thereby distorting the results of the experiment. Outside buyers might live on the fringes of the test market area and receive TV advertisements—intended only for those in the test area—that offer a lower price, a special rebate, or some other incentive to buy a product. Their purchases will indicate that the particular sales-stimulating factor being tested is more effective than actually is the case.

In some cases, test markets may be so different, and the behavior of consumers in those markets so different, that a relatively small experimental effect is difficult to detect. This problem can be dealt with by careful matching of test markets and other similar strategies designed to ensure a high degree of equivalency of test units.

Finally, in some situations, no appropriate geographic area or group of people may be available to serve as a control group. This may be the case in a test of industrial products, whose very small number of purchasers are concentrated geographically. An attempt to test a new product among a subset of such purchasers would almost certainly be doomed to failure.

Selected Experimental Designs

This section presents examples of pre-experimental, true experimental, and quasi-experimental designs.[9] In outlining these experimental designs, we will use the system of notation introduced earlier.

Pre-Experimental Designs

pre-experimental designs
Designs that offer little or no control over extraneous factors.

Pre-experimental designs are research designs that do not include basic elements required in a true experimental design. Because of their simplicity, they may make sense in certain situations, but they may be difficult to interpret. Studies using **pre-experimental designs** generally are difficult to interpret because such designs offer little or no control over the influence of extraneous factors. As a result, these studies often are not much better than descriptive studies when it comes to making causal inferences. With these designs, the researcher has little control over aspects of exposure to the treatment variable (such as to whom and when) and measurements. However, these designs frequently are used in commercial test marketing because they are simple and inexpensive. They are useful for suggesting new hypotheses but do not offer strong tests of existing hypotheses. The reasons for this will be clear after you review the discussion of pre-experimental designs that follows.

one-shot case study design
Pre-experimental design with no pretest observations, no control group, and an after measurement only.

One-Shot Case Study Design   The **one-shot case study design** involves exposing test units (people or test markets) to the treatment variable for some period of time and then taking a measurement of the dependent variable. Using standard notation, the design is shown as follows:

$$X \qquad O_1$$

There are two basic weaknesses in this design. No pretest observations are made of the test units that will receive the treatment, and no control group of test units that did not receive the treatment is observed. As a result of these deficiencies, the design does not deal with the effects of any of the extraneous variables discussed previously. Therefore, the design lacks internal validity and, most likely, external validity as well. This design is useful for suggesting causal hypotheses but does not provide a strong test of such hypotheses. Many test markets for new products (not previously on the market) are based on this design because it is simpler and less costly.

One-Group Pretest–Posttest Design

The **one-group pretest–posttest design** is the design employed most frequently for testing changes in established products or marketing strategies. The fact that the product was on the market before the change provides the basis for the pretest measurement (O_1). The design is shown symbolically as follows:

$$O_1 \qquad X \qquad O_2$$

Pretest observations are made of a single group of subjects or a single test unit (O_1) that then receives the treatment. Finally, a posttest observation is made (O_2). The treatment effect is estimated by $O_2 - O_1$.

History is a threat to the internal validity of this design because an observed change in the dependent variable might be caused by an event that took place outside the experiment between the pretest and posttest measurements. In laboratory experiments, this threat can be controlled by insulating respondents from outside influences. Unfortunately, this type of control is impossible in field experiments.

Maturation is another threat to this type of design. An observed effect might be caused by the fact that subjects have grown older, smarter, more experienced, or the like between the pretest and the posttest.

This design has only one pretest observation. As a result, the researcher knows nothing of the pretest trend in the dependent variable. The posttest score may be higher because of an increasing trend of the dependent variable in a situation where this effect is not the treatment of interest.

Bias can creep into any design, as discussed next in the Global Research box.

> **one-group pretest–posttest design**
> Pre-experimental design with pre- and postmeasurements but no control group.

GLOBAL RESEARCH

What Happens When Your Selection Bias Is the Interviewer's Gender?

In creating an experimental design to test variables in a market research strategy, selection bias usually means a threat to validity because the test group is too different from the desired target population the researcher wants to probe. But what if the selection bias starts with the market researcher's gender? What impact might that have on the experimental validity? Recently, German researchers found that surveys sent by women or with women's names get better responses than men's.

Stefan Althoff is a marketing researcher manager for Lufthansa Technik in Hamburg, Germany. In 2004, his department started an online customer survey. They received a very low response. A week later they sent out reminders, but the writer signing the letter was named Julia. The response rate jumped to 30 percent. For many of the subsequent online surveys, Lufthansa Technik had women sign their e-mail surveys and reminders, and anecdotally the researchers had the impression respondents read and completed the surveys faster than before when men had signed them. They called this the Anita Effect—the impact of a sender's gender on response.

In January 2006, Althoff and colleagues ran an in-house employee survey at Lufthansa

Technik regarding intranet usage. Their sample was two groups of 105 men each in which one group got a mailed invitation to participate from a female, one from a male. The response rate for the 210 men was 80 percent, but for the men receiving invitations from the female sender, it was 83.9 percent and from the male sender, it was only 74.3 percent.

In March 2006, Althoff and his associates tested the Anita Effect again, this time with a survey of registered users of UNIpark and associated with the academic market. Althoff split 460 users into four groups and asked them to evaluate UNIpark's Web site homepage and the utility of Globalpark's online survey software. Althoff and crew (which included a woman researcher) varied the gender of the

e-mail invitations, but the results were significant: "The response rate was higher from the group that received an invitation mailed from a female sender," Althoff commented.[10]

Questions

1. What types of possible (even if subtle) bias might result from male respondents answering an e-mail survey sent or signed by a female?

2. Althoff planned to test the impact of different women's names on response rate. Consider which three female names might be the most attractive and least attractive to male respondents.

True Experimental Designs

> **true experimental design**
> Research using an experimental group and a control group, to which test units are randomly assigned.

In a **true experimental design,** the experimenter randomly assigns treatments to randomly selected test units. In our notation system, the random assignment of test units to treatments is denoted by (R). Randomization is an important mechanism that makes the results of true experimental designs more valid than the results of pre-experimental designs. True experimental designs are superior because randomization takes care of many extraneous variables. The principal reason for choosing randomized experiments over other types of research designs is that they clarify causal inference.[11] Two true experimental designs are discussed in this section: before and after with control group design and after-only with control group design.

> **before and after with control group design**
> True experimental design that involves random assignment of subjects or test units to experimental and control groups and pre- and postmeasurements of both groups.

Before and After with Control Group Design   The **before and after with control group design** can be presented symbolically as follows:

$$\text{Experimental Group:}\quad (R)\quad\quad O_1\quad\quad X\quad\quad O_2$$
$$\text{Control Group:}\quad\quad\;\; (R)\quad\quad O_3\quad\quad\quad\quad\;\; O_4$$

Because the test units in this design are randomly assigned to the experimental and control groups, the two groups can be considered equivalent. Therefore, they are likely to be subject to the same extraneous causal factors, except for the treatment of interest in the experimental group. For this reason, the difference between the pre- and postmeasurements of the control group $(O_4 - O_3)$ should provide a good estimate of the effect of all the extraneous influences experienced by each group. The true impact of the treatment variable X can be known only when the extraneous influences are removed from the difference between the pre- and postmeasurements of the experimental group. Thus, the true impact of X is estimated by $(O_2 - O_1) - (O_4 - O_3)$. This design generally controls for all but two major threats to validity: mortality and history.

Mortality is a problem if units drop out during the study and these units differ systematically from the ones that remain. This results in a selection bias because the experimental and control groups are composed of different subjects at the posttest than at the pretest. History will be a problem in those situations where factors other than the

EXHIBIT 8.1 Examples of True Experimental Designs

Situation: California Tan wants to measure the sales effect of a point-of-purchase display. The firm is considering two true experimental designs.

After-Only with Control Group Design	Before and After with Control Group Design

After-Only with Control Group Design

Basic design:

Experimental Group: (R) X O_1
Control Group: (R) O_2

Sample: Random sample of stores that sell their products. Stores are randomly assigned to test and control groups. Groups can be considered equivalent.

Treatment (X): Placing the point-of-purchase display in stores in the experimental group for 1 month.

Measurements (O_1, O_2): Actual sales of company's brand during the period that the point-of-purchase displays are in test stores.

Comments:

Because of random assignment of stores to groups, the test group and control group can be considered equivalent. Measure of the treatment effect of X is $O_1 - O_2$. If $O_1 = 125,000$ units and $O_2 = 113,000$ units, then treatment effect = 12,000 units.

Before and After with Control Group Design

Basic design:

Experimental Group: (R) O_1 X O_2
Control Group: (R) O_3 O_4

Sample: Same as after-only design.

Treatment (X): Same as after-only design.

Measurements (O_1 to O_4):

O_1 and O_2 are pre- and postmeasurements for the experimental group;
O_3 and O_4 are the same for the control group.

Results:

$O_1 = 113,000$ units
$O_2 = 125,000$ units
$O_3 = 111,000$ units
$O_4 = 118,000$ units

Comments:

Random assignment to groups means that the groups can be considered equivalent.

Because groups are equivalent, it is reasonable to assume that they will be equally affected by the same extraneous factors.

The difference between pre- and postmeasurements for the control group ($O_4 - O_3$) provides a good estimate of the effects of all extraneous factors on both groups. Based on these results, $O_4 - O_3 = 7,000$ units. The estimated treatment effect is $(O_2 - O_1) - (O_4 - O_3) = (125,000 - 113,000) - (118,000 - 111,000) = 5,000$ units.

treatment variable affect the experimental group but not the control group, or vice versa. Examples of this design and the after-only with control group design are provided in Exhibit 8.1.

After-Only with Control Group Design The **after-only with control group design** differs from the static-group comparison design (the pre-experimental design with nonequivalent groups) in regard to the assignment of the test units. In the static-group comparison design, test units are not randomly assigned to treatment groups. As a result, it is possible for the groups to differ in regard to the dependent variable before presentation of the treatment. The after-only with control group design deals with this shortcoming; it can be shown symbolically as follows:

Experimental Group: (R) X O_1
Control Group: (R) O_2

Notice that the test units are randomly (R) assigned to experimental and control groups. This random assignment should produce experimental and control groups that are approximately equal in regard to the dependent variable before presentation of the treatment to the experimental group. It can reasonably be assumed that test unit mortality (one of the threats to internal validity) will affect each group in the same way.

after-only with control group design
True experimental design that involves random assignment of subjects or test units to experimental and control groups, but no premeasurement of the dependent variable.

Considering this design in the context of the sun tan lotion example described in Exhibit 8.1, we can see a number of problems. Events other than the treatment variable may have occurred during the experimental period in one or a few stores in the experimental group. If a particular store in the experimental group ran a sale on certain other products and, as a result, had a larger than average number of customers in the store, sun tan lotion sales might have increased because of the heavier traffic. Events such as these, which are store-specific (history), may distort the overall treatment effect. Also, there is a possibility that a few stores may drop out during the experiment (mortality threat), resulting in selection bias because the stores in the experimental group will be different at the posttest.

Quasi-Experiments

When designing a true experiment, the researcher often must create artificial environments to control independent and extraneous variables. Because of this artificiality, questions are raised about the external validity of the experimental findings. Quasi-experimental designs have been developed to deal with this problem. They generally are more feasible in field settings than are true experiments.

In **quasi-experiments**, the researcher lacks complete control over the scheduling of treatments or must assign respondents to treatments in a *nonrandom* fashion. These designs frequently are used in marketing research studies because cost and field constraints often do not permit the researcher to exert direct control over the scheduling of treatments and the randomization of respondents. Examples of quasi-experiments are interrupted time-series designs and multiple time-series designs.

Interrupted Time-Series Designs **Interrupted time-series designs** involve repeated measurement of an effect both before and after a treatment is introduced that "interrupts" previous data patterns. Interrupted time-series experimental designs can be shown symbolically as follows:

$$O_1 \qquad O_2 \qquad O_3 \qquad O_4 \qquad X \qquad O_5 \qquad O_6 \qquad O_7 \qquad O_8$$

A common example of this type of design in marketing research involves the use of consumer purchase panels. A researcher might use such a panel to make periodic measurements of consumer purchase activity (the Os), introducing a new promotional campaign (the X) and examining the panel data for an effect. The researcher has control over the timing of the promotional campaign but cannot be sure when the panel members were exposed to the campaign or whether they were exposed at all.

This design is very similar to the one-group pretest–posttest design

$$O_1 \qquad X \qquad O_2$$

However, time-series experimental designs have greater interpretability than the one-group pretest–posttest design because the many measurements allow more understanding of extraneous variables. If, for example, sales of a product were on the rise and a new promotional campaign were introduced, the true effect of this campaign could not be estimated if a pretest–posttest design were used. However, the rising trend in sales would be obvious if a number of pretest and posttest observations had been made. Time-series designs help determine the underlying trend of the dependent variable and provide better interpretability in regard to the treatment effect.

The interrupted time-series design has two fundamental weaknesses. The primary weakness is the experimenter's inability to control history. Although maintaining a careful log of all possibly relevant external happenings can reduce this problem, the researcher has no way of determining the appropriate number and timing of pretest and posttest observations.

quasi-experiments
Studies in which the researcher lacks complete control over the scheduling of treatments or must assign respondents to treatments in a nonrandom manner.

interrupted time-series design
Research in which repeated measurement of an effect "interrupts" previous data patterns.

The other weakness of this design comes from the possibility of interactive effects of testing and evaluation apprehension resulting from the repeated measurements taken on test units. For example, panel members may become "expert" shoppers or simply become more conscious of their shopping habits. Under these circumstances, it may be inappropriate to make generalizations to other populations.

Multiple Time-Series Designs If a control group can be added to an interrupted time-series design, then researchers can be more certain in their interpretation of the treatment effect. This design, called the **multiple time-series design,** can be shown symbolically as follows:

> Experimental Group: O_1 O_2 O_3 X O_4 O_5 O_6
>
> Control Group: O_1 O_2 O_3 O_4 O_5 O_6

⊃ **multiple time-series design**
Interrupted time-series design with a control group.

The researcher must take care in selecting the control group. For example, if an advertiser were testing a new advertising campaign in a test city, that city would constitute the experimental group and another city that was not exposed to the new campaign would be chosen as the control group. It is important that the test and control cities be roughly equivalent in regard to characteristics related to the sale of the product (e.g., competitive brands available).

Test Markets

A common form of experimentation used by marketing researchers is the test market. The term **test market** is used rather loosely to refer to any research that involves testing a new product or change in an existing marketing strategy (e.g., product, price, place promotion) in a single market, group of markets, or region of the country through the use of experimental or quasi-experimental designs.[12]

⊃ **test market**
Real world testing of a new product or some element of the marketing mix using an experimental or quasi-experimental design.

New product introductions play a key role in a firm's financial success or failure. The conventional wisdom in the corporate world is that new products will have to be more profitable in the future than they were in the past because of higher levels of competition and a faster pace of change. Estimates of new product failure rates vary all over the place and range to more than 90 percent.

As you probably already recognize, test market studies have the goal of helping marketing managers make better decisions about new products and additions or changes to existing products or marketing strategies. A test market study does this by providing a real-world test for evaluating products and marketing programs. Marketing managers use test markets to evaluate proposed national programs with many separate elements on a smaller, less costly scale. The basic idea is to determine whether the estimated profits from rolling the product out on a national basis justify the potential risks. Test market studies are designed to provide information in regard to the following issues:

- ☐ Estimates of market share and volume.

- ☐ The effects that the new product will have on sales of similar products (if any) already marketed by the company. This is referred to as the *cannibalization rate.*

- ☐ Characteristics of consumers who buy the product. Demographic data will almost surely be collected, and lifestyle, psychographic, and other types of classification data may also be collected. This information is useful in helping the firm refine the marketing strategy for the product. For example, knowing the demographic characteristics of

Lifestyle data are often collected to find out about the characteristics of possible consumers. This information helps a firm refine the marketing strategy for its product. What might lifestyle data reveal about consumers who would purchase this iPhone?

Sean Gallup/Getty Images

likely purchasers will help in developing a media plan that will effectively and efficiently reach target customers. Knowing the psychographic and lifestyle characteristics of target customers will provide valuable insights into how to position the product and the types of promotional messages that will appeal to them.

☐ The behavior of competitors during the test. This may provide some indication of what competitors will do if the product is introduced nationally.

Types of Test Markets

The vast majority of test markets can be categorized into four types—traditional, scanner or electronic, controlled, and simulated.[13] The *traditional or standard test market* involves testing the product and other elements of the marketing mix through a firm's regular channels of distribution. Traditional test markets take a relatively long time (six months or more), are costly, and immediately tip one's hand to the competition. Some have argued that the traditional test market provides the best read on how a product and the associated marketing mix will actually do if introduced because it provides the best analog of the real marketplace. However, some of the other options, discussed below, may provide very good estimates at a fraction of the cost, more quickly and without giving the competition advance warning regarding what a company is planning to do.

Scanner or electronic test markets are markets where scanner panel research firms have panels of consumers who carry scannable cards for use in buying particular products, especially those sold through grocery stores. These panels permit the researcher to analyze the characteristics of those consumers who buy and those who don't buy the test products. Purchase/nonpurchase by individual panel participants can be related to their detailed demographic data, past purchase history, and, in some cases, media viewing habits. Firms offering scanner panels include ACNielsen and Information Resources. This approach offers speed, lower cost, and some degree of security regarding the marketing strategy or changes in strategy we are considering. The major criticism of this approach to test marketing relates to what some argue is its unrepresentative sampling: those who agree to participate in these panels may not be representative of the broader populations of consumers in these markets and other markets.

Controlled test markets are managed by research suppliers who ensure that the product is distributed through the agreed upon types and numbers of distributors. Research suppliers who offer controlled test markets, such as ACNielsen, pay distributors to provide the required amount of shelf space for test products. Research suppliers carefully monitor sales of the product in these controlled test markets. They enable companies to get their products into test more quickly, often supply more realistic levels of distribution, and provide better monitoring of product movement.

STMs (simulated test markets) are just what the name implies—simulations of the types of test markets noted above. As such, they can normally be conducted more quickly than the other two approaches, at a lower cost, and produce results that are, in most cases, highly predictive of what will actually happen. In these simulated test markets, a more limited amount of information is used in conjunction with mathematical models that include estimates of the effects of different marketing variables that can be adjusted to fit the situation. A number of different companies, including ACNielsen (Bases), Harris Interactive (Litmus), and Synovate (MarkeTest), offer these services, and each one has special features. However, they all share the following elements:

- A sample of consumers is selected based on the expected or known characteristics of the target consumer for the test product.
- Consumers sampled are recruited to come to a central location testing facility to view commercials for the test product and competitive products.
- Consumers are then given the opportunity to purchase the test product in the actual marketplace or in a simulated store environment.
- Purchasers are contacted after they have had time to use the product. They are asked how likely they are to repurchase and for their evaluations of the product.
- The above information is used with the proprietary model of the STM company to generate estimates of sales volume, market share, and other key market metrics.[14]

Costs of Test Marketing

Test marketing is expensive. A simple two-market test can cost a bare minimum of $1 million and probably much more. A long-running, more complex test can cost in the tens of millions of dollars. These estimates refer only to direct costs, which may include the following:

- Production of commercials
- Payments to an advertising agency for services
- Media time, charged at a higher rate because of low volume
- Syndicated research information
- Customized research information and associated data analysis
- Point-of-purchase materials
- Coupons and sampling
- Higher trade allowances to obtain distribution[15]

Many *indirect costs* are also associated with test marketing, including the following:

- Cost of management time spent on the test market
- Diversion of sales activity from existing products
- Possible negative impact of a test market failure on other products with the same family brand
- Possible negative trade reactions to products if the firm develops a reputation for not doing well
- Cost of letting competitors know what the firm is doing, thereby allowing them to develop a better strategy or beat the firm to the national market[16]

Test markets are expensive, and, as a result, they should be used only as the last step in a research process that has shown the new product or strategy has potential. In some situations, it may be cheaper to go ahead and launch the product, even if it fails.

Decision to Conduct Test Marketing

From the preceding discussion, you can see that test markets offer at least two important benefits to the firm conducting the test.[17]

- First and foremost, the test market provides a vehicle by which the firm can obtain a good estimate of a product's sales potential under realistic market conditions.

A researcher can develop estimates of the product's national market share on the basis of these test results and use this figure to develop estimates of future financial performance for the product.

☐ Second, the test should identify weaknesses of the product and the proposed marketing strategy for the product and give management an opportunity to correct any weaknesses. It is much easier and less expensive to correct these problems at the test market stage than after the product has gone into national distribution.

These benefits must be weighed against a number of costs and other negatives associated with test markets.[18] The financial costs of test markets are not insignificant. And test markets give competitors an early indication of what the firm is planning to do. They thus share the opportunity to make adjustments in their marketing strategy; or, if the idea is simple and not legally protected, they may be able to copy the idea and move into national distribution faster than the original firm can.

Four major factors should be taken into account in determining whether to conduct a test market:

1. Weigh the cost and risk of failure against the probability of success and associated profits. If estimated costs are high and you are uncertain about the likelihood of success, then you should lean toward doing a test market. On the other hand, if both expected costs and the risk of product failure are low, then an immediate national rollout without a test market may be the appropriate strategy.

2. Consider the likelihood and speed with which competitors can copy your product and introduce it on a national basis. If the product can be easily copied, then it may be appropriate to introduce the product without a test market.

3. Consider the investment required to produce the product for the test market versus the investment required to produce the product in the quantities necessary for a national rollout. In cases where the difference in investment required is very small, it may make sense to introduce the product nationally without a test market. However, in cases where a very large difference exists between the investment required to produce the product for test market and that required for a national rollout, conducting a test market before making a decision to introduce the product nationally makes good sense.

4. Consider how much damage an unsuccessful new product launch would inflict on the firm's reputation. Failure may hurt the firm's reputation with other members of the channel of distribution (retailers) and impede the firm's ability to gain their cooperation in future product launches.

Steps in a Test Market Study

Once the decision has been made to conduct test marketing, a number of steps must be carried out if we are to achieve a satisfactory result.

Step One: Define the Objective   As always with these kinds of lists, the first step in the process is to define the objectives of the test. Typical test market objectives include the following:

☐ Develop share and volume estimates

☐ Determine the characteristics of people who are purchasing the product

☐ Determine frequency and purpose of purchase

☐ Determine where (retail outlets) purchases are made

☐ Measure the effect of sales of the new product on sales of similar existing products in the line

Step Two: Select a Basic Approach

After specifying the objectives of the test market exercise, the next step is to decide on the appropriate type of test market, given the stated objectives.

Earlier in the chapter, we discussed the characteristics, advantages, and disadvantages of four types of test markets:

☐ Traditional or standard test market

☐ Scanner or electronic test market

☐ Controlled test market

☐ Simulated test market (STM) (See Practicing Marketing Research on page 237 for more discussion of STMs.)

The decision regarding which type of test market to use in a given situation depends on how much time you have, how much budget you have, and how important it is to keep the competition in the dark about what you are planning to do.

Selecting markets for a test is an important decision. Significant regional differences should be considered in choosing cities as test markets. To find some readily apparent regional differences between Seattle and Miami, visit www.ci.seattle.wa.us and www.miami.com.

Corbis Digital Stock (top and bottom)

Step Three: Develop Detailed Test Procedures After the objectives and a basic approach for the test have been developed, the researcher must develop a detailed plan for conducting the test. Manufacturing and distribution decisions must be made to ensure that adequate product is available and that it is available in most stores of the type that sell that particular product class. In addition, the detailed marketing plan to be used for the test must be specified. The basic positioning approach must be selected, the actual commercials must be developed, a pricing strategy must be chosen, a media plan must be developed, and various promotional activities must be specified.

GLOBAL RESEARCH

Best Global Test Markets? Danes Are Quick, Koreans Love Tech

If you want to reach the world's most innovative customers, try Denmark for your next test market in global marketing, says the Danish weekly, *Mandag Morgen*.

The claim is supported by the findings of a major market research initiative of European markets conducted by American and European universities, whose numbers included Professor Gerard Tellis, a prominent market researcher at the University of Southern California. Danish consumers are quicker to adopt new products than all other Europeans and even Americans or Chinese, the study found. The Danes are also more open to new ideas, an essential foundation for trying new products.

It takes only 3.3 years from product launch to widespread sales and market entrenchment in Denmark, compared to Germany, France, or England, where it might take two to three times longer, or up to 9.3 years in Portugal, the study said. Companies that release new products in Denmark's climate of quick uptake have the advantage of being able to improve or adjust them faster based on results there before committing themselves to an expensive multination product rollout.[19]

If it's brand-new wireless Internet services and applications, or equipment and services pertaining to the telecom infrastructure, South Korea, the most wired nation in Asia and the hotbed for digital or online innovations, is *the* test market for high tech, says *BusinessWeek*. Two-thirds of the population's 16 million households have broadband Internet service, and 68 percent already have advanced cell phones capable of high-speed data transmission. Korea offers global test marketers a "rapid uptake" of the newest types of wireless and Internet products and a "mass" of consumers already versed in this technology and in formats that are not even that familiar to high-tech Americans. As with Denmark, uptake and consumer response for new tech products promise to be delivered fast in digitized South Korea.[20]

Denmark may be an all-purpose test marketing bellwether and South Korea may be the tech marketer's paradise, but you'll still need to tailor your approach to local customs, language, habits of perception, and cultural preferences for success. Mary Beth Lake, chief of global product design and development for Synovate of Chicago, a major marketing research firm, stresses that companies engaged in global marketing need to "localize their product offerings in ways that are culturally acceptable." She has three recommendations in this regard.

First, study and master the particularities of the country's language usage. She calls this *vocabulary elicitation* and advises market researchers to compile a dictionary on how consumers in the target country use and define products. What is "creaminess in the mouth" for a North American to describe a beverage's taste impact is "milk feel" to the Japanese. The North American term does not compute in Japanese food experience, just as "milk feel" may leave us speechless.

Second, perform a one-on-one analysis at the level of individual consumers. Study the reaction of the potential customers to the product in conditions approximating how it will be when they actually use it on their own, says Lake. Take software marketed for children or elementary school use. Testing here involves interviewing the students, observing them on closed-circuit television, and evaluating their experience as they follow directions for using the software in a real classroom.

Third, Lake adds, don't overlook traditional qualitative analysis. Interview groups of potential consumers to find out how they perceive and describe the products; look into whether your proposed imagery and message style will work in that specific cultural context, and if not,

find ways to adjust it to fit the cognitive framework. Modify the packaging if necessary to reinforce the adjusted message. Follow these three steps, says Lake, to fine-tune your culture-specific test marketing.[21]

Questions

1. Identify and discuss other examples of culture-specific references that are taken for granted in the United States but that would seem strange or incomprehensible in other countries.

2. Identify three cutting-edge high-tech products (e.g., in the category of new products like iPhone, Kindle, or flat-screen televisions) and devise a test market approach for Danish customers.

Step Four: Select Test Markets   The selection of markets for the test is an important decision. A number of factors must be taken into account in making this decision. First there are the overall standards[22]:

☐ There should be a minimum of two test markets, in addition to a control market, for an existing national brand or a minimum of three markets for testing a new brand.

☐ The markets selected should be geographically dispersed; if the brand is a regional brand, the markets should cover several dispersed markets within that region.

☐ Markets should be demographically representative of the United States, unless, for instance, a pronounced ethnic skew is desirable for a specific brand.

☐ Depending on the product purchase cycle, the test should be run for at least 6 months, up to 12 months, before the results can be considered reliably projectable. If the product is purchased infrequently, it is advisable to run the test for even longer than a year.

☐ The market must have a variety of media outlets, including at least four television stations, cable penetration no more than 10 percent above or below the U.S. average, at least four radio stations, a dominant local newspaper with daily and Sunday editions, a Sunday supplement with a syndicated edition, or a local supplement of similar quality.

☐ There should be a dominant newspaper in the market or a dominant newspaper in each city the market encompasses.

☐ The market should be as reflective as possible of the U.S. population or regional population if that is more appropriate for the particular test.

See the Global Research on page 234 for discussion of what makes a good global test market.

Step Five: Execute the Plan   Once the plan is in place, the researcher can begin execution. At this point, a key decision has to be made: how long should the test run? The average test runs for 6 to 12 months. However, shorter and longer tests are not uncommon. The test must run long enough for an adequate number of repeat purchase cycles to be observed in order to provide a measure of the "staying power" of a new product or marketing program. The shorter the average period is, the shorter the test needs to be. Cigarettes, soft drinks, and packaged goods are purchased every few days, whereas such products as shaving cream and toothpaste are purchased only every few months. The latter products would require a longer test. Whatever the product type, the test must be continued until the repeat purchase rate stabilizes. The percentage of people making repeat purchases tends to drop for some period of time before reaching a relatively constant level. Repeat purchase rate is critical to the process of estimating ultimate sales of the product. If the test is ended too soon, sales will be overestimated.

Two other considerations in determining the length of the test relate to the expected speed of competitor reaction and the costs of running the test. If there is reason to expect that competitors will react quickly to the test marketing (introduce their own versions of the new product), then the test should be as short as possible. Minimizing the length of the test reduces the amount of time competitors have to react. Finally, the value of additional information to be gained from the test must be balanced against the cost of continuing to run the test. At some point, the value of additional information will be outweighed by its cost.

Step Six: Analyze the Test Results   The data produced by an experiment should be evaluated throughout the test period. However, after completion of the experiment, a more careful and thorough evaluation of the data must be performed. This analysis will focus on four areas:

- ☐ *Purchase data.* The purchase data are often the most important data produced by an experiment. The levels of initial purchase (trial) throughout the course of the experiment provide an indication of how well the advertising and promotion program worked. The repeat rate (percentage of initial triers who made second and subsequent purchases) provides an indication of how well the product met the expectations created through advertising and promotion. Of course, the trial and repeat purchase results provide the basis for estimating sales and market share if the product was distributed nationally.

- ☐ *Awareness data.* How effective were the media expenditures and media plan in creating awareness of the product? Do consumers know how much the product costs? Do they know its key features?

General Mills used the "rolling rollout" when it introduced MultiGrain Cheerios to the public. Visit www.generalmills.com to find out what new products the company may be introducing.

Copyright John Wiley & Sons, Inc.

PRACTICING MARKETING RESEARCH

Quick Scans of Product-Specific Test Markets

Some locations just seem to specialize in favorable conditions for selected test market trials, such as for high-end beer, premium vodkas, or Brazilian steakhouses.

Miller Brewing Company of Milwaukee, Wisconsin, decided to test market three kinds of low-calorie, craft-style light beers in only four cities starting in 2008, including Minneapolis, Minnesota; Charlotte, North Carolina; San Diego, California; and Baltimore, Maryland. Their goal was to establish a new category for light craft-style beers and to capitalize on three noticeable trends in the beer industry: the shift toward lighter beers (fewer calories and carbohydrates), more variety, and what's called premiumization—high-end, quality-perceived offerings. It's a solid idea because craft beer sales for 2006 were up 17.8 percent, and those four cities have the right combination of demographics to warrant the test market.[23]

Fuller's, a London brewery founded in 1711, selected Denver, Colorado, as the premium United States locale to test market its high-end London Pride beer. Why Denver? The area is home to a hefty quantity of beer drinkers who prefer the high-end brews and presumably won't mind spending $8 for a London Pride six-pack. People there, research has found, are "friendly" to premium or craft-style beers. Even better, craft beer commands a 10 percent market share in Colorado, putting it third in the nation. Fuller's marketing approach included radio ads that trolled for the golf and outdoors-focused types who are more the "microbrew set," the company said.[24]

Anheuser-Busch is test-running its Purus vodka, distilled in Italy and fetching $35 a bottle retail, in Boston, New York, Washington, and Annapolis. Why there? The company wants to attract the "modern luxury connoisseur" to their organic wheat-based Purus, and they want to test-position it in those cities' most exclusive lounges and restaurants as well as in a handful of specialty groceries and liquor stores. Again, there's evidence of sober thinking behind the approach: U.S. sales of upper-end or ultra-premium vodkas more than doubled between 2003 and 2006. Typical consumers? Young drinkers, aged 21 to 30, who care more about image than price.[25]

What U.S. city did International Restaurant Concepts of Lakewood, Colorado, select to test market its Tucanos Brazilian Grill steakhouse? Provo, Utah. At first glance, Provo's demographics would seem against it: of its 100,000 residents, 87 percent are white and only 10 percent Hispanic, so where's the market for Tucanos's *churrascaria*? It turns out that because Provo is the home of Brigham Young University and runs a missionary training center for the Church of the Latter-Day Saints, many of the thousands of Mormon students sent out in the field have been posted to Brazil. In addition, the university population comprises many international students—all of which generates an ethnically diverse and language-rich community and good test market.[26]

Questions

1. What characteristics do the cities of Minneapolis, Charlotte, San Diego, and Baltimore possess that make them good markets for introducing premium-level beers?

2. How would you tailor a test market experimentation for Brazilian cuisine in a Mormon-saturated region whose members nonetheless are well-traveled and versed in Brazilian foods?

☐ *Competitive response.* Ideally, the responses of competitors should be monitored during the period of the test market. For example, competitors may try to distort test results by offering special promotions, price deals, and quantity discounts. Their actions may provide some indication of what they will do if the product moves into national distribution and some basis for estimating the effect of these actions on their part.

☐ *Source of sales.* If the product is a new entry in an existing product category, it is important to determine where sales are coming from. In other words, which brands did the people who purchased the test product previously purchase? This information provides a true indication of real competitors. If the firm has an existing brand in the market, it also indicates to what extent the new product will take business from existing brands and from the competition.

Based on the evaluation, a decision will be made to improve the marketing program or the product, drop the product, or move the product into national or regional distribution.

Other Types of Product Tests

In addition to traditional test marketing and STMs, there are other means by which companies can gauge a product's potential. One alternative is a *rolling rollout*, which usually follows a pretest. A product is launched in a certain region rather than in one or two cities. Within a matter of days, scanner data can provide information on how the product is doing. The product can then be launched in additional regions; ads and promotions can be adjusted along the way to a national introduction. General Mills has used this approach for products such as MultiGrain Cheerios.

Another alternative is to try a product out in a foreign market before rolling it out globally. Specifically, one or a few countries can serve as a test market for a continent or even the world. This *lead country strategy* has been used by Colgate-Palmolive Company. In 1991, the company launched Palmolive Optims shampoo and conditioner in the Philippines, Australia, Mexico, and Hong Kong. Later, the products were rolled out in Europe, Asia, Latin America, and Africa.

Some marketers think that classic test marketing will make a comeback. It may be that for totally new products, more thorough testing will be necessary, whereas for other types of product introductions, such as line extensions, an alternative approach is more appropriate.

SUMMARY

Experimental research provides evidence of whether a change in an independent variable causes some predictable change in a dependent variable. To show that a change in *A* likely caused an observed change in *B*, one must show three things: concomitant variation, appropriate time order of occurrence, and the elimination of other possible causal factors. Experiments can be conducted in a laboratory or a field setting. The major advantage of conducting experiments in a laboratory is that the researcher can control extraneous factors. However, in marketing research, laboratory settings often do not appropriately replicate the marketplace. Experiments conducted in the actual marketplace are called field experiments. The major difficulty with field experiments is that the researcher cannot control all the other factors that might influence the dependent variable.

In experimentation, we are concerned with internal and external validity. Internal validity refers to the extent to which competing explanations of the experimental results observed can be ruled out. External validity refers to the extent to which causal relationships measured in an experiment can be generalized to other settings. Extraneous variables are other independent variables that may affect the dependent variable and thus stand in the way of the ability to conclude that an observed change in the dependent variable was due to the effect of the experimental, or treatment, variable. Extraneous factors include history, maturation, instrument variation, selection bias, mortality, testing effects, and regression to the mean. Four basic approaches are used to control extraneous factors: randomization, physical control, design control, and statistical control.

In an experimental design, the researcher has control over and manipulates one or more independent variables. Nonexperimental designs, which involve no manipulation, are referred to as *ex post facto* research. An experimental design includes four elements: the treatment, subjects, a dependent variable that is measured, and a plan or procedure for dealing with extraneous causal factors. An experimental effect is the effect of the treatment variable on the dependent variable.

Experiments have an obvious advantage in that they are the only type of research that can demonstrate the existence and nature of causal relationships between variables of interest. Yet the amount of actual experimentation done in marketing research is limited because of the high cost of experiments, security issues, and implementation problems. There is evidence to suggest that the use of experiments in marketing research is growing.

Pre-experimental designs offer little or no control over the influence of extraneous factors and are thus generally difficult to interpret. Examples include the one-shot case study design and the one-group pretest–posttest design. In a true experimental design, the researcher is able to eliminate all extraneous variables as competitive hypotheses to the treatment. Examples of true experimental designs are the before and after with control group design and the after-only with control group design.

In quasi-experiments, the researcher has control over data collection procedures but lacks complete control over the scheduling of treatments. The treatment groups in a quasi-experiment normally are formed by assigning respondents to treatments in a non-random fashion. Examples of quasi-experimental designs are the interrupted time-series design and the multiple time-series design.

Test marketing involves testing a new product or some element of the marketing mix by using experimental or quasi-experimental designs. Test markets are field experiments, and they are extremely expensive to conduct. The steps in conducting a test market study include defining the objectives for the study, selecting a basic approach to be used, developing detailed procedures for the test, selecting markets for the test, executing the plan, and analyzing the test results.

KEY TERMS & DEFINITIONS

experiment Research approach in which one variable is manipulated and the effect on another variable is observed.

causal research Research designed to determine whether a change in one variable likely caused an observed change in another.

concomitant variation Statistical relationship between two variables.

appropriate time order of occurrence Change in an independent variable occurring before an observed change in the dependent variable.

elimination of other possible causal factors Hard to prove that something else did not cause change in *B*.

laboratory experiments Experiments conducted in a controlled setting.

field experiments Tests conducted outside the laboratory in an actual environment, such as a marketplace.

internal validity Extent to which competing explanations for the experimental results observed can be ruled out.

external validity Extent to which causal relationships measured in an experiment can be generalized to outside persons, settings, and times.

history Intervention, between the beginning and end of an experiment, of outside variables or events that might change the dependent variable.

maturation Changes in subjects occurring during the experiment that are not related to the experiment but that may affect subjects' response to the treatment factor.

instrument variation Changes in measurement instruments (e.g., interviewers or observers) that might affect measurements.

selection bias Systematic differences between the test group and the control group due to a biased selection process.

mortality Loss of test units or subjects during the course of an experiment, which may result in a nonrepresentativeness.

testing effect Effect that is a by-product of the research process itself.

regression to the mean Tendency of subjects with extreme behavior to move toward the average for that behavior during the course of an experiment.

randomization Random assignment of subjects to treatment conditions to ensure equal representation of subject characteristics.

physical control Holding constant the value or level of extraneous variables throughout the course of an experiment.

design control Use of the experimental design to control extraneous causal factors.

statistical control Adjusting for the effects of confounded variables by statistically adjusting the value of the dependent variable for each treatment condition.

experimental design Test in which the researcher has control over and manipulates one or more independent variables.

treatment variable Independent variable that is manipulated in an experiment.

experimental effect Effect of the treatment variable on the dependent variable.

contamination Inclusion in a test of a group of respondents who are not normally there—for example, buyers from outside the test market who see an advertisement intended only for those in the test area and who enter the area to purchase the product being tested.

pre-experimental designs Designs that offer little or no control over extraneous factors.

one-shot case study design Pre-experimental design with no pretest observations, no control group, and an after measurement only.

one-group pretest–posttest design Pre-experimental design with pre- and postmeasurements but no control group.

true experimental design Research using an experimental group and a control group, to which test units are randomly assigned.

before and after with control group design True experimental design that involves random assignment of subjects or test units to experimental and control groups and pre- and postmeasurements of both groups.

after-only with control group design True experimental design that involves random assignment of subjects or test units to experimental and control groups, but no premeasurement of the dependent variable.

quasi-experiments Studies in which the researcher lacks complete control over the scheduling of treatments or must assign respondents to treatments in a nonrandom manner.

interrupted time-series design Research in which repeated measurements of an effect "interrupts" previous data patterns.

multiple time-series design An interrupted time-series design with a control group.

test market Testing of a new product or some element of the marketing mix using an experimental or quasi-experimental design.

(Team Exercise)

1. Divide the class into as many as six groups, as appropriate. Each group will have the task of recommending a test market design and addressing the associated questions for one of the following scenarios.

   ☐ Design a test of a new pricing strategy for orange juice concentrate. The brand is an established brand, and we are only interested in testing the effect of a 5 percent price increase and a 5 percent decrease. All other elements of the marketing mix will remain the same.

   ☐ A soft drink company has determined in taste tests that consumers prefer the taste of their diet product when sweetened with Splenda in comparison to Equal. Now they are interested in determining how the new sweetener will play in the marketplace. Design a test market that will achieve this goal.

   ☐ A national pizza chain wants to test the effect on sales of four different discount coupons. Design a test that will do this in a way that gives a clear read. Your focus should be on the effect on sales volume. Financial analysis after the test results are in will address the revenue and profit impact.

   ☐ A national value-priced hotel chain needs to understand the business impact of including a free buffet style breakfast to guests. Design and justify a test that will do this.

   ☐ A credit card company needs to test its strategy for attracting college students to its card. It is going to continue using booths in student unions and other high-traffic campus locations. It has been offering free CDs from a list to those who sign up for its card, but since other card companies are using this approach, the company wants to try some alternatives. It is considering free MP3 downloads from iTunes and t-shirts featuring popular music groups. Design a test that will tell the company which option to choose if its goal is to increase signups by the largest amount.

2. Tico Taco, a national chain of Mexican fast-food restaurants, has developed the "Super Sonic Taco," which is the largest taco in the market and sells for $1.19. Tico Taco has identified its target customers for this new product as men under 30 who are not concerned about health issues, such as fat content or calories. It wants to test the product in at least four regional markets before making a decision to introduce it nationally. What criteria would you use to select test cities for this new product? Which cities would you recommend using? Why would you recommend those cities?

3. Of the primary data-collection techniques available to the researcher (survey, observation, experiment), why is the experiment the only one that can provide conclusive evidence of causal relationships? Of the various types of experiments, which type or types provide the best evidence of causation or noncausation?

4. What are some important independent variables that must be dealt with in an experiment to test consumer reactions to a pilot for a new TV series? Explain why those variables are important.

5. Managers of the student center at your university or college are considering three alternative brands of frozen pizza to be offered on the menu. They want to offer only one of the three and want to find out which brand students prefer. Design an experiment to determine which brand of pizza the students prefer.

6. Night students at the university or college are much older than day students. Introduce an explicit control for day versus night students in the preceding experiment.

7. Why are quasi-experiments much more popular in marketing research than true experiments?

8. How does history differ from maturation? What specific actions might you take to deal with each in an experiment?

9. A manufacturer of microwave ovens has designed an improved model that will reduce energy costs and cook food evenly throughout. However, this new model will increase the product's price by 30 percent because of extra components and engineering design changes. The company wants to determine what effect the new model will have on sales of its microwave ovens. Propose an appropriate experimental design that can provide the desired information for management. Why did you select this design?

10. Discuss various methods by which extraneous causal factors can be controlled.

11. Discuss the alternatives to traditional test marketing. Explain their advantages and disadvantages.

WORKING THE NET

1. Go to *www.claritas.com/claritas/psychographics.jsp* for information on six psychographics methodologies and evaluate them for application to a test market.

2. Visit *www.questionpro.com/akira/showLibrary.do?categoryID=16&mode=1* to take a psychographics profile with 269 focused questions distributed into 15 categories. What kind of consumer are you? How would you design a test market to attract a customer like yourself?

3. Consult *www.city-data.com* Research city demographics for Cedar Rapids, Iowa; Eau Claire, Wisconsin; and Grand Junction, Colorado, to evaluate why *Advertising Age* (2005) ranked them among the top seven most popular test market sites in the United States for matching the average American demographic profile.

REAL-LIFE RESEARCH • 8.1

Millennium Marketing Research Simulated Test Market

The best way to test the efficacy of a proposed new product is to test market it. That is, to test the product, along with its complete marketing mix, in selected markets that are representative of the entire market where a full-scale launch would take place. The test market results should, of course, be predictive of the results that will actually occur. But even with test marketing, some marketers are surprised when the launch results do not match the test-marketing results. Often, the problem is the marketer, who didn't launch the new product in exactly the manner tested.

Test marketing is expensive, and marketers often will not undertake it for that reason. Thus, they simply launch the product without any test marketing, hoping that it will be a success, that their "instincts" about the product are good. The simulated test market is another approach to testing that reduces cost and time while still providing estimates of sales for new products. The simulated test market approach used by Millennium Marketing Research is described later in this discussion.

When we conduct a simulated test market (at much, much less than the $1 million we had to pay some years ago), we ordinarily select five cities that are representative of the market where the product would be launched. Then, in each city, we select a mall that has a high incidence of those who constitute the new product's target market. Within each mall, we set up a simulated store (in a vacant facility), which is stocked with products from the product category being tested (including the client's new product, of course).

An interviewer then qualifies (target market characteristics) passers-by and invites them to participate in a marketing research study that will take about 15 minutes of their time. Those who agree to participate are then asked to view a portfolio of advertisements (which may be print media advertisements or 30-second television advertisements). After viewing the portfolio of advertisements, participants are asked to indicate which advertisements they recalled having viewed. In this way, we get a measure of the extent to which the advertisement generated "unaided" awareness of the new product.

Then participants are given Millennium Marketing Dollars, with which they can "purchase" product from the simulated store, at no cost to them. In this way, they can "purchase" the new product being tested or any of the competing products. Thus, we get a measure of the extent to which trial is achieved for the new product. At the same time, we have some indication of the relative contribution made by the advertisement and the packing (and point-of-purchase) materials in achieving that level of trial.

Subsequently, we give those participants who "purchased" the new product the opportunity to purchase additional product on two more occasions, at a price that is lower than they would ordinarily pay in a real store.

While a Millennium Marketing simulated test market does not permit one to evaluate one's entire marketing mix, it provides a basis for estimating awareness, trial, and adoption before launch, and in a very cost-effective fashion.

Questions

1. How does the approach described in the case differ from more traditional test markets?
2. What are the advantages and disadvantages of the simulated test market approach described? Explain.
3. It was noted that the approach does not permit one to evaluate one's entire market mix and that it provides a basis of estimating awareness, trial, and adoption before launch in a very cost-effective fashion.
   a. Why do they say that the approach does not permit you to evaluate all marketing mix elements? Do you agree?
   b. How could the test be modified to address other marketing mix elements? Indicate how you would address at least one other element of the marketing mix.
   c. How does the methodology used by Millennium provide a basis for estimating awareness, trial, and adoption?
   d. Do you think participant behavior in the test will be consistent with their behavior in the actual marketplace? Why do you say that?

Jon Riley/Getty Images

THE CONCEPT OF MEASUREMENT AND ATTITUDE SCALES

		LEARNING OBJECTIVES
→	1.	To understand the concept of measurement.
→	2.	To understand the four levels of scales and their typical usage.
→	3.	To explore the concepts of reliability and validity.
→	4.	To become familiar with the concept of scaling.
→	5.	To learn about the various types of attitude scales.
→	6.	To examine some basic considerations in selecting a type of scale.
→	7.	To realize the importance of attitude measurement scales in management decision making.

Luth Research's IndicatorEDG conducts a quarterly online study surveying a total of 6,000 respondents around the world. The survey focuses on general well-being and happiness (see Exhibit 9.1). With increasing interactions between the members of the global village, the nascent trends in the local market have subtle but intrinsic differences. Children and family are notably more important to the Chinese and Scandinavians than to people from other regions. While people from Western countries strive for physical fitness and active lifestyles, those from China and Japan value good health in a general sense. A good marriage also remains in the top five ingredients for happiness, but is more essential to Americans and Canadians.

When it comes to the specific things that make us happy, we are globally similar; we draw the most satisfaction from our family life, which is a dramatic shift from 20 years ago when satisfaction was associated primarily with success in the professional realm. Work life is becoming a markedly low priority as a source of happiness in the lives of consumers around the globe.

Although people's satisfaction with their residency and community is comparable across countries, people from the United Kingdom and Europe are more inclined to live in another country and Americans are the least inclined to do so.[1]

As you can see, the construct of happiness may encompass many dimensions. What may seem like a simple notion on the surface, happiness, requires a rigorous process in order to be properly measured. What is measurement? How does one determine the reliability and validity of the information? What are the various ways to measure attitude? Why is it useful to measure attitudes? What factors should be considered in creating an attitude scale? These questions will be addressed in this chapter.

EXHIBIT 9.1   Top Five Picks for Definition of Happiness

Happiness (Ranking 1 = Most Selected)	U.S.	U.K.	India	Canada	Europe (mainland)	Scandinavia	China	Japan
Being physically fit and active throughout my life	2	2	1	1	1	2	5	3
Enjoyment, fun, and laughter throughout my life	4	4				5	3	5
Good health throughout my life				5		1	2	1
Having a wonderful and lasting marriage	2	3	4	2	5	3	4	
Having children and a happy family	5	5	5	4	4	1	1	
Having enough time and money to be content	1	1	3	3	2	2		2
Having enough time to enjoy all that life has to offer	3		2	3	3	1	1	4
Having good friends and good times						4		

Source of happiness (Ranking 1 = Most Happy)	U.S.	U.K.	India	Canada	Europe (mainland)	Scandinavia	China	Japan
My current residence	3	2	2	3	2	3	3	1
My community	2	3	3	2	3	2	4	3
My family life	1	1	1	1	1	1	1	2
My romantic life	5	4	4	5	5	5	2	5
My work life	6	6	6	6	6	6	5	6
My social life	4	5	5	4	4	4	6	4

Source: "Happiness, As Defined by the World," *Quicks Marketing Research Review* (May 2007), p. 10.

The Measurement Process

> **measurement**
> Process of assigning numbers or labels to persons, objects, or events in accordance with specific rules for representing quantities or qualities of attributes.

> **rule**
> Guide, method, or command that tells a researcher what to do.

Measurement is the process of assigning numbers or labels to persons, objects, or events in accordance with specific rules for representing quantities or qualities of attributes. Measurement, then, is a procedure used to assign numbers that reflect the amount of an attribute possessed by a person, object, or event. Note that it is not the person, object, or event that is being measured, but rather its attributes. A researcher, for example, does not measure a consumer per se but rather measures that consumer's attitudes, income, brand loyalty, age, and other relevant factors.

The concept of rules is key to measurement. A **rule** is a guide, a method, or a command that tells a researcher what to do. For example, a rule of measurement might state, "Assign the numbers 1 through 5 to people according to their disposition to do household chores. If they are extremely willing to do any and all household chores, assign them a 1. If they are not willing to do any household chores, assign them a 5." The numbers 2, 3, and 4 would be assigned based on the *degree* of their willingness to do chores, as it relates to the absolute end points of 1 and 5.

A problem often encountered with rules is a lack of clarity or specificity. Some things are easy to measure because rules are easy to create and follow. The measurement of gender, for example, is quite simple, as the researcher has concrete criteria to apply in assigning a 1 for a male and a 2 for a female. Unfortunately, many characteristics of interest to a marketing researcher—such as brand loyalty, purchase intent, and total family income—are much harder to measure because of the difficulty of devising rules to assess the true value of these consumer attributes.

Creating a measurement scale begins with determining the level of measurement desirable or possible. Exhibit 9.2 describes the four basic levels of measurement: nominal, ordinal, interval, and ratio. A **scale** is a set of symbols or numbers so constructed that the symbols or numbers can be assigned by a rule to the individuals (or their behaviors or attitudes) to whom the scale is applied. The assignment on the scale is indicated by the individual's possession of whatever the scale is supposed to measure. Thus, a salesperson who feels he knows exactly how he is supposed to interact with customers would mark *very certain* for that item.

> **scale**
> Set of symbols or numbers so constructed that the symbols or numbers can be assigned by a rule to the individuals (or their behaviors or attitudes) to whom the scale is applied.

Nominal Level of Measurement

> **nominal scales**
> Scales that partition data into mutually exclusive and collectively exhaustive categories.

Nominal scales are among those most commonly used in marketing research. A nominal scale partitions data into categories that are mutually exclusive and collectively exhaustive, implying that every bit of data will fit into one and only one category and that all data will fit somewhere on the scale. The term *nominal* means "name-like," indicating that the numbers assigned to objects or phenomena are naming or classifying them but have no true number value; that is, the numbers cannot be ordered, added, or divided. The numbers are simply labels or identification numbers and nothing else. Examples of two nominal scales follow:

Gender:	(1) Male	(2) Female	
Geographic area:	(1) Urban	(2) Rural	(3) Suburban

The only quantifications in numerical scales are the number and percentage of objects in each category—for example, 50 males (48.5 percent) and 53 females (51.5 percent). Computing a mean of 2.4 for geographic area would be meaningless; only the mode, the value that appears most often, would be appropriate.

EXHIBIT 9.2	The Four Basic Levels of Measurement			
Level	Basic Empirical Description*	Operations	Typical Descriptive Typical Usage	Typical Descriptive Statistics
Nominal	Uses numerals to identify objects, individuals, events, or groups	Determination of equality/inequality	Classification (male/ female; buyer/ nonbuyer)	Frequency counts, percentages/modes
Ordinal	In addition to identification, provides information about the relative amount of some characteristic possessed by an event, object, etc.	Determination of greater or lesser	Rankings/ratings (preferences for hotels, banks, etc.; social class; ratings of foods based on fat content, cholesterol)	Median (mean and variance metric)
Interval	Possesses all the properties of nominal and ordinal scales plus equal intervals between consecutive points	Determination of equality of intervals	Preferred measure of complex concepts/ constructs (temperature scale, air pressure scale, level of knowledge about brands)	Mean/variance
Ratio	Incorporates all the properties of nominal, ordinal, and interval scales plus an absolute zero point	Determination of equality of ratios	Preferred measure when precision instruments are available (sales, number of on-time arrivals, age)	Geometric mean/ harmonic mean

*Because higher levels of measurement contain all the properties of lower levels, higher level scales can be converted into lower level ones (i.e., ratio to interval or ordinal or nominal, or interval to ordinal or nominal, or ordinal to nominal).
Source: Adapted from S.S. Stevens, "On the Theory of Scales of Measurement," *Science*, 103 (June 7, 1946), pp. 677–680.

Ordinal Level of Measurement

Ordinal scales have the labeling characteristics of nominal scales plus an ability to order data. Ordinal measurement is possible when the transitivity postulate can be applied. (A *postulate* is an assumption that is an essential prerequisite to carrying out an operation or line of thinking.) The *transitivity postulate* is described by the notion that "if *a* is greater than *b*, and *b* is greater than *c*, then *a* is greater than *c*." Other terms that can be substituted for *is greater than* are *is preferred to*, *is stronger than*, and *precedes*. An example of an ordinal scale follows:

> **ordinal scales**
> Scales that maintain the labeling characteristics of nominal scales and have the ability to order data.

> Please rank the following online dating services from 1 to 5, with 1 being the most preferred and 5 the least preferred.
>
> www.AmericanSingles.com   _____
> www.eharmony.com   _____
> www.yahoopersonals.com   _____
> www.greatexpectations.com   _____
> www.friendfinder.com   _____

Ordinal numbers are used strictly to indicate rank order. The numbers do not indicate absolute quantities, nor do they imply that the intervals between the numbers are equal. For example, a person ranking fax machines might like Toshiba only slightly more

Commonly used temperature scales are based on equal intervals and an arbitrary zero point. Marketing researchers often prefer interval scales because they can measure how much more of a trait one consumer has than another.

Copyright John Wiley & Sons, Inc.

interval scales
Scales that have the characteristics of ordinal scales, plus equal intervals between points to show relative amounts; they may include an arbitrary zero point.

than Savin and view Ricoh as totally unacceptable. Such information would not be obtained from an ordinal scale.

Because ranking is the objective of an ordinal scale, any rule prescribing a series of numbers that preserves the ordered relationship is satisfactory. In other words, AmericanSingles could have been assigned a value of 30; eharmony, 40; YahooPersonals, 27; GreatExpectations, 32; and FriendFinder, 42. Or any other series of numbers could have been used, as long as the basic ordering was preserved. In the case just cited, FriendFinder is 1; eHarmony 2; GreatExpectations 3; AmericanSingles 4; and YahooPersonals 5. Common arithmetical operations such as addition and multiplication cannot be used with ordinal scales. The appropriate measure of central tendency is the mode or the median. A percentile or quartile measure is used for measuring dispersion.

A controversial (yet rather common) use of ordinal scales is to rate various characteristics. In this case, the researcher assigns numbers to reflect the relative ratings of a series of statements, then uses these numbers to interpret relative distance. Recall that the marketing researchers examining role ambiguity used a scale ranging from *very certain* to *very uncertain*. The following values were assigned:

(1)	(2)	(3)	(4)	(5)
Very Certain	**Certain**	**Neutral**	**Uncertain**	**Very Uncertain**

If a researcher can justify the assumption that the intervals are equal within the scale, then the more powerful parametric statistical tests can be applied. (Parametric statistical tests will be discussed in Chapters 13 and 14.) Indeed, some measurement scholars argue that equal intervals should be normally assumed.

The best procedure would seem to be to treat ordinal measurements as though they were interval measurements but to be constantly alert to the possibility of gross inequality of intervals. As much as possible about the characteristics of the measuring tools should be learned. Much useful information has been obtained by this approach, with resulting scientific advances in psychology, sociology, and education. In short, it is unlikely that researchers will be led seriously astray by heeding this advice, if they are careful in applying it.[2]

Interval Level of Measurement

Interval scales contain all the features of ordinal scales with the added dimension that the intervals between the points on the scale are equal. The concept of temperature is based on equal intervals. Marketing researchers often prefer interval scales over ordinal scales because they can measure how much of a trait one consumer has (or does not have) over another. An interval scale enables a researcher to discuss differences separating two objects. The scale possesses properties of order and difference but with an arbitrary zero point. Examples are the Fahrenheit and Celsius scales; the freezing point of water is zero on one scale and 32 degrees on the other.

The arbitrary zero point of interval scales restricts the statements that a researcher can make about the scale points. One can say that 80°F is hotter than 32°F or that 64°F is 16° cooler than 80°F. However, one cannot say that 64°F is twice as warm as 32°F. Why? Because the zero point on the Fahrenheit scale is arbitrary. To understand this point, consider the transformation of the two Fahrenheit temperatures to Celsius using the formula Celsius = $(F-32)(5/9)$; 32°F equals 0°C, and 64°F equals 17.8°C. The statement we made about the Fahrenheit temperatures (64° is twice as warm as 32°) does not hold for Celsius. The same would be true of rankings of online dating services on an interval scale. If YahooPersonals had received a 20 and GreatExpectations a 10, we cannot say that YahooPersonals is liked twice as much as GreatExpectations, because a point defining the absence of liking has not been identified and assigned a value of zero on the scale.

Interval scales are amenable to computation of an arithmetic mean, standard deviation, and correlation coefficients. The more powerful parametric statistical tests such as t tests and F tests can be applied. In addition, researchers can take a more conservative approach and use nonparametric tests if they have concern about the equal intervals assumption.

Ratio Level of Measurement

Ratio scales have all the characteristics of those scales previously discussed as well as a meaningful absolute zero or origin. Because there is universal agreement as to the location of the zero point, comparisons among the magnitudes of ratio-scaled values are acceptable. Thus, a ratio scale reflects the actual amount of a variable. Physical characteristics of a respondent such as age, weight, and height are examples of ratio-scaled variables. Other ratio scales are based on area, distance, money values, return rates, population counts, and lapsed periods of time.

> ▷ **ratio scales**
> Scales that have the characteristics of interval scales, plus a meaningful zero point so that magnitudes can be compared arithmetically.

Because some objects have none of the property being measured, a ratio scale originates at a zero point with absolute empirical meaning. For example, an investment (albeit a poor one) can have no rate of return, or a census tract in New Mexico could be devoid of any persons. An absolute zero implies that all arithmetic operations are possible, including multiplication and division. Numbers on the scale indicate the actual amounts of the property being measured. A large bag of McDonald's french fries weighs 8 ounces and a regular bag at Burger King weighs 4 ounces; thus, a large McDonald's bag of fries weighs twice as much as a regular Burger King bag of fries.

Evaluating the Reliability and Validity of the Measurement

An ideal marketing research study would provide information that is accurate, precise, lucid, and timely. Accurate data imply accurate measurement, or $M = A$, where M refers to measurement and A stands for complete accuracy. In marketing research, this ideal is rarely, if ever, achieved. Instead,

$$M = A + E$$

where E = errors

Errors can be either random or systematic, as noted in Chapter 5. Systematic error results in a constant bias in the measurements caused by faults in the measurement instrument or process. For example, if a faulty ruler (on which one inch is actually one and a half inches) is used in Pillsbury's test kitchens to measure the height of chocolate cakes baked with alternative recipes, all cakes will be recorded at less than their actual height. *Random error* also influences the measurements but not systematically. Thus, random error is transient in nature. A person may not answer a question truthfully because he is in a bad mood that day.

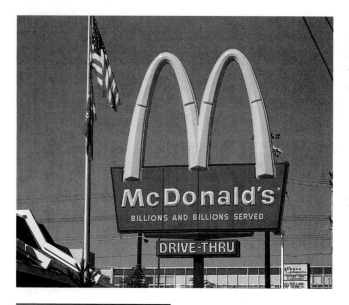

Two scores on a measurement scale can differ for a number of reasons. McDonald's may score higher on one person's survey than on another person's because of real differences in perceptions of the service or because of a variety of random or systematic errors. The reliability and validity of the type of measurement should always be checked.

Copyright John Wiley & Sons, Inc.

Two scores on a measurement scale can differ for a number of reasons.[3] Only the first of the following eight reasons does not involve error. A researcher must determine whether any of the remaining seven sources of measurement differences are producing random or systematic error.

1. *A true difference in the characteristic being measured.* A perfect measurement difference is solely the result of actual differences. For example, John rates McDonald's service as 1 (excellent) and Sandy rates its service as 4 (average), and the variation is due only to actual attitude differences.

2. *Differences due to stable characteristics of individual respondents,* such as personality, values, and intelligence. Sandy has an aggressive, rather critical personality, and she gives no one and nothing the benefit of the doubt. She actually was quite pleased with the service she received at McDonald's, but she expects such service and so gave it an average rating.

3. *Differences due to short-term personal factors,* such as temporary mood swings, health problems, time constraints, or fatigue. Earlier on the day of the study, John had won $400 in a "Name That Tune" contest on a local radio station. He stopped by McDonald's for a burger after he picked up his winning check. His reply on the service quality questionnaire might have been quite different if he had been interviewed the previous day.

4. *Differences caused by situational factors,* such as distractions or others present in the interview situation. Sandy was giving her replies while trying to watch her 4-year-old nephew, who was running amok on the McDonald's playground; John had his new fiancée along when he was interviewed. Replies of both people might have been different if they had been interviewed at home while no other friend or relative was present.

5. *Differences resulting from variations in administering the survey.* Interviewers can ask questions with different voice inflections, causing response variation. And because of such factors as rapport with the interviewee, manner of dress, sex, or race, different interviewers can cause responses to vary. Interviewer bias can be as subtle as a nodding of the head. One interviewer who tended to nod unconsciously was found to bias some respondents. They thought that the interviewer was agreeing with them when he was, in fact, saying, "Okay, I'm recording what you say—tell me more."

6. *Differences due to the sampling of items included in the questionnaire.* When researchers attempt to measure the quality of service at McDonald's, the scales and other questions used represent only a portion of the items that could have been used. The scales created by the researchers reflect their interpretation of the construct (service quality) and the way it is measured. If the researchers had used different words or if items had been added or removed, the scale values reported by John and Sandy might have been different.

7. *Differences due to a lack of clarity in the measurement instrument.* A question may be ambiguous, complex, or incorrectly interpreted. A survey that asked "How far do you live from McDonald's?" and then gave choices "(1) less than 5 minutes, (2) 5 to 10 minutes," and so forth, would be ambiguous; someone walking would undoubtedly take longer to get to the restaurant than a person driving a car or riding a bike. This topic is covered in much greater detail in Chapter 10.

8. *Differences due to mechanical or instrument factors.* Blurred questionnaires, lack of space to fully record answers, missing pages in a questionnaire, incorrect computer keystrokes, or a balky pen can result in differences in responses.

Reliability

A measurement scale that provides consistent results over time is reliable. If a ruler consistently measures a chocolate cake as 9 inches high, then the ruler is said to be reliable. Reliable scales, gauges, and other measurement devices can be used with confidence and with the knowledge that transient and situational factors are not interfering with the measurement process. Reliable instruments provide stable measures at different times under different conditions. A key question regarding reliability is "If we measure some phenomenon over and over again with the same measurement device, will we get the same or highly similar results?" An affirmative answer means that the device is reliable.

Thus, **reliability** is the degree to which measures are free from random error and, therefore, provide consistent data. The less error there is, the more reliable the observation is, so a measurement that is free of error is a correct measure. A reliable measurement, then, does not change when the concept being measured remains constant in value. However, if the concept being measured does change in value, the reliable measure will indicate that change. How can a measuring instrument be unreliable? If your weight stays constant at 150 pounds but repeated measurements on your bathroom scale show your weight to fluctuate, the scale's lack of reliability may be due to a weak spring.

There are three ways to assess reliability: test–retest, the use of equivalent forms, and internal consistency.

Test–Retest Reliability
Test–retest reliability is obtained by repeating the measurement with the same instrument, approximating the original conditions as closely as possible. The theory behind test–retest is that if random variations are present, they will be revealed by differences in the scores between the two tests. **Stability** means that very few differences in scores are found between the first and second administrations of the test; the measuring instrument is said to be stable. For example, assume that a 30-item department store image measurement scale was administered to the same group of shoppers at two different times. If the correlation between the two measurements was high, the reliability would be assumed to be high.

There are several problems with test–retest reliability. First, it may be very difficult to locate and gain the cooperation of respondents for a second testing. Second, the first measurement may alter a person's response on the second measurement. Third, environmental or personal factors may change, causing the second measurement to change.

Equivalent Form Reliability
The difficulties encountered with the test–retest approach can be avoided by creating equivalent forms of a measurement instrument. For example, assume that the researcher is interested in identifying inner-directed versus outer-directed lifestyles. Two questionnaires can be created containing measures of inner-directed behavior (see Exhibit 9.3) and measures of outer-directed behavior. These measures should receive about the same emphasis on each questionnaire. Thus, although the questions used to ascertain the lifestyles are different on the two questionnaires, the number of questions used to measure each lifestyle should be approximately equal. The recommended interval for administering the second equivalent form is two weeks, although in some cases the two forms are given one after the other

reliability
Degree to which measures are free from random error and, therefore, provide consistent data.

test–retest reliability
Ability of the same instrument to produce consistent results when used a second time under conditions as similar as possible to the original conditions.

stability
Lack of change in results from test to retest.

EXHIBIT 9.3	Statements Used to Measure Inner-Directed Lifestyles

I often don't get the credit I deserve for things I do well.
I try to get my own way regardless of others.
My greatest achievements are ahead of me.
I have a number of ideas that someday I would like to put into a book.
I am quick to accept new ideas.
I often think about how I look and what impression I am making on others.
I am a competitive person.
I feel upset when I hear that people are criticizing or blaming me.
I'd like to be a celebrity.
I get a real thrill out of doing dangerous things.
I feel that almost nothing in life can substitute for great achievement.
It's important for me to be noticed.
I keep in close touch with my friends.
I spend a good deal of time trying to decide how I feel about things.
I often think I can feel my way into the innermost being of another person.
I feel that ideals are powerful motivating forces in people.
I think someone can be a good person without believing in God.
The Eastern religions are more appealing to me than Christianity.
I feel satisfied with my life.
I enjoy getting involved in new and unusual situations.
Overall, I'd say I'm happy.
I feel I understand where my life is going.
I like to think I'm different from other people.
I adopt a commonsense attitude toward life.

> **equivalent form reliability**
> Ability of two very similar forms of an instrument to produce closely correlated results.

or simultaneously. **Equivalent form reliability** is determined by measuring the correlation of the scores on the two instruments.

There are two problems with equivalent forms that should be noted. First, it is very difficult, and perhaps impossible, to create two totally equivalent forms. Second, if equivalence can be achieved, it may not be worth the time, trouble, and expense involved. The theory behind the equivalent forms approach to reliability assessment is the same as that of the test–retest. The primary difference between the test–retest and the equivalent forms methods is the testing instrument itself. Test–retest uses the same instrument, whereas the equivalent forms approach uses a different, but highly similar, measuring instrument.

> **internal consistency reliability**
> Ability of an instrument to produce similar results when used on different samples during the same time period to measure a phenomenon.

> **split-half technique**
> Method of assessing the reliability of a scale by dividing the total set of measurement items in half and correlating the results.

Internal Consistency Reliability   **Internal consistency reliability** assesses the ability to produce similar results when different samples are used to measure a phenomenon during the same time period. The theory of internal consistency rests on the concept of equivalence. *Equivalence* is concerned with how much error may be introduced by using different samples of items to measure a phenomenon; it focuses on variations at one point in time among samples of items. A researcher can test for item equivalence by assessing the homogeneity of a set of items. The total set of items used to measure a phenomenon, such as inner-directed lifestyles, is divided into two halves; the total scores of the two halves are then correlated. Use of the **split-half technique** typically calls for scale items to be randomly assigned to one half or the other. The problem with this method is that the estimate of the coefficient of reliability is totally dependent on how the items were split. Different splits result in different correlations when, ideally, they should not.

To overcome this problem, many researchers now use the *Cronbach alpha technique*, which involves computing mean reliability coefficient estimates for all possible ways of splitting a set of items in half. A lack of correlation of an item with other items in the scale is evidence that the item does not belong in the scale and should be omitted. One limitation of the Cronbach alpha is that the scale items require equal intervals. If this criterion cannot be met, another test called the KR-20 can be used. The *KR-20 technique* is applicable for all dichotomous or nominally scaled items.

Validity

Recall that the second characteristic of a good measurement device is validity. **Validity** addresses the issue of whether what the researcher was trying to measure was actually measured. When Pontiac brought out the Aztek, research told them that the car would sell between 50,000 and 70,000 units annually despite the controversial styling. After selling only 27,000 cars per year, the model was discontinued in 2005. Unfortunately, the research measuring instrument was not valid. The validity of a measure refers to the extent to which the measurement instrument and procedure are free from both systematic and random error. Thus, a measuring device is valid only if differences in scores reflect true differences on the characteristic being measured rather than systematic or random error. You should recognize that a necessary precondition for validity is that the measuring instrument be reliable. An instrument that is not reliable will not yield consistent results when measuring the same phenomenon over time.

> **validity**
> The degree to which what the researcher was trying to measure was actually measured.

A scale or other measuring device is basically worthless to a researcher if it lacks validity because it is not measuring what it is supposed to. On the surface, this seems like a rather simple notion, yet validity often is based on subtle distinctions. Assume that your teacher gives an exam that he has constructed to measure marketing research knowledge, and the test consists strictly of applying a number of formulas to simple case problems. A friend receives a low score on the test and protests to the teacher that she "really understands marketing research." Her position, in essence, is that the test was not valid. She maintains that, rather than measuring knowledge of marketing research, the test measured memorization of formulas and the ability to use simple math to find solutions. The teacher could repeat the exam only to find that student scores still fell in the same order. Does this mean that the protesting student was incorrect? Not necessarily; the teacher may be systematically measuring the ability to memorize rather than a true understanding of marketing research.

Unlike the teacher attempting to measure marketing research knowledge, a brand manager is interested in successful prediction. The manager, for example, wants to know if a purchase intent scale successfully predicts trial purchase of a new product. Thus, validity can be examined from a number of different perspectives, including face, content, criterion-related, and construct validity (see Exhibit 9.4).

Face Validity **Face validity** is the weakest form of validity. It is concerned with the degree to which a measurement seems to measure what it is supposed to. It is a judgment call by the researcher, made as the questions are designed. Thus, as each question is scrutinized, there is an implicit assessment of its face validity. Revisions enhance the face validity of the question until it passes the researcher's subjective evaluation. Alternatively, *face validity* can refer to the subjective agreement of researchers, experts, or people familiar with the market, product, or industry that a scale logically appears to be accurately reflecting what it is supposed to measure.[4] A straightforward question such as "What is your age?" followed by a series of age categories generally is agreed to have face validity. Most scales used in marketing research attempt to measure attitudes or behavioral intentions, which are much more elusive.

> **face validity**
> Degree to which a measurement seems to measure what it is supposed to measure.

EXHIBIT 9.4	Assessing the Validity of a Measurement Instrument
Face validity	The degree to which a measurement instrument seems to measure what it is supposed to, as judged by researchers.
Content validity	The degree to which measurement items represent the universe of the concept under study.
Criterion-related validity	The degree to which a measurement instrument can predict a variable that is designated a criterion.
	a. Predictive validity: The extent to which a future level of a criterion variable can be predicted by a current measurement on a scale.
	b. Concurrent validity: The extent to which a criterion variable measured at the same point in time as the variable of interest can be predicted by the measurement instrument.
Construct validity	The degree to which a measurement instrument confirms a hypothesis created from a theory based on the concepts under study.
	a. Convergent validity: The degree of association among different measurement instruments that purport to measure the same concept.
	b. Discriminant validity: A measure of the lack of association among constructs that are supposed to be different.

> **content validity**
> Representativeness, or sampling adequacy, of the content of the measurement instrument.

Content Validity   **Content validity** is the representativeness, or sampling adequacy, of the content of the measurement instrument. In other words, does the scale provide adequate coverage of the topic under study? Say that McDonald's has hired you to measure its image among adults 18 to 30 years of age who eat fast-food hamburgers at least once a month. You devise the following scale:

Modern building	1	2	3	4	5	Old-fashioned building
Beautiful landscaping	1	2	3	4	5	Poor landscaping
Clean parking lots	1	2	3	4	5	Dirty parking lots
Attractive signs	1	2	3	4	5	Unattractive signs

A McDonald's executive would quickly take issue with this scale, claiming that a person could evaluate McDonald's on this scale and never have eaten a McDonald's hamburger. In fact, the evaluation could be made simply by driving past a McDonald's. The executive could further argue that the scale lacks content validity because many important components of image—such as the quality of the food, cleanliness of the eating area and restrooms, and promptness and courtesy of service—were omitted.

The determination of content validity is not always a simple matter. It is very difficult, and perhaps impossible, to identify all the facets of McDonald's image. Content validity ultimately becomes a judgmental matter. One could approach content validity by first carefully defining precisely what is to be measured. Second, an exhaustive literature search and focus groups could be conducted to identify all possible items for inclusion on the scale. Third, a panel of experts could be asked their opinions on whether an item should be included. Finally, the scale could be pretested and an open-ended question asked that might identify other items to be included. For example, after a more refined image scale for McDonald's has been administered, a follow-up question could be "Do you have any other thoughts about McDonald's that you would like to express?" Answers to this pretest question might provide clues for other image dimensions not previously considered.

> **criterion-related validity**
> Degree to which a measurement instrument can predict a variable that is designated a criterion.

Criterion-Related Validity   **Criterion-related validity** examines the ability of a measuring instrument to predict a variable that is designated a criterion. Suppose that we wish to devise a test to identify marketing researchers who are exceptional at moderating

A politician is interested in what issues those likely to vote perceive as important. The predictive validity of the politician's measures may determine whether or not he or she is elected.

Mark Richards/PhotoEdit

focus groups. We begin by having impartial marketing research experts identify from a directory of researchers those they judge to be best at moderating focus groups. We then construct 300 items to which all the group moderators are asked to reply yes or no, such as "I believe it is important to compel shy group participants to speak out" and "I like to interact with small groups of people." We then go through the responses and select the items that the "best" focus group moderators answered one way and the rest of the moderators answered the other way. Assume that this process produces 84 items, which we put together to form what we shall call the Test of Effectiveness in Focus Group Moderating (TEFGM). We feel that this test will identify good focus group moderators. The criterion of interest here is the ability to conduct a good focus group. We might explore further the criterion-related validity of TEFGM by administering it to another group of moderators, each of whom has been designated as either "best" or "not as good." Then we could determine how well the test identifies the section to which each marketing researcher is assigned. Thus, criterion-related validity is concerned with detecting the presence or absence of one or more criteria considered to represent constructs of interest.

Two subcategories of criterion-related validity are predictive validity and concurrent validity. **Predictive validity** is the extent to which a future level of a criterion variable can be predicted by a current measurement on a scale. A voter-motivation scale, for example, is used to predict the likelihood that a person will vote in the next election. A savvy politician is not interested in what the community as a whole perceives as important problems but only in what persons who are likely to vote perceive as important problems. These are the issues that the politician would address in speeches and advertising. Another example of predictive validity is the extent to which a purchase intent scale for a new Pepperidge Farm pastry predicts actual trial of the product.

Concurrent validity is concerned with the relationship between the predictor variable and the criterion variable, both of which are assessed at the same point in time—for example, the ability of a home pregnancy test to accurately determine whether a woman is pregnant right now. Such a test with low concurrent validity could cause a lot of undue stress.

> **predictive validity**
> Degree to which a future level of a criterion variable can be forecast by a current measurement scale.

> **concurrent validity**
> Degree to which another variable, measured at the same point in time as the variable of interest, can be predicted by the measurement instrument.

construct validity
Degree to which a measurement instrument represents and logically connects, via the underlying theory, the observed phenomenon to the construct.

Construct Validity   Construct validity, though not often consciously addressed by many marketing researchers on a day-to-day basis, is extremely important to marketing scientists. Assessing construct validity involves understanding the theoretical foundations underlying the obtained measurements. A measure has **construct validity** if it behaves according to the theory behind the prediction. Purchase behavior can be observed directly; someone either buys product A or does not. Yet scientists have developed constructs on lifestyle, involvement, attitude, and personality that help explain why someone does or does not purchase something. These constructs are largely unobservable. Researchers can observe behavior related to the constructs—that is, the purchase of a product. However, they cannot observe the constructs themselves—such as an attitude. Constructs help scientists communicate and build theories to explain phenomena.[5]

You might think of construct validity as a "labeling" issue. When you measure a notion (construct) called "high involvement," is that what you are really measuring? Viewed in a slightly different manner, when a researcher claims construct validity, he or she essentially has a theory of how phenomena, people, and measures relate to each other (and other theoretical terms). In other words, the researcher offers us a theoretical pattern. When the researcher claims construct validity, he or she is claiming that the observed pattern in a research project corresponds to the theoretical pattern. In this instance, how the researcher thought the world works is how it works.

Although construct validity is presented here with various other types of validity, it really stands above all others. Why? Because construct validity relates back to the very essence of what you are trying to measure. If your research lacks construct validity, little else matters.[6]

Two statistical measures of construct validity are convergent and discriminant validity. **Convergent validity** reflects the degree of correlation among different measures that purport to measure the same construct. **Discriminant validity** reveals the lack of—or low—correlation among constructs that are supposed to be different. Assume that we develop a multi-item scale that measures the propensity to shop at discount stores. Our theory suggests that this propensity is caused by four personality variables: high level of self-confidence, low need for status, low need for distinctiveness, and high level of adaptability. Furthermore, our theory suggests that propensity to shop at discount stores is not related to brand loyalty or high-level aggressiveness.

convergent validity
Degree of correlation among different measurement instruments that purport to measure the same construct.

discriminant validity
Measure of the lack of association among constructs that are supposed to be different.

Evidence of construct validity exists if our scale does the following:

☐ Correlates highly with other measures of propensity to shop at discount stores, such as reported stores patronized and social class (convergent validity)

☐ Has a low correlation with the unrelated constructs of brand loyalty and a high level of aggressiveness (discriminant validity)

All the types of validity discussed here are somewhat interrelated in both theory and practice. Predictive validity is obviously very important on a scale to predict whether a person will shop at a discount store. A researcher developing a discount store patronage scale probably would first attempt to understand the constructs that provide the basis for prediction. The researcher would put forth a theory about discount store patronage—that, of course, is the foundation of construct validity. Next, the researcher would be concerned with which specific items to include on the discount store patronage scale and whether these items relate to the full range of the construct. Thus, the researcher would ascertain the degree of content validity. The issue of criterion-related validity could be addressed in a pretest by measuring scores on the discount store patronage scale and actual store patronage.

Reliability and Validity—A Concluding Comment

The concepts of reliability and validity are illustrated in Exhibit 9.5. Situation 1 shows holes all over the target, which could be caused by the use of an old rifle, being a poor

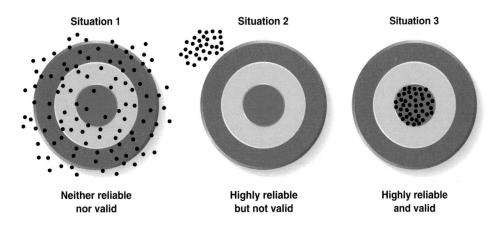

Exhibit 9.5

Illustrations of Possible Reliability and Validity Situations in Measurement

shot, or many other factors. This complete lack of consistency means there is no reliability. Because the instrument lacks reliability, thus creating huge errors, it cannot be valid. Measurement reliability is a necessary condition for validity.

Situation 2 denotes a very tight pattern (consistency), but the pattern is far removed from the bull's-eye. This illustrates that an instrument can have a high level of reliability (little variance) but lack validity. The instrument is consistent, but it does not measure what it is supposed to measure. The shooter has a steady eye, but the sights are not adjusted properly. Situation 3 shows the reliability and validity that researchers strive to achieve in a measurement instrument; it is on target with what the researcher is attempting to measure.

Scaling Defined

The term **scaling** refers to procedures for attempting to determine quantitative measures of subjective and sometimes abstract concepts. It is defined as a procedure for assigning numbers (or other symbols) to properties of an object in order to impart some numerical characteristics to the properties in question. Actually, numbers are assigned to *indicants* of the properties of objects. The rise and fall of mercury in a glass tube (a thermometer) is an indicant of temperature variations.

A scale is a measurement tool. Scales are either unidimensional or multidimensional. **Unidimensional scales** are designed to measure only one attribute of a concept, respondent, or object. Thus, a unidimensional scale measuring consumers' price sensitivity might include several items to measure price sensitivity, but combined into a single measure; all interviewees' attitudes are then placed along a linear continuum, called *degree of price sensitivity*. **Multidimensional scales** are based on the premise that a concept, respondent, or object might be better described using several dimensions. For example, target customers for Jaguar automobiles may be defined in three dimensions: level of wealth, degree of price sensitivity, and appreciation of fine motor cars.

Advice on what makes a good scale is given in the following Practicing Marketing Research box.

scaling
Procedures for assigning numbers (or other symbols) to properties of an object in order to impart some numerical characteristics to the properties in question.

unidimensional scales
Scales designed to measure only one attribute of a concept, respondent, or object.

multidimensional scales
Scales designed to measure several dimensions of a concept, respondent, or object.

Attitude Measurement Scales

Measurement of attitudes relies on less precise scales than those found in the physical sciences and hence is much more difficult. Because an attitude is a construct that exists in the mind of the consumer, it is not directly observable—unlike, for example, weight in the physical sciences. In many cases, attitudes are measured at the nominal or ordinal

PRACTICING MARKETING RESEARCH

What Makes a Good Scale?

Kunal Gupta, Jamie Baker-Prewitt, and Jeff Miller, all of Burke Marketing Research, discuss the popularity of itemized rating scales and the properties of any good scale.

The prevalent use of itemized rating scales is not surprising because . . .

☐ They are fairly easy to construct.

☐ Marketing research studies that have used such scales abound, and scales from such studies can be easily duplicated or adapted for new research.

☐ They enable respondents to express their attitudes and opinions in common and simple words, or through the use of numerical values.

Properties of a Good Scale

While there is no single, itemized scale that works well under all situations, it is important to recognize that the chosen scale must meet certain overall criteria. These criteria help to ensure that responses are being measured and reported in a reliable and valid manner. In particular, good scales should:

☐ Be easy to understand by respondents.

☐ Discriminate well between respondent perceptions.

☐ Be easy to interpret.

☐ Have minimal response bias.

☐ Be easy to administer.

☐ Be credible and useful.

Thus, marketing researchers should strive to design scales that perform well against the maximum number of these criteria rather than search for a universally applicable, one-size-fits-all scale.[7]

Questions

1. How does a researcher know if he or she has created a good scale? Are any of the factors above more important than others?

---

level. Some more sophisticated scales enable the marketing researcher to measure at the interval level. One must be careful not to attribute the more powerful properties of an interval scale to the lower-level nominal or ordinal scales.

Graphic Rating Scales

> **graphic rating scales**
> Measurement scales that include a graphic continuum, anchored by two extremes.

Graphic rating scales offer respondents a graphic continuum, typically anchored by two extremes. Exhibit 9.6 depicts three types of graphic rating scales that might be used to evaluate La-Z-Boy recliners. Scale A represents the simplest form of a graphic scale. Respondents are instructed to mark their response on the continuum. After respondents have done so, scores are ascertained by dividing the line into as many categories as desired and assigning a score based on the category into which the mark has been placed. For example, if the line were 6 inches long, every inch might represent a category. Scale B offers the respondent slightly more structure by assigning numbers along the scale.

Responses to graphic rating scales are not limited to simply placing a mark on a continuum, as scale C illustrates. Scale C has been used successfully by many researchers to speed up self-administered interviews. Respondents are asked to touch the thermometer on the computer screen that best depicts their feelings.

Graphic rating scales can be constructed easily and are simple to use. They enable a researcher to discern fine distinctions, assuming that the rater has adequate discriminatory abilities. Numerical data obtained from the scales are typically treated as interval data.

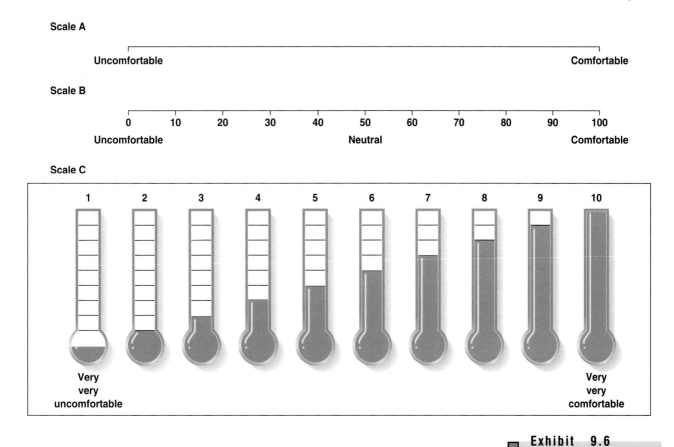

Exhibit 9.6

Three Types of Graphic Rating Scales

One disadvantage of graphic rating scales is that overly extreme anchors tend to force respondents toward the middle of the scale. Also, some research has suggested that such scales are not as reliable as itemized rating scales.

Itemized Rating Scales

Itemized rating scales are similar to graphic rating scales, except that respondents must select from a limited number of ordered categories rather than placing a mark on a continuous scale. (Purists would argue that scale C in Exhibit 9.6 is an itemized rating scale.) Exhibit 9.7 shows some examples of itemized rating scales taken from nationwide marketing research surveys. Starting items are rotated on each questionnaire to eliminate the order bias that might arise from starting with the same item each time.

Scale A was used by a dot-com company in determining what features and services it should add to its website. Scale B was used in measuring satisfaction with an online travel site. Scale C was used by an e-commerce music retailer to better understand how people select a music website. Scale D was also an Internet survey, conducted by a producer of customer relationship management software. Examples of other itemized rating scales are shown in Exhibit 9.8.

Although itemized rating scales do not allow for the fine distinctions that can be achieved in a graphic rating scale, they are easy to construct and administer. And the definitive categories found in itemized rating scales usually produce more reliable ratings.

When a researcher, for some reason, is interested in the most extreme position views, he or she may elect to use a two-stage format. Research has shown that a two-stage format can provide better data quality in detecting extreme views than a single-stage itemized rating scale. Following is an example of the two-stage approach.[8]

itemized rating scales Measurement scales in which the respondent selects an answer from a limited number of ordered categories.

Exhibit 9.7

Itemized Rating Scales Used in Internet and Mall Surveys

If offered, how likely would you be to use the following areas on this site?

Scale A

a. Auctions
Not at all likely to use ○1 ○2 ○3 ○4 ○5 ○6 ○7 **Extremely likely to use**

b. Fee-based education tools
Not at all likely to use ○1 ○2 ○3 ○4 ○5 ○6 ○7 **Extremely likely to use**

c. Event registration
Not at all likely to use ○1 ○2 ○3 ○4 ○5 ○6 ○7 **Extremely likely to use**

d. Online shopping markets
Not at all likely to use ○1 ○2 ○3 ○4 ○5 ○6 ○7 **Extremely likely to use**

e. Recruiting
Not at all likely to use ○1 ○2 ○3 ○4 ○5 ○6 ○7 **Extremely likely to use**

f. Research subscription
Not at all likely to use ○1 ○2 ○3 ○4 ○5 ○6 ○7 **Extremely likely to use**

g. Trading community
Not at all likely to use ○1 ○2 ○3 ○4 ○5 ○6 ○7 **Extremely likely to use**

h. Training/seminars
Not at all likely to use ○1 ○2 ○3 ○4 ○5 ○6 ○7 **Extremely likely to use**

Scale B

Submitting a Request for a Hotel Reservation

We'd like to get your feedback regarding your experience in submitting a request for a hotel reservation at our website today. Please rate your satisfaction with each of the following aspects of *fasthotels.com* based on **your experience this visit**.

	Very Satisfied 1	2	3	4	Very Dissatisfied 5
Ability to access the offer page	○	○	○	○	○
Ability to locate hotel information	○	○	○	○	○
Ability to locate city information	○	○	○	○	○
Clarity of how the bonus program works	○	○	○	○	○
Clarity of the purchase agreement	○	○	○	○	○

Please rate the extent to which you are satisfied that *Fasthotels.com* **has communicated** each of the following to you during this visit:

	Very Satisfied 1	2	3	4	Very Dissatisfied 5
Your hotel reservation is/will be nonchangeable	○	○	○	○	○
Your hotel reservation is/will be nonrefundable	○	○	○	○	○

How **satisfied** would you say you were with **this visit** to *Fasthotels.com*?

○ Very satisfied
○ Satisfied
○ Somewhat satisfied
○ Neither satisfied nor dissatisfied
○ Somewhat dissatisfied
○ Dissatisfied
○ Very dissatisfied

Scale C

What factors influence your choice of music websites? (Rate the importance of each item.)

	Not at All Important				Very Important
Customer benefits or rewards for shopping	○	○	○	○	○
Customer service or delivery options	○	○	○	○	○
Ease of use of website	○	○	○	○	○
Low prices	○	○	○	○	○
Real-time audio sampling of CDs	○	○	○	○	○
Reviews and artist information	○	○	○	○	○

Scale D

How interested would you be in obtaining additional information about this customer relationship management solution for your business?

○ Extremely interested   ○ Somewhat interested   ○ Not at all interested
○ Very interested   ○ Not very interested

How likely is it that your business will invest in this type of customer relationship management solution within the next 12 months?

○ Extremely likely   ○ Somewhat likely   ○ Not at all likely
○ Very likely   ○ Not very likely

EXHIBIT 9.8   Selected Itemized Rating Scales

Characteristic of Interest	Rating Choices				
Purchase Intent	Definitely will buy	Probably will buy	Probably will not buy	Definitely will not buy	
Level of Agreement	Strongly agree	Somewhat agree	Neither agree nor disagree	Somewhat disagree	Strongly disagree
Quality	Very good	Good	Neither good nor bad	Fair	Poor
Dependability	Completely dependable	Somewhat dependable	Not very dependable	Not dependable at all	
Style	Very stylish	Somewhat stylish	Not very stylish	Completely unstylish	
Satisfaction	Completely satisfied	Somewhat satisfied	Neither satisfied nor dissatisfied	Somewhat dissatisfied	Completely dissatisfied
Cost	Extremely expensive	Expensive	Neither expensive nor inexpensive	Slightly inexpensive	Very inexpensive
Ease of Use	Very easy to use	Somewhat easy to use	Not very easy to use	Difficult to use	
Color Brightness	Extremely bright	Very bright	Somewhat bright	Slightly bright	Not bright at all
Modernity	Very modern	Somewhat modern	Neither modern nor old-fashioned	Somewhat old-fashioned	Very old-fashioned

Traditional One-Stage Format

"How effective do you believe Senator Foghorn is in having your money stay in the community?"

Very effective	Somewhat effective	Somewhat ineffective	Very ineffective	Don't know
4	3	2	1	0

Two-Stage Format

"How effective do you believe Senator Foghorn is in having your money stay in the community?"

How *effective*?
- ☐ Effective
- ☐ Ineffective
- ☐ No opinion

Would that be *very* or *somewhat*?
- ☐ Very
- ☐ Somewhat

Rank-Order Scales

> **noncomparative scales** Measurement scales in which judgment is made without reference to another object, concept, or person.

> **rank-order scales** Measurement scales in which the respondent compares two or more items and ranks them.

> **comparative scales** Measurement scales in which one object, concept, or person is compared with another on a scale.

Itemized and graphic scales are considered to be **noncomparative scales** because the respondent makes a judgment without reference to another object, concept, or person. **Rank-order scales**, on the other hand, are **comparative scales** because the respondent is asked to compare two or more items and rank each item. Rank-order scales are widely used in marketing research for several reasons. They are easy to use and give ordinal measurements of the items evaluated. Instructions are easy to understand, and the process typically moves at a steady pace. Some researchers claim that rank-order scales force respondents to evaluate concepts in a realistic manner. Exhibit 9.9(a) illustrates a series of rank-order scales taken from a study on eye shadows. Exhibit 9.9(b) shows an online scale on automobile resale value percentage rank-order scale.

Rank-order scales possess several disadvantages. If all of the alternatives in a respondent's choice set are not included, the results could be misleading. For example, a respondent's first choice on all dimensions in the eye shadow study might have been Wet'n'Wild, which was not included. A second problem is that the concept being ranked may be completely outside a person's choice set, thus producing meaningless data. Perhaps a respondent doesn't use eye shadow and feels that the product isn't appropriate for any woman. Another limitation is that the scale gives the researcher only ordinal data. Nothing is learned about how far apart the items stand or how intensely the respondent feels about the ranking of an item. Finally, the researcher does not know why the respondent ranked the items as he or she did.

Q-Sorting

> **Q-sorting** Measurement scale employing a sophisticated form of rank ordering using card sorts.

Q-sorting is basically a sophisticated form of rank ordering. A respondent is given cards listing a set of objects—such as verbal statements, slogans, product features, or potential customer services—and asked to sort them into piles according to specified

(a) Eye Shadow Scales

Please rank the following eye shadows, with 1 being the brand that best meets the characteristic being evaluated and 6 the worst brand on the characteristic being evaluated. The six brands are listed on card C. (HAND RESPONDENT CARD C.) Let's begin with the idea of having high-quality compacts or containers. Which brand would rank as having the highest quality compacts or containers? Which is second? (RECORD BELOW.)

	Q.48. Having High-Quality Container	Q.49. Having High-Quality Applicator	Q.50. Having High-Quality Eye Shadow
Avon	_____	_____	_____
Cover Girl	_____	_____	_____
Estee Lauder	_____	_____	_____
L'Oreal	_____	_____	_____
Natural Wonder	_____	_____	_____
Revlon	_____	_____	_____

Card C		
Avon	Cover Girl	Estee Lauder
L'Oreal	Natural Wonder	Revlon

(b) Car Resale Value Scale

Based on your personal experience or what you have seen, heard or read, please rank the following car brands according to the resale value percentage—that is, the brand that enables you to recover the largest dollar amount (percentage) of your original purchase price of the vehicle.

Place a "1" next to the brand that has the highest resale value percentage, a "2" next to the brand that has the next highest resale value percentage, and so forth. Remember, no two cars can have the same ranking.

_____ Chevrolet
_____ Toyota
_____ BMW
_____ Ford

rating categories. For example, the cards might each describe a feature that could be incorporated into a new automobile design, and the respondent might be asked to sort the cards according to how well he or she likes the potential feature. Q-sorts usually contain a large number of cards—from 60 to 120 cards. For statistical convenience, the respondent is instructed to put varying numbers of cards in several piles, the whole making up a normal statistical distribution.

Here is a Q-sort distribution of 90 items:

Excellent Feature										**Poor Feature**
3	4	7	10	13	16	13	10	7	4	3
10	9	8	7	6	5	4	3	2	1	0

This is a rank-order continuum from Excellent Feature (10) to Poor Feature (0), with varying degrees of approval and disapproval between the extremes.

The numbers 3, 4, 7, . . . , 7, 4, 3 are the numbers of cards to be placed in each pile. The numbers below the line are the values assigned to the cards in each pile. That is, the three cards on the left (Excellent Feature) are each assigned 10, the four cards in the next pile are assigned 9, and so on through the distribution, to the three cards on the extreme right (Poor Feature), which are assigned 0. The center pile, containing 16 cards, is a neutral pile. The respondent is told to put into the neutral pile cards that are left over after other choices have been made; these include cards that seem ambiguous or about which he or she cannot make a decision. In brief, this Q-sort will contain 11 piles of varying numbers of cards, and the cards in each pile will be assigned a value from 0 through 10. A Q-sort can be used to determine the relative ranking of items by individuals and to identify clusters of individuals who exhibit the same preferences. These clusters may then be analyzed as a potential basis for market segmentation. Thus, Q-sorts have a much different objective than other types of scaling—the goal is to uncover groups of individuals who possess similar attitudes.

Paired Comparisons

> **paired comparison scales**
> Measurement scales that ask the respondent to pick one of two objects in a set, based on some stated criteria.

Paired comparison scales ask a respondent to pick one of two objects from a set, based on some stated criteria. The respondent, therefore, makes a series of paired judgments between objects. Exhibit 9.10 shows a paired comparison scale used in a national study for sun care products. Only part of the scale is shown; the data collection procedure typically requires the respondent to compare all possible pairs of objects.

Paired comparisons overcome several problems of traditional rank-order scales. First, it is easier for people to select one item from a set of two than to rank a large set of data. Second, the problem of order bias is overcome; there is no pattern in the ordering of items or questions to create a source of bias. On the negative side, because all possible pairs are evaluated, the number of paired comparisons increases geometrically as the number of objects to be evaluated increases arithmetically. Thus, the number of objects to be evaluated should remain fairly small to prevent interviewee fatigue.

Exhibit 9.10

Paired Comparison Scale for Sun Care Products

Here are some characteristics used to describe sun care products in general. Please tell me which characteristic in each pair is more important to you when selecting a sun care product.

a. Tans evenly	**b.** Tans without burning
a. Prevents burning	**b.** Protects against burning and tanning
a. Good value for the money	**b.** Goes on evenly
a. Not greasy	**b.** Does not stain clothing
a. Tans without burning	**b.** Prevents burning
a. Protects against burning and tanning	**b.** Good value for the money
a. Goes on evenly	**b.** Tans evenly
a. Prevents burning	**b.** Not greasy

Constant Sum Scales

To avoid long lists of paired items, marketing researchers use **constant sum scales** more often than paired comparisons. Constant sum scales require the respondent to divide a given number of points, typically 100, among two or more attributes based on their importance to him or her. Respondents must value each item relative to all other items. The number of points allocated to each alternative indicates the ranking assigned to it by the respondent, as well as the relative magnitude of each alternative as perceived by the respondent. A constant sum scale used in a national study of tennis sportswear is shown in Exhibit 9.11. Another advantage of the constant sum scale over a rank-order or paired comparison scale is that if the respondent perceives two characteristics to have equal value, he or she can so indicate.

A major disadvantage of this scale is that the respondent may have difficulty allocating the points to total 100 if there are a lot of characteristics or items. Most researchers feel that 10 items is the upper limit on a constant sum scale.

> **constant sum scales**
> Measurement scales that ask the respondent to divide a given number of points, typically 100, among two or more attributes, based on their importance to him or her.

Semantic Differential Scales

The semantic differential was developed by Charles Osgood, George Suci, and Percy Tannenbaum.[9] The focus of their original research was on the measurement of meaning of an object to a person. The object might be a savings and loan association, and the meaning its image among a certain group of people.

The construction of a **semantic differential scale** begins with determination of a concept to be rated, such as the image of a company, brand, or store. The researcher selects dichotomous (opposite) pairs of words or phrases that could be used to describe the concept. Respondents then rate the concept on a scale (usually 1 to 7). The mean of the responses for each pair of adjectives is computed, and the means are plotted as a profile, or image.

Exhibit 9.12 is an actual profile of an Arizona savings and loan association as perceived by noncustomers with family incomes of $80,000 and above. A quick glance shows that the firm is viewed as somewhat old-fashioned, with rather plain facilities. It is viewed as well-established, reliable, successful, and probably very nice to deal with. The institution has parking problems and perhaps entry and egress difficulties. Its advertising is viewed as dismal.

> **semantic differential scales**
> Measurement scales that examine the strengths and weaknesses of a concept by having the respondent rank it between dichotomous pairs of words or phrases that could be used to describe it; the means of the responses are then plotted as a profile, or image.

Exhibit 9.11

Constant Sum Scale Used in Tennis Sportswear Study

Below are seven characteristics of women's tennis sportswear. Please allocate 100 points among the characteristics such that the allocation represents the importance of each characteristic to you. The more points that you assign to a characteristic, the more important it is. If the characteristic is totally unimportant, you should not allocate any points to it. When you've finished, please double-check to make sure that your total adds to 100.

Characteristics of Tennis Sportswear	Number of Points
Is comfortable to wear	_____
Is durable	_____
Is made by well-known brand or sports manufacturers	_____
Is made in the United States	_____
Has up-to-date styling	_____
Gives freedom of movement	_____
Is a good value for the money	_____
	100 points

The semantic differential is a quick and efficient means of examining the strengths and weaknesses of a product or company image versus those of the competition. More importantly, however, the semantic differential has been shown to be sufficiently reliable and valid for decision making and prediction in marketing and the behavioral sciences.[10] Also, the semantic differential has proved to be statistically robust (generalizable from one group of subjects to another) when applied to corporate image research.[11] This makes possible the measurement and comparison of images held by interviewees with diverse backgrounds.

Although these advantages have led many researchers to use the semantic differential as an image measurement tool, it is not without disadvantages. First, the semantic differential suffers from a lack of standardization. It is a highly generalized technique that must be adapted for each research problem. There is no single set of standard scales, and hence the development of customized scales becomes an integral part of the research.

The number of divisions on the semantic differential scale also presents a problem. If too few divisions are used, the scale is crude and lacks meaning; if too many are used, the scale goes beyond the ability of most people to discriminate. Researchers have found the seven-point scale to be the most satisfactory.

Another disadvantage of the semantic differential is the *halo effect*. The rating of a specific image component may be dominated by the interviewee's overall impression of the concept being rated. Bias may be significant if the image is hazy in the respondent's mind. To partially counteract the halo effect, the researcher should randomly reverse scale adjectives so that all the "good" ones are not placed on one side of the scale and the "bad" ones on the other. This forces the interviewee to evaluate the adjectives before responding. After the data have been gathered, all the positive adjectives are placed on one side and the negative ones on the other to facilitate analysis.

In analysis of a seven-point semantic differential scale, care must be taken in interpreting a score of 4. A response of 4 indicates one of two things—the respondent either

Exhibit 9.12

Semantic Differential Profile of an Arizona Savings and Loan Association

Adjective 1	Mean of Each Adjective Pair							Adjective 2
	1	2	3	4	5	6	7	
Modern								Old-fashioned
Aggressive								Defensive
Friendly								Unfriendly
Well-established								Not well-established
Attractive exterior								Unattractive exterior
Reliable								Unreliable
Appeals to small companies								Appeals to big companies
Makes you feel at home								Makes you feel uneasy
Helpful services								Indifferent to customers
Nice to deal with								Hard to deal with
No parking or transportation problems								Parking or transportation problems
My kind of people								Not my kind of people
Successful								Unsuccessful
Ads attract a lot of attention								Haven't noticed ads
Interesting ads								Uninteresting ads
Influential ads								Not influential

is unable to relate the given pair of adjectives to the concept or is simply neutral or indifferent. Image studies frequently contain a large number of 4 responses. This phenomenon tends to pull the profiles toward the neutral position. Thus, the profiles lack clarity, and little distinction appears.

Stapel Scales

The **Stapel scale** is a modification of the semantic differential. A single adjective is placed in the center of the scale, which typically is a 10-point scale ranging from +5 to −5. The technique is designed to measure both the direction and the intensity of attitudes simultaneously. (The semantic differential, on the other hand, reflects how closely the descriptor adjective fits the concept being evaluated.) An example of a Stapel scale is shown in Exhibit 9.13.

The primary advantage of the Stapel scale is that it enables the researcher to avoid the arduous task of creating bipolar adjective pairs. The scale may also permit finer discrimination in measuring attitudes. A drawback is that descriptor adjectives can be phrased in a positive, neutral, or negative vein, and the choice of phrasing has been shown to affect the scale results and the person's ability to respond.[12] The Stapel scale has never had much popularity in commercial research and is used less frequently than the semantic differential.

Likert Scales

The **Likert scale** is another scale that avoids the problem of developing pairs of dichotomous adjectives. The scale consists of a series of statements expressing either a favorable or an unfavorable attitude toward the concept under study. The respondent is asked to indicate the level of her or his agreement or disagreement with each statement by assigning it a numerical score. The scores are then totaled to measure the respondent's attitude.

Exhibit 9.14 shows two Likert scales for an Internet game site targeted toward teenagers. Scale A measures attitudes toward the registration process; scale B evaluates users' attitudes toward advertising on the website.

> **Stapel scales**
> Measurement scales that require the respondent to rate, on a scale ranging from +5 to −5, how closely and in what direction a descriptor adjective fits a given concept.

> **Likert scales**
> Measurement scales in which the respondent specifies a level of agreement or disagreement with statements expressing either a favorable or an unfavorable attitude toward the concept under study.

Exhibit 9.13

Stapel Scale Used to Measure a Retailer's Website

+5	+5
+4	+4
+3	+3
+2	+2
+1	+1
Cheap Prices	Easy to Navigate
−1	−1
−2	−2
−3	−3
−4	−4
−5	−5

Select a "plus" number for words you think describe the website accurately. The more accurately you think the word describes the website, the larger the "plus" number you should choose. Select a "minus" number for words you think do not describe the website accurately. The less accurately you think the word describes the website, the larger the "minus" number you should choose. Therefore, you can select any number from +5 for words you think are very accurate all the way to −5 for words you think are very inaccurate.

Exhibit 9.14

Likert Scales Used by an Internet Game Site

Scale A

How did you feel about the registration process when you became a new user?

	Strongly disagree	Somewhat disagree	Neutral	Somewhat agree	Strongly agree
The registration was simple.	○	○	○	○	○
The registration questions were "nonthreatening."	○	○	○	○	○
Registration here will protect my privacy.	○	○	○	○	○
The registration did not take a long time to complete.	○	○	○	○	○
The registration informed me about the site.	○	○	○	○	○

Scale B

How do you feel about the following statements?

	Strongly disagree	Somewhat disagree	Neutral	Somewhat agree	Strongly agree
Allowing companies to advertise on the Internet allows me to access free services.	○	○	○	○	○
I do not support advertising on this site even though it provides me with free entertainment.	○	○	○	○	○
There is extremely too much advertising on the Internet.	○	○	○	○	○
There is extremely too much advertising on this site.	○	○	○	○	○
It's easy for me to ignore the advertising on this site and just play the game.	○	○	○	○	○

With the Likert scale, the respondent is required to consider only one statement at a time, with the scale running from one extreme to the other. A series of statements (attitudes) can be examined, yet there is only a single set of uniform replies for the respondent to choose from.

Rensis Likert created this scale to measure a person's attitude toward concepts (e.g., unions), activities (e.g., swimming), and so forth. He recommended the following steps in building the scale:

1. The researcher identifies the concept or activity to be scaled.

2. The researcher assembles a large number of statements (75 to 100) concerning the public's sentiments toward the concept or activity.

3. Each test item is classified by the researcher as generally "favorable" or "unfavorable" with regard to the attitude under study. No attempt is made to scale the items; however, a pretest is conducted that involves the full set of statements and a limited sample of respondents.

4. In the pretest, the respondent indicates agreement (or not) with *every* item, checking one of the following direction-intensity descriptors:
   a. Strongly agree
   b. Agree
   c. Undecided
   d. Disagree
   e. Strongly disagree

5. Each response is given a numerical weight (e.g., 5, 4, 3, 2, 1).

6. The individual's *total attitude score* is represented by the algebraic summation of weights associated with the items checked. In the scoring process, weights are assigned so that the direction of attitude— favorable to unfavorable—is consistent over items. For example, if 5 were assigned to "strongly agree" for favorable items, 5 should be assigned to "strongly disagree" for unfavorable items.

7. After seeing the results of the pretest, the researcher selects only those items that appear to discriminate well between high and low *total* scorers. This may be done by first finding the highest and lowest quartiles of subjects on the basis of *total* score and then comparing the mean differences on each *specific* item for these high and low groups (excluding the middle 50 percent of subjects).

8. The 20 to 25 items finally selected are those that have discriminated "best" (i.e., exhibited the greatest differences in mean values) between high and low total scorers in the pretest.

9. Steps 3 through 5 are then repeated in the main study.

People's attitudes toward activities like snowboarding can be measured using Likert scales.

Corbis Stock Market

Likert created the scale so that a researcher could look at a summed score and tell whether a person's attitude toward a concept was positive or negative. For example, the maximum favorable score on a 20-item scale would be 100; therefore, a person scoring 92 would be presumed to have a favorable attitude. Of course, two people could both score 92 and yet have rated various statements differently. Thus, specific components of their overall attitude could differ markedly. For example, if respondent A strongly agreed (5) that a particular bank had good parking and strongly disagreed (1) that its loan programs were the best in town and respondent B had the exact opposite attitude, both would have summed scores of 6.

In the world of marketing research, Likert-like scales are very popular. They are quick and easy to construct and can be administered by telephone or via the Internet. Commercial researchers rarely follow the textbook-like process just outlined. Instead, the scale usually is developed jointly by a client project manager and a researcher. Many times, the scale is created following a focus group.

Purchase Intent Scales

> **purchase intent scales**
> Scales used to measure a respondent's intention to buy or not buy a product.

Perhaps the single scale used most often in marketing research is the **purchase intent scale**. The ultimate issue for marketing managers is, Will they buy the product or not? If so, what percentage of the market can I expect to obtain? The purchase intent question normally is asked for all new products and services and product and service modifications, by manufacturers, retailers, and even nonprofit organizations.[13]

During new product development, the purchase intent question is first asked during concept testing to get a rough idea of demand. The manager wants to quickly eliminate potential turkeys, take a careful look at those products for which purchase intent is moderate, and push forward the products that seem to have star potential. At this stage, investment is minimal and product modification or concept repositioning is an easy task. As the product moves through development, the product itself, promotion strategy, price levels, and distribution channels become more concrete and focused. Purchase intent is evaluated at each stage of development, and demand estimates are refined. The crucial go–no go decision for national or regional rollout typically comes after test marketing. Immediately before test marketing, commercial researchers have another critical stage of evaluation. Here, the final or near-final version of the product is placed in consumers' homes in test cities around the country. After a period of in-home use (usually two to six weeks), a follow-up survey is conducted among participants to find out their likes and dislikes, how the product compares with what they use now, and what they would pay for it. The critical question near the end of the questionnaire is purchase intent.

Question 21 in Exhibit 9.15 is a purchase intent question taken from a follow-up study on in-home placement of a fly trap. The trap consisted of two 3-inch disks held about one-quarter inch apart by three plastic pillars; it looked somewhat like a large, thin yo-yo. The trap contained a pheromone to attract the flies and a glue that would remain sticky for six months. Supposedly, the flies flew in but never out. Centered on the back side of one of the disks was an adhesive tab so that the disk could be attached to a kitchen window. The concept was to eliminate flies in the kitchen area without resorting to a pesticide. Question 22 was designed to aid in positioning the

---

Exhibit 9.15

Purchase Intent Scale and Related Questions for In-Home Product Placement of Fly Traps

21. If a set of three traps sold for approximately $3.00 and was available in the stores where you normally shop, would you:

	(51)
definitely buy the set of traps	1
probably buy	2
probably not buy	3
definitely not buy	4

22. Would you use the traps (a) instead of or (b) in addition to existing products?

	(52)
instead of	1
in addition to	2

23. Would you recommend this product to your friends?

	(53)
definitely	1
probably	2
probably not	3
definitely not	4

product, and question 23 traditionally was used by the manufacturer as a double-check on purchase intent. If 60 percent of the respondents claimed that they definitely would buy the product and 90 percent said they definitely would not recommend the product to their friends, the researcher would question the validity of the purchase intent.

The purchase intent scale has been found to be a good predictor of consumer choice of frequently purchased and durable consumer products.[14] The scale is very easy to construct, and consumers are simply asked to make a subjective judgment of their likelihood of buying a new product. From past experience in the product category, a marketing manager can translate consumer responses on the scale to estimates of purchase probability. Obviously, everyone who "definitely will buy" the product will not do so; in fact, a few who state that they definitely will not buy actually will buy the product. The manufacturer of the fly trap is a major producer of both pesticide and nonpesticide pest control products. Assume that, based on historical follow-up studies, the manufacturer has learned the following about purchase intent of nonpesticide home-use pest-control products:

☐ 63 percent of the "definitely will buy" actually purchase within 12 months.

☐ 28 percent of the "probably will buy" actually purchase within 12 months.

☐ 12 percent of the "probably will not buy" actually purchase within 12 months.

☐ 3 percent of the "definitely will not buy" actually purchase within 12 months.

Suppose that the fly trap study resulted in the following:

☐ 40 percent—definitely will buy

☐ 20 percent—probably will buy

☐ 30 percent—probably will not buy

☐ 10 percent—definitely will not buy

Assuming that the sample is representative of the target market,

$$(0.4)(63\%) + (0.2)(28\%) + (0.3)(12\%) + (0.1)(3\%)$$
$$= 35.7\% \text{ market share}$$

Most marketing managers would be deliriously happy about such a high market share prediction for a new product. Unfortunately, because of consumer confusion, the product was killed after the in-home placement despite the high prediction.

It is not uncommon for marketing research firms to conduct studies containing a purchase intent scale in cases where the client does not have historical data to use as a basis for weighing the results. A reasonable but conservative estimate would be 70 percent of the "definitely will buy," 35 percent of the "probably will buy," 10 percent of the "probably will not buy," and zero of the "definitely will not buy."[15] Higher weights are common in the industrial market.

Some companies use the purchase intent scale to make go–no go decisions in product development without reference to market share. Typically, managers simply add the "definitely will buy" and "probably will buy" percentages and compare that total to a predetermined go–no go threshold. Combining "definitely" and "probably" is referred to as a top two box score. One consumer goods manufacturer, for example, requires a box score of 80 percent or higher at the concept testing stage and 65 percent for a product to move from in-home placement tests to test marketing.

The Net Promoter Score (NPS)

> **Net Promoter Score (NPS)**
> Begins with a 10-point scale on likelihood to recommend. Next, the difference between promoters and dissuaders is computed.

In his December 2003 *Harvard Business Review* article, "The One Number You Need to Grow," Frederick Reichheld asserted that the only research question a company needs to answer is, "How likely are you to recommend our company to a friend or colleague?" (see Exhibit 9.15, question 23). This approach is commonly referred to as the **Net Promoter Score (NPS)** because the likelihood-to-recommend data collected are used to compute the difference between brand promoters and dissuaders; it promises both simplicity and insight.[16]

Many researchers would agree that this concept has merit as a trailing snapshot of what customers think about a brand at a specific time. In fact, most practitioners and academics believe that advocacy is an important outcome of customers' experiences with a brand because as customers' satisfaction increases, so does their likelihood of recommending a brand. However, many business leaders are beginning to mistakenly believe that the NPS metric is the only measure that predicts financial performance.

In 2007, a group of researchers from J.D. Power and Associates and two academic researchers conducted an extensive study on the NPS concept.[17] Their findings showed that NPS using the likelihood-to-recommend question was not critical and that different scales actually yield very similar outcomes. The researchers examined data from 26,944 customers and 64 brands in the auto insurance, investment banking, airlines, and rental car industries. The actual "likelihood question" was a 10-point scale in all studies but one. This was compared with other voice-of-the-customer scales including:

- [ ] Overall satisfaction, the 10-point single-item scale that provides the data for computing:
  - [ ] *Net delighted (ND),* derived from a 10-point overall satisfaction scale where ND equals percentage outstanding (10) minus displeased (scores 1–5)
  - [ ] *Net satisfied (NS),* derived from a 10-point overall satisfaction scale where NS equals percentage satisfied or delighted (top-two box) minus displeased (scores 1–5)
- [ ] Customer satisfaction index, the multi-item index that captures customers' experience ratings across various aspects of the product or service, including both the people providing it and the process by which it is provided
- [ ] Commitment, a four-item scale capturing the degree to which customers feel committed to the brand
- [ ] Likelihood to recommend, the 4-point scale underlying the NPS described previously (with an 11-point version also included for the full-service investment industry)[18]

The research results found that there was more than one way to look at customer behavior and its impact on financial performance. Other measures, including those cited above, are equally valid in correlating with financial performance.[19]

Scale Conversions[20]

A considerable amount of voice-of-the-customer (VOC), also called customer satisfaction studies, is collected using tracking studies. Tracking studies simply follow changes in consumers' attitudes and purchase behavior over time. For example, VOC research may be conducted every quarter or every six months. Sometimes situations arise in firms, such as policy changes, that require changes in the VOC research methodology. One such change is moving from one scale (say, 5-point) to another scale (say, 10-point). There could be many reasons for that kind of change, but it raises the obvious question: How can data collected using the two scales be compared?

The objective is to aid the researcher in comparing data that are measured in different ways and make informed decisions. The underlying assumption here is that the scale

EXHIBIT 9.16	Box Score Distributions for Four Scales				
Scale	Top 1	Top 2	Top 3	Top 4	Top 5
5-point	20%	40%			
7-point	14%	28%	42%		
10-point	10%	20%	30%	40%	
11-point	9%	18%	27%	36%	45%

wording is sufficiently comparable that scale conversions can be attempted. Although several techniques can be used for scale conversion, we will examine a simple, straightforward method here.

In the scale equivalence approach, no attempt is made to modify the data in any way. Instead, the focus is on identifying the appropriate way of reporting that would enable scores to become comparable. This wouldn't be applicable in all situations and is useful primarily in situations where "boxed" scores (top-two box, top-three box, etc.) are reported.

Consider four scales (in terms of scale points) that are commonly used in marketing research: 5-point, 7-point, 10-point, and 11-point scales. Often, the results of a study using these kinds of scales are reported using boxed scores. Questions then relate to how a study using a 5-point scale and reporting on "top-two box" scores can be translated when the new scale has, say, 7 points. In the approach of scale equivalence, we look at the proportion of a scale each scale point covers.

For example, each scale point on a 5-point scale covers 20 percent of the scale. That is, if we were generating completely random data to respond to this scale, we would expect approximately 20 percent of the responses to be 1, 20 percent to be 2, and so on. Therefore, a top-two box score would cover 40 percent of the scale points on a 5-point scale. Similarly, for a 7-point scale, each scale point accounts for approximately 14 percent of the scale, and top-two box scores would account for about 28 percent of the scale points. Exhibit 9.16 shows the box score distributions for the four scales.

The boxed numbers show, for example, that a top-two box score on a 5-point scale accounts for approximately the same proportion of the scale as a top-three box score on a 7-point scale, or top-four box score on a 10-point scale (approximately 40 percent). Hence, when data using these scales are to be compared, the relevant number of top boxes could be used. More generally, Exhibit 9.17 provides (approximate) conversions for boxed scores among the four scales. A "?" indicates that a simple conversion is not available.

EXHIBIT 9.17	Approximate Conversions for Boxed Scores among Four Scales		
11-Point Scale	10-Point Scale	7-Point Scale	5-Point Scale
?	Top-4 Box	Top-3 Box	Top-2 Box
Top-3 Box	Top-3 Box	Top-2 Box	?
Top-2 Box	Top-2 Box	?	Top Box

Considerations in Selecting a Scale

> **balanced scales**
> Measurement scales that have the same number of positive and negative categories.

> **nonbalanced scales**
> Measurement scales that are weighted toward one end or the other of the scale.

Past research has indicated that the YMCA has an overall positive image. This means that a nonbalanced scale with more positive gradients than negative can be used in future research about the YMCA. Go to www.ymca.com to see how the YMCA is using research to reach new customers.

YMCA of Greater Cincinnati

Most nonimage studies include a purchase intent scale. But many other questions arise in selecting a scale. Considerations include the nature of the construct being measured, type of scale, balanced versus nonbalanced scale, number of scale categories, and forced versus nonforced choice.

The Nature of the Construct Being Measured

A basic check of the appropriateness of a scale is confirmation that it is drawn directly from the overall objective of the research study. The scope of the research objectives has a fundamental effect on the manner in which scales are used for survey measurement. This was clearly demonstrated in the Net Promoter Score discussion.

Type of Scale

Most commercial researchers lean toward scales that can be administered over the telephone or via the Internet, to save interviewing expense. Ease of administration and development also are important considerations. For example, a rank-order scale can be quickly created, whereas developing a semantic differential (rating) scale is often a long and tedious process. The client's decision-making needs are always of paramount importance. Can the decision be made using ordinal data, or must the researcher provide interval information? Researchers also must consider the respondents, who usually prefer nominal and ordinal scales because of their simplicity. Ultimately, the choice of which type of scale to use will depend on the problem at hand and the questions that must be answered. It is not uncommon to find several types of scales in one research study. For example, an image study for a grocery chain might have a ranking scale of competing chains and a semantic differential to examine components of the chain's image.

Marketing researchers sometimes borrow scales directly from other studies or Internet sites. Many online survey sites have libraries of scales available. (See surveymonkey.com; custominsight.com; surveysystem.com; and express.perseus.com).There are also several scale handbooks that facilitate the appropriate measures and encourage researchers to standardize on previously developed and validated measures.[21] This makes the research stream more cumulative. Marketing researchers often find that these borrowed scales work just fine. Sometimes, however, they don't work very well.

A marketing researcher should fully understand the nature of the construct that was measured, the scope of the measurement, and the content and phrasing of the scale items for relevance to a new population before borrowing a scale. In sum, the caveat is "borrow with caution."[22]

Balanced versus Nonbalanced Scales

A **balanced scale** has the same number of positive and negative categories; a **nonbalanced scale** is weighted toward one end or the other. If the researcher expects a wide range of opinions, then a balanced scale probably is in order. If past research or a preliminary study has determined that most opinions are positive, then using a scale with more positive gradients than negative ones will enable the researcher to ascertain the degree of positiveness toward the concept being researched. We have conducted a series of studies for the YMCA and know that its overall image is positive. Thus, we used the following categories to track the YMCA's image: (1) outstanding, (2) very good, (3) good, (4) fair, (5) poor.

Number of Scale Categories

The number of categories to be included in a scale is another issue that must be resolved by the marketing researcher. If the number of categories is too small—for example, good, fair, poor—the scale is crude and lacks richness. A 3-category scale does not reveal the intensity of feeling that, say, a 10-category scale offers. Yet, a 10-category scale may go beyond a person's ability to accurately discriminate among categories. Research has shown that rating scales with either 5 or 7 points are the most reliable.[23]

With an even number of scale categories, there is no neutral point. Without a neutral point, respondents are forced to indicate some degree of positive or negative feelings on an issue. Persons who are truly neutral are not allowed to express their neutrality. On the other hand, some marketing researchers say that putting a neutral point on a scale gives the respondent an easy way out, allowing the person with no really strong opinion to avoid concentrating on his or her actual feelings. Of course, it is rather unusual for any individual to be highly emotional about a new flavor of salad dressing, a package design, or a test commercial for a pickup truck!

Forced versus Nonforced Choice

As mentioned in the discussion of semantic differential scales, if a neutral category is included, it typically will attract those who are neutral and those who lack adequate knowledge to answer the question. Some researchers have resolved this issue by adding a "Don't know" response as an additional category. For example, a semantic differential might be set up as follows:

Friendly	1	2	3	4	5	6	7	**Unfriendly**	Don't Know
Unexciting	1	2	3	4	5	6	7	**Exciting**	Don't Know

A "Don't know" option, however, can be an easy out for the lazy respondent.

If it has a neutral point, a scale without a "Don't know" option does not force a respondent to give a positive or negative opinion. A scale without a neutral point or a "Don't know" option forces even those persons with no information about an object to state an opinion. The argument for forced choice is that the respondent has to concentrate on his or her feelings. The arguments against forced choice are that inaccurate data are recorded and that some respondents may refuse to answer the question. A questionnaire that continues to require respondents to provide an opinion when, in fact, they lack the necessary information to do so can create ill will and result in early termination of the interview.

Attitude Measures and Management Decision Making

So far in this chapter we have discussed the nature of attitudes, various types of measurement scales, and some considerations in creating a scale. We now turn our attention to making attitude research more valuable for management decision making.

In the wide spectrum of features of a product or brand, there are some that predispose consumers to action (that is, to preference for the product, to actual purchase, to making recommendations to friends, and so on) and others that do not. Attitudes that are most

> **determinant attitudes**
Those consumer attitudes most closely related to preferences or to actual purchase decisions.

closely related to preference or to actual purchase decisions are said to be **determinant attitudes**. Other attitudes—no matter how favorable—are not determinant. Obviously, marketers need to know which features lead to attitudes that "determine" buying behavior, for these are the features around which marketing strategy must be built.[24]

With reference to determinant attitudes, Nelson Foote, manager of the consumer and public relations research program for General Electric, commented: "In the electrical appliance business, we have been impressed over and over by the way in which certain characteristics of products come to be taken for granted by consumers, especially those concerned with basic functional performance or with values like safety."

"If these values are missing in a product, the user is extremely offended," he said. "But if they are present, the maker or seller gets no special credit or preference because, quite logically, every other maker and seller is assumed to be offering equivalent values. In other words, the values that are salient in decision making are the values that are problematic—that are important, to be sure, but also those which differentiate one offering from another."

In proprietary studies evaluating such automobile attributes as power, comfort, economy, appearance, and safety, for example, consumers often rank safety as first in importance. However, these same consumers do not see various makes of cars as differing widely with respect to safety; therefore, safety is not a determinant feature in the actual purchase decision. This fact should rightly lead the company to concentrate on raising its performance in features other than safety. However, if safety is totally ignored, the brand may soon be perceived as being so unsafe that it loses some of its share of the market. At this point, safety would achieve determinance, a quality it would hold until concentration on safety by the "unsafe" company brought its product back into line with those of other companies.

To identify determinant attitudes and discern their relative degree of determinance, researchers must go beyond the scaling of respondents' attitudes. The study design must include a methodology for measuring determinance, for it will not naturally develop in the course of scaling. There are three major approaches to identifying determinant attitudes: (1) direct questioning, (2) indirect questioning, and (3) observation.

Direct Questioning

The most obvious way to approach determinant attitudes is to ask consumers directly what factors they consider important in a purchasing decision. Through direct questioning, respondents may be asked to explain their reasons for preferring one product or brand over another. Or they may be asked to rate their "ideal brand" for a given product in terms of several product attributes so that a model profile can be constructed (see the discussion of semantic differential scales).

This approach has the appeal of seeming to get directly to the issue of "Why do you buy?" Unfortunately, it rests on two very questionable assumptions: (1) respondents know why they buy or prefer one product over another, and (2) they will willingly explain what these reasons are.

Another direct questioning approach is "dual questioning," which involves asking two questions concerning each product attribute that might be determinant. Consumers are first asked what factors they consider important in a purchasing decision and then asked how they perceive these factors as differing among the various products or brands.

Exhibits 9.18 and 9.19 illustrate this approach through ratings of attitudes toward savings and loan associations, given during a survey of the general public in the Los

EXHIBIT 9.18	Importance Ratings of Savings and Loan Characteristics	
Benefit or Claim		**Average Ratings***
Safety of money		1.4
Interest rate earned		1.6
Government insurance		1.6
Financial strength		2.0
Ease of withdrawing money		2.0
Management ability		2.0
Attitude of personnel		2.1
Speed/efficiency of service		2.2
Compounding frequency		2.2
Branch location convenience		2.3
Time required to earn interest		2.3
Parking convenience		2.4
Years in business		2.5
Other services offered		3.1
Building/office attractiveness		3.4
Premiums offered		4.0

*1—extremely important; 2—very important; 3—fairly important; 4—slightly important, etc.
Source: James Myers and Mark Alpert, "Determinant Buying Attitudes: Meaning and Measurement," *Marketing Management* (Summer 1997), p. 52. Reprinted by permission of the American Marketing Association.

EXHIBIT 9.19	Difference Ratings of Savings and Loan Characteristics			
Benefit or Claim	**Big Difference**	**Small Difference**	**No Difference**	**Don't Know**
Years in business	53%	31%	10%	6%
Financial strength	40	32	22	6
Parking convenience	37	35	22	6
Safety of money	36	15	47	2
Management ability	35	26	27	12
Government insurance	35	11	51	3
Branch location convenience	34	36	28	2
Attitude of personnel	34	28	33	5
Interest rate earned	33	30	35	2
Speed/efficiency of service	32	28	35	5
Ease of withdrawing money	29	18	48	5
Compounding frequency	28	36	31	5
Time required to earn interest	26	34	33	7
Building/office attractiveness	24	44	30	2
Other services offered	21	34	29	16
Premiums offered	15	36	38	11

Source: James Myers and Mark Alpert, "Determinant Buying Attitudes: Meaning and Measurement," *Marketing Management* (Summer 1997), p. 53. Reprinted by permission of the American Marketing Association.

Angeles area. (The various benefits or claims are ranked in descending order in each exhibit so that comparisons between the exhibits can be made more easily.) Notice that some items are high in rated importance but are not thought to differ much among the various savings and loan associations (for example, safety of money, interest rate earned). Thus, while safety of money is ranked first in importance, about half of all respondents feel there is no difference among savings and loan associations in terms of safety; therefore, safety of funds is probably not a determinant feature. Conversely, some items show big differences among the various associations but are considered to be of relatively little importance in determining the choice of a savings and loan (for example, years in business, parking convenience).

On the other hand, "interest rate earned" has a very high importance ranking, and far fewer respondents feel there is no difference among the various associations relative to interest rate. Financial strength is rated somewhat lower in importance but is second highest in terms of the difference between associations. Therefore, financial strength appears to be relatively determinant of attitudes. Similarly, the researcher can proceed through the rest of the ratings to identify those attitudes that seem to influence the choice among various savings and loans most strongly and thus, presumably, are determinant attitudes.

Indirect Questioning

Another approach to identifying determinant attitudes is indirect questioning, of which there are many forms. Recall from Chapter 4 that indirect questioning is any interviewing approach that does not directly ask respondents to indicate the reasons why they bought a product or service or which features or attributes are most important in determining choice.

Observation

A third technique for identifying buying motives is observation research (see Chapter 7). For example, in one study, supermarket shoppers were observed, and detailed reports were recorded of their movements and statements while interacting with certain products on display in several different stores. The authors drew conclusions concerning who does the shopping, the influence of children and adult males on purchasing decisions, the effect of pricing, where brand choices seem to be made, and how much package study is involved. One of the findings of this study was that shoppers seemed to reject certain candy packaging in favor of other packaging. This finding suggests that package design might be a determinant feature, though by no means the only one.[25] (The disadvantages of observation research were discussed in Chapter 7.)

Choosing a Method for Identifying Determinant Attitudes

Direct questioning, indirect questioning, and observation each have some limitations in identifying determinant attitudes. Therefore, the marketing researcher should use two or more of the techniques. Convergent findings will offer greater assurance that the attitudes identified are indeed determinant attitudes. Several statistical tools can aid the researcher in this process; they will be discussed in Chapters 13 & 14.

SUMMARY ☐

Measurement consists of using rules to assign numbers or labels to objects in such a way as to represent quantities or qualities of attributes. A measurement rule is a guide, a method, or a command that tells a researcher what to do. Accurate measurement requires rules that are both clear and specific.

There are four basic levels of measurement: nominal, ordinal, interval, and ratio. A nominal scale partitions data into categories that are mutually exclusive and collectively exhaustive. The numbers assigned to objects or phenomena have no true numerical meaning; they are simply labels. Ordinal scales have the labeling characteristics of nominal scales plus an ability to order data. Interval scales contain all the features of ordinal scales with the added dimension that the intervals between the points on the scale are equal. Interval scales enable the researcher to discuss differences separating two objects. They are amenable to computation of an arithmetic mean, standard deviation, and correlation coefficients. Ratio scales have all the characteristics of previously discussed scales as well as a meaningful absolute zero or origin, thus permitting comparison of the absolute magnitude of the numbers and reflecting the actual amount of the variable.

Measurement data consist of accurate information and errors. Systematic error results in a constant bias in the measurements. Random error also influences the measurements but is not systematic; it is transient in nature. Reliability is the degree to which measures are free from random error and therefore provide consistent data. There are three ways to assess reliability: test–retest, internal consistency, and use of equivalent forms. Validity addresses whether the attempt at measurement was successful. The validity of a measure refers to the extent to which the measurement device or process is free from both systematic and random error. Types of validity include face, content, criterion-related, and construct validity.

The term *scaling* refers to procedures for attempting to determine quantitative measures of subjective and sometimes abstract concepts. It is defined as a procedure for assigning numbers or other symbols to properties of an object in order to impart some numerical characteristics to the properties in question. Scales are either unidimensional or multidimensional. A unidimensional scale is designed to measure only one attribute of a concept, respondent, or object. Multidimensional scaling is based on the premise that a concept, respondent, or object might be better described using several dimensions.

One type of scale is called a graphic rating scale. Respondents are presented with a graphic continuum, typically anchored by two extremes. Itemized rating scales are similar to graphic rating scales except that respondents must select from a limited number of categories rather than placing a mark on a continuous scale. A rank-order scale is a comparative scale because respondents are asked to compare two or more items with each other. Q-sorting is a sophisticated form of rank ordering. Respondents are asked to sort a large number of cards into piles of predetermined size according to specified rating categories. Paired comparison scales ask the respondent to pick one of two objects from a set, based on some stated criteria. Constant sum scales require the respondent to divide a given number of points, typically 100, among two or more attributes, based on their importance to him or her. Respondents must value each item relative to all other items. The number of points allocated to each alternative indicates the ranking assigned to it by the respondent.

The semantic differential was developed to measure the meaning of an object to a person. The construction of a semantic differential scale begins with determination of a concept to be rated, such as a brand image; then the researcher selects dichotomous pairs of words or phrases that could be used to describe the concept. Respondents then rate the concept on a scale, usually 1 to 7. The mean of the responses is computed for each pair of adjectives, and the means are plotted as a profile, or image. In the Stapel scale, a single adjective is placed in the center of the scale. Typically, a Stapel scale is designed to simultaneously measure both the direction and the intensity of attitudes. The Likert scale is another scale that avoids the problem of developing pairs of dichotomous adjectives. The scale consists of a series of statements expressing either a favorable or an unfavorable attitude toward the concept under study. The respondent is asked to indicate the level of his or her agreement or disagreement with each statement by assigning it a numerical score. Scores are then totaled to measure the respondent's attitude.

The scale that is used most often and perhaps is most important to marketing researchers is the purchase intent scale. This scale is used to measure a respondent's intention to buy or not buy a product. The purchase intent question usually asks a person to state whether he would definitely buy, probably buy, probably not buy, or definitely not buy the product under study. The purchase intent scale has been found to be a good predictor of consumer choice of frequently purchased consumer durable goods. A variation of purchase intent is the Net Promoter Score, which is typically computed using a 10-point scale that asks "if" you would recommend the product/service to a friend. The creator of the concept claims it is all that management needs to predict future financial performance. Subsequent research has found other measures to be just as valid, however.

Sometimes it is necessary to do scale conversions in tracking studies when, over time, the number of points on a scale changes. Scale equivalence can be created when box scores are used as evaluation measures.

Several factors should be considered in selecting a particular scale for a study. The first is the type of scale to use: rating, ranking, sorting, or purchase intent. Next, consideration must be given to the use of a balanced scale versus a nonbalanced scale. The number of categories also must be determined. A related factor is whether to use an odd or even number of categories. Finally, the researcher must consider whether to use forced or nonforced choice sets.

Attitudes that predispose consumers to action are called determinant attitudes. Marketing researchers need to identify which attitudes, of all those measured, are determinant. This can be accomplished by direct questioning, indirect questioning, and observation research.

KEY TERMS & DEFINITIONS

measurement Process of assigning numbers or labels to persons, objects, or events in accordance with specific rules for representing quantities or qualities of attributes.

rule Guide, method, or command that tells a researcher what to do.

scale Set of symbols or numbers so constructed that the symbols or numbers can be assigned by a rule to the individuals (or their behaviors or attitudes) to whom the scale is applied.

nominal scales Scales that partition data into mutually exclusive and collectively exhaustive categories.

ordinal scales Scales that maintain the labeling characteristics of nominal scales and have the ability to order data.

interval scales Scales that have the characteristics of ordinal scales, plus equal intervals between points to show relative amounts; they may include an arbitrary zero point.

ratio scales Scales that have the characteristics of interval scales, plus a meaningful zero point so that magnitudes can be compared arithmetically.

reliability Degree to which measures are free from random error and, therefore, provide consistent data.

test–retest reliability Ability of the same instrument to produce consistent results when used a second time under conditions as similar as possible to the original conditions.

stability Lack of change in results from test to retest.

equivalent form reliability Ability of two very similar forms of an instrument to produce closely correlated results.

internal consistency reliability Ability of an instrument to produce similar results when used on different samples during the same time period to measure a phenomenon.

split-half technique Method of assessing the reliability of a scale by dividing the total set of measurement items in half and correlating the results.

validity Degree to which what the researcher was trying to measure was actually measured.

face validity Degree to which a measurement seems to measure what it is supposed to measure.

content validity Representativeness, or sampling adequacy, of the content of the measurement instrument.

criterion-related validity Degree to which a measurement instrument can predict a variable that is designated a criterion.

predictive validity Degree to which a future level of a criterion variable can be forecast by a current measurement scale.

concurrent validity Degree to which another variable, measured at the same point in time as the variable of interest, can be predicted by the measurement instrument.

construct validity Degree to which a measurement instrument represents and logically connects, via the underlying theory, the observed phenomenon to the construct.

convergent validity Degree of correlation among different measurement instruments that purport to measure the same construct.

discriminant validity Measure of the lack of association among constructs that are supposed to be different.

scaling Procedures for assigning numbers (or other symbols) to properties of an object in order to impart some numerical characteristics to the properties in question.

unidimensional scales Scales designed to measure only one attribute of a concept, respondent, or object.

multidimensional scales Scales designed to measure several dimensions of a concept, respondent, or object.

graphic rating scales Measurement scales that include a graphic continuum, anchored by two extremes.

itemized rating scales Measurement scales in which the respondent selects an answer from a limited number of ordered categories.

noncomparative scales Measurement scales in which judgment is made without reference to another object, concept, or person.

rank-order scales Measurement scales in which the respondent compares two or more items and ranks them.

comparative scales Measurement scales in which one object, concept, or person is compared with another on a scale.

Q-sorting A measurement scale employing a sophisticated form of rank ordering using card sorts.

paired comparison scales Measurement scales that ask the respondent to pick one of two objects in a set, based on some stated criteria.

constant sum scales Measurement scales that ask the respondent to divide a given number of points, typically 100, among two or more attributes, based on their importance to him or her.

semantic differential scales Measurement scales that examine the strengths and weaknesses of a concept by having the respondent rank it between dichotomous pairs of words or phrases that could be used to describe it; the means of the responses are then plotted as a profile, or image.

Stapel scales Measurement scales that require the respondent to rate, on a scale ranging from $+5$ to -5, how closely and in what direction a descriptor adjective fits a given concept.

Likert scales Measurement scales in which the respondent specifies a level of agreement or disagreement with statements expressing either a favorable or an unfavorable attitude toward the concept under study.

purchase intent scales Scales used to measure a respondent's intention to buy or not buy a product.

Net Promoter Score (NPS) Begins with a 10-point scale on likelihood to recommend.

Next, the differences between promoters and dissuaders is computed.

balanced scales Measurement scales that have the same number of positive and negative categories.

nonbalanced scales Measurement scales that are weighted toward one end or the other of the scale.

determinant attitudes Those consumer attitudes most closely related to preferences or to actual purchase decisions.

QUESTIONS FOR REVIEW & CRITICAL THINKING

1. What is measurement?
2. Differentiate among the four types of measurement scales, and discuss the types of information obtained from each.
3. How does reliability differ from validity? Give examples of each.
4. Give an example of a scale that would be reliable but not valid. Also give an example of a scale that would be valid but not reliable.
5. What are three methods of assessing reliability?
6. What are three methods of assessing validity?
7. Discuss some of the considerations in selecting a rating, ranking, or purchase intent scale.
8. Compare and contrast the semantic differential scale, Stapel scale, and Likert scale. Under what conditions would a researcher use each one?
9. Develop a purchase intent scale for students eating at the university's cafeteria. How might the reliability and validity of this scale be measured? Why do you think purchase intent scales are so popular in commercial marketing research?
10. When might a researcher use a graphic rating scale rather than an itemized rating scale?
11. What is the difference between a rating and a ranking? Which is best for attitude measurement? Why?
12. What are determinant attitudes, and why are they important?
13. Do you think that the Net Promoter Score is sufficient to predict financial performance?
14. Explain the concept of scale equivalence.

(Team Exercise) 15. Divide the class into teams. Each team should create five adjective pairs of phrases that could be used in a semantic differential to measure the image of your college or university. The instructor will then aggregate the suggestions into a single semantic differential. Each team member should then conduct five interviews with students not in the class. The data can then be analyzed later in the term when statistical analysis is covered.

WORKING THE NET

1. Go to a Web search engine and look up "validity and reliability." Describe to the class the new insights you gain into these important concepts.
2. SRIC-BI (Stanford Research Institute Consulting-Business Intelligence) is a spinoff of the Stanford Research Institute. One of its most popular products is called VALS

(Values and Life Style Survey). SRIC-BI uses VALS to segment the marketplace on the basis of personality traits that drive consumer behavior. VALS is used in all phases of the marketing mix. The survey categorizes consumers into one of eight personality types. GEOVALS applies the power of VALS to local marketing efforts by identifying the concentration of the VALS consumer group residing within a specific block group or zip code.

Go to *www.sric-bi.com*, then click on the VALS SURVEY link. Next, click on "Take the survey."

1. Explain the theory behind the creation of VALS.
2. Do you agree with your VALS classification? Learn more by going to "The VALS Types" link.
3. What kind of scale was used in the survey? Could other types of scales have been used?
4. Explain how a marketer could use GEOVALS.

Coffee Culture as a Global Phenomenon

Consumers the world over, according to research agency Synovate, are highly in favor of coffee giants and the vast array of choices they offer. In a study that sought to illuminate coffee culture around the globe, Synovate spoke to 5,806 respondents in the United States, UK, France, Brazil, Hong Kong, Singapore, Serbia, Morocco, and Australia. Overall, 76 percent of respondents agreed that "large multinational coffee chains are good because they expand choices for consumers."

For many, however, it's clearly a trade-off between enjoyment and principles, with 28 percent also agreeing that these "large multinational chains have negatively impacted local culture." According to the survey, a huge 74 percent of Moroccans agree that coffee from large international chains is of better quality than coffee from small, independent shops. Next came Hong Kongers at 50 percent, closely followed by Brazilians. Surprisingly, Australians and Americans showed particularly low agreement on this score (11 percent and 14 percent, respectively), suggesting that these nations are more likely to support the "little guys."

When asked whether these chains have negatively impacted local culture, Moroccans again answered yes in the largest numbers, a paradox that suggests an element of moral conflict in their coffee choices. At the opposite end of the spectrum, however, only 11 percent of Hong Kongers and 20 percent of Serbians felt this was an issue. "Asians don't have the almost automatic negative reaction to big business that Westerners seem to have. They are much more accepting and tolerant of big companies. Perhaps this finding says more about the West than about Asia," says Jill Telford, Synovate managing director at Hong Kong.

What is the favorite type of coffee bought outside the home? While preferences vary from country to country, it seems that the majority of us prefer the simpler things in life. Almost half of the U.S. respondents would opt for regular coffee, along with some two out of five Brazilians and French and about a third of Brits and Singaporeans. Meanwhile, the cappuccino is king in Australia (45 percent), while Moroccans love their lattés (38 percent). Unsurprisingly, espresso is relatively popular in France, while mocha seems to go down better in Singapore and Hong Kong than anywhere else.

When asked which coffee shop or café first comes to mind for quality ready-to-drink coffee, a majority of respondents from Hong Kong and the United States mentioned

Starbucks. The ubiquitous coffee giant was also cited by a significant proportion of Brits and Singaporeans.

In France, however, unspecified bars, restaurants, or cafés were top of minds, with Starbucks cited by a mere 2 percent. The top result for Australians was Gloria Jean at 32 percent, while two in five Serbians mentioned Nescafé.

The Australian finding makes sense to Synovate Serbia's Milica Vulicevic: "Ready-to-drink coffee is very expensive for people in Serbia—the country is suffering economically, and considering that people here easily drink five to 10 coffees a day, most will opt for instant."

It seems that the English (63 percent), Australians (70 percent), and particularly the Moroccans (90 percent) are glugging coffee the entire day. The Asian markets, however, hold the fewest caffeine lovers, with only 21 percent of Hong Kongers and 44 percent of Singaporeans reliant on their morning coffee and as little as 12 percent and 31 percent, respectively, admitting to drinking coffee throughout the day.

Finally, it seems that the "coffee culture" as typified (or perhaps accelerated) by popular American sitcoms is very much alive and well in the markets surveyed. Unsurprisingly, 78 percent of respondents overall prefer to buy coffee from a café that has an inviting atmosphere. Moreover, four out of five Serbians, two-thirds of Moroccans, and nearly two-thirds of the French say that the main reason for going to a coffee chain shop or café is to hang out with friends, rather than for the coffee itself. Ironically, Americans came lowest on this score—only 14 percent gave the above response versus an average of 44 percent across all countries.[26]

Questions

1. Create a graphic rating scale for preference for instant coffee.
2. Create an itemized rating scale for coffee covering taste, sociability, cost, and quality.
3. Create a rank-order preference scale for mocha, espresso, latté, medium regular coffee, mild regular coffee, and cappuccino. Create a constant sum scale using the same coffees.
4. Create a Stapel scale using the additional factors in question 2.
5. Create a Likert scale for coffee using your own adjectives.

Mark Leibowitz/Masterfile

QUESTIONNAIRE DESIGN

LEARNING OBJECTIVES

1.	To understand the role of the questionnaire in the data collection process.
2.	To become familiar with the criteria for a good questionnaire.
3.	To learn the process for questionnaire design.
4.	To become knowledgeable about the three basic forms of questions.
5.	To learn the necessary procedures for successful implementation of a survey.
6.	To understand how software and the Internet are influencing questionnaire design.
7.	To understand the impact of the questionnaire on data-collection costs.

For any survey-based marketing research project, the questionnaire is the heart of the process. It serves as the bridge between the objectives on one end and the analysis and conclusions on the other. You look to the research objectives to determine what questions need to be asked to get the information necessary to meet those objectives. The answers to the questions you ask become the raw input for the analysis. You obviously can't address any issue for which you do not have responses. All too often we look at surveys and the analysis done with survey results and scratch our heads, wondering why did they ask this or that? In recent surveys reviewed by the authors, we have found many examples of bad questionnaire design:

- ☐ Using language that is likely to be misunderstood or misinterpreted by the respondent (e.g., Do you currently receive RSS feeds from any sources on your computer?).

- ☐ Bad sequencing of questions (e.g., putting detailed demographic questions at the start of the survey before you have established rapport with the respondents will likely turn them off and lead them to terminate the survey).

- ☐ Using a question that in fact includes two questions (double-barreled questions), but only providing for a single response (e.g., Please indicate your satisfaction with the friendliness and knowledge of the customer service rep to whom you spoke.).

- ☐ Using biasing wording (e.g., How often do you eat at downscale restaurants such as Applebee's?).

And, there are many, many other common questionnaire mistakes that we will discuss in this chapter.

At a high level, the questionnaire design is more art than science. However, when dealing with questionnaire specifics, such as how to ask certain types of questions, there is plenty of science in the form of methodological research that has been conducted by academics and marketing research professionals. In this chapter, we will provide both overall guidance regarding questionnaire design and best practices for handling specific issues based on the findings of methodological research studies.

Role of a Questionnaire

Every form of survey research relies on the use of a questionnaire, the common thread in almost all data-collection methods. A **questionnaire** is a set of questions designed to generate the data necessary to accomplish the objectives of the research project; it is a formalized schedule for collecting information from respondents. You have most likely seen or even filled out a questionnaire recently. Creating a good questionnaire requires both hard work and imagination.

A questionnaire standardizes the wording and sequencing of questions and imposes uniformity on the data-gathering process. Every respondent sees or hears the same words; every interviewer asks identical questions. Without such standardization, interviewers could ask whatever they wanted, and researchers would be left wondering whether respondents' answers were a consequence of interviewer influence or interpretation; a valid basis for comparing respondents' answers would not exist. The jumbled mass of data would be unmanageable from a tabulation standpoint. In a very real sense, then, the questionnaire is a control device, but it is a unique one, as you will see.

The questionnaire (sometimes referred to as an *interview schedule* or *survey instrument*) plays a critical role in the data-collection process. An elaborate sampling plan, well-trained interviewers, proper statistical analysis techniques, and good editing and coding are all for naught if the questionnaire is poorly designed. Improper

> **questionnaire**
> Set of questions designed to generate the data necessary to accomplish the objectives of the research project; also called an *interview schedule* or *survey instrument*.

design can lead to incomplete information, inaccurate data, and, of course, higher costs. The questionnaire is the production line of marketing research. It is here that the product, be it good or bad, is created. The questionnaire is the tool that creates the basic product (respondent information).

Exhibit 10.1 illustrates the pivotal role of the questionnaire. It is positioned between survey objectives (drawn from the manager's problem) and respondent information. In this position, it must translate the objectives into specific questions to solicit the required information from respondents.

Assume that Swatch is considering the development of a child's wristwatch. The timepiece would have a plastic casing with printed circuits inside. Swatch's engineering staff believes that it can come up with a watch that will withstand the potential abuse from the normal activities of a child between 8 and 13 years old. Preliminary marketing research is called for to determine the acceptability of the watch to the target market. One objective is to determine children's reactions to the watch. The marketing researchers must translate the objectives into language understandable to child respondents, as an 8-year-old child probably won't be able to respond to questions that use such terms as *acceptability*, *efficiency*, and *likelihood of purchase*.

This example illustrates the pivotal role of the questionnaire: It must translate the survey objectives into a form understandable to respondents and "pull" the requisite information from them. At the same time, it must recover their responses in a form that can be easily tabulated and translated into findings and recommendations that will satisfy a manager's information requirements. Questionnaires also play a key role in survey costs, which will be discussed in detail later in the chapter.

Exhibit 10.1

Questionnaire's Pivotal Role in the Research Process

Criteria for a Good Questionnaire

To design a good questionnaire, the researchers must consider a number of issues: does it provide the necessary decision-making information for management? Does it consider the respondent? Does it meet editing, coding, and data processing requirements?

Does It Provide the Necessary Decision-Making Information?

The primary role of any questionnaire is to provide the information required for management decision making. Any questionnaire that fails to provide important insights for management or decision-making information should be discarded or revised. Therefore, the managers who will be using the data should always approve the questionnaire. By signing off on the questionnaire, the manager is saying, "Yes, this instrument will supply the data I need to reach a decision." If the manager does not sign off, then the marketing researcher must continue to revise the questionnaire.

Does It Consider the Respondent?

As companies have recognized the importance of marketing research, the number of surveys taken annually has mushroomed. Poorly designed, confusing, and lengthy surveys have literally turned off thousands of potential respondents. It is estimated that more than 60 percent of all persons contacted refuse to participate in surveys.

A questionnaire should always fit the respondent. Though parents typically purchase cereal, children often make the decision about what kind to buy. A taste-test questionnaire for children should be worded in language they can understand.

The researcher designing a questionnaire must consider not only the topic and the type of respondent, but the interviewing environment and questionnaire length as well. Respondents will answer somewhat longer questionnaires when they are interested in the topic and when they perceive that they will have little difficulty in responding to the questions.

A questionnaire should be designed explicitly for the intended respondents. For example, although a parent typically is the purchaser of cold cereals, the child, either directly or indirectly, often makes the decision as to which brand. Thus, a taste-test questionnaire about cold cereals should be formulated in children's language. On the other hand, a survey about *purchasing* cold cereals should be worded in language suitable for adult interviewees. One of the most important tasks of questionnaire design is to fit the questions to the prospective respondent. The questionnaire designer must strip away any marketing jargon and business terminology that may be misunderstood by the respondent. In fact, it is best to use simple, everyday language, as long as the result is not insulting or demeaning to the respondent.

Does It Meet Editing and Coding Requirements?

Once the information has been gathered, it will have to be edited and then coded for data processing. A questionnaire should be designed with these later processes in mind.

Editing refers to going through each questionnaire to make certain that skip patterns were followed and required questions were filled out. The **skip pattern** is the sequence in which questions are asked, based on a respondent's answer. Exhibit 10.2 shows a clearly defined skip pattern from question 4a to question 5a for persons who answer "No" to question 4a.

Most marketing research data analysis software automatically catches coding errors. Computer-aided telephone interviewing (CATI) and Internet software programs take care of skip patterns automatically. Flexibility is programmed into a questionnaire in two ways:

▷ **editing**
Going through each questionnaire to ensure that skip patterns were followed and the required questions filled out.

▷ **skip pattern**
Sequence in which questions are asked, based on a respondent's answer.

- ☐ Branching takes the participant to a different set of questions based on the answer that is given to a prior question. This could be a "simple skip," in which questions are skipped because they would not be relevant to the respondent, or could be "dynamic branching," in which one of many possible sets of questions is presented to the participant depending on the way that he or she responded to a question.

Exhibit 10.2

Example of a Questionnaire Skip Pattern

4a. Do you usually use a cream rinse or a hair conditioner on your child's hair?
(1) ( ) No (SKIP to 5a)   (2) ( ) Yes (ASK Q. 4b)

4b. Is that a cream rinse that you pour on or a cream rinse that you spray on?
(1) ( ) Cream rinse that you pour on
(2) ( ) Cream rinse that you spray on

4c. About how often do you use a cream rinse or a hair conditioner on your child's hair? Would you say less than once a week, once a week, or more than once a week?
(1) ( ) Less than once a week
(2) ( ) Once a week
(3) ( ) More than once a week

5a. Thinking of the texture of your child's hair, is it. . . . (READ LIST)
(1) ( ) Fine   (2) ( ) Coarse   (3) ( ) Regular

5b. What is the length of your child's hair? (READ LIST)
(1) ( ) Long   (2) ( ) Medium   (3) ( ) Short

☐ Piping integrates responses from a question into later questions. A participant could be asked to type an answer to an open-ended question, and the text of that answer could be incorporated into the wording of the next question.

In mall and telephone interviews, replies to all open-ended questions (which ask respondents to answer in their own words) are recorded verbatim by the interviewer (see later discussion). Sometimes the responses are then **coded** by listing the answers from a number of randomly selected completed questionnaires; however, if at all possible, responses to open-ended questions should be precoded. Those responses occurring with the greatest frequency are listed on a coding sheet (such as the one in Exhibit 10.3), which the editor uses to code all other responses to the open-ended question. Today, sophisticated neural network systems software is decreasing the necessity for manually coding responses to open-ended questions.

Low survey participation rates are discussed in the feature on page 291.

In summary, a questionnaire serves many masters. First, it must accommodate all the research objectives in sufficient depth and breadth to satisfy the information requirements

> **coding**
> The process of grouping and assigning numeric codes to the various responses to a question.

EXHIBIT 10.3	Coding Sheet for the Question "What Is Your Occupation?"
Category	**Code**
Professional/technical	1
Manager/official/self-employed	2
Clerical/sales	3
Skilled worker	4
Service worker	5
Unskilled laborer	6
Farm operator or rancher	7
Unemployed or student	8
Retired	9

PRACTICING MARKETING RESEARCH

Are Heavy Responders Taking All the Market Research Surveys?

Did you ever wonder why you never seem to get polled for a consumer survey? That's because survey contact and participation rates are lower than researchers thought and possibly only about 5 percent of the population take them. Can this 5 percent be screened out of future polls? Unfortunately, asking people if they took surveys before does not guarantee accurate data.

These were the findings of Barbara Bickart, marketing professor at Rutgers—the State University of New Jersey, and David Schmittlein, marketing professor at the University of Pennsylvania. Their meta-study presented a statistical model for estimating survey contact and response across the United States, and they obtained these results by analyzing survey responses to the question of how often a person had taken a survey. The researchers relied on the published results of surveys already conducted by the Council for Marketing and Opinion Research (CMOR) and Market Facts, Inc.

The evidential matter is fraught with paradox, they found, for if a consumer is willing to take a survey, and some quite enjoy this, that in itself skews the data. A 1995 CMOR telephone survey of 4,800 people generated 1,920 actual participants (40 percent). Researchers found that 45.3 percent of survey respondents said they took part in a survey in the past year, and 20 percent said they had taken three or more surveys. However, the 1,920 respondents did not actually represent the "desired universe" for the survey because their willingness to take part showed they were "particularly accessible" to surveys and thereby not representative of the general population.

Further complicating data matters is that Bickart and Schmittlein took exception to CMOR's data. CMOR reported that 50.6 percent of Americans were not contacted, 15.6 percent were contacted once, 9.0 percent twice, 13.0 percent between three and five times, and 11.8 percent six or more. But, Bickart and Schmittlein claimed, on the basis of their own statistical model, the number of people who didn't take a survey in one year was actually 40 percent greater than the CMOR data suggested, and the number of adults polled heavily (six or more times in a year) was 40 percent lower than CMOR estimated.

They found that "unadjusted estimates" (i.e., the CMOR raw data) of the number of Americans taking polls are "severely biased." This means that even if your survey factors in lots of demographic variables, the final respondents may still come from the "same small fraction" of population. In a given year, between 20 to 23 percent of adults account for all survey responses, and 4 to 5 percent of heavy responders account for more than 50 percent of them. "They are being surveyed almost once a month and are providing most of the country's survey data." It seems unlikely such "extreme concentration" of respondents produces an accurate market picture, they concluded.[1]

Questions

1. Devise some screening questions to accurately eliminate survey "heavy responders."
2. Are there other ways around the heavy responder quandary or should market researchers be content to work with this presumed 5 percent?

of the manager. Next, it must "speak" to the respondent in understandable language and at the appropriate intellectual level. Furthermore, it must be convenient for the interviewer to administer, and it must allow the interviewer to quickly record the respondent's answers. At the same time, the questionnaire must be easy to edit and check for completeness. It also should facilitate coding. Finally, the questionnaire must be translatable into findings that respond to the manager's original questions.

Tips for designing questionnaires to improve response rates are covered in the feature below.

Questionnaire Design Process

Designing a questionnaire involves a series of logical steps, as shown in Exhibit 10.4. The steps may vary slightly when performed by different researchers, but all researchers tend to follow the same general sequence. Committees and lines of authority can complicate the process, so it is wise to clear each step with the individual who has the ultimate authority for the project. This is particularly true for the first step: determining survey objectives, resources, and constraints. Many work hours have been wasted because a researcher developed a questionnaire to answer one type of question and the "real" decision maker wanted something entirely different. It also should be noted that the design process itself—specifically, question

Exhibit 10.4

Questionnaire Design Process

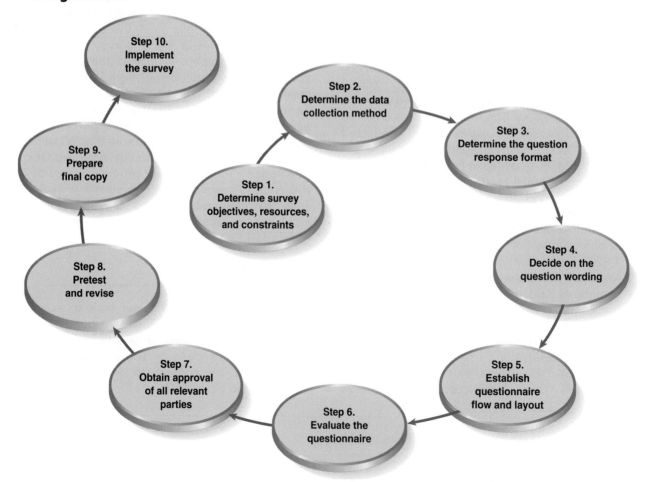

wording and format—can raise additional issues or unanswered questions. This, in turn, can send the researcher back to step one for a clearer description of the information sought.

Step One: Determine Survey Objectives, Resources, and Constraints

The research process often begins when a marketing manager, brand manager, or new product development specialist has a need for decision-making information that is not available. In some firms, it is the manager's responsibility to evaluate all secondary sources to make certain that the needed information has not already been gathered. In other companies, the manager leaves all research activities, primary and secondary, to the research department. The discussion of uses of marketing research in Chapter 1 covers this issue in more detail.

Although a brand manager may initiate the research request, everyone affected by the project—including the assistant brand manager, the group product manager, and even the marketing manager—should provide input into exactly what data are needed. **Survey objectives** (outlining the decision-making information required) should be spelled out as clearly and precisely as possible. If this step is completed carefully and thoroughly, the rest of the process will follow more smoothly and efficiently.

> **survey objectives**
> Outline of the decision-making information sought through the questionnaire.

Step Two: Determine the Data-Collection Method

Given the variety of ways in which survey data can be gathered, such as via the Internet, telephone, mail, or self-administration, the research method will have an impact on questionnaire design. An in-person interview in a mall will have constraints (such as a time limitation) not encountered with an Internet questionnaire. A self-administered questionnaire must be explicit and is usually rather short; because no interviewer will be present, respondents will not have the opportunity to clarify a question. A telephone interview may require a rich verbal description of a concept to make certain the respondent understands the idea being discussed. In contrast, an Internet survey can show the respondent a picture or video or demonstrate a concept.

Step Three: Determine the Question Response Format

Once the data-collection method has been determined, a decision must be made regarding the types of questions to be used in the survey. Three major types of questions are used in marketing research: open-ended, closed-ended, and scaled-response questions.

Open-Ended Questions   **Open-ended questions** are those to which the respondent replies in her or his own words. In other words, the researcher does not limit the response choices.

Often, open-ended questions require probes from the interviewer. In a *probe*, the interviewer encourages the respondent to elaborate or continue the discussion. The interviewer may say, "Is there anything else?" or "Would you elaborate on that?" in order to clarify the respondent's interests, attitudes, and feelings. Computers are playing an increasingly important role in analyzing and recording probes to open-ended questions.

> **open-ended questions**
> Questions to which the respondent replies in her or his own words.

Open-ended questions offer several advantages to the researcher. They enable respondents to give their general reactions to questions like the following:

1. What advantages, if any, do you think ordering from an e-retailer company offers compared with buying from local retail outlets? (*Probe:* What else?)

2. Why do you have one or more of your rugs or carpets professionally cleaned rather than cleaning them yourself or having someone else in the household clean them?

3. What do you think is most in need of improvement here at the airport?

4. What is there about the color of _____ [product] that makes you like it the best? (*Probe:* What color is that?)

5. Why do you say that brand [the one you use most often] is better?

Each of the preceding questions was taken from a different nationwide survey covering five products and services. Note that open-ended questions 2 and 4 are part of a skip pattern. Before being asked question 2, the respondent has already indicated that he or she uses a professional carpet cleaning service and does not depend on members of the household.

Open-ended responses have the advantage of providing the researcher with a rich array of information. The respondent's answers are based on his or her personal frame of reference and described in real-world terminology rather than laboratory or marketing jargon. Often, this is helpful in designing promotion themes and campaigns; it enables copywriters to use the consumer's language. This rich array of information can now be captured even in computer-assisted interviews and Internet surveys.

The inspection of open-ended responses also can serve as a means of interpreting closed-ended questions. Analysis often sheds additional light on the motivations or attitudes behind closed-ended response patterns. It is one thing to know that color ranks second in importance out of five product attributes—but it might be much more valuable to know why color is important. For example, a recent study of mobile home park residents identified a great deal of dissatisfaction with the trash pick-up service, but further inspection of the open-ended responses uncovered the reason: neighbors' dogs were allowed to run free and were overturning the receptacles.

Similarly, open-ended questions may suggest additional alternatives not listed in a closed-ended response format. For example, a previously unrecognized advantage of using an e-retail company might be uncovered in responses to question 1. A closed-ended question on the same subject would not have this advantage.

One manufacturer for which the authors consult always ends product placement questionnaires with the following: "Is there anything else that you would like to tell us about the product that you have tried during the past three weeks?" This probe seeks any final tidbit of information that might provide additional insight for the researcher.

Alexa Smith, president of Research Department in New York City, suggests several open-ended questions that can be asked for greater insights in the accompanying Practicing Marketing Research box.

Open-ended questions are not without their problems. Editing and coding can consume great amounts of time and money if done manually. Editing open-ended responses requires collapsing the many response alternatives into some reasonable number. If too many categories are used, data patterns and response frequencies may be difficult to interpret. Even if a proper number of categories is used, editors may still have to interpret what the interviewer has recorded and force the data into a category. If the categories are too broad, the data may be too general and important meaning may be lost.

A related problem of open-ended questions is the potential for interviewer bias. Although training sessions continually stress the importance of verbatim recording of open-ended questions, interviewers in the field often take shortcuts. Also, slow writers may unintentionally miss important comments. Good probes that ask "Can you tell me a little more?" or "Is there anything else?" are helpful in dealing with this problem. Good examples of open-ended questions are provided in the feature on page 296.

Precoding open-ended questions can partially overcome these problems. Assume that this question was to be asked in a food study: "What, if anything, do you normally add to a taco that you have prepared at home, besides meat?" Coding categories for this open-ended question might be as follows:

Response	Code
Avocado	1
Cheese (Monterey Jack, cheddar)	2
Guacamole	3
Lettuce	4
Mexican hot sauce	5
Olives (black or green)	6
Onions (red or white)	7
Peppers (red or green)	8
Pimento	9
Sour cream	0
Other	X

These answers would be listed on the questionnaire, and a space would be provided to write in any nonconforming reply in the "Other" category. In a telephone interview, the question would still qualify as open-ended because the respondents would not see the

Useful Open-Ended Questions

Here are some open-ended questions, often overlooked, that lead to greater insight:

☐ **What would it take to get you to use or buy a product or service?** Such a question is useful at the end of a focus group or in-depth interview. At minimum, it can provide a handy summation of the findings that have gone before. It can also serve as a forum for problems and issues that have not yet surfaced. In a study about children's magazines developed in Europe, for example, the respondents said the text would need to be simplified and the illustrations improved for the magazines to be acceptable for children in the United States.

☐ **What is the best thing about the product, service, or promotion?** This question yields far more than the typical "What do you like about it?" question and can be useful as an addition to the traditional "likes" question. A food company had developed a frozen breakfast item that did not seem to be winning any awards for quality and taste. But asking what respondents liked about the food item yielded little because respondents were dissatisfied with the product. By asking what the *best* thing about it was, however, the company found it was "the idea." Many of the participants in the study were working mothers and longed for a quick and convenient hot breakfast item they could provide for their families. Based on answers to a question on simple likes, the whole idea might have been thrown out, but based on "the best thing," the client knew the company was on to something and that the product just needed taste and quality improvements.

☐ **What is the worst thing about the product, service, or promotion?** The corollary to "the best thing," this question also often

yields surprising answers. Respondents who talked about going to the dentist responded rationally to what they disliked, including pain, expense, and insecurity about their personal experience. When asked, "What is the worst thing that can happen when you go to the dentist?" many said, "You could die!" Dying in the dentist's chair is a rare occurrence, but the response taught the study's sponsor something about the level of fear people were dealing with.

☐ **Main idea registration.** At the least, the researcher needs to know if respondents have the correct understanding of an idea. Asking for main idea registration is often a good shortcut to identifying communications problems with a concept that would otherwise impede acceptance of an idea. Sometimes the executional elements of a concept can provide a sticking point that can be distracting. A quick fix may be either to verbally correct the misunderstanding or to rewrite the concepts in between focus groups or interviews. If respondents do not understand the intended message, they often find it difficult to answer a question about whether anything is confusing or hard to understand.

☐ **How would friends and close associates relate to this idea?** Sometimes an idea or a concept can be so blatant that it causes a consumer backlash. This can happen when a company tries to create an upscale, status-conscious image for its product or service. In this case, consumers will indicate something to the effect that they would never be so snobbish as to relate to the idea. When this happens, the merit of the strategy can become apparent if the question is moved into the third person, such as "Do you know friends and associates who would relate to this idea?" If respondents say "yes," then the researcher can determine what friends and associates would like about the idea. In telling how their friends and associates would relate to the idea, consumers are really talking about themselves in a more socially sanctioned way. A surprising number of clients are not aware of this and tend to pass the moderator admonishing notes about just wanting to know what respondents themselves think.

☐ **What do you do just before you use a product or service?** Elderly women were asked this question in the context of reading

their favorite magazine and how special the experience was when they explained that they take their shoes off, put on their favorite slippers, change into comfortable clothes, and go off by themselves to read the magazine. Reading the magazine was something they did entirely for themselves, and the publisher learned that the magazine was truly a valued companion to these women.[2]

categories and the interviewer would be instructed not to divulge them. Precoding necessitates that the researcher have sufficient familiarity with previous studies of a similar nature to anticipate respondents' answers. Otherwise, a pretest with a fairly large sample is needed.

Open-ended questions may be biased toward the articulate interviewee. A person with elaborate opinions and the ability to express them may have much greater input than a shy, inarticulate, or withdrawn respondent. Yet, both might be equally likely prospective consumers of a product.

Suppose an editor confronted the following responses to the taco question: "I usually add a green, avocado-tasting hot sauce." "I cut up a mixture of lettuce and spinach." "I'm a vegetarian; I don't use meat at all. My taco is filled only with guacamole." How should the editor code these?

A basic problem with open-ended questions lies in the interpretation-processing area. A two-phase judgment must be made. First, the researcher must decide on an appropriate set of categories, and then each response must be evaluated to determine into which category it falls.

A final difficulty with open-ended questions is their inappropriateness on some self-administered questionnaires. With no interviewer there to probe, respondents may give a shallow, incomplete, or unclear answer. On a self-administered questionnaire without precoded choices, answers to the taco question might read "I use a little bit of everything" or "I use the same things they use in restaurants." These answers would have virtually no value to a researcher.

Closed-Ended Questions   A **closed-ended question** requires the respondent to make a selection from a list of responses. The primary advantage of closed-ended questions is simply the avoidance of many of the problems associated with open-ended questions. Reading response alternatives may jog a person's memory and generate a more realistic response. Interviewer bias is eliminated because the interviewer is simply clicking a box, circling a category, recording a number, or punching a key. Because the option of expounding on a topic is not given to a respondent, there is no bias toward the articulate. Finally, coding and data entry can be done automatically with questionnaire software programs.

It is important to realize the difference between a precoded open-ended question and a multiple-choice question. A precoded open-ended question allows the respondent to answer in a freewheeling format; the interviewer simply checks coded answers as they are given. Probing is used, but a list is never read. If the answer given is not one of the precoded ones, it is written verbatim in the "Other" column. In contrast, a closed-ended question requires that a list of alternatives be read by the respondent or interviewer.

Traditionally, marketing researchers have separated closed-ended questions into two types: **dichotomous questions**, with a two-item response option; **multiple-choice** (or multichotomous) **questions**, with a multi-item response option.

closed-ended questions
Questions that require the respondent to choose from a list of answers.

dichotomous questions
Closed-ended questions that ask the respondents to choose between two answers.

multiple-choice questions
Closed-ended questions that ask the respondent to choose among several answers; also called *multichotomous questions.*

Dichotomous Questions. In a dichotomous question, the two response categories are sometimes implicit. For instance, the implicit response options to the question "Did you buy gasoline for your automobile in the last week?" are "Yes" and "No." Even if the respondent says, "I rented a car last week, and they filled it up for me. Does that count?" the question would still be classified as dichotomous. A few examples of dichotomous questions follow:

1. Did you heat the Danish roll before serving it?
   Yes   1
   No   2

2. The federal government doesn't care what people like me think.
   Agree   1
   Disagree   2

3. Do you think that inflation will be greater or less than it was last year?
   Greater than   1
   Less than   2

Because the respondent is limited to two fixed alternatives, dichotomous questions are easy to administer and tabulate and usually evoke a rapid response. Many times, a neutral response option is added to dichotomous questions; if it is omitted, interviewers may jot down "DK" for "Don't know" or "NR" for "No response."

The "don't know" response has raised some concerns as telephone surveys have migrated to the Internet.

Dichotomous questions are prone to a large amount of measurement error. Because alternatives are polarized, the wide range of possible choices between the poles is omitted. Thus, appropriate wording is critical to obtaining accurate responses. Questions phrased in a positive form may well result in opposite answers from questions expressed in a negative form. For example, responses may depend on whether "Greater than" or "Less than" is listed first. These problems can be overcome by using a split ballot technique: one-half of the questionnaires have "Greater than" listed first, and the other half have "Less than" first. This procedure helps reduce potential order bias.

Another problem with the dichotomous question is that responses frequently fail to communicate any intensity of feeling on the part of the respondent. In some cases, like the gasoline purchasing example, the matter of intensity does not apply. But in some instances, strong feelings about an issue may be lost in the dichotomous response form. If the gasoline purchasing interview continued with the question "Would you purchase gasoline priced $1.00 per gallon above current prices if you were guaranteed twice the miles per gallon?" responses would likely range in intensity from "No; absolutely not" to "You bet!"

Multiple-Choice Questions. With multiple-choice questions, replies do not have to be coded as they do with open-ended questions, but the amount of information provided is more limited. The respondent is asked to give one alternative that correctly expresses his or her opinion or, in some instances, to indicate all alternatives that apply. Some examples of multiple-choice questions follow:

1. I'd like you to think back to the last footwear of any kind that you bought. I'll read you a list of descriptions and would like for you to tell me into which category it falls. (READ LIST AND CHECK THE PROPER CATEGORY)

Dress and/or formal	1	Specialized athletic shoes	4
Casual	2	Boots	5
Canvas-trainer-gym shoes	3		

2. (HAND RESPONDENT CARD) Please look at this card and tell me the letter that indicates the age group to which you belong.

A. Under 17 — 1   D. 35–49 years — 4
B. 17–24 years — 2   E. 50–64 years — 5
C. 25–34 years — 3   F. 65 and over — 6

3. In the last three months, have you used Noxzema Skin Cream . . . (CHECK ALL THAT APPLY)

as a facial wash? — 1
for moisturizing the skin? — 2
for treating blemishes? — 3
for cleansing the skin? — 4
for treating dry skin? — 5
for softening skin? — 6
for sunburn? — 7
for making the facial skin smooth? — 8

Question 1 from a mall intercept interview may not cover all possible alternatives and, thus, may not capture a true response. Where, for example, would an interviewer record work shoes? The same thing can be said for question 3. Not only are all possible alternatives not included, but respondents cannot elaborate or qualify their answers. The problem could be easily overcome by adding an "Any other use?" alternative to the question.

The multiple-choice question has two additional disadvantages. First, the researcher must spend time generating the list of possible responses. This phase may require brainstorming or intensive analysis of focus group tapes or secondary data. Second, the researcher must settle on a range of possible answers. If the list is too long, the respondent may become confused or lose interest. A related problem with any list is *position bias*. Respondents typically will choose either the first or the last alternative, all other things being equal. When Internet questionnaire software and CATI systems are used, however, position bias is eliminated by automatically rotating response order.

Scaled-Response Questions

The last response format to be considered is **scaled-response questions**, which are closed-ended questions where the response choices are designed to capture intensity of feeling. Consider the following questions:

> **scaled-response questions** Closed-ended questions in which the response choices are designed to capture the intensity of the respondent's feeling.

1. Now that you have used the product, would you say that you would buy it or not? (CHECK ONE)
Yes, would buy it
No, would not buy it

2. Now that you have used the product, would you say that you . . . (CHECK ONE)
definitely would buy it?
probably would buy it?
might or might not buy it?
probably would not buy it?
definitely would not buy it?

The first question fails to capture intensity. It determines the direction ("Yes" versus "No"), but it cannot compare with the second question in completeness or sensitivity of response. The latter also has the advantage of being ordinal in nature.

A primary advantage of using scaled-response questions is that scaling permits measurement of the intensity of respondents' answers. Also, many scaled-response forms incorporate numbers that can be used directly as codes. Finally, the marketing researcher can use much more powerful statistical tools with some scaled-response questions (see Chapter 14).

The most significant problems with scaled-response questions arise from respondent misunderstanding. Scaled questions sometimes tax respondents' abilities to remember and answer. First, the questionnaire must explain the response category options; then, the respondent must translate these options into his or her own frame of reference. Interviewers usually are provided with a detailed description of the response categories allowed and often are instructed to have the respondent state that he or she understands the scale before they ask any questions. Take a look at Exhibit 10.5 for examples of a telephone interviewer's instructions to respondents. In the case of self-administered questionnaires or Internet surveys, the researcher often presents the respondent with an example of how to respond to a scale as part of the instructions.

Step Four: Decide on the Question Wording

Once the marketing researcher has decided on the specific types of questions and the response formats, the next task is the actual writing of the questions. Wording specific questions can require a significant investment of the researcher's time unless questionnaire software or a survey website like Vovici is used. Four general guidelines about the wording of questions are useful to bear in mind: (1) The wording

Exhibit 10.5

Sample Telephone Interviewer's Instructions for a Scaled-Response Question Form

Example 1

I have some statements that I will read to you. For each one, please indicate whether you "strongly agree," "agree," "disagree," "strongly disagree," or have no opinion. I will read the statement, and you indicate *your* opinion as accurately as possible. Are the instructions clear?

(IF THE RESPONDENT DOES NOT UNDERSTAND, REPEAT RESPONSE CATEGORIES. THEN GO ON TO READ STATEMENTS AND RECORD RESPONSES. CIRCLE RESPONDENT'S OPINION IN EACH CASE.)

Example 2

Now I'm going to read you a list of statements that may or may not be important to you in deciding where to shop for computer equipment. Let's use your telephone keypad as a scale. Number 1 would mean "definitely disagree," and number 6 would mean "definitely agree." Or you can pick any number in between that best expresses your feelings.

Let's begin. To what extent do you agree or disagree that (INSERT STATEMENT) is an important aspect when deciding where to shop for computer equipment?

Example 3

Now I shall read a list of statements about automotive servicing that may or may not be important to you when servicing your car.

Let's use your telephone dial as a scale. . . .
Number 1 would mean you *disagree completely* with the statement.
Number 2 would mean you *disagree* with the statement.
Number 3 would mean you *somewhat disagree* with the statement.
Number 4 would mean you *somewhat agree* with the statement.
Number 5 would mean you *agree* with the statement.
Number 6 would mean you *agree completely* with the statement.

Do you have any questions about the scale?

1. To what extent do you agree or disagree that (INSERT STATEMENT) is a feature you consider when selecting a place to have your car serviced?

must be clear, (2) the wording must not bias the respondent, (3) the respondent must be able to answer the questions, and (4) the respondent must be willing to answer the questions.

Make Sure the Wording Is Clear Once the researcher has decided that a question is absolutely necessary, the question must be stated so that it means the same thing to all respondents. Ambiguous terminology—for example, "Do you live within five minutes of here?" or "Where do you usually shop for clothes?"—should be avoided. The respondent's answer to the first question will depend on such factors as mode of transportation (maybe the respondent walks), driving speed, and perceptions of elapsed time. (The interviewer would do better to display a map with certain areas delineated and ask whether the respondent lives within the area outlined.) The second question depends on the type of clothing being purchased and the meaning of the word "Where."

    Clarity also calls for the use of reasonable terminology. A questionnaire is not a vocabulary test. Jargon should be avoided, and verbiage should be geared to the target audience. The question "What is the level of efficacy of your preponderant dishwashing liquid?" probably would be greeted by a lot of blank stares. It would be much simpler to ask "Are you (1) very satisfied, (2) somewhat satisfied, or (3) not satisfied with your current brand of dishwashing liquid?" Words with precise meanings, universal usage, and minimal connotative confusion should be selected. When respondents are uncertain about what a question means, the incidence of "No response" answers increases.

    A further complication in wording questions is the need to tailor the language to the target respondent group, whether it is lawyers or construction laborers. This advice may seem painfully obvious, but there are instances in which failure to relate to respondents' frames of reference has been disastrous. A case in point is the use of the word *bottles* (or *cans*) in this question: "How many bottles of beer do you drink in a normal week?" Because in some southern states beer is sold in 32-, 12-, 8-, 7-, 6-, and even 4-ounce bottles, a "heavy" drinker (defined as someone who consumes eight bottles of beer per week) may drink as little as 32 ounces while a "light" drinker (defined as someone who consumes up to three bottles) may actually drink as much as 96 ounces.

    Clarity can be improved by stating the purpose of the survey at the beginning of the interview. To put the questions in the proper perspective, the respondent needs to understand the nature of the study and what is expected of him or her but not necessarily who is sponsoring the project.

    To achieve clarity in wording, the researcher should avoid asking two questions in one, sometimes called a *double-barreled question*. For example, "How did you like the taste and texture of the coffee cake?" should be broken into two questions, one concerning taste and the other texture. Each question should address only one aspect of evaluation.

> **clarity in wording**
> Avoid ambiguous terminology, use reasonable, vernacular language adjusted to the target group, and ask only one question at a time.

Avoid Biasing the Respondent Questions such as "Do you often shop at lower-class stores like Super Shop?" and "Have you purchased any high-quality Black & Decker tools in the past six months?" show an obvious **bias**. Leading questions, such as "Weren't you pleased with the good service you received last night at the Holiday Inn?" is also quite obviously biased. However, bias may be much more subtle than that illustrated in these examples.

    Sponsor identification early in the interviewing process can distort answers. An opening statement such as "We are conducting a study on the quality of banking for Northeast National Bank and would like to ask you a few questions" should be avoided. Similarly, it

> **respondent biasing**
> Leading questions that give away the research goal or sponsor identity.

GLOBAL RESEARCH

Survey Bias from Ethnicity and Gender of Interviewers and Respondents

Does it make a difference if you're an Hispanic male answering survey questions from an Anglo woman? Definitely, says Cynthia Webster, marketing professor at Mississippi State University. Will this produce survey bias? Yes.

To prove it, she assembled four groups of interviewers, including 19 Anglo women, 20 Anglo men, 22 Hispanic women, and 18 Hispanic men. All of them were in the age bracket 31 to 45. Using a questionnaire consisting of 50 closed-ended and four open-ended queries, which took 20 minutes to administer, the interviewers polled several hundred appropriate respondents as identified in a shopping mall.

Webster found that respondent ethnicity "interacted strongly" with interviewer ethnicity and provided "overwhelming support" for what she called a general deference theory. Specifically, that means that both Anglo and Hispanic respondents "significantly" biased or adjusted their responses when presented with items related to the interviewer's culture. For example, Hispanic men assigned themselves a higher socioeconomic status when the interviewer was an Hispanic female or Anglo man. They enhanced their image when questioned by an Hispanic

woman or Anglo male. Respondents deferred to interviewers of opposite ethnicity only when the questions were about the respondent's culture, Webster noted.

Gender differences in respondent behavior were notable, too. Men made a much bigger effort to respond when the interviewer was female, but in these circumstances they also tended to put themselves in a higher social class, thereby skewing the accuracy of the data. Men also distorted their answers on sensitive questions when interviewed by women. Women did not. Their responses were unaffected by the interviewer's gender; the women produced a higher response quality than men and as interviewers omitted fewer items. Hispanic men, Webster noted, tend to exhibit a traditional sex-role orientation and are easily influenced (and thus potentially biased) by women in an interviewer or respondent situation.[3]

Questions

1. Does Webster's data mean you may best avoid survey bias with Hispanics by using interviewers of their same ethnicity and gender?

2. Since women outshop men and tend to be more open to new products, should market surveys only include women respondents?

---

will not take long, for example, for a person to recognize that the survey is being conducted for Miller beer if, after the third question, every question is related to this product.

> **respondent's question answering ability**
> Factors affecting this ability include lack of required information, forgetfulness, or incomplete recall ability.

Consider the Respondent's Ability to Answer the Questions In some cases, a respondent may never have acquired the **information needed to answer the question**. For example, a husband may not know which brand of sewing thread is preferred by his wife, and respondents will know nothing about a brand or store that they have never encountered. A question worded so as to imply that the respondent should be able to answer it will often elicit a reply that is nothing more than a wild guess. This creates measurement error, since uninformed opinions are being recorded.

Another problem is forgetfulness. For example, you probably cannot remember the answers to all these questions: What was the name of the last movie you saw in a theater?

Who were the stars? Did you have popcorn? How many ounces were in the container? What price did you pay for the popcorn? Did you purchase any other snack items? Why or why not? The same is true for the typical respondent. Yet a brand manager for Mars, Incorporated wants to know what brand of candy you purchased last, what alternative brands you considered, and what factors led you to the brand selected. Because brand managers want answers to these questions, market researchers ask them. This, in turn, creates measurement error. Often respondents will give the name of a well-known brand, like Milky Way or Hershey. In other cases, respondents will mention a brand that they often purchase, but it may not be the last brand purchased.

To avoid the problem of a respondent's inability to recall, the researcher should keep the referenced time periods relatively short. For example, if the respondent says "Yes" to the question "Did you purchase a candy bar within the past seven days?" then brand and purchase motivation questions can be asked. A poor question like "How many movies have you rented in the past year to view at home on your DVD?" might be replaced with the following:

a. How many movies have you rented in the past month to view on your DVD?

b. Would you say that, in the last month, you rented more movies, fewer movies, or about the average number of movies you rent per month? (IF "MORE" or "LESS," ASK THE FOLLOWING QUESTION)

c. What would you say is the typical number of movies you rent per month?

Here are two questions from actual marketing research studies. The first is from a mail survey and the second from a telephone survey. Question 1: In the past three months, how much have you spent on movies you saw advertised in the newspaper? Most people haven't a clue as to how much they have spent on movies in the last three months unless it is "nothing." And they certainly don't recall which of the movies were advertised where. Also, what if the respondent bought tickets for the whole family? Question 2: Of your last ten drinks of scotch, how many were at home? At a friend's? At a restaurant? At a bar or tavern? A light scotch drinker may have consumed ten drinks over a period of not less than two years! Maybe he carries around a scotch intake logbook, but it's doubtful.

The above questions are bad, but the questions below, from a real mail panel survey, were written by either a careless questionnaire designer or one who lives quite differently from most of us. Question: How many times in an average day do you apply your usual underarm product? One to two times per day? Three to four times per day? Five to six times per day? More than six times per day? Question: How many times in an average day do you shower/bathe? One time per day? Two times per day? Three times per day? Four times per day? Five or more times per day? Good grooming is important, but perhaps these questions are over the line.

Consider the Respondent's Willingness to Answer the Question
A respondent may have a very good memory, yet not be **willing** to give a truthful reply. If an event is perceived as embarrassing, sensitive in nature, threatening, or divergent from the respondent's self-image, it is likely either not to be reported at all or to be distorted in a socially desirable direction.

> **respondent's willingness to answer** Embarrassing, sensitive, or threatening questions or questions divergent from respondent's self-image may cause them to refuse to answer.

Embarrassing questions that deal with topics such as borrowing money, personal hygiene, sexual activities, and criminal records must be phrased carefully to minimize measurement error. One technique is to ask the question in the third person—for example, "Do you think that most people charge more on their credit cards than they should? Why?" By generalizing the question to "most people," the researcher may be able to learn more about individual respondents' attitudes toward credit and debt.

Another method for soliciting embarrassing information is for the interviewer to state, prior to asking the question, that the behavior or attitude is not unusual—for example, "Millions of Americans suffer from hemorrhoids; do you or any member of your family suffer from this problem?" This technique, called *using counterbiasing statements*, makes embarrassing topics less intimidating for respondents to discuss. Issues related to biases related to interviewer and respondent ethnicity and gender are discussed in the Global Research box on page 302.

Step Five: Establish Questionnaire Flow and Layout

After the questions have been properly formulated, the next step is to sequence them and develop a layout for the questionnaire. Questionnaires are not constructed haphazardly; there is a logic to the positioning of each section (see Exhibit 10.6). Experienced marketing researchers are well aware that good questionnaire development is the key to obtaining a completed interview. A well-organized questionnaire usually elicits answers that are more carefully thought out and detailed. Researcher wisdom has led to the following general guidelines concerning questionnaire flow.

Use Screening Questions to Identify Qualified Respondents Most marketing research employs some type of quota sampling. Only qualified respondents are interviewed, and specific minimum numbers (quotas) of various types of qualified respondents may be sought. For example, a food products study generally has quotas of users of specific brands, a magazine study screens for readers, and a cosmetic study screens for brand awareness.

EXHIBIT 10.6	**How a Questionnaire Should Be Organized**		
Location	**Type**	**Examples**	**Rationale**
Screeners	Qualifying questions	"Have you been snow skiing in the past 12 months?" "Do you own a pair of skis?"	The goal is to identify target respondents.
First few questions	Warm-ups	"What brand of skis do you own?" "How many years have you owned them?"	Easy-to-answer questions show the respondent that the survey is simple.
First third of questions	Transitions	"What features do you like best about the skis?"	Questions related to research objectives require slightly more effort.
Second third	Difficult and complicated questions	"Following are 10 characteristics of snow skis. Please rate your skis on each characteristic, using the scale below."	The respondent has committed to completing the questionnaire.
Last third	Classifying and demographic questions	"What is the highest level of education you have attained?"	The respondent may leave some "personal" questions blank, but they are at the end of the survey.

Exhibit 10.7

Screening
Questionnaire That
Seeks Men 15 Years
of Age and Older
Who Shave at Least
Three Times a Week
with a Blade Razor

Hello. I'm from Data Facts Research. We are conducting a survey among men, and I'd like to ask you a few questions.

1. Do you or does any member of your family work for an advertising agency, a marketing research firm, or a company that manufactures or sells shaving products?

(TERMINATE)   Yes ( )
(CONTINUE WITH Q. 2)   No ( )

2. How old are you? Are you . . . (READ LIST)

(TERMINATE)   Under 15 yrs. old? ( )

(CHECK QUOTA CONTROL FORM—IF QUOTA GROUP FOR   15 to 34 yrs. old? ( )
WHICH THE RESPONDENT QUALIFIES *IS NOT* FILLED,
CONTINUE, IF QUOTA GROUP *IS* FILLED, THEN TERMINATE.)   Over 34 yrs. old? ( )

3. The last time you shaved, did you use an electric razor or a razor that uses blades?

(TERMINATE)   Electric Razor ( )

(CONTINUE WITH Q. 4)   Blade Razor ( )

4. How many times have you shaved in the past seven days?
(IF LESS THAN THREE TIMES, TERMINATE. IF THREE OR MORE TIMES, CONTINUE WITH THE MAIN QUESTIONNAIRE.)

Screeners (screening questions) may appear on the questionnaire, or a screening questionnaire may be filled out for everyone who is interviewed. Any demographics obtained provide a basis against which to compare persons who qualify for the full study. A long screening questionnaire can significantly increase the cost of the study, as more information must be obtained from every contact with a respondent. But it may provide important data on the nature of nonusers, nontriers, and persons unaware of the product or service being researched. Short screening questionnaires, such as the one in Exhibit 10.7, quickly eliminate unqualified persons and enable the interviewer to move immediately to the next potential respondent.

Most importantly, screeners provide a basis for estimating the costs of a survey. A survey in which all persons are qualified to be interviewed is going to be much cheaper to conduct than one with a 5 percent incidence rate. Many surveys are placed with field services at a flat rate per completed questionnaire. The rate is based on a stated average interview time and incidence rate. Screeners are used to determine whether, in fact, the incidence rate holds true in a particular city. If it does not, the flat rate is adjusted accordingly.

Tips on writing good screeners can be found in the accompanying Practicing Marketing Research box.

screeners
Questions used to identify appropriate respondents.

Begin with a Question That Gets the Respondent's Interest After introductory comments and screens to find a qualified respondent, the initial questions should be simple, interesting, and nonthreatening. To open a questionnaire with an income or age question could be disastrous. These are often considered threatening and immediately put the respondent on the defensive. The initial question should be easy to answer without much forethought.

Ask General Questions First Once the interview progresses beyond the opening warm-up questions, the questionnaire should proceed in a logical fashion. First, general questions are asked to get the person thinking about a concept, company, or type of product; then the questionnaire moves to the specifics. For example, a questionnaire on

PRACTICING MARKETING RESEARCH

Some Problems and Potential Solutions with Screening Questions

Based on the recommended methods for screening, a researcher who has the unfortunate task of conducting a phone survey of bus commuters who earn over $50,000 a year and live in ZIP Code 23456 might start the survey by asking if the person on the phone earns over $50,000 a year, lives in zip code 23456, and has commuted to work by bus in the past week. Such a method might be used despite the fact that researchers usually ask about income at the end of the survey, after some rapport has been established.

While having to screen for three characteristics may be an extreme example for a phone survey, needing to screen for multiple characteristics is very common when recruiting for focus groups. In fact, a review of 68 recent focus group screeners used by clients of Continental Research found an income screener on the first page of over 70 percent of them.

Sometimes researchers can reduce the number of screening questions or eliminate them altogether by narrowing the initial sample frame. In the above example, the need to ask for zip code could be eliminated by using a sampling frame that contains only households in the desired zip code. Similarly, if the researcher purchased a list of people living in that zip code who earned over $50,000 a year, then two of the "screeners" could be asked at the end of the survey as confirmation questions (anticipating a very high incidence). While only one screening question, bus ridership, would be necessary, one does have to weigh any possible biases caused by the list source.

Some problem screeners and solutions created by Continental Research of Norfolk, Virginia, are as follows.

Career Choice Survey

The purpose of this telephone survey was to learn more about how women between ages 20 and 29 made certain career decisions. To minimize costs, the questionnaire started with:

> Hello, I'm with Acme Research in (city). We're doing a survey this evening with women in their twenties.
>
> **IF MALE SAY:** Does anyone in your home fit this description? (Get female, repeat introduction)
>
> **IF FEMALE SAY:** May I ask your age?

At the close of the first evening of interviewing, we found a female in the age group in only 23 (12.8 percent) of 180 households contacted. Researchers began to suspect that some people were using the screening criteria to politely end the interview. The survey was revised by placing three opinion questions after a brief introduction. The newly revised survey read:

> Hello, I'm with Acme Research in (city). We're doing a brief opinion survey this evening.
>
> **IF MALE SAY:** We alternate who we ask for in our surveys; may I speak with an adult female?
>
> **IF FEMALE SAY:** Do you think that employees should be allowed to smoke in ALL workplaces, SOME, or in NO workplaces?
>
> **(THEN, TWO OTHER OPINION ITEMS WERE ASKED BEFORE THE AGE QUESTION.)**

Using this survey format, we found that the improved incidence rate was 26.6 percent. The difference was found to be statistically significant.

Pet Product Survey

A client who was considering creating an infomercial for a pet product had identified his target market as dog and/or cat owners who held a major credit card. He wanted these prospects to evaluate various features of his new product. To minimize cost, the questionnaire started with:

1. *Hello, I'm with (company). We're doing a survey this evening with pet owners, do you have a dog or cat?*

2. *And do you have a major credit card such as MasterCard or VISA?*

Based on other research done previously, the client said that we should expect an incidence rate of between 30 and 40 percent. Unfortunately, the incidence rate we found when using this survey format was only 8.9 percent.

To help account for the lower-than-expected incidence rate, we split the sample frame and reworded some surveys as follows:

1. *Hello, I'm with (company). We're doing a brief lifestyle survey tonight and we'd like to know how many refrigerators and televisions you have in your home.*

2. *Do you have a DVD?*

3. *Do you have a dog or cat?*

4. *Do you have more than one car?*

5. *Do you have a major credit card?*

By the end of the project, the incidence rate was 11.4 percent using the first, more direct questioning method and 31.8 percent using the second, more indirect technique. The difference between these two percentages was found to be statistically significant.[4]

---

shampoo might begin with "Have you purchased a hair spray, hair conditioner, or hair shampoo within the past six weeks?" Then it would ask about the frequency of shampooing, brands purchased in the past three months, satisfaction and dissatisfaction with brands purchased, repurchase intent, characteristics of an "ideal" shampoo, respondent's hair characteristics, and finally demographics.

Ask Questions That Require "Work" in the Middle   Initially, the respondent will be only vaguely interested in and understanding of the nature of the survey. As the interest-building questions transpire, momentum and commitment to the interview will build. When the interview shifts to questions with scaled-response formats, the respondent must be motivated to understand the response categories and options. Alternatively, questions might necessitate some recall or opinion formation on the part of the respondent. Established interest and commitment must sustain the respondent in this part of the interview.

Insert "Prompters" at Strategic Points   Good interviewers can sense when a respondent's interest and motivation sag and will attempt to build them back up. However, it is always worthwhile for the questionnaire designer to insert **prompters**, short encouragements at strategic locations in the questionnaire. These may be simple statements such as "There are only a few more questions to go" or "This next section will be easier." Encouraging words may also be inserted as part of an introduction to a section: "Now that you have helped us with those comments, we would like to ask a few more questions."

> **prompters**
> Short encouraging statements to rebuild respondent interest.

Position Sensitive, Threatening, and Demographic Questions at the End   As mentioned earlier, the objectives of a study sometimes necessitate questions on topics about which respondents may feel uneasy. These topics should be covered near the end of the questionnaire to ensure that most of the questions are answered before the respondent becomes defensive or breaks off the interview. Another argument for placing sensitive questions toward the end is that by the time these questions are asked, interviewees have been conditioned to respond. In other words, the respondent has settled into a pattern of seeing or hearing a question and giving an answer.

Allow Plenty of Space for Open-Ended Responses   An open-ended question that allows half a line for a reply usually will receive a reply of that length and nothing more. Generally speaking, three to five lines of blank space are deemed sufficient for open-ended replies. The researcher must judge how much detail is desirable in an open-ended reply. "Which department store did you visit most recently?" requires much less answer space than the follow-up question "What factors were most important in your decision to go to [name of department store]?"

Put Instructions in Capital Letters   To avoid confusion and to clarify what is a question and what is an instruction, all instructions should be in capital letters— for example, "IF 'YES' TO QUESTION 13, SKIP TO QUESTION 17." Capitalizing helps bring the instructions to the interviewer's or respondent's attention.

Use a Proper Introduction and Closing   Every questionnaire must have an introduction and closing. The Council for Marketing and Opinion Research (CMOR) has developed a model survey introduction and closing based on research findings from a number of different studies. CMOR recommends the following:[5]

Model Introduction/Opening

- ☐ In order to gain the trust of the respondent, the interviewer should provide his or her first name or agreed upon contact name. Providing a last name is optional but is recommended for business-to-business studies or surveys involving professionals such as those in the medical field.
- ☐ Provide the name of the company that the interviewer represents and the name of the client/sponsor of the research whenever possible.
- ☐ Explain the nature of the study topic/subject matter in general terms.
- ☐ State, as early in the interview as possible, that no selling will be involved as a result of the call.
- ☐ The respondent should be told in the introduction the approximate length of the survey.
- ☐ It is recommended as standard practice to obtain two-party consent to monitoring/ recording; that is, both the respondent and the interviewer should be informed that the call might be monitored/recorded for quality control purposes.
- ☐ Reinforce the fact that the respondent's time is appreciated/valued.
- ☐ Invite the respondent to participate in the survey, determine if the interview time is convenient, and, if not, offer an alternative callback time and date to complete the survey.

Hello, my name is _____ and I'm calling from (company). Today/Tonight we are calling to gather opinions regarding (general subject), and are not selling anything. This study will take approximately (length) and may be monitored (and recorded) for quality purposes. We would appreciate your time. May I include your opinions?

Model Closing

- ☐ At the conclusion of the survey, thank the respondent for his or her time.
- ☐ Express the desired intention that the respondent had a positive survey experience and will be willing to participate in future market research projects.
- ☐ Remind the respondent that his or her opinions do count.

Thank you for your time and cooperation. I hope this experience was a pleasant one and you will participate in other marketing research projects in the future. Please remember that your opinion counts! Have a good day/evening.

Alternative: Participate in collecting respondent satisfaction data to improve survey quality.

Thank you very much for taking part in this survey. Because consumers like you are such a valued part of what we do, I'd like you to think about the survey you just participated in. On a scale from 1 to 10 where 10 means "it was a good use of my time," and 1 means "it was not a good use of my time," which number between 1 and 10 best describes how you feel about your experience today? That's all the questions I have. Please remember that your opinion counts! Have a good day/evening!

Step Six: Evaluate the Questionnaire

Once a rough draft of the questionnaire has been designed, the marketing researcher is obligated to take a step back and critically evaluate it. This phase may seem redundant, given the careful thought that went into each question. But recall the crucial role played by the questionnaire. At this point in the questionnaire development, the following issues should be considered: (1) Is the question necessary? (2) Is the questionnaire too long? (3) Will the questions provide the information needed to accomplish the research objectives?

Is the Question Necessary?   Perhaps the most important criterion for this phase of questionnaire development is the **necessity** for a given question. Sometimes researchers and brand managers want to ask questions because "they were on the last survey we did like this" or because "it would be nice to know." Excessive numbers of demographic questions are very common. Asking for education data, numbers of children in multiple age categories, and extensive demographics on the spouse simply is not warranted by the nature of many studies.

Each question must serve a purpose. Unless it is a screener, an interest generator, or a required transition, it must be directly and explicitly related to the stated objectives of the particular survey. Any question that fails to satisfy at least one of these criteria should be omitted.

necessary questions Pertain directly to the stated survey objectives or are screeners, interest generators, or required transitions.

Is the Questionnaire Too Long?   At this point, the researcher should role-play the survey, with volunteers acting as respondents. Although there is no magic number of interactions, the length of time it takes to complete the questionnaire should be averaged over a minimum of five trials. Any questionnaire to be administered in a mall or over the telephone should be a candidate for cutting if it averages longer than 20 minutes. Sometimes mall-intercept interviews can run slightly longer if an incentive is provided to the respondent. Most Internet surveys should take less than 15 minutes to complete.

Common incentives are movie tickets, pen and pencil sets, and cash or checks. The use of incentives often actually lowers survey costs because response rates increase and terminations during the interview decrease. If checks are given out instead of cash, the canceled checks can be used to create a list of survey participants for follow-up purposes.

A technique that can reduce the length of questionnaires is called a split-questionnaire design. It can be used when the questionnaire is long and the sample size is large. The questionnaire is split into one core component (such as demographics, usage patterns, and psychographics) and a number of subcomponents. Respondents complete the core component plus a randomly assigned subcomponent.

Will the Questions Provide the Information Needed to Accomplish the Research Objectives? The researcher must make certain that sufficient numbers and types of questions are contained within the questionnaire to meet the decision-making needs of management. A suggested procedure is to carefully review the written objectives for the research project and then write each question number next to the objective that the particular question will address. For example, question 1 applies to objective 3, question 2 to objective 2, and so forth. If a question cannot be tied to an objective, the researcher should determine whether the list of objectives is complete. If the list is complete, the question should be omitted. If the researcher finds an objective with no questions listed beside it, appropriate questions should be added.

Step Seven: Obtain Approval of All Relevant Parties

After the first draft of the questionnaire has been completed, copies should be distributed to all parties who have direct authority over the project. Practically speaking, managers may step in at any time in the design process with new information, requests, or concerns. When this happens, revisions are often necessary. It is still important to get final approval of the first draft even if managers have already intervened in the development process.

> ⬦ **approval by managers**
> Managerial review approval after questionnaire drafting to prevent false starts and expensive later redrafts.

Managerial approval commits management to obtaining a body of information via a specific instrument (questionnaire). If the question is not asked, the data will not be gathered. Thus, questionnaire approval tacitly reaffirms what decision-making information is needed and how it will be obtained. For example, assume that a new product questionnaire asks about shape, material, end use, and packaging. By approving the form, the new product development manager is implying, "I know what color the product will be" or "It is not important to determine color at this time."

Step Eight: Pretest and Revise

When final managerial approval has been obtained, the questionnaire must be pretested. No survey should be conducted without a pretest. Moreover, a pretest does not mean that one researcher is administering the questionnaire to another researcher. Ideally, a pretest is done by the best interviewers who will ultimately be working on the job and is administered to target respondents for the study. In a **pretest**, researchers look for misinterpretations by respondents, lack of continuity, poor skip patterns, additional alternatives for precoded and closed-ended questions, and general respondent reaction to the interview. The pretest should be conducted in the same mode as the final interview—that is, if the study is to be an Internet survey, then the pretest should be too.

> ⬦ **pretest**
> Trial run of a questionnaire.

After completion of the pretest, any necessary changes should be made. Managerial approval should then be re-obtained before going forward. If the original pretest results in extensive design and question alterations, a second pretest is in order. Effects of national differences are discussed in the feature on page 316.

Step Nine: Prepare Final Questionnaire Copy

Even the final copy phase does not allow the researcher to relax. Precise instructions for skip patterns, numbering, and precoding must be set up, and the results proofread. In a mail survey, compliance and subsequent response rates may be affected positively by a professional-looking questionnaire. For telephone interviews, the copy is typically read from a computer screen. Survey software for online interviews often lets the designer choose backgrounds, formats, and so forth.

Step Ten: Implement the Survey

Completion of the questionnaire establishes the basis for obtaining the desired decision-making information from the marketplace. Most mall and telephone research interviewing is conducted by field service firms. It is the firm's job to complete the interviews and send them back to the researcher. In essence, field services are the in-person interviewers, the production line of the marketing research industry. A series of forms and procedures must be issued with the questionnaire to make certain that the field service firm gathers the data correctly, efficiently, and at a reasonable cost. Depending on the data collection method, these may include supervisor's instructions, interviewer's instructions, screeners, call record sheets, and visual aids.

Supervisor's Instructions   As mentioned above, mall, focus group, and some other types of research are handled by field services. This necessitates supervisor's instructions. **Supervisor's instructions** inform the field services firm of the nature of the study, start and completion dates, quotas, reporting times, equipment and facility requirements, sampling instructions, number of interviewers required, and validation procedures. In addition, detailed instructions are required for any taste test that involves food preparation. Quantities typically are measured and cooked using rigorous measurement techniques and devices.

> **supervisor's instructions** Written directions to the field service firm on how to conduct the survey.

A vital part of any study handled by a field service, supervisor's instructions establish the parameters for conducting the research. Without clear instructions, the interview may be conducted 10 different ways in 10 different cities. A sample page from a set of supervisor's instructions is shown in Exhibit 10.8.

Field Management Companies

Conducting fieldwork is much easier today than it was in years past. The stereotypical "kitchen table" field service firm is passing into history. In its place are companies that specialize in field management. **Field management companies**, such as QFact, On-Line Communications, and Direct Resource, generally provide questionnaire formatting, screener writing, development of instructional and peripheral materials, shipping services, field auditing, and all coordination of data collection, coding, and tab services required for the project. On completion of a study, they typically submit a single, comprehensive invoice for the project. Generally lean on staff, these companies provide the services clients need without attempting to compete with the design and analytical capabilities of full-service companies and ad agency research staffs.

> **field management companies** Firms that provide such support services as questionnaire formatting, screener writing, and coordination of data collection.

A number of full-service companies and qualitative professionals have discovered that using field management companies can be cost-effective; it can increase productivity by allowing them to take on more projects while using fewer of their internal resources. Several qualitative researchers have developed ongoing relationships with field management companies, whose personnel function as extensions of the consultant's staff, setting up projects and freeing up the researcher to conduct groups, write reports, and consult with clients.

Of course, like any other segment of the research industry, field management has its limitations. By definition, field management companies generally do not have design and analytical capabilities. This means that their clients may, on occasion, need to seek other providers to meet their full-service needs. In addition, experience, services, and standards vary tremendously from firm to firm. It's advisable to carefully screen prospective companies and check references. These limitations notwithstanding, field management companies provide a way for researchers to increase their productivity in a cost-effective manner, while maintaining the quality of the information on which their company's decisions and commitments are based.

Exhibit 10.8

Sample Page of Supervisor's Instructions for a Diet Soft Drink Taste Test

Purpose	To determine from diet soft drink users their ability to discriminate among three samples of Diet Dr Pepper and give opinions and preferences between two of the samples
Staff	3–4 experienced interviewers per shift
Location	One busy shopping center in a middle to upper-middle socioeconomic area. The center's busiest hours are to be worked by a double shift of interviewers.
	In the center, 3–4 private interviewing stations are to be set up and a refrigerator and good counterspace made available for product storage and preparation.
Quota	192 completed interviews broken down as follows:
	A minimum of 70 Diet Dr Pepper users
	A maximum of 122 other diet brand users
Project materials	For this study, you are supplied the following:
	250 Screening Questionnaires
	192 Study Questionnaires
	4 Card A's
Product/preparation	For this study, our client shipped to your refrigerated facility 26 cases of soft drink product. Each case contains 24 10-oz. bottles—312 coded with an *F* on the cap, 312 with an *S*.
	Each day, you are to obtain from the refrigerated facility approximately 2–4 cases of product—1–2 of each code. Product must be transported in coolers and kept refrigerated at the location. It should remain at approximately 42°F.
	In the center, you are to take one-half of the product coded *F* and place the #23 stickers on the bottles. The other half of the *F* product should receive #46 stickers.
	The same should be done for product *S*—one-half should be coded #34, the other half #68. A supervisor should do this task before interviewing begins. Interviewers will select product by *code number*. Code number stickers are enclosed for this effort.
	Each respondent will be initially testing three product samples as designated on the questionnaire. Interviewers will come to the kitchen, select the three designated bottles, open and pour 4 oz. of each product into its corresponding coded cup. The interviewer should cap and *refrigerate* leftover product when finished pouring and take only the three *cups* of product on a tray to respondent.

Impact of the Internet on Questionnaire Development

As with most other aspects of marketing research, the Internet has affected questionnaire development and use in several ways. For example, a marketing research company can now create a questionnaire and send it as an e-mail attachment to management for comments and approval; once approved, it can be placed on the client's server to be used as an Internet survey. Or researchers can simply use an Internet company like Vovici, Inquisite, SSI Web, or many others to create a survey on the Internet.

Vovici, for example, is a leading Internet self-service questionnaire-building site. It allows marketing researchers to create online surveys quickly and then view real-time results anytime and anywhere, using remote access. The advantage is that the marketing research client has no questionnaire software to install, and no programming or administration is required. All operations are automated and performed through the Vovici website. This includes survey design, respondent invitation, data collection, analysis, and results reporting.

Software for Questionnaire Development

Sawtooth Software offers some of the most widely used analytical and questionnaire development software in the world. The systems are both powerful and easy to use. SSI's online interviewing product is called SSI Web. Exhibit 10.9 illustrates the kinds of questions that can be used with SSI Web. Some of the capabilities of SSI Web are:

- ☐ **Easy-to-use, template-based authoring on the researcher's own PC**
- ☐ **Randomization of pages, questions, and response options**
- ☐ **Data piping**
- ☐ **Constructed (dynamic) lists**:
  One of the most powerful aspects of SSI Web is the ability to create custom lists of response options. These lists are defined by rules you specify and are customized to each respondent, based on the respondent's answers. The following example demonstrates how a constructed list might be used.

Which cities have you visited?

- ☒ Seattle
- ☐ Portland
- ☒ San Diego
- ☒ Denver
- ☐ Dallas

⟶

Out of all the cities that you visited, which is your favorite?

- ○ Seattle
- ○ San Diego
- ○ Denver

In the global market of today, a product may be tested in many countries at the same time. The need for questionnaires in several different languages has grown considerably in the last decade.

Alex Farnsworth/The Image Works

Exhibit 10.9

Types of Questions That Can Be Used with SSI Web

Single Select Response (radio) question type

If you had the opportunity to visit one of the following cities, which one would you choose?
○ Seattle
○ Hong Kong
○ Miami
○ Paris

Multiple Select Response (checkbox) question type

Please select all of the activities you enjoy:

☐ Shopping   ☐ Walking
☐ Bowling   ☐ Skiing
☐ Swimming   ☐ Golfing
☐ Kayaking   ☐ Other (please specify)
☐ Bird Watching   ☐ None of these

Single Select Response (combo box) question type

Which is your favorite holiday?

(Holidays are listed in drop-down box.)

The Numeric question type. A response from 0 to 100 is required.

How old are you? ☐

Open-end (multiple-line) question type

In the box below tell us about where you grew up.

Grid question type. This grid has select questions (radio buttons) specified for the rows.

Please tell us how likely you are to participate in each activity over the next 3 months.

	Not Likely		Somewhat Likely		Very Likely
Shopping	○	○	○	○	○
Bowling	○	○	○	○	○
Swimming	○	○	○	○	○
Kayaking	○	○	○	○	○
Bird Watching	○	○	○	○	○

Grid question type. This example shows the flexibility in grids by demonstrating how different question types can be set for each row.

Please answer the following questions about the electronic products displayed below.

Which items do you own?	☐	☐	☐	☐
Which is your favorite?	○	○	○	○
How much would you pay for each?	$	$	$	$

Ranking question type

Please rank the top three activities that you enjoy.
- ☐ Shopping
- ☐ Bowling
- ☐ Swimming
- ☐ Kayaking
- ☐ Bird Watching

Constant Sum question type

Given a budget of $3,000, please specify how much you would spend for each holiday.
- ☐ Easter
- ☐ 4th of July
- ☐ Halloween
- ☐ Thanksgiving
- ☐ Christmas
- ☐ New Years
- ☐ Total (Total is automatically computed each time numbers are entered into a holiday box.)

Free Format question type. The Free Format question type allows researchers to specify their own HTML to create custom questions.

Personal Information

First Name: _____

Last Name: _____

Street Address: _____

_____

City: _____ State: _____ Zip: _____ - _____

Gender: ○ Male   ○ Female

Interests: ☐ **Walking**
   ☐ **Running**
   ☐ **Hiking**
   ☐ **Swimming**
   ☐ **Eating**

Exhibit 10.9

Types of Questions That Can Be Used with SSI Web
(continued)
Source: Sawtooth Software, Inc.

- ☐ **Automatic question response verification**
  Questions must be answered before moving to the next question.

- ☐ **Powerful skip logic**
  SSI Web makes it easy to add skip logic (branching) within your survey. Skips can be executed with the page loads (pre-skips) or after it has been submitted (post-skips). That means respondents can receive pages that only include the subset of questions that apply to them, and respondents can skip pages that are not relevant.

- ☐ **Quota control**

- ☐ **Foreign language character support**

- ☐ **Questionnaire preview and testing on local PC**

- ☐ **Ability to create your own custom questions with HTML and "Free Format" question type**

- ☐ **Power users may insert HTML, JavaScript, or Perl**

GLOBAL RESEARCH

Survey Contamination from National Differences in Response Styles

Do people in different countries have characteristic and different styles of responding to questions? They do, report Hans Baumgartner, marketing professor at Pennsylvania State University, and Jan-Benedict E. M. Steenkamp, professor of international marketing research at Tilburg University in the Netherlands. Response styles, or non-content-based ways of responding, or simply, response biases, can contaminate questionnaire ratings and threaten the validity of research conclusions.

The researchers used a sample of 10,477 people drawn from 11 European Union countries and presented them a questionnaire with queries about their consumer behavior, response to media, demographics, and 60 attitudinal statements. These questions, using a 5-point Likert scale from "strongly agree" to "strongly disagree," focused on respondent attitudes about product choice, advertising response, new product openness, health awareness, susceptibility to deal offers, and more.

The researchers identified five response styles: (1) agreement tendency, regardless of content; (2) disagreement tendency or habitual negativity; (3) tendency to endorse extreme responses; (4) tendency to respond either wide or narrow compared to the mean; and (5) tendency to use the middle-scale category due to presumed indecision, evasiveness, or indifference.

The results showed that across the 11 countries variance in scale scores due to response style ranged from 0 percent to 29 percent, with an average of 8 percent. A few categories were especially susceptible to distortion from response style; these included health consciousness (average of 22 percent variance), consumer ethnocentrism (16 percent), quality consciousness (14 percent), and environmental consciousness (12 percent). Response styles are thus "a source of systematic measurement error" that can threaten the validity of conclusions drawn from the data and produce "seriously biased conclusions."[7]

Questions

1. How would you screen potential respondents who exhibit the disagreement tendency or habitual negativity?
2. Come up with a series of survey questions that compensate for response bias where the respondent is clearly indecisive or evasive.

☐ **Respondent restart (without cookies)**

☐ **Similar look across different browsers, including Mac and legacy browsers**

☐ **Automatic respondent password generation, or import from text file**

☐ **Link to/from other online interviewing systems and websites**

☐ **Online administrative module for real-time reports, download, and data management**

☐ **Exports to common formats (including Excel, SPSS), with label[6]**

Today's global marketers offer a variety of products to their customers throughout the world. Many times, a new product concept is tested simultaneously in a number of different countries, requiring questionnaires in a variety of languages.

Costs, Profitability, and Questionnaires

A discussion of questionnaires would not be complete without mentioning their impact on **costs and profitability**. Marketing research suppliers typically bid against one another for a client's project. A supplier who overestimates costs will usually lose the job to a lower-cost competitor. In all survey research, the questionnaire and incidence rate (see Chapter 5) are the core determinants of a project's estimated costs. When one of America's largest research suppliers examined costs and bids for all of its projects conducted by central-location telephone interviewing, it found that it had overestimated project costs 44 percent of the time during a recent 18-month period. The resulting overbidding had translated into millions of dollars of lost sales opportunities.

To avoid overbidding, managers must better understand questionnaire costs. In one central-location telephone study with a 50 percent incidence rate and calls lasting an average of 15 minutes, M/A/R/C/ a large international marketing research firm, found that only 30 percent of the data-collection costs involved asking the questions. Seventy percent of the data-collection costs were incurred trying to reach a qualified respondent.[8]

Exhibit 10.10 depicts the numerous roadblocks an interviewer can encounter trying to get a completed interview. Each roadblock adds to the costs. M/A/R/C/ for example, has found that simply adding a security screener to a questionnaire can increase the cost of interviewing by as much as 7 percent.

Another major source of extra cost in survey research is premature termination of interviews. People terminate interviews for four major reasons: the subject matter, redundant or difficult-to-understand questions, questionnaire length, and changing the subject during an interview. People like to talk about some subjects and not others. For example, the subject of gum is no problem, but bringing up mouthwash results in many terminations. Exhibit 10.11 reveals that a 20+-minute interview on gum results in few terminations (actual data). However, many people terminate a mouthwash interview within

> **questionnaire costs and profitability**
Factors affecting costs and profits include overestimating, overbidding, incidence rate, roadblocks to completed interviews, and premature interview terminations.

EXHIBIT 10.10 — **Difficulties in Finding a Qualified Respondent in a Central-Location Telephone Interview**

1. Failed Attempts
   - Busy
   - No answer
   - Answering machine
   - Business number
   - Phone/language problem
   - Discontinued line
2. Cooperation Problems
   - Respondent not at home
   - Respondent refused to be interviewed
3. Screener Determines Respondent Not Eligible
   - Failed security test (works for marketing research firm, advertising agency, or the client)
   - Doesn't use the product
   - Demographic disqualification (wrong gender, age, etc.)
   - Quota filled (For example, survey has a quota of 500 users of Tide and 500 users of other clothes washing powders. Interviewer already has 500 Tide users; the current respondent uses Tide.)
4. Respondent Terminated during Interview

Exhibit 10.11

Actual Respondent Termination Patterns for Interviews in Three Different Product Categories

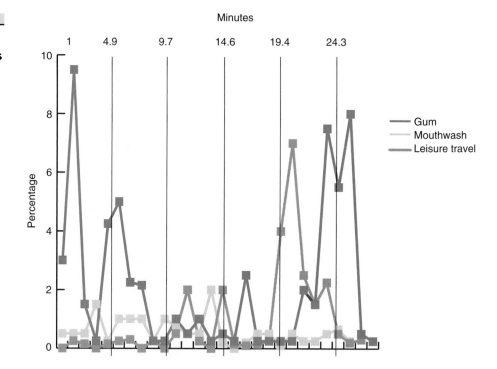

3 minutes or in the 19- to 22-minute range. Terminations of a leisure travel interview don't become a serious problem until the interview reaches 20 minutes in length. Terminations usually mean that the interview must be redone and all the time spent interviewing the respondent was wasted. However, preliminary research has found that callbacks on terminated interviews can sometimes result in a completed interview.[9] (The same research on callbacks to persons who originally refused to be surveyed was not productive.)

Once managers understand the actual costs of data collection, they should be in a better position to bid on jobs with a high degree of cost accuracy. Better information should result in less overbidding and therefore more contracts.

SUMMARY

The questionnaire plays a critical role in the data-collection process. The criteria for a good questionnaire may be categorized as follows: (1) providing the necessary decision-making information, (2) fitting the respondent, and (3) meeting editing, coding, and data processing requirements.

The process of developing a questionnaire is a sequential one:

Step One. Determine survey objectives, resources, and constraints.

Step Two. Determine the data-collection method.

Step Three. Determine the question response format.

Step Four. Decide on the question wording.

Step Five. Establish questionnaire flow and layout.

Step Six. Evaluate the questionnaire.

Step Seven. Obtain approval of all relevant parties.

Step Eight. Pretest and revise.

Step Nine. Prepare final questionnaire copy.

Step Ten. Implement the survey.

The three different types of questions—open-ended, closed-ended, and scaled-response questions—each have advantages and disadvantages. In establishing the wording and positioning of questions within the questionnaire, the researcher must try to ensure that the wording is clear and does not bias the respondent and that the respondent will be able and willing to answer the questions.

During the implementation of survey research, procedures must be followed to ensure that the data are gathered correctly, efficiently, and at a reasonable cost. These include preparing supervisor's instructions, interviewer's instructions, screeners, call record sheets, and visual aids. Many research organizations are now turning to field management companies to actually conduct the interviews.

Questionnaire software and the Internet are having a major impact on survey design. Vovici, SSI Web, and others enable researchers to go to the website and create online surveys.

The role of the questionnaire in survey research costs can be a decisive one. If a research firm overestimates data-collection costs, chances are that it will lose the project to another supplier. Most data-collection costs are associated not with conducting the actual interview, but with finding a qualified respondent. A respondent's propensity to terminate an interview, which can be costly, is often based on the nature of the topic discussed.

KEY TERMS & DEFINITIONS

questionnaire Set of questions designed to generate the data necessary to accomplish the objectives of the research project; also called an *interview schedule* or *survey instrument*.

editing Going through each questionnaire to ensure that skip patterns were followed and the required questions were filled out.

skip pattern Sequence in which questions are asked, based on a respondent's answer.

coding Process of grouping and assigning numeric codes to the various responses to a question.

survey objectives Outline of the decision-making information sought through the questionnaire.

open-ended questions Questions to which the respondent replies in her or his own words.

closed-ended questions Questions that require the respondent to choose from a list of answers.

dichotomous questions Closed-ended questions that ask the respondent to choose between two answers.

multiple-choice questions Closed-ended questions that ask the respondent to choose among several answers; also called *multichotomous questions*.

scaled-response questions Closed-ended questions in which the response choices are designed to capture the intensity of the respondent's feeling.

clarity in wording Avoid ambiguous terminology, use reasonable, vernacular language adjusted to the target group, and ask only one question at a time.

respondent biasing Leading questions that give away the research goal or sponsor identity.

respondent's question answering ability Factors affecting this ability include lack of required information, forgetfulness, or incomplete recall ability.

respondent's willingness to answer Embarrassing, sensitive, or threatening questions or questions divergent from respondent's self-image may cause them to refuse to answer.

screeners Questions used to identify appropriate respondents.

prompters Short encouraging statements to rebuild respondent interest.

necessary questions Pertain directly to the stated survey objectives or are screeners, interest generators, or required transitions.

approval by managers Managerial review and approval after questionnaire drafting to prevent false starts and expensive later redrafts.

pretest Trial run of a questionnaire.

supervisor's instructions Written directions to the field service firm on how to conduct the survey.

field management companies Firms that provide such support services as questionnaire formatting, screener writing, and coordination of data collection.

questionnaire costs and profitability Factors affecting costs and profits include overestimating, overbidding, incidence rate, roadblocks to completed interviews, and premature interview terminations.

QUESTIONS FOR REVIEW & CRITICAL THINKING

1. Explain the role of the questionnaire in the research process.

2. How do respondents influence the design of a questionnaire? Give some examples (e.g., questionnaires designed for engineers, baseball players, army generals, migrant farmworkers).

3. Discuss the advantages and disadvantages of open-ended questions and closed-ended questions.

4. Assume that you are developing a questionnaire about a new sandwich for McDonald's. Use this situation to outline the procedure for designing a questionnaire.

5. Give examples of poor questionnaire wording, and explain what is wrong with each question.

6. Once a questionnaire has been developed, what other factors need to be considered before the questionnaire is put into the hands of interviewers?

7. Why is pretesting a questionnaire important? Are there some situations in which pretesting is not necessary?

8. Design three open-ended and three closed-ended questions to measure consumers' attitudes toward BMW automobiles.

9. What's wrong with the following questions?
   a. How do you like the flavor of this high-quality Maxwell House coffee?
   b. What do you think of the taste and texture of this Sara Lee coffee cake?
   c. We are conducting a study for Bulova watches. What do you think of the quality of Bulova watches?

10. What do you see as the major advantages of using a field management company? What are the drawbacks?

11. Discuss the advantages and disadvantages of Web-based questionnaires.

(Team Exercise) 12. Divide the class into groups of four or five. Next, match the groups evenly into supplier and client teams. The instructor will then pair a client team with a supplier team. Each client team should pick some aspect of the university such as student housing, student transportation, sports, sororities, fraternities, food on campus, or some other aspect of student life. Next, the client team should create

four management objectives for their topic and construct a questionnaire to meet the management objectives. In addition, the questionnaire should include the following demographics: age, gender, major, and others determined by your instructor. Once the client team approves the questionnaire, both the client and supplier team members should complete 10 interviews each. The results should then be presented to the class. *Note:* this data can be formatted into SPSS for more detailed analysis later in the text.

WORKING THE NET

1. Visit *www.vovici.com* and take a series of free online surveys and evaluate the programs, questions, approach, assumptions, and results. *Note:* Vovici was formerly known as Perseus.
2. Log on to *www.surveymonkey.com* and *www.inquisite.com* and consider how suitable, or not, their online polling software would be for conducting market research for new customers for iPhone.
3. See what it's like to be at the receiving end of an online survey; take one or two surveys at *www.greenfield.com* and click on "Take a Survey."

Singles Dinner Club

REAL-LIFE RESEARCH • 10.1

For the past five years Amy West has worked for Bill Jackson, owner of a local chain of pet stores in the Albuquerque–Santa Fe area. Both Amy and Bill have been divorced for several years and seem to have adjusted to the "single life." Over a casual lunch one day, Bill observed that, overall, his lifestyle was very pleasant, but he found it difficult to meet interesting, exciting, and compatible women. The single's bar scene just did not seem to provide the right atmosphere, and the kind of person he wanted to meet didn't frequent "single's bars." Amy echoed a similar frustration when attempting to meet men. She also noted that dating services, particularly the online ones, seemed "too clinical."

Bill decided to explore the situation a little further. He found that the number of one-person households had increased by over 20 percent during the last decade, yet the total population had risen only a fraction of that. Also, there are 3 million women in the 30 to 40 age bracket who have never been married. Furthermore, the divorce rate had increased substantially for this group.

Armed with these data, Bill decided that there must be many other single professional people like Amy and himself who would like to meet compatible singles. Thus, the Singles Dinner Club was born. The initial membership fee was $100, for which the member received the right to attend the club's dinners. An e-mail newsletter was sent out every month detailing where the meals would be held (once a week), the price, and the menu. Bill chose four different types of restaurants each month, with prices ranging from $35 to $80 per meal. The price did not include cocktails, but was a complete dinner, from appetizer to dessert. Bill and Amy negotiated cost with restaurants and marked up the discounted price by 30 percent.

Bill and Amy arranged the seating with name cards at each place to ensure people saw new faces each week. To encourage mixing, a cocktail hour was held before each meal. Often groups would get together after dinner and go dancing.

In the first few months of operation, the club exceeded Bill's wildest expectations. Four months after opening, membership reached 550 persons. Bill had hoped to have 1,000 members after two and one-half years. Despite the initial success, several factors began to bother Bill:

1. The average attendance per week was only 42 persons.
2. The average age seemed to be about 45; young people came once and then did not return for months.
3. The women usually outnumbered the men three to one.
4. Some people had told Bill that they did not seem to be getting a good value for their money, which could be significant when the annual renewal time rolled around.

Bill decided that perhaps the club should branch out in new directions (e.g., guided tours, movie previews, dances, wine tastings, dancing lessons), but he was not sure what to do. He also hoped to address the problems just outlined.

Questions

1. Prepare a mail questionnaire that will provide ideas for Bill and Amy in diversifying their club.
2. Write the cover letter to accompany the questionnaire.

© Fog City Productions/Age Fotostock America, Inc.

BASIC SAMPLING ISSUES

LEARNING OBJECTIVES

1.	To understand the concept of sampling.
2.	To learn the steps in developing a sampling plan.
3.	To understand the concepts of sampling error and nonsampling error.
4.	To understand the differences between probability samples and nonprobability samples.
5.	To understand sampling implications of surveying over the Internet.

There are many parallels between sampling for marketing research and sampling for political polls. One key difference is that with political polls Election Day comes, people vote, and we see the results and can compare them to the predictions made by pollsters. The fact that we see a high degree of accuracy in predicting election results from polls supports the basic idea that a small but carefully chosen sample can accurately estimate the behavior of millions. Zogby International, headed by John Zogby, is a public opinion and political polling firm. The following issues addressed by John Zogby (JZ) provide valuable insights on basic sampling issues:[1]

Why don't you ever call me or my friends? None of my friends or those in my circle agree with the polls!

JZ: "Phone numbers are chosen purely by random, ensuring that every household in the U.S. (or wherever we are polling) have as much chance of being selected as any other. With tens of millions of adults in the U.S., it is still rather easy to be missed—but stay in there and maybe stay home more often. You probably have more of a chance of being called than having a visit by Ed McMahon."

How can polls be so accurate when you only ask such a small number of people?

JZ: "It's pure probability and statistics. The same theory is involved as when you take a blood test and the clinician draws only a small sample rather than draining all the blood out of your body."

What is a "margin of error"?

JZ: "The margin of sampling error means that if we do the same poll 100 times, in 95 cases out of 100, we will get the same results plus or minus a certain percentage. Generally, a sample of 400 gives you a MOE of $\pm 5\%$, 600 gets you $\pm 4\%$, 1,000 gets $\pm 3\%$. We need to be sure our sampling is random and scientific. It all relates to probability and statistics. If there are a million marbles in a jar, some black and some white—how best do I determine the number of each color, short of counting every marble? If I draw 1,000 out at random, chances are I will get the same numbers of each 95 times out of 100 within a margin of error of $\pm 3\%$. However, there are other sources of survey error—for example, how questions are phrased, etc."

I've heard so many conflicting stories—is Zogby International a Republican pollster, a Democratic pollster, or an Independent pollster?

JZ: "We are independent and nonpartisan. I am personally a Democrat, but the firm does a lot of work for media (like Reuters America, *New York Post*, *St. Louis Post Dispatch*, etc.) and we work for both parties."

Where do you poll for Zogby America? What regions, area codes, or time zones?

JZ: "If we are polling the U.S., we poll from a sample drawn from all households with telephones in 48 states. We, like others, do not poll Hawaii or Alaska because of time differences and because Republican Alaska cancels out Democratic Hawaii. As well, out of a sample of 1,000 likely voters there would only be a total of 1 from both states (combined)."

Can I be put on a list so that you can call me for a future poll?

JZ: "I'm sorry but our polls must be random. As soon as we 'place' people in our pool of respondents we run the risk of skewing results."

I read a lot of polls and yours is so different from the others—what makes your answers so different (and accurate)?

JZ: "We poll only likely voters who are different from just all adults. In addition, we poll all day long—9 a.m. to 9 p.m. local time (to the region we're calling). Finally, we apply weighting for party identification to ensure that there is no built-in Democratic bias in our sampling."

This chapter addresses the issues commented on by Mr. Zogby above and many others.

Concept of Sampling

> **sampling**
> Process of obtaining information from a subset of a larger group.

Sampling refers to the process of obtaining information from a subset (a sample) of a larger group (the universe or population). A user of marketing research then takes the results from the sample and makes estimates of the characteristics of the larger group. The motivation for sampling is to be able to make these estimates more quickly and at a lower cost than would be possible by any other means. It has been shown time and again that sampling a small percentage of a population can result in very accurate estimates. An example that you are probably familiar with is polling in connection with a presidential election. Most major polls use samples of 1,000 to 1,500 people to make predictions regarding the voting behavior of tens of millions of people, and their predictions have proven to be remarkably accurate.

The key to making accurate predictions about the characteristics or behavior of a large population on the basis of a relatively small sample lies in the way in which individuals are selected for the sample. It is critical that they be selected in a scientific manner, which ensures that the sample is representative—that it is a true miniature of the population. All of the major types of people who make up the population of interest should be represented in the sample in the same proportions in which they are found in the larger population. This sounds simple, and as a concept, it is simple. However, achieving this goal in sampling from a human population is not easy. The issue of cell-phone-only households is covered in the feature on page 327.

Population

> **population**
> Entire group of people about whom information is needed; also called *universe* or *population of interest*.

In discussions of sampling, the terms *population* and *universe* are often used interchangeably.[2] In this textbook, we will use the term *population*. The **population**, or *population of interest*, is the entire group of people about whom the researcher needs to obtain information. One of the first steps in the sampling process is defining the population of interest. This often involves defining the target market for the product or service in question.

Consider a product concept test for a new nonprescription cold symptom relief product, such as Contac. You might take the position that the population of interest includes everyone, because everyone suffers from colds from time to time. Although this is true, not everyone buys a nonprescription cold symptom relief product when he or she gets a cold. In this case, the first task in the screening process would be to determine whether people have purchased or used one or more of a number of competing brands during some time period. Only those who had purchased or used one of these brands would be included in the population of interest.

Defining the population of interest is a key step in the sampling process. There are no specific rules to follow in defining the population of interest. What the researcher must do is apply logic and judgment in addressing the basic issue: Whose opinions are needed in order to satisfy the objectives of the research? Often, the definition of the population is based on the characteristics of current or target customers.

Sample versus Census

> **census**
> Collection of data obtained from or about every member of the population of interest.

In a **census**, data are obtained from or about every member of the population of interest. Censuses are seldom employed in marketing research, as populations of interest to marketers normally include many thousands or even millions of individuals. The cost and time required to collect data from a population of this magnitude are so great that censuses are usually out of the question. It has been demonstrated repeatedly that a relatively small

PRACTICING MARKETING RESEARCH

Cell Phone Only Households—The Need to Broaden the Polling Sample

So many Americans now use cell phones, and sometimes exclusively, that not to include them in public opinion polls is to court data inaccuracy. In 2003, cell phone only households numbered only 3 percent of the total in the United States, but in 2007, that number had jumped to 16 percent, and at least 60 percent of households have at least one cell phone. The polling standard of course has been random sampling of landlines because these are tied to households and are geographically fixed. With cell phones, it's all different.

Cell phones are not geographically based but tied to an individual who could be anywhere. If you poll somebody on his cell phone, what do you put down for his location to fit your sampling frame? That's assuming the cell phone holder will even talk to you because why would they want to waste valuable minutes taking a 20-minute poll? Complicating matters is that federal law mandates that pollsters manually dial the cell phone users; they can't automate it through computers. But given the increasing incidence of exclusive cell phone use, not to include those users is to skew the data by misrepresenting the desired sampling frame. A "truly representative sample," critics say, now must include homes that only have cell phones, only have landlines, or have both.

Surveys show that people who only use cell phones currently tend to be young; 50 percent of cell phone only users are under 30, unmarried, and politically liberal, and many are Hispanic (14 percent) or low-income renters living in cities— certainly a viable demographic sample itself. In contrast, in the total population only 21 percent are younger than 30, and in landline households, only 14 percent; only 29 percent of cell users are married compared to 57 percent of landliners. A 2006 study by the Pew Researcher Center reported that not including cell phone only users had only a "minimal" impact on the results; on a political poll with nine questions, weighting the respondents to include cell phone only people changed the results by only 1 percent.[3]

But a lot can change in two years. In early 2008, media critics and bloggers were challenging the validity of political polls because they didn't include cell phone only households. Researchers estimate that by the end of 2008, the U.S. percentage of cell phone only households will be about 25 percent. That's probably why CBS News is already including about 2 percent of cell phone only users in their research polls. The general consensus among researchers is that until that day when Internet polling yields a reasonable sampling frame, public opinion researchers will have to include cell phones in their standard telephone polling.[4]

Questions

1. Given the likelihood that cell phone users will not want to use valuable minutes taking your poll, what incentives might you offer them?

2. Discuss the feasibility of a cell phone only household taking a poll by way of text messaging, which theoretically should use up fewer minutes.

---

but carefully chosen sample can very accurately reflect the characteristics of the population from which it is drawn. A **sample** is a subset of all the members of a population. Information is obtained from or about a sample and used to make estimates about various

 sample
Subset of all the members of a population of interest.

characteristics of the total population. Ideally, the sample from or about which information is obtained is a representative cross section of the total population.

Although censuses are used infrequently in marketing research, there are instances in which they are appropriate and feasible. For example, a census may be useful to an industrial products firm that has only a small number of customers for some highly specialized product it sells. In such a situation, it may be possible to obtain information from the entire population of customers.

Note that the popular belief that a census provides more accurate results than a sample is not necessarily true. In a census of a human population, there are many impediments to actually obtaining information from every member of the population. The researcher may not be able to obtain a complete and accurate list of the entire population, or certain members of the population may refuse to provide information. Because of these barriers, the ideal census is seldom attainable, even with very small populations. You may have read or heard about these types of problems in connection with the 1990 and 2000 U.S. Census.[5]

Developing a Sampling Plan

The process of developing an operational sampling plan can be summarized by the seven steps shown in Exhibit 11.1. These steps are defining the population, choosing a data-collection method, identifying a sampling frame, selecting a sampling method, determining sample size, developing operational procedures, and executing the sampling plan.

Step One: Define the Population of Interest

The basic issue in developing a sampling plan is to specify the characteristics of those individuals or things (for example, customers, companies, stores) from whom or about whom information is needed to meet the research objectives. The population of interest is often

Exhibit 11.1

Developing a Sampling Plan

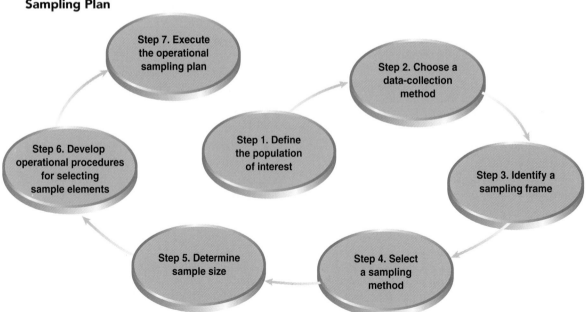

PRACTICING MARKETING RESEARCH

Driver's Licenses and Voter Registration Lists as Sampling Frames

Medical researchers at the University of North Carolina at Chapel Hill wanted to provide the most representative sampling frame for a population-based study of the spread of HIV among heterosexual African Americans living in eight rural North Carolina counties. They found that the list of driver's licenses for men and women aged 18 to 59 gave them the "best coverage" and a "more nearly complete sampling frame" for this population, one that permitted "efficient sampling," followed by voter registration lists. It far exceeded all census lists and at least four other available population lists.

Telephone directories, for example, are inadequate because they do not publish unlisted numbers, thereby eliminating people from the study. Medicare lists only tally the elderly, disabled, or those with diagnosed diseases. Motor vehicle registries only cover people who own cars, and random-digit dialing does not tell a researcher whether or not the person called belongs to the targeted demographic subset. Census lists are not good enough either, the researchers found, because the driver's license file often exceeded in

number the projected population based on the census, highlighting its inaccuracy. Furthermore, the list of registered drivers was superior to voter registration lists in identifying men in the desired population inasmuch as fewer men were registered to vote than women.

In 1992, other medical researchers had employed driver's license lists as a sampling frame for their studies of bladder and breast cancer among adult blacks. But in 1994, a congressional act restricted the release of driver's license lists to applications for statistical analysis but not direct contact of license holders. Unfortunately for market researchers, subsequent congressional, judicial review, and legislation at the state level in selected states have kept this sampling frame methodology in a state of uncertainty and flux.[6]

Questions

1. What kinds of usable data could a statistical analysis of driver's license lists generate, and how would you go about the study?
2. Identify two other market research categories in which driver's license lists would excel in providing accurate data.

specified in terms of geographic area, demographic characteristics, product or service usage characteristics, and/or awareness measures (see Exhibit 11.2). In surveys, the question of whether a particular individual does or does not belong to the population of interest is often dealt with by means of screening questions. Even with a list of the population and a sample from that list, researchers still need screening questions to qualify potential respondents. Exhibit 11.3 provides a sample sequence of screening questions.

In addition to defining who will be included in the population of interest, researchers should also define the characteristics of individuals who should be excluded. For example, most commercial marketing research surveys exclude some individuals for so-called security reasons. Very frequently, one of the first questions on a survey asks whether the respondent or anyone in the respondent's immediate family works in marketing research, advertising, or the product or service area at issue in the survey (see, for example, question 5 in Exhibit 11.3). If the individual answers "Yes" to this question, the interview is terminated. This type of question is called a *security question* because those

EXHIBIT 11.2	Some Bases for Defining the Population of Interest
Geographic Area	What geographic area is to be sampled? This is usually a question of the client's scope of operation. The area could be a city, a county, a metropolitan area, a state, a group of states, the entire United States, or a number of countries.
Demographics	Given the objectives of the research and the target market for the product, whose opinions, reactions, and so on are relevant? For example, does the sampling plan require information from women over 18, women 18–34, or women 18–34 with household incomes over $35,000 per year who work and who have preschool children?
Usage	In addition to geographic area and/or demographics, the population of interest frequently is defined in terms of some product or service use requirement. This is usually stated in terms of use versus nonuse or use of some quantity of the product or service over a specified period of time. The following examples of use screening questions illustrate the point: ■ Do you drink five or more cans, bottles, or glasses of diet soft drinks in a typical week? ■ Have you traveled to Europe for vacation or business purposes in the past two years? ■ Have you or has anyone in your immediate family been in a hospital for an overnight or extended stay in the past two years?
Awareness	The researcher may be interested in surveying those individuals who are aware of the company's advertising, to explore what the advertising communicated about the characteristics of the product or service.

who work in the industries in question are viewed as security risks. They may be competitors or work for competitors, and managers do not want to give them any indication of what their company may be planning to do.

There may be reasons to exclude individuals for other reasons. For example, the Dr Pepper Company might wish to do a survey among individuals who drink five or more cans, bottles, or glasses of soft drink in a typical week but do not drink Dr Pepper, because the company is interested in developing a better understanding of heavy soft drink users who do not drink its product. Therefore, researchers would exclude those who drank one or more cans, bottles, or glasses of Dr Pepper in the past week.

Step Two: Choose a Data-Collection Method

The selection of a data-collection method has implications for the sampling process.

- Mail surveys suffer from biases associated with low response rates (which are discussed in greater detail later in this chapter).

- Telephone surveys have a less significant problem with nonresponse, but suffer from call screening technologies used by potential respondents and the fact that some people have mobile phones only.

- Internet surveys have problems with professional respondents (discussed in Chapter 6) and the fact that the panel or e-mail lists used often do not provide appropriate representation of the population of interest.

> **sampling frame**
> List of population elements from which units to be sampled can be selected or a specified procedure for generating such a list.

Step Three: Identify a Sampling Frame

The third step in the process is to identify the **sampling frame**, which is a list of the members or elements of the population from which units to be sampled are to be selected. Identifying the sampling frame may simply mean specifying a procedure for

Hello. I'm _____ with _____ Research. We're conducting a survey about products used in the home. May I ask you a few questions?

1. Have you been interviewed about any products or advertising in the past 3 months?

    Yes   (TERMINATE AND TALLY)

    No   (CONTINUE)

2. Which of the following hair care products, if any, have you used in the past month? (HAND PRODUCT CARD TO RESPONDENT; CIRCLE ALL MENTIONS)

        1 Regular shampoo

        2 Dandruff shampoo

        3 Creme rinse/instant conditioner

        4 "Intensive" conditioner

    (INSTRUCTIONS: IF "4" IS CIRCLED—SKIP TO Q. 4 AND CONTINUE FOR "INTENSIVE" QUOTA; IF "3" IS CIRCLED BUT NOT "4"—ASK Q. 3 AND CONTINUE FOR "INSTANT" QUOTA)

3. You said that you have used a creme rinse/instant conditioner in the past month. Have you used either a creme rinse or an instant conditioner in the past week?

    Yes (used in the past week)   (CONTINUE FOR "INSTANT" QUOTA)

    No (not used in past week)   (TERMINATE AND TALLY)

4. Into which of the following groups does your age fall? (READ LIST, CIRCLE AGE)

        X   Under 18   (CHECK AGE QUOTAS)

        1   18–24

        2   25–34

        3   35–44

        X   45 or over

5. Previous surveys have shown that people who work in certain jobs may have different reactions to certain products. Now, do you or does any member of your immediate family work for an advertising agency, a marketing research firm, a public relations firm, or a company that manufactures or sells personal care products?

    Yes   (TERMINATE AND TALLY)

    No   (CONTINUE)

(IF RESPONDENT QUALIFIES, INVITE HIM OR HER TO PARTICIPATE AND COMPLETE NAME GRID BELOW)

generating such a list. In the ideal situation, the list of population members is complete and accurate. Unfortunately, there usually is no such list. For example, the population for a study may be defined as those individuals who have spent two or more hours on the Internet in the past week; there can be no complete listing of these individuals. In such instances, the sampling frame specifies a procedure that will produce a representative sample with the desired characteristics. Thus, there seldom is a perfect correspondence between the sampling frame and the population of interest.

For example, a telephone book might be used as the sample frame for a telephone survey sample in which the population of interest was all households in a particular city. However, the telephone book does not include households that do not have telephones

The population for a study must be defined. For example, a population for a study may be defined as those individuals who have spent two or more hours on the Internet in the past week.

PhotoDisc, Inc./Getty Images

➤ **random-digit dialing**
Method of generating lists of telephone numbers at random.

➤ **probability samples**
Samples in which every element of the population has a known, nonzero likelihood of selection.

➤ **nonprobability samples**
Samples in which specific elements from the population have been selected in a nonrandom manner.

or those with unlisted numbers. It is well established that those with listed telephone numbers are significantly different from those with unlisted numbers in regard to a number of important characteristics. Subscribers who voluntarily unlist their phone numbers are more likely to be renters, live in the central city, have recently moved, have larger families, have younger children, and have lower incomes than their counterparts with listed numbers.[7] There are also significant differences between the two groups in terms of purchase, ownership, and use of certain products.

Unlisted numbers are more prevalent in the western United States, in metropolitan areas, among nonwhites, and among those in the 18 to 34 age group. These findings have been confirmed in a number of studies.[8] The extent of the problem is suggested by the data in Exhibit 11.4. The implications are clear: if representative samples are to be obtained in telephone surveys, researchers should use procedures that will produce samples including appropriate proportions of households with unlisted numbers. One possibility is **random-digit dialing**, which generates lists of telephone numbers at random. This procedure can become fairly complex. Fortunately, companies such as Survey Sampling offer random-digit samples at a very attractive price. Details on the way such companies draw their samples can be found at www.surveysampling.com/products_samples.php. Developing an appropriate sampling frame is often one of the most challenging problems facing the researcher.[9] Sample frame issues are illustrated in the feature on page 329.

Step Four: Select a Sampling Method

The fourth step in developing a sampling plan is selection of a sampling method, which will depend on the objectives of the study, the financial resources available, time limitations, and the nature of the problem under investigation. The major alternative sampling methods can be grouped under two headings: probability sampling methods and nonprobability sampling methods.

Probability samples are selected in such a way that every element of the population has a known, nonzero likelihood of selection.[10] Simple random sampling is the best known and most widely used probability sampling method. With probability sampling, the researcher must closely adhere to precise selection procedures that avoid arbitrary or biased selection of sample elements. When these procedures are followed strictly, the laws of probability hold, allowing calculation of the extent to which a sample value can be expected to differ from a population value. This difference is referred to as *sampling error*.

Nonprobability samples are those in which specific elements from the population have been selected in a nonrandom manner. *Nonrandomness* results when population elements are selected on the basis of convenience—because they are easy or inexpensive to reach. *Purposeful nonrandomness* occurs when a sampling plan systematically excludes or overrepresents certain subsets of the population. For example, if a sample designed to solicit the opinions of all women over the age of 18 were based on a telephone survey conducted during the day on weekdays, it would systematically exclude working women. See Practicing Marketing Research on page 334.

EXHIBIT 11.4	Household Phone Statistics by State in 2004

STATE	Population 1–Jan–04	Households 1–Jan–04	Estimated Telephone Households	% with Phone	RDD Listed Households	% Listed
Alabama	4,517,136	1,822,088	1,748,531	96%	1,259,537	72%
Alaska	655,899	234,433	227,749	97%	151,271	66%
Arizona	5,719,160	2,167,325	2,097,004	97%	1,013,547	48%
Arkansas	2,741,511	1,093,223	1,036,476	95%	717,435	69%
California	35,979,311	12,227,339	12,059,310	99%	5,570,852	46%
Colorado	4,625,293	1,797,550	1,774,673	99%	992,864	56%
Connecticut	3,507,246	1,357,133	1,342,738	99%	952,701	71%
Delaware	827,856	323,359	319,312	99%	211,755	66%
Washington DC	560,725	256,560	250,276	98%	141,585	57%
Florida	17,342,822	7,255,877	7,115,986	98%	4,741,206	67%
Georgia	8,836,255	3,380,788	3,284,648	97%	2,146,325	65%
Hawaii	1,272,696	429,724	421,464	98%	229,768	55%
Idaho	1,388,573	507,623	498,526	98%	324,410	65%
Illinois	12,725,117	4,736,295	4,597,367	97%	2,540,032	55%
Indiana	6,230,346	2,465,349	2,396,774	97%	1,550,538	65%
Iowa	2,949,245	1,174,389	1,154,652	98%	796,270	69%
Kansas	2,733,795	1,074,016	1,044,740	97%	688,755	66%
Kentucky	4,140,891	1,704,528	1,629,916	96%	1,065,731	65%
Louisiana	4,505,373	1,755,361	1,685,873	96%	1,199,469	71%
Maine	1,315,211	550,163	543,327	99%	421,225	78%
Maryland	5,574,702	2,117,321	2,085,320	98%	1,314,780	63%
Massachusetts	6,457,204	2,519,388	2,496,407	99%	1,676,116	67%
Michigan	10,121,382	3,984,102	3,884,355	97%	2,536,569	65%
Minnesota	5,101,284	2,027,904	2,006,263	99%	1,398,406	70%
Mississippi	2,892,228	1,103,166	1,034,634	94%	737,337	71%
Missouri	5,737,314	2,318,958	2,254,844	97%	1,490,840	66%
Montana	922,368	373,148	363,002	97%	240,299	66%
Nebraska	1,748,000	693,868	681,030	98%	432,229	63%
Nevada	2,315,504	880,502	863,425	98%	377,145	44%
New Hampshire	1,303,425	508,725	503,462	99%	369,832	73%
New Jersey	8,707,156	3,199,381	3,143,179	98%	1,956,163	62%
New Mexico	1,892,304	724,405	685,442	95%	380,692	56%
New York	19,254,372	7,204,879	7,072,175	98%	4,685,488	66%
North Carolina	8,517,110	3,462,050	3,367,113	97%	2,161,991	64%
North Dakota	631,440	259,937	255,318	98%	178,358	70%
Ohio	11,459,952	4,663,484	4,565,767	98%	2,648,643	58%
Oklahoma	3,530,711	1,411,715	1,349,700	96%	874,190	65%
Oregon	3,602,559	1,418,021	1,396,212	98%	763,708	55%
Pennsylvania	12,392,109	4,937,535	4,871,855	99%	2,986,805	61%
Rhode Island	1,084,664	429,549	423,612	99%	263,950	62%
South Carolina	4,188,493	1,663,078	1,599,303	96%	1,072,268	67%
South Dakota	767,184	301,193	292,737	97%	205,286	70%
Tennessee	5,888,107	2,394,744	2,328,315	97%	1,550,987	67%
Texas	22,508,240	8,216,915	7,982,006	97%	5,064,309	63%
Utah	2,387,580	770,119	759,317	99%	457,713	60%
Vermont	622,165	252,576	248,941	99%	202,284	81%
Virginia	7,480,156	2,955,415	2,897,759	98%	1,883,563	65%
Washington	6,204,912	2,416,587	2,385,477	99%	1,293,432	54%
West Virginia	1,811,363	761,032	726,246	95%	496,642	68%
Wisconsin	5,505,083	2,222,958	2,188,750	98%	1,620,450	74%
Wyoming	503,630	202,957	196,722	97%	126,481	64%
USA	293,687,162	112,708,735	110,138,030	98%	68,162,232	62%

Source: Survey Sampling, Inc., July 2005.

PRACTICING MARKETING RESEARCH

Why This Online Sample Was Not a Probability Sample

Harris Interactive, world-renowned for its Harris Polls, published the results of its 2005 Telecommunications Report in June 2005. The study had been conducted online in April 2005 using a sample of 1,088 adults (18 and older). Its results showed that 10 percent of U.S. adults now use wireless or cellular phones exclusively and have abandoned their connection to traditional phones.

In their methodology discussion, Harris Interactive researchers noted that they had weighted the demographics of their sampling pool, in terms of gender, race or ethnicity, educational level, religious affiliation, income, and sexual orientation, to match that of the total U.S. population. They further weighted the data, using propensity score weighting, to adjust for the respondents' propensity to be online.

Harris Interactive researchers explained that theoretically, using a probability sample of this size, they could be 95 percent certain their sampling error was ±3 percent. But some skepticism is in order, they added, because the sampling error for people saying they have disconnected their conventional phone systems (420 respondents) is ±3 percent.

Complicating the picture is that the additional sources of error involved in polls such as this ultimately are more problematic for the accuracy of the final data than anything a theoretical calculation of sampling error would indicate. Specifically, these sources of error include nonresponse (a respondent refusing to be interviewed), the way a question is worded or the order in which questions are presented, and the style, even the fact, of weighting. "It is impossible to quantify the errors that may result from these factors," the researchers said.[12]

Probability samples offer several advantages over nonprobability samples, including the following:

☐ The researcher can be sure of obtaining information from a representative cross section of the population of interest.

☐ Sampling error can be computed.

☐ The survey results can be projected to the total population. For example, if 5 percent of the individuals in a probability sample give a particular response, the researcher can project this percentage, plus or minus the sampling error, to the total population.

On the other hand, probability samples have a number of disadvantages, the most important of which is that they are usually more expensive than nonprobability samples of the same size. The rules for selection increase interviewing costs and professional time spent in signing and executing the sample design.[11]

The disadvantages of nonprobability samples are essentially the reverse of the advantages of probability samples:

☐ The researcher does not know the degree to which the sample is representative of the population from which it was drawn.

☐ Sampling error cannot be computed.

☐ The results cannot and should not be projected to the total population.

Exhibit 11.5

Classification of Sampling Methods

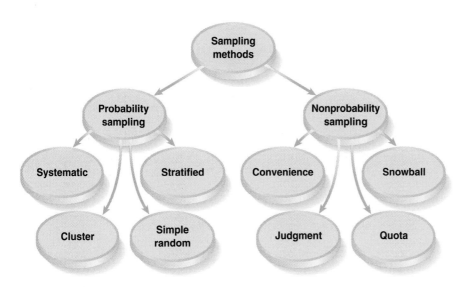

Given the disadvantages of nonprobability samples, you may wonder why they are used so frequently by marketing researchers. The reasons for their use relate to their inherent advantages, which include the following:

- Nonprobability samples cost less than probability samples. Lower costs have considerable appeal in those situations where accuracy is not of critical importance. Exploratory research is an example of such a situation.

- Nonprobability samples ordinarily can be gathered more quickly than probability samples can.

- Nonprobability samples of the population are reasonably representative if collected in a careful, thorough manner.[13]

In addition to choosing between probability and nonprobability sampling methods, the researcher must choose among sampling procedures. These choices are summarized in Exhibit 11.5 and discussed in greater detail later in the chapter.

Step Five: Determine Sample Size

Once a sampling method has been chosen, the next step is to determine the appropriate **sample size**. (The issue of sample size determination is covered in detail in Chapter 12.) In the case of nonprobability samples, researchers tend to rely on such factors as available budget, rules of thumb, and number of subgroups to be analyzed in their determination of sample size. However, with probability samples, researchers use formulas to calculate the sample size required, given target levels of *acceptable error* (the difference between sample result and population value) and *levels of confidence* (the likelihood that the confidence interval—sample result plus or minus the acceptable error—will take in the true population value). As noted earlier, the ability to make statistical inferences about population values based on sample results is the major advantage of probability samples.

sample size
The identified and selected population subset for the survey, chosen because it represents the entire group.

Step Six: Develop Operational Procedures for Selecting Sample Elements

The operational procedures to be used in selecting sample elements in the data-collection phase of a project should be developed and specified, whether a probability or a nonprobability sample is being used.[14] However, the procedures are much more critical to

Source: From "Belden Associates Interviewer Guide," reprinted by permission. The complete guide is over 30 pages long and contains maps and other aids for the interviewer.

Exhibit 11.6

Example of Operational Sampling Plan

In the instructions that follow, reference is made to follow your route around a block. In cities, this will be a city block. In rural areas, a block is a segment of land surrounded by roads.

1. If you come to a dead end along your route, proceed down the opposite side of the street, road, or alley, traveling in the other direction. Continue making right turns, where possible, calling at every third occupied dwelling.
2. If you go all the way around a block and return to the starting address without completing four interviews in listed telephone homes, attempt an interview at the starting address. (This should seldom be necessary.)
3. If you work an entire block and do not complete the required interviews, proceed to the dwelling on the opposite side of the street (or rural route) that is *nearest* the starting address. Treat it as the next address on your Area Location Sheet and interview that house only if the address appears next to an "X" on your sheet. If it does not, continue your interviewing to the left of that address. Always follow the right turn rule.
4. If there are no dwellings on the street or road opposite the starting address for an area, circle the block opposite the starting address, following the right turn rule. (This means that you will circle the block following a clockwise direction.) Attempt interviews at every third dwelling along this route.
5. If, after circling the adjacent block opposite the starting address, you do not complete the necessary interviews, take the next block found, *following a clockwise direction*.
6. If the third block does not yield the dwellings necessary to complete your assignment, proceed to as many blocks as necessary to find the required dwellings; follow a clockwise path around the primary block.

the successful execution of a probability sample, in which case they should be detailed, clear, and unambiguous and should eliminate any interviewer discretion regarding the selection of specific sample elements. Failure to develop a proper operational plan for selecting sample elements can jeopardize the entire sampling process. Exhibit 11.6 provides an example of an operational sampling plan.

Step Seven: Execute the Operational Sampling Plan

The final step in the sampling process is execution of the operational sampling plan. This step requires adequate checking to ensure that specified procedures are followed.

Sampling and Nonsampling Errors

> **population parameter**
> A value that accurately portrays or typifies a factor of a complete population, such as average age or income.

Consider a situation in which the goal is to determine the average gross income of the members of a particular population.[15] If the researcher could obtain accurate information about all members of the population, he or she could simply compute the population parameter average gross income. A **population parameter** is a value that defines a true characteristic of a total population. Assume that μ (the population parameter, average gross income) is $42,300. As already noted, it is almost always impossible to measure an entire population (take a census). Instead, the researcher selects a sample and makes inferences about population parameters from sample results. In this case, the researcher might take a sample of 400 from a population of

250,000. An estimate of the average age of the members of the population $(\overline{X})$ would be calculated from the sample values. Assume that the average gross income of the sample members is $41,100. A second random sample of 400 might be drawn from the same population, and the average again computed. In the second case, the average might be $43,400. Additional samples might be chosen, and a mean calculated for each sample. The researcher would find that the means computed for the various samples would be fairly close but not identical to the true population value in most cases.

The accuracy of sample results is affected by two general types of error: sampling error and nonsampling (measurement) error. The following formula represents the effects of these two types of error on estimating a population mean:

$$\overline{X} = \mu \pm \epsilon_s \pm \epsilon_{ns}$$

where
$\overline{X}$ = sample mean
μ = true population mean
ϵ_s = sampling error
ϵ_{hs} = nonsampling, or measurement, error

Sampling error results when the sample selected is not perfectly representative of the population. There are two types of sampling error: administrative and random. *Administrative error* relates to the problems in the execution of the sample—that is, flaws in the design or execution of the sample that cause it to not be representative of the population. These types of error can be avoided or minimized by careful attention to the design and execution of the sample. *Random sampling error* is due to chance and cannot be avoided. This type of error can be reduced, but never totally eliminated, by increasing the sample size. **Nonsampling**, or measurement **error**, includes all factors other than sampling error that may cause inaccuracy and bias in the survey results.

> **sampling error**
> Error that occurs because the sample selected is not perfectly representative of the population.

> **nonsampling error**
> All errors other than sampling error; also called *measurement error.*

Probability Sampling Methods

As discussed earlier, every element of the population has a known and equal likelihood of being selected for a probability sample. There are four types of probability sampling methods: simple random sampling, systematic sampling, stratified sampling, and cluster sampling.

Simple Random Sampling

Simple random sampling is the purest form of probability sampling. For a simple random sample, the known and equal probability is computed as follows:

$$\text{Probability of selection} = \frac{\text{Sample size}}{\text{Population size}}$$

For example, if the population size is 10,000 and the sample size is 400, the probability of selection is 4 percent:

$$.04 = \frac{400}{10,000}$$

If a sampling frame (listing of all the elements of the population) is available, the researcher can select a **simple random sample** as follows:

simple random sample
Probability sample selected by assigning a number to every element of the population and then using a table of random numbers to select specific elements for inclusion in the sample.

1. Assign a number to each element of the population. A population of 10,000 elements would be numbered from 1 to 10,000.

2. Using a table of random numbers (such as Table 1 in the Appendix, "Statistical Tables"), begin at some arbitrary point and move up, down, or across until 400 (sample size) numbers between 1 and 10,000 have been chosen. The numbers selected from the table identify specific population elements to be included in the sample.

Simple random sampling is appealing because it seems easy and meets all the necessary requirements of a probability sample. It guarantees that every member of the population has a known and equal chance of being selected for the sample. Simple random sampling begins with a current and complete listing of the population. Such listings, however, are extremely difficult, if not impossible, to obtain. Simple random samples can be obtained in telephone surveys through the use of random-digit dialing. They can also be generated from computer files such as customer lists; software programs are available or can be readily written to select random samples that meet all necessary requirements.

Systematic Sampling

systematic sampling
Probability sampling in which the entire population is numbered and elements are selected using a skip interval.

Because of its simplicity, **systematic sampling** is often used as a substitute for simple random sampling. It produces samples that are almost identical to those generated via simple random sampling.

To obtain a systematic sample, the researcher first numbers the entire population, as in simple random sampling. Then the researcher determines a *skip interval* and selects names based on this interval. The skip interval can be computed very simply through use of the following formula:

$$\text{Skip interval} = \frac{\text{Population size}}{\text{Sample size}}$$

For example, if you were using a local telephone directory and had computed a skip interval of 100, every 100th name would be selected for the sample. The use of this formula would ensure that the entire list was covered.

A random starting point should be used in systematic sampling. For example, if you were using a telephone directory, you would need to draw a random number to determine the page on which to start—say, page 53. You would draw another random number to determine the column to use on that page—for example, the third column. You would draw a final random number to determine the actual starting element in that column—say, the 17th name. From that beginning point, you would employ the skip interval until the desired sample size had been reached.

The main advantage of systematic sampling over simple random sampling is economy. Systematic sampling is often simpler, less time-consuming, and less expensive to use than simple random sampling. The greatest danger lies in the possibility that hidden patterns within the population list may inadvertently be pulled into the sample. However, this danger is remote when alphabetical listings are used.

Stratified Sampling

Stratified samples are probability samples that are distinguished by the following procedural steps:

1. The original, or parent, population is divided into two or more mutually exclusive and exhaustive subsets (for example, male and female).

2. Simple random samples of elements from the two or more subsets are chosen independently of each other.

> **stratified sample**
> Probability sample that is forced to be more representative through simple random sampling of mutually exclusive and exhaustive subsets.

Although the requirements for a stratified sample do not specify the basis on which the original or parent population should be separated into subsets, common sense dictates that the population be divided on the basis of factors related to the characteristic of interest in the population. For example, if you are conducting a political poll to predict the outcome of an election and can show that there is a significant difference in the way men and women are likely to vote, then gender is an appropriate basis for stratification. If you do not do stratified sampling in this manner, then you do not get the benefits of stratification, and you have expended additional time, effort, and resources for no benefit. With gender as the basis for stratification, one stratum, then, would be made up of men and one of women. These strata are mutually exclusive and exhaustive in that every population element can be assigned to one and only one (male or female) and no population elements are unassignable. The second stage in the selection of a stratified sample involves drawing simple random samples independently from each stratum.

Researchers prefer stratified samples over simple random samples because of their potential for greater statistical efficiency.[16] That is, if two samples are drawn from the same population—one a properly stratified sample and the other a simple random sample—the stratified sample will have a smaller sampling error. Also, reduction of a sampling error to a certain target level can be achieved with a smaller stratified sample. Stratified samples are statistically more efficient because one source of variation has been eliminated.

If stratified samples are statistically more efficient, why are they not used all the time? There are two reasons. First, the information necessary to properly stratify the sample frequently may not be available. For example, little may be known about the demographic characteristics of consumers of a particular product. To properly stratify the sample and to get the benefits of stratification, the researcher must choose bases for stratification that yield significant differences between the strata in regard to the measurement of interest. When such differences are not identifiable, the sample cannot be properly stratified. Second, even if the necessary information is available, the potential value of the information may not warrant the time and costs associated with stratification.

A stratified sample may be appropriate in certain cases. For example, if a political poll is being conducted to predict who will win an election, a difference in the way men and women are likely to vote would make gender an appropriate basis for stratification.

PhotoDisc, Inc./Getty Images

In the case of a simple random sample, the researcher depends entirely on the laws of probability to generate a representative sample of the population. With stratified sampling, the researcher, to some degree, forces the sample to be representative by making sure that important dimensions of the population are represented in the sample in their true population proportions. For example, the researcher may know that although men and women are equally likely to be users of a particular product, women are much more likely to be heavy users. In a study designed to analyze consumption patterns of the product, failure to properly represent women in the sample would result in a biased view of consumption patterns. Assume that women make up 60 percent of the population of interest and men account for 40 percent. Because of sampling fluctuations, a properly executed simple random sampling procedure might produce a sample made up of 55 percent women and 45 percent men. This is the same kind of error you would obtain if you flipped a coin 10 times. The ideal result of 10 coin tosses would be five heads and five tails, but more than half the time you would get a different result. In similar fashion, a properly drawn and executed simple random sample from a population made up of 60 percent women and 40 percent men is not likely to consist of exactly 60 percent women and 40 percent men. However, the researcher can force a stratified sample to have 60 percent women and 40 percent men.

Three steps are involved in implementing a properly stratified sample:

1. *Identify salient (important) demographic or classification factors*—factors that are correlated with the behavior of interest. For example, there may be reason to believe that men and women have different average consumption rates of a particular product. To use gender as a basis for meaningful stratification, the researcher must be able to show with actual data that there are significant differences in the consumption levels of men and women. In this manner, various salient factors are identified. Research indicates that, as a general rule, after the six most important factors have been identified, the identification of additional salient factors adds little in the way of increased sampling efficiency.[17]

2. *Determine what proportions of the population fall into the various subgroups under each stratum* (for example, if gender has been determined to be a salient factor, determine what proportion of the population is male and what proportion is female). Using these proportions, the researcher can determine how many respondents are required from each subgroup. However, before a final determination is made, a decision must be made as to whether to use proportional allocation or disproportional, or optimal, allocation.

Under **proportional allocation**, the number of elements selected from a stratum is directly proportional to the size of the stratum in relation to the size of the population. With proportional allocation, the proportion of elements to be taken from each stratum is given by the formula n/N, where n = the size of the stratum and N = the size of the population.

Disproportional, or **optimal**, **allocation** produces the most efficient samples and provides the most precise or reliable estimates for a given sample size. This approach requires a double weighting scheme. Under this scheme, the number of sample elements to be taken from a given stratum is proportional to the relative size of the stratum and the standard deviation of the distribution of the characteristic under consideration for all elements in the stratum. This scheme is used for two reasons. First, the size of a stratum is important because those strata with greater numbers of elements are more important in determining the population mean. Therefore, such strata should have more weight in deriving estimates of population parameters. Second, it makes sense that relatively more elements should be drawn from those strata having larger standard deviations (more variation) and relatively fewer elements should be drawn from those strata having smaller standard deviations. Allocating relatively more of the sample to those strata where the potential for sampling error is greatest (largest standard deviation) is cost-effective and improves the overall accuracy of the estimates. There is no difference between proportional

> **proportional allocation**
> Sampling in which the number of elements selected from a stratum is directly proportional to the size of the stratum relative to the size of the population.

> **disproportional, or optimal, allocation**
> Sampling in which the number of elements taken from a given stratum is proportional to the relative size of the stratum and the standard deviation of the characteristic under consideration.

allocation and disproportional allocation if the distributions of the characteristic under consideration have the same standard deviation from stratum to stratum.[18]

3. *Select separate simple random samples from each stratum.* This process is implemented somewhat differently than traditional simple random sampling. Assume that the stratified sampling plan requires that 240 women and 160 men be interviewed. The researcher will sample from the total population and keep track of the number of men and women interviewed. At some point in the process, when 240 women and 127 men have been interviewed, the researcher will interview only men until the target of 160 men is reached. In this manner, the process generates a sample in which the proportion of men and women conforms to the allocation scheme derived in step 2.

Stratified samples are not used as often as one might expect in marketing research. The reason is that the information necessary to properly stratify the sample is usually not available in advance. Stratification cannot be based on guesses or hunches but must be based on hard data regarding the characteristics of the population and the relationship between these characteristics and the behavior under investigation. Stratified samples are frequently used in political polling and media audience research. In those areas, the researcher is more likely to have the information necessary to implement the stratification process.

Cluster Sampling

The types of samples discussed so far have all been single unit samples, in which each sampling unit is selected separately. In the case of **cluster samples**, the sampling units are selected in groups.[19] There are two basic steps in cluster sampling:

> **cluster sample**
> Probability sample in which the sampling units are selected from a number of small geographic areas to reduce data collection costs.

1. The population of interest is divided into mutually exclusive and exhaustive subsets.
2. A random sample of the subsets is selected.

If the sample consists of all the elements in the selected subsets, it is called a *one-stage cluster sample.* However, if the sample of elements is chosen in some probabilistic manner from the selected subsets, the sample is a *two-stage cluster sample.*

Both stratified and cluster sampling involve dividing the population into mutually exclusive and exhaustive subgroups. However, in stratified samples the researcher selects a sample of elements from each subgroup, while in cluster samples, the researcher selects a sample of subgroups and then collects data either from all the elements in the subgroup (one-stage cluster sample) or from a sample of the elements (two-stage cluster sample).

All the probability sampling methods discussed to this point require sampling frames that list or provide some organized breakdown of all the elements in the target population. Under cluster sampling, the researcher develops sampling frames that specify groups or clusters of elements of the population without actually listing individual elements. Sampling is then executed by taking a sample of the clusters in the frame and generating lists or other breakdowns for only those clusters that have been selected for the sample. Finally, a sample is chosen from the elements of the selected clusters.

The most popular type of cluster sample is the area sample, in which the clusters are units of geography (for example, city blocks). A researcher, conducting a door-to-door survey in a particular metropolitan area, might randomly choose a sample of city blocks from the metropolitan area, select a sample of clusters, and then interview a sample of consumers from each cluster. All interviews would be conducted in the clusters selected, dramatically reducing interviewers' travel time and expenses. Cluster sampling is considered to be a probability sampling technique because of the random selection of clusters and the random selection of elements within the selected clusters.

GLOBAL RESEARCH

Area Sampling Frame Used to Tally Livestock Population for Disease Control

Veterinarians in Gauteng Province of South Africa wanted to assess livestock population for potential outbreak and control of diseases in the animal population. But the country had no census or baseline data of livestock numbers or distribution, and even a reliable list of farmers or landowners was not available. A census would be too expensive, so they used an area sampling frame to get the numbers they needed.

The researchers started with the various known land parcel layers (31); reclassified them into five classes; merged them into a single continuous layer of land parcels; and then stratified this list to cut back on the variance of animal numbers in the study. This enabled them to calculate the sample size from which they randomly selected land parcels (out of six strata based on parcel size, and totaling 1.7 million hectares) for the four-month questionnaire survey. Finally, using these data, they prepared estimations for spatial and density distributions per species of Gauteng's livestock population, obtaining results which the researchers believed were reliable, successful, and cost-effective in contrast with the alternative, a province-wide census.

The area frame sampling approach produced excellent results for cattle, sheep, pigs, dogs, and cats, but did not work as well for goats, donkeys, poultry, game, ostriches, or mules. The distribution plots of these six categories were distorted, the researchers noted, because of extreme counts (poultry: 360,163) in some land parcels. The best results typically came from livestock whose numbers were midrange or at the mean, such as cattle (60,954), sheep (17,801), pigs (6,393), and dogs/cats (7,008); results were less good for animals whose numbers were low (donkeys: 234) or rare (mules: 43). The area sampling frame produced a reliable distribution atlas for Gauteng livestock, showing areas where medical resources should be concentrated in times of livestock emergencies.[20]

Questions

1. Identify two instances in which using the area frame sampling approach might be the only cost-effective means for gathering information about humans.

2. Come up with a way in which a desired population, such as chickens, whose numbers, as in this study, are high to extreme, might be more accurately factored into an area frame sampling approach.

> **multistage area sampling** Geographic areas selected for national or regional surveys in progressively smaller population units, such as counties, then residential blocks, then homes.

Cluster sampling assumes that the elements in a cluster are as heterogeneous as those in the total population. If the characteristics of the elements in a cluster are very similar, then that assumption is violated and the researcher has a problem. In the city-block sampling just described, there may be little heterogeneity within clusters because the residents of a cluster are very similar to each other and different from those of other clusters. Typically, this potential problem is dealt with in the sample design by selecting a large number of clusters and sampling a relatively small number of elements from each cluster.

Another possibility is **multistage area sampling,** or **multistage area probability sampling**, which involves three or more steps. Samples of this type are used for national surveys or surveys that cover large regional areas. Here, the researcher randomly selects geographic areas in progressively smaller units. For example, a statewide door-to-door survey might include the following steps:

1. Choose counties within the state to make sure that different areas are represented in the sample. Counties should be selected with a probability proportional to the number of sampling units (households) within the county. Counties with a larger number of households would have a higher probability of selection than would counties with a smaller number of households.

2. Select residential blocks within those counties.

3. Select households within those residential blocks.

From the standpoint of statistical efficiency, cluster samples are generally less efficient than other types of probability samples. In other words, a cluster sample of a certain size will have a larger sampling error than a simple random sample or a stratified sample of the same size. To see the greater cost efficiency and lower statistical efficiency of a cluster sample, consider the following example. A researcher needs to select a sample of 200 households in a particular city for in-home interviews. If she selects these 200 households via simple random sampling, they will be scattered across the city. Cluster sampling might be implemented in this situation by selecting 20 residential blocks in the city and randomly choosing 10 households on each block to interview. It is easy to see that interviewing costs will be dramatically reduced under the cluster sampling approach. Interviewers do not have to spend as much time traveling and their mileage is dramatically reduced. In regard to sampling error, however, you can see that simple random sampling has the advantage. Interviewing 200 households scattered across the city increases the chance of getting a representative cross section of respondents. If all interviewing is conducted in 20 randomly selected blocks within the city, certain ethnic, social, or economic groups might be missed or over- or underrepresented.

As noted previously, cluster samples are, in nearly all cases, statistically less efficient than simple random samples. It is possible to view a simple random sample as a special type of cluster sample, in which the number of clusters is equal to the total sample size, with one sample element selected per cluster. At this point, the statistical efficiency of the cluster sample and that of the simple random sample are equal. From this point on, as the researcher decreases the number of clusters and increases the number of sample elements per cluster, the statistical efficiency of the cluster sample declines. At the other extreme, the researcher might choose a single cluster and select all the sample elements from that cluster. For example, he or she might select one relatively small geographic area in the city where you live and interview 200 people from that area. How comfortable would you be that a sample selected in this manner would be representative of the entire metropolitan area where you live? An unusual area sampling example is provided in the feature on page 342.

The most popular type of cluster sample is the area sample in which the clusters are units of geography (for example, city blocks). Cluster sampling is considered to be a probability sampling technique because of the random selection of clusters and the random selection of elements within the selected clusters.

PhotoDisc, Inc./Getty Images

Nonprobability Sampling Methods

In a general sense, any sample that does not meet the requirements of a probability sample is, by definition, a nonprobability sample. We have already noted that a major disadvantage of nonprobability samples is the inability to calculate sampling error for them. This suggests the even greater difficulty of evaluating the overall quality of non-probability samples. How far do they deviate from the standard required of probability samples? The user of data from a nonprobability sample must make this assessment, which should be based on a careful evaluation of the methodology used to generate the nonprobability sample. Is it likely that the methodology employed will generate a cross section of individuals from the target population? Or is the sample hopelessly biased in some particular direction? These are the questions that must be answered. Four types of nonprobability samples are frequently used: convenience, judgment, quota, and snowball samples.

Convenience Samples

> **convenience samples**
> Nonprobability samples based on using people who are easily accessible.

Convenience samples are primarily used, as their name implies, for reasons of convenience. Companies such as Frito-Lay often use their own employees for preliminary tests of new product formulations developed by their R&D departments. At first, this may seem to be a highly biased approach. However, these companies are not asking employees to evaluate existing products or to compare their products with a competitor's products. They are asking employees only to provide gross sensory evaluations of new product formulations (for example, saltiness, crispness, greasiness). In such situations, convenience sampling may represent an efficient and effective means of obtaining the required information. This is particularly true in an exploratory situation, where there is a pressing need to get an inexpensive approximation of true value.

Some believe that the use of convenience sampling is growing at a faster rate than the growth in the use of probability sampling.[21] The reason is the growing availability of databases of consumers in low-incidence and hard-to-find categories. For example, suppose a company has developed a new athlete's foot remedy and needs to conduct a survey among those who suffer from the malady. Because these individuals make up only 4 percent of the population, researchers conducting a telephone survey would have to talk with 25 people to find 1 individual who suffered from the problem. Purchasing a list of individuals known to suffer from the problem can dramatically reduce the cost of the survey and the time necessary to complete it. Although such a list might be made up of individuals who used coupons when purchasing the product or sent in for manufacturers' rebates, companies are increasingly willing to make the trade-off of lower cost and faster turnaround for a lower-quality sample. Exhibit 11.7 provides some examples of the more than 3,000 lists available from Survey Sampling, Incorporated.

Judgment Samples

> **judgment samples**
> Nonprobability samples in which the selection criteria are based on the researcher's judgment about representativeness of the population under study.

The term **judgment sample** is applied to any sample in which the selection criteria are based on the researcher's judgment about what constitutes a representative sample. Most test markets and many product tests conducted in shopping malls are essentially judgment sampling. In the case of test markets, one or a few markets are selected based on the judgment that they are representative of the population as a whole. Malls are selected for product taste tests based on the researcher's judgment that the particular malls attract a reasonable cross section of consumers who fall into the target group for the product being tested.

Quota Samples

> **quota samples**
> Nonprobability samples in which quotas, based on demographic or classification factors selected by the researcher, are established for population subgroups.

Quota samples are typically selected in such a way that demographic characteristics of interest to the researcher are represented in the sample in target proportions. Thus, many people confuse quota samples and stratified samples. There are, however, two key differences

Exhibit 11.7

Examples from the Activities List of Survey Sampling, Incorporated

Sports/Boating/Fishing/Outdoor Activities

Bicycling	Outdoor Enthusiast
Boating: Power	Outdoor Recreation
Boating: Sailing	Outdoor Sports Lover
Bow Hunting	Physical Fitness
Camping	Running/Jogging
Cycling	Sailing
Environmental Concerns	Scuba Diving
Exercise Equipment	Snow Boarding
Fishing	Snow Skiing
Fly Fishing	Soccer
Golf	Sports
Hiking	Sports Cards
Horseback Riding	Sports Equipment
Hunting/Shooting	Sports Items
Motorcycles, Interest in	Tennis
Motorcycling, Participation in	Walking for Health
NASCAR Enthusiast	Watching Sports on TV

between a quota sample and a stratified sample. First, respondents for a quota sample are not selected randomly, as they must be for a stratified sample. Second, the classification factors used for a stratified sample are selected based on the existence of a correlation between the factor and the behavior of interest. There is no such requirement in the case of a quota sample. The demographic or classification factors of interest in a quota sample are selected on the basis of researcher judgment.

Snowball Samples

In **snowball samples**, sampling procedures are used to select additional respondents on the basis of referrals from initial respondents. This procedure is used to sample from low-incidence or rare populations—that is, populations that make up a very small percentage of the total population.[22] The costs of finding members of these rare populations may be so great that the researcher is forced to use a technique such as snowball sampling. For example, suppose an insurance company needed to obtain a national sample of individuals who have switched from the indemnity form of healthcare coverage to a health maintenance organization in the past six months. It would be necessary to sample a very large number of consumers to identify 1,000 that fall into this population. It would be far more economical to obtain an initial sample of 200 people from the population of interest and have each of them provide the names of an average of four other people to complete the sample of 1,000.

The main advantage of snowball sampling is a dramatic reduction in search costs. However, this advantage comes at the expense of sample quality. The total sample is likely to be biased because the individuals whose names were obtained from those sampled in the initial phase are likely to be very similar to those initially sampled. As a result, the sample may not be a good cross section of the total population. There is general agreement that some limits should be placed on the number of respondents obtained through referrals, although there are no specific rules regarding what these limits should be. This approach may also be hampered by the fact that respondents may be reluctant to give referrals. An approach used when snowballing did not work is described in the Practice Marketing Research feature on page 346.

> **snowball samples**
> Nonprobability samples in which additional respondents are selected based on referrals from initial respondents.

PRACTICING MARKETING RESEARCH

E-Mail Surveys of WebSite Usage—When Snowballing Fails to Snowball

Elaine Peterson, librarian and professor at Montana State University Libraries at Bozeman, Montana, wanted to evaluate user response and opinion regarding the school's popular digital library called the Montana Natural Resource Information System (NRIS). This highly visited website (1 million hits per month) presents information about plants, animals, and water status, as well as maps for the area. She used the snowball sampling approach in two stages: in-person interviews followed up a year later by e-mail surveys of the same respondents. In particular, Peterson wanted to see if snowball sampling would be successful if the survey were based exclusively on e-mail.

In the first round, Peterson interviewed 47 people representing 37 relevant organizations, either in person or on the telephone, expending about 45 minutes per interview. She found the respondents willing to provide references for colleagues. But a year later, after the NRIS website had been improved, Peterson got a surprise.

Of the same respondents, only 32 percent answered the e-mail survey, and all were reluctant to provide the names of colleagues for the snowball sample given in that format.

"The solicitation of names for potential participants, a key component of snowball sampling, proved to be more difficult with the e-mail survey," she observed. Using e-mails to get more names through snowball sampling was the most time-consuming activity in the e-mail survey, so that even though telephone interviews might seem to take longer, they produced better results in terms of usable new names. "The e-mail survey," Peterson said, "is not the best option for digital library evaluations."[23]

Questions

1. Come up with some plausible inducements or assurances for people receiving the e-mail survey to provide snowball references of friends.

2. What is the inherent difference between a telephone interview and e-mail survey as regards an interviewee feeling comfortable giving names?

Internet Sampling

The advantages of Internet interviewing are compelling:

☐ *Target respondents can complete the survey at their convenience*—late at night, over the weekend, and at any other convenient time.

☐ *Data collection is inexpensive.* Once basic overhead and other fixed costs are covered, interviewing is essentially volume-insensitive. Thousands of interviews can be conducted at an actual data collection cost of less than $1 per survey. This low cost may, to some extent, be offset by the need to use incentives to encourage responses. By comparison, a 10-minute telephone interview targeting people who make up 50 percent of the population may cost $15 or more per survey. Data entry and data processing costs are dramatically reduced because respondents essentially do the data entry for the researcher.

☐ *The interview can be administered under software control*, which allows the survey to follow skip patterns and do other "smart" things.

□ *The survey can be completed quickly.* Hundreds or thousands of surveys can be completed in a day or less.[24]

Unfortunately, there is no large body of scientific research regarding the representativeness of Internet samples, as there is for other data-collection approaches. Those who have carefully evaluated Internet surveying are most concerned that the pool of people available in cyberspace does not correctly represent the general population. The group of Internet respondents tend to be richer, whiter, more male, and more tech-savvy.[25] The biases are becoming less pronounced over time as the percentage of the population connected to the Internet increases.[26] However, the nonrepresentativeness of Internet respondents will exist for some time into the future. This general problem is compounded by the fact that no comprehensive and reliable source of e-mail addresses exists.

Companies such as Survey Sampling, Incorporated are busily building e-mail databases, but the problems are great. For example, although SSI claims to have 7 million e-mail addresses in its database, this number is small in relation to the total U.S. population. The problem is compounded by the fact that e-mail addresses are easily and frequently changed as people switch jobs, change Internet service providers, and open or close accounts at Yahoo!, Hotmail, and other e-mail providers. This means that any list of e-mail addresses will be constantly changing. For the foreseeable future, it will be virtually impossible to get an inclusive sampling frame of e-mail addresses for almost any generalized population, such as new car buyers, new home buyers, people with cable TV service, or fast-food consumers.

In some cases, researchers recruit samples of consumers via Internet bulletin board postings or banner advertising on search engines (Yahoo!, Google, Hotbot, and others). Once again, the biases are obvious. Those who do not use the Internet have no chance of being included in the sample, even though they might be part of the target population. Among Internet users, consumers who do not visit the sites in question or who do not visit those sites during the time that the banner ads are running have no chance of being included in the sample. In addition, those who visit the sites infrequently have less chance of being included than those who visit them frequently.

Finally, research firms such as Harris Black and Greenfield Online tout the fact that they have developed large panels of individuals who have responded to their solicitations and have agreed to accept and complete e-mail surveys.[27] Again, the biases are fairly obvious, and the lack of representativeness of their panels can be clearly seen. These firms counter criticism by claiming that they weight survey results to make them representative. For example, suppose a population is known to be 60 percent female and 40 percent male. If an Internet survey produces a sample that is 70 percent male and 30 percent female, the results can be weighted to align them with the known population proportions. However, this approach fails to recognize that other biases may lurk below the surface and only be distorted by such weighting.

There are cases where Internet surveys, with all their other inherent advantages, may produce excellent samples. Those cases involve situations where the client organization or the researcher has e-mail addresses for all members of a particular population. For example, high-technology firms such as Texas Instruments may have lists of essentially all individuals who make decisions regarding the purchase of their products for incorporation in other products. These industrial buyers are probably fairly heavy users of the Internet, both at home and at work. Selecting a true random sample of all members of such a population is relatively easy. At minimal cost, all the individuals can be sent invitations to participate and reminders to complete the survey. Response rates in excess of 70 percent are not uncommon for surveys of this type, especially if incentives are offered to encourage responses. Internet surveys are an emerging form of data collection that will probably become dominant at some point in the future. Their advantages are numerous and compelling. However, until the sampling issues discussed in this chapter can be resolved, the results of Internet surveys will be suspect because of lack of survey representativeness.

SUMMARY

The population, or universe, is the total group of people in whose opinions one is interested. A census involves collecting desired information from every member of the population of interest. A sample is simply a subset of a population. The steps in developing a sampling plan are as follows: define the population of interest, choose the data-collection method, identify the sampling frame, select the sampling method, determine sample size, develop and specify an operational plan for selecting sampling elements, and execute the operational sampling plan. The sampling frame is a list of the elements of the population from which the sample will be drawn or a specified procedure for generating the list.

In probability sampling methods, samples are selected in such a way that every element of the population has a known, nonzero likelihood of selection. Nonprobability sampling methods select specific elements from the population in a nonrandom manner. Probability samples have several advantages over nonprobability samples, including reasonable certainty that information will be obtained from a representative cross section of the population, a sampling error that can be computed, and survey results that can be projected to the total population. However, probability samples are more expensive than nonprobability samples and usually take more time to design and execute.

The accuracy of sample results is determined by both sampling and nonsampling error. Sampling error occurs because the sample selected is not perfectly representative of the population. There are two types of sampling error: random sampling error and administrative error. Random sampling error is due to chance and cannot be avoided; it can only be reduced by increasing sample size.

Probability samples include simple random samples, systematic samples, stratified samples, and cluster samples. Nonprobability samples include convenience samples, judgment samples, quota samples, and snowball samples. At the present time, Internet samples tend to be convenience samples. That may change in the future as better e-mail sampling frames become available.

KEY TERMS & DEFINITIONS

sampling Process of obtaining information from a subset of a larger group.

population Entire group of people about whom information is needed; also called *universe* or *population of interest*.

census Collection of data obtained from or about every member of the population of interest.

sample Subset of all the members of a population of interest.

sampling frame List of population elements from which units to be sampled can be selected or a specified procedure for generating such a list.

random-digit dialing Method of generating lists of telephone numbers at random.

probability samples Samples in which every element of the population has a known, nonzero likelihood of selection.

nonprobability samples Samples in which specific elements from the population have been selected in a nonrandom manner.

sample size The identified and selected population subset for the survey, chosen because it represents the entire group.

population parameter A value that accurately portrays or typifies a factor of a complete population, such as average age or income.

sampling error Error that occurs because the sample selected is not perfectly representative of the population.

nonsampling error All error other than sampling error; also called *measurement error*.

simple random sample Probability sample selected by assigning a number to every element of the population and then using a table of random numbers to select specific elements for inclusion in the sample.

systematic sampling Probability sampling in which the entire population is numbered and elements are selected using a skip interval.

stratified sample Probability sample that is forced to be more representative though simple random sampling of mutually exclusive and exhaustive subsets.

proportional allocation Sampling in which the number of elements selected from a stratum is directly proportional to the size of the stratum relative to the size of the population.

disproportional, or optimal, allocation Sampling in which the number of elements taken from a given stratum is proportional to the relative size of the stratum and the standard deviation of the characteristic under consideration.

cluster sample Probability sample in which the sampling units are selected from a number of small geographic areas to reduce data collection costs.

multistage area sampling Geographic areas selected for national or regional surveys in progressively smaller population units, such as counties, then residential blocks, then homes.

convenience samples Nonprobability samples based on using people who are easily accessible.

judgment samples Nonprobability samples in which the selection criteria are based on the researcher's personal judgment about representativeness of the population under study.

quota samples Nonprobability samples in which quotas, based on demographic or classification factors selected by the researcher, are established for population subgroups.

snowball samples Nonprobability samples in which additional respondents are selected based on referrals from initial respondents.

QUESTIONS FOR REVIEW & CRITICAL THINKING

1. What are some situations in which a census would be better than a sample? Why are samples usually employed rather than censuses?

2. Develop a sampling plan for examining undergraduate business students' attitudes toward Internet advertising.

3. Give an example of a perfect sampling frame. Why is a telephone directory usually not an acceptable sampling frame?

4. Distinguish between probability and nonprobability samples. What are the advantages and disadvantages of each? Why are nonprobability samples so popular in marketing research?

5. Distinguish among a systematic sample, a cluster sample, and a stratified sample. Give examples of each.

6. What is the difference between a stratified sample and a quota sample?

7. American National Bank has 1,000 customers. The manager wishes to draw a sample of 100 customers. How could this be done using systematic sampling? What would be the impact on the technique, if any, if the list were ordered by average size of deposit?

8. Do you see any problem with drawing a systematic sample from a telephone book, assuming that the telephone book is an acceptable sample frame for the study in question?

9. Describe snowball sampling. Give an example of a situation in which you might use this type of sample. What are the dangers associated with this type of sample?

10. Name some possible sampling frames for the following:
    a. Patrons of sushi bars
    b. Smokers of high-priced cigars
    c. Snowboarders
    d. Owners of DVD players
    e. People who have visited one or more countries in Europe in the last year
    f. People who emigrated to the United States within the last two years
    g. People with allergies

11. Identify the following sample designs:
    a. The names of 200 patrons of a casino are drawn from a list of visitors for the last month, and a questionnaire is administered to them.
    b. A radio talk show host invites listeners to call in and vote yes or no on whether handguns should be banned.
    c. A dog food manufacturer wants to test a new dog food. It decides to select 100 dog owners who feed their dogs canned food, 100 who feed their dogs dry food, and 100 who feed their dogs semimoist food.
    d. A poll surveys men who play golf to predict the outcome of a presidential election.

WORKING THE NET

1. In 2008, Greenfield Online released a new survey methodology called Real-Time Sampling for rollout in European markets. Visit *www.greenfield.com* and evaluate this system; see how it might improve the accuracy and scope of global market research.

2. Throughout 2008, Knowledge Networks worked in conjunction with the Associated Press and Yahoo! to repeatedly poll 2,230 people (from random telephone sampling) about likely election results and political preferences. Visit *www.knowledgenetworks.com* and evaluate their methodology and ultimate accuracy (or inaccuracy) on this topic.

REAL-LIFE RESEARCH • 11.1

Texas Field Research

Texas Field Research (TFR) has been commissioned by the National Association of Dry Cleaners to determine the following:

- Why do people select one dry cleaner over another?
- Do customers know or care if a dry cleaning establishment is a member of the association?

- What services, beyond dry cleaning, would customers like to receive from their dry cleaner?

TFR underbid four other research firms to obtain the contract from the Dry Cleaning Institute. In fact, their bid was about 30 percent less than the next lowest bid. The primary method by which TFR was able to lower its cost was the sampling methodology selected. In its proposal, TFR stated that college students would be used to gather the survey data. The company said that it would randomly select 20 colleges from across the United States and contact the chairperson of the Marketing Department at each school. The chairperson would be asked to submit a list of 10 students who would be interested in earning extra money. Next, the field service director for TFR would contact the students individually. TFR's goal was to identify 5 students at each school who would ultimately complete 10 interviews each.

When the students were contacted by the field director, they were told that they would be given $5 for each completed interview. The only screening requirement was that the person interviewed had to have spent at least $10 on dry cleaning within the past month. In fact, the TFR field director told the students that the easiest thing to do would be to go to the Student Center during lunch time and go from table to table asking people who might be interested in being interviewed.

Questions

1. How would you describe this sampling methodology?
2. What problems do you see arising from this technique?
3. Suggest an alternative sampling method that might give the Dry Cleaning Institute a much better picture of the information it desired.

iStockphoto

SAMPLE SIZE DETERMINATION

LEARNING OBJECTIVES

→	1.	To learn the financial and statistical issues in the determination of sample size.
→	2.	To discover methods for determining sample size.
→	3.	To gain an appreciation of a normal distribution.
→	4.	To understand population, sample, and sampling distributions.
→	5.	To distinguish between point and interval estimates.
→	6.	To recognize problems involving sampling means and proportions.

One of the authors was recently asked to review a survey project conducted for a company that sells to the 65 and older population. Many of the survey results did not ring true to the decision makers in the company and were not consistent with the findings of other surveys they had conducted.

It did not take long to identify the problem. The marketing research firm that conducted the surveys specialized in conducting surveys via the Internet. They used a well-known Internet panel company as the source of the sample. Comparing the demographic characteristics of the survey respondents to the demographic characteristics of the 65 and over population from the U.S. Census, we quickly found a number of serious discrepancies. The most striking discrepancy related to the education level of survey respondents. Fifty-two percent of the people responding from the Internet panel reported that they had a college degree or more in terms of education. This compares to a figure of 16 percent from the U.S. Census. Compared to the population that they wanted to represent for the study (all people 65 years of age or older), they had more than three times as many people with a college education or more. This had serious implications for the research findings in that many questions covered attitudes and opinions about a range of topics, and it is known that those attitudes and opinions tend to differ by level of education. As you might expect, usage of the Internet by those 65 and over has lagged usage levels for those under 65 years of age. Review of a few studies of the 65 and over Internet population shows that Internet users in this group tend to have higher levels of income and higher incomes than those who do not.

Although the sample was relatively large, the fact that it was not representative of the population of interest made it meaningless. Worse yet, if the client had acted on the results, they likely would have made serious blunders. We cannot stress enough that the way a sample is chosen is much more important than the size of the sample. In this case, the research firm computed sampling error in the standard way and reported an error level of ±2 percent with 95 percent confidence. However, the sampling error calculations assume that the sample has been drawn in a way that assures that it is representative of the population. In this case, that was not a correct assumption, and it was inappropriate to use the sampling error calculation formulas presented in this chapter.

Determining Sample Size for Probability Samples

The process of determining sample size for probability samples involves financial, statistical, and managerial issues. As a general rule, the larger the sample is, the smaller the sampling error. However, larger samples cost more money, and the resources available for a project are always limited. Although the cost of increasing sample size tends to rise on a linear basis (double the sample size, almost double the cost), sampling error decreases at a rate equal to the square root of the relative increase in sample size. If sample size is quadrupled, data-collection cost is almost quadrupled, but the level of sampling error is reduced by only 50 percent.

Managerial issues must be reflected in sample size calculations. How accurate do estimates need to be, and how confident must managers be that true population values are included in the chosen confidence interval? Some cases require high levels of precision (small sampling error) and confidence that population values fall in the small range of sampling error (the confidence interval). Other cases may not require the same level of precision or confidence.

Budget Available

The sample size for a project is often determined, at least indirectly, by the budget available. Thus, it is frequently the last project factor determined. A brand manager may have

$50,000 available in the budget for a new product test. After deduction of other project costs (e.g., research design, questionnaire development, data processing), the amount remaining determines the size of the sample that can be surveyed. Of course, if the dollars available will not produce an adequate sample size, then management must make a decision: either additional funds must be found, or the project should be canceled.

Although this approach may seem highly unscientific and arbitrary, it is a fact of life in a corporate environment. Financial constraints challenge the researcher to develop research designs that will generate data of adequate quality for decision-making purposes at low cost. This "budget available" approach forces the researcher to explore alternative data-collection approaches and to carefully consider the value of information in relation to its cost. The Practicing Marketing Research feature on page 355 explains why you can't be too stingy on sample size.

Rule of Thumb

Potential clients may specify in the RFP (request for proposal) that they want a sample of 200, 400, 500, or some other size. Sometimes, this number is based on desired sampling error. In other cases, it is based on nothing more than past experience. The justification for the specified sample size may boil down to a "gut feeling" that a particular sample size is necessary or appropriate.

If the researcher determines that the sample size requested is not adequate to support the objectives of the proposed research, then she or he has a professional responsibility to present arguments for a larger sample size to the client and let the client make the final decision. If the client rejects arguments for a larger sample size, then the researcher may decline to submit a proposal based on the belief that an inadequate sample size will produce results with so much error that they may be misleading.[1]

Number of Subgroups Analyzed

In any sample size determination problem, consideration must be given to the number and anticipated size of various subgroups of the total sample that must be analyzed and about which statistical inferences must be made. For example, a researcher might decide that a sample of 400 is quite adequate overall. However, if male and female respondents must be analyzed separately and the sample is expected to be 50 percent male and 50 percent female, then the expected sample size for each subgroup is only 200. Is this number adequate for making the desired statistical inferences about the characteristics of the two groups? If the results are to be analyzed by both sex and age, then the problem gets even more complicated.

Assume that it is important to analyze four subgroups of the total sample: men under 35, men 35 and over, women under 35, and women 35 and over. If each group is expected to make up about 25 percent of the total sample, a sample of 400 will include only 100 respondents in each subgroup. The problem is that as sample size gets smaller, sampling error gets larger, and it becomes more difficult to tell whether an observed difference between two groups is a real difference or simply a reflection of sampling error.

Other things being equal, the larger the number of subgroups to be analyzed, the larger the required total sample size. It has been suggested that a sample should provide, at a minimum, 100 or more respondents in each major subgroup and 20 to 50 respondents in each of the less important subgroups.[4]

Traditional Statistical Methods

You probably have been exposed in other classes to traditional approaches for determining sample size for simple random samples. These approaches are reviewed in this chapter.

PRACTICING MARKETING RESEARCH

Factors to Consider in Determining Optimal Sample Size

If your survey starts with the correct sample size, this increases the chances that your findings will be accurate and will correctly reflect the target population, says Bonnie W. Eisenfeld, an independent marketing research consultant working in Philadelphia, Pennsylvania. She offers a number of practical suggestions for qualitative researchers who may want excellent results without having to delve into all the mathematics:

1. Make your sample size large enough that you can discern patterns in consumer behavior or attitudes.

2. Make your sample size large enough so you can see important differences between the segments and subgroups.

3. Avoid bias in creating your sampling and ensure that each person in the target population has an equal chance of inclusion in the sample.

4. Be wary of using convenience samples based on repeaters or referred friends; this can produce sampling bias and may exclude good recruits.

5. Don't be seduced by the seeming need to obtain a huge population to create a proportional sample. You are as likely to derive sound conclusions from a sample population of 1,000 as from 1,000,000.

6. Offer desirable incentives to survey participants, knowing that the higher or better the incentive, in most cases, the better the response.

7. Minimize sampling error and having your study fall off the mark by using a larger size sample; this generates a smaller sampling error while offering higher precision and data accuracy.

8. If in doubt on ideal sample size, consult a statistician.[2]

Or you may enjoy the benefits of a sample size table produced by statistical method but not requiring any mathematical input or even statistician consultation on your part to put to use. Paul C. Boyd of Research Advisors in Franklin, Massachusetts, used statistical formulas to produce a practical sample size table that suggests the ideal sample size for a population and a desired margin of error and confidence interval. Boyd realized that many market researchers only have to deal with the "unnecessarily complex" issues of population size for samples on an occasional basis. So might there be an easier way than slogging through formulas? There is: Boyd's sample size table.

Say your desired market population is 3,500 people and you want a 95 percent confidence level. The variables lie in the desired margin of error (MOE) results. If you are comfortable with a 5 percent MOE, then get 346 people in your sample; for a 3.5 percent MOE, then use 641; for 2.5 percent, 1,068; and for 1.0 percent, 2,565. If you're shooting even higher, for a 99 percent confidence level, then for the same target population, use 558 people in your sample for a 5 percent MOE; 977 for a 3.5 percent MOE; 1,510 for 2.5 percent; and 2,890 for 1.0 percent.

The cautious approach, Boyd suggests, is to avoid the lower confidence levels (95 percent) and lower MOEs (5 percent) if your reason is solely to reduce the size of the sample. The confidence level should be based, he says, with an eye on the likely consequences if you draw the wrong market conclusions based on sampling error. Similarly, he advises determining your MOE on the utility of the interval constructed while keeping in mind the fact that interval width is twice the margin of error. To view the entire table online, go to: www.research-advisors.com/tools/SampleSize.htm.[3]

Questions

1. Are there any circumstances or research topics where using a preset table for sample size would be inadvisable or produce distorted data?

2. How will using convenience sampling with repeaters or referred friends produce sampling bias or exclude potentially good survey recruits?

Three pieces of information are required to make the necessary calculations for a sample result:

☐ An estimate of the population standard deviation

☐ The acceptable level of sampling error

☐ The desired level of confidence that the sample result will fall within a certain range (result ± sampling error) of true population values

With these three pieces of information, the researcher can calculate the size of the simple random sample required.[5]

Normal Distribution

General Properties

The normal distribution is crucial to classical statistical inference. There are several reasons for its importance. First, many variables encountered by marketers have probability distributions that are close to the normal distribution. Examples include the number of cans, bottles, or glasses of soft drink consumed by soft drink users, the number of times that people who eat at fast-food restaurants go to such restaurants in an average month, and the average hours per week spent viewing television. Second, the normal distribution is useful for a number of theoretical reasons; one of the more important of these relates to the central limit theorem. According to the **central limit theorem,** for any population, regardless of its distribution, the distribution of sample means or sample proportions approaches a normal distribution as sample size increases. The importance of this tendency will become clear later in the chapter. Third, the normal distribution is a useful approximation of many other discrete probability distributions. If, for example, a researcher measured the heights of a large sample of men in the United States and plotted those values on a graph, a distribution similar to the one shown in Exhibit 12.1 would result. This distribution is a **normal distribution,** and it has a number of important characteristics, including the following:

⇒ **central limit theorem**
Idea that a distribution of a large number of sample means or sample proportions will approximate a normal distribution, regardless of the distribution of the population from which they were drawn.

⇒ **normal distribution**
Continuous distribution that is bell-shaped and symmetric about the mean; the mean, median, and mode are equal.

1. The normal distribution is bell-shaped and has only one mode. The mode is a measure of central tendency and is the particular value that occurs most frequently. (A bimodal, or two-mode, distribution would have two peaks or humps.)

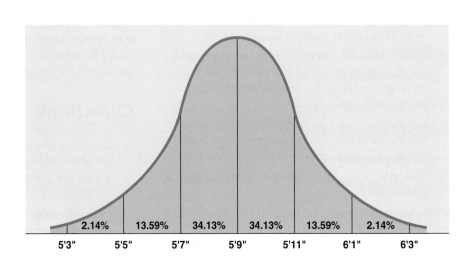

■ **Exhibit 12.1**

Normal Distribution for Heights of Men

	2.14%	13.59%	34.13%	34.13%	13.59%	2.14%	
5'3"	5'5"	5'7"	5'9"	5'11"	6'1"	6'3"	

2. The normal distribution is symmetric about its mean. This is another way of saying that it is not skewed and that the three measures of central tendency (mean, median, and mode) are all equal.

3. A particular normal distribution is uniquely defined by its mean and standard deviation.

4. The total area under a normal curve is equal to one, meaning that it takes in all observations.

5. The area of a region under the normal distribution curve between any two values of a variable equals the probability of observing a value in that range when an observation is randomly selected from the distribution. For example, on a single draw, there is a 34.13 percent chance of selecting from the distribution shown in Exhibit 12.1 a man between 5′7″ and 5′9″ in height.

6. The area between the mean and a given number of standard deviations from the mean is the same for all normal distributions. The area between the mean and plus or minus one standard deviation takes in 68.26 percent of the area under the curve, or 68.26 percent of the observations. This **proportional property of the normal distribution** provides the basis for the statistical inferences we will discuss in this chapter.

Standard Normal Distribution

Any normal distribution can be transformed into what is known as a standard normal distribution. The **standard normal distribution** has the same features as any normal distribution. However, the mean of the standard normal distribution is always equal to zero, and the standard deviation is always equal to one. The probabilities provided in Table 2 in the Appendix are based on a standard normal distribution. A simple transformation formula, based on the proportional property of the normal distribution, is used to transform any value X from any normal distribution to its equivalent value Z from a standard normal distribution:

$$Z = \frac{\text{Value of the variable} - \text{Mean of the variable}}{\text{Standard deviation of the variable}}$$

Symbolically, the formula can be stated as follows:

$$Z = \frac{X - \mu}{\sigma}$$

where X = value of the variable

μ = mean of the variable

σ = standard deviation of the variable

The areas under a standard normal distribution (reflecting the percent of all observations) for various Z values (**standard deviations**) are shown in Exhibit 12.2. The standard normal distribution is shown in Exhibit 12.3.

> **proportional property of the normal distribution**
> Feature that the number of observations falling between the mean and a given number of standard deviations from the mean is the same for all normal distributions.

> **standard normal distribution**
> Normal distribution with a mean of zero and a standard deviation of one.

> **standard deviation**
> Measure of dispersion calculated by subtracting the mean of the series from each value in a series, squaring each result, summing the results, dividing the sum by the number of items minus 1, and taking the square root of this value.

EXHIBIT 12.2	Area under Standard Normal Curve for Z Values (Standard Deviations) of 1, 2, and 3
Z Values (Standard Deviation)	**Area under Standard Normal Curve (%)**
1	68.26
2	95.44
3	99.74

Exhibit 12.3

Standard Normal Distribution

Note: The term Pr(Z) is read "the probability of Z."

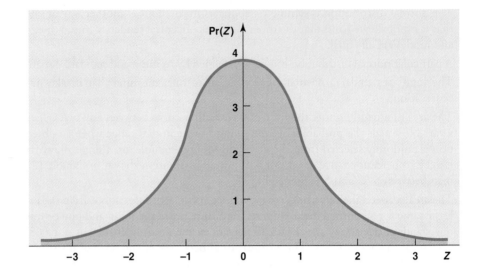

Population and Sample Distributions

> **population distribution**
> Frequency distribution of all the elements of a population.

> **sample distribution**
> Frequency distribution of all the elements of an individual sample.

The purpose of conducting a survey based on a sample is to make inferences about the population, not to describe the sample. The population, as defined earlier, includes all possible individuals or objects from whom or about which information is needed to meet the objectives of the research. A sample is a subset of the total population.

A **population distribution** is a frequency distribution of all the elements of the population. It has a mean, usually represented by the Greek letter μ, and a standard deviation, usually represented by the Greek letter σ.

A **sample distribution** is a frequency distribution of all the elements of an individual (single) sample. In a sample distribution, the mean is usually represented by $\overline{X}$ and the standard deviation is usually represented by S.

Sampling Distribution of the Mean

> **sampling distribution of the mean**
> Theoretical frequency distribution of the means of all possible samples of a given size drawn from a particular population; it is normally distributed.

At this point, it is necessary to introduce a third distribution, the sampling distribution of the sample mean. Understanding this distribution is crucial to understanding the basis for our ability to compute sampling error for simple random samples. The **sampling distribution of the mean** is a conceptual and theoretical probability distribution of the means of all possible samples of a given size drawn from a given population. Although this distribution is seldom calculated, its known properties have tremendous practical significance. Actually deriving a distribution of sample means involves drawing a large number of simple random samples (for example, 25,000) of a certain size from a particular population. Then, the means for the samples are computed and arranged in a frequency distribution. Because each sample is composed of a different subset of sample elements, all the sample means will not be exactly the same. If the samples are sufficiently large and random, then the resulting distribution of sample means will approximate a

EXHIBIT 12.4	Notation for Means and Standard Deviations of Various Distributions	
Distribution	**Mean**	**Standard Deviation**
Population	μ	σ
Sample	$\overline{X}$	S
Sampling	$\mu_{\overline{x}} = \mu$	$S_{\overline{x}}$

normal distribution. This assertion is based on the central limit theorem, which states that as sample size increases, the distribution of the means of a large number of random samples taken from virtually any population approaches a normal distribution with a mean equal to μ and a standard deviation (referred to as *standard error*) $S_{\overline{x}}$, where $n =$ sample size and

$$S_{\overline{x}} = \frac{\sigma}{\sqrt{n}}$$

The **standard error of the mean** $(S_{\overline{x}})$ is computed in this way because the variance, or dispersion, within a particular distribution of sample means will be smaller if it is based on larger samples. Common sense tells us that with larger samples individual sample means will, on the average, be closer to the population mean.

▶ **standard error of the mean** Standard deviation of a distribution of sample means.

It is important to note that the central limit theorem holds regardless of the shape of the population distribution from which the samples are selected. This means that, regardless of the population distribution, the sample means selected from the population distribution will tend to be normally distributed.

The notation ordinarily used to refer to the means and standard deviations of population and sample distributions and sampling distribution of the mean is summarized in Exhibit 12.4. The relationships among the population distribution, sample distribution, and sampling distribution of the mean are shown graphically in Exhibit 12.5.

Basic Concepts

Consider a case in which a researcher takes 1,000 simple random samples of size 200 from the population of all consumers who have eaten at a fast-food restaurant at least once in the past 30 days. The purpose is to estimate the average number of times these individuals eat at a fast-food restaurant in an average month.

If the researcher computes the mean number of visits for each of the 1,000 samples and sorts them into intervals based on their relative values, the frequency distribution shown in Exhibit 12.6 might result. Exhibit 12.7 graphically illustrates these frequencies in a histogram, on which a normal curve has been superimposed. As you can see, the histogram closely approximates the shape of a normal curve. If the researcher draws a large enough number of samples of size 200, computes the mean of each sample, and plots these means, the resulting distribution will be a normal distribution. The normal curve shown in Exhibit 12.7 is the sampling distribution of the mean for this particular

Exhibit 12.5

Relationships of the Three Basic Types of Distribution

Source: Adapted from *Statistics, A Fresh Approach,* 4th ed., by D. H. Sanders et al. © 1990 McGraw-Hill, Inc. Reprinted with permission of the McGraw-Hill Companies.

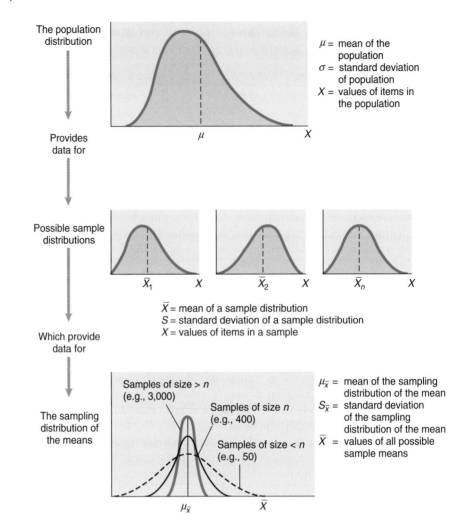

problem. The sampling distribution of the mean for simple random samples that are large (30 or more observations) has the following characteristics:

- ☐ The distribution is a normal distribution.
- ☐ The distribution has a mean equal to the population mean.
- ☐ The distribution has a standard deviation (the standard error of the mean) equal to the population standard deviation divided by the square root of the sample size:

$$\sigma_{\bar{x}} = \frac{\sigma}{\sqrt{n}}$$

This statistic is referred to as the standard error of the mean (instead of the standard deviation) to indicate that it applies to a distribution of sample means rather than to the standard deviation of a sample or a population. Keep in mind that this calculation applies *only* to a simple random sample. Other types of probability samples (for example, stratified samples and cluster samples) require more complex formulas for computing standard error. Note that this formula does not account for any type of bias, including nonresponse bias discussed in the feature on page 362.

EXHIBIT 12.6	Frequency Distribution of 1,000 Sample Means: Average Number of Times Respondent Ate at a Fast-Food Restaurant in the Past 30 Days	
Number of Times	**Frequency of Occurrence**	
2.6–3.5	8	
3.6–4.5	15	
4.6–5.5	29	
5.6–6.5	44	
6.6–7.5	64	
7.6–8.5	79	
8.6–9.5	89	
9.6–10.5	108	
10.6–11.5	115	
11.6–12.5	110	
12.6–13.5	90	
13.6–14.5	81	
14.6–15.5	66	
15.6–16.5	45	
16.6–17.5	32	
17.6–18.5	16	
18.6–19.5	9	
Total	1000	

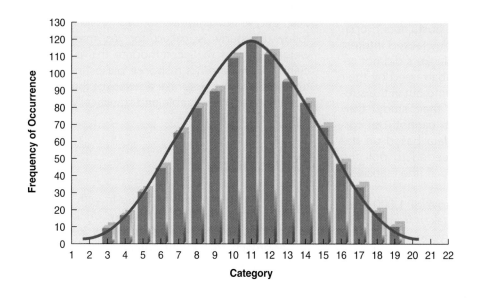

Exhibit 12.7

Actual Sampling Distribution of Means for Number of Times Respondent Ate at Fast-Food Restaurant in Past 30 Days

GLOBAL RESEARCH

Nonresponse Bias in a Dutch Alcohol Consumption Study

The fact that some people fail to respond to a poll or respond only selectively to certain questions, ignoring others, can distort the accuracy of a survey. Market researchers call this nonresponse bias, and researchers at the Addiction Research Institute in Rotterdam, The Netherlands, concluded it can be a serious problem. In fact, response rates to surveys in The Netherlands had dropped from 80 percent in the 1980s to 60 percent at the end of the 1990s, and was still continuing to decline, all of it leading to a smaller sample size and accuracy loss in population estimates. People who don't respond to polls may have relevant characteristics different from responders.

In 2002, the researchers reviewed the results of a study done in 1999 on alcohol usage. Their research assumption was that abstainers probably didn't respond because they lacked interest in the subject and excessive drinkers did not respond because they were embarrassed by their usage. This hypothesis was borne out in the subsequent study. In designing their study, they knew that nonresponse bias cannot be corrected simply by weighting data based on demographic variables. They needed to poll the nonrespondents and evaluate if their answers differed from responders.

Originally, a random sample of 1,000 people, aged 16 to 69 years, was taken from the city registry of Rotterdam. Everyone received a mailed questionnaire about their alcohol consumption. After two reminders were sent, the response rate was 44 percent. For the follow-up study, the researchers chose 25 postal areas in Rotterdam and a secondary sample of 310 people. Of these, 133 had already responded to the first survey, and 177 did not, so these two groups were called primary respondents and

primary nonrespondents, respectively. Members of the latter group were approached in person by the researchers in a series of five in-person attempts to conduct the interview at their homes. In the end, 48 primary nonrespondents could not be reached, leaving a final sample size for primary nonrespondents of 129.

Both groups were asked the same two questions: (1) do you ever drink alcohol?; and (2) do you ever drink six or more alcoholic beverages in the same day? The net response rate from the nonrespondents to both questions was 52 percent—in other words, even more nonresponse (48 percent) was encountered in the follow-up study.

More importantly, the Dutch researchers discovered, first, that alcohol abstainers were underrepresented, but frequent, excessive drinkers were not; second, that the underrepresentation of abstainers was greater among women than men, greater for those older than 35, and greater for those who were Dutch versus other nationalities; and third, that a thorough nonresponse follow-up study is called for (as mentioned, weighting data to accommodate this is insufficient) to evaluate nonresponse biases in any future studies. The potential answers of those who don't answer are valuable and statistically necessary for any study.[6]

Questions

1. The nonresponse bias came in with the extremes (abstainers and heavy drinkers) regarding alcohol use. Is there any weighting approach that might compensate for these two important groups of nonresponders so that a follow-up study would not be needed?

2. For the 48 percent who failed to respond to the second study, would a mailed questionnaire, insuring privacy, be worth the expense in terms of the improvement in statistical accuracy it might generate?

Making Inferences on the Basis of a Single Sample

In practice, there is no call for taking all possible random samples from a particular population and generating a frequency distribution and histogram like those shown in Exhibits 12.6 and 12.7. Instead, the researcher wants to take one simple random sample and make statistical inferences about the population from which it was drawn. The question is, what is the probability that any one simple random sample of a particular size will produce an estimate of the population mean that is within one standard error (plus or minus) of the true population mean? The answer, based on the information provided in Exhibit 12.2, is that there is a 68.26 percent probability that any one sample from a particular population will produce an estimate of the population mean that is within plus or minus one standard error of the true value, because 68.26 percent of all sample means fall in this range. There is a 95.44 percent probability that any one simple random sample of a particular size from a given population will produce a value that is within plus or minus two standard errors of the true population mean, and a 99.74 percent probability that such a sample will produce an estimate of the mean that is within plus or minus three standard errors of the population mean.

Point and Interval Estimates

The results of a sample can be used to generate two kinds of estimates of a population mean: point and interval estimates. The sample mean is the best **point estimate** of the population mean. Inspection of the sampling distribution of the mean shown in Exhibit 12.7 suggests that a particular sample result is likely to produce a mean that is relatively close to the population mean. However, the mean of a particular sample could be any one of the sample means shown in the distribution. A small percentage of these sample means are a considerable distance from the true population mean. The distance between the sample mean and the true population mean is the sampling error.

Given that point estimates based on sample results are exactly correct in only a small percentage of all possible cases, interval estimates generally are preferred. An **interval estimate** is a particular interval or range of values within which the true population value

> **point estimate**
> Particular estimate of a population value.

> **interval estimate**
> Interval or range of values within which the true population value is estimated to fall.

The sampling distribution of the proportion is used to estimate the percentage of the population that watches a particular television program.

is estimated to fall. In addition to stating the size of the interval, the researcher usually states the probability that the interval will include the true value of the population mean. This probability is referred to as the **confidence level** and the interval is called the **confidence interval.**

Interval estimates of the mean are derived by first drawing a random sample of a given size from the population of interest and calculating the mean of that sample. This sample mean is known to lie somewhere within the sampling distribution of all possible sample means, but exactly where this particular mean falls in that distribution is not known. There is a 68.26 percent probability that this particular sample mean lies within one standard error (plus or minus) of the true population mean. Based on this information, the researcher states that he or she is 68.26 percent confident that the true population value is equal to the sample value plus or minus one standard error. This statement can be shown symbolically, as follows:

> **confidence level**
> Probability that a particular interval will include the true population value; also called *confidence coefficient*.

> **confidence interval**
> Interval that, at the specified confidence level, includes the true population value.

$$\bar{X} - 1\sigma_{\bar{x}} \leq \mu \leq \bar{X} + 1\sigma_{\bar{x}}$$

By the same logic, the researcher can be 95.44 percent confident that the true population value is equal to the sample estimate ± 2 (technically 1.96) standard errors, and 99.74 percent confident that the true population value falls within the interval defined by the sample value ± 3 standard errors.

These statements assume that the standard deviation of the population is known. However, in most situations, this is not the case. If the standard deviation of the population were known, by definition the mean of the population would also be known, and there would be no need to take a sample in the first place. Because information on the standard deviation of the population is lacking, its value is estimated based on the standard deviation of the sample.

Sampling Distribution of the Proportion

Marketing researchers frequently are interested in estimating proportions or percentages rather than or in addition to estimating means. Common examples include estimating the following:

- ☐ The percentage of the population that is aware of a particular ad
- ☐ The percentage of the population that accesses the Internet one or more times in an average week
- ☐ The percentage of the population that has visited a fast-food restaurant four or more times in the past 30 days
- ☐ The percentage of the population that watches a particular television program

In situations in which a population proportion or percentage is of interest, the sampling distribution of the proportion is used.

The **sampling distribution of the proportion** is a relative frequency distribution of the sample proportions of a large number of random samples of a given size drawn from a particular population. The sampling distribution of a proportion has the following characteristics:

> **sampling distribution of the proportion**
> Relative frequency distribution of the sample proportions of many random samples of a given size drawn from a particular population; it is normally distributed.

- ☐ It approximates a normal distribution.
- ☐ The mean proportion for all possible samples is equal to the population proportion.

☐ The standard error of a sampling distribution of the proportion can be computed with the following formula:

$$S_p = \sqrt{\frac{P(1 - P)}{n}}$$

where
S_p = standard error of sampling distribution of proportion

P = estimate of population proportion

n = sample size

Consider the task of estimating the percentage of all adults who have purchased something over the Internet in the past 90 days. As in generating a sampling distribution of the mean, the researcher might select 1,000 random samples of size 200 from the population of all adults and compute the proportion of all adults who have purchased something over the Internet in the past 90 days for all 1,000 samples. These values could then be plotted in a frequency distribution, and this frequency distribution would approximate a normal distribution. The estimated standard error of the proportion for this distribution can be computed using the formula provided earlier.

For reasons that will be clear to you after you read the next section, marketing researchers have a tendency to prefer dealing with sample size problems as problems of estimating proportions rather than means.

Determining Sample Size

Problems Involving Means

Consider once again the task of estimating how many times the average fast-food restaurant user visits a fast-food restaurant in an average month. Management needs an estimate of the average number of visits to make a decision regarding a new promotional campaign that is being developed. To make this estimate, the marketing research manager for the organization intends to survey a simple random sample of all fast-food users. The question is, what information is necessary to determine the appropriate sample size for the project? The formula for calculating the required sample size for problems that involve the estimation of a mean is as follows:[7]

$$n = \frac{Z^2 \sigma^2}{E^2}$$

where
Z = level of confidence expressed in standard errors

σ = population standard deviation

E = acceptable amount of sampling error

Three pieces of information are needed to compute the sample size required:

1. The acceptable or allowable level of sampling error E.
2. The acceptable level of confidence Z. In other words, how confident does the researcher want to be that the specified confidence interval includes the population mean?
3. An estimate of the population standard deviation σ.

> **allowable sampling error**
> Amount of sampling error the researcher is willing to accept.

The level of confidence Z and **allowable sampling error** E for this calculation must be set by the researcher in consultation with his or her client. As noted earlier, the level of confidence and the amount of error are based not only on statistical criteria, but also on financial and managerial criteria. In an ideal world, the level of confidence would always be very high and the amount of error very low. However, because this is a business decision, cost must be considered. An acceptable trade-off among accuracy, level of confidence, and cost must be developed. High levels of precision and confidence may be less important in some situations than in others. For example, in an exploratory study, you may be interested in developing a basic sense of whether attitudes toward your product are generally positive or negative. Precision may not be critical. However, in a product concept test, you would need a much more precise estimate of sales for a new product before making the potentially costly and risky decision to introduce that product in the marketplace. The fact that margin of error is not well understood is illustrated by the feature on page 367.

> **population standard deviation**
> Standard deviation of a variable for the entire population.

Making an estimate of the **population standard deviation** presents a more serious problem. As noted earlier, if the population standard deviation were known, the population mean also would be known (the population mean is needed to compute the population standard deviation), and there would be no need to draw a sample. How can the researcher estimate the population standard deviation before selecting the sample? One or some combination of the following four methods might be used to deal with this problem:

1. *Use results from a prior survey.* In many cases, the firm may have conducted a prior survey dealing with the same or a similar issue. In this situation, a possible solution to the problem is to use the results of the prior survey as an estimate of the population standard deviation.

2. *Conduct a pilot survey.* If this is to be a large-scale project, it may be possible to devote some time and some resources to a small-scale pilot survey of the population. The results of this pilot survey can be used to develop an estimate of the population standard deviation that can be used in the sample size determination formula.

3. *Use secondary data.* In some cases, secondary data can be used to develop an estimate of the population standard deviation.

4. *Use judgment.* If all else fails, an estimate of the population standard deviation can be developed based solely on judgment. Judgments might be sought from a variety of managers in a position to make educated guesses about the required population parameters.

It should be noted that after the survey has been conducted and the sample mean and sample standard deviation have been calculated, the researcher can assess the accuracy of the estimate of the population standard deviation used to calculate the required sample size. At this time, if appropriate, adjustments can be made in the initial estimates of sampling error.[8]

Let's return to the problem of estimating the average number of fast-food visits made in an average month by users of fast-food restaurants:

☐ After consultation with managers in the company, the marketing research manager determines that an estimate is needed of the average number of times that fast-food consumers visit fast-food restaurants. She further determines that managers believe that a high degree of accuracy is needed, which she takes to mean that the estimate should be within .10 (one-tenth) of a visit of the true population value. This value (.10) should be substituted into the formula for the value of E.

- In addition, the marketing research manager decides that, all things considered, she needs to be 95.44 percent confident that the true population mean falls in the interval defined by the sample mean plus or minus E (as just defined). Two (technically, 1.96) standard errors are required to take in 95.44 percent of the area under a normal curve. Therefore, a value of 2 should be substituted into the equation for Z.

- Finally, there is the question of what value to insert into the formula for σ. Fortunately, the company conducted a similar study one year ago. The standard deviation in that study for the variable—the average number of times a fast-food restaurant was visited in the past 30 days—was 1.39. This is the best estimate of σ available. Therefore, a value of 1.39 should be substituted into the formula for the value of σ. The calculation follows:

$$
\begin{aligned}
n &= \frac{Z^2 \sigma^2}{E^2} \\
&= \frac{2^2 (1.39)^2}{(.10)^2} \\
&= \frac{4(1.93)}{.01} \\
&= \frac{7.72}{.01} \\
&= 772
\end{aligned}
$$

Based on this calculation, a simple random sample of 772 is necessary to meet the requirements outlined.

PRACTICING MARKETING RESEARCH

Harris Poll on "Margin of Error" Finds It Is Widely Misunderstood

A Harris poll of 1,052 adults interviewed over the telephone found that 52 percent of Americans misunderstand or have wrong beliefs about what pollsters mean by margin of error. The pollsters also discovered that Americans presume a level of accuracy that no statistician could ever meet. Harris Interactive, which does not use the phrase "margin of error" in any of its poll results, conducted the poll in October 2007.

The Harris poll revealed that 52 percent of adults understand the phrase "the margin of error being plus or minus 3 percent" to mean that all the survey results are accurate to within a maximum of 3 percent error considering all types of possible error. This is a mistaken belief, Harris observes. They found that 66 percent believe that "margin of error" factors in errors are produced by how the questions are worded. This is also a wrong belief. Furthermore, 45 percent assume "margin of error" takes into account mistakes made while developing a representative base or weighting errors, interviewer errors, or errors resulting from where the questions are placed in a survey. It doesn't, Harris says.

Only 12 percent of people polled understand that "margin of error" is supposed to address only sampling error. Overall, 56 percent reported that the phrase does not make it clear that the calculation it refers to leaves out all error sources except for sampling error on a purely random sample. This same 56 percent stated that margin of error calculations should include all possible sources of error, not just sampling error.

Harris does not use the phrase "margin of error" because it believes the phrase is inherently misleading. At least four types of error are possible in any survey, including errors due to nonresponse, question wording or order, interviewers, or weighting. It's impossible to calculate all the possible sources of error, Harris adds. The study highlights how Americans realize polls are not infallible even if they misunderstand some terms, yet Harris was surprised to find

these same Americans (52 percent) still prefer use of the phrase "margin of error" in the publishing of poll results.[9]

Questions

1. Should "margin of error" still be used in reporting polls, should its meaning or scope be broadened, or should additional qualifications be added to show that poll results are fallible?

2. Suggest another sampling poll Harris Interactive might conduct that would clarify an important topic or assumption in market research.

Problems Involving Proportions

Now let's consider the problem of estimating the proportion or percentage of all adults who have purchased something via the Internet in the past 90 days. The goal is to take a simple random sample from the population of all adults to estimate this proportion.[10]

☐ As in the problem involving fast-food users, the first task in estimating the population mean on the basis of sample results is to decide on an acceptable value for E. If, for example, an error level of ± 4 percent is acceptable, a value of .04 should be substituted into the formula for E.

☐ Next, assume that the researcher has determined a need to be 95.44 percent confident that the sample estimate is within ± 4 percent of the true population proportion. As in the previous example, a value of 2 should be substituted into the equation for Z.

☐ Finally, in a study of the same issue conducted one year ago, 5 percent of all respondents indicated they had purchased something over the Internet in the past 90 days. Thus, a value of .05 should be substituted into the equation for P.

The resulting calculations are as follows:

$$n = \frac{Z^2[P(1 - P)]}{E^2}$$
$$= \frac{2^2[.05(1 - .05)]}{.04^2}$$
$$= \frac{4(.0475)}{.0016}$$
$$= \frac{.19}{.0016}$$
$$= 119$$

Given the requirements, a random sample of 475 respondents is required. It should be noted that, in one respect, the process of determining the sample size necessary to estimate a proportion is easier than the process of determining the sample size necessary to estimate a mean: If there is no basis for estimating P, the researcher can make what is sometimes referred to as the most pessimistic, or worst-case, assumption regarding the value of P. Given the values of Z and E, what value of P will require the largest possible sample? A value of .50 will make the value of the expression $P(1 - P)$ larger than any possible value of P. There is no corresponding most pessimistic assumption that the researcher can make regarding the value of σ in problems that involve determining the sample size necessary to estimate a mean with given levels of Z and E.

Determining Sample Size for Stratified and Cluster Samples

The formulas for sample size determination presented in this chapter apply only to simple random samples. There also are formulas for determining required sample size and sampling error for other types of probability samples such as stratified and cluster samples. Although many of the general concepts presented in this chapter apply to these other types of probability samples, the specific formulas are much more complicated.[11] In addition, these formulas require information that frequently is not available or is difficult to obtain. For these reasons, sample size determination for other types of probability samples is beyond the scope of this introductory text.

Population Size and Sample Size

You may have noticed that none of the formulas for determining sample size takes into account the size of the population in any way. Students (and managers) frequently find this troubling. It seems to make sense that one should take a larger sample from a larger population. But this is not the case. Normally, there is no direct relationship between the size of the population and the size of the sample required to estimate a particular population parameter with a particular level of error and a particular level of confidence. In fact, the size of the population may have an effect only in those situations where the size of the sample is large in relation to the size of the population. One rule of thumb is that an adjustment should be made in the sample size if the sample size is more than 5 percent of the size of the total population. The normal presumption is that sample elements are drawn independently of one another (**independence assumption**). This assumption is justified when the sample is small relative to the population. However, it is not appropriate when the sample is a relatively large (5 percent or more) proportion of the population. As a result, the researcher must adjust the results obtained with the standard formulas. For example, the formula for the standard error of the mean, presented earlier, is as follows:

> **independence assumption** Assumption that sample elements are drawn independently.

$$\sigma_{\bar{x}} = \frac{\sigma}{\sqrt{n}}$$

For a sample that is 5 percent or more of the population, the independence assumption is dropped, producing the following formula:

$$\sigma_{\bar{x}} = \frac{\sigma}{\sqrt{n}} \sqrt{\frac{N - n}{N - 1}}$$

▶ **finite population correction factor (FPC)**
An adjustment to the required sample size that is made in cases where the sample is expected to be equal to 5 percent or more of the total population.

The factor $(N - n)/(N - 1)$ is referred to as the **finite population correction factor (FPC).**

In those situations in which the sample is large (5 percent or more) in relation to the population, the researcher can appropriately reduce the required sample size using the FPC. This calculation is made using the following formula:

$$n' = \frac{nN}{N + n - 1}$$

where n' = revised sample size

n = original sample size

N = population size

If the population has 2,000 elements and the original sample size is 400, then

$$n' = \frac{400(2000)}{2000 + 400 - 1} = \frac{800,000}{2399}$$

$$= 333$$

With the FPC adjustment, a sample of only 333 is needed, rather than the original 400.

The key is not the size of the sample in relation to the size of the population, but whether the sample selected is truly representative of the population. Empirical evidence shows that relatively small but carefully chosen samples can quite accurately reflect characteristics of the population. Many well-known national surveys and opinion polls, such as the Gallup Poll and the Harris Poll, are based on samples of fewer than 2,000. These polls have shown that the behavior of tens of millions of people can be predicted quite accurately using samples that are minuscule in relation to the size of the population.

Determining How Many Sample Units Are Needed

Regardless of how the target sample size is determined, the researcher is confronted with the practical problem of figuring out how many sampling units (telephone numbers, addresses, and so on) will be required to complete the assignment. For example, if the target final sample size is 400, then obviously more than 400 telephone numbers will be needed to complete a telephone survey.

Some of the numbers on the list will be disconnected, some people will not qualify for the survey because they do not meet the requirements for inclusion in the population, and some will refuse to complete the survey. These factors affect the final estimate of the number of phone numbers, which may be used to place an order with a sample provider, such as Survey Sampling, Incorporated, or to ask the client for customer names and phone numbers for a satisfaction survey. This estimate must be reasonably accurate because the researcher wants to avoid paying for more numbers than are needed; on the other hand, the researcher doesn't want to run out of numbers during the survey and have to wait for more.

PRACTICING MARKETING RESEARCH

Estimating with Precision How Many Phone Numbers Are Needed

Calculating how many phone numbers are needed for a project may seem like a difficult task, but following a few basic rules can make it simple. The formula used by Survey Sampling, Inc (SSI) to calculate sample size involves four factors: (1) the number of completed interviews needed, (2) the working phone (or "reachable") rate, (3) the incidence rate, and (4) the contact/completion rate.

Completed Interviews

The number of completed interviews is based on the sample size calculation formula for simple random samples. It is the final sample size you want to achieve.

Working Phone Rate

The working phone rate varies with the sampling methodology used. An SSI RDD sample yields a 60 percent working phone rate. That is a good number to use in the formula for estimation purposes.

Incidence Rate

The incidence rate is the percentage of contacts that will qualify for the interview. Or put another way, what percentage of people who answer the phone (or reply to your mail questionnaire) will pass your screening questions? Accurate incidence data are critical to determining proper sample size. An incidence figure that is too high will leave you short of sample once your study is in the field.

Contact/Completion Rate

The last factor is the contact/completion rate. SSI defines this rate as the percentage of people who, once they qualify for your study, will agree to cooperate by completing the interview. There are several important elements you should consider when trying to reasonably estimate the completion rate:

☐ Contact rate
☐ Length of interview
☐ Sensitivity of topic
☐ Time of year
☐ Number of attempts/callbacks
☐ Length of time in the field

Provided that the interview is short (less than 10 minutes) and nonsensitive in nature, sufficient callbacks are scheduled, and the study will be in the field for an adequate period of time, SSI estimates a 30 percent completion rate. The completion rate should be adjusted according to the specifications of each study. If the subject matter is sensitive or the interview is long, the completion rate should be reduced. If the length of time in the field is less than one week, SSI recommends increasing the sample size by at least 20 percent.

An Example

Suppose you wish to complete 300 interviews in the United Kingdom. Using a random-digit sample, you can expect a working phone rate of 60 percent. Start by dividing the number of completed interviews you need (300) by the working phone rate (.60), to yield 500. You need to reach heavy soft drink users (17 percent of adults), and you estimate that 30 percent of the people contacted will complete the interview. Divide 500 by the incidence rate for the group under study (.17) and then by the completion rate (.30). This calculation shows you need 9,804 phone numbers to complete this survey.[12]

If you wish to complete 300 interviews in the United Kingdom, you need to determine the contact/completion rate in order to figure out how many calls will actually have to be made to complete the survey.

Image State

Estimating the number of sample units needed for a telephone sample is covered in the feature on page 371.

Statistical Power

> **statistical power**
> Probability of not making a type II error.

Although it is standard practice in marketing research to use the formulas presented in this chapter to calculate sample size, these formulas all focus on *type I error*, or the error of concluding that there is a difference when there is not a difference. They do not explicitly deal with *type II error*, or the error of saying that there is no difference when there is a difference. The probability of not making a type II error is called **statistical power**.[13] The standard formulas for calculating sample size implicitly assume a power of 50 percent. For example, suppose a researcher is trying to determine which of two product concepts has stronger appeal to target customers and wants to be able to detect a 5 percent difference in the percentages of target customers who say that they are very likely to buy the products. The standard sample size formulas indicate that a sample size of approximately 400 is needed for each product test. By using this calculation, the researcher implicitly accepts the fact that there is a 50 percent chance of incorrectly concluding that the two products have equal appeal.

Exhibit 12.8 shows the sample sizes required, at an alpha (probability of incorrectly rejecting the null hypothesis) of 0.05, for specific levels of power and specific levels of

EXHIBIT 12.8	**Sample Size Required to Detect Differences between Proportions from Independent Samples at Different Levels of Power and an Alpha of 0.05**					
Difference to Detect	**Power**					
	50%	**60%**	**70%**	**75%**	**80%**	**90%**
0.01	19,205	24,491	30,857	34,697	39,239	52,530
0.05	766	977	1,231	1,384	1,568	2,094
0.10	190	242	305	343	389	518
0.15	83	106	133	150	169	226

differences between two independent proportions. Formulas are available to permit power calculations for any level of confidence; however, they are somewhat complex and will not help you understand the basic concept of power. Programs available on the Internet can be used to make these calculations. To reproduce the numbers in Exhibit 12.8, go to www.dssresearch.com/SampleSize/default.asp and do the following:

☐ Click on the Two-Sample Using Percentage Values option under Sample Size.

☐ Enter the Sample 1 Percentage and the Sample 2 Percentage in the boxes so that the figures entered reflect the differences you want to be able to detect and the values are in the expected range. These figures are set at the 50 percent level (value of p in the standard sample size formula).

☐ Below those boxes, enter the Alpha and Beta Error Levels. Alpha is the value you would use for E in the standard sample size formula, and beta is the probability of incorrectly failing to reject the null hypothesis of no difference when a real difference exists. Power is equal to $1 -$ beta.

☐ Click on the Calculate Sample Size button at the bottom of the screen for the answer.

SUMMARY ☐

Determining sample size for probability samples involves financial, statistical, and managerial considerations. Other things being equal, the larger the sample is, the smaller the sampling error. In turn, the cost of the research grows with the size of the sample.

There are several methods for determining sample size. One is to base the decision on the funds available. In essence, sample size is determined by the budget. Although seemingly unscientific, this approach is often a very realistic one in the world of corporate marketing research. The second technique is the so-called rule of thumb approach, which essentially involves determining the sample size based on a gut feeling or common practice. Samples of 300, 400, or 500 are often listed by the client in a request for proposal. A third technique for determining sample size is based on the number of subgroups to be analyzed. Generally speaking, the more subgroups that need to be analyzed, the larger is the required total sample size.

In addition to these methods, there are a number of traditional statistical techniques for determining sample size. Three pieces of data are required to make sample size calculations: an estimate of the population standard deviation, the level of sampling error that the researcher or client is willing to accept, and the desired level of confidence that the sample result will fall within a certain range of the true population value.

Crucial to statistical sampling theory is the concept of the normal distribution. The normal distribution is bell-shaped and has only one mode. It also is symmetric about its mean. The standard normal distribution has the features of a normal distribution; however, the mean of the standard normal distribution is always equal to zero, and the standard deviation is always equal to one. The transformation formula is used to transform any value X from any normal distribution to its equivalent value Z from a standard normal distribution. The central limit theorem states that the distribution of the means of a large number of random samples taken from virtually any population approaches a normal distribution with a mean equal to μ and a standard deviation equal to $S_{\bar{x}}$, where

$$S_{\bar{x}} = \frac{\sigma}{\sqrt{n}}$$

The standard deviation of a distribution of sample means is called the standard error of the mean.

When the results of a sample are used to estimate a population mean, two kinds of estimates can be generated: point and interval estimates. The sample mean is the best point estimate of the population mean. An interval estimate is a certain interval or range of values within which the true population value is estimated to fall. Along with the magnitude of the interval, the researcher usually states the probability that the interval will include the true value of the population mean—that is, the confidence level. The interval is called the confidence interval.

The researcher who is interested in estimating proportions or percentages rather than or in addition to means uses the sampling distribution of the proportion. The sampling distribution of the proportion is a relative frequency distribution of the sample proportions of a large number of random samples of a given size drawn from a particular population. The standard error of a sampling distribution of proportion is computed as follows:

$$S_p = \sqrt{\frac{P(1-P)}{n}}$$

The following are required to calculate sample size: the acceptable level of sampling error E, the acceptable level of confidence Z, and an estimate of the population standard deviation σ. The formula for calculating the required sample size for situations that involve the estimation of a mean is as follows:

$$n = \frac{Z^2\sigma^2}{E^2}$$

The following formula is used to calculate the required sample size for problems involving proportions:

$$n = \frac{Z^2[P(1-P)]}{E^2}$$

Finally, statistical power is the probability of not making a type II error. A type II error is the mistake of saying that there is not a difference when there is a difference. The standard sample size formula implicitly assumes a power of 50 percent. It may be important to use different levels of power depending on the nature of the decision in question.

KEY TERMS & DEFINITIONS

central limit theorem Idea that a distribution of a large number of sample means or sample proportions will approximate a normal distribution, regardless of the distribution of the population from which they were drawn.

normal distribution Continuous distribution that is bell-shaped and symmetric about the mean; the mean, median, and mode are equal.

proportional property of the normal distribution Feature that the number of observations falling between the mean and a given number of standard deviations from the mean is the same for all normal distributions.

standard normal distribution Normal distribution with a mean of zero and a standard deviation of one.

standard deviation Measure of dispersion calculated by subtracting the mean of the series from each value in a series, squaring each result, summing the results, dividing the sum by the number of items minus 1, and taking the square root of this value.

population distribution Frequency distribution of all the elements of a population.

sample distribution Frequency distribution of all the elements of an individual sample.

sampling distribution of the mean Theoretical frequency distribution of the means of all possible samples of a given size drawn from a particular population; it is normally distributed.

standard error of the mean Standard deviation of a distribution of sample means.

point estimate Particular estimate of a population value.

interval estimate Interval or range of values within which the true population value is estimated to fall.

confidence level Probability that a particular interval will include the true population value; also called *confidence coefficient*.

confidence interval Interval that, at the specified confidence level, includes the true population value.

sampling distribution of the proportion Relative frequency distribution of the sample proportions of many random samples of a given size drawn from a particular population; it is normally distributed.

allowable sampling error Amount of sampling error the researcher is willing to accept.

population standard deviation Standard deviation of a variable for the entire population.

independent assumption Assumption that sample elements are drawn independently.

finite population correction factor (FPC) Adjustment to the required sample size that is made in cases where the sample is expected to be equal to 5 percent or more of the total population.

statistical power Probability of not making a type II error.

QUESTIONS FOR REVIEW & CRITICAL THINKING

1. Explain how the determination of sample size is a financial, statistical, and managerial issue.
2. Discuss and give examples of three methods that are used in marketing research for determining sample size.
3. A marketing researcher analyzing the fast-food industry noticed the following: The average amount spent at a fast-food restaurant in California was $3.30, with a standard deviation of $0.40. Yet in Georgia, the average amount spent at a fast-food restaurant was $3.25, with a standard deviation of $0.10. What do these statistics tell you about fast-food consumption patterns in these two states?
4. Distinguish among population, sample, and sampling distributions. Why is it important to distinguish among these concepts?
5. What is the finite population correction factor? Why is it used? When should it be used?
6. Assume that previous fast-food research has shown that 80 percent of the consumers like curly french fries. The researcher wishes to have a standard error of 6 percent or less and be 95 percent confident of an estimate to be made about curly french fry consumption from a survey. What sample size should be used for a simple random sample?
7. You are in charge of planning a chili cook-off. You must make sure that there are plenty of samples for the patrons of the cook-off. The following standards have been set: a confidence level of 99 percent and an error of less than 4 ounces per cooking team. Last year's cook-off had a standard deviation in amount of chili cooked of 3 ounces. What is the necessary sample size?

8. Based on a client's requirements of a confidence interval of 99.74 percent and acceptable sampling error of 2 percent, a sample size of 500 is calculated. The cost to the client is estimated at $20,000. The client replies that the budget for this project is $17,000. What are the alternatives?

9. A marketing researcher must determine how many telephone numbers she needs to order from a sample provider to complete a survey of ATM users. The goal is to complete 400 interviews with ATM users. From past experience, she estimates that 60 percent of the phone numbers provided will be working phone numbers. The estimated incidence rate (percentage of people contacted who are ATM users) is 43 percent. Finally, she estimates from previous surveys that 35 percent of the people contacted will agree to complete the survey. How many telephone numbers should she order?

WORKING THE NET

1. Log on to *http://research-advisors.com/documents/SampleSize-web.xls* to get a download of an Excel spreadsheet for a sample size table. The spreadsheet enables users to change the margin of error, confidence level, and population size. Experiment with different combinations.

2. For an online statistical power calculator, go to: *www.dssresearch.com/toolkit/spcalc/power.asp* Estimate the statistical power (type II error or beta error) for existing survey projects.

3. Use the sample size calculator online at *www.dssresearch.com/toolkit/sscalc/size.asp* to work out these problems. What size samples are needed for a statistical power of 70 percent in detecting a difference of 5 percent between the estimated percentages of recent CD buyers in two independent samples? Assume an expected percentage in the range of 50 percent and an alpha error of 5 percent.

REAL-LIFE RESEARCH • 12.1

Sky Meals

Sky Meals is the second largest airline caterer in the United States, providing nearly all the meals for passengers of the three largest airlines and several smaller commuter airlines. As part of a Total Quality Management (TQM) program, one of its clients, Continental Airlines, has recently met with representatives of Sky Meals to discuss a customer satisfaction program it is planning to implement.

Continental plans to interview a sample of its customers four times a year. In the survey, it intends to ask customers to rate the quality of meals provided on a 1-to-10 scale, where 1 means poor and 10 means excellent. It has just completed a benchmark study of 1,000 customers. In that study, meals received an average rating of 8.7 on the 10-point scale, with a standard deviation of 1.65. Continental has indicated that it wants Sky Meals to guarantee a level of satisfaction of 8.5 in the first quarterly survey, to be conducted in three months. For its quarterly surveys, Continental plans to use a sample size of 500. In the new contract with Sky Meals, Continental wants to include a clause that will penalize Sky Meals $25,000 for each one-tenth of a point it falls below an average of 8.5 on the next satisfaction survey.

Questions

1. What is the 95.44 percent confidence interval for the estimated satisfaction level in the benchmark survey? What is the 99.74 percent confidence interval?

2. Assume that the upcoming first-quarter satisfaction survey shows an average rating of 8.4 on satisfaction with meals. Compute the 95.44 percent confidence interval and the 99.74 confidence interval.

3. If you were negotiating for Sky Meals, how would you respond to Continental regarding the penalty clause?

SPSS EXERCISES FOR CHAPTER 12

Exercise #1: Sample Size Determination Using the Sample Means Method SPSS-H1

1. Go to the Wiley Web site at *www.wiley.com/college/mcdaniel* and download the *Segmenting the College Student Market for Movie Attendance database* to SPSS windows. Using the *Segmenting the College Student Market for Movie Attendance* database, <u>assume that the most important items in the survey are in question #5,</u> which has nine movie items in which respondents rate their relative importance (download a copy of the *Segmenting the College Student Market for Movie Attendance* questionnaire). Notice the computer coding for each of the variables, which is the same as that in the *variable view* option on the SPSS Data Editor.

2. The Sample Means method of sample size determination consists of:
    i. required confidence level (z)
    ii. level of tolerable error (e)
    iii. estimated population variance (σ)
    iv. estimated sample size (n)
    v. *Formula:* $n = (z^2 * \sigma^2)/e^2$

3. Of the various methods of deriving sample size, estimated population standard deviation can be estimated based on prior studies, expert judgment, or by conducting a pilot sample. For this problem, we are going to estimate population standard deviation using a ***pilot sample.*** To do this you will use only the first 200 cases in the *Segmenting the College Student Market for Movie Attendance* database. Invoke the *data/select cases* sequence to select the first 200 cases in the database. We are assuming that these are responses to a pilot sample, and we will use them to estimate the needed sample size.

4. Use the *analyze/descriptive statistics/descriptive* sequence to compute the standard deviation for variables Q5a–Q5i. We are assuming that each of the nine variables is equally important with respect to the research objective.

5. From your knowledge of sample size determination, you should know that the variable to select for sample size determination is the one with <u>the largest standard deviation</u>. Select that variable.

Answer the following questions:

1. Which of the nine movie theater items had the largest standard deviation?
    _____

2. Invoke the sample means method of sample size determination to make the necessary computations for each of the following:
    a. Compute sample size given the following:
        i.   required confidence level (Z) is 95.44%.
        ii. tolerable error (e) is .1 or 1/10 of a response point.
        iii. standard deviation (σ) = _____
        iv. sample size (n) = _____
    b. Compute sample size given the following:
        i.   required confidence level (Z) is 99.72%.
        ii. tolerable level (e) is .1 or 1/10 of a response point.
        iii. standard deviation (σ) = _____
        iv. sample size (n) = _____

3. How do your computed sample sizes in the problems above compare to the total number of cases in the *Segmenting the College Student Market for Movie Attendance* database?
    _____

4. We are going to assume that the objective of our research concerning students attendance at movies can be expressed as a dichotomy (greater or lesser, etc.); for example, it doesn't matter how much one group attends movies over another group, but just *who* attends the most. To accomplish this we can use the much less complicated *sample proportions* formula. We are going to assume that we have no prior studies, hence, in the sample proportions formula P = .5 and (1 − P) = .5. **You will not need SPSS to assist you with this computation.**
    a. Compute sample size given the following:
        i.   required confidence level (Z) is 95.44%.
        ii. tolerable error (e) is .05 or accuracy within 5% of the true population mean.
        iii. standard deviation P = .5 and (1 − P) = .5
        iv. sample size (n) = _____
    b. Compute sample size given the following:
        i.   required confidence level (Z) is 99.72%.
        ii. tolerable error (e) is .03 or accuracy within 3% of the true population mean.
        iii. standard deviation P = .5 and (1 − P) = .5
        iv. sample size (n) = _____

Exercise #2: Determining the Reliability/Confidence of Sample Results

1. In the subsequent exercise the objective will not be to determine the needed sample size, but to evaluate the confidence level of results derived from the entire *Segmenting the College Student Market for Movie Attendance* database. To evaluate this type of confidence, using the sample means formula, solve for Z instead of n. Hence, use the formula $Z^2 = n * e^2/\sigma^2$. Then take the square root of Z^2. Go to the normal

distribution table in the appendix of your text to determine the confidence level associated with the database. For the sample proportions formula, solve for Z using the formula $Z^2 = (n * e^2)/[P(1 - P)]$, then take the square root of Z^2.

2. For this problem again assume that question 5 has the most important questions in the questionnaire, with respect to the research objectives. Using the *analyze/descriptive statistics/descriptives* sequence, compute the standard deviation for variables Q5a–Q5i. We are assuming that each of the nine variables are equally important with respect to the research objective. <u>Again, choose the variable with the largest standard deviation</u> to input into the analysis.

3. Given the preceding, compute the confidence level associated with the *Segmenting the College Student Market for Movie Attendance* database, given the following:
   1. a. tolerable error is .1 or 1/10 of a response point
      b. sample size = 500
      c. standard deviation _____
   2. Confidence Level = _____ %
   3. How do the results in 2, above compare to the results in 2, of the sample size determination problem?

   _____

4. <u>Sample Proportions Formula</u>: Given the information below, compute the confidence level associated with the *Segmenting the College Student Marketing for Movie Attendance* database. **You will not need SPSS to make this computation.**
   1. a. tolerable error is .05 or 5%
      b. sample size = 500
      c. standard deviation P = .5 and (1 − P) = .5
   2. Confidence Level = _____ %
   3. How do the results in this problem compare to the confidence level in the question above? _____

Justin Horricks/Stockphoto.

DATA PROCESSING, FUNDAMENTAL DATA ANALYSIS, AND THE STATISTICAL TESTING OF DIFFERENCES

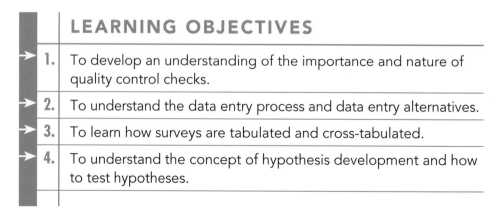

LEARNING OBJECTIVES

1.	To develop an understanding of the importance and nature of quality control checks.
2.	To understand the data entry process and data entry alternatives.
3.	To learn how surveys are tabulated and cross-tabulated.
4.	To understand the concept of hypothesis development and how to test hypotheses.

Stephanie Benson, of Technology Decisions, is the firm's account executive for Dell Computer. She recently submitted a proposal to Dell for a project involving the processing of 20,000 to 25,000 questionnaires to be collected by Dell personnel from attendees at a series of high-tech trade shows over the next six months. On this project, she will be working directly with the manager from the sales group responsible for Dell's trade show activities, Jill Jackson. Benson did not take this into account when she wrote her proposal. Normally, she worked with marketing research department staff, who would interface between her and the managers for whom the research was being done. Knowing that these marketing researchers were well acquainted with editing, coding, data entry, and tabulation procedures, she did not cover those topics in any depth in her proposal.

She has just received a lengthy e-mail from Jackson who says she likes the price quoted and the sample report included in the proposal. However, Benson can see that Jackson is a process-oriented person who wants lots of details regarding how various things will be done. Jill Jackson's questions, taken from her e-mail, follow:

- ☐ Will the questionnaires be checked for logical consistency, accuracy, and completeness before they are entered into electronic files? How will this be done? What quality checks are built into this process?

- ☐ I'm assuming that no data entry will be done until questionnaires have been checked as suggested above. Is that assumption correct?

- ☐ As you know from the sample questionnaire, the survey has seven open-ended questions. This information is very important to us. We intend to use feedback from the trade show attendees—they are either customers or people we would like to have as customers—to guide us in developing a number of sales and marketing initiatives. Therefore, it is important that we get an accurate and complete summarization of these comments. Obviously, there are far too many questionnaires for us to read and somehow summarize ourselves. In your proposal, you refer to the "coding" of open-ended questions. I have only a very general idea of what that means. What does it mean to "code" open-ended questions? How do you go about it? Outline the process. What quality control checks are built into the process? Finally, can we [management] have some input in shaping how comments are coded?

- ☐ In your proposal, you say you will enter data from the paper questionnaires after completion of the coding process. I'm assuming that you're talking about transferring the data from the paper questionnaire to an electronic file. How will this be done? What quality control procedures are built into this process so that I can be assured that the data in the electronic file accurately reflect the original responses on the paper questionnaires?

- ☐ You refer to cross tabulations in your proposal. What are cross tabulations, and how are they produced? I know they are tables of some sort. Can we have input into the design of those tables?

- ☐ Finally, is there some way that we could have access to our data over the Internet? Having access to the tables would be okay, but we really would like to be able to have access to the data and a tool that would permit us to generate any tables that we might want to produce. Is this possible?

This chapter will offer answers to Jackson's questions by providing all of the background and tools needed to perform these important tasks. The seemingly mechanical data processing activities are a critical bridge between the data-collection and data-analysis phases of a project.

You should be able to give her the answers after you read this chapter.

Overview of the Data Analysis Procedure

Once data collection has been completed and questionnaires have been returned, the researcher may be facing anywhere from a few hundred to several thousand interviews, each ranging from a few pages to 20 or more pages. We recently completed a study involving 1,300 questionnaires of 10 pages each. The 13,000 pages amounted to a stack of paper nearly 3 feet high. How should a researcher transform all the information contained on 13,000 pages of completed questionnaires into a format that will permit the summarization necessary for detailed analysis? At one extreme, the researcher could read all the interviews, make notes while reading them, and draw some conclusions from this review of the questionnaires. The folly of this approach is fairly obvious. Instead of this haphazard and inefficient approach, professional researchers follow a five-step procedure for data analysis:

Step One: Validation and editing (quality control)
Step Two: Coding
Step Three: Data entry
Step Four: Logical cleaning of data
Step Five: Tabulation and statistical analysis

Step One: Validation and Editing

The purpose of the first step is twofold. The researcher wants to make sure that all the interviews actually were conducted as specified (validation) and that the questionnaires have been filled out properly and completely (editing).

Validation

> **validation**
> Process of ascertaining that interviews actually were conducted as specified.

First, the researcher must determine, to the extent possible, that each of the questionnaires to be processed represents a valid interview. Here, we are using the term *valid* in a different sense than in Chapter 9. In Chapter 9, *validity* was defined as the extent to which what was being measured was actually measured. In this chapter, **validation** is defined as the process of ascertaining that interviews were conducted as specified. In this context, no assessment is made regarding the validity of the measurement. The goal of validation is solely to detect interviewer fraud or failure to follow key instructions. You may have noticed that the various questionnaires presented throughout the text almost always have a place to record the respondent's name, address, and telephone number. This information is seldom used in any way in the analysis of the data; it is collected only to provide a basis for validation.

Professional researchers know that interviewer cheating does happen. Various studies have documented the existence and prevalence of interviewer falsification of several types. For this reason, validation is an integral and necessary step in the data processing stage of a marketing research project.

After all the interviews have been completed, the research firm recontacts a certain percentage of the respondents surveyed by each interviewer. Typically, this percentage ranges from 10 to 20 percent. If a particular interviewer surveyed 50 people and the research firm normally validates at a 10 percent rate, 5 respondents surveyed by that interviewer would be recontacted by telephone. Telephone validation typically answers four questions:

1. Was the person actually interviewed?

2. Did the person who was interviewed qualify to be interviewed according to the screening questions on the survey? For example, the interview may have required that the

PRACTICING MARKETING RESEARCH

Tips to Avoid Interview Fraud at the Level of the Data-Collection Company

Market researchers have a grasp of the possibility of interviewer falsification of field data, but what happens when an entire data-collection company fabricates data?

In 2003, the Smoke-Free Homes Research Project, which was run out of the University of Prince Edward Island in Canada, learned that its data-collection agency had cheated. The Project had hired the firm to conduct 1,410 telephone interviews of households, then a year later, another 1,410 homes. The survey firm completed the data sets on time, but soon, during an examination of the results, project administrators discovered "inexplicable inconsistencies" in the data collected in year 2 of the survey.

They found that the data-collection company had fabricated many interviews by copying and pasting parts or all of genuine interviews to generate the number called for. When the administrators looked again at the results of the first year's data, they discovered additional glaring evidence of cheating, "similar, but more cunningly concealed fabricated data." In all, 23 percent of the surveys from both years were fraudulent.

Knowing convincingly that survey fraud originating at a level beyond the individual interviewer is a real problem, the researchers devised a "menu of options" that market researchers could usefully incorporate to prevent or at least detect interviewer fraud at the data company level. Here are some of their practical tips:

1. Don't contract with companies whose managers or staff also do for-profit telephone promotions, sales, or customer service.
2. Create survey centers within a university context where research is an integral part of the intellectual culture.
3. Engage a third-party or security consultant to supervise the making of deals with research bidders.
4. Scrutinize the researcher's references, previous clients, and sources.
5. Pay on a time-spent basis, not for numbers of finished surveys.
6. Spread out data collection between two companies.
7. Discuss explicitly in advance of the project the general problem of interview cheating with the data collection company.
8. Include open-ended questions, which are hard to fabricate, and record all data collected to discourage the likelihood of made-up data.
9. Require an operator signature for each finished interview.
10. Develop a certification and registration system for data managers.[1]

Questions

1. What "inexplicable inconsistencies" would you look for in evaluating whether a data collection company had fabricated the interviews?
2. If you contracted data collection on a time-spent basis, how would you ensure the collection agency was not fabricating labor hours?

---

person being interviewed come from a family with an annual household income of $25,000 or more. On validation, the respondent would again be asked whether the annual household income for his or her family was $25,000 or more per year.

3. Was the interview conducted in the required manner? For example, a mall survey should have been conducted in the designated mall. Was this particular respondent

A mall survey should be conducted in the designated mall. An important part of data analysis is validating that the data were gathered as specified.

PhotoDisc, Inc./Getty Images.

≽ editing
Process of ascertaining that questionnaires were filled out properly and completely.

≽ skip pattern
Sequence in which later questions are asked, based on a respondent's answer to an earlier question or questions.

interviewed in the mall, or was she or he interviewed at some other place, such as a restaurant or someone's home?

4. Did the interviewer cover the entire survey? Sometimes interviewers recognize that a potential respondent is in a hurry and may not have time to complete the entire survey. If respondents for that particular survey are difficult to find, the interviewer may be motivated to ask the respondent a few questions at the beginning and a few questions at the end and then fill out the rest of the survey without the respondent's input. Validation for this particular problem would involve asking respondents whether they were asked various questions from different points in the interview.

Validation also usually involves checking for other problems. For example: Was the interviewer courteous? Did the interviewer speculate about the client's identity or the purpose of the survey? Does the respondent have any other comments about the interviewer or the interview experience?

The purpose of the validation process, as noted earlier, is to ensure that interviews were administered properly and completely. Researchers must be sure that the research results on which they are basing their recommendations reflect the legitimate responses of target individuals.

Editing

Whereas validation involves checking for interviewer cheating and failure to follow instructions, **editing** involves checking for interviewer and respondent mistakes. Paper questionnaires usually are edited at least twice before being submitted for data entry. First, they may be edited by the field service firm that conducted the interviews, and then they are edited by the marketing research firm that hired the field service firm to do the interviewing. CATI, Internet, and other software-driven surveys have built-in logical checking. The editing process for paper surveys involves manual checking for a number of problems, including the following:

1. *Whether the Interviewer Failed to Ask Certain Questions or Record Answers for Certain Questions.* In the questionnaire shown in Exhibit 13.1, no answer was recorded for question 19. According to the structure of the questionnaire, this question should have been asked of all respondents. Also, the respondent's name does not give a clear indication of gender. The purpose of the first edit—the field edit—is to identify these types of problems when there is still time to recontact the respondent and determine the appropriate answer to questions that were not asked. This may also be done at the second edit (by the marketing research firm), but in many instances there is not time to recontact the respondent and the interview has to be discarded.

2. *Whether Skip Patterns Were Followed.* According to the **skip pattern** in question 2 in Exhibit 13.1 if the answer to this question is "Very unlikely" or "Don't know," the interviewer should skip to question 16. The editor needs to make sure that the interviewer followed instructions. Sometimes, particularly during the first few interviews in a particular study, interviewers get mixed up and skip when they should not or fail to skip when they should.

3. *Whether the Interviewer Paraphrased Respondents' Answers to Open-Ended Questions.* Marketing researchers and their clients usually are very interested in the responses to open-ended questions. The quality of the responses, or at least what was recorded, is an excellent indicator of the competence of the interviewer who recorded them. Interviewers are trained to record responses verbatim and not to paraphrase or insert

Exhibit 13.1

Sample Questionnaire

Consumer Survey
Cellular Telephone Survey Questionnaire

Long Branch—Asbury, N.J.

Date ___1-05-09___   (01-03) _001_

Respondent Telephone Number _____201-555-2322_____

Hello. My name is ___Sally___ with POST Research. May I please speak with the male or female head of the household?

(IF INDIVIDUAL NOT AVAILABLE, RECORD NAME AND CALLBACK INFORMATION ON SAMPLING FORM.)

(WHEN MALE/FEMALE HEAD OF HOUSEHOLD COMES TO PHONE): Hello, my name is _____, with POST Research. Your number was randomly selected, and I am not trying to sell you anything. I simply want to ask you a few questions about a new type of telephone service.

1. First, how many telephone calls do you make during a typical day?

                                                                                                        (04)

0–2 1
3–5 2
6–10 . . . . .③
11–15 4
16–20 5
More than 20 6
Don't know 7

Now, let me tell you about a new service called cellular mobile telephone service, which is completely wireless. You can get either a portable model that may be carried in your coat pocket or a model mounted in any vehicle. You will be able to receive calls and make calls, no matter where you are. Although cellular phones are wireless, the voice quality is similar to your present phone service. This is expected to be a time-saving convenience for household use.

This new cellular mobile phone service may soon be widely available in your area.

2. Now, let me explain to you the cost of this wireless service. Calls will cost 26 cents a minute plus normal toll charges. In addition, the monthly minimum charge for using the service will be $7.50 and rental of a cellular phone will be about $40. Of course, you can buy the equipment instead of leasing it. At this price, do you think you would be very likely, somewhat likely, somewhat unlikely, or very unlikely to subscribe to the new phone service?

                                                                                                        (05)

Very likely 1
Somewhat likely . . . . .②
Somewhat unlikely 3
Very unlikely . . . .(GO TO QUESTION 16) 4
Don't know . . . .(GO TO QUESTION 16) 5

INTERVIEWER—IF "VERY UNLIKELY" OR "DON'T KNOW," GO TO QUESTION 16.

3. Do you think it is likely that your employer would furnish you with one of these phones for your job?

                                                                                                        (06)

No . . . .(GO TO QUESTION 5) 1
Don't know . . . .(GO TO QUESTION 5) 2
Yes . . . .(CONTINUE) . . . . .③

INTERVIEWER—IF "NO" OR "DON'T KNOW," GO TO QUESTION 5; OTHERWISE CONTINUE.

4. If your employer did furnish you with a wireless phone, would you also purchase one for household use?

                                                                                                        (07)

Yes . . . .(CONTINUE) . . . . .①
No . . . .(GO TO QUESTION 16) 2
Don't know . . . .(GO TO QUESTION 16) 3

5. Please give me your best estimate of the number of mobile phones your household would use (write in "DK" for "Don't know").

Number of Units _____ _01_ _____ (08–09)

■ **Exhibit 13.1**

Sample Questionnaire
(continued)

6. Given that cellular calls made or received will cost 26 cents a minute plus normal toll charges during weekdays, how many calls on the average would you expect to make in a typical weekday?

RECORD NUMBER _____06_____ (10–11)

7. About how many minutes would your average cellular call last during the week?

RECORD NUMBER _____05_____ (12–13)

8. Weekend cellular calls made or received will cost 8 cents per minute plus normal toll charges. Given this, about how many cellular calls on the average would you expect to make in a typical Saturday or Sunday?

RECORD NUMBER _____00_____ (14–15)

9. About how many minutes would your average cellular call last on Saturday or Sunday?

RECORD NUMBER _____ (16–17)

10. You may recall from my previous description that two types of cellular phone units will be available. The vehicle phone may be installed in any vehicle. The portable phone will be totally portable—it can be carried in a briefcase, purse, or coat pocket. The totally portable phones may cost about 25 percent more and may have a more limited transmitting range in some areas than the vehicle phone. Do you think you would prefer portable or vehicle phones if you were able to subscribe to this service?

(18)
Portable 1
Vehicle . . . . .②
Both 3
Don't know 4

11. Would you please tell me whether you, on the average, would use a mobile phone about once a week, less than once a week, or more than once a week from the following geographic locations.

	Less Than Once a Week	Once a Week	More Than Once a Week	Never	
Monmouth County	1	2	③	4	(19)
(IF "NEVER," SKIP TO QUESTION 16)					
Sandy Hook	1	2	3	④	(20)
Keansburg	1	2	3	④	(21)
Atlantic Highlands	1	2	③	4	(22)
Matawan-Middletown	①	2	3	4	(23)
Red Bank	①	2	3	4	(24)
Holmdel	1	2	③	4	(25)
Eatontown	1	②	3	4	(26)
Long Branch	1	2	3	④	(27)
Freehold	1	2	3	④	(28)
Manalapan	1	2	3	④	(29)
Cream Ridge	1	2	3	④	(30)
Belmar	1	2	3	④	(31)
Point Pleasant	1	2	③	4	(32)

I'm going to describe to you a list of possible extra features of the proposed cellular service. Each option I'm going to describe will cost not more than $3.00 a month per phone. Would you please tell me if you would be very interested, interested, or uninterested in each feature:

	Very Interested	Interested	Uninterested
12. Call forwarding (the ability to transfer any call coming in to your mobile phone to any other phone).	①	2	3 (33)
13. No answer transfer (service that redirects calls to another number if your phone is unanswered).	1	2	③ (34)

Exhibit 13.1

Sample Questionnaire
(continued)

	Very Interested	Interested	Uninterested
14. Call waiting (a signal that another person is trying to call you while you are using your phone).	1	②	3 (35)
15. Voice mailbox (a recording machine that will take the caller's message and relay it to you at a later time. This service will be provided at $5.00 per month).	1	2	③ (36)

16. What is your age group? (READ BELOW)

(37)

Under 25 1
25–44 . . . . .②
45–64 3
65 and over 4
Refused, no answer, or don't know 5

17. What is your occupation?

(38)

Manager, official, or proprietor . . . . .①
Professional (doctors, lawyers, etc.) 2
Technical (engineers, computer programmers, draftsmen, etc.) 3
Office worker/clerical 4
Sales 5
Skilled worker or foreman 6
Unskilled worker 7
Teacher 8
Homemaker, student, retired 9
Not now employed X
Refused . . . . .Y

18. Into which category did your total family income fall in 2008? (READ BELOW)

(39)

Under $15,000 1
$15,000-$24,999 2
$25,000-$49,999 3
$50,000-$74,999 4
$75,000 and over . . . . .⑤
Refused, no answer, don't know 6

19. (INTERVIEWER—RECORD SEX OF RESPONDENT):

(40)

Male 1
Female 2

20. May I have your name? My office calls about 10 percent of the people I talk with to verify that I have conducted the interview.

Gave name . . . . .①
Refused 2

Jordan Beasley
Name

Thank you for your time. Have a good day.

Exhibit 13.2

Recording of Open-Ended Questions

A. Example of Improper Interviewer Recording of Response to an Open-Ended Question

Question: Why do you go to Burger King most often among fast food/quick service restaurants? (PROBE)

Response recorded:
The consumer seemed to think Burger King had better tasting food and better quality ingredients.

B. Example of Interviewer Failure to Probe a Response

Question: Same as Part A.

Only response recorded:
Because I like it.

C. Example of Proper Recording and Probing

Question: Same as Part A.

Response recorded:
Because I like it. (P)[*] I like it, and I go there most often because it is the closest place to where I work. (AE)[**] No.

---

[*](P) is an interviewer mark indicating he or she has probed a response.

[**](AE) is interviewer shorthand for "Anything else?" This gives the respondent an opportunity to expand on the original answer.

their own language. They also are instructed to probe the initial response. The first part of Exhibit 13.2 shows an example of an interviewer's paraphrasing and interpretation of a response to an open-ended question. The second part of Exhibit 13.2 shows the result of interviewer failure to probe a response. The response is useless from a decision-making perspective. It comes as no surprise that the respondent goes to Burger King most often because he likes it. The third part of Exhibit 13.2 shows how an initial meaningless response can be expanded to a useful response by means of proper probing. A proper probe to the answer "Because I like it" would be "Why do you like it?" or "What do you like about it?" The respondent then indicates that he goes there most often because it is the fast-food restaurant most convenient to his place of work.

The person doing the editing must make judgment calls in regard to substandard responses to open-ended questions. She or he must decide at what point particular answers are so limited as to be useless and whether respondents should be recontacted.

The editing process is extremely tedious and time-consuming. (Imagine for a moment reading through 13,000 pages of interviews!) However, it is a very important step in the processing of survey responses.

Step Two: Coding

 coding
Process of grouping and assigning numeric codes to the various responses to a question.

Coding refers to the process of grouping and assigning numeric codes to the various responses to a particular question. Most questions on surveys are closed-ended and precoded, meaning that numeric codes have been assigned to the various responses on the questionnaire. All answers to closed-ended questions should be precoded, as they are in question 1 on the questionnaire in Exhibit 13.1. Note that each answer has a numeric code to its right; the answer "0–2" has the code 1, the answer "3–5" has the code 2, and so on. The interviewer can record the response by circling the numeric code next to the answer given by the respondent. In this case, the respondent's answer was seven calls per day. The code 3 next to the category "6–10" (calls per day) is circled.

Open-ended questions create a coding dilemma. They were phrased in an open-ended manner because the researcher either had no idea what answers to expect or wanted a richer response than is possible with a closed-ended question. As with editing, the process of coding responses to open-ended questions is tedious and time-consuming. In addition, the procedure is to some degree subjective.[2] For these reasons, researchers tend to avoid open-ended questions unless they are absolutely necessary.

Coding Process

The process of coding responses to open-ended questions includes the following steps:

1. *List Responses.* Coders at the research firm prepare lists of the actual responses given to each open-ended question on a particular survey. In studies of a few hundred respondents, all responses may be listed. With larger samples, responses given by a sample of respondents are listed. The listing of responses may be done as part of the editing process or as a separate step, often by the same individuals who edited the questionnaires.

2. *Consolidate Responses.* A sample list of responses to an open-ended question is provided in Exhibit 13.3. Examination of this list indicates that a number of the responses can be interpreted to mean essentially the same thing; therefore, they can be appropriately consolidated into a single category. This process of consolidation might yield the list shown in Exhibit 13.4. Consolidating requires a number of subjective decisions—for example, does response number 4 in Exhibit 13.3 belong in category 1 or should it have its own category? These decisions typically are made by a qualified research analyst and may involve client input.

EXHIBIT 13.3	Sample of Responses to Open-Ended Question

Question: Why do you drink that brand of beer? (BRAND MENTIONED IN ANSWER TO PREVIOUS QUESTION)

Sample responses:
1. Because it tastes better.
2. It has the best taste.
3. I like the way it tastes.
4. I don't like the heavy taste of other beers.
5. It is the cheapest.
6. I buy whatever beer is on sale. It is on sale most of the time.
7. It doesn't upset my stomach the way other brands do.
8. Other brands give me headaches. This one doesn't.
9. It has always been my brand.
10. I have been drinking it for over 20 years.
11. It is the brand that most of the guys at work drink.
12. All my friends drink it.
13. It is the brand my wife buys at the grocery store.
14. It is my wife's/husband's favorite brand.
15. I have no idea.
16. Don't know.
17. No particular reason.

EXHIBIT 13.4	Consolidated Response Categories and Codes for Open-Ended Responses from Beer Study

Response Category Descriptor	Response Items from Exhibit 13.3 included	Assigned Numeric Code
Tastes better/like taste/tastes better than others	1, 2, 3, 4	1
Low/lower price	5, 6	2
Does not cause headache, stomach problems	7, 8	3
Long-term use, habit	9, 10	4
Friends drink it/influence of friends	11, 12	5
Wife/husband drinks/buys it	13, 14	6

3. *Set Codes.* A numeric code is assigned to each of the categories on the final consolidated list of responses. Code assignments for the sample beer study question are shown in Exhibit 13.4.

4. *Enter Codes.* After responses have been listed and consolidated and codes set, the last step is the actual entry of codes. This involves several substeps:

   a. Read responses to individual open-ended questions on questionnaires.
   b. Match individual responses with the consolidated list of response categories, and determine the appropriate numeric code for each response.
   c. Write the numeric code in the appropriate place on the questionnaire for the response to the particular question (see Exhibit 13.5) or enter the appropriate code in the database electronically.[3]

Here's an example of the process, using the listing of responses shown in Exhibit 13.3 and the consolidation and setting of codes shown in Exhibit 13.4.

☐ You turn to the first questionnaire and read this response to the question "Why do you drink that brand of beer?": "Because it's cheaper."

☐ You compare this response with the consolidated response categories and decide that it best fits into the "Low/lower price" category. The numeric code associated with this category is 2 (see Exhibit 13.4).

☐ You enter the code in the appropriate place on the questionnaire (see Exhibit 13.5).

Automated Coding Systems

With CATI and Internet surveys, data entry and coding are completely eliminated for closed-ended questions. However, when the text of open-ended questions is electronically captured, a coding process is still required. A number of developments are making it likely that the tedious coding process for open-ended questions will soon be replaced with computer-based systems requiring limited high-level human intervention and decision making.[4]

EXHIBIT 13.5	Example Questionnaire Setup for Open-Ended Questions

37. Why do you drink that brand of beer? (BRAND MENTIONED IN PREVIOUS QUESTION)?

(48) ___2

Because it's cheaper. (P) Nothing. (AE) Nothing.

PRACTICING MARKETING RESEARCH

Text Analytics Software Streamlines Coding Open-Ended Responses

As market researchers well know, the major shortcoming of open-ended questions in a survey is the postinterview coding. Opinion-based answers do not easily lend themselves to simple numerical coding. It is very expensive, in terms of time and effort, to categorize individualized responses, and it tends to limit survey size so as to avoid this complication during data processing.

Keyword-based search software helps the human analysis of open-ended responses, but typically this kind of software cannot deal with the variety of unstructured responses. Each answer must be interpreted by an analyst at an average cost of $2.00 to $5.00 per question.

A Text Analytics software program called Content Analyst offers an automated way to code open-ended responses and cut costs (and processing time) by about 50 percent. This makes it feasible to conduct in-depth surveys of 100,000, for example, asking many open-ended questions without concern for the prohibitive postinterview cost of coding. The software automates the laborious analysis of conceptual information and the processing and interpretation of large volumes of open-ended data. The product is made by Content Analyst Company, LLC, of Reston, Virginia (www.contentanalyst.com).

"It's taking us in the direction of concept-based coding rather than keyword coding, and that's a significant advance," comments Justin Greeves of Worthlin Worldwide, an opinion research company based in MacLean, Virginia, that uses the software. The approach, Greeves adds, takes us one step closer to the "automation of human-level analysis." The software also shifts the focus from coding answers to a higher-value interpretation of results. "The open ends reveal the voice of the customer," so that their different and unstructured answers are no longer a problem but a source of greater, more valuable market information.[5]

The TextSmart module of SPSS is one example of the automated coding systems. Algorithms based on semiotics are at the heart of these systems and show great promise for speeding up the coding process, reducing its cost, and increasing its objectivity. Basically, these algorithms use the power of computers to search for patterns in open-ended responses and in group responses, based on certain keywords and phrases.

Step Three: Data Entry

Once the questionnaires have been validated, edited, and coded, it's time for the next step in the process—data entry. We use the term **data entry** here to refer to the process of converting information to a form that can be read by a computer. This process requires a data entry device, such as a PC, and a storage medium, such as a hard (magnetic) disk.

> **data entry**
> Process of converting information to an electronic format.

Intelligent Entry Systems

Most data entry is done by means of intelligent entry systems. With **intelligent data entry,** the information entered is checked for internal logic. Intelligent entry systems can be programmed to avoid certain types of errors at the point of data entry, such as invalid or wild codes and violation of skip patterns.

> **intelligent data entry**
> Form of data entry in which the information being entered into the data entry device is checked for internal logic.

Consider question 2 on the questionnaire in Exhibit 13.1. The five valid answers have the associated numeric codes 1 through 5. An intelligent data entry system programmed for valid codes would permit the data entry operator to enter only one of these codes in the field reserved for the response to this question. If the operator attempts to enter a code other than those defined as valid, the device will inform the data entry operator in some manner that there is a problem. The data entry device, for example, might beep and display a message on the screen that the entered code is invalid. It will not advance to the next appropriate field until the code has been corrected. Of course, it is still possible to incorrectly enter a 3 rather than the correct answer 2. Referring again to question 2, note that if the answer to the question is "Very unlikely" or "Don't know," then the data entry operator should skip to question 16. An intelligent data entry device will make this skip automatically.

The Data Entry Process

The validated, edited, and coded questionnaires have been given to a data entry operator seated in front of a personal computer. The data entry software system has been programmed for intelligent entry. The actual data entry process is ready to begin. Usually, the data are entered directly from the questionnaires, because experience has shown that a large number of errors are introduced when questionnaire data are transposed manually to coding sheets. Going directly from the questionnaire to the data entry device and associated storage medium is much more accurate and efficient. To better understand the mechanics of the process, look again at Exhibit 13.1.

- ☐ In the upper right-hand corner of the questionnaire, the number 001 is written. This number uniquely identifies the particular questionnaire, which should be the first questionnaire in the stack that the data entry operator is preparing to enter. This number is an important point of reference because it permits the data entry staff to refer back to the original document if any errors are identified in connection with the data input.

- ☐ To the left of the handwritten number 001 is (01–03). This tells the data entry operator that 001 should be entered into fields 01–03 of the data record. Throughout the questionnaire, the numbers in parentheses indicate the proper location on the data record for the circled code for the answer to each question. Question 1 has (04) associated with the codes for the answers to the question. Thus, the answer to this question would be entered in field 04 of the data record. Now, take a look at the open-ended question in Exhibit 13.5. As with closed-ended questions, the number in parentheses refers to the field on the data record where the code or codes for the response to this question should be entered. Note the number 2 written in to the right of (48); a 2 should be entered in field 48 of the data record associated with this questionnaire.

Exhibit 13.1 clearly illustrates the relationship between the layout of the questionnaire, in terms of codes (numbers associated with different answers to questions) and fields (places on the data record where the code is entered), and the layout of the data record.

Scanning

As all students know, the scanning of documents (test scoring sheets) has been around for decades. It has been widely used in schools and universities as an efficient way to capture and score responses to multiple-choice questions. However, until more recently, its use in marketing research has been limited. This limited use can be attributed to two factors: setup costs and the need to record all responses with a No. 2 pencil. Setup costs include the cost of special paper, special ink in the printing process, and very precise placement of the bubbles for recording responses. The break-even point, at which the savings in data entry costs exceeded the setup costs, was in the 10,000 to 12,000 survey range. Therefore, for most surveys, scanning was not feasible.

However, changes in **scanning technology** and the advent of personal computers have changed this equation. Today, questionnaires prepared with any one of a number of Windows word-processing software packages and printed on a laser printer or by a standard printing process can be readily scanned, using the appropriate software and a scanner attached to a personal computer. In addition, the latest technology permits respondents to fill out the survey using almost any type of writing implement (any type of pencil, ballpoint pen, or ink pen). This eliminates the need to provide respondents with a No. 2 pencil and greatly simplifies the process of mailing surveys. Finally, the latest technology does not require respondents to carefully shade the entire circle or square next to their response choices; they can put shading, a check mark, an X, or any other type of mark in the circle or square provided for the response choice.[6]

As a result of these developments, the use of scannable surveys is growing dramatically. An analyst who expects more than 400 to 500 surveys to be completed will find scannable surveys to be cost-effective.

Though no reliable volume figures are available, it is an accepted fact that the amount of survey data being captured electronically is increasing. For example, electronic data capture is used in computer-assisted telephone interviewing, Internet surveys, and TouchScreen kiosk surveys.

> **scanning technology**
> Form of data entry in which responses on questionnaires are read in automatically by the data entry device.

Step Four: Logical Cleaning of Data

At this point, the data from all questionnaires have been entered and stored in the computer that will be used to process them. It is time to do final error checking before proceeding to the tabulation and statistical analysis of the survey results. Many colleges have one or more statistical software packages available for the tabulation and statistical analysis of data, including SAS (Statistical Analysis System) and SPSS (Statistical Package for the Social Sciences), which have proven to be the most popular mainframe computer statistical packages. Most colleges have personal computer versions of SPSS and SAS, in addition to other PC statistical packages. The number of other PC packages is large and growing.

Regardless of which computer package is used, it is important to do a final computerized error check of the data, or what is sometimes referred to as **logical cleaning of data**. This may be done through error checking routines and/or marginal reports.

Some computer programs permit the user to write **error checking routines**. These routines include a number of statements to check for various conditions. For example, if a particular field on the data records for a study should be coded with only a 1 or a 2, a logical statement can be written to check for the presence of any other code in that field. Some of the more sophisticated packages generate reports indicating how many times a particular condition was violated and the data records on which it was violated. With this list, the user can refer to the original questionnaires and determine the appropriate values.

Exhibit 13.6 illustrates the **marginal report,** another approach to machine cleaning often used for error checking. The first row of this report lists the fields of the data record. The columns show the frequency with which each possible value was encountered in each field. For example, the second row in Exhibit 13.6 shows that in field 111 of the data record

> **logical cleaning of data**
> Final computerized error check of data.

> **error checking routines**
> Computer programs that accept instructions from the user to check for logical errors in the data.

> **marginal report**
> Computer-generated table of the frequencies of the responses to each question, used to monitor entry of valid codes and correct use of skip patterns.

EXHIBIT 13.6		Sample Marginal Report (Marginal Counts of 300 Records)												
FIELD	1	2	3	4	5	6	7	8	9	10	11	12	BL	TOT
111	100	100	1	0	0	0	0	0	0	99	0	0	0	300
112	30	30	30	30	30	30	30	30	30	0	0	0	0	300
113	30	30	30	30	30	30	30	30	30	30	0	0	0	300
114	67	233	0	0	0	0	0	0	0	0	0	0	0	300
115	192	108	0	0	0	0	0	0	0	0	0	0	0	300
116	108	190	0	0	0	0	0	0	0	0	0	2	0	300
117	13	35	8	0	2	136	95	7	2	0	0	0	2	298
118	0	0	0	0	0	0	0	0	0	0	0	2	298	2
119	29	43	12	1	2	48	50	6	4	1	0	0	104	196
1111	6	16	6	1	1	10	18	4	2	0	0	0	236	64
1113	3	4	1	1	0	1	2	0	1	0	0	0	288	12
1115	0	0	0	1	1	0	0	2	0	0	0	0	296	4
1117	24	2	22	0	1	239	9	2	0	0	0	0	1	299
1118	0	0	0	0	0	0	0	0	0	0	0	0	299	1
1119	4	49	6	0	0	81	117	5	2	0	0	0	36	264
1120	0	0	0	0	0	0	0	0	0	0	0	36	264	36
1121	5	60	6	0	0	84	116	4	3	1	0	0	21	279
1122	0	0	0	0	0	0	0	0	0	0	0	21	279	21
1123	118	182	0	0	0	0	0	0	0	0	0	0	0	300
1124	112	187	0	0	0	0	0	0	0	0	0	0	1	299
1125	47	252	0	0	0	0	0	0	0	0	0	1	0	300
1126	102	198	0	0	0	0	0	0	0	0	0	0	0	300
1127	5	31	5	1	0	33	31	9	1	0	0	0	184	116
1128	0	0	0	0	0	0	0	0	0	0	0	2	298	2
1129	0	3	1	0	0	4	8	2	1	0	0	0	281	19
1131	7	16	3	0	2	60	21	3	0	0	0	0	188	112
1133	1	3	1	0	0	2	3	1	0	0	0	0	289	11

for this study there are 100 "1" punches, 100 "2" punches, 1 "3" punch, and 99 "10" punches. This report permits the user to determine whether inappropriate codes were entered and whether skip patterns were properly followed. If all the numbers are consistent, there is no need for further cleaning. However, if logical errors (violated skip patterns and impossible codes) are detected, then the appropriate original questionnaires must be located and the corrections made in the computer data file. Note that these procedures cannot identify situations in which an interviewer or data entry operator incorrectly entered a 2 for a "no" response instead of a 1 for a "yes" response.

This is the final error check in the process. When this step is completed, the computer data file should be ready for tabulation and statistical analysis. Exhibit 13.7 shows the data for the first 50 respondents (out of a total of 400) for the study associated with the questionnaire shown in Exhibit 13.1. Note that the apparent gaps in the data are a result of the skip called for in question 4. Also note that the gender data (noted as missing earlier) for respondent 001 has been filled in with a 2 for female based on information obtained by recontacting the respondent.

Step Five: Tabulation and Statistical Analysis

The survey results have been stored in a computer file and are free of logical data entry and interviewer recording errors. The next step is to tabulate the survey results.

EXHIBIT 13.7	Printout of Data for the First 50 Respondents for Cellular Telephone Survey

```
001323101060500    23443113244444313232152

00224                                23412
00334                                49622
00414                                36221
00524                                33312
00634                                22612
00714                                21321
008221  02040503103342324444344442222929321
00925                                36311
01044                                23311
0116131024005033013423444443443322330321
012622  0140072007334444444444444132330511
013221  01060306032313123333233221232216211
01424                                29321
01514                                40121
01624                                22612
01774                                20622
01854                                34621
01924                                25212
02024                                23622
02114                                16611
02214                                36211
02314                                15611
024131    001010041022133444444444442229611
02524                                26621
026131  0101030203124221422244414223222611
02724                                10122
02814                                59622
02924                                39622
03024                                49611
03134                                53621
03234                                32622
03321       01       1244444444444444211220211
03424                                32622
035311  041030043013313113111313121120121
036232303010502013344144333442442323220622
03724                                37622
03814                                40121
03934                                30121
04024                                16121
04124                                26311
04264                                26411
04324                                20321
04414                                26311
04524                                19321
04634                                19222
04724                                29621
04824                                31422
04924                                33121
05014                                21311
```

One-Way Frequency Tables

➤ one-way frequency table
Table showing the number of respondents choosing each answer to a survey question.

The most basic tabulation is the **one-way frequency table,** which shows the number of respondents who gave each possible answer to each question. An example of this type of table appears in Exhibit 13.8. This table shows that 144 consumers (48 percent) said they would choose a hospital in St. Paul, 146 (48.7 percent) said they would choose a hospital in Minneapolis, and 10 (3.3 percent) said they didn't know which location they would choose. A printout is generated with a one-way frequency table for every question on the survey. In most instances, a one-way frequency table is the first summary of survey results seen by the research analyst. In addition to frequencies, these tables typically indicate the percentage of those responding who gave each possible response to a question.

An issue that must be dealt with when one-way frequency tables are generated is what base to use for the percentages for each table. There are three options for a base:

1. *Total Respondents.* If 300 people are interviewed in a particular study and the decision is to use total respondents as the base for calculating percentages, then the percentages in each one-way frequency table will be based on 300 respondents.

2. *Number of People Asked the Particular Question.* Because most questionnaires have skip patterns, not all respondents are asked all questions. For example, suppose question 4 on a particular survey asked whether the person owned any dogs and 200 respondents indicated they were dog owners. Since questions 5 and 6 on the same survey were to be asked only of those individuals who owned a dog, questions 5 and 6 should have been asked of only 200 respondents. In most instances, it would be appropriate to use 200 as the base for percentages associated with the one-way frequency tables for questions 5 and 6.

3. *Number of People Answering the Question.* Another alternative base for computing percentages in one-way frequency tables is the number of people who actually answered a particular question. Under this approach, if 300 people were asked a particular question but 28 indicated "Don't know" or gave no response, then the base for the percentages would be 272.

Ordinarily, the number of people who were asked a particular question is used as the base for all percentages throughout the tabulations, but there may be special cases in which other bases are judged appropriate Exhibit 13.9 is a one-way frequency table in which three different bases are used for calculating percentages.

EXHIBIT 13.8	**One-Way Frequency Table**

Q.30 If you or a member of your family were to require hospitalization in the future, and the procedure could be performed in Minneapolis or St. Paul, where would you choose to go?

	Total
Total	300 100%
To a hospital in St. Paul	144 48.0%
To a hospital in Minneapolis	146 48.7%
Don't know/no response	10 3.3%

EXHIBIT 13.9	One-Way Frequency Table Using Three Different Bases for Calculating Percentages

Q.35 Why would you not consider going to St. Paul for hospitalization?

	Total[a] Respondents	Total Asked	Total Answering
Total	300	64	56
	100%	100%	100%
They aren't good/service poor	18	18	18
	6%	28%	32%
St. Paul doesn't have the services/equipment that Minneapolis does	17	17	17
	6%	27%	30%
St. Paul is too small	6	6	6
	2%	9%	11%
Bad publicity	4	4	4
	1%	6%	7%
Other	11	11	11
	4%	17%	20%
Don't know/no response	8	8	
	3%	13%	

[a]A total of 300 respondents were surveyed. Only 64 were asked this question because in the previous question those respondents said they would not consider going to St. Paul for hospitalization. Only 56 respondents gave an answer other than "Don't know".

Some questions, by their nature, solicit more than one response from respondents. For example, consumers might be asked to name all brands of vacuum cleaners that come to mind. Most people will be able to name more than one brand. Therefore, when these answers are tabulated, there will be more responses than respondents. If 200 consumers are surveyed and the average consumer names three brands, then there will be

The base for each percentage must be determined before one-way frequency tables are run. If a survey question asks whether the person has a dog and 200 respondents indicate that they do, further questions designated for dog owners should have only 200 respondents.

Corbis Digital Photo.

EXHIBIT 13.10	Percentages for a Multiple-Response Question Calculated on the Basis of Total Respondents and Total Responses	

Q.34 To which of the following towns and cities would you consider going for hospitalization?

	Total Respondents	Total Responses
Total	300	818
	100%	100%
Minneapolis	265	265
	88.3%	32.4%
St. Paul	240	240
	80.0%	29.3%
Bloomington	112	112
	37.3%	13.7%
Rochester	92	92
	30.7%	11.2%
Minnetonka	63	63
	21.0%	7.7%
Eagan	46	46
	15.3%	5.6%

200 respondents and 600 answers. The question is, should percentages in frequency tables showing the results for these questions be based on the number of respondents or the number of responses? Exhibit 13.10 shows percentages calculated using both bases. Most commonly, marketing researchers compute percentages for multiple-response questions on the basis of the number of respondents, reasoning that the client is primarily interested in the proportion of people who gave a particular answer.

Cross Tabulations

> **cross tabulation**
> Examination of the responses to one question relative to the responses to one or more other questions.

Cross tabulations are likely to be the next step in analysis. They represent a simple-to-understand, yet powerful, analytical tool. Many marketing research studies go no further than cross tabulations in terms of analysis. The idea is to look at the responses to one question in relation to the responses to one or more other questions. Exhibit 13.11 shows a simple cross tabulation that examines the relationship between cities consumers are willing to consider for hospitalization and their age. This cross tabulation includes frequencies and percentages, with the percentages based on column totals. This table shows an interesting relationship between age and likelihood of choosing Minneapolis or St. Paul for hospitalization. Consumers in successively older age groups are increasingly likely to choose St. Paul and increasingly less likely to choose Minneapolis.

Following are a number of considerations regarding the setup of cross tabulation tables and the determination of percentages within them:

☐ The previous discussion regarding the selection of the appropriate base for percentages applies to cross tabulation tables as well.

☐ Three different percentages may be calculated for each cell in a cross tabulation table: column, row, and total percentages. Column percentages are based on the column total, row percentages are based on the row total, and total percentages

---

EXHIBIT 13.11 | Sample Cross Tabulation

Q.30 If you or a member of your family were to require hospital-ization in the future, and the procedure could be performed in Minneapolis or St. Paul, where would you choose to go?

	Total	Age 18–34	35–54	55–64	65 or Over
Total	300	65	83	51	100
	100%	100%	100%	100%	100%
To a hospital in St. Paul	144	21	40	25	57
	48.0%	32.3%	48.2%	49.0%	57.0%
To a hospital in Minneapolis	146	43	40	23	40
	48.7%	66.2%	48.2%	45.1%	40.0%
Don't know/no response	10	1	3	3	3
	3.3%	1.5%	3.6%	5.9%	3.0%

are based on the table total. Exhibit 13.12 shows a cross tabulation table in which the frequency and all three of the percentages are shown for each cell in the table.

☐ A common way of setting up cross tabulation tables is to use columns to represent factors such as demographics and lifestyle characteristics, which are expected to be predictors of the state of mind, behavior, or intentions data shown as rows of the table. In such tables, percentages usually are calculated on the basis of column

---

EXHIBIT 13.12 | Cross Tabulation Table with Column, Row, and Total Percentages[a]

Q.34 To which of the following towns and cities would you consider going for hospitalization?

	Total	Male	Female
Total	300	67	233
	100.0%	100.0%	100.0%
	100.0%	22.3%	77.7%
	100.0%	22.3%	77.7%
St. Paul	265	63	202
	88.3%	94.0%	86.7%
	100.0%	23.6%	76.2%
	88.3%	21.0%	67.3%
Minneapolis	240	53	187
	80.0%	79.1%	80.3%
	100.0%	22.1%	77.9%
	80.0%	17.7%	62.3%
Bloomington	112	22	90
	37.3%	32.8%	38.6%
	100.0%	19.6%	80.4%
	37.3%	7.3%	30.0%

[a]Percentages listed are column, row, and total percentages, respectively.

PRACTICING MARKETING RESEARCH

Six Practical Tips for Easier Cross Tabulations

Cross tabulation is a valuable method of mining further data and significance and teasing out unsuspected relationships from your basic survey data. Here are six practical tips to improve your cross tabulation gleanings from Custom Insight, a provider of Web-based survey software located in Carson City, Nevada (www.custominsight.com).

1. **Make hypotheses.** Probably you already have one or two hunches about what the data might yield in cross tabulation. Articulate your initial hypotheses and use them as a starting point for cross tabulation.

2. **Look for what is not there.** After you observe what the data manifestly shows, examine it for what it doesn't show, that is, relationships that you may have assumed to be real or substantive. For example, if your hypothesis postulates that people with higher incomes plan to make more purchases, the data may actually refute that and thus reveal a new set of data—that affluent people are not planning to spend.

3. **Scrutinize for the obvious.** Some relationships among the data may be obvious (e.g., age and student status). Finding these evident connections early on will validate your results and inspire greater confidence that your survey interviewers did a competent job.

4. **Keep your mind open.** Don't be tied to your hypotheses and assumptions. You may see data relationships that you hadn't expected and that are not congruent with your hypotheses. Think about the data from this new angle and formulate new hypotheses to account for them.

5. **Trust the data.** If your results don't match your initial expectations, maybe they're wrong, not the data. Study the data for new relationships even if they contradict your starting hypotheses.

6. **Watch the *n*.** Small totals should raise suspicions, and if you have few respondents in a given category, do not trust the data or look for stronger trends first before drawing final conclusions. For example, your study shows that 38 percent of people under age 15 want a particular product, except that only 8 people comprise that 38 percent. Better is the fact that 88 percent of people under 15 are students. Even though the number of respondents is minimal, the relationship exhibited by the data (88 percent) is much stronger and can be trusted.[7]

---

totals. This approach permits easy comparisons of the relationship between, say, lifestyle characteristics and expected predictors such as sex or age. For example, in Exhibit 13.11 this approach facilitates examination of how people in different age groups differ in regard to the particular factor under examination.

Cross tabulations provide a powerful and easily understood approach to the summarization and analysis of survey research results. However, it is easy to become swamped by the sheer volume of computer printouts if a careful tabulation plan has not been developed. The cross tabulation plan should be created with the research objectives and hypotheses in mind. Because the results of a particular survey might be cross tabulated in an almost endless number of ways, it is important for the analyst to exercise judgment and select from all the possibilities only those cross tabulations that are truly responsive to the research objectives of the project. Spreadsheet programs such as Excel and nearly all statistics packages (SAS, SPSS, SYSTAT, STATISTICA) can generate cross tabulations.

A complex cross tabulation, generated using the UNCLE software package, is shown in Exhibit 13.13. UNCLE was designed with the special needs of marketing researchers in mind and is widely used in the marketing research industry. As indicated, this more complex table is sometimes referred to as a *stub and banner table*. The column headings are the banner and the row titles are the stub. In this single table, the relationship between marital status and each of seven other variables is explored. Cross tabulation can be produced in Excel, but it is a cumbersome process.

Graphic Representations of Data

You have probably heard the saying "One picture is worth a thousand words." Graphic representations of data use pictures rather than tables to present research results. Results—particularly key results—can be presented most powerfully and efficiently through graphs.

Marketing researchers have always known that important findings identified by cross tabulation and statistical analysis could be best presented graphically. However, in the early years of marketing research, the preparation of graphs was tedious, difficult, and time-consuming. The advent of personal computers, coupled with graphics software and laser printers, has changed all of this. Spreadsheet programs such as Excel have extensive graphics capabilities, particularly in their Windows versions. In addition, programs designed for creating presentations, such as PowerPoint, permit the user to generate a wide variety of high-quality graphics with ease. With these programs, it is possible to do the following:

☐ Quickly produce graphs
☐ Display those graphs on the computer screen
☐ Make desired changes and redisplay
☐ Print final copies on a laser or inkjet printer

All of the graphs shown in this section were produced using a personal computer, a laser printer, and a graphics software package.

Line Charts

Line charts are perhaps the simplest form of graphs. They are particularly useful for presenting a given measurement taken at several points over time. Exhibit 13.14 shows monthly sales data for Just Add Water, a retailer of women's swimwear. The results reveal similar sales patterns for 2001 and 2002, with peaks in June and generally low sales in January through March and September through December. Just Add Water is evaluating the sales data to identify product lines that it might add to improve sales during those periods.

Pie Charts

Pie charts are another type of graph that is frequently used. They are appropriate for displaying marketing research results in a wide range of situations. Exhibit 13.15 shows radio music preferences gleaned from a survey of residents of several Gulf Coast metropolitan areas in Louisiana, Mississippi, and Alabama. Note the three-dimensional effect produced by the software.

EXHIBIT 13.13 A Stub and Banner Table

North Community College—Anywhere, U.S.A.
Q.1c. Are you single, married, or formerly married?

	Total	Zones			Gender		Age		
		1	2	3	M	F	18–34	35–54	55 and Over
Total	300	142	103	55	169	131	48	122	130
	100%	100%	100%	100%	100%	100%	100%	100%	100%
Married	228	105	87	36	131	97	36	97	95
	76%	74%	84%	65%	78%	74%	75%	80%	73%
Single	5	1	2	2	4	1	2	1	2
	2%	1%	2%	4%	2%	1%	4%	1%	2%
Formerly married	24	11	10	3	12	12	3	9	12
	8%	8%	10%	5%	7%	9%	6%	7%	9%
Refused to answer	43	25	4	14	22	21	7	15	21
	14%	18%	4%	25%	13%	16%	15%	12%	16%

Exhibit 13.14

Line Chart for Sales of Women's Swimwear

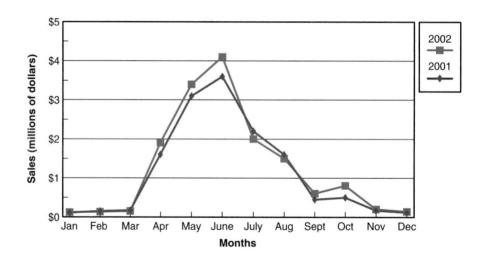

Exhibit 13.15

Three-Dimensional Pie Chart for Types of Music Listened to Most Often

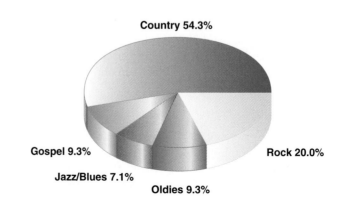

	Race			Family Profile		Vote History		Registered Voter	
	White	Black	Other	Child <18 years	Child >18 years	2–3 Times	4 Times or More	Yes	No
	268	28	4	101	53	104	196	72	228
	100%	100%	100%	100%	100%	100%	100%	100%	100%
	207	18	3	82	39	80	148	58	170
	77%	64%	75%	81%	74%	77%	76%	81%	75%
	5	—	—	—	—	2	3	1	4
	2%	—	—	—	—	2%	2%	1%	2%
	18	6	—	5	6	10	14	3	21
	7%	21%	—	5%	11%	10%	7%	4%	9%
	38	4	1	14	8	12	31	10	33
	14%	14%	25%	14%	15%	12%	16%	14%	14%

Bar Charts

Bar charts may be the most flexible of the three types of graphs discussed in this section. Anything that can be shown in a line graph or a pie chart also can be shown in a bar chart. In addition, many things that cannot be shown—or effectively shown—in other types of graphs can be readily illustrated in bar charts. Four types of bar charts are discussed here.

1. *Plain bar chart.* As the name suggests, plain bar charts are the simplest form of bar chart. The same information displayed in the pie chart in Exhibit 13.15 is shown in the bar chart in Exhibit 13.16. Draw your own conclusions regarding whether the pie chart or the bar chart is the more effective way to present this information. Exhibit 13.16 is a traditional two-dimensional chart. Many of the software packages available today can take the same information and present it

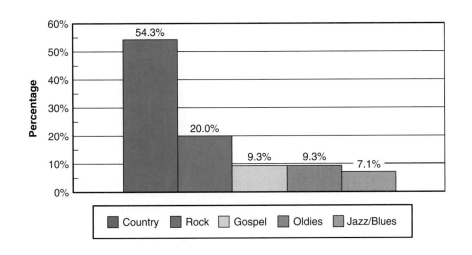

Exhibit 13.16

Simple Two-Dimensional Bar Chart for Types of Music Listened to Most Often

PRACTICING MARKETING RESEARCH

Expert Tips on Making Bad Graphics Every Time

He may sound tongue-in-cheek, but information visualization expert Juan C. Dürsteler thinks the funny approach to teaching data graphic design can be effective. Ideally, a reader's reaction to an excellent graphic should be an exclamation as to how interesting the data are. But often data graphics fail to work that way. Dürsteler, who earned his Ph.D. from the Universidad Politécnica de Catalunya in Spain in computer-assisted design systems, adapts and comments on the design specifications of Howard Wainer laid down in his book, *Visual Revelations* (Lawrence Erlbaum, 1997). Dürsteler assigns them to two primary categories of misapproach: (1) occultation and (2) inconsistency. Follow these approaches, and your data graphics, he assures us, will be terrible.

Occultation: This means, simply, hide everything important and avoid showing the relevant data. Specifically, Dürsteler offers six recommendations under this topic to ensure your design is terrible:

- Reduce to a minimum the data density (put miniscule data on a large chart).
- Minimize the data/ink ratio (use a little ink for the data but lots for the axis, reference grid, and labels).
- Hide the key differences (use a scale that makes them hard to see).
- Display the data out of proper context (omit previous supporting data).

- Put a lot of attention on the trivial (ensure that what catches one's attention is not the key conclusion).
- Make sure your labels are hard to read, incomplete, and unclear (there are lots of ways to achieve this: be original).

Inconsistency: Employ inconsistent techniques in your data codification and graphic presentation, change tactics and emphases in midstream, Dürsteler notes, and you'll be on your way to achieving this technique for bad graphics:

- Ignore the codification (make the lengths or data areas nonproportional to its values).
- Focus your codes in one dimension, next represent them in many (codify the lengths, and then show areas or volumes).
- Shift your regularity in the middle of the axis (for example, start with steps of eight years, then end up with one-year steps).
- Contrast the values between curves or alter the situation regarding the origin of the data so you cannot compare in the same conditions (stacked bar charts are good for this).[8]

Questions

1. Come up with two more ways to hide data and two more ways to be inconsistent in presenting data graphics.
2. Find three examples of inept data graphics from either academic or mainstream published sources and analyze how they fail.

---

with a three-dimensional effect, as shown in Exhibit 13.17. Again, decide for yourself which approach is visually more appealing and interesting.

2. *Clustered bar chart.* The clustered bar chart is one of three types of bar charts useful for showing the results of cross tabulations. The radio music preference results are cross tabulated by age in Exhibit 13.18 the graph shows that country music is mentioned most often as the preferred format by those over 35 and those 35 or under. The graph also shows that rock music is a close second for those 35 or under

and is least frequently mentioned by those over 35. The results suggest that if the target audience is those in the 35 or under age group, then a mix of country and rock music is appropriate. A focus on country music probably would be the most efficient approach for those over 35.

3. *Stacked bar chart.* Like clustered bar charts, stacked bar charts are helpful in graphically representing cross tabulation results. The same music preference data shown in Exhibit 13.18 are presented as a stacked bar chart in Exhibit 13.19.

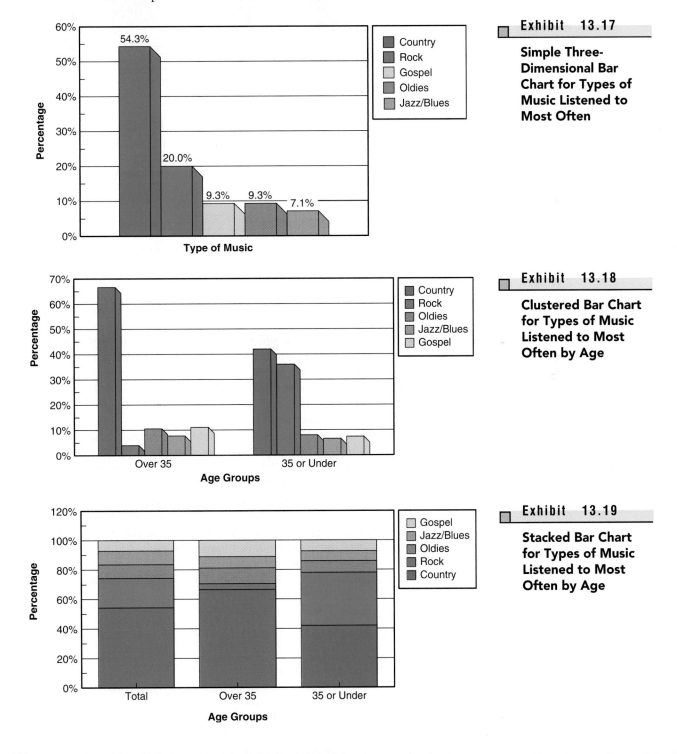

Exhibit 13.17

Simple Three-Dimensional Bar Chart for Types of Music Listened to Most Often

Exhibit 13.18

Clustered Bar Chart for Types of Music Listened to Most Often by Age

Exhibit 13.19

Stacked Bar Chart for Types of Music Listened to Most Often by Age

Exhibit 13.20

Multiple-Row, Three-Dimensional Bar Chart for Types of Music Listened to Most Often by Age

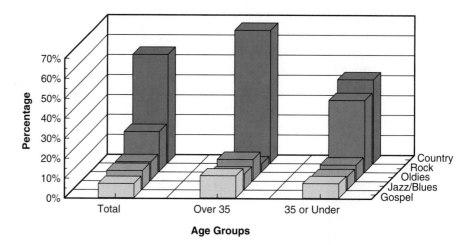

4. *Multiple-row, three-dimensional bar chart.* This type of bar chart provides what we believe to be the most visually appealing way of presenting cross tabulation information. The same music preference data displayed in Exhibit 13.18 and 13.19 are presented in a multiple-row, three-dimensional bar chart in Exhibit 13.20.

Descriptive Statistics

Descriptive statistics are the most efficient means of summarizing the characteristics of large sets of data. In a statistical analysis, the analyst calculates one number or a few numbers that reveal something about the characteristics of large sets of data.

Measures of Central Tendency

Before beginning this section, you should review the types of data scales presented in Chapter 9. Recall that there are four basic types of measurement scales: nominal, ordinal, interval, and ratio. Nominal and ordinal scales are sometimes referred to as nonmetric scales, whereas interval and ratio scales are called metric scales. Many of the statistical procedures discussed in this section and in following sections require metric scales, whereas others are designed for nonmetric scales.

> **mean**
> Sum of the values for all observations of a variable divided by the number of observations.

The three measures of central tendency are the arithmetic mean, median, and mode. The **mean** is properly computed only from interval or ratio (metric) data. It is computed by adding the values for all observations for a particular variable, such as age, and dividing the resulting sum by the number of observations. With survey data, the exact value of the variable may not be known; it may be known only that a particular case falls in a particular category. For example, an age category on a survey might be 18 to 34 years of age. If a person falls into this category, the person's exact age is known to be somewhere between 18 and 34. With grouped data, the midpoint of each category is multiplied by the number of observations in that category, the resulting totals are summed, and the total is then divided by the total number of observations. This process is summarized in the following formula:

$$\overline{X} = \frac{\sum_{i=1}^{h} f_i X_i}{n}$$

where
f_i = frequency of the i th class
X_i = midpoint of that class
h = number of classes
n = total number of observations

The **median** can be computed for all types of data except nominal data. It is calculated by finding the value below which 50 percent of the observations fall. If all the values for a particular variable were put in an array in either ascending or descending order, the median would be the middle value in that array. The median is often used to summarize variables such as income when the researcher is concerned that the arithmetic mean will be affected by a small number of extreme values and, therefore, will not accurately reflect the predominant central tendency of that variable for that group.

median
Value below which 50 percent of the observations fall.

The **mode** can be computed for any type of data (nominal, ordinal, interval, or ratio). It is determined by finding the value that occurs most frequently. In a frequency distribution, the mode is the value that has the highest frequency. One problem with using the mode is that a particular data set may have more than one mode. If three different values occur with the same level of frequency and that frequency is higher than the frequency for any other value, then the data set has three modes. The mean, median, and mode for sample data on beer consumption are shown in Exhibit 13.21.

mode
Value that occurs most frequently.

Measures of Dispersion

Frequently used measures of dispersion include standard deviation, variance, and range. Whereas measures of central tendency indicate typical values for a particular variable, measures of dispersion indicate how spread out the data are. The dangers associated with relying only on measures of central tendency are suggested by the example shown in Exhibit 13.22. Note that average beer consumption is the same in both markets—3 cans/bottles/glasses. However, the standard deviation is greater in market two, indicating more dispersion in the data. Whereas the mean suggests that the two markets are the same, the added information provided by the standard deviation indicates that they are different.

EXHIBIT 13.21 Mean, Median, and Mode for Beer Consumption Data

A total of 10 beer drinkers (drink one or more cans, bottles, or glasses of beer per day on the average) were interviewed in a mall-intercept study. They were asked how many cans, bottles, or glasses of beer they drink in an average day.

Respondent	Number of Cans/Bottles/Glasses per Day
1	2
2	2
3	3
4	2
5	5
6	1
7	2
8	2
9	10
10	1

Mode = 2 cans/bottles/glasses
Median = 2 cans/bottles/glasses
Mean = 3 cans/bottles/glasses

| EXHIBIT 13.22 | Measures of Dispersion and Measures of Central Tendency |

Consider the beer consumption data presented in Exhibit 13.21. Assume that interviewing was conducted in two markets. The results for both markets are shown.

Respondent	Number of Cans/ Bottles/Glasses Market One	Number of Cans/ Bottles/Glasses Market Two
1	2	1
2	2	1
3	3	1
4	2	1
5	5	1
6	1	1
7	2	1
8	2	3
9	10	10
10	1	10
Mean	3	3
Standard deviation	2.7	3.7

Occupation is an example of a categorical variable. The only results that can be reported for a variable of this type are the frequency and the relative percentage with which each category was encountered.

Corbis Stock Market.

The formula for computing the standard deviation for a sample of observations is as follows:

$$S = \sqrt{\frac{\sum_{i=1}^{n}(X_i - \overline{X})^2}{n-1}}$$

where
S = sample standard deviation
X_i = value of the ith observation
$\overline{X}$ = sample mean
n = sample size

The variance is calculated by using the formula for standard deviation with the square root sign removed. That is, the sum of the squared deviations from the mean is divided by the number of observations minus 1. Finally, the range is equal to the maximum value for a particular variable minus the minimum value for that variable.

Percentages and Statistical Tests

In performing basic data analysis, the research analyst is faced with the decision of whether to use measures of central tendency (mean, median, mode) or percentages (one-way frequency tables, cross tabulations). Responses to questions either are categorical or take the form of continuous variables. Categorical variables such as "Occupation" (coded 1 for professional/managerial, 2 for clerical, etc.) limit the analyst to reporting the frequency and relative percentage with which each category was encountered. Variables such as age can be continuous or categorical, depending on how the information was obtained. For example, an interviewer can ask people their actual age or ask them which category (under 35, 35 or older) includes their age. If actual age data are available, mean age can be readily computed. If categories are used, one-way frequency tables and cross tabulations are the most obvious choices for analysis. However, continuous data can be put into categories, and means can be estimated for categorical data by using the formula for computing a mean for grouped data (presented earlier).

Finally, statistical tests are available that can indicate whether two means—for example, average expenditures by men and average expenditures by women at fast-food restaurants—or two percentages differ to a greater extent than would be expected by chance (sampling error) or whether there is a significant relationship between two variables in a cross tabulation table.

Evaluating Differences and Changes

The issue of whether certain measurements are different from one another is central to many questions of critical interest to marketing managers. Some specific examples of managers' questions follow:

- ☐ Our posttest measure of top-of-mind awareness is slightly higher than the level recorded in the pretest. Did top-of-mind awareness really increase, or is there some other explanation for the increase? Should we fire or commend our agency?

- ☐ Our overall customer satisfaction score increased from 92 percent three months ago to 93.5 percent today. Did customer satisfaction really increase? Should we celebrate?

- ☐ Satisfaction with the customer service provided by our cable TV system in Dallas is, on average, 1.2 points higher on a 10-point scale than is satisfaction with the customer service provided by our cable TV system in Cincinnati. Are customers in Dallas really more satisfied? Should the customer service manager in Cincinnati be replaced? Should the Dallas manager be rewarded?

- ☐ In a recent product concept test, 19.8 percent of those surveyed said they were very likely to buy the new product they evaluated. Is this good? Is it better than the results we got last year for a similar product? What do these results suggest in terms of whether to introduce the new product?

- ☐ A segmentation study shows that those with incomes of more than $30,000 per year frequent fast-food restaurants 6.2 times per month on average. Those with incomes of $30,000 or less go an average of 6.7 times. Is this difference real—is it meaningful?

- ☐ In an awareness test, 28.3 percent of those surveyed have heard of our product on an unaided basis. Is this a good result?

These are the eternal questions in marketing and marketing research. Although considered boring by some, statistical hypothesis testing is important because it helps researchers get closer to the ultimate answers to these questions. We say "closer" because certainty is never achieved in answering these questions in marketing research.

Statistical Significance

The basic motive for making statistical inferences is to generalize from sample results to population characteristics. A fundamental tenet of statistical inference is that it is possible for numbers to be different in a mathematical sense but not significantly different in a statistical sense. For example, suppose cola drinkers are asked to try two cola drinks in a blind taste test and indicate which they prefer; the results show that 51 percent prefer one test product and 49 percent prefer the other. There is a mathematical difference in the results, but the difference would appear to be minor and unimportant. The difference probably is well within the range of accuracy of researchers' ability to measure taste preference and thus probably is not significant in a statistical sense. Three different concepts can be applied to the notion of differences when we are talking about results from samples:

- ☐ *Mathematical differences.* By definition, if numbers are not exactly the same, they are different. This does not, however, mean that the difference is either important or statistically significant.

- ☐ *Statistical significance.* If a particular difference is large enough to be unlikely to have occurred because of chance or sampling error, then the difference is statistically significant.

- ☐ *Managerially important differences.* One can argue that a difference is important from a managerial perspective only if results or numbers are sufficiently different. For example, the difference in consumer responses to two different packages in a test market might be statistically significant but yet so small as to have little practical or managerial significance.[9]

This chapter covers different approaches to testing whether results are statistically significant.

Hypothesis Testing

> **hypothesis**
> Assumption or theory that a researcher or manager makes about some characteristics of the population under study.

A **hypothesis** is an assumption or guess that a researcher or manager makes about some characteristic of the population being investigated. The marketing researcher is often faced with the question of whether research results are different enough from the norm that some element of the firm's marketing strategy should be changed. Consider the following situations.

- ☐ The results of a tracking survey show that awareness of a product is lower than it was in a similar survey conducted six months ago. Are the results significantly lower? Are the results sufficiently low enough to call for a change in advertising strategy?

- ☐ A product manager believes that the average purchaser of his product is 35 years of age. A survey is conducted to test this hypothesis, and the survey shows that the average purchaser of the product is 38.5 years of age. Is the survey result different enough from the product manager's belief to cause him to conclude that his belief is incorrect?

- ☐ The marketing director of a fast-food chain believes that 60 percent of her customers are female and 40 percent are male. She does a survey to test this hypothesis and finds that, according to the survey, 55 percent are female and 45 percent are male. Is this result sufficiently different enough from her original theory to permit her to conclude that her original theory was incorrect?

All of these questions can be evaluated with some kind of statistical test. In hypothesis testing, the researcher determines whether a hypothesis concerning some characteristic of the population is likely to be true, given the evidence. A statistical hypothesis test allows us to calculate the probability of observing a particular result if the stated hypothesis is actually true.[10]

There are two basic explanations for an observed difference between a hypothesized value and a particular research result. Either the hypothesis is true and the observed difference is likely due to sampling error, or the hypothesis is false and the true value is some other value.

Steps in Hypothesis Testing

Five steps are involved in testing a hypothesis. First, the hypothesis is specified. Second, an appropriate statistical technique is selected to test the hypothesis. Third, a decision rule is specified as the basis for determining whether to reject or fail to reject (FTR) the null hypothesis H_0. Please note that we did not say "reject H_0 or accept H_0." Although a seemingly small distinction, it is an important one. The distinction will be discussed in greater detail later on. Fourth, the value of the test statistic is calculated and the test is performed. Fifth, the conclusion is stated from the perspective of the original research problem or question.

Step One: Stating the Hypothesis   Hypotheses are stated using two basic forms: the null hypothesis H_0 and the alternative hypothesis H_a. The null hypothesis H_0 (sometimes called the *hypothesis of the status quo*) is the hypothesis that is tested against its complement, the alternative hypothesis H_a (sometimes called the *research hypothesis of interest*). Suppose the manager of Burger City believes that his operational procedures will guarantee that the average customer will wait two minutes in the drive-in window line. He conducts research, based on the observation of 1,000 customers at randomly selected stores at randomly selected times. The average customer observed in this study spends 2.4 minutes in the drive-in window line. The null hypothesis and the alternative hypothesis might be stated as follows:

- ☐ Null hypothesis H_0: Mean waiting time $\neq 2$ minutes
- ☐ Alternative hypothesis H_a: Mean waiting time $= 2$ minutes

PRACTICING
MARKETING RESEARCH

Why We Need Statistical Tests of Differences

A 13-year-old spent 4.5 hours searching through the Internet for a workable definition of statistically significant. He needed the definition for his science class. Finally, he came upon Ask A Scientist, a feature sponsored by the Argonne National Laboratory, Division of Educational Programs for grades K–12. Dr. Ali Khounsary of the laboratory volunteered to answer the student's question.

Say you have a new drug to treat cancer and you try it on sick rats. You apply the drug to 100 sick rats and notice that 20 get well. Does this mean the drug works? Although it seemingly cured 20 rats, perhaps they could have recovered on their own, without the drug. Now

you test the drug on 200 sick rats, randomly selected. Divide these 200 rats into two groups of 100 each. Treat one group with the actual drug and the other with a fake or placebo drug. The person administering the real and fake drugs will not know which pills are which.

After a while, see how many rats have recovered. If 20 taking the real drug and only 5 from the placebo group are cured, then you would comfortably feel that the drug really works. But if 18 rats taking the placebo actually survived, then you would not be sure that the new drug had any effect because the difference between the two survival rates, 20 on the real drug, 18 on the placebo, is not very big.

Statistical tests provide a basis for determining whether differences are greater or not greater than we would expect due to chance.[11]

It should be noted that the null hypothesis and the alternative hypothesis must be stated in such a way that both cannot be true. The idea is to use the available evidence to ascertain which hypothesis is more likely to be true.

Step Two: Choosing the Appropriate Test Statistic   As you will see in the following sections of this chapter, the analyst must choose the appropriate statistical test, given the characteristics of the situation under investigation. A number of different statistical tests, along with the situations where they are appropriate, are discussed in this chapter. Exhibit 13.23 provides a guide to selecting the appropriate test for various situations. All the tests in this table are covered in detail later in this chapter.

Step Three: Developing a Decision Rule   Based on our previous discussions of distributions of sample means, you may recognize that one is very unlikely to get a sample result that is exactly equal to the value of the population parameter. The problem is determining whether the difference, or deviation, between the actual value of the sample mean and its expected value based on the hypothesis could have occurred by chance (5 times out of 100, for example) if the statistical hypothesis is true. A decision rule, or standard, is needed to determine whether to reject or fail to reject the null hypothesis. Statisticians state such decision rules in terms of significance levels.

The significance level (α) is critical in the process of choosing between the null and alternative hypotheses. The level of significance—.10, .05, or .01, for example—is the probability that is considered too low to justify acceptance of the null hypothesis.

Consider a situation in which the researcher has decided that she wants to test a hypothesis at the .05 level of significance. This means that she will reject the null hypothesis if the test indicates that the probability of occurrence of the observed result (for example, the difference between the sample mean and its expected value) because of chance or sampling error is less than 5 percent. Rejection of the null hypothesis is equivalent to supporting the alternative hypothesis.

Step Four: Calculating the Value of the Test Statistic   In this step, the researcher does the following:

☐ Uses the appropriate formula to calculate the value of the statistic for the test chosen

☐ Compares the value just calculated to the critical value of the statistic (from the appropriate table), based on the decision rule chosen

☐ Based on the comparison, determines to either reject or fail to reject the null hypothesis H_0

Step Five: Stating the Conclusion   The conclusion summarizes the results of the test. It should be stated from the perspective of the original research question.

Types of Errors in Hypothesis Testing

Hypothesis tests are subject to two general types of errors, typically referred to as type I error and type II error. A **type I error** involves rejecting the null hypothesis when it is, in fact, true. The researcher may reach this incorrect conclusion because the observed difference between the sample and population values is due to sampling error. The researcher must decide how willing she or he is to commit a type I error. The probability of committing a type I error is referred to as the *alpha* (α) *level*. Conversely, $1-\alpha$ is the probability of making a correct decision by not rejecting the null hypothesis when, in fact, it is true.

type I error (α error) Rejection of the null hypothesis when, in fact, it is true.

EXHIBIT 13.23	Statistical Tests and Their Users				
Area of Application	Subgroups or Samples	Level Scaling	Test	Special Requirements	Example
Hypotheses about frequency distribution	One	Nominal	χ^2	Random sample	Are observed differences in the numbers of people responding to three different promotions likely/not likely due to chance?
	Two or more	Nominal	χ^2	Random sample, independent samples	Are differences in the numbers of men and women responding to a promotion likely/not likely due to chance?
Hypotheses about means	One (large sample)	Metric (interval or ratio)	Z test for one mean	Random sample, $n \geq 30$	Is the observed difference between a sample estimate of the mean and some set standard or expected value of the mean likely/not likely due to chance?
	One (small sample)	Metric (interval or ratio)	t test for one mean	Random sample, $n < 30$	Same as for small sample above
	Two (large sample)	Metric (interval or ratio)	Z test for one mean	Random sample, $n \geq 30$	Is the observed difference between the means for two subgroups (mean income for men and women) likely/not likely due to chance?
	Three or more	Metric (interval or ratio)	One-way ANOVA	Random sample	Is the observed variation between means for three or more subgroups (mean expenditures on entertainment for high-, moderate-, and low-income people) likely/not likely due to chance?
Hypotheses about proportions	One (large sample)	Metric (interval or ratio)	Z test for one proportion	Random sample, $n \geq 30$	Is the observed difference between a sample estimate of proportion (percentage who say they will buy) and some set standard or expected value likely/not likely due to chance?
	Two (large sample)	Metric (interval or ratio)	Z test for two proportions	Random sample, $n \geq 30$	Is the observed difference between estimated percentages for two subgroups (percentage of men and women who have college degrees) likely/not likely due to chance?

A **type II error** involves failing to reject the null hypothesis when it actually is false. A type II error is referred to as a *beta* (β) *error*. The value $1 - \beta$ reflects the probability of making a correct decision in rejecting the null hypothesis when, in fact, it is false. The four possibilities are summarized in Exhibit 13.24.

As we consider the various types of hypothesis tests, keep in mind that when a researcher rejects or fails to reject the null hypothesis, this decision is never made with

type II error (β error)
Failure to reject the null hypothesis when, in fact, it is false.

EXHIBIT 13.24	Type I and Type II Errors	
Actual State of the Null Hypothesis	**Fail to Reject H$_0$**	**Reject H$_0$**
H$_0$ is true	Correct $(1-\alpha)$	Type I error (α)
H$_0$ is false	Type II error (β)	Correct $(1-\beta)$

100 percent certainty. There is a probability that the decision is correct and there is a probability that the decision is not correct. The level of α is set by the researcher, after consulting with his or her client, considering the resources available for the project, and considering the implications of making type I and type II errors. However, the estimation of β is more complicated and is beyond the scope of our discussion. Note that type I and type II errors are not complementary; that is, $\alpha+\beta \neq 1$.

It would be ideal to have control over n (the sample size), α (the probability of a type I error), and β (the probability of a type II error) for any hypothesis test. Unfortunately, only two of the three can be controlled. For a given problem with a fixed sample size, n is fixed, or controlled. Therefore, only one of α and β can be controlled.

Assume that for a given problem you have decided to set $\alpha = .05$. As a result, the procedure you use to test H$_0$ versus H$_a$ will reject H$_0$ when it is true (type I error) 5 percent of the time. You could set $\alpha = 0$ so that you would never have a type I error. The idea of never rejecting a correct H$_0$ sounds good. However, the downside is that β (the probability of a type II error) is equal to 1 in this situation. As a result, you will always fail to reject H$_0$ when it is false. For example, if $\alpha = 0$ in the fast-food service time example, where H$_0$ is mean waiting time = 2 minutes, then the resulting test of H$_0$ versus H$_a$ will automatically fail to reject H$_0$ (mean waiting time = 2 minutes) whenever the estimated waiting time is any value other than 2 minutes. If, for example, we did a survey and determined that the mean waiting time for the people surveyed was 8.5 minutes, we would still fail to reject (FTR) H$_0$. As you can see, this is not a good compromise. We need a value of α that offers a more reasonable compromise between the probabilities of the two types of errors. Note that in the situation in which $\alpha = 0$ and $\beta = 1$, $\alpha+\beta = 1$. As you will see later on, this is not true as a general rule.

The value of α selected should be a function of the relative importance of the two types of errors. Suppose you have just had a diagnostic test. The purpose of the test is to determine whether you have a particular medical condition that is fatal in most cases. If you have the disease, a treatment that is painless, inexpensive, and totally without risk will cure the condition 100 percent of the time. Here are the hypotheses to be tested:

H$_0$: Test indicates that you do not have the disease.
H$_a$: Test indicates that you do have the disease.

Thus,

$\alpha = P$(rejecting H$_0$ when it is true)
= (test indicates that you have the disease when you do not have it)
$\beta = P$(FTR H$_0$ when in fact it is false)
= P(test indicates that you do not have the disease when you do have it)

Clearly, a type I error (measured by α) is not nearly as serious as a type II error (measured by β). A type I error is not serious because the test will not harm you if you are well. However, a type II error means that you will not receive the treatment you need even though you are ill.

The value of β is never set in advance. When α is made smaller, β becomes larger. If you want to minimize type II error, then you choose a larger value for α in order to make β smaller. In most situations, the range of acceptable values for α is .01 to .1.

In the case of the diagnostic test situation, you might choose a value of α at or near .1 because of the seriousness of a type II error. Conversely, if you are more concerned about type I errors in a given situation, then a small value of α is appropriate. For example, suppose you are testing commercials that were very expensive to produce, and you are concerned about the possibility of rejecting a commercial that is really effective. If there is no real difference between the effects of type I and type II errors, as is often the case, an α value of .05 is commonly used.

Accepting H_0 versus Failing to Reject (FTR) H_0

Researchers often fail to make a distinction between accepting H_0 and failing to reject H_0. However, as noted earlier, there is an important distinction between these two decisions. When a hypothesis is tested, H_0 is presumed to be true until it is demonstrated to be likely to be false. In any hypothesis testing situation, the only other hypothesis that can be accepted is the alternative hypothesis H_a. Either there is sufficient evidence to support H_a (reject H_0) or there is not (fail to reject H_0). The real question is whether there is enough evidence in the data to conclude that H_a is correct. If we fail to reject H_0, we are saying that the data do not provide sufficient support of the claim made in H_a—not that we accept the statement made in H_0.

One-Tailed versus Two-Tailed Test

Tests are either one-tailed or two-tailed. The decision as to which to use depends on the nature of the situation and what the researcher is trying to demonstrate. For example, when the quality control department of a fast-food organization receives a shipment of chicken breasts from one of its vendors and needs to determine whether the product meets specifications in regard to fat content, a one-tailed test is appropriate. The shipment will be rejected if it does not meet minimum specifications. On the other hand, the managers of the meat company that supplies the product should run two-tailed tests to determine two factors. First, they must make sure that the product meets the minimum specifications of their customer before they ship it. Second, they want to determine whether the product exceeds specifications because this can be costly to them. If they are consistently providing a product that exceeds the level of quality they have contracted to provide, their costs may be unnecessarily high.

The classic example of a situation requiring a two-tailed test is the testing of electric fuses. A fuse must trip, or break contact, when it reaches a preset temperature or a fire may result. On the other hand, you do not want the fuse to break contact before it reaches the specified temperature or it will shut off the electricity unnecessarily. The test used in the quality control process for testing fuses must, therefore, be two-tailed.

PRACTICING MARKETING RESEARCH

Why in Medicine a Two-Tailed Test Is Preferable to a One-Tailed Test

The one-tailed hypothesis test in clinical research can seem very attractive, efficient, low-cost, and productive, yet it has some hidden problems. Lemuel A. Loye, MD, and Alan T. N. Tita, MD, physicians at the University of Texas and Baylor College of Medicine, respectively, argue that ethical researchers should studiously avoid one-tailed or one-sided testing in medical research for both ethical and cost-efficiency reasons. Why? Because a one-tailed test of a drug, for example, assumes that the drug will be safe and so the test produces no surprises and only demonstrates an unknown level of efficacy—and it will do so with a lower cost and smaller sample size.

In fact, however, that's simply not the case, as the doctors explain. In the 1990s, Dr. Loye was part of a research effort called the Cardiac Arrhythmia Suppression Trial (CAST), which used one-tailed testing of a prescription drug that was supposed to stop irregular heartbeats. CAST researchers assumed unquestioningly that this was the likely result; as it turned out, it wasn't. A lot of people died from the drug, far more than any statistical projection expected.

This incident highlights the shortcomings of one-tailed testing in medicine, say Loye and Tita: it excludes the possibility of harmful effect or negative result because the test cannot distinguish a harmful effect from a null effect (that no action or change happened). The one-tailed test does not allow researchers to draw the correct conclusions if they are proved wrong by the actual results, if the drug is harmful.

The medical community needs assurance that an injury or a negative result is not due to sampling error, and normally this assurance would come from measuring type I error. The trouble here is that one cannot tell what type I error is associated with a harmful finding in a one-tailed test exclusively designed to show only one result—that of benefit. The one-tailed test yields less "strength of evidence" for a positive result than a two-tailed test, and that may jeopardize patient health and lead to patient harm.

One-tailed testing has other limitations in medical research, too. One advantage often proposed in its favor is the reduced sample size required. This is a fallacy, Loye and Tita point out, because 79 percent of the observations needed in a two-tailed test are also needed in a one-tailed test that treats the same subject or drug. Thus any reduction in sample size that is achieved is modest at best.

Furthermore, if the one-tailed test produces a negative result, unanticipated by the test design, retesting is required. A two-tailed study in the first place needs only 63 percent of the total sample size for two separate one-tailed tests and of course avoids the necessity of test repetition. Finally, the two-sided test is "ultimately more informative" when faced with an unexpected outcome and can prevent subsequent patient exposure to or harm from interventions otherwise (wrongly) greenlighted by a one-tailed test.[12]

Questions

1. Are there any circumstances in clinical research where a one-tailed test would be ethically justified?

2. Are there any situations in market research where a one-tailed test might yield data that could lead to harmful effects or conclusions?

The quality control department of a fast-food organization would probably do a one-tailed test to determine whether a shipment of chicken breasts met product specifications. However, a two-tailed test would probably be done by the managers of the meat company that supplied the chicken breasts.

PhotoDisc, Inc./Getty Images.

Example of Performing a Statistical Test

Income is an important determinant of the sales of luxury cars. Lexus North America (LNA) is in the process of developing sales estimates for the Southern California market, one of its key markets. According to the U.S. Census, the average annual family income in the market is $55,347. LNA has just completed a survey of 250 randomly selected households in the market to obtain other measures needed for its sales forecasting model. The recently completed survey indicates that the average annual family income in the market is $54,323. The actual value of the population mean (μ) is unknown. This gives us two estimates of μ: the census result and the survey result. The difference between these two estimates could make a substantial difference in the estimates of Lexus sales produced by LNA's forecasting model. In the calculations, the U.S. Census Bureau estimate is treated as the best estimate of (μ)

LNA decides to statistically compare the census and survey estimates. The statistics for the sample are

$$\overline{X} = \$54{,}323$$
$$S = \$4{,}323$$
$$n = 250$$

The following hypotheses are produced:

$$H_0: \mu = \$55{,}347$$
$$H_a: \mu \neq \$55{,}347$$

The decision makers at LNA are willing to use a test that will reject H_0 when it is correct only 5 percent of the time ($\alpha = .05$). This is the significance level of the test.

LNA will reject H_0 if $|\bar{X}-\$55,347|$ is larger than can be explained by sampling error at $\alpha = .05$.

Standardizing the data so that the result can be directly related to Z values in Exhibit 2 in the Appendix, we have the following criterion:

Reject H_0 if $|\bar{X}-\$55,347/S/\sqrt{n}|$ is larger than can be explained by sampling error at $\alpha = .05$. This expression can be rewritten as

$$\left|\frac{\bar{X}-\$55,347}{S/\sqrt{n}}\right| > k$$

What is the value of k? If H_0 is true and the sample size is large (≥ 30), then (based on the central limit theorem) X approximates a normal random variable with

$$\text{Mean} = \mu = \$55,347$$
$$\text{Standard deviation} = \frac{S}{\sqrt{n}}$$

That is, if H_0 is true, $(\bar{X}-\$55,347)/(S/\sqrt{n})$ approximates a standard normal variable Z for samples of 30 or larger with a mean equal to 0 and a standard deviation equal to 1.

We will reject H_0 if $|Z| > k$. When $|Z| > k$, either $Z > k$ or $Z < -k$, as shown in Exhibit 13.25. Given that

$$P(|Z| > k) = .05$$

the total shaded area is .05, with .025 in each tail (two-tailed test). The area between 0 and k is .475. Referring to Exhibit 2 in the Appendix, we find that $k = 1.96$. Therefore, the test is

$$\text{Reject } H_0 \text{ if } \left|\frac{\bar{X}-\$55,347}{S/\sqrt{n}}\right| > 1.96$$

Exhibit 13.25

Shaded Area Is Significance Level α

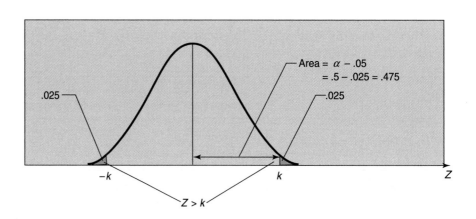

and FTR H_0 otherwise. In other words,

$$\text{Reject } H_0 \text{ if } \left| \frac{\bar{X}-\$55,347}{S/\sqrt{n}} \right| > 1.96 \text{ or if } \left| \frac{\bar{X}-\$55,347}{S/\sqrt{n}} \right| < 1.96$$

The question is, is $\bar{X} = \$54,323$ far enough away from \$55,347 for LNA to reject H_0? The results show that

$$Z = \frac{\bar{X}-\$55,347}{S/\sqrt{n}}$$
$$= \frac{\$54,323-\$55,347}{\$4,322/\sqrt{250}} = -3.75$$

Because $-3.75 < -1.96$, we reject H_0. On the basis of the sample results and $\alpha = .05$, the conclusion is that the average household income in the market is not equal to \$55,347. If H_0 is true ($\mu = \$55,347$), then the value of $\bar{X}$ obtained from the sample (\$54,323) is 3.75 standard deviations to the left of the mean on the normal curve for $\bar{X}$. A value of $\bar{X}$ this far away from the mean is very unlikely (probability is less than .05). As a result, we conclude that H_0 is not likely to be true, and we reject it.

Commonly Used Statistical Hypothesis Tests

A number of commonly used statistical hypothesis tests of differences are presented in the following sections. Many other statistical tests have been developed and are used, but a full discussion of all of them is beyond the scope of this text.

The distributions used for comparing the computed and tabular values of the statistics are the Z distribution, the t distribution, the chi-square (χ^2) distribution, and the F distribution. The tabular values for these distributions appear in Exhibits 2, 3, 4, and 5 of the Appendix.

Independent versus Related Samples

In some cases, one needs to test the hypothesis that the value of a variable in one population is equal to the value of that same variable in another population. Selection of the appropriate test statistic requires the researcher to consider whether the samples are independent or related. **Independent samples** are those in which measurement of the variable of interest in one sample has no effect on measurement of the variable in the other sample. It is not necessary that there be two different surveys, only that the measurement of the variable in one population has no effect on the measurement of the variable in the other population. In the case of **related samples,** measurement of the variable of interest in one sample may influence measurement of the variable in another sample.

If, for example, men and women were interviewed in a particular survey regarding their frequency of eating out, there is no way that a man's response could affect or change the way a woman would respond to a question in the survey. Thus, this would be an example of independent samples. On the other hand, consider a situation in which the researcher needed to determine the effect of a new advertising campaign on consumer

independent samples
Samples in which measurement of a variable in one population has no effect on measurement of the variable in the other.

related samples
Samples in which measurement of a variable in one population may influence measurement of the variable in the other.

PRACTICING MARKETING RESEARCH

A Simple Field Application of Chi-Square Goodness of Fit

Say you are a marketing manager and you want to know if an observed pattern of frequencies differs from an expected pattern. The best test for addressing this question is the chi-square test of goodness of fit in which only one categorical variable is involved. Here's how to apply it in a case of packaging color design.

As a marketing manager you have five colors to choose from for your packaging design, but you can only use one. Which one does the market prefer? Obviously, you want to know this before you debut the product. You do a random sampling of 400 consumers and ask them, getting these results:

Package Color	Consumer Preference
Red	70
Blue	106
Green	80
Pink	70
Orange	74
Total	**400**

The results suggest that people prefer blue, but you need to be sure that this seeming preference for blue is not a chance result. Your null hypothesis posits that all colors are preferred equally, but your alternative hypothesis says they are not equally preferred. In the calculations, note that in terms of the null hypothesis for equal preference for all colors, the expected frequencies for all colors will equal 80. The chi-square value is 11.40 calculated per the standard formula. The results are below.

Because the critical value of chi-square at the 0.5 level of significance (5 percent probability of incorrectly rejecting the null hypothesis) for 4 degrees of freedom is 9.488, you can eliminate the null hypothesis. You can conclude that consumers do not equally prefer all colors but in fact like blue the best. As marketing manager, you can introduce your product in a blue package and do so confident that it is the best option of those available to you.[13]

Package Color	Observed Frequencies (O)	Expected Frequencies (E)	(O−E)	$\chi^2 = \sum \left(\dfrac{(O-E)^2}{E} \right)$
Red	70	80	100	1.25
Blue	106	80	676	8.45
Green	80	80	0	0.00
Pink	70	80	100	1.25
Orange	74	80	36	0.45
Total	**400**	**400**	—	**11.40**

awareness of a particular brand. To do this, the researcher might survey a random sample of consumers before introducing the new campaign and then survey the same sample of consumers 90 days after the new campaign was introduced. These samples are not independent. The measurement of awareness 90 days after the start of the campaign may be affected by the first measurement.

Degrees of Freedom

Many of the statistical tests discussed in this chapter require the researcher to specify *degrees of freedom* in order to find the critical value of the test statistic from the table for that statistic. The number of degrees of freedom is the number of observations in a statistical problem that are not restricted or are free to vary.

The number of degrees of freedom (d.f.) is equal to the number of observations minus the number of assumptions or constraints necessary to calculate a statistic. Consider the problem of adding five numbers when the mean of the five numbers is known to be 20. In this situation, only four of the five numbers are free to vary. Once four of the numbers are known, the last value is also known (can be calculated) because the mean value must be 20. If four of the five numbers were 14, 23, 24, and 18, then the fifth number would have to be 21 to produce a mean of 20. We would say that the sample has $n-1$ or 4 degrees of freedom. It is as if the sample had one less observation—the inclusion of degrees of freedom in the calculation adjusts for this fact.

p Values and Significance Testing

For the various tests discussed in this chapter, a standard—a level of significance and associated critical value of the statistics—is established, and then the value of the statistic is calculated to see whether it beats that standard. If the calculated value of the statistic exceeds the critical value, then the result being tested is said to be statistically significant at that level.

However, this approach does not give the exact probability of getting a computed test statistic that is largely due to chance. The calculations to compute this probability, commonly referred to as the **p value,** are tedious to perform by hand. Fortunately, they are easy for computers. The *p* value is the most demanding level of statistical (not managerial) significance that can be met, based on the calculated value of the statistic. Computer statistical packages usually use one of the following labels to identify the probability that the distance between the hypothesized population parameter and the observed test statistic could have occurred due to chance:

p value
> **p value**
> Exact probability of getting a computed test statistic that is due to chance. The smaller the *p* value, the smaller the probability that the observed result occurred by chance.

☐ *p* value
☐ ≤ PROB
☐ PROB =

The smaller the *p* value, the smaller is the probability that the observed result occurred by chance (sampling error).

Once the questionnaires have been returned from the field, a five-step process takes place. These steps are (1) validation and editing, which are quality control checks, (2) coding, (3) data entry, (4) logical cleaning of data, and (5) tabulation and statistical analysis. The first step in the process, making sure that the data have integrity, is critical. Otherwise, the age-old adage is true: "Garbage in, garbage out." Validation involves determining with as much certainty as possible that each questionnaire is, in fact, a valid interview. A valid interview in this sense is one that was conducted in an appropriate manner. The objective of validation is to detect interviewer fraud or failure to follow key instructions. Validation is accomplished by recontacting a certain percentage of the respondents surveyed by each interviewer. Any surveys found to be fraudulent are eliminated from the database. After the validation process is completed, editing begins. Editing involves checking for interviewer and respondent mistakes—making certain that all required questions were answered, that skip patterns were followed properly, and that responses to open-ended questions were accurately recorded.

Upon completion of the editing, the next step is to code the data. Most questions on surveys are closed-ended and precoded, which means that numeric codes already have been assigned to the various responses on the questionnaire. With open-ended questions, the researcher has no idea in advance what the responses will be. Therefore, the coder must establish numeric codes for response categories by listing actual responses to open-ended questions and then consolidating those responses and assigning numeric codes to the consolidated categories. Once a coding sheet has been created, all questionnaires are coded using the coding sheet categories.

The next step is data entry. Today, most data entry is done by means of intelligent entry systems that check the internal logic of the data. The data typically are entered directly from the questionnaires. New developments in scanning technology have made a more automated approach to data entry cost-effective for smaller projects.

Logical cleaning of data is a final, computerized error check of the data, performed through the use of error checking routines and/or marginal reports. Error checking routines indicate whether or not certain conditions have been met. A marginal report is a type of frequency table that helps the user determine whether inappropriate codes were entered and whether skip patterns were properly followed.

The final step in the data analysis process is tabulation of the data. The most basic tabulation involves a one-way frequency table, which indicates the number of respondents who gave each possible answer to each question. Generating one-way frequency tables requires the analyst to determine a basis for percentages.

Statistical measures provide an even more powerful way to analyze data sets. The most commonly used statistical measures are those of central tendency: the arithmetic mean, median, and mode. The arithmetic mean is computed only from interval or ratio data by adding the values for all observations of a particular variable and dividing the resulting sum by the number of observations. The median can be computed for all types of data except nominal data by finding the value below which 50 percent of the observations fall. The mode can be computed for any type of data by simply finding the value that occurs most frequently. The arithmetic mean is, by far, the most commonly used measure of central tendency.

In addition to central tendency, researchers often want to have an indication of the dispersion of the data. Measures of dispersion include standard deviation, variance, and range.

The purpose of making statistical inferences is to generalize from sample results to population characteristics. Three important concepts applied to the notion of differences are mathematical differences, managerially important differences, and statistical significance.

A hypothesis is an assumption or theory that a researcher or manager makes about some characteristic of the population being investigated. By testing, the researcher determines whether a hypothesis concerning some characteristic of the population is valid. A statistical hypothesis test permits the researcher to calculate the probability of observing the particular result if the stated hypothesis actually were true. In hypothesis testing, the first step is to specify the hypothesis. Next, an appropriate statistical technique should be selected to test the hypothesis. Then, a decision rule must be specified as the basis for determining whether to reject or fail to reject the hypothesis. Hypothesis tests are subject to two types of errors called type I (α error) and type II (β error). A type I error involves rejecting the null hypothesis when it is, in fact, true. A type II error involves failing to reject the null hypothesis when the alternative hypothesis actually is true. Finally, the value of the test statistic is calculated, and a conclusion is stated that summarizes the results of the test.

validation Process of ascertaining that interviews actually were conducted as specified.

editing Process of ascertaining that questionnaires were filled out properly and completely.

skip pattern Sequence in which later questions are asked, based on a respondent's answer to an earlier question.

coding Process of grouping and assigning numeric codes to the various responses to a question.

data entry Process of converting information to an electronic format.

intelligent data entry Form of data entry in which the information being entered into the data entry device is checked for internal logic.

scanning technology Form of data entry in which responses on questionnaires are read in automatically by the data entry device.

logical cleaning of data Final computerized error check of data.

error checking routines Computer programs that accept instructions from the user to check for logical errors in the data.

marginal report Computer-generated table of the frequencies of the responses to each question, used to monitor entry of valid codes and correct use of skip patterns.

one-way frequency table Table showing the number of respondents choosing each answer to a survey question.

cross tabulation Examination of the responses to one question relative to the responses to one or more other questions.

mean Sum of the values for all observations of a variable divided by the number of observations.

median Value below which 50 percent of the observations fall.

mode Value that occurs most frequently.

hypothesis Assumption or theory that a researcher or manager makes about some characteristics of the population under study.

type I error (α error) Rejection of the null hypothesis when, in fact, it is true.

type II error (β error) Failure to reject the null hypothesis when, in fact, it is false.

independent samples Samples in which measurement of a variable in one population has no effect on measurement of the variable in the other.

related samples Samples in which measurement of a variable in one population may influence measurement of the variable in the other.

***p* value** Exact probability of getting a computed test statistic that is due to chance. The smaller the *p* value, the smaller the probability that the observed result occurred by chance.

1. What is the difference between measurement validity and interview validation?
2. Assume that Sally Smith, an interviewer, completed 50 questionnaires. Ten of the questionnaires were validated by calling the respondents and asking them one opinion question and two demographic questions over again. One respondent claimed that his age category was 30–40, when the age category marked on the questionnaire was 20–30. On another questionnaire, in response to the question "What is the most important problem facing our city government?" the interviewer had written, "The city council is too eager to raise taxes." When the interview was validated, the respondent said, "The city tax rate is too high." As a validator, would

you assume that these were honest mistakes and accept the entire lot of 50 interviews as valid? If not, what would you do?

3. What is meant by the editing process? Should editors be allowed to fill in what they think a respondent meant in response to open-ended questions if the information seems incomplete? Why or why not?

4. Give an example of a skip pattern on a questionnaire. Why is it important to always follow the skip patterns correctly?

5. It has been said that, to some degree, coding of open-ended questions is an art. Would you agree or disagree? Why? Suppose that, after coding a large number of questionnaires, the researcher notices that many responses have ended up in the "Other" category. What might this imply? What could be done to correct this problem?

6. What is the purpose of logical cleaning data? Give some examples of how data can be logically cleaned. Do you think that logical cleaning is an expensive and unnecessary step in the data tabulation process? Why or why not?

7. It has been said that a cross tabulation of two variables offers the researcher more insightful information than does a one-way frequency table. Why might this be true? Give an example.

8. Illustrate the various alternatives for using percentages in one-way frequency tables. Explain the logic of choosing one alternative method over another.

9. Explain the differences among the mean, median, and mode. Give an example in which the researcher might be interested in each of these measures of central tendency.

10. Explain the notions of mathematical differences, managerially important differences, and statistical significance. Can results be statistically significant and yet lack managerial importance? Explain your answer.

11. Describe the steps in the procedure for testing hypotheses. Discuss the difference between a null hypothesis and an alternative hypothesis.

12. Distinguish between a type I error and a type II error. What is the relationship between the two?

WORKING THE NET

1. Which conference in the National Football League is more fun to watch? To compare the average total offense yardage for teams from the NFC with that for teams from the AFC, go to *(http://www.ufl.com.)* Select "Stars" and then "Total Offense." Conduct a *t*-test comparing the two means to determine if the difference is statistically significant.

2. What kinds of publications can you obtain to assist your marketing research efforts? To find out, go to *http://www.marketingtools.com*.

REAL-LIFE RESEARCH • 13.1

California Fitness, Inc.

Joe McDaniel and Fred Clark have known each other since college, and have regularly worked out together and participated in sports leagues. The two friends therefore decided that a natural business for them would be a fitness center. The question immediately arose as to what kind of individual they should target for their new center. Secondary research showed that the percentage of Americans who do not exercise at all varies significantly by age and income. Only 33 percent of adults aged 25 to 34 do not take part at least occasionally in one of seven common exercise activities, compared with 59 percent of people aged 55 and older who do not exercise. Also, only 32 percent of people in households with incomes of $50,000 or more do not take part, at least occasionally, in one of the seven fitness activities. This compares with 59 percent of people with household incomes below $15,000.

The percentage of people who do not participate in fitness activities is greatest among those with the least education. Based on this information, Joe and Fred decided to target consumers 35 to 54 years of age who are slightly upscale socioeconomically. The next question was related to the design for the interior of the center. Should it have a male orientation, a female orientation, or both? Also, what kinds of activities appeal more to men or women? Exhibit 13.26 shows the number of males and females 35 to 54 years of age who exercise regularly.

EXHIBIT 13.26	Frequent Participants in Fitness Activities by Gender, 2007 (number of participants and nonparticipants)		
		Sex	
Participation Status	Total	Male	Female
Participate	699	320	379
Do not participate	501	280	221

Questions

1. Determine if there is a significant difference at the .05 level between males and females.

2. What would you recommend to the owners in terms of atmosphere for the center? Should it be oriented toward males or females?

SPSS EXERCISES FOR CHAPTER 13

Exercise #1: Logical Cleaning of Data

1. Go to the Wiley Web site at *www.wiley.com/college/mcdaniel* and download the "*Segmenting the College Student Market for Movie Attendance*" database to SPSS Windows. This database will have several errors for you to correct. In the SPSS Data Editor, go to the *variable view* option and notice the **computer coding** for each variable.

2. Also from the Wiley Web site, download a copy of the "*Segmenting the College Student Market for Movie Attendance*" questionnaire. Notice the computer coding for each of the variables; which is the same as that in the *variable view* option on the SPSS Data Editor. This information will be important in finding errors in the database.

3. In the SPSS Data Editor, invoke the *analyze/descriptive statistics/frequencies* sequence to obtain frequencies for all of the variables in the database.

4. From the SPSS Viewer *output screen*, determine which variables have input errors. Summarize the errors using the template below as a guide.

Questionnaire Number	Variable Containing Error	Incorrect Value	Correct Value

Going back to the *data view* screen of the *SPSS Data Editor.*

5. Another possible source of errors is in question 8. Notice that in this question the sum of the answers should be 100 percent. Create a summated variable for question 8 (Q8a+Q8b+Q8c+Q8d) to check for errors by invoking the *transform/compute* sequence. Now, compute a frequency distribution for Q8sum. The values that are not "100" indicate an input error. (Such an error could be the result of the respondent not totaling percentages to 100, but for this logical cleaning exercise, the assumption is that it is an input error.) Summarize the errors using the template above.

6. Once you have completed summarizing the variables containing errors, go back to the *data view* screen of the *SPSS Data Editor*. Position the cursor on each of the variables containing errors. Use the *ctrl-f* function to find the questionnaire numbers where the errors occurred. At this point, you will need the corrected database, or the database with no errors. Your professor has access to this database with no errors. After getting the corrected database, finish filling in the table in part 4 above with the correct values. Then make the changes in your database, so that you have a database with no errors. Be sure to resave your database after correcting it for errors.

7. After logically cleaning your data, rerun the *analyze/descriptive statistics/frequencies* sequence to obtain frequencies for your corrected database.

8. You will use the results of this exercise to answer the questions in Exercises #2 and #4.

Exercise #2: Analysis of Data with Frequency Distributions

If you did not complete Exercise #1, you will need the corrected database from your professor. After getting the corrected database, use the *analyze/descriptive statistics/frequencies* sequence to obtain frequency distributions for all of the variables in your database except the questionnaire number (QNO).

If you completed Exercise #1, you will have a corrected database, which consists of frequency distributions for each of the variables in the database.
Answer the following questions.

1. What percentage of all respondents attended at least one movie in the past year? _____%

2. What percentage of all respondents *never buy food items* at a movie? _____%

3. Produce a table indicating the percentage of all respondents that consider each of the movie theater items in question 5 of the questionnaire *very important*. List the top five movie items in descending order (start with the movie items that have the highest percentage of *very important* responses).

For Example:

Movie Item	Percentage of Respondents
Movie item with the highest percentage	75.0%
Movie item with the 2nd highest percentage, etc.	39.2%

4. What percentage of respondents consider the "newspaper" a *very important* source of information about movies playing at movie theaters? _____%

5. What percentage of respondents consider the "Internet" a *very unimportant* source of information about movies playing at movie theaters? _____%

6. By observing the distribution of responses for Q8a, Q8b, Q8c, and Q8d, which is the most popular *purchase option* for movie theater tickets? _____

7. Produce a table listing in descending order the percentage of respondents that consider each of the movie theater information sources (Q7) *very important*.

For Example:

Movie Theater Information Sources	Percentage of Respondents Indicating Very Important
Internet	55%
Newspaper	31%

Exercise #3: Analysis of Data with Descriptive Statistics

If you did not complete Exercises #1 or #2, you will need the corrected database from your professor. The objective of this exercise is to analyze data using measures of central tendency and measures of dispersion. To analyze means and standard deviations, use the *analyze/descriptive statistics/descriptives* sequences. To analyze medians and modes, use the *analyze/descriptive statistics/frequencies* sequence, and select *statistics*. You will see the box with all three measures of central tendency (mean, median and mode).

On the questionnaire, question 5 utilizes a four-point itemized rating scale (illustrated below). This scale is balanced and can be assumed to yield interval scale/metric data. Given the preceding, invoke SPSS to calculate the mean and standard deviation for all of the variables in question 5 (Q5a–Q5i).

Very Unimportant	Somewhat Unimportant	Somewhat Important	Very Important
1	2	3	4

Answer the following questions.

1. Using only the **mean** for each of the variables, which of the movie theater items was considered "most important"? _____

survey solutions XP

2. Using only the **standard deviation** for each of the variables, for which question was there the greatest amount of agreement? _____ Hint: Least amount of dispersion regarding the response to the movie item

3. Questions 4 and 6 utilize multiple choice questions which yield nonmetric data, but which is ordinal scale. The appropriate measures of central tendency for nonmetric data are the median and the mode.

   a. What is the *median* response for question 4, concerning the amount a person spends on food/drink items at a movie? _____

Never Buy Food Items at Movies (0)	Up to $7.49 (1)	$7.50 to $14.99 (2)	$15.00 or More (3)

   b. Concerning question 6, the distance a person would drive to see a movie on a "big screen," what is the *mode* of that distribution of responses?

Zero (0)	1 to 9 Miles (1)	11 to 24 Miles (2)	25 to 49 Miles (3)	50+ Miles (4)

4. In this question the objective will be to compare the results of median and mean responses for Q3.

   a. Mean response: _____
   b. Median response: _____
   c. Standard deviation: _____
   d. Minimum response: _____
   e. Maximum response: _____

5. When the responses to a question contain extreme values, the mean response can lie in the upper or lower quartile of the response distribution. In such a case, the median value would be a better indicator of an average response than the mean value. Given the information you obtained from answering item 4 above, is the mean or median a better representative of the "average" response to Q3?

   _____
   _____
   _____

Exercise #4: Analysis of Demographic Characteristics Using Charts

If you completed Exercise #1 and/or Exercise #2 you will have the information to complete this exercise.

If you did not complete either Exercise #1 or #2, you will need to get a corrected soft drink database from your professor. After getting the database, use the *analyze/descriptive*

surveysolutions XP

statistics/frequencies sequence to obtain frequency distributions for the demographic questions (questions 11–14).

Answer the following questions.

1. Display the demographic data for each of the four demographic variables in tables.
2. For each demographic variable, illustrate the table results using some type of graphic representation of the data (pie charts, line charts, or bar charts).

Note: Some students who are proficient in Excel may want to paste their databases into an Excel spreadsheet for the geographical depiction of the demographic variables.

Exercise #5: Analyzing Data Using Cross Tabulation Analysis

Note: If you did not complete any of the SPSS exercises in Chapter 13 thus far, you will need a corrected database from your professor.

Use the *analyze/descriptive statistics/crosstab* sequence to obtain cross tabulated results. In addition, click on the "cell" icon and make sure the *observed, expected, total, row,* and *column* boxes are checked. Then, click on the "statistics" icon and check the *chi-square* box. Once you run the analysis, on the output for the chi–square analysis, you will only need the *Pearson chi-square statistic* to assess whether or nor the results of the cross tab are statistically significant.

In this exercise we are assessing whether or not persons who attend movies at movie theaters are demographically different from those who do not. Invoke the cross tab analysis for the following pairs of variables:

a. Q1 & Q11
b. Q1 & Q12
c. Q1 & Q13
d. Q1 & Q14

Answer questions 1–6 <u>using only the sample data. Do not consider</u> the results of the *chi-square test.*

1. What % of males do not attend movies at movie theaters? _____%
2. What % of all respondents are African American and do not attend movies at movie theaters? _____%
3. What % of respondents not attending movies at movie theaters are in the 19–20 age category? _____%
4. Which classification group is most likely to attend movies at movie theaters? _____
5. Which age category is least likely to attend movies at a movie theater? _____
6. Are Caucasians less likely to attend movie theaters than African Americans? _____

For question 7, the objective is to determine whether the people who go to and don't go to movies are significantly different in a statistical sense in their demographic characteristics. We do this by using the results of the *chi-square test for independent samples.*

7. Evaluate the chi-square statistic in each of your cross tab tables. Construct a table to summarize the results. For example:

Variables	Pearson Chi-Square	Degrees of Freedom	Asymp sig.	Explanation
Q1 (attend or not attend movies at movie theaters & Q12 (gender)	2.71	1	.10	We can be 90% confident that based on our sample results, males differ significantly from females in their tendency to attend or not attend movies at movie theaters.

Exercise #6: T/Z Test for Independent Samples

Use the *analyze/compare means/independent samples t-test* sequence to complete this exercise. This exercise compares males and females regarding the information sources they utilize to search for information about movies at movie theaters. SPSS calls the variable in which the means are being computed the *test variable,* and the variable in which we are grouping responses the *grouping variable.*

Note: In statistics, if a sample has less than 30 observations or cases, then we invoke a *t* test. If there are 30 or more cases, we invoke a *z* test, as *the t test values and z test values are virtually the same, hence SPSS refers only to a t test.*

Answer the following questions.
The result of the *t* test generates a table of **group statistics**, which is based only on the **sample** data. The other output table generated by the *t* test has statistical data from which we can determine whether or not the sample results can be generalized to the population from which the sample data was drawn. If the *t* test is significant, then we can use the group statistics to determine the specifics of the computed results. For example, a significant *t* test may tell us that males differ from females regarding the importance they place on the newspaper as an information source, but the group statistics tell us "who" considers it most important.

From our *sample data,* can we generalize our results to the population by saying that males differ from females regarding the importance they place on various information sources to get information about movies at movie theaters by:

1. the newspaper (Q7a)?
2. the Internet (Q7b)?
3. phoning in to the movie theater for information (Q7c)?

4. the television (Q7d)?

5. friends or family (Q7e)?

You may want to use the template below to summarize your *t* test results. For example:

Variables	Variance Prob. of Sig. Diff.	Means Prob. of Sig. Diff.	Interpretation of Results
Q12 (gender) & Q7a (newspaper)	.000	.035	96.5% confident that based on our sample results, males differ significantly from females concerning the importance they place on the newspaper as an information source about movies at movie theaters (**means test**). 100% confident that males and females were significantly different regarding to the variance of response within each gender (**variance test**).

Exercise #7: ANOVA Test for Independent Samples

Invoke the *analyze/compare means/One-Way ANOVA* sequence to invoke the ANOVA test to complete this exercise. This exercise compares the responses of freshman, sophomores, juniors, seniors, and graduate students to test for significant differences in the importance placed on several movie theater items. For the ANOVA test, SPSS calls the variable in which means are being computed the *independent variable* and the variable in which we are grouping responses the *factor variable*. Be sure to click the *options* icon and check *descriptives* so that the output will produce the mean responses by student classification for the sample data.

As with the *t* test, the ANOVA test produces a table of *descriptives* based on sample data. If our ANOVA test is significant, the *descriptives* can be used to determine, for example, which student classification places the most importance on comfortable seats.

Answer the following questions.
From our sample data, can we generalize our results to the population by saying that there are significant differences across the <u>classification of students</u> by the importance they place on the following movie theater items?

1. video arcade at the movie theater (Q5a)

2. soft drinks and food items (Q5b)

3. plentiful restrooms (Q5c)

4. comfortable chairs (Q5d)

5. auditorium-type seating (Q5e)

6. size of the movie theater screens (Q5f)

7. quality of the sound system (Q5g)

8. number of screens at a movie theater (Q5h)

9. clean restroom (Q5i)

10. Using only the *descriptive statistics*, which classification group (Q13) places the least amount of importance on clean restrooms (Q5i)? _____

11. Using only the *descriptive statistics*, which classification group (Q13) places the greatest amount of importance on quality of sound system (Q5i)? _____

Summarize the results of your ANOVA analysis using a table similar to the one below.

Variables	Degrees of Freedom	F Value	Probability of Insignificance	Interpretation of Results
Q5a (importance of a video arcade) & Q13 (student classification)	4.461	12.43	.001	99.9% confident that based on the sample results, students differ significantly by classification concerning the importance placed on there being a video arcade at the movie theater.

Robert Stainforth/Alamy

BIVARIATE CORRELATION AND REGRESSION

LEARNING OBJECTIVES

1.	To comprehend the nature of correlation analysis.
2.	To understand bivariate regression analysis.
3.	To become aware of the coefficient of determination R^2.
4.	To understand Spearman rank-order correlation.

In consulting work, it is not uncommon to find clients who want to use simple tools such as bivariate correlation and regression to explore the relationship between important marketing variables such as sales and advertising. Recently, we worked with an electronics chain on this issue. The marketing manager observed that traffic in the company's stores tended to increase on the weekends based, he claimed, on their newspaper advertising. Some of his colleagues were not convinced that there was a direct relationship between the amount of newspaper advertising and weekend traffic in their stores.

The company's directors wanted to perform additional analysis to determine whether a relationship existed between the amount of newspaper advertising and store traffic on the weekends, and if there was a relationship, to ascertain the nature and extent of that relationship. Their thinking at this point was that bivariate correlation and regression analyses might be the right tools for this analysis. Indeed, some initial runs showed a high correlation between the amount of advertising and store traffic on the weekends. This finding was based on looking at daily traffic and advertising expenses for the last 90 days. The data included weekday and weekend traffic and advertising figures.

Do you think that they are correct in this line of thinking? Can the high correlations be relied on as proof of the advertising/store traffic relationship? Why do you agree or disagree? Is there a better way to address this issue?

In this chapter, we will cover techniques that will permit you to evaluate the relationships between two variables.

Bivariate Analysis of Association

In many marketing research studies, the interests of the researcher and manager go beyond issues that can be addressed by the statistical testing of differences discussed in Chapter 13. They may be interested in the degree of association between two variables. Statistical techniques appropriate for this type of analysis are referred to as **bivariate techniques**. When more than two variables are involved, the techniques employed are known as *multivariate techniques*.

When the degree of association between two variables is analyzed, the variables are classified as the **independent** (predictor) **variable** and the **dependent** (criterion) **variable**. Independent variables are those that are believed to affect the value of the dependent variable. Independent variables such as price, advertising expenditures, or number of retail outlets may, for example, be used to predict and explain sales or market share of a brand—the dependent variable. Bivariate analysis can help provide answers to questions such as the following: How does the price of our product affect its sales? What is the relationship between household income and expenditures on entertainment?

It must be noted that none of the techniques presented in this chapter can be used to prove that one variable caused an observed change in another variable. They can be used only to describe the nature of statistical relationships between variables.

The analyst has a large number of bivariate techniques from which to choose. This chapter discusses two procedures that are appropriate for metric (ratio or internal) data—bivariate regression and Pearson's product-moment correlation. Other statistical procedures that can be used for analyzing the statistical relationship between two variables include the two-group *t* test, chi-square analysis of crosstabs or contingency tables, and ANOVA (analysis of variance) for two groups.

> **bivariate techniques**
> Statistical methods of analyzing the relationship between two variables.

> **independent variable**
> Variable believed to affect the value of the dependent variable.

> **dependent variable**
> Variable expected to be explained or caused by the independent variable.

Bivariate Regression

> ⟫ **bivariate regression analysis**
> Analysis of the strength of the linear relationship between two variables when one is considered the independent variable and the other the dependent variable.

Bivariate regression analysis is a statistical procedure appropriate for analyzing the relationship between two variables when one is considered the dependent variable and the other the independent variable. For example, a researcher might be interested in analyzing the relationship between sales (dependent variable) and advertising (independent variable). If the relationship between advertising expenditures and sales can be accurately captured by regression analysis, the researcher can use the resulting model to predict sales for different levels of advertising. When the problem involves using two or more independent variables (for example, advertising and price) to predict the dependent variable of interest, multiple regression analysis is appropriate.

Nature of the Relationship

> ⟫ **scatter diagram**
> Graphic plot of the data with dependent variable on the *Y* (vertical) axis and the independent variable on the *X* (horizontal) axis. Shows the nature of the relationship between the two variables, linear or nonlinear.

One way to study the nature of the relationship between the dependent and the independent variable is to plot the data in a **scatter diagram**. The dependent variable Y is plotted on the vertical axis, whereas the independent variable X is plotted on the horizontal axis. By examining the scatter diagram, one can determine whether the relationship between the two variables, if any, is linear or curvilinear. If the relationship appears to be linear or close to linear, linear regression is appropriate. If a nonlinear relationship is shown in the scatter diagram, curve-fitting nonlinear regression techniques are appropriate. These techniques are beyond the scope of this discussion.

Exhibit 14.1 depicts several kinds of underlying relationships between the X (independent) and Y (dependent) variables. Scatter diagrams (a) and (b) suggest a positive linear relationship between X and Y. However, the linear relationship shown in (b) is not as strong as that portrayed in (a); there is more scatter in the data shown in (b). Diagram (c) shows a perfect negative, or inverse, relationship between variables X and Y. An example might be the relationship between price and sales. As price goes up, sales go down. As price goes down, sales go up. Diagrams (d) and (e) show nonlinear relationships between the variables; appropriate curve-fitting techniques should be used to mathematically describe these relationships. The scatter diagram in (f) shows no relationship between X and Y.

Example of Bivariate Regression

Stop 'N Go recently conducted a research effort designed to measure the effect of vehicular traffic past a particular store location on annual sales at that location. To control

Bivariate regression analysis can help answer such questions as "How does advertising affect sales?"

Michael Milia/Retna

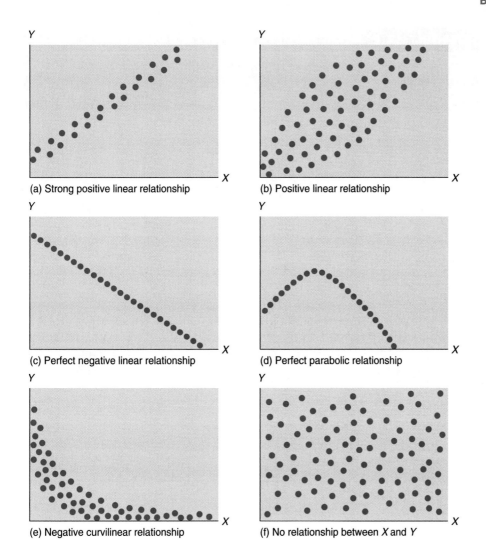

Exhibit 14.1

Types of Relationships Found in Scatter Diagrams

(a) Strong positive linear relationship

(b) Positive linear relationship

(c) Perfect negative linear relationship

(d) Perfect parabolic relationship

(e) Negative curvilinear relationship

(f) No relationship between X and Y

for other factors, researchers identified 20 stores that were virtually identical on all other variables known to have a significant effect on store sales (for example, square footage, amount of parking, demographics of the surrounding neighborhood). This particular analysis is part of an overall effort by Stop 'N Go to identify and quantify the effects of various factors that affect store sales. The ultimate goal is to develop a model that can be used to screen potential sites for store locations and select, for actual purchase and store construction, the ones that will produce the highest level of sales.

After identifying the 20 sites, Stop 'N Go took a daily traffic count for each site over a 30-day period. In addition, from internal records, the company obtained total sales data for each of the 20 test stores for the preceding 12 months (see Exhibit 14.2).

A scatterplot of the resulting data is shown in Exhibit 14.3. Visual inspection of the scatterplot suggests that total sales increase as average daily vehicular traffic increases. The question now is how to characterize this relationship in a more explicit, quantitative manner. Another bivariate regression example is provided in the feature on page 439.

EXHIBIT 14.2	Annual Sales and Average Daily Vehicular Traffic	
Store Number (i)	Average Daily Vehicular Count in Thousands (X_i)	Annual Sales in Thousands of Dollars (Y_i)
1	62	1121
2	35	766
3	36	701
4	72	1304
5	41	832
6	39	782
7	49	977
8	25	503
9	41	773
10	39	839
11	35	893
12	27	588
13	55	957
14	38	703
15	24	497
16	28	657
17	53	1209
18	55	997
19	33	844
20	29	883

Exhibit 14.3

Scatterplot of Annual Sales by Traffic

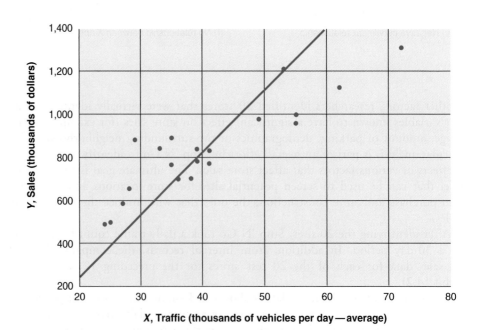

PRACTICING MARKETING RESEARCH

Bivariate Regression Analysis Shows Higher Cancer Rates among California Farm Workers

Bivariate regression is a valuable statistical tool that is used widely in many fields, including medicine. As the text explains, the application of this statistical approach is to analyze the relationship and changes in relationship between two variables in which one is the dependent and the other the independent factor.

Recently, epidemiologists with the Cancer Registry of Central California in Fresno investigated whether new pesticides being used in California agriculture were producing more cancers among female farm workers routinely exposed to them. In the researchers' use of bivariate regression analysis, the cancer rate was the dependent variable (the factor the researchers hoped would be explained or caused by the independent variable), and exposure to new pesticides was the independent variable (the factor believed to be causing the value of the dependent variable).

California, as the leading agricultural state in America, uses 25 percent of all pesticides consumed in the country each year—approximately 120 million pounds. Researchers Paul. K. Mills and Richard Yang subjected data for the years 1988–2000 from the California Cancer Registry (a list based on population that monitors cancer incidence) to regression analysis, and also used data on pesticide use in California for 1970–1988. They wanted to see if Hispanic female farm workers showed a higher incidence of cancer, especially of the breast, from pesticide exposure. They used the negative binomial (NB) regression model because its use was well-indicated by "evidence of overdispersion in the data" and because "the goodness of fit was found to be much better" with the NB approach than with the standard Poisson model. The results were given as incidence rate ratios (IRRs), at 95 percent confidence intervals.

Mills and Yang performed regression analysis of data on pesticide use per county (California has 58 counties), focusing on two classes of pesticides, namely, organochlorines (eight types) and triazine herbicides (two types). Hispanic females represented the main study population since they are heavily represented in California agriculture (81 percent of all women employed in California agriculture), but the researchers controlled the study for age, socioeconomic status, and fertility rates, as previous studies had shown that these were risk factors for cancer susceptibility or incidence in this specific population. In short, they studied the relationship of pesticide use per county with new cancer incidence.

Mills and Yang found that during 1988–1999, a total of 23,513 female Latinas were diagnosed with breast cancer and that this incidence was positively associated with the amount of two specific types of organochlorines they had been exposed to, but not to the triazine herbicides, increasing the risk of breast cancer development by up to 18 percent. These high levels of elevated cancer risk did not change when the researchers subjected the other risk factors, such as age, socioeconomic status, and fertility, to multivariate analysis.[1]

Questions

1. Are there other ways to configure this experiment in terms of which factors are the dependent and independent variables?

2. How would you structure the bivariate correlation to handle different volumes of the pesticides applied during the same time period?

Least-Squares Estimation Procedure The least-squares procedure is a fairly simple mathematical technique that can be used to fit data for X and Y to a line that best represents the relationship between the two variables. No straight line will perfectly represent every observation in the scatterplot. This is reflected in discrepancies between the actual values (dots on the scatter diagram) and predicted values (values indicated by the line). Any straight line fitted to the data in a scatterplot is subject to error. A number of lines could be drawn that would seem to fit the observations in Exhibit 14.3.

The least-squares procedure results in a straight line that fits the actual observations (dots) better than any other line that could be fitted to the observations. Put another way, the sum of the squared deviations from the line (squared differences between dots and the line) will be lower for this line than for any other line that can be fitted to the observations.

The general equation for the line is $Y = a + bX$. The estimating equation for regression analysis is

$$Y = \hat{a} + \hat{b}X + e$$

where $Y =$ dependent variable, annual sales in thousands of dollars

$\hat{a} =$ estimated Y intercept for regression line

$\hat{b} =$ estimated slope of regression line, regression coefficient

$X =$ independent variable, average daily vehicular traffic in thousands of vehicles

$e =$ error, difference between actual value and value predicted by regression line

Values for $\hat{a}$ and $\hat{b}$ can be calculated from the following equations:

$$\hat{b} = \frac{\sum X_i Y_i - n\bar{X}\,\bar{Y}}{\sum X_i^2 - n(\bar{X})^2}$$

$$\hat{a} = \bar{Y} - \hat{b}\bar{X}$$

where $\bar{X} =$ mean value of X

$\bar{Y} =$ mean value of Y

$n =$ sample size (number of units in the sample)

With the data from Exhibit 14.4, $\hat{b}$ is calculated as follows:

$$\hat{b} = \frac{734{,}083 - 20(40.8)(841.3)}{36{,}526 - 20(40.8)^2} = 14.7$$

The value of $\hat{a}$ is calculated as follows:

$$\hat{a} = \overline{Y} - \hat{b}\overline{X}$$
$$= 841.3 - 14.72(40.8) = 240.9$$

Thus, the estimated regression function is given by

$$\hat{Y} = \hat{a} + \hat{b}X$$
$$= 240.9 + 14.7(X)$$

where $\hat{Y}$ (Y hat) is the value of the estimated regression function for a given value of X.

According to the estimated regression function, for every additional 1,000 vehicles per day in traffic (X), total annual sales will increase by \$14,720 (estimated value of b). The value of $\hat{a}$ is 240.9. Technically, $\hat{a}$ is the estimated value of the dependent variable (Y, or annual sales) when the value of the independent variable (X, or average daily vehicular traffic) is zero.

EXHIBIT 14.4		Least-Squares Computation			
Store	X	Y	X²	Y²	XY
1	62	1,121	3,844	1,256,641	69,502
2	35	766	1,225	586,756	26,810
3	36	701	1,296	491,401	25,236
4	72	1,304	5,184	1,700,416	93,888
5	41	832	1,681	692,224	34,112
6	39	782	1,521	611,524	30,498
7	49	977	2,401	954,529	47,873
8	25	503	625	253,009	12,575
9	41	773	1,681	597,529	31,693
10	39	839	1,521	703,921	32,721
11	35	893	1,225	797,449	31,255
12	27	588	729	345,744	15,876
13	55	957	3,025	915,849	52,635
14	38	703	1,444	494,209	26,714
15	24	497	576	247,009	11,928
16	28	657	784	431,649	18,396
17	53	1,209	2,809	1,461,681	64,077
18	55	997	3,025	994,009	54,835
19	33	844	1,089	712,336	27,852
20	29	883	841	779,689	25,607
Sum	816	16,826	36,526	15,027,574	734,083
Mean	40.8	841.3			

Steps that you need to go through to do the bivariate regression problem shown in the book are provided below along with the output produced. Use the data set **Bivregex**, which you can download from the Web site for the text.

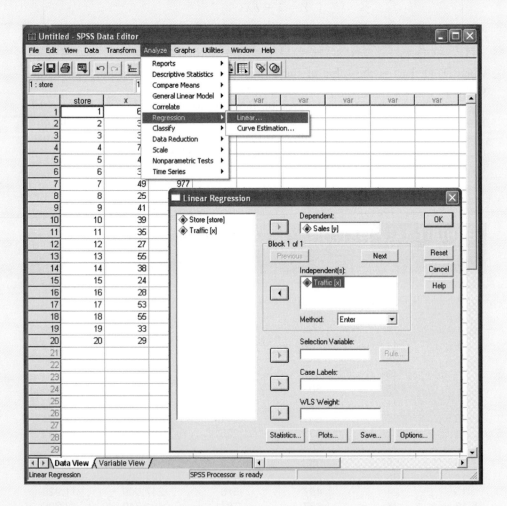

Steps in SPSS

1. Select *Analyze → Regression → Linear*.
2. Move **y** to Dependent.
3. Move **x** to Independent(s).
4. Click OK.

SPSS Output for Regression

Regression

Variables Entered/Removed[b]

Model	Variables Entered	Variables Removed	Method
1	Traffic[a]	.	Enter

a. All requested variables entered.

b. Dependent Variable: Sales

Model Summary

Model	R	R Square	Adjusted R Square	Std. Error of the Estimate
1	.896[a]	.803	.792	97.640

a. Predictors: (Constant). Traffic

ANOVA[b]

Model		Sum of Squares	df	Mean Square	F	Sig.
1	Regression	700255.40	1	700255.399	73.451	.000[a]
	Residual	171604.80	18	9533.600		
	Total	871860.20	19			

a. Predictors: (Constant). Traffic

b. Dependent Variable: Sales

Coefficients[a]

Model		Unstandardized Coefficients		Standardized Coefficients		
		B	Std. Error	Beta	t	Sig.
1	(Constant)	240.857	73.383		3.282	.004
	Traffic	14.717	1.717	.896	8.570	.000

a. Dependent Variable: Sales

Regression Line   Predicted values for Y, based on calculated values for $\hat{a}$ and $\hat{b}$, are shown in Exhibit 14.5. In addition, errors for each observation $(Y - \hat{Y})$ are shown. The regression line resulting from the $\hat{Y}$ values is plotted in Exhibit 14.6.

Strength of Association: R^2   The estimated regression function describes the nature of the relationship between X and Y. Another important factor is the strength of the relationship between the variables. How widely do the actual values of Y differ from the values predicted by the model?

EXHIBIT 14.5		Predicted Values and Errors for Each Observation				
Store	X	Y	$\hat{Y}$	$Y - \hat{Y}$	$(Y - \hat{Y})^2$	$(Y - \bar{Y})^2$
1	62	1,121	1,153.3	−32.2951	1,043	78,232
2	35	766	755.9	10.05716	101	5,670
3	36	701	770.7	−69.6596	4,852	19,684
4	72	1,304	1,300.5	3.537362	13	214,091
5	41	832	844.2	−12.2434	150	86
6	39	782	814.8	−32.8098	1,076	3,516
7	49	977	962.0	15.02264	226	18,414
8	25	503	608.8	−105.775	11,188	114,447
9	41	773	844.2	−71.2434	5,076	4,665
10	39	839	814.8	24.19015	585	5
11	35	893	755.9	137.0572	18,785	2,673
12	27	588	638.2	−50.2088	2,521	64,161
13	55	957	1,050.3	−93.2779	8,701	13,386
14	38	703	800.1	−97.0931	9,427	19,127
15	24	497	594.1	−97.0586	9,420	118,542
16	28	657	652.9	4.074415	17	33,966
17	53	1,209	1,020.8	188.1556	35,403	135,203
18	55	997	1,050.3	−53.2779	2,839	24,242
19	33	844	726.5	117.4907	13,804	7
20	29	883	667.6	215.3577	46,379	1,739
Sum	816	16,826	16,826	0	171,605	871,860
Mean	40.8	841				

> **coefficient of determination**
> Percentage of the total variation in the dependent variable explained by the independent variable.

The **coefficient of determination**, denoted by R^2, is the measure of the strength of the linear relationship between X and Y. The coefficient of determination measures the percentage of the total variation in Y that is "explained" by the variation in X. The R^2 statistic ranges from 0 to 1. If there is a perfect linear relationship between X and Y (all

Exhibit 14.6

Least-Squares Regression Line Fitted to Sample Data

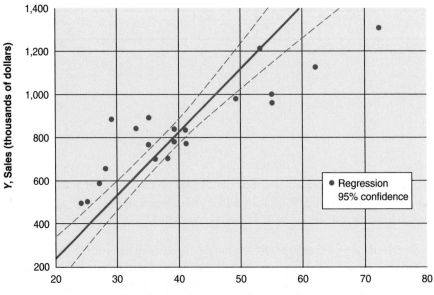

Y, Sales (thousands of dollars) — vertical axis
X, Traffic (thousands of vehicles per day—average) — horizontal axis

- Regression
- 95% confidence

the variation in Y is explained by the variation in X), then R^2 equals 1. At the other extreme, if there is no relationship between X and Y, then none of the variation in Y is explained by the variation in X, and R^2 equals 0.

$$R^2 = \frac{\text{Explained variation}}{\text{Total variation}}$$

where

Explained variation = Total variation − Unexplained variation

The coefficient of determination for the Stop 'N Go data example is computed as follows. [See Exhibit 14.5 for calculation of $(Y - \hat{Y})^2$ and $(Y - \bar{Y})^2$.]

$$R^2 = \frac{\text{Total variation} - \text{Unexplained variation}}{\text{Total variation}}$$
$$= 1 - \frac{\text{Unexplained variation}}{\text{Total variation}}$$
$$= 1 - \frac{\sum_{i=1}^{n}(Y_i - \hat{Y}_i)^2}{\sum_{i=1}^{n}(Y_i - \bar{Y})^2}$$
$$= 1 - \frac{171,605}{871,860} = .803$$

Of the variation in Y (annual sales), 80 percent is explained by the variation in X (average daily vehicular traffic). There is a very strong linear relationship between X and Y.

Statistical Significance of Regression Results In computing R^2, the total variation in Y was partitioned into two component sums of squares:

Total variation = Explained variation + Unexplained variation

The total variation is a measure of variation of the observed Y values around their mean $\bar{Y}$. It measures the variation of the Y values without any consideration of the X values.

Total variation, known as the *total sum of squares* (SST), is given by

$$SST = \sum_{i=1}^{n}(Y_i - \bar{Y})^2 = \sum_{i=1}^{n}Y_i^2 - \left(\frac{\sum_{i=1}^{n}Y_i^2}{n}\right)$$

The explained variation, or the **sum of squares due to regression** (SSR), is given by

sum of squares due to regression
Variation explained by the regression.

$$SSR = \sum_{i=1}^{n}(\hat{Y}_i - \bar{Y})^2 = a\sum_{i=1}^{n}Y_i + b\sum_{i=1}^{n}X_iY_i - \left(\frac{\sum_{i=1}^{n}Y_i}{n}\right)^2$$

Exhibit 14.7

Measures of Variation in a Regression

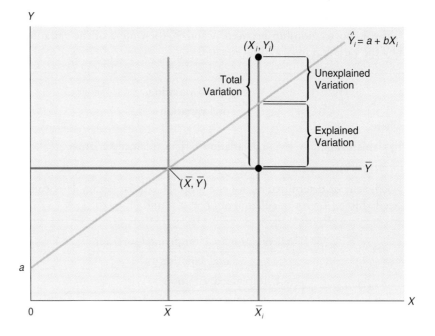

Exhibit 14.7 depicts the various measures of variation (that is, sum of squares) in a regression. SSR represents the differences between Y_i (the values of Y predicted by the estimated regression equation) and $\overline{Y}$ (the average value of Y). In a well-fitting regression equation, the variation explained by regression (SSR) will represent a large portion of the total variation (SST). If $Y_i = \hat{Y}_i$ at each value of X, then a perfect fit has been achieved. All the observed values of Y are then on the computed regression line. Of course, in that case, SSR $\neq$ SST.

The unexplained variation, or **error sum of squares** (SSE), is obtained from

> **error sum of squares**
> Variation not explained by the regression.

$$SSE = \sum_{i=1}^{n} (Y_i - \hat{Y}_i)^2 = \sum_{i=1}^{n} Y_i^2 - a \sum_{i=1}^{n} Y_i - b \sum_{i=1}^{n} X_i Y_i$$

In studying the relationship between vehicular traffic and sales, the coefficient of determination may be used to measure the percent of the total variation.

PhotoDisc, Inc./Getty Images

EXHIBIT 14.8	Analysis of Variance			
Source of Variation	Degrees of Freedom	Sum of Squares	Mean Square	F Statistic
Regression (explained)	1	SSR	$MSR = \dfrac{SSR}{1}$	$F = \dfrac{MSR}{MSE}$
Residual (unexplained)	$n - 2$	SSE	$MSE = \dfrac{SSE}{n-2}$	
Total	$n - 1$	SST		

In Exhibit 14.7, note that SSE represents the residual differences (error) between the observed and predicted Y values. Therefore, the unexplained variation is a measure of scatter around the regression line. If the fit were perfect, there would be no scatter around the regression line and SSE would be zero.

Hypotheses Concerning Overall Regression   Here we, as the researchers, are interested in hypotheses regarding the computed R^2 value for the problem. Is the amount of variance explained in the result (by our model) significantly greater than we would expect due to chance? Or, as with the various statistical tests discussed in Chapter 13, to what extent can we rule out sampling error as an explanation of the results? Analysis of variance (an F test) is used to test the significance of the results.

An analysis of variance table is set up as shown in Exhibit 14.8. The computer output for our example appears in Exhibit 14.9. The breakdowns of the total sum of squares and associated degrees of freedom are displayed in the form of an analysis of variance (ANOVA) table. We use the information in this table to test the significance of the linear relationship between Y and X. As noted previously, an F test will be used for this purpose. Our hypotheses are as follows:

☐ Null hypothesis H_0: There is no linear relationship between X (average daily vehicular traffic) and Y (annual sales).

☐ Alternative hypothesis H_a: There is a linear relationship between X and Y.

As in other statistical tests, we must choose α. This is the likelihood that the observed result occurred by chance, or the probability of incorrectly rejecting the null hypothesis. In this case, we decide on a standard level of significance: $\alpha = .05$. In other words, if the calculated value of F exceeds the tabular value, we are willing to accept a 5 percent chance of incorrectly rejecting the null hypothesis. The value of F, or the F ratio, is computed as follows (see Exhibit 14.9):

$$F = \frac{MSR}{MSE}$$
$$= \frac{700,255}{9,534} = 73.5$$

We will reject the null hypothesis if the calculated F statistic is greater than or equal to the table, or critical, F value. The numerator and denominator degrees of freedom for this F ratio are 1 and 18, respectively. As noted earlier, it was decided that an alpha level of .05 ($\alpha = .05$) should be used.

EXHIBIT 14.9	Regression Analysis Output

STAT. MULTIPLE REGRESS.	Regression Summary for Dependent Variable: Y R = .89619973 R^2 = .80317395 Adjusted R^2 = .79223917 $F(1,18)$ = 73.451 p <.00000 Std. Error of estimate: 97.640

N = 20	BETA	St. Err. of BETA	B	St. Err. of B	$t(18)$	p-level
Intercpt			240.8566	73.38347	3.282164	.004141
X	.896200	.104570	14.7168	1.71717	8.570374	.000000

The table, or critical, value of F with 1 (numerator) and 18 (denominator) degrees of freedom at α = .05 is 4.49 (see Exhibit 5 in the Appendix). Because the calculated value of F is greater than the critical value, we reject the null hypothesis and conclude that there is a significant linear relationship between the average daily vehicular traffic (X) and annual sales (Y). This result is consistent with the high coefficient of determination R^2 discussed earlier.

Hypotheses about the Regression Coefficient b   Finally, we may be interested in making hypotheses about b, the regression coefficient. As you may recall, b is the estimate of the effect of a one-unit change in X on Y. The hypotheses are as follows:

- Null hypothesis H$_0$: b = 0.
- Alternative hypothesis H$_a$: $b \neq 0$.

The appropriate test is a t test, and, as you can see from the last line of Exhibit 14.9, the computer program calculates the t value (8.57) and the p value (probability of incorrectly rejecting the null hypothesis of .0000). See Chapter 13 for a more detailed discussion of p values. Given the α criterion of .05, we would reject the null hypothesis in this case.

Correlation Analysis

Correlation for Metric Data: Pearson's Product–Moment Correlation

> **correlation analysis**
> Analysis of the degree to which changes in one variable are associated with changes in another.

> **Pearson's product–moment correlation**
> Correlation analysis technique for use with metric data.

Correlation is the degree to which changes in one variable (the dependent variable) are associated with changes in another. When the relationship is between two variables, the analysis is called simple, or bivariate, **correlation analysis**. With metric data, **Pearson's product–moment correlation** may be used.

In our example of bivariate regression, we used the coefficient of determination R^2 as a measure of the strength of the linear relationship between X and Y. Another descriptive measure, called the *coefficient of correlation R*, describes the degree of association between X and Y. It is the square root of the coefficient of determination with the appropriate sign (+ or −):

$$R = \pm\sqrt{R^2}$$

The value of R can range from −1 (perfect negative correlation) to +1 (perfect positive correlation). The closer R is to ±1, the stronger the degree of association between X and Y. If R is equal to zero, then there is no association between X and Y.

GLOBAL RESEARCH

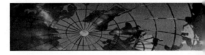

Rethinking the Applicability of Pearson's Product–Moment Correlation

Is Pearson's product–moment correlation the best way to test reliability between a test and its retest scores? Maybe not, say Miaofen Yen, PhD, RN, and Li-Hua Lo, PhD, RN, both professors at National Cheng Jung University in Tainan, Taiwan. In statistics, the authors explain, the reliability of a measure means "the proportion of the observed score variance due to the true scores, that is, the ratio of true score variance to total score variance." Typically, statisticians use the Pearson correlation to calculate the reliability of results from test to retest, especially in nursing research, which is the domain of the authors. But research shows that this method has three limitations.

First, Pearson's calculation is designed to show the relationship between two variables, but it is inappropriate to apply this correlation to two data sets from the same variable. Second, when multiple tests are employed, it's hard to discern variations from test to test; when one concept is measured three times, generating three scores, one cannot create correlation coefficients for all three scores at the same time. Third, Pearson's is unable to detect systematic errors even though test and retest scores may be "perfectly correlated," as Yen and Lo say.

An alternative approach called intraclass correlation, or ICC, and also known as generalizing coefficient, addresses these three limitations. Three issues need to be borne in mind when using ICC: first, the study design should focus on reliability, not correlation; second, the

correct statistical model must be selected—either a one-way or a two-way random model depending on study conditions; and third, the number of measures in the study must be carefully considered.

Miaofen Yen and Li-Hua Lo demonstrated the strength of ICC on a study of competence for breast self-examination. The study looked at perceived competence and perceived barriers to the self-exam. The doctors engaged 10 nurses to complete the research study twice over a two-week period, polling them on 20 questions, each with a 5-point scale. Then they used ICC to run the test–retest reliability gauge. The calculations produced two ICC coefficients: the first was a single measure ICC (0.640), and the second was an average measure ICC (0.781). But it was the first result that the researchers found most applicable because in practical terms they would only give the test once.

The ICC value of 0.640 was close to the Pearson's value of 0.643, but ICC showed its merit in the area of discerning systematic error. When a systematic error of 12 points was introduced, the two resulting coefficients were found to be different. Pearson's was 0.643 and ICC was 0.554, demonstrating ICC's greater sensitivity to systematic error and its suitability for test–retest reliability.[2]

Questions

1. Find several published examples of test–retest reliability studies done with Pearson's product–moment correlation and evaluate whether ICC would have given better results.

2. Why is Pearson's correlation unable to accurately reflect systematic errors, and how does ICC better accommodate this function?

If we had not been interested in estimating the regression function, we could have computed R directly from the data for the convenience store example, using this formula:

$$
\begin{aligned}
R &= \frac{n\Sigma XY - (\Sigma X)(\Sigma Y)}{\sqrt{[n\Sigma X^2 - (\Sigma X)^2][n\Sigma Y^2 - (\Sigma Y)^2]}} \\
&= \frac{20(734{,}083) - (816)(16{,}826)}{\sqrt{[20(36{,}526) - (816)^2][20(15{,}027{,}574) - (16{,}826)^2]}} \\
&= .896
\end{aligned}
$$

In this case, the value of R indicates a positive correlation between the average daily vehicular traffic and annual sales. In other words, successively higher levels of sales are associated with successively higher levels of traffic.

SPSS JUMP START FOR CORRELATION

Steps that you need to go through to do the correlation problem shown in the book are provided below along with the output produced. Use the data set **Correx**, which you can download from the Web site for the text.

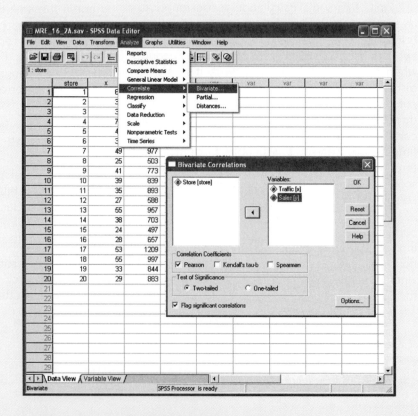

Steps in SPSS

1. Select *Analyze → Correlate → Bivariate*.
2. Move **x** to Variables.
3. Move **y** to Variables.
4. Click OK.

SPSS Output for Correlation

Correlations

Correlations

		Traffic	Sales
Traffic	Pearson Correlation	1	.896**
	Sig. (2-tailed)	.	.000
	N	20	20
Sales	Pearson Correlation	.896**	1
	Sig. (2-tailed)	.000	.
	N	20	20

**. Correlation is significant at the 0.01 level

GLOBAL RESEARCH

Pearson's Product–Moment Correlation Fine-Tunes Medical Statistics

Pearson's product–moment correlation is an appropriate statistical tool for cases involving a comparison between two variables, *X* and *Y*, with metric data. It produces a coefficient, called *r*, which results from dividing the covariance of two variables by the product of their standard deviations. It measures the degree of a linear relationship between two variables, indicating this as a range of +1 to −1.

Statisticians may thank an English professor named Karl Pearson (1857–1936) for this calculation. In 1911, Pearson founded the Department of Applied Statistics at University College in London, England, the first academic statistics department in the world. Since then, researchers in many fields, especially medicine, have relied on Pearson's to fine-tune their data, as the following medical example vividly shows.

Chronic Fatigue Syndrome Studies

Researchers at the Human Performance Laboratory and Department of Internal Medicine at Vrije Universiteit Brussel in Brussels, Belgium, assembled a test group of 427 women with clinically diagnosed Chronic Fatigue Syndrome (CFS) and a control group of 204 age-matched women with sedentary lifestyles to participate in an exercise program to test heart rate. The women used a stationary ergometric bicycle and pedaled for 8 to 12 minutes as their oxygen levels, heart rate, and other physical parameters were monitored.

The researchers used the Pearson's calculation to study variations in the associations between variables within each group (test and control). They also employed Pearson's to discern any differences in the exercise parameters between the two groups. The purpose was to yield a better understanding of how exercise capacity varied between both groups. As the data show, Pearson's provided clear-cut correlations.

The calculation showed, for example, the correlation differences in terms of workload at anaerobic threshold (WAT, reduced oxygen intake) for maximum heart rate was 0.37 for CFS women compared to 0.70 for control-group sedentary women. It also showed that the maximum respiratory quotient for CFS women was positively associated with WAT ($r = 0.26$; $P < .001$ [P = difference]) and negatively associated with HRAT (heart rate at anaerobic threshold: $r = 0.15$; $P < .01$). Among women in the control group, the maximum respiratory quotient was positively correlated with the resting heart rate, ($r = 0.17$; $P < .02$) and negatively correlated with WAT ($r = 0.24$; $P < .002$).

Overall, Pearson's showed that "variation in heart rate was strongly related to changes in exercise capacity in patients with CFS." The researchers state that theirs was the first large-scale study to assess exercise capacity in a large population of CFS sufferers; the report, aided by Pearson's correlation, validated the belief that people with CFS have significantly reduced exercise capacity, sometimes up to 50 percent.[3]

Questions

1. Explain the statistical operating principle that accounts for Pearson's ability to clearly show differences between the two groups as reflected in the r values.

2. Is there an r value, possibly on the high side, that would seem suspect if reported for this study?

SUMMARY

The techniques used to analyze the relationship between variables taken two at a time are called bivariate analyses. Bivariate regression analysis allows a single dependent variable to be predicted from knowledge about a single independent variable. One way to examine the underlying relationship between a dependent and an independent variable is to plot them on a scatter diagram. If the relationship appears to be linear, then linear regression analysis may be used. If it is curvilinear, then curve-fitting techniques should be applied. The general equation for a straight line fitted to two variables is given by

$$Y = a + bX$$

where Y = dependent variable
X = independent variable
a = Y intercept
b = amount Y increases with each unit increase in X

Both a and b are unknown and must be estimated. This process is known as simple linear regression analysis. Bivariate least-squares regression analysis is a mathematical technique for fitting a line to measurements of the two variables X and Y. The line is fitted so that the algebraic sum of deviations of the actual observations from the line is zero and the sum of the squared deviations is less than it would be for any other line that might be fitted to the data.

The estimated regression function describes the nature of the relationship between X and Y. In addition, researchers want to know the strength of the relationship between the variables. This is measured by the coefficient of determination, denoted by R^2. The coefficient of determination measures the percent of the total variation in Y that is "explained" by the variation in X. The R^2 statistic ranges from 0 to 1. An analysis of variance (ANOVA) approach also can be used for regression analysis. The total variation is known as the total sum of squares (SST). The explained variation, or the sum of squares due to regression (SSR), represents the variability explained by the regression. The unexplained variation is called the error sum of squares (SSE).

Correlation analysis is the measurement of the degree to which changes in one variable are associated with changes in another. Correlation analysis will tell the researcher whether the variables are positively correlated, negatively correlated, or independent.

KEY TERMS & DEFINITIONS

bivariate techniques Statistical methods of analyzing the relationship between two variables.

independent variable Variable believed to affect the value of the dependent variable.

dependent variable Variable expected to be explained or caused by the independent variable.

bivariate regression analysis Analysis of the strength of the linear relationship between two variables when one is considered the independent variable and the other the dependent variable.

scatter diagram Graphic plot of the data with dependent variable on the Y (vertical) axis and the independent variable on the X (horizontal) axis. Shows the nature of the relationship between the two variables, linear or nonlinear.

coefficient of determination Percentage of the total variation in the dependent variable explained by the independent variable.

sum of squares due to regression Variation explained by the regression.

error sum of squares Variation not explained by the regression.

correlation analysis Analysis of the degree to which changes in one variable are associated with changes in another.

Pearson's product–moment correlation Correlation analysis technique for use with metric data.

QUESTIONS FOR REVIEW & CRITICAL THINKING

1. Give an example of a marketing problem for which use of each of the two procedures listed in question 1 would be appropriate.
2. A sales manager of a life insurance firm administered a standard multiple-item job satisfaction scale to all the members of the firm's salesforce. The manager then correlated (Pearson's product-moment correlation) job satisfaction score with years of school completed for each salesperson. The resulting correlation was .11. On the basis of this analysis, the sales manager concluded: "A salesperson's level of education has little to do with his or her job satisfaction." Would you agree or disagree with this conclusion? Explain the basis for your position.
3. What purpose does a scatter diagram serve?
4. Explain the meaning of the coefficient of determination. What does this coefficient tell the researcher about the nature of the relationship between the dependent and independent variables?

5. It has been observed in the past that when an AFC team wins the Super Bowl, the stock market rises in the first quarter of the year in almost every case. When an NFC team wins the Super Bowl, the stock market falls in the first quarter in most cases. Does this mean that the direction of movement of the stock market is caused by which conference wins the Super Bowl? What does this example illustrate?

6. The following table gives data collected by a convenience store chain for 20 of its stores.

Column 1: ID number for each store

Column 2: Annual sales for the store for the previous year in thousands of dollars

Column 3: Average number of vehicles that pass the store each day, based on actual traffic counts for one month

Column 4: Total population that lives within a 2-mile radius of the store, based on 1990 census data

Column 5: Median family income for households within a 2-mile radius of the store, based on 2000 census data

Store ID No.	Annual Sales (thousands of dollars)	Average Daily Traffic	Population in 2-Mile Radius	Average Income In Area
1	$1,121	61,655	17,880	$28,991
2	$ 766	35,236	13,742	$14,731
3	$ 595	35,403	19,741	$ 8,114
4	$ 899	52,832	23,246	$15,324
5	$ 915	40,809	24,485	$11,438
6	$ 782	40,820	20,410	$11,730
7	$ 833	49,147	28,997	$10,589
8	$ 571	24,953	9,981	$10,706
9	$ 692	40,828	8,982	$23,591
10	$1,005	39,195	18,814	$15,703
11	$ 589	34,574	16,941	$ 9,015
12	$ 671	26,639	13,319	$10,065
13	$ 903	55,083	21,482	$17,365
14	$ 703	37,892	26,524	$ 7,532
15	$ 556	24,019	14,412	$ 6,950
16	$ 657	27,791	13,896	$ 9,855
17	$1,209	53,438	22,444	$21,589
18	$ 997	54,835	18,096	$22,659
19	$ 844	32,916	16,458	$12,660
20	$ 883	29,139	16,609	$11,618

Answer the following:
a. Which of the other three variables is the best predictor of sales? Compute correlation coefficients to answer the question.
b. Do the following regressions:
   1. Sales as a function of average daily traffic
   2. Sales as a function of population in a 2-mile radius
c. Interpret the results of the two regressions.

7. Interpret the following:
   a. $Y = .11 + .009X$, where Y is the likelihood of sending children to college and X is family income in thousands of dollars. Remember: It is family income in *thousands*.
      1. According to our model, how likely is a family with an income of $100,000 to send their children to college?
      2. What is the likelihood for a family with an income of $50,000?
      3. What is the likelihood for a family with an income of $17,500?
      4. Is there some logic to the estimates? Explain.
   b. $Y = .25 - .0039X$, where Y is the likelihood of going to a skateboard park and X is age.
      1. According to our model, how likely is a 10-year-old to go to a skateboard park?
      2. What is the likelihood for a 60-year-old?
      3. What is the likelihood for a 40-year-old?
      4. Is there some logic to the estimates? Explain.

8. The following ANOVA summary data are the result of a regression with sales per year (dependent variable) as a function of promotion expenditures per year (independent variable) for a toy company.

$$F = \frac{MSR}{MSE} = \frac{34,276}{4,721}$$

The degrees of freedom are 1 for the numerator and 19 for the denominator. Is the relationship statistically significant at $\alpha = .05$? Comment.

WORKING THE NET

1. For an informative and practical tutorial with examples and graphs on different regression models with count data (including Poisson, negative binomial, zero-inflated count models, and others), visit: *www.ats.ucla.edu/STAT/stata/seminars/count_presentation/count.htm*.
2. For a free online statistical calculator to work with the Pearson's product–moment correlation, see: *www.wessa.net*.

REAL-LIFE RESEARCH • 14.1

Axcis Athletic Shoes

Fred Luttrell is the new product development manager for Axcis Athletic Shoe Company. He recently completed consumer testing of 12 new shoe concepts. As part of this test, a panel of consumers was asked to rate the 12 shoe concepts on two attributes, overall quality and style. A 10-point scale was used with anchors at 10 = best possible and 1 = worst possible.

The panel of 20 consumers met as a group and came up with the ratings as a group. Fred believes that there is a relationship between the style ratings and the overall quality ratings. He believes that shoes receiving higher ratings on style also will tend to receive higher ratings on overall quality. The ratings results for the 12 shoe concepts are as follows.

Shoe Model	Style Rating	Quality Rating	Shoe Model	Style Rating	Quality Rating
1	9	8	7	9	7
2	7	7	8	7	9
3	6	8	9	8	6
4	9	9	10	10	9
5	8	7	11	6	5
6	5	5	12	9	10

Questions

1. Which of the statistical procedures covered in this chapter is appropriate for addressing Fred's theory? Why would you choose that technique over the other?

2. Use the technique that you chose to determine whether Fred's theory is supported by the statistical evidence. State the appropriate null and alternative hypotheses. Is Fred's theory supported by the statistical evidence? Why or why not?

 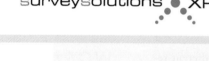

SPSS EXERCISES FOR CHAPTER 14

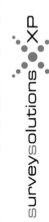

Note: If you did not complete any of the SPSS exercises in Chapter 13, you will need a corrected database from your professor.

Exercise #1: Bivariate Regression

Use the *analyze/regression/linear* sequence to invoke bivariate regression analysis. This exercise attempts to explain the variation in the *number of movies the respondent attends in an average month* (Q3). Hence, **Q3** is the **dependent variable**. Invoke the bivariate regression procedure for the following pairs of variables:

1. Q3 and Q5d (movie theater item—importance of comfortable chairs)
2. Q3 and Q5e (movie theater item—auditorium type seating)
3. Q3 and Q7a (movie theater information source—newspaper)
4. Q3 and Q7b (movie theater information source—Internet)
5. Q3 and Q7c (movie theater information source—phone in for information)
6. Q3 and Q9 (self-perception of how physically active)
7. Q3 and Q10 (self-perception of how socially active)

surveysolutions XP

Summarize the results of the bivariate regression analysis by filling in tables similar to the following ones.

Model	Regression coefficient	t	Sig.
Constant			
Q5d			
Q5e, etc.			

Variables	Model R^2	Model F-value	Sig.
Q5d			
Q5e, etc.			

1. At the 95 percent level of confidence, which of the regression models (list the pairs of variables) are significant (list the dependent variables)?

2. *Interpretation of the regression coefficients:* Use the following table to summarize the regression coefficient, b, in each of the seven regression models.

Model	Regression Coefficient b	t	Sig. of b	Interpretation of the Regression Coefficient b
Example Q3 & Q5b	.244	4.147	.000	A one-unit increase in Q5b is associated with a .244 increase in monthly movie attendance

3. Using the regression results, compute Y(Q3) if Q5d = 4. _____
4. Using the regression results, compute Y(Q3) if Q7c = 2. _____
5. Using the regression results, compute Y(Q3) if Q9 = 3. _____
6. Which of the seven models in the bivariate regression analysis explained the most variation in Q3 (*hint: R^2*)? _____
7. In which of the seven models does the independent variable's regression coefficient cause the largest change in Q3 for a one unit change in the independent variable? _____

Exercise #2: Pearson's Product–Moment Correlation

Use the *analyze/correlate/bivariate* sequence to invoke bivariate correlation analysis. This exercise utilizes the metric correlation technique (Pearson's), which requires that both variables in the bivariate analysis be of at least interval measurement scale. The objective of this exercise is to examine the association between various pairs of variables.

Invoke the bivariate correlation procedure utilizing the Pearson coefficient to evaluate the association between the following pairs of variables:

a. Q3 and Q8a (purchase option for movie tickets—Internet)
b. Q9 (self-perception of how physically active) and Q10 (self-perception of how socially active)
c. Q8a (purchase option for movie tickets—Internet) and Q7b (importance of the Internet as a source of information about movies at movie theaters)
d. Q5b (movie theater item—importance of soft drinks and food items) and Q9 (self-perception of how physically active)
e. Q5h (movie theater item—number of screens at a movie theater) and Q10 (self-perception of how socially active)

With the results of the bivariate correlation using the Pearson coefficient, fill in a table similar to the following.

Variables	Pearson Coefficient (include ±)	Probability of an insignificant correlation in the population (based on the sample results)	Interpretation of the results

Questions to Answer: (Assume a significant relationship requires at least a **95 percent** level of confidence.)

1. Of the five correlations computed, which pair of variables had the strongest association? _____

2. Of the three correlations computed, which pair of variables had the weakest association? _____

3. Do people who perceive themselves as more physically active have a greater or lesser need for food and drink at a movie theater? _____

4. Are people who use the Internet to purchase movie tickets more or less likely to use the Internet to get information about movies at movie theaters? _____

© It Stock Free/Age Fotostock America, Inc.

COMMUNICATING RESEARCH RESULTS AND MANAGING MARKETING RESEARCH

LEARNING OBJECTIVES

1.	To become aware of the primary purposes of a research report.
2.	To learn how to organize and prepare a research report.
3.	To learn how to make a personal presentation.
4.	To understand the effective use and communication of marketing research information.
5.	To understand what clients want from a marketing research supplier or department.
6.	To learn about managing a marketing research supplier organization.
7.	To become familiar with marketing research outsourcing.
8.	To gain insights into the unique management issues of managing a corporate marketing research department.
9.	To see what marketing research departments are doing to gain a more strategic role in the corporation.
10.	To examine how corporations are measuring the contribution of marketing research to the organization.

Here's a common scenario troubling many excellent researchers: Your research group is too successful. You've been head of your research department for more than a year and are worried. Things have been going very well since you took over—maybe too well. While research was sometimes an afterthought under your predecessor, you have worked hard to make your research indispensable. By having in-depth project planning conversations and using project approval forms, you have made sure that each research design fits client needs and objectives. By using state-of-the-art research methodologies and best-in-class suppliers, you have made sure that your methodologies and analyses are the best possible. By coaching your staff and hiring experienced people with a range of skills, you have several senior people in your department who think and act like consultants. And they are able to work with your clients to plan the research objectives, as well as the actions to be taken when the research is completed.

More and more clients have noticed the improvements, and they are asking for more and more research. In fact, your research volume has nearly doubled in the last year. You are being invited to participate in top management meetings, as well as in the firm's strategic planning.

So what's the problem? There's too much work, and too few resources are available. Your staff is rapidly burning out. They are starting to skip staff meetings and are too busy to build relationships among themselves or with clients between projects. When you manage to break away to attend conferences, you and your staff find yourselves working your BlackBerrys—instead of building your skills and connections. You have streamlined your basic research processes by simplifying project sign-offs, using preferred suppliers, creating report and presentation templates, and blueprinting work flow—but there is no more "fat" in your work that you can cut.

Clients keep asking you for more work. And when you politely say you are working at capacity right now, they respond by saying that they are willing to pay for the projects they want. You are simply drowning and are afraid that your work quality will soon suffer if you don't do something quickly.[1]

The above scenario, described by two marketing research consultants, cries out for better management. In this chapter we will explore how to effectively manage marketing research. This process begins with effectively communicating the research results. We will cover this important topic first. We will then examine research management from the perspective of both the research supplier and the corporate research department.

The Research Report

A good researcher is anticipating the report almost from the time she writes the proposal for a project, before she even has the business. The genesis of the report and the researcher's thinking are the objectives provided by the client in the request for proposal (RFP). Along with any background information provided with the RFP or developed as part of the process of preparing the proposal, the objectives give the researcher insight into the client's thinking and needs. What problem/opportunity is the client organization facing? What resources and competencies can it bring to bear on the problem or opportunity? What decisions is the client facing, and what information is it going to need to make those decisions in the most effective manner? If the researcher does not get a handle on these issues, then that failure will be reflected in the resulting proposal, and she probably will not get the job to begin with.

Given that we are about to write the report, we have to assume that the researcher did understand the client's needs and wrote a proposal, including a detailed methodology, that resonated with the client to the extent that she was chosen to do the work over the other competitors.

The research objectives, the decisions to be made based on the research, and a vision of the analysis and the report to be written should have guided the researcher through the design and execution of the research. For a survey-based project, the development of the questionnaire, in particular, should have been based on continuous reference to the research objectives. Now, we have the data, it has been cross-tabulated, statistical testing has been performed, extensive statistical analysis has been conducted, and the researcher and her team have spent time sifting through all of this information and relating it back to the original objectives and the decisions associated with those objectives. This process could go on and on, but deadlines in the schedule push the process to a conclusion, often faster than we would like.

The researcher has a tremendous amount of information—piles of crosstabs, reams of statistical analyses, tons of notes, and an assortment of other pieces of information. The challenge is: How to package all of this in a coherent report that efficiently and effectively communicates the key findings and the decision implications of those findings? We like to think of this process as one of trying to figure out how to tell a story. Before you can tell a story, you have to have a pretty good idea of where the story is going to end up. All the analysis brings one to that conclusion. Once you know or have ascertained the key points that you want to make, it becomes much easier to map out what you need to get across to your readers to bring them to that same conclusion.

It is important that a research firm have a consistent style for reporting. This puts all analysts on the same page so that even a glance at a report will tell clients it was produced by a certain research firm. Having said all this, we must admit that when a client has a different internal standard for reporting, it is sometimes necessary to follow a different approach than the one recommended above. In some cases, the client may even dictate that the research supplier produce the report on the client's PowerPoint template according to the client's style rules.

Organizing the Report

The traditional research report follows an outline like the following one:

1. **Title Page.** The title page should be dominated by the name of the project. Other elements that should be included are the name of the client organization, name of the research firm, and date of the report.

2. **Table of Contents.** This should not exceed one page and should list the major sections of the report along with the page numbers on which they start. It is a convenience for the reader and, often, the researcher in that it permits quick reference for finding specific information in the report.

3. **Executive Summary.** This is perhaps the most difficult part of the report to write because it must succinctly cover the key findings and any recommendations that flow from those findings. Not all reports include recommendations. Whether they include recommendations depends on the nature of the research, what is expected from the research firm, and what the research found. However, all research reports should include key findings. What makes it tough to do the executive summary is that it should be short (two to four pages at a maximum), and many researchers find it very difficult to summarize the massive amount of information available to them in just two to four pages. It is easy to be long winded, but it is difficult to be compact in your summarization. The executive summary should not summarize every single

finding but should focus on those findings that are important and relevant to the goals of the research.

4. **Background.** The background sets the context for the research and addresses such things as the overall goal of the research, the decisions that need to be made, the company's strength and weaknesses regarding the issue in question, and other similar information. It should not be more than one or two pages. Again, it is often difficult to compress a lot of information down to its essentials.

5. **Methodology.** Here we should discuss how the research was done and why it was done that way. Issues that need to be addressed include who was interviewed, why did we interview those people, how were they interviewed (for example, telephone survey, mail survey, Internet survey, or some hybrid of these methods), why were they interviewed in that manner, how were people selected, what type of sampling methodology did we use, whether the sample is a representative sample, how many people did we interview, how were the completed surveys processed, what special statistical procedures were used and why did we use those procedures, and so forth. It is not necessary that this section be long—one to two pages is appropriate. If it is necessary to address some technical elements of the methodology in a more extensive manner, then more detailed information on, for example, statistical procedures used should be provided in an appendix.

6. **Findings.** This is typically the longest section of the report and should summarize results for almost every question on the survey.

7. **Appendixes.** This final section of the report provides a number of supporting items such as a copy of the questionnaire, a set of cross tabulations for every question on the survey (client can look up specific issues not addressed in the findings), and other supporting material such as detailed technical information on special research procedures and techniques.

Interpreting the Findings

The most difficult task for individuals who are writing a research report for the first time is interpreting the findings to arrive at conclusions and then using these conclusions to formulate recommendations. The **executive summary** is the portion of the report that explains what the research found, what the data mean, and what action, if any, should be taken, based on the research. The difficulties of this process are completely understandable, given that the marketing researcher is often inundated with piles of computer printouts, stacks of questionnaires, hundreds of pages of cross tabulations, the results of hundreds of statistical tests, pages and pages of statistical analysis printouts, and a scratch pad full of notes on the project. There is, however, a systematic method that the researcher can follow to draw conclusions.

> **executive summary**
> Portion of a research report that explains why the research was done, what was found, what those findings mean, and what action, if any, management should undertake.

The research objectives and background stated early in the marketing research process should serve as the primary guide for interpreting findings and drawing conclusions. These objectives should have been stated as specifically as possible, perhaps even with an explicit priority rank for each objective. Although the questionnaire should have been designed to touch on all facets of the objectives, specific bits of information about any one objective may be spread across the questionnaire. Computer printouts often contain information in statistical order rather than in the order in which managers will use the data. Consequently, the researcher's first task is to pull together all the printouts and results that pertain to each of the various objectives. A system will evolve as the researcher focuses attention on the objectives one at a time.

For example, assume that Burger King is reconsidering its breakfast menu. An objective of its breakfast research study is "to determine the feasibility of adding (1) bagels and cream cheese, (2) a western omelette, or (3) French toast." All cross tabulations and one-dimensional tables referring to these food items should be brought together. Generally, the researcher first examines the one-dimensional tables to get the overall picture—that is, understand which of the three breakfast items was most preferred. Next, cross tabulations are analyzed to obtain a better understanding of the overall data—that is, to get a clear view of which age group is most likely to prefer French toast.

Conclusions are generalizations that answer the questions raised by the research objectives or otherwise satisfy the objectives. These conclusions are derived through the process of *induction,* or generalizing from small pieces of information. The researcher should try to merge the information and then paraphrase it in a few descriptive statements that generalize the results. In short, the conclusion of a research report should be a statement or series of statements that communicate the results of the study to the reader but would not necessarily include any of the data derived from the statistical analysis.

conclusions
Generalizations that answer the questions raised by the research objectives or otherwise satisfy the objectives.

Format of the Report

The format and preparation of marketing research reports have changed dramatically over the last 15 years. The pressure to find more efficient and effective ways to communicate research results has pushed researchers toward a heavy reliance on presentation software to tell their stories. Microsoft's PowerPoint totally dominates the market today.

A typical marketing research report tells its story with pictures or graphics. This is what clients expect and what the researcher is expected to deliver. It is not unusual for clients to specify that they want graphics-based reports in their RFPs. Research reports that might have included 50 or more pages of text and a handful of graphs in the past are now presented in a limited amount of text, perhaps just a few pages if it were all strung together, and 20 or 30 pages of graphs and tables. This approach enables time-pressed executives to quickly grasp the story and the key findings and move ahead to conclusions and recommendations. Most clients today just want a copy of the PowerPoint presentation instead of a long, detailed traditional report.

Graphics, text boxes, bulleted lists, and the like are used to interpret the meaning of various graphs. Examples of pages from a report prepared using presentation software are provided in Exhibits 15.1 through 15.9.

Formulating Recommendations

Recommendations are gained from the process of deduction. The marketing researcher applies the conclusions to specific areas in order to make suggestions for marketing strategies or tactics. A recommendation usually focuses on how the client can gain a differential advantage. A *differential advantage* is a true benefit offered by a potential marketing mix that the target market cannot obtain anywhere else (for example, American Airlines having exclusive U.S. carrier landing rights at a foreign airport).

recommendations
Conclusions applied to marketing strategies or tactics that focus on a client's achievement of differential advantage.

In some cases, a marketing researcher must refrain from making specific recommendations and instead fall back on more general ones. For example, the marketing researcher might not have sufficient information about the resources and experience base of the company or about the decision maker to whom the report is being directed. Or the researcher may have been notified that the recommendations will be determined by the decision maker. Under these circumstances, the researcher offers conclusions and stops at that point.

The final report represents the culmination of the research effort. The quality of the report and its recommendations often determine whether a client will return to a supplier. Within a corporation, an internal report prepared by a research department may have less impact, but a history of preparing excellent reports may lead to merit salary increases and, ultimately, promotion for a research staff member.

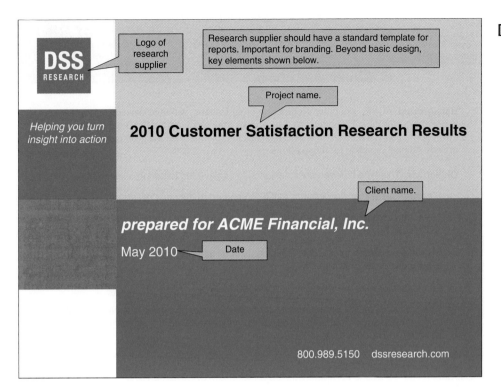

Exhibit 15.1

Sample Title Slide

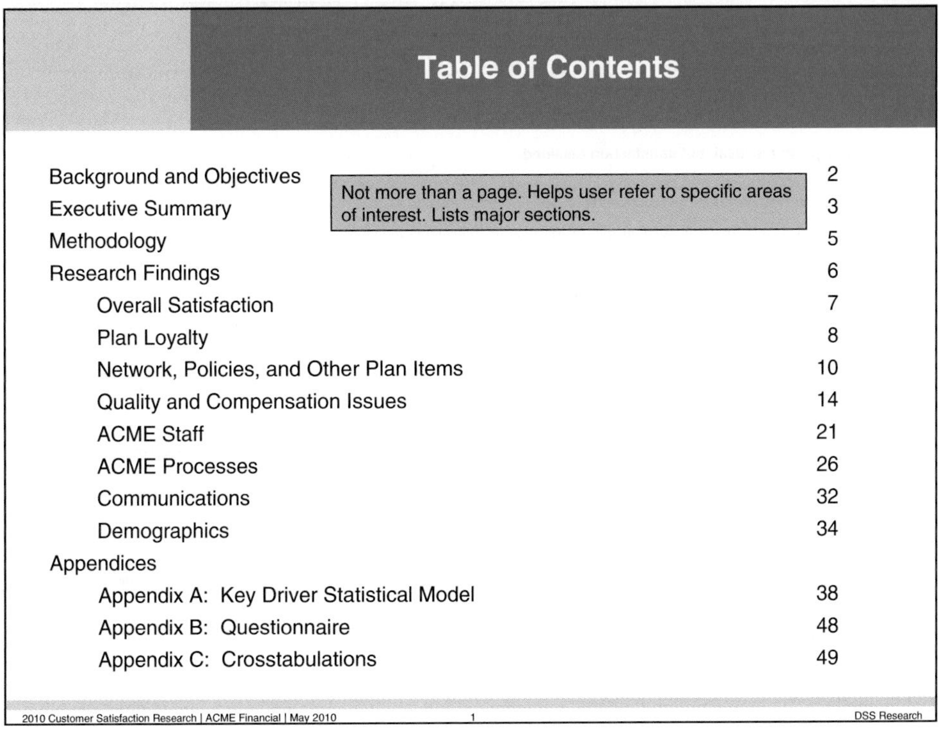

Exhibit 15.2

Sample Table of Contents

Exhibit 15.3

Sample Background and Objective

Keep it concise. Put key objectives in bulleted list.

Background and Objectives

Background. ACME, like other progressive organizations, wants to develop a program to assess customer satisfaction with the services they receive from the organization. This information will be used in ACME's quality improvement efforts. The goal is to provide rational direction for those efforts.

Objectives. This type of research is designed to achieve the following objectives:

- Measure overall satisfaction with ACME compared to the competition.

- Measure customer satisfaction with ACME's new Web site where all transactions with ACME can be handled.

- Measure satisfaction with specific elements of all other programs and services provided to customers by ACME.

- Identify major reasons for satisfaction/dissatisfaction.

- Evaluate and classify program and service elements on the basis of their importance to customers and ACME's perceived performance of ACME (i.e., identify areas of strength and opportunities for improvement).

Exhibit 15.4

Sample First Page of Executive Summary

Focus on key findings, not just reiteration of detailed results.

Executive Summary

The majority are loyal, but satisfaction declined.

- Four out of five customers see their relationship with ACME continuing on a long-term basis. Over half are categorized as secure or favorable and can be considered loyal to ACME.

- Two-thirds report they are satisfied with ACME in 2008. However, this is a significant decline from 80.1% in 2008.

- ACME overall satisfaction and loyalty measures are significantly lower than the National Average.

Heavy Users are highly satisfied; Light Users less so.

- Heavy users report significantly higher satisfaction than light users and are more likely to see their relationship with ACME continuing on a long-term basis.

- Although only a small percentage of customers is categorized as alienated, Light Users make up a higher proportion of this group.

ACME processes are primary areas of strength.

- Both the customer service and application processes are identified through key driver analysis as areas of strength for ACME.

- Satisfaction with the billing process continues an upward trend. Ratings are on par with the National Average and significantly higher than 200x.

Staff ratings remain strong, with knowledge a key asset.

- The majority of customers are satisfied with all aspects related to ACME staff. About four out of five are satisfied with staff knowledge, the area of highest satisfaction across all staff levels.

- Although still high, relatively lower staff ratings are associated with accessibility related measures. Key driver analysis identifies ease of reaching staff as an opportunity for improvement.

Exhibit 15.5

Sample Methodology Slide

Explain what was done in a simple, straightforward manner.

Methodology

Questionnaire. DSS was responsible for developing the survey instrument. ACME approved the final draft of the questionnaire. A copy of the mail survey instrument used is provided in Appendix B.

Methodology employed. Eligible respondents included a list of customers provided by ACME. The sample design is as follows:

	2010			2009			2008		
	Heavy Users	Light Users	Overall	Heavy Users	Light Users	Overall	Heavy Users	Light Users	Overall
Completed surveys	52	60	**112**	101	71	**172**	87	71	**158**
Mailed surveys	200	200	**400**	200	200	**400**	200	200	**400**
Returned undeliverable surveys	NA	NA	**4**	NA	NA	**8**	NA	NA	**14**
Response rate	26.0%	30.0%	**28.0%**	50.5%	35.5%	**43.0%**	43.5%	35.5%	**39.5%**
Adjusted response rate**	NA	NA	**28.3%**	NA	NA	**43.9%**	NA	NA	**40.9%**
Sample error*	NA	NA	**±7.9%**	NA	NA	**±5.6%**	NA	NA	**±6.1%**
Initial survey mailed	February 28, 2010			March 7, 2009			February 28, 2008		
Second survey mailed	March 21, 2010			March 28, 2009			March 21, 2008		
Last day to accept surveys	April 27, 2010			May 2, 2009			April 25, 2008		

Data collection. All data were collected by DSS Research.

Data processing and analysis. DSS processed all completed surveys and analyzed the results. A complete set of survey tabulations is provided in Appendix C of this report.

* At 95% confidence, using the most pessimistic assumption regarding variance (p=0.5).
** Excludes undeliverables.

Exhibit 15.6

Graphics Make Communication More Efficient

Slide takeaways summarize key points.

Plan loyalty

Over half of customers are categorized as secure or favorable and can be considered loyal to ACME. Another one in four is at risk though not necessarily dissatisfied. Only a small percentage is categorized as alienated; however specialists make up a greater proportion of this group.

Loyalty Analysis

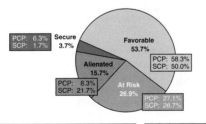

| PCP: | 6.3% |
| SCP: | 1.7% |

Secure 3.7%

Favorable 53.7%

| PCP: | 58.3% |
| SCP: | 50.0% |

Alienated 15.7%

At Risk 26.9%

| PCP: | 8.3% |
| SCP: | 21.7% |

| PCP: | 27.1% |
| SCP: | 26.7% |

National Average	
Secure:	11.8%
Favorable:	61.1%
At risk:	21.4%
Alienated:	5.6%

Questions used to determine "loyalty":

- Q13 -Overall, how satisfied are you with ACME? *Very satisfied, satisfied, dissatisfied, very dissatisfied*
- Q15 -Would you recommend ACME to your patients who asked your advice about which managed care plan to join? *Definitely yes, probably yes, probably not, definitely not*
- Q16 -Would you recommend ACME to a physician who was interested in contracting with a managed care plan? *Definitely yes, probably yes, probably not, definitely not*
- Q17 -I see my relationship with ACME continuing on a long-term basis. *Strongly agree, agree, disagree, strongly disagree*

Definitions of groups:

- **Secure** –Top box answer on all four questions. Very satisfied and loyal to ACME.
- **Favorable** –Top-two-box answer on all four questions (but not top box on all four). Satisfied and fairly loyal to ACME.
- **At Risk**–Bottom-two-box answer on one, two or three (but not all) of the four questions. Not necessarily satisfied and has questionable loyalty to ACME.
- **Alienated**–Bottom-two-box answer on all four questions. Dissatisfied and likely to leave ACME.

Exhibit 15.7

**Multiple Graphics
Provide Summary
on a Topic**

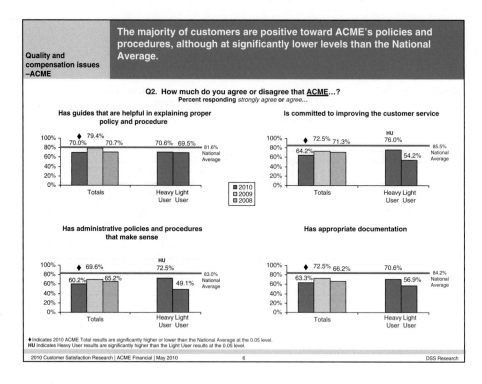

Exhibit 15.8

**Graphic and Table
Work Together**

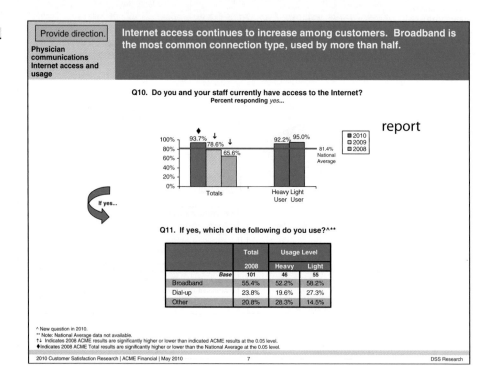

Exhibit 15.9

Graphic and Text Tell How to Interpret Statistical Results

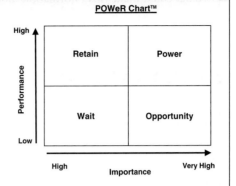

Key Driver Statistical Model
POWeR Chart ™

Classification Matrix. The importance and performance results for each item in the model are plotted in a matrix like the one shown to the right. This matrix provides a quick summary of what is most important to customers and how ACME is doing on those items. The matrix is divided into four quadrants. The quadrants are defined by the point where the medians of the importance and performance scales intersect. The four quadrants can be interpreted as follows:

- *Power.* These items are very important to customers and ACME's performance levels on these items are high. Promote and leverage your strengths in this quadrant.

- *Opportunity.* Items in this quadrant are very important to customers, but ACME's performance is below average. Focus your resources on improving processes that underlie these items and look for significant improvements in your satisfaction scores.

- *Wait.* Though still important to customers, these items are somewhat less important than those that fall on the right hand of the chart. Relatively speaking, ACME's performance is low on these items. Dealing with these items can wait until more important items have been dealt with.

- *Retain.* Items in this quadrant are also somewhat less important to customers, but ACME's performance is above average. Simply maintain your performance on these items.

2010 Customer Satisfaction Research | ACME Financial | May 2010   8   DSS Research

The Presentation

Clients may expect a presentation of the research results. A presentation serves many purposes. It requires that the interested parties assemble and become reacquainted with the research objectives and methodology. It also brings to light any unexpected events or findings and highlights the research conclusions. In fact, for some decision makers in the company, the presentation will be their *only* exposure to the findings; they will never read the report. Other managers may only skim the written report, using it as a memory-recall trigger for points made in the presentation. In short, effective communication in the presentation is absolutely critical.

Making a Presentation

An effective presentation is tailored to the audience. It takes into account the receivers' frame of reference, attitudes, prejudices, educational background, and time constraints. The speaker must select words, concepts, and illustrative figures to which the audience can relate. A good presentation allows time for questions and discussion.

One reason presentations are sometimes inadequate is that the speaker lacks an understanding of the barriers to effective communication. A second factor is that the speaker fails to recognize or admit that the purpose of many research reports is persuasion. *Persuasion* does not imply stretching or bending the truth, but rather using research findings to reinforce conclusions and recommendations. In preparing a presentation, the researcher should keep the following questions in mind:

- ☐ What do the data really mean?
- ☐ What impact do they have?

☐ What have we learned from the data?

☐ What do we need to do, given the information we now have?

☐ How can future studies of this nature be enhanced?

☐ What could make this information more useful?

Presentations on the Internet

With PowerPoint, publishing presentations to the Web is easier than ever. Publication to the Web enables individuals to access the presentation, regardless of where they are or when they need to access it. In addition, researchers can present results at multiple locations on the Internet. The steps are very simple:

1. Open your presentation in PowerPoint. To see what your slides will look like on the Web, choose "Web Page Preview" from the "File" menu. After you have made any edits, choose "Save as Web Page" from the same menu.

2. The "Save As" dialog box allows you to change the title of your presentation to whatever you want displayed in the title bar of your visitor's browser.

3. The "Publish" button takes you to the "Publish as Web Page" dialog box, where you can customize your presentation.

4. The "Web Options" dialog box lets you specify the way your published file will be stored on the Web server and whether to update internal links to these files automatically.

We now turn our attention from making effective presentations to managing the marketing research function.

Marketing Research Supplier Management

What Do Clients Want?

Managing a marketing research supplier organization involves understanding what clients want and expect, maintaining good communications with the client, effectively managing the research process, and good time management, cost management, and client profitability management. If a marketing research department in a large organization is conducting its own research, then it will also face these same managerial issues. If it farms out its research, then good management requires selecting the right vendor. A research department must also try to become less of an "order taker" and play a greater role in the marketing decision-making process within the organization.

Market Directions, a marketing research firm in Kansas City, Missouri, asked marketing research clients across the United States to rate the importance of several statements about research companies and research departments. Replies from a wide range of industries are summarized in the following top-10 list:

1. Maintains client confidentiality

2. Is honest

3. Is punctual

4. Is flexible

5. Delivers against project specifications
6. Provides high-quality output
7. Is responsive to the client's needs
8. Has high quality-control standards
9. Is customer oriented in interactions with client
10. Keeps the client informed throughout a project.[2]

The two most important factors, confidentiality and honesty, are ethical issues, which were covered earlier in the text. The remaining issues relate to managing the research function and maintaining good communication.

Communication

The key to good supplier–client relations is excellent communication. Every project should have a liaison who serves as a communication link between the supplier and the client. In large firms, this individual may be an account executive or project manager, while in small firms, he or she may be an owner or a partner. But, whatever the job title, the liaison must communicate accurately, honestly, and frequently with the client.

Before a project begins, the communication liaison should go over the project objectives, methodology, and timing with the client to make certain that there are no misunderstandings. The client should then sign off on the questionnaire, thereby agreeing that the questionnaire is sufficient to gather the raw data needed to accomplish the research objectives.

John Colias, vice-president of M/A/R/C Research, says the following about communication between a research supplier and its client:

When a company hires a market research firm to design a study, the supplier must operate as part of the team of researchers and marketers. To be an effective member of the team, the supplier must also intimately understand the marketing questions. This understanding results from interactive dialogue among the researcher, marketer, and the supplier about the marketing questions and business decisions. Such a dialogue crystallizes the research objectives into concrete deliverables that directly influence business decisions.[3]

The liaison must ascertain how often the client wants progress reports. At a minimum, these reports should be issued weekly. The report should cover the status of the project, unusual problems encountered, and, if it is a cost-plus project, expenses incurred to date. *Cost-plus* refers to actual costs plus an additional markup to cover overhead. Cost-plus projects are typically found in situations where a research department of a large corporation, such as General Foods, conducts a project for another department.

Managing the Research Process

Research management has seven important goals beyond excellent communication: building an effective organization, assurance of data quality, adherence to time schedules, cost control, client profitability management, and staff management and development.

Organizing the Supplier Firm Traditionally, most marketing research firms were organized around functions. Large suppliers, for example, may have separate departments for sampling, questionnaire programming, field, coding, tabulation, statistics,

> **research management**
> Overseeing the development of excellent communication systems, data quality, time schedules, cost controls, client profitability, and staff development.

and sales. Even the client service staff may be separate from those who manage projects and write questionnaires and reports. Each of these departments has a head who is expert in the functions of that department and manages work assignments within the department. Projects flow from department to department.

A functional form of organization allows technical people to perform backroom tasks such as programming and data analysis and the "people people" to handle project management and client contact. It provides for knowledgeable supervision, so that, for example, beginners in sample design are working under the direction of veteran experts. It permits the development of good work processes and quality standards, so that tasks are performed consistently. It lets the difficulty of a given project be matched with the skill of the person doing it, so that routine work is given to junior staff and the most complex tasks are reserved for the expert. This matching of work and skill levels leads to happier staff and lower project costs.

Yet functional organizations are not without their problems. Department staff can become focused on the execution of their task, to the detriment of the whole process and the client. Departmental standards and scheduling policies may take on lives of their own, optimizing the efficiency and quality of a department's work but making timely completion of the whole project difficult. By becoming removed from client contact, departments can become inwardly oriented, viewing clients as problems rather than the source of their livelihood. Interdepartmental communication and scheduling can become time-consuming and flawed, as project managers or operations schedulers negotiate each project's schedule with a series of independent department heads. Each department may feel that it is performing perfectly, yet the whole process viewed from the outside can seem rigid, bureaucratic, and ineffective.

In response to problems like these, some companies are organizing by teams. They are breaking up functional departments and organizing their staff into units based around client groups or research types. These teams include people with all or most of the skills necessary to complete a study from beginning to end. A typical team might include several client service/project management people, a field director, a questionnaire programmer, and a tab specwriter. Staff are frequently cross-trained in multiple functions. The team is almost always headed by a senior staff member with a client service or project management background.

There are many variations on this theme. Within the teams, work may remain specialized (the specwriter does the tables), or there can be extensive cross-training (everyone does tables). Highly specialized functions (such as statistical analysis) that are carried out by one or two experts may remain as functional departments, available to all. A hybrid approach is also possible, where some functions are moved within the teams, while others (such as field management) remain as separate departments.

Because each client group controls its own resources, scheduling and communication are easier. With no department heads or central scheduling to go through, the group head directly prioritizes the work of everyone working on his or her projects.

Technical and operations personnel become closer to clients and more aligned with their needs. By reducing the organizational distance between the client and these staff members, it is easier for them to appreciate the client's situation and focus on serving his or her needs.

Staff may develop more flexibility and broader skills. Cross-training and cross-assignment of work are easier when all the people involved report to the same person.[4]

Effective time management is becoming increasingly important in all aspects of professional life. One requirement of research management is to keep a project on the schedule specified by the client.

PhotoDisc, Inc./Getty Images

Data Quality Management   Perhaps the most important objective of research management is to ensure the quality or integrity of the data produced by the research process. You have probably heard announcers on television say, "The poll had a margin of error of 3 percent." Some problems and implicit assumptions are associated with this statement. First, you learned in the discussion of sampling error in Chapter 13 that this statement is missing an associated level of confidence. In other words, how confident are the pollsters that the poll has a margin of error of 3 percent? Are they 68.26 percent confident, 95.44 percent confident, 99.74 percent confident, or confident at some other level? Second, this statement does not make clear that the margin of error applies only to *random sampling error*. The implicit, or unstated, assumption is that there are no other sources of error, that all other sources of error have been effectively dealt with by the research design and procedures, or that all other sources of error have been effectively randomized by taking summary measures across the entire sample. By definition, error is random when there are just as many errors in one direction as in the other direction, leaving overall measures, such as averages, unaffected. Marketing research managers can help assure high-quality data by having policies and procedures in place to minimize sources of error (see Chapter 5).

A recent Harris poll found that there are a lot of misperceptions about error out there. After surveying 1,052 U.S. adults, Harris reported the following:

- ☐ Fifty-two percent of all adults believe, wrongly, that statements about "the margin of error being plus or minus 3 percent" mean that "all of the results of the survey are accurate to within a maximum of 3 percent given all types of error."

- ☐ A 66 percent majority of adults believes, wrongly, that the phrase "margin of error" includes calculation of errors caused by "how the questions are worded."

- ☐ Large minorities believe, wrongly, that the calculation of the margin of error includes errors in developing a representative base or weighting errors (45 percent), mistakes made by interviewers (45 percent), and errors because of where the questions are placed in the survey (40 percent).

- ☐ Only 12 percent of the public agrees that the words "margin of error" should only address one specific source of error, sampling error—as they almost always do.

- ☐ A 56 percent majority believes that statements about margin of error do not make it clear that this calculation excludes all sources of error except for sampling error for a pure random sample.[5]

Marketing researchers must not only attempt to minimize error, but must also do a better job of explaining the term *margin of error*. Simply saying "a survey statistic has a margin of error of plus or minus 3 percent" gives a false impression of accuracy to the typical audience. Readers should be informed of other possible sources of error, such as interviewer bias or question wording, even if it is not feasible, or practical, to calculate these errors.

Also, managers must have in place procedures to ensure the careful proofing of all text, charts, and graphs in written reports and other communications provided to the client. Mistakes may mislead a client into making the wrong decision. Suppose the data suggest purchase intent at 18 percent, but the report shows 81 percent; this typographical mistake could easily lead to an incorrect decision. If the client finds even small mistakes, the credibility of the researcher and all of the research findings may be brought into serious question. The rule of thumb is to never provide information to the client that has not been very carefully checked.

Time Management   A second goal of research management is to keep the project on schedule. Time management is important in marketing research because clients often have a specified time schedule that they must meet. For example, it may be absolutely imperative that the research results be available on March 1 so that they can be presented at the quarterly meeting of the new product committee. The findings will affect whether the test product will receive additional funding for development.

Two problems that can play havoc with time schedules are inaccuracies in estimates of the incidence rate and the interview length. A lower-than-expected incidence rate will require more interviewing resources than originally planned to get the job done on time. If the research manager does not have idle resources to devote to the project, then it will take longer to complete. The same is true for a longer-than-anticipated interview.

Recall that the *incidence rate* is the percentage of persons or households out of the general population that fit the qualifications to be interviewed in a particular study. Often, estimates of incidence rate are based not on hard-and-fast data but on data that are incomplete, known to be relatively inaccurate, or dated. Incidence rate problems cannot only increase the amount of time required to complete the sample for the project but also negatively affect the costs of the data-collection phase of the research.

The project manager must have early information regarding whether or not a project can be completed on time. If a problem exists, the manager must first determine whether anything can be done to speed up the process. Perhaps training additional interviewers would help expedite completion of the survey. Second, the researcher must inform the client that the project is going to take longer than expected. The researcher can then explore with the client whether a time extension is possible or what changes the client might be willing to make to get the project completed on the original time schedule. For example, the client might be willing to reduce the total sample size or shorten the length of the interview by eliminating questions that are judged to be less critical. Thus, it is very important that the system be structured so that both the researcher and the client are alerted to potential problems within the first few days of the project.

Time management, like cost control, requires that systems be put in place to inform management as to whether or not the project is on schedule. Policies and procedures must be established to efficiently and quickly solve schedule problems and promptly notify the client about the problem and potential solutions.

Cost Management   In comparison to data quality and time management, cost management is straightforward. All it requires is adherence to good business practices, such as procedures for cost tracking and control. In particular, good procedures for cost control include the following elements:

- ☐ Systems that accurately capture data collection and other costs associated with the project on a daily basis.

- ☐ Daily reporting of costs to the communication liaison. Ideally, reports should show actual costs in relation to budget.

- ☐ Policies and practices in the research organization that require the liaison to communicate the budget picture to clients and to senior managers at the research company.

- ☐ Policies and practices that quickly identify over-budget situations and then find causes and seek solutions.

If the project is over budget because the client provided information that proved to be erroneous (for example, incidence rate, interview length), then it is imperative that the client be offered options early in the process: a higher cost, smaller sample size, shorter interview, or some combination of these. If the firm waits until the project is complete to communicate this problem to the client, the client is likely to say, "You should have told me sooner—there is nothing I can do now." In this situation, the firm will probably have to swallow the cost overrun.

Outsourcing One way that research firms are cutting costs is outsourcing. The term **outsourcing** as used in this text is having personnel in another country perform some, or all, of the functions involved in a marketing research project. When a research firm sets up a wholly-owned foreign subsidiary, it is called **captive outsourcing**. Simple outsourcing is where a domestic research company enters into a relationship with a foreign company that provides a variety of marketing research functions. For example, Cross-Tab Services of Mumbai, India, offers online survey programming, data processing, data analysis, and other services. Other services that are beginning to be outsourced are data management and panel management. A number of issues need to be considered when one is outsourcing, as shown in Exhibit 15.10.

India is most likely the world leader in marketing research outsourcing firms. Over 110 marketing research outsourcing firms in India (noncaptive) employ over 9,000 people.[6] The country's revenues from marketing research outsourcing are expected to reach $800 million by 2012.[7]

Client Profitability Management While marketing research departments may be able to focus on doing "on-demand" projects for internal clients, marketing research suppliers have to think about profitability. The old adage that 20 percent of the clients generate 80 percent of the profits is often true.

Custom Research Incorporated (CRI), of Minneapolis, realized a few years back that it had too many clients—or too few good ones.[8] The company divided its clients into four categories based on the client's perceived value to CRI's bottom line (see

outsourcing
Having personnel in another country perform some, or all, of the functions involved in a marketing research project.

captive outsourcing
When a research firm creates a wholly-owned foreign facility for outsourcing.

EXHIBIT 15.10	Outsourcing Issues
Issues	**Management Strategies**
Confidentiality	Proper confidentiality and data security agreements need to be signed with third-party providers and senior personnel of captive centers. Frequent audits are also recommended to ensure compliance.
Infrastructure	It is important that the destination country and the city selected within the country have access to required infrastructure such as power, bandwidth, good connectivity through airports, hotel facilities for visits by customer's team, and of course talented workers.
Quality of deliverables	Careful documentation is important for processes executed in any location, but they are doubly important in the case of offshore outsourcing. Also, proper systems and protocols must be laid down for communication between teams in the client country and in the vendor country.
Domain knowledge	It is important to ensure that the senior members of the team in the offshore location have a strong domain understanding of market research and do not have just an IT or data processing background.
Cultural issues	It is necessary to understand the culture of the offshore location and the sensitivities of the people. Cultural misunderstandings can cause misgivings and can affect the quality of work.
Job losses in the client country and associated negative publicity for the agency	Good people can be retained and be provided jobs in other roles in the same agency in order to fuel the growth that will result from the cost savings realized. It is important to have a proper PR initiative to explain the benefits of offshoring to the economy of the client country. (Economic studies have shown that in the long term offshoring leads to greater benefits for the economy of the client country and actually creates more jobs.)
Employee liability	This risk is not an issue if one outsources to third-party providers. If one is going the captive route, then it is important to carefully study the employment laws of the destination country to ensure no legal conflicts.

Source: Ashwin Mittal and Kedar Sohoni, "A Brief Guide to Oursourcing," *Quirk's Marketing Research Review* (November 2005), p. 70.

Exhibit 15.11

CRI's Client Profitability Analysis

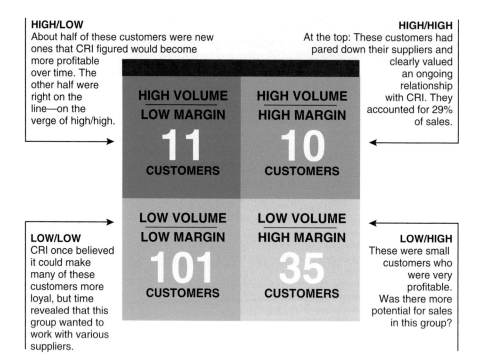

HIGH/LOW
About half of these customers were new ones that CRI figured would become more profitable over time. The other half were right on the line—on the verge of high/high.

HIGH/HIGH
At the top: These customers had pared down their suppliers and clearly valued an ongoing relationship with CRI. They accounted for 29% of sales.

| HIGH VOLUME LOW MARGIN 11 CUSTOMERS | HIGH VOLUME HIGH MARGIN 10 CUSTOMERS |
| LOW VOLUME LOW MARGIN 101 CUSTOMERS | LOW VOLUME HIGH MARGIN 35 CUSTOMERS |

LOW/LOW
CRI once believed it could make many of these customers more loyal, but time revealed that this group wanted to work with various suppliers.

LOW/HIGH
These were small customers who were very profitable. Was there more potential for sales in this group?

Exhibit 15.11). Only 10 of CRI's 157 customers fell into the most desirable category (generating a high dollar volume and a high profit margin). Another 101 customers contributed very little to the top or bottom line. In short, CRI was spending too much time and too many valuable employee resources on too many unprofitable customers.

In assessing which customers to keep, CRI calculated the profit for each one by subtracting all direct costs and selling expenses from the total revenues brought into CRI by that customer for the year. That is, CRI asked, "What costs would we not incur if this customer went away?" The cutoff points for high and low scores were purely subjective; they corresponded to CRI's goals for profit volume and profit margin. CRI management decided that it had to systematically drop a large number of old customers and carefully screen potential new customers. CRI's screening questions for new customers are shown in Exhibit 15.12.

Using the customer's analysis, CRI went from 157 customers and $11 million in revenue to 78 customers and $30 million in revenue. Most importantly, profits more than doubled. Managers had calculated they'd need to reap about 20 to 30 percent more business from some two dozen companies to help make up for the roughly 100 customers they planned to "let go" within two years. This was accomplished by building a close personal relationship with the clients that remained. The process involved CRI's researching the industry, the client company, and its research personnel to fully understand the client's needs. For each client, CRI created a Surprise and Delight plan to deliver a "value-added" bonus to the client. For example, Dow Brands received some complimentary software that CRI knew the company needed. This one-on-one relationship marketing has been the key to CRI's success.

Staff Management and Development   The primary asset of any marketing research firm is its people. Proprietary techniques and models can help differentiate a marketing research company, but eventually its success depends on the professional nature of its staff and their determination to deliver a quality product. Consequently, recruiting and retaining a competent, enthusiastic staff are crucial and constant management challenges.

EXHIBIT 15.12	Screening Questions Used by CRI and the Rationale for Each Question
Question	**Rationale**
How did you hear about us?	A bad answer: "I found you in the Yellow Pages." Unlike many companies, CRI doesn't ask this question so that it can decide how to divvy up the marketing dollars. "If someone finds us in the Yellow Pages, they have no reason to use us over anyone else," CRI cofounder Judy Corson explains. A good answer: "A colleague of mine worked with you at another company."
What kind of work is it (in terms of industry or scope)?	More than anything, the answer reveals whether the caller is trying to price a quick, one-time project or one that's totally outside CRI's realm. If so, the caller is referred to an indirect competitor.
What's your budget?	That's akin to asking someone how much money he or she makes, but the prospect's response to a ballpark guess on the cost of the project helps CRI ascertain what the client has in mind.
What are your decision criteria?	CRI knows that it doesn't fare well in blind bidding or in drawn-out, committee-style decisions, so it's interested in dealing with callers who have some level of decision-making power—and assiduously avoids getting involved in anything that smells like a bidding war.
Whom are we competing against for your business?	CRI likes to hear the names of its chief rivals, a half-dozen large companies, including the M/A/R/C Group, Market Facts, and Burke Marketing Research.
Why are you thinking of switching?	"There's a two-edged sword here," explains cofounder Jeff Pope. "Clients that are hard to break into are better because they don't switch too easily. But you need a way to get in—so a legitimate need for a new supplier is OK." Each month only 2 or 3 of 20 to 30 callers answer enough questions correctly to warrant more attention. So why spend time with the rest? "Do unto others. . . . You never know where people will go."

Source: Susan Greco, "Choose or Lose," *INC.* (December 1998), pp. 57–59, 62–66.

Kathleen Knight is president and CEO of BAIGlobal, Incorporated, a Tarrytown, New York, marketing research firm. She offers several suggestions for staff development in a research firm:

1. *Create an environment that encourages risk taking, experimentation, and responsibility.* The benefits to the research firm, such as new service development, new techniques, and business growth, outweigh any potential risks. However, employees need to feel that they will be supported in taking risks. New ideas and different business approaches need to be treated with respect and given room to develop.

2. *Foster recognition and accountability.* Recognize good effort and reward it. One of the best forms of reward is visibility within the company. Make sure that everyone knows when an outstanding job was done and that excellence matters.

3. *Provide job autonomy within a certain structure.* Marketing research is a technical science, and the numbers have to add up. But it also is a business, and projects have to generate money to pay the bills. Within these boundaries, there are many different ways to get the job done. Let employees put their personal stamp on a project and they will feel like true partners in their work.

4. *Attract and support people with entrepreneurial attitudes.* Set business goals and management parameters; then let the staff determine the path to take to get the job done. This allows each person to leverage his or her own abilities and achieve the highest level of success.

5. *Connect rewards to a business result.* Providing open financial data to researchers seems to create a business consciousness that is exciting for all. Often, very talented researchers know little about the financial dynamics of the industry. They welcome the chance to learn and thus become more accountable for bottom-line results.

6. *Open your financial books.* Research firms can provide senior employees with full financial information to let them know how well they are doing across the months and years. The bottom line is the best aggregate measure of performance—individually, as a group, and as a firm. Opening the books establishes a common mission and goal across the organization.

7. *Offer diversity within your organization.* It's fun and exciting to learn new products, serve new clients, and work with a new research team. A chance at a new position is often the spark someone needs to really do well within a firm. And the possibility of this kind of job change seems to add to the satisfaction that employees feel. If you pay attention to individuals and create a career path across disciplines within your organization, it's more likely that talented researchers will stay.

8. *Provide clear promotional paths.* Employees like to know how they can advance and want to feel some control over their careers. Clear criteria and expectations go a long way toward helping researchers feel comfortable. In the marketing research business, the best training is as an apprentice, working with senior researchers doing interesting work. Talented people will grow and prosper where the expectations are that senior managers will be mentors, that junior staff will learn, and that excellent work produced together will lead to everyone's career advancement.[9]

Managing a Marketing Research Department

A manager of a marketing research department within a corporation faces a different set of issues from a research supplier. Among these issues are effective spending of the research budget, prioritizing projects for the corporation, retaining skilled staff, selecting the right research suppliers, moving the marketing research function to a more strategic role in the firm, and measuring return on investment for marketing research.

Allocating the Research Department Budget[10]

No matter who controls the research project budget, it's important to spend money and (most importantly) research staff time wisely. That is especially important when the clients (new product development managers or brand managers) fund each project and cannot understand why the marketing research department doesn't have the staff time to do whatever they want. In that case, many research heads are learning how to prioritize projects. There are several effective ways to accomplish that.

A research study found that only about 20 percent of research projects are focused on strategically important issues. The other 80 percent of projects are focused on tactical issues, such as setting prices, advertising, distributing products, or adding new features to existing products. Researchers and clients agree that they would prefer to spend more time on the strategic issues, such as identifying promising new markets or developing new products and services.[11]

For example, one research group took it upon itself to improve its firm's new product development process by bringing together experts from marketing research, marketing, research and development, manufacturing, and sales to design a new process.

Another research group head learned to facilitate strategic planning (an ad hoc effort in her firm), so that she could help her executive team plan when cross-functional action was needed.

Several research heads said that they try to meet with their clients annually before budgeting season begins to talk about what research issues will be most important to clients in the coming year. Both parties then agree on the vital projects for the coming year and on how much time or money to allocate to them. While everyone admits that unforeseen circumstances almost always force the plans to be altered, having an annual plan enables a manager to adapt quickly and be flexible.

Many department heads say that they believe it's important for the research group to have a discretionary budget for important projects. That is considered especially important if research projects are usually funded by the clients. One new director of research used the discretionary budget to study why demand for his organization's main product appeared to be dropping in the face of a changing industry. Another researcher paid for a project on store designs because he felt that the designs were probably holding back sales—and he was right. Still another group paid to learn scenario planning and used it to help clients pick options for new-product testing.

Prioritize Projects

Estimating the financial return from a research project is a great way to rationalize spending across projects because it provides a quantitative methodology that helps clients identify "must-have" versus "nice-to-have" projects. It is not only an effective way of turning away less important work; it also helps strengthen relations with clients because it shows that researchers are thinking about their bottom line, too. We will present a way to measure return on investment (ROI) for marketing research, created by research consultants Diane Schmalensee and A. Dawn Lesh, later in the chapter.

Estimating the return on investment (ROI) for a given project has several advantages. First, estimating the expected returns on research before beginning work may help: Focus the research on important research objectives and clarify client needs; differentiate projects that are likely to be implemented (and thus have a higher ROI) from those that may not lead to action; clarify how much money and time it is worth spending on a project given its expected financial payoff.

Second, measuring the payoff of research does not end during the planning stages: Ideally, researchers check back with their clients after the work is completed to validate the actual payoff. This permits researchers and clients to learn how accurate the original ROI estimate was as well as how to improve future estimates.

Finally, having ROI discussions with clients both before and after projects is a great way to show that the research function is a partner with its clients—sharing client objectives and spending research monies effectively. This process has the added benefit of allowing overworked research staff to shrink or delay less important research.

Retaining Skilled Staff

When researchers are feeling overworked and finding it difficult to meet client needs without sacrificing their personal time needs, they begin to burn out and think about working elsewhere. Losing a skilled staff member can damage a research group: It means more work for the remaining staff members, and it can leave a hole in valuable client relationships. It is especially important to recognize and reward hard-working staff members. How can this be done? Research shows that staff members of marketing research departments value doing interesting and fulfilling work, getting recognition for a job well done, and earning adequate pay.[12]

A few techniques for retaining key research staff are as follows:

1. Conduct regular performance reviews that give continuing feedback on a job well done—or offer ways to improve. Many staff members think their bosses play favorites during performance reviews. So department heads try to use clear performance criteria for each position and offer objective appraisals for everyone.

2. Offer public recognition for great work. Some groups mention great work during staff meetings; post client comments on a "wall of fame" in the department; have bosses send personal letters to staff members at home, praising their work; hold pizza parties for teams that have performed "above and beyond"; or simply have the head of the department stop by a staff member's office to offer congratulations and thanks.

3. Give differential pay raises that recognize superior performance. While across-the-board, uniform pay increases are often used (because they are the easiest to administer), they do not recognize the high performers—and they allow the lower performers to believe they are doing adequate work.

4. Vary the work. In order to keep everyone interested, some research groups identify one-off projects and then allow staff members to volunteer for them. Examples of special projects could include a project that will feed into the firm's strategic plans, formation of a high-visibility cross-functional team, or a project that uses a new technique or addresses an unusually interesting topic.[13]

Selecting the Right Marketing Research Suppliers

Once the nature, scope, and objectives of the project have been determined, the next step is to assess the capabilities of alternative suppliers. Some research vendors have a particular area of specialization. Some firms specialize in advertising or customer satisfaction research, while others are devoted to a particular technique (for example, conjoint analysis or market segmentation) or data-collection method (for example, mall intercepts, mail surveys, or Internet panels).

A research department manager should beware of firms committed to a particular technique and/or data-collection method, as they are more likely to "force" the department's research project into their particular model, rather than tailor the research to fit the specific needs of the research department's project.

Research department managers must consider the size of the firms in their decision. The size of the vendor is an extremely important decision criterion. It is important not to overwhelm a small firm with an enormous project, and, conversely, a small project may not get the proper attention at a large firm.

The general rule is to favor the smallest firm consistent with the scope of the project. However, any project that is 30 percent or more of a marketing research supplier's annual revenues may be too large for that firm to handle effectively.

The research department manager should establish, up front, the individual who will be managing the project. It should be determined in advance who would be responsible for the day-to-day management of the project; that is, will it be the person who "sold" the project or a project director hundreds of miles away? If the contact becomes unavailable, will competent support staff be available?

The research department manager needs to become acquainted with the backgrounds of the potential vendors. There are some general questions that every potential vendor should be asked to determine the stability of the company and its qualifications to complete the project in a satisfactory manner. These questions would include:

☐ How long has the vendor been in business?

☐ For what other companies has the vendor conducted research projects? Remember it is imperative to request references and check them for each firm.

☐ What are the academic backgrounds and experience of those persons who will be working on the project, that is, the project director, field director, data processing manager, and so forth? Does the composition of the project team strike the right balance between top-level management and technical researchers and analysts?

☐ Does the success of the project depend on the capabilities of a subcontractor? If the marketing research supplier will be subcontracting any elements of the project, it is important that the subcontractor and his or her qualifications be identified.

Also, the research manager should review the quality control standards of each potential vendor. The validity of the results of any research project is dependent on the quality control measures practiced by the vendor. For example, on telephone studies, what are the procedures with respect to callbacks, monitoring, and validation? It is prudent to avoid firms that do not practice generally accepted practices in their operations.

The reputations of the firms must be considered in the decision. Reputation is important, but a department should not pay a larger premium for it. However, some situations may require the services of a prestigious research firm because a company plans to publicize the results, or use them in advertisements, so having the best reputation available may actually be a good investment. For example, Dell touts its standings in J.D. Power Customer Satisfaction surveys.

Finally, a manager should avoid letting price be the sole determining factor in the selection. When reviewing proposals, price should be the last item to be considered.[14]

Moving Marketing Research into a Decision-Making Role

A more strategic managerial question regarding the marketing research department is the role and importance of marketing research in the managerial decision-making process. The researchers' challenge is to shed their long-held traditional role as a support function, one that reacts to requests from project and new product development managers and then focuses on producing the numbers but not on their meaning to the business.

"There's a gap between what research believes it's capable of providing and what top management perceives it can get from research," says Larry Stanek, senior associate of the Hartman Group, located in Bellevue, Washington. "Researchers believe they have answers critical to decision making, while management views research as having the data but maybe not the insight to drive business."[15]

Experts agree that, to earn the ear of senior management, researchers must move beyond the task of simply crunching numbers and churning out results; they need to understand the underlying business issues at stake and adjust the information they gather and how they analyze it. They also must reach out to other departments, building relationships and a better understanding of the issues companywide. "We need to evolve just from doing research to doing insights," says Peter Daboll, chief of insights for Sunnyvale, California-based Yahoo! Inc. "If you want to be at the table you have to be senior. [To be senior means to] go from collecting, collating and presenting to anticipating, reconciling and recommending. . . . [Executives] want the freaking answer, not the tool to give them the answer."[16]

Experts also suggest that researchers should spend more time discussing the decisions that need to be made with the results before designing and conducting a study—to avoid a that's-nice-to-know-but-I-really-need-this-*other*-information response from management. And when it comes to reporting results, researchers must translate the numbers into specific recommendations and even link the findings to other data that management typically uses to make decisions. Not surprisingly, researchers agree that securing a seat at the table not only demands strong analytical abilities, but also so-called softer skills in persuasion, communication, and presentation.

"I strongly emphasize that while [the research managers and associates] may be in my official marketing research department—it's my insistence that they view themselves as members of the business team" first and foremost, says Daryl Papp, Lilly's director of U.S. market research. He adds that about half of his department comprises professionals who come from areas of marketing other than research for a several-year "broadening assignment" to learn about the company's businesses. Papp believes that having marketing researchers sit side by side with other colleagues who aspire to high-level management helps contribute to the business-oriented mentality in his department.[17]

Most firms rely on marketing research departments to provide data to the brand marketing and sales teams so that successes can be achieved in many areas, including new product launches, brand management and stewardship, the efficiency of marketing operations, and advertising effectiveness. In this context, the marketing researcher participates on a team charged with accomplishing an objective for the firm. The great majority of a firm's marketing research activities fall into this category. At this stage, the question of whether the objective or initiative has merit is already decided. The marketing researcher helps the team make decisions about the most efficient and effective ways to spend its limited marketing funds to achieve the greatest result. This is not limited to new product initiatives. These activities include tracking studies, usage and attitude studies, copy testing and advertising research, sales promotion evaluation, sales analysis, strategic positioning studies, and many more.[18]

In order to influence senior management, the marketing researcher needs to move beyond fulfilling research assignments designed to avoid failure or enable success. When marketing researchers look beyond already-generated ideas and already-created products, services, ads, or distribution channels, their strategic value increases. And this begins to attract management's attention. Management places high value on this activity because companies need growth, which has become exceedingly hard to achieve. At its best, marketing research redefines business strategy by using data in novel ways to create a sustainable competitive advantage (see Exhibit 15.13).[19]

To keep management's attention during strategic presentations, Barry Jennings, marketing research manager for Dell Computer, offers an excellent tip. Jennings says that researchers can best sell their data to executives when they explicitly present their research as relaying the voice of the customer. "So often we use words like 'respondent' or 'participant,' but they are all customers. (When you say) 'customers say' this or that—then the C-level listens because they can then put a dollar value on them. . . . Putting it in their language makes a huge, huge difference," he says. "The customer needs a seat at the table."[20]

Measuring Marketing Research's Return on Investment (ROI)

The old view of marketing as an art form disappeared long ago. In its place is the notion of strict accountability. Marketing expenditures become investments, with performance measures coming from the world of finance. So it has become increasingly fashionable in large corporations to demand that marketing research prove its worth. The approach that is gaining in popularity is ROI. Recall that ROI is simply the after-tax income from an investment divided by the dollar amount of the investment. Several arguments can be made against using ROI to measure the value of marketing research to an organization.

First, ROI is theoretically flawed because it divides the profit return by the expenditure instead of subtracting it. All reputable bottom-line metrics, such as profit, cash

EXHIBIT 15.13	A Researcher's Route to the Table		
	Area of Influence	**Key Contribution**	**How**
On the Management Radar	Transforming the Business	Discovering new and better business strategies	Innovating with data.
	Discovering Opportunities	Finding new opportunities or products to become passionate about	Using data to spot the next trend. Assessing failures and learning from them. Helping creators to innovate through better input from the marketplace.
Below the Management Radar	Enabling Success	Serving as a passionate member of the team	Researching the market and customers to improve marketing for existing products. Using research to achieve greatest leverage at lowest cost. Overcoming obstacles to shorten time lines. Finding conclusions faster.
	Avoiding Failure	Remaining objective so team passion can be channeled into the right initiatives	At minimum, preventing the firm from making errors. Proving the potential of great new ideas. Quickly and accurately predicting marketplace success.

Source: John Huppertz, "Passion vs. Dispassion," *Marketing Research* (Summer 2003), p. 21.

flow, payback, and shareholder value, subtract expenditure from income. Dividing one into the other distorts the result.

Second, ROI was invented to compare alternative uses of capital, based on their projected percentage return on that capital. Market research (MR), however, is usually a stream of costs that continue for the purposes of comparison in each and every year. Market research is rarely an investment in the true sense of the word.

Third, improving ROI tends to suboptimize expenditure. Most investments have diminishing profit returns. The early profits give the greatest ROI, but maximizing productivity (i.e., total profit return) requires more expenditure beyond that. Would you rather, at the same low level of risk, have a 100 percent return on $2 or an 80 percent return on $1,000? This objection arises directly from the division rather than subtraction anomaly.

Fourth, ROI usually focuses on the short term and does not consider the effects on the marketing asset (brand equity) or the dynamic development of marketing over longer time periods.

Fifth, the purpose of the ROI ratio is to compare alternative expenditures. Research is not really an alternative to the elements of the marketing mix it should control. Such a comparison does not contrast like with like. Internal information, such as the management accounts or budgets, is a closer comparison as it fights with marketing metrics for space on the dashboard used by top management to help drive the business. And yet when did anyone call for the ROI on the internal accounting function?[21]

Despite the negatives, the growing popularity of ROI deserves further examination into how it can be operationalized. Two approaches are ROI Lite and ROI Complete created by Dawn Lesh, president of New York-based A. Dawn Lesh International, and Diane Schmalensee, president of Schmalensee Partners in Chestnut Hill, Massachusetts.[22]

ROI Lite   To measure ROI Lite, MR asks the client for two estimates during pre-project planning:

1. The anticipated dollar value of the decision that will be based on the research.
2. The anticipated increase in confidence of making the "right" decision. For example, instead of saying a decision is worth $10 million, a client might say it's worth $8 million to $12 million. Or a client could say he or she expects his or her confidence to rise 40 to 60 percent.

With the answers to these questions, MR can calculate the expected ROI Lite using the following formula.

$$\text{ROI Lite} = \frac{\$ \text{ Value} \times \text{Increased Confidence}}{\text{Cost of Research}}$$

For example, assume a firm has to decide which of five creative approaches to use in a $2 million advertising campaign.

☐   Since it is uncertain how the advertising will affect sales, the firm decides to use the $2 million campaign cost as the value estimate.

☐   No one knows which of the five approaches is best, so the confidence of randomly picking the best one is only 20 percent.

☐   The firm believes that after the research it will be 80 percent confident of making the best decision (an increase of 60 percent).

☐   The cost of the copy testing is $250,000.

$$\text{ROI Lite} = \frac{\$2\text{M} \times 60\%}{\$250\text{K}} = \frac{\$1.2\text{M}}{\$250\text{K}} = 480\%$$

This ROI Lite discussion can help determine how much to invest in the research. If the dollar value of a decision is small or the expected decrease in uncertainty is low, then the budget should be kept small. After the research is completed, MR meets again with the client to revise the ROI Lite estimate in light of what was learned.

ROI Complete   ROI Complete is similar to ROI Lite except that it adds the concept of the likelihood of taking action. MR and the client discuss the estimated likelihood of taking action with and without the research. If the firm usually acts without research, then MR may not be able to raise the likelihood of acting, and the firm should not spend much money on the research. However, if the firm seldom acts without research, then the research is more valuable.

The following equation is used:

$$\text{ROI Complete} = \frac{\$ \text{ Value} \times \text{Increased Confidence} \times \text{Increased Likelihood of Acting}}{\text{Cost of Research}}$$

For example, suppose the decision is whether or not to enter a new market.

☐ Costs (including research, manufacturing, and marketing) are estimated to be $20 million, and potential revenue is estimated at $50 million in the first year. The client and MR agree to use the first year's net income of $30 million as the expected dollar value. (Note that a few sophisticated MR departments calculate the net present value of the continuing revenue stream, but we have kept the example simple.)

☐ The executives know that entering a new market is risky. They are only 10 percent confident of making the right decision without research. With the research, they estimate that they will be 70 percent confident—an increase of 60 percent.

☐ The executives often act without research. The estimated likelihood of acting without research (based on past history) is 50 percent. They expect this would rise to 80 percent after the research—an increase of 30 percent.

☐ The cost of the research is $1 million.

☐ The firm decides to go forward with the research because there will be an anticipated positive 540 percent ROI by the end of the first year.

$$\text{ROI Complete} = \frac{\$30M \times 60\% \times 30\%}{\$1M} = \frac{\$5.4M}{\$1M} = 540\%$$

After the research is completed, MR and the client recalculate ROI.

What if the research says the firm should not enter the market? In that case, the research still has a positive ROI since it saves the firm from investing in a losing venture. Using the previous example, suppose that the research made the firm 80 percent certain it would lose its $20 million investment. Before the research, the firm was 50 percent likely to act and make a losing decision, which means the return on the research is 800 percent:

$$\text{Actual ROI} = \frac{\$20M \times 80\% \times 50\%}{\$1M} = \frac{\$8M}{\$1M} = 800\%$$

What if the research convinces the firm to avoid the market it originally preferred (as shown above) but to invest in an alternative market that would generate a new profit of $30 million in the first year? Assume the firm is 70 percent confident that the alternative is the best one (an increase of 60 percent since it had only 10 percent confidence in it before the research). Also assume that the research increases the likelihood of actually entering a new market by 30 percent. Then the ROI is even higher:

$$\text{Actual ROI} = \frac{(\$20M \times 80\% \times 50\%) + (\$30M \times 60\% \times 30\%)}{\$1M}$$

$$= \frac{\$8M + \$5.4M}{\$1M} = 1,340\%$$

What if the client decides not to act even though the research projects a positive outcome? This often happens when there are changes in leadership or other uses for the capital. In that case, ROI is 0 percent, but the postresearch discussion makes clear that this is the client's choice and not MR's fault.

It's not always easy to ask clients how likely they are to take action. Sometimes firms commission research simply to bless a decision that has already been made. Or firms may expect the research to increase their knowledge without necessarily leading to action. Examples of this would be new segmentation research or customer satisfaction tracking. In these cases, the likelihood of acting and the dollar value would depend entirely on what was learned. One MR director said, "Just like estimating the return on IT investments, there are so many assumptions necessary that you can never be sure your estimate will be close. For some kinds of exploratory research, you don't know until you're done whether or not it will produce anything of financial value." Because these discussions are difficult, some MR groups prefer to use ROI Lite rather than ROI Complete.[23]

SUMMARY

The six primary sections of a contemporary marketing research report are, in order: the table of contents, background and objectives, executive summary, methodology, findings, and appendixes with supporting information.

The primary objectives of the marketing research report are to state the specific research objectives, explain why and how the research was done, present the findings of the research, and provide conclusions and recommendations. Most of these elements are contained in the executive summary. The conclusions do not necessarily contain statistical numbers derived from the research but rather generalize the results in relation to the stated objectives. Nor do conclusions suggest a course of action. This is left to the recommendations, which direct the conclusions to specific marketing strategies or tactics that would place the client in the most positive position in the market.

The marketing research report of today makes heavy use of graphics to present key findings. For most researchers, PowerPoint is the software of choice for creating research reports. In terms of mechanics, reports minimize the use of words, feed information to clients in "minibites," and make extensive use of bulleted charts and graphics. In addition to the written report which is often nothing more than a copy of the PowerPoint presentation, a presentation of research results is often required. It is common for research reports to be published on the Internet by the client or by the researcher at the client's request. This has the advantage of making the results available to individuals worldwide in the client's organization. The Internet can also be used to support simultaneous presentation of the research results in multiple locations.

Supplier research marketing management has six important goals beyond excellent communication: creation of an effective organization, assurance of data quality, adherence to time schedules, cost control, client profitability management, and staff management and development. Many research firms are transitioning to a team-based organization from the traditional functional organizational structure. Marketing research managers can help assure high-quality data by attempting to minimize sources of error. Researchers should also strive for better client and audience understanding of the margin of error concept. Time management requires a system to notify management of potential problems and policies to solve behind-schedule problems both efficiently and quickly. Cost management demands good cost-tracking and cost control processes. Client profitability management requires that the marketing research supplier determine how much each client contributes to the researcher's overall profitability. Unprofitable clients should be dropped; marginally profitable clients should be developed into high-profit clients or dropped. The supplier should use relationship marketing to build a solid, increasingly profitable long-term relationship with clients identified as high-profit contributors. Finally, staff management and development requires that employees be encouraged to take risks and assume responsibility, be recognized for a job well done, and be offered job autonomy, financial rewards tied to business results, new challenges, and a clear career path.

A trend embraced by both research suppliers and departments is marketing research outsourcing. Outsourcing can be a source of cost reduction and also often save time. Most outsourcing by American firms is to India. Outsource firms offer programming, data processing, data analysis, data management, and panel management. Some important issues when considering outsourcing are confidentiality, infrastructure, quality of deliverables, domain, knowledge, culture considerations, potential negative publicity from job losses, and employee liability.

A manager of a marketing research department within a corporation faces a different set of issues than from a research supplier. Among these are effective spending of the research budget, prioritizing projects for the corporation, retaining skilled staff, selecting the right research suppliers, moving the marketing research function to a more strategic role in the firm, and measuring return on investment for marketing research.

One technique for prioritizing projects is to focus first on strategic projects and then the tactical. This is also true for allocating the corporate research budget. Also, projects should be funded that have the highest potential ROI. Ways to retain key staff are to offer interesting and fulfilling work, recognizing someone for a job well done, and offering competitive pay.

A manager of a corporate research department must develop methodologies and skills for selecting the right research suppliers. This includes assessing competing supplier capabilities and reviewing the quality controls of each supplier.

The objective of many research departments is to move from being simply data collectors to partners in the strategic decision process. The chapter makes a number of suggestions on how to make this a reality. Finally, a number of corporations are now measuring the ROI on marketing research. This tool, when applied to marketing research, is controversial.

KEY TERMS & DEFINITIONS

executive summary Portion of a research report that explains why the research was done, what was found, what those findings mean, and what action, if any, management should undertake.

conclusions Generalizations that answer the questions raised by the research objectives or otherwise satisfy the objectives.

recommendations Conclusions applied to marketing strategies or tactics that focus on a client's achievement of differential advantage.

research management Overseeing the development of excellent communication systems, data quality, time schedules, cost controls, client profitability, and staff development.

outsourcing Having personnel in another country perform some, or all, of the functions involved in a marketing research project.

captive outsourcing When a research firm creates a wholly-owned foreign facility for outsourcing.

QUESTIONS FOR REVIEW & CRITICAL THINKING

1. What are the roles of the research report? Give examples.
2. Why should research reports contain executive summaries? What should be contained in an executive summary?
3. Should a survey presentation say, "the margin of effort is plus or minus 3 percent"? If not, what problem does it present?
4. Describe four different ways a manager can help ensure high data quality.

5. What policies need to be put in place to ensure that research projects are handled in a timely manner? What steps should be taken if a project falls behind schedule?

6. How can a research supplier develop its employees?

7. Should every firm conduct a client profitability study? Why?

8. Is outsourcing beneficial to the marketing research industry? Why or why not?

9. What are some issues to consider when planning to outsource? Are some more important than others?

10. How should one allocate a corporate marketing research budget? Is this the only way?

11. What is an acceptable method of prioritizing research projects in a research department?

12. What should marketing research do in order to play a more strategic role in the organization?

13. Assume that a company is trying to determine whether to enter a new market. The estimated first year's revenue is $2.2 million. Because management knows a little about this market, they are 20 percent confident that they can make the right decision without research. With research, they will be 80 percent confident. The estimated likelihood of moving into the market without research is 40 percent. This figure would rise to 80 percent after the research. The cost of the research is $400,000. What is the ROI after the first year?

WORKING THE NET

1. Go to *http://www.gallup.com* and examine some of the special reports on American opinions, such as those found under "Social Issues and Policy." Do these reports meet the criteria discussed in the text for good marketing research reports? Why or why not?

2. Go to *http://www.presentersuniversity.com*. Describe the different ways this organization can help an individual become a more effective speaker.

3. Go to *www.worldopinion.com* or *www.Quirks.com* and find an article on managing marketing research firms. Summarize this article for the class.

4. Go to Google, or another search engine, and look up "marketing research outsourcing." Present your findings to the class.

REAL-LIFE RESEARCH • 15.1

Maxwell Research Considers Outsourcing to Cross-Tab in India

Maxwell Research, a full-service research firm located in Austin, Texas, specializes in custom research. The firm has grown dramatically in recent years, serving primarily the hospitality, travel, and consumer package goods industries. Mike Maxwell, CEO and founder, says that the firm's success is attributable to providing outstanding service to their clients. Maxwell doesn't have "black-box" copyrighted models or huge Internet panels; instead he has a razor-like focus on its clients. The firm has a unique key-account program for its 15 top accounts. Each key account manager must reside in the city where the key account is located in order to be available 24/7. Mike believes face-to-face contact the moment a key client calls or has a problem is the best method for having excellent customer relationship management.

While sales have increased a minimum of 20 percent annually since 2000, net profits have not. In fact, the net profit margin has fallen in each of the last three years. Last year it dropped 6 percent. Mike knew that his labor-intensive, customer-oriented approach was part of the problem. His attitude has been, "let's overstaff if necessary to make sure that we can meet clients' deadlines during crunch times." Now, Mike is rethinking his strategy.

One possible approach to lowering labor costs is outsourcing. He has heard good things about a company located in India called Cross-Tab. The firm also has an office in Bellevue, Washington. An examination of Cross-Tab's website reveals the following about Cross-Tab:

Why Cross-Tab

Orientation

Cross-Tab is a full-service market research agency that also provides outsourcing services for market research and data analytics processes to global marketing and market research organizations. The team has deep knowledge of market research data and its implications. We are able to utilize this knowledge to add substantial value to our outsourcing engagements. We continuously keep ourselves updated and abreast of global research trends and best practices. We are active members of key global industry bodies such as ESOMAR, CASRO, MRSI, and AMA and adhere to their respective codes.

Experience

We have experience across all areas of research, including:

Online surveys, CATI, and PAPI; small ad-hoc projects as well as large multicountry projects; qualitative and quantitative studies; business and consumer research.

Working with national and global clients, we have experience in managing large-volume data projects. We can integrate and harness data from a variety of sources and platforms:

- ☐ Transaction data
- ☐ System-generated data
- ☐ Multiproject/multiwave/multicountry data

We have developed expertise in key statistical and scripting tools like SAS, SPSS, Wincross, Quantum, Confirmit, MRInterview, NetMR, and many more.

People

Our team is equipped with the knowledge, resources, and domain expertise to effectively execute each client's business mandates. Every member of the working team has relevant expertise and experience in research, analysis, advertising and marketing industry, having worked with companies such as 3M, Cap Gemini, DDB, EuroRSCG, Gallup, GE Analytics, IDC, IMRB, JWT, NFO, Nestlé, and TNS.

Every team member goes through training programs to remain updated on market research's best practices. Our outsourcing services team has an excellent understanding of the role and contribution of each outsourced activity within the entire market research process.[24]

Questions

1. What do you think about Mike's labor-intensive focus on customer service? What are the advantages and disadvantages?

2. What are the advantages and disadvantages for Maxwell Research to engage in outsourcing?

3. What are some key issues Maxwell needs to resolve before it signs an outsourcing agreement?

4. Will outsourcing solve Maxwell's ROI problem? What might happen to sales revenue?

ENDNOTES

Chapter 1

1. Karl Hellman and Stephen Whitelaw, "The Middle Ground of Untapped Profits," *Marketing Management* (July/August 2005), pp. 44–47.
2. *www.marketingpower.com* (October 25, 2007).
3. "Are Pre-Movie Commercials a Cure for Ad Zapping?" *Quirk's Marketing Research Review* (June 2007), p. 8.
4. "Understanding Discontinuous Opportunities," *Marketing Research* (Fall 1999), p. 9.
5. "Oscar Mayer Prepares a Better Bacon Package," *Brandweek* (June 11, 2007), p. 11.
6. "Roll Out the Blue Carpet," *Business 2.0* (May 2007), pp. 53–54.
7. "Satisfaction Not Guaranteed," *Business Week* (June 19, 2006), p. 33.
8. "Why Some Customers Are More Equal Than Others," *Fortune* (September 19, 1994), pp. 215–224.
9. Sunil Gupta, Donald Lehmann, and Jennifer Ames Stuart, "Valuing Customers," *Journal of Marketing Research* (February 2004), pp. 7–18.
10. "Soup on the Front Burner," *Brandweek* (March 27, 2006), pp. 20–21.
11. Michael Fielding, "Resorts' email Alerts Revive Flat Business on Slopes," *Marketing News* (March 1, 2005), pp. 17–18.
12. *www.websiteoptimization.com* (July 10, 2007).
13. *www.marketingresearchtech.com* (July 6, 2007); also see "Compare and Contrast," *Quirk's Marketing Research Review* (June 2007), pp. 26–30.
14. William D. Neal, "Getting Serious about Marketing Research," *Marketing Research* (Summer 2002), pp. 24–28.
15. "Young Financial Services Consumers Still Want the Personal Touch," *Quirk's Marketing Research Review* (June 2007), p. 90.

Appendix 1-B

1. These ethical theories are from: Catherine Rainbow, "Descriptions of Ethical Theories and Principles," *www.bio.davidson.edu/people/Kabernd/Indep/carainbow.htm* (June 22, 2005).
2. David Haynes, "Respondent Goodwill Is a Cooperative Activity," *Quirk's Marketing Research Review* (February 2005), pp. 30–32.
3. "New York State Sues Survey Firm for Allegedly Tricking Students," *Wall Street Journal* (August 30, 2002), p. B4.
4. Shelby Hunt, Lawrence Chonko, and James Wilcox, "Ethical Problems of Marketing Researchers," *Journal of Marketing Research* (August 1984), p. 314. Reprinted by permission of the American Marketing Association.
5. Terry Grapentine, "You Can't Take the Human Nature out of Black Boxes," *Marketing Research* (Winter 2004), pp. 20–22.
6. "The Code of Marketing Research Standards," *www.mra-net.org/pdf/expanded_code.pdf* (June 29, 2005).
7. Diane Bowers, "New Requirement for Research: Privacy Assurance and Professional Accountability," *CASRO Journal* (2002), pp. 115–116.
8. "Professional Researcher Certification," *http://www.mra-net.org* (June 29, 2005).

Chapter 2

1. Tara Hutton, "My Cell Phone, My Life," *Quirk's Marketing Research Review* (February 2006), pp. 22–25.
2. Terry H. Grapentine and Dianne Weaver, "Business Goals Are Key to Proper Marketing Research," *Marketing News* (September 15, 2006), pp. 28–31.
3. "Meet the Aggregators," *Brandweek* (May 30, 2005), p. 25.
4. Paul Conner, "Defining the Decision Purpose of Research," *Marketing News* (June 9, 1997), p. H15. Reprinted by permission of the American Marketing Association.
5. Terry H. Grapentine and Dianne Weaver, "Business Goals Are Key to Proper Marketing Research."
6. Todd Wasserman, "K-C Tries Seeing Things From Consumer's POV," *Brandweek* (September 5, 2005), p. 6.
7. Joseph Rydholm, "What Do Clients Want from a Research Firm?" *Marketing Research Review* (October 1995), p. 82.
8. Fred Luthans and Janet K. Larsen, "How Managers Really Communicate," *Human Relations 39* (1986), pp. 161–178; and Harry E. Penley and Brian Hawkins, "Studying Interpersonal Communication in Organizations: A Leadership Application," *Academy of Management Journal 28* (1985), pp. 309–326.
9. Matthew Harrison, "Learning the Language," *Marketing Research* (Winter 2006), pp. 11–16.
10. Rohit Deshpande and Scott Jeffries, "Attitudes Affecting the Use of Marketing Research in Decision Making: An Empirical Investigation," in *Educators' Conference Proceedings*, Series 47, edited by Kenneth L. Bernhardt et al. (Chicago: American Marketing Association, 1981), pp. 1–4.
11. Rohit Deshpande and Gerald Zaltman, "Factors Affecting the Use of Market Information: A Path Analysis," *Journal of Marketing Research 19* (February 1982), pp. 14–31; Rohit Deshpande, "A Comparison of Factors Affecting Researcher and Manager Perceptions of Market Research Use," *Journal of Marketing Research 21* (February 1989), pp. 32–38; Hanjoon Lee, Frank Acito, and Ralph Day, "Evaluation and Use of Marketing Research by Decision Makers: A Behavioral Simulation," *Journal of Marketing Research 24* (May 1987), pp. 187–196; and Michael Hu, "An Experimental Study of Managers' and Researchers' Use of Consumer Market Research," *Journal of the Academy of Marketing Science 14* (Fall 1986), pp. 44–51.
12. Rohit Deshpande and Gerald Zaltman, "A Comparison of Factors Affecting Use of Marketing Information in Consumer and Industrial Firms," *Journal of Marketing Research 24* (February 1987), pp. 114–118.
13. Sonia Reyes, "Health Marketing Messages Not Always on the Mark," *Brandweek* (March 27, 2006), p. 18.

Chapter 3

1. "Values and Trends amongst the Boomer Generation" (London: Research International Qualitative), 2005.
2. "Survey Says: BtoB Database Marketers Are All Grown Up," *BtoB* (October 8, 2007), p. 26.
3. "A Potent New Tool for Selling Database Marketing," *BusinessWeek* (September 5, 1994), pp. 56–62.
4. Joan Raymond, "Home Field Advantage," *American Demographics* (April 2001), pp. 34–36.
5. "What've You Done for Us Lately?" *BusinessWeek* (April 23, 1999), pp. 24–34.
6. "Looking for Patterns," *Wall Street Journal* (June 21, 1999), pp. R16, R20.
7. Kevin Delaney and Emily Steel, "Firm Mines Offline Data to Target Online Ads," *Wall Street Journal* (October 17, 2007), pp. Bl, B2.
8. Ibid.
9. The Acxiom story is from Delaney and Steel, "Firm Mines Offline Data to Target Online

Ads," *Wall Street Journal* (October 17, 2007), pp. Bl, B2.

10. *www.privacy.org* (October 17, 2007).

11. "The Great Data Heist," *Fortune* (May 16, 2005). pp. 66–75.

12. "ChoicePoint to Exit Non-FCRA. Consumer-Sensitive Data Markets," (*www.choicepoint .com*) (March 4, 2005).

13. "On My Mind: The Privacy Hoax: Consumers Say They Care about Internet Privacy But Don't Act That Way. Let the Market Rule," *Forbes* (October 14, 2002), pp. 42–44.

14. Donna Gillin and Jane Sheppard, "The Fallacy of Gelling Paid for Your Opinions," *Marketing Research* (Fall 2003), p. 8.

15. The section on GIS has been updated by Joshua Been, The University of Texas at Arlington.

16. Case Study—Avon Products (November 2004), *www.tactician.com/News/News_CS_ AVON1104.asp*

17. Catherine Greenman, "Turning a Map into a Layer Cake of Information," *New York Times*, January 20, 2000, Thursday, Late Edition—Final, Section G.

18. Amy Cortese, "Is Your Business in the Right Spot? *Business 2.0* (May 2004), pp. 76–77.

19. "Sanitized for Your Perfection," *Brandweek* (January 9, 2006), p. 17.

Chapter 4

1. Michael Myser, "Marketing Made Easy," *Business 2.0* (June 2006), pp. 43–45.

2. "ESOMAR Unveils Top Line Results from 25 Global Marketing Research Report," ESOMAR (June 2007).

3. "Focus Groups Illuminate Quantitative Research," *Marketing News* (September 23, 1996), p. 41.

4. Steve Richardson, "Respondents Lie and Good Ideas Die," *Quirk's Marketing Research Review* (May 2007), pp. 48–54. The 2007 estimates are the authors'.

5. "Motives Are as Important as Words When Group Describes a Product," *Marketing News* (August 28, 1987), p. 49.

6. John Houlahan, "In Defense of the Focus Group," *Quirk's Marketing Research Review* (October 2003), pp. 16, 84.

7. Alison Stein Wellner, "The New Science of Focus Groups," *American Demographics* (March 2003), pp. 29–33.

8. Ibid., p. 32.

9. Ken Berwitz, "Not So Stupid, Recruiting Tricks," *Quirk's Marketing Research Review* (December 2002), pp. 40–43.

10. Peter Tuckel, Elaine Leppo, and Barbara Kaplan, "Focus Groups under Scrutiny," *Marketing Research* (June 1992), pp. 12–17; see also "Break These Three Focus Group

Rules," *Quick's Marketing Research Review* (December 1999), pp. 50–53.

11. Marilyn Rausch, "Qualities of a Beginning Moderator," *Quirk's Marketing Research Review* (December 1996), p. 24. Reprinted by permission of *Quirk's Marketing Research Review*; also see: Tom Neveril, "Ten Qualities for Qualitative Researchers," *Quirk's Marketing Research Review* (June 2004), pp. 18–21.

12. Jim Eschrich, "Establishing a Comfort Level," *Quirk's Marketing Research Review* (April 2002), pp. 44–47.

13. Yvonne Martin Kidd, "A Look at Focus Group Moderators Through the Client's Eyes," *Quirk's Marketing Research Review* (May 1997), pp. 22–26. Reprinted by permission of *Quirk's Marketing Research Review*.

14. Dennis Rook, "Out of Focus Groups," *Marketing Research* (Summer 2003), pp. 10–15.

15. Jacob Brown, "For Best Results, Plan Ahead," *Quirk's Marketing Research Review* (November 2005), pp. 44–47.

16. B. G. Yovovich, "Focusing on Consumers' Needs and Motivations," *Business Marketing* (March 1991), pp. 13–14. Reprinted with permission of *Business Marketing*. Copyright Crain Communications Inc., 1991.

17. Ibid.

18. Ibid.

19. "Survey Finds Acceptance of Focus Group Video Transmission," *Quirk's Marketing Research Review* (July/August 2006), pp. 18–20.

20. Naomi Henderson, "Art and Science of Effective In-Depth Qualitative Interviews," *Quirk's Marketing Research Review* (December 1998), pp. 24–31; reprinted by permission; "Dangerous Intersections," *Marketing News* (February 28, 2000), p. 18; and "Go In-Depth with Depth Interviews," *Quirk's Marketing Research Review* (April 2000), pp. 36–40.

21. Henderson, "Art and Science of Effective In-Depth Qualitative Interviews," p. 26.

22. Gerald Berstell and Denise Nitterhouse, "Asking All the Right Questions," *Marketing Research* (Fall 2001), pp. 15–20.

23. "One-on-Ones Put the Quality in Qualitative," *Quirk's Marketing Research Review* (November 2006), pp. 16–18.

24. Jennifer Haid, "Understand the Mind of the Market," *Quirk's Marketing Research Review* (December 2004), pp. 26–31.

25. "Toward a Broader Definition," *Quirk's Marketing Research Review* (May 2006), p. 64.

26. The material on analogies is from: Andrew Cutler, "What's the Real Story?" *Quirk's Marketing Research Review* (December 2006), pp. 38–45.

27. The material on personification is from Cutler, "What's the Real Story?"

28. Ronald Lieber, "Storytelling: A New Way to Get Closer to Your Customer," *Fortune* (February 3, 1997), pp. 102–110; see also "Marketers Seek the Naked Truth in Consumers' Psyches," *Wall Street Journal* (May 30, 1997), pp. B1, B13; for details on Zaltman's technique, see Gwendolyn Catchings-Castello, "The ZMET Alternative," *Marketing Research* (Summer 2000), pp. 6–12.

29. Anna Lilleegen, "A Storied Destination," *Quirk's Marketing Research Review* (November 2005), pp. 24–29.

Chapter 5

1. "Now Playing: Grills Gone Wild," *Quirk's Marketing Research Review* (July/August 2007), p. 8.

2. "Research Department As Bellwether?" *Quirk's Marketing Research Review* (June 2005), p. 8.

3. Patricia E. Moberg, "Biases in Unlisted Phone Numbers," *Journal of Advertising Research* 22 (August–September 1982), p. 55.

4. Reprinted with permission from the *Respondent Cooperation and Industry Image Survey* (New York: Council for Marketing and Opinion Research, 2003), p. 2; also see Joseph Rydholm, "A Cooperative Effort on Cooperation," *Quirk's Marketing Research Review* (November 2006), pp. 137–138.

5. Matthew Harrison, "Learning the Language," *Marketing Research* (Winter 2006), pp. 11–16.

6. *www.mrsi.com/instore.html* (June 11, 2005).

7. "Phone Surveys Skewed by Cell-Only Homeowners," *Quirk's Marketing Research Review* (October 2007), pp. 10, 86.

8. Ibid.

9. Ibid.

10. Ibid.

11. David Whitlark and Michael Gearts, "Phone Surveys: How Well Do Respondents Represent Average Americans" *Marketing Research* (Fall 1998), pp. 13–17; see also "This Is Not a Sales Call," *Quirk's Marketing Research Review* (May 2000), pp. 32–34.

12. Ibid.

13. For a high-tech variation of the self-administered questionnaire see John Weisberg, "The MCAPI Primer," *Quirk's Marketing Research Review* (February 2003), pp. 24–34; see also Karl Feld and Steven Wygant, "E-interviewers Add Human Touch to Web-based Research," *Quirk's Marketing Research Review* (July–August 2000), pp. 36–41.

14. "Mail Surveys—The Right Alternative," *Quirk's Marketing Research Review* (July–August 2005), p. 18.

15. SurveySpot Panel, April 2004.

Chapter 6

1. "Waiter, My Portion's Too Big," *Quirk's Marketing Research Review* (July/August 2007), p. 12.
2. Kira Signer and Andy Korman, "One Billion and Growing," *Quirk's Marketing Research Review* (July/August 2006), pp. 62–67.
3. Ibid.
4. Conversation with Craig Stevens, EVP of e-Rewards Market Research, based on company research (November 2, 2007); also see "Market Research," *Marketing News* (September 15, 2007), p. 16.
5. Ibid.
6. Tim Macer and Sheila Wilson, "Online Makes More Inroads," *Quirk's Marketing Research Review* (February 2007), pp. 50–58.
7. This section is from *www.lib.berkeley.edu/TeachingLib/Guides/Internet/Strategies.html*.
8. This section is adapted from Nick Wingfield, "A Marketer's Dream," *Wall Street Journal* (December 7, 1998), p. R20.
9. Ibid.
10. Kate Maddox, "Virtual Panels Add Real Insight for Marketers," *Advertising Age* (June 29, 1998), pp. 34, 40; and "Turning the Focus Online," *Marketing News* (February 28, 2000), p. 15; see also "The Hows, Whys, Whens and Wheres of Online Focus Groups," *MRA Alert* (December 1999), p. 21, and "Online Group Messaging," *Marketing News* (September 1, 2007), p. 24.
11. Hy Mariampolski and Pat Sabena, "Qualitative Research Develops in China," *Quirk's Marketing Research Review* (December 2002), pp. 44–49.
12. *www.channelM2.com* (November 5, 2007).
13. Vauhini Vara, "Researchers Mine Web for Focus Groups," *Wall Street Journal* (November 17, 2007), p. B3E.
14. Berni Stevens, "Best Practices for Online Qualitative Research," *Quirk's Marketing Research Review* (July/August 2007), pp. 34–42.
15. Gregory S. Heist, "Beyond Brand Building," *Quirk's Marketing Research Review* (July/August 2007), pp. 62–67.
16. Ibid.
17. Ibid.
18. Ibid.
19. Chris Yalonis, "The Revolution in e-Research," *CASRO Marketing Research Journal* (1999), pp. 131–133; "The Power of On-line Research," *Quirk's Marketing Research Review* (April 2000), pp. 46–48; Bill MacElroy, "The Need for Speed," *Quirk's Marketing Research Review* (July–August 2002), pp. 22–27; Cristina Mititelu, "Internet Surveys: Limits and Beyond Limits," *Quirk's Marketing Research Review* (January 2003), pp. 30–33; Nina Ray, "Cybersurveys Come of Age," *Marketing Research* (Spring 2003), pp. 32–37; "Online Market Research Booming, According to Survey," *Quirk's Marketing Research Review* (January 2005); Roger Gates, "Internet Data Collection So Far," speech given to Kaiser Permanente (May 2005); and Gabe Gelb, "Online Options Change Biz a Little—And a Lot," *Marketing News* (November 1, 2006), pp. 23–24.
20. Gates, "Internet Data Collection So Far."
21. Lee Smith, "Online Research's Time Has Come as a Proven Methodology," *CASRO Journal* (2002), pp. 45–50.
22. Bill MacElroy, "International Growth of Web Survey Activity," *Quirk's Marketing Research Review* (November 2000), pp. 48–51.
23. "Tips Offer Better Response Rates, Engaging Surveys," *Marketing News* (April 1, 2007), p. 28.
24. Jamin Brazil, Aaron Jue, Chandra Mulkins, and Jayme Plunkett, "Capture Their Interest," *Quirk's Marketing Research Review* (July/August 2006), pp. 46–54.
25. Ibid.
26. Giselle Lederman, "Formatting Your Internet Survey," *Quirk's Marketing Research Review* (January 2007), pp. 34–36.
27. "Timing Appears to Be Everything with Survey Invitations," *Quirk's Marketing Research Review* (March 2007), p. 8.
28. *www.comscore.com/custom-research/sample.asp*. Also referenced by Mary Beth Weber, Sigma Validation at AMA 2005 Marketing Research Conference, Boston (September 25–28, 2005), "Why Validate Internet Research?"
29. Birgi Martin, "Research-to-Go," *Quirk's Marketing Research Review* (November 2007), pp. 68–72.
30. Ibid.
31. Ibid.
32. Ibid.
33. "Industry Split over Net Research Group," *Marketing News* (June 5, 2000), pp. 5, 8.
34. Joseph Rydholm, "However They Can, Grocery Shoppers Just Want to Save Money," *Quirk's Marketing Research Review* (June 2006), pp. 117–118.

Chapter 7

1. Jeff Borden, "Bertolli's Big Bite," *Marketing News* (October 1, 2007), pp. 12–15.
2. E. W. Webb, D. T. Campbell, K. D. Schwarts, and L. Sechrest, *Unobtrusive Measures: Nonreaction Research in the Social Sciences* (Chicago: Rand McNally, 1966), pp. 113–114.
3. Alison Stein Wellner, "Watch Me Now," *American Demographics* (October 2002), pp. S1–S8; and Robert Kozinets, "The Field behind the Screen: Using Netnography for Marketing Research in Online Communities," *Journal of Marketing Research* (February 2002), pp. 61–72.
4. "The Chocolate War," *Marketing Research* (Winter 2005), p. 4.
5. Richard Durante and Michael Feehan, "Watch and Learn," *Marketing Research* (Winter 2005), pp. 11–15.
6. Ibid.
7. See Clynton Taylor, "What's All the Fuss About?" *Quirk's Marketing Research Review* (December 2003), pp. 40–45.
8. Wellner, "Watch Me Now."
9. "The Science of Desire," *Business Week* (June 5, 2006), p. 104.
10. Ibid.
11. Ibid.
12. "P&G's Teaching an Old Dog New Tricks," *Fortune* (May 31, 2004), p. 172.
13. Martha C. Rivera, "An Enriching Process," *Quirk's Marketing Research Review* (November 2005), pp. 30–37.
14. Jerry Thomas, "Worth a Thousand Words," *Decision Analyst Flyer* (2006).
15. "Mystery Shopper," *Smart Money* (December 2005), p. 98.
16. Ibid.
17. Randall Brandt, "Improve the Customer Experience," *Quirk's Marketing Research Review* (January 2006), p. 68.
18. Ron Welty, "21st Century Mystery Shopping," *Quirk's Marketing Research Review* (January 2005), pp. 78–81.
19. "Family of Toy Testers Plays Recurring Role at Fisher-Price," *Wall Street Journal* (December 21, 2004), pp. A1, A8.
20. Rebecca Gardyn, "What's on Your Mind?" *American Demographics* (April 2000), pp. 31–33.
21. John Cacioppo and Richard Petty, "Physiological Responses and Advertising Effects," *Psychology and Marketing* (Summer 1985), pp. 115–126; and Jack Shimell, "Testing Ads Using Galvanic Skin Response Measurements," *Quirk's Marketing Research Review* (March 2002), pp. 46–55.
22. "An Eyeball Test for Better Ads," *Business 2.0* (March 2007), p. 34.
23. Andy Rasking, "A Face Any Business Can Trust," *Business 2.0* (December 2003), pp. 58–60.
24. Ibid; also see Dan Hill, "What Lies Beneath," *Quirk's Marketing Research Review* (October 2006), pp. 68–74.
25. *www.nielsenoutdoor.com* (October 28, 2007).
26. *www.pretesting.com* (June 2005).
27. Jon Gertner, "Our Ratings, Ourselves," *New York Times* (April 10, 2005), p. D12.
28. Linda Dupree and John Bosarge, "Media on the Move: How to Measure In-and-Out-of-Home Media Consumption," *ACNielsen Trends & Insights*. Downloaded on March 9, 2005.

29. "Arbitron-Nielsen Venture Shows Promise," *Wall Street Journal* (February 27, 2007), p. B4.

30. Laurence Gold, "The Coming of Age of Scanner Data," *Marketing Research* (Winter 1993), pp. 20–23.

31. The material on Information Resources Incorporated is from its public relations department on its website (October 28, 2007).

32. "IRI Enhances BehaviorScan," *IRI News Release* (October 29, 2001).

33. IRI website, "Custom Store Tracking," April 4, 2003.

34. IRI website, "Syndicated Store Tracking," April 4, 2003.

35. "The Online Numbers Game," *Fortune* (September 3, 2007), p. 18.

36. Ibid.

37. "Cyberstalking Your Customers," *Business 2.0* (September 2007), pp. 24–25.

38. Ibid.

39. "The Quest for the Perfect Online Ad," *Business 2.0* (March 2007), pp. 88–93.

40. "How Marketers Hone Their Aim Online," *Wall Street Journal* (June 19, 2007), p. B6.

41. "The Click-Through Puzzle Solved," *Business 2.0* (June 2007), pp. 26–28.

42. Rich Bruner, "The Decade in Online Advertising," *www.doubleclick.com* (April 2005).

43. Ibid.

44. Raymond R. Burke, "Virtual Shopping: Breakthrough in Marketing Research," *Harvard Business Review* (March/April 1996), pp. 120–131.

45. Ellen Byron, "A Virtual View of the Store Aisle," *Wall Street Journal* (October 3, 2007), pp. B1, B12.

46. Ibid.

47. Ibid.

48. Ibid.

49. Ibid.

50. Constantine von Hoffman, "Masters of Funky Flex," *Brandweek* (September 25, 2006), pp. 23–24.

Chapter 8

1. Thomas D. Cook and Donald T. Campbell, *Experimentation: Design Analysis Issues for Field Settings* (Chicago: Rand McNally, 1979).

2. See Claire Selltiz et al., *Research in Social Relations*, rev. ed. (New York: Holt, Rinehart and Winston, 1959), pp. 80–82.

3. A good example of a laboratory experiment is described in Caroll Mohn, "Simulated-Purchase 'Chip' Testing vs. Trade-Off Conjoint Analysis—Coca-Cola's Experience." *Marketing Research* (March 1990), pp. 49–54.

4. A. G. Sawyer, "Demand Artifacts in Laboratory Experiments in Consumer Research," *Journal of Consumer Research 2* (March 1975), pp. 181–201; and N. Giges,

"No Miracle in Small Miracle: Story Behind Failure," *Advertising Age* (August 1989), p. 76.

5. John G. Lynch, "On the External Validity of Experiments in Consumer Research," *Journal of Consumer Research 9* (December 1982), pp. 225–239.

6. Richard C. Becherer, DBA, Lawrence M. Richard, PhD, and James B. Wiley, PhD, "Predicting Market Behavior: Are Psychographics Really Better?" *Journal of the Academy of Marketing Science* (Spring 1977, Vol. 5, No. 2), pp. 75–84.

7. For a more detailed discussion of this and other experimental issues, see Thomas D. Cook and Donald T. Campbell, "The Design and Conduct of Quasi-Experiments and True Experiments in Field Settings," in M. Dunnette, ed., *Handbook of Industrial and Organizational Psychology* (Skokie, IL: Rand McNally, 1978).

8. Ibid.

9. For further discussion of the characteristics of various types of experimental designs, see Donald T. Campbell and Julian C. Stanley, *Experimental and Quasi-Experimental Design for Research* (Chicago: Rand McNally, 1966); see also Richard Bagozzi and Youjar Ti, "On the use of Structural Equation Models in Experimental Design," *Journal of Marketing Research 26* (August 1989), pp. 225–270.

10. Stefan Althoff, "Does the Survey Sender's Gender Matter?" *Quirk's Marketing Research Review* (February 2007, Vol. XXI, No. 2) pp. 24,26.

11. Thomas D. Cook and Donald T. Campbell, *Quasi-Experimentation: Design and Analysis Issues for Field Settings* (Boston: Houghton Mifflin, 1979), p. 56.

12. T. Karger, "Test Marketing as Dress Rehearsals," *Journal of Consumer Marketing 2* (Fall 1985), pp. 49–55; Tim Harris, "Marketing Research Passes Toy Marketer Test," *Advertising Age* (August 24, 1987), pp. 1,8; John L. Carefoot, "Marketing and Experimental Designs in Marketing Research: Uses and Misuses," *Marketing News* (June 7, 1993), p. 21; and Jim Miller and Sheila Lundy, "Test Marketing Plugs into the Internet," *Consumer Insights* (Spring 2002), p. 23.

13. Jay Klompmaker, G. David Hughes, and Russell I. Haley, "Test Marketing in New Product Development," *Harvard Business Review* (May–June 1976), p. 129; and N. D. Cadbury, "When, Where and How to Test Market," *Harvard Business Review* (May–June 1985), pp. 97–98.

14. Churchill, G. A., Jr. (2001). *Basic Marketing Research*, 4th ed. Fort Worth, TX: The Dryden Press, pp. 144–145.

15. Jay Klompmaker, G. David Hughes, and Russell I. Haley, "Test Marketing in New

Product Development," *Harvard Business Review* (May–June 1976), p. 129; and N. D. Cadbury, "When, Where and How to Test Market," *Harvard Business Review* (May–June 1985), pp. 97–98.

16. Ibid.

17. Joseph Rydholm, "To Test or Not to Test," *Quirk's Marketing Research Review* (February 1992), pp. 61–62.

18. "Test Marketing Is Valuable, but It's Often Abused," *Marketing News* (January 2, 1987), p. 40.

19. "Denmark, the World's Best Test Market," *Copenhagen Capacity* (November 23, 2005) online at: *www.copcap.com/com/composite-9206.htm*

20. "South Korea: Tech's Test Market," *Business Week* (March 4, 2003) online edition: *www.businessweek.com/technology/content/mar 2003/tc2003034 4357 tc105.htm*

21. Deborah L. Vence, "Proper Message, Design in Global Markets Require Tests," *Marketing News* (September 1, 2006) pp. 18–25.

22. "Guide to Test Market Selection and Planning," *Creative Marketing* (2000).

23. "Miller to Test Market Low-Cal Craft Beers in Minneapolis," *Minneapolis-St. Paul Business Journal* (December 14, 2007).

24. Roger Fillion, "Denver Test Market for Beer Ads," *Rocky Mountain News* (July 4, 2006).

25. Jeremiah McWilliams, "Anheuser-Busch Test Markets New Vodka Brand," *St. Louis Post-Dispatch* (November 27, 2007).

26. Dina Berta, "Utah City Turns Out to be Best Test Market for Brazilian Concept," *Nation's Restaurant News* (September 22, 2003).

Chapter 9

1. "Happiness, As Defined by the World," *Quirk's Marketing Research Review* (May 2007), p. 10.

2. F. N. Kerlinger, *Foundations of Behavioral Research*, 3rd ed. (New York: Rinehart and Winston, 1986), p. 403; see also Mel Crask and R. J. Fox, "An Exploration of the Internal Properties of Three Commonly Used Research Scales," *Journal of Marketing Research Society* (October 1987), pp. 317–319.

3. Adapted from Claire Selltiz, Laurence Wrightsman, and Stuart Cook, *Research Methods in Social Relations,* 3rd ed. (New York: Holt Rinehart and Winston, 1976), pp. 164–168.

4. See David Hardesty and William Bearden, "The Use of Expert Judges in Scale Development: Implications for Improving Face Validity of Measures of Unobservable Constructs," *Journal of Business Research* (February 2004), pp. 98–107.

5. See Edward McQuarrie, "Integration of Construct and External Validity by Means of

Proximal Similarity: Implications for Laboratory Experiments in Marketing," *Journal of Business Research* (February 2004), pp. 142–153.

6. Adapted from: William Trochim, *Research Methods Knowledge Base, www.atomicdog.com/trochim* (October 20, 2006).

7. Kunal Gupta, Jamie Baker-Prewitt, and Jeff Miller, "Scaling: The Never Ending Debate," *CASRO Journal* (2001), pp. 125–129.

8. Gerald Albaum, Catherine Roster, Julie H. Yu, and Robert D. Rogers, "Simple Rating Scale Formats: Exploring Extreme Response," *International Journal of Market Research 49*, no. 5 (2007), pp. 633–649.

9. For an excellent discussion of the semantic differential, see Charles E. Osgood, George Suci, and Percy Tannenbaum, *The Measurement of Meaning* (Urbana: University of Illinois Press, 1957).

10. Ibid., pp. 140–153, 192, 193; see also William D. Barclay, "The Semantic Differential as an Index of Brand Attitude," *Journal of Advertising Research 4* (March 1964), pp. 30–33.

11. Theodore Clevenger, Jr., and Gilbert A. Lazier, "Measurement of Corporate Images by the Semantic Differential," *Journal of Marketing Research 2* (February 1965), pp. 80–82.

12. Michael J. Etzel, Terrell G. Williams, John C. Rogers, and Douglas J. Lincoln, "The Comparability of Three Stapel Forms in a Marketing Setting," in Ronald F. Bush and Shelby D. Hunt, eds., *Marketing Theory: Philosophy of Science Perspectives* (Chicago: American Marketing Association, 1982), pp. 303–306.

13. An excellent article on purchase intent is: Pierre Chandon, Vicki Morwitz, and Werner Reinartz, "Do Intentions Really Predict Behavior? Self Generated Validity Effects in Survey Research," *Journal of Marketing* (April 2005), pp. 1–14.

14. Albert Bemmaor, "Predicting Behavior from Intention-to-Buy Measures: The Parametric Case," *Journal of Marketing Research* (May 1995), pp. 176–191.

15. We use a more conservative set of weights than those recommended by Linda Jamieson and Frank Bass, "Adjusting Stated Intention Measures to Predict Trial Purchase of New Products: A Comparison of Models and Methods," *Journal of Marketing Research* (August 1989), pp. 336–345.

16. Frederick Reichheld, "The One Number That You Need to Grow," *Harvard Business Review* (December 2003), pp. 46–57.

17. Adriana Gigliotti, Jay Meyers, Neil A. Morgan, Gina Pingitore and Lopo L. Rego, "NPS Not the Only Way," *Marketing News* (September 15, 2007), pp. 48–52.

18. Ibid.

19. Ibid.

20. This section on scale conversions is from Rajan Sambandam, "Scale Conversions," *Quirk's Marketing Research Review* (December 2006), pp. 22–28.

21. William O. and Richard G. Netemeyer, *Handbook of Marketing Scales*, 2nd ed. (Newbury Park, CA: Sage Publications, 1999), pp. 1–9.

22. Brian Engelland, Bruce Alford, and Ron Taylor, "Cautions and Precautions on the Use of Borrowed Scales in Marketing Research," *Proceedings: Society for Marketing Advances* (November 2001).

23. J. A. Krosnick and L. R. Fabrigar, "Designing Rating Scales for Effective Measurement in Surveys," in L. Lybert, M. Collins, L. Decker, E. Deleeuw, C. Dippo, N. Schwarz, and D. Trewing, eds., *Survey Measurement and Process Quality* (New York: Wiley-Interscience, 1997). Also see Madhubalan Viswanathan, Seymore Sudman, and Michael Johnson, "Maximum Versus Meaningful Discrimination in Scale Response: Implications for Validity Measurement of Consumer Perceptions about Products," *Journal of Business Review* (February 2004), pp. 108–124.

24. This section is based on James H. Myers and Mark I. Alpert, "Determinant Buying Attitudes: Meaning and Management," *Marketing Management* (Summer 1997), pp. 50–56.

25. William Wells and Leonard Lo Scruto, "Direct Observation of Purchasing Behavior," *Journal of Marketing Research* (August 1996), pp. 42–51.

26. "Coffee Culture: A Global Phenomenon?" *Quirk's Marketing Research Review* (December 2006), p. 10.

Chapter 10

1. Barbara Bickart and David Schmittlein, "The Distribution of Survey Contact and Participation in the United States: Constructing a Survey-Based Estimate," *Journal of Marketing Research* (May 1999, Vol. 36, No. 2), pp. 286–294.

2. Alexa Smith, "Ask Overlooked Questions for Greater Insights," *Marketing News* (September 15, 2003), pp. 27–28.

3. Cynthia Webster, "Hispanic and Anglo Interviewer and Respondent Ethnicity and Gender: The Impact on Survey Response Quality," *Journal of Marketing Research* (February 1996, Vol. 33, No. 1), pp. 62–72.

4. Nanci Glassman and Myron Glassman, "Screening Questions," (Fall 1998), pp. 276–230. Reprinted with permission from the American Marketing Association.

5. *www.CMOR.org* (June 15, 2005).

6. *www.sawtooth.com* (June 15, 2005).

7. Hans Baumgartner and Jan-Benedict E. M. Steenkamp, "Response Styles in Marketing Research: A Cross-National Investigation," *Journal of Marketing Research* (May 2001, Vol. 38, No. 2), pp. 143–156.

8. Internal company documents supplied to the authors by M/A/R/C, Inc.

9. Internal company documents supplied to the authors by M/A/R/C, Inc.

Chapter 11

1. "Frequently Asked Questions," *Zogby International* (February 2, 2007), zogby.com/about/faq.cfm.

2. For excellent discussions of sampling, see Seymour Sudman, *Applied Sampling* (New York: Academic Press, 1976), and L. J. Kish, *Survey Sampling* (New York: John Wiley and Sons, 1965).

3. "The Cell Phone Challenge to Survey Research," *The Pew Research Center for the People and the Press* (May 15, 2006), people-press.org/reports/display.php3?Report1D-276.

4. Megan Thee, "Cellphones Challenge Poll Sampling," *The New York Times* (December 7, 2007), *www.nytimes.com*.

5. "Report of the President's Blue Ribbon Panel on the Census," *American Statistical Association* (2003); Brad Edmondson, "The Cliffhanger Census," *American Demographics* (January 1998), p. 2.

6. A. Adimora Adaora, MD., Victor J. Schoenbach, PhD., et al., "Driver's License and Voter Registration Lists as Population-Based Sampling Frames for Rural African Americans," *Annals of Epidemiology* (August 2001, Vol. 11, No. 60), pp. 385–388.

7. S. Sudman, *Applied Sampling*, pp. 63–67.

8. G. J. Glasser and G. D. Metzger, "Random-Digit Dialing as a Method of Telephone Sampling," *Journal of Marketing Research 9* (February 1972), pp. 59–64; and S. Roslow and L. Roslow, "Unlisted Phone Subscribers Are Different," *Journal of Advertising 12* (August 1972), pp. 59–64.

9. Charles D. Cowan, "Using Multiple Sample Frames to Improve Survey Coverage, Quality, and Costs," *Marketing Research* (December 1991), pp. 66–69.

10. James McClove and P. George Benson, *Statistics for Business and Economics* (San Francisco: Dellen Publishing, 1988), pp. 184–185; and "Probability Sampling in the Real World," *CATI NEWS* (Summer 1993), pp. 1, 4–6; Susie Sangren, "Survey and Sampling in an Imperfect World," *Quirk's Marketing Research Review* (April 2000), pp. 16, 66–69.

11. R. J. Jaeger, "Sampling in Education and the Social Sciences," (New York: Longman, 1984), pp. 28–35.

12. "Nearly One in Ten U.S. Adults Use Wireless Phones Exclusively and Land-line Displacement Expected To Grow," *Harris Interactive* (June 27, 2005), *www.harrisinteractive.com/news/allnewsbydate.asp?NewsID=943*

13. R. J. Jaeger, "Sampling in Education and the Social Sciences," (New York: Longman, 1984), pp. 28–35.

14. Lewis C. Winters, "What's New in Telephone Sampling Technology?" *Marketing Research* (March 1990), pp. 80–82; and "A Survey Researcher's Handbook of Industry Terminology and Definitions," (Fairfield, CT: Survey Sampling, Inc. 1992), pp. 3–20.

15. For discussions of related issues, see John E. Swan, Stephen J. O'Connor, and Seug Doug Lee, "A Framework for Testing Sampling Bias and Methods of Bias Reduction in a Telephone Survey," *Marketing Research* (December 1991), pp. 23–34; Charles D. Cowan, "Coverage Issues in Sample Surveys: A Component of Measurement Error," *Marketing Research* (June 1991), pp. 65–68; and Susie Sangren, "Survey and Sampling in an Imperfect World."

16. For an excellent discussion of stratified sampling, see William G. Cochran, "Sampling Techniques," (2nd ed., New York: John Wiley and Sons, 1963); and Susie Sangren, "Survey and Sampling in an Imperfect World."

17. Sudman, "Applied Science," pp. 110–121.

18. Ibid.

19. Earl R. Babbie, "The Practice of Social Research", 2nd ed., Belmont, CA: Wadsworth Publishing, 1979, p. 167.

20. Craig von Hagen, "Using an Area Sampling Frame to Calculate Livestock Statistics in the Gauteng Province, South Africa, within a GIS," *Directions Magazine* (Winnetka, IL: Directions Media, August 20, 2002), *www.directionsmag.com/article.php?article_id=241&trv=1*

21. "Convenience Sampling Outpacing Probability Sampling," (Fairfield, CT: Survey Sampling, Inc. March 1994) p. 4.

22. Leo A. Goodman, "Snowball Sampling," *Annuals of Mathematical Statistics* 32 (1961), pp. 148–170.

23. Elaine Peterson, "Evaluation of Digital Libraries Using Snowball Sampling," *First Monday—Peer-Reviewed Journal on the Internet* (May 2005, Vol. 10, No. 5), *www.firstmonday.org/Issues/issue10_5/peterson*; Elaine Peterson and Vicky York, "User Evaluation of the Montana Natural Resource Information System (NRIS)," *D-Lib Magazine* (July/August 2003, Vol. 9, No. 7/8), *www.dlib.org/dlib/july03/peterson/07peterson.html*.

24. Douglas Rivers, "Fulfilling the Promise of the Web," *Quirk's Marketing Research Review* (February 2000), pp. 34–41.

25. Roger Gates and Michael Foytik, "Implementing an HRA on the Internet: Lessons Learned," *Society of Prospective Medicine* (October 1998).

26. Beth Clarkson, "Research and the Internet: A Winning Combination," *Quirk's Marketing Research Review* (July 1999), pp. 46–51.

27. Gates and Foytik, "Implementing an HRA on the Internet."

Chapter 12

1. Tom McGoldrick, David Hyatt, and Lori Laffin. "How Big Is Big Enough?" *Marketing Tools* (May 1998), pp. 54–58.

2. Bonnie W. Eisenfeld, "Sampling for Qualitative Researchers," *Quirk's Marketing Research Review* No. 3 (March 2007), pp. 18, 20.

3. Paul C. Boyd, "A Sample Size Table," *Quirk's Marketing Research Review* (December 2006 Vol. XX, No. 11), pp. 30–31.

4. McGoldrick et al., "How Big Is Big Enough?" pp. 54–58.

5. Lafayette Jones, "A Case for Ethnic Sampling," *Promo* (October 1, 2000), p. 12.

6. M. H. Vivienne, C. J. Lahaut, et al., "Non-Response Bias in a Sample Survey on Alcohol Consumption," *Alcohol & Alcoholism* (2002, Vol. 37, No. 3), pp. 256–260.

7. Gang Xu, "Estimating Sample Size for a Descriptive Study in Quantitative Research," *Quirk's Marketing Research Review* (June 1999), pp. 14, 52–53.

8. Susie Sangren, "A Simple Solution to Nagging Questions about Survey, Sample Size and Validity," *Quirk's Marketing Research Review* (January 1999), pp. 18, 53.

9. "'Margin of Error,' When Used by Pollsters, Is Widely Misunderstood and Confuses Most People," The Harris Poll #113 (November 13, 2007), *www.harrisinteractive.com/harris_poll/index.asp?PID=832*

10. Gang Xu, "Estimating Sample Size for a Descriptive Study in Quantitative Research."

11. For discussions of these techniques, see Bill Williams, *A Sampler on Sampling*, (New York: John Wiley & Sons, 1978); and Richard Jaeger, *Sampling in Education and the Social Sciences* (New York: Longman, 1984).

12. Survey Sampling, Inc., "Estimate Sample Size with Precision," *The Frame* (January 1999), p. 1.

13. David Anderson, Dennis Sweeney, and Thomas Williams, *Statistics for Business and Economics*, 4th ed., (St. Paul, MN: West Publishing, 1990), pp. 355–357.

Chapter 13

1. Lorraine H. Begley, et al. "Preventing Data Fabrication in Telephone Survey Research," *Journal of Research Administration* (July 1, 2004, Vol. 36, No. 2).

2. Joseph Rydholm, "Dealing with Those Pesky Open-Ended Responses," *Quirk's Marketing Research Review* (February 1994), pp. 70–79.

3. Raymond Raud and Michael A. Fallig, "Automating the Coding Process with Neural Networks," *Quirk's Marketing Research Review* (May 1993), pp. 14–16, 40–47.

4. For information on semiotics, see Paul Cobley, Litza Jansz, and Richard Appignanesi, *Introducing Semiotics* (Melbourne Australia Totem Books, 1997); Marcel Danesi, *Of Cigarettes, High Heels and Other Interesting Things: An Introduction to Semiotics* (New York: St. Martin's Press, 1998); and Umberto Eco, *Semiotics and the Philosophy of Languages* (Bloomington: Indiana University Press, 1986).

5. *Content Analyst Report 1*, No. 2 (July 1, 2004), *www.contentanalyst.com/update/report02/feature.html*.

6. Joseph Rydholm, "Scanning the Seas: Scannable Questionnaires Give Princess Cruises Accuracy and Quick Turnaround," *Quirk's Marketing Research Review* (May 1993), pp. 38–42.

7. "Cross Tabulation," Custom Insight (2005), at: *www.custominsight.com/articles/crosstbsample.asp*.

8. Carl James Schwarz, "Graphical Design," Course Notes for Statistics 301 (1998), at: *www.math.sfu.cal-cschwarz/Stat-301/Handouts/node7.html*.

9. Hank Zucker, "What is Significance?" *Quirk's Marketing Research Review* (March 1994), pp. 12, 14; Gordon A. Wyner, "How High is Up?" *Marketing Research* (Fall 1993), pp. 42–43; Gordon A. Wyner, "The Significance of Marketing Research," *Marketing Research* (Fall 1993), pp. 43–45; and Patrick M. Baldasare and Vikas Mittel, "The Use, Misuse and Abuse of Significance," *Quirk's Marketing Research Review* (November 1994), pp. 16, 32.

10. Thomas T. Semon, "Probability a Perennial Problem for Gamblers—and Also for Researchers." *Marketing News* (January 1999), p. 11

11. Dr. Ali Khounsary, "What is Statically Significant?" *Ask a Scientist*, Mathematics Archives (1999), Argonne National Laboratory, Department of Energy, *www.newton.dep.anl.gov/askasci/math99/math99052.htm*.

12. Lemuel A. Moye, MD, PhD, and Alan T. N. Tita, MD, MPH, "Defending the Rationale for the Two-Tailed Test in Clinical Research," *Circulation* (2002: Vol. 105), pp. 3062–3065.

13. P.K. Viswanathan, "Glimpses into Application of Chi-Square Tests in Marketing," at: *http://davidmlane.com/hyperstat/viswanathan/chi_square_marketing.html*

Chapter 14

1. P. K. Mills and R. Yang, "Regression Analysis of Pesticide Use and Breast Cancer Incidence in California Latinas," *Journal of Environmental Health* (January–February 2006: Vol. 68, No. 6), pp. 15–22.

2. Miaofen Yen and Li-Hua Lo, "Examining Test-Retest Reliability: An Intra-Class Correlation Approach," *Nursing Research* (January–February 2002: Vol. 51, No. 1), pp. 59–62.

3. Pascale de Becker, PhD. and Johan Roeykens, PT., et al., "Exercise Capacity in Chronic Fatigue Syndrome," *Archives of Internal Medicine* (November 27, 2000: Vol. 160), pp. 3270–3277.

Chapter 15

1. Diane Schmalensee and A. Dawn Lesh, "Creating Win-Win Relationships," *Marketing Research* (Winter 2007), pp. 16–21.

2. Joseph Rydholm, "What Do Clients Want from a Research Firm?" *Quirk's Marketing Research Review* (October 1996), p. 80.

3. John Walters and John Colias, "The Simple Secret to Effective Market Research," *CASRO Journal* (2002), pp. 65–66.

4. The material on organizing a supplier firm is from: Michael Mitrano, "Supplier Side: Organizing Your Company—Are Project Teams the Answer?" *Quirk's Marketing Research Review* (April 2002), pp. 20, 68.

5. Joseph Rydholm, "No Margin for Margin of Error," *Quirk's Marketing Research Review* (February 2008), pp. 117–118.

6. "Market Research Outsourcing—The India Growth Story," bporesearch@valuenotes.blz (February 19, 2008).

7. Ibid.

8. Susan Greco, "Choose or Lose." Reprinted with permission from *Inc.* magazine, February 2001. Copyright 1998 by Gruner & Jahr USA Publishing.

9. Kathleen Knight, "Finding and Retaining Research Staff: A Perspective," *Quirk's Marketing Research Review* (February 1998), pp. 18, 54. Reprinted by permission.

10. The sections on allocating the research budget, prioritizing projects, and retaining skilled staff are from Schmalensee and Lesh, "Creating Win-Win Relationships."

11. Ibid.

12. Ibid.

13. Ibid.

14. This section is adapted from Richard Snyder, *Quirk's Marketing Research Review* (November 2002), pp. 62–65.

15. Dana James, "Establish Your Place at the Table," *Marketing News* (September 16, 2002), pp. 1, 19–20; Keith Malo, "Raising Research's Profile," *Quirk's Marketing Research Review* (October 2007), pp. 76–85; and Michael Carlon, "Moving from Validation to Inspiration," *Quirk's Marketing Research Review* (October 2007), pp. 80–81.

16. Allison Enright, "Give 'em What They Need," *Marketing News* (February 1, 2008), p. 30.

17. Ibid.; also see Natalie Jobity and Jeff Scott, "Practices Make Perfect—Improving Research and Consulting Through Collaboration," *CASRO Journal* (2002), pp. 19–24.

18. John Huppertz, "Passion vs. Dispassion," *Marketing Research* (Summer 2003), pp. 17–21.

19. Ibid.

20. Enright, "Give 'em What They Need."

21. Tim Ambler, "Differing Dimensions," *Marketing Research* (Fall 2004), pp. 8–13.

22. This section of ROI is from A. Dawn Lesh and Diane Schmalensee, "Measuring Returns of Research," *Marketing Research* (Fall 2004), pp. 22–27.

23. Ibid.

24. www.cross-tab.com (February 20, 2008).

INDEX